H A N D B O O K

Associated Press

The Associated Press Broadcast News Handbook
Incorporating the AP Libel Manual
by Brad Kalbfeld

ISBN: 0-917360-15-x

Library of Congress Cataloging in Publication Data:

Kalbfeld, Brad, 1954-
    The Associated Press broadcast news handbook:
incorporating the AP libel manual / by Brad Kalbfeld — 2nd
ed.

        p.   cm.

    Rev. ed. of: Associated Press broadcast news hand-
book / James R. Hood. 1982

        1. Journalism—style manuals. 2. Broadcast journal-
ism. 3. Libel and slander—United States. I. Hood, James R.,
1994- Associated Press broadcast news handbook. II.
Associated Press. III. Title. IV. Title: AP broadcast services
handbook
PN4783.H57 1997
808'.06607—dc21   97-17715
                                                        CIP

DEDICATION

To the memory of Oliver Gramling, founder and longtime head of AP Broadcast Services.

Without him, this book and the standards it represents might very well not exist.

Table of Contents

Acknowledgments

No book is created in a vacuum, but few grow as directly from another as this one.

Parts 2 and 3 of *The Associated Press Broadcast News Handbook* are based to a large extent on *The Associated Press Stylebook and Libel Manual.* The first editions of that book were edited by Eileen Alt Powell and Howard Angione; later editions were edited by the late Christopher W. French and by Norm Goldstein. Parts 2 and 3 of this book would not have been possible without their groundwork.

James Williams, AP vice president and director of Broadcast Services, is the person who did the most to make sure we had a second edition. He encouraged me to thoroughly rewrite the 1982 edition, which had clearly become outdated.

Louis D. Boccardi, AP's president and chief executive officer, and William Ahearn, AP vice president and executive editor, both lent their support to the project.

Laura Baker brought her incredible eye for detail to the job of proofreading the final product.

Many others made contributions as well, among them Eugene Kim, who helped me research quotations, and Evelyn Cassidy, who assisted with the book's design. Among those who read the manuscript and offered suggestions were Greg Crowley, Bob Feldman, Steve Katz, Dave Lubeski, George Mayo, Sue Mosher, Lee Perryman and Mark Smith. Barbara Worth made a particular contribution in this regard.

And finally, my personal thanks to Jane Kalbfeld, who helped keep the material organized and, in the process, found new meaning in the phrase "cut and paste."

BRAD KALBFELD
Washington, D.C.

Introduction to the Second Edition

Many things have changed since the AP first published its *Broadcast News Handbook* in early 1982.

Computerized text editing, once limited to the large news agencies, has spread to television and radio stations across the country.

The television industry has been revolutionized by the miniaturization of cameras and recorders. What was considered an impossibility just a few years ago—the one-person crew—is reality in many places.

What's more, the videotape those smaller crews are shooting is now available to virtually everyone—almost instantaneously, due to the invention of satellite news gathering.

When the first *Handbook* was published, broadcast television was the dominant provider of visual news. AM radio was still thriving, although FM certainly was thought to be the audio medium of the future. Few people thought about layoffs, reductions in network news budgets or the wholesale closing of radio news departments.

The television audience has fragmented in the face of cable, pay-per-view and, most recently, DBS. FM dominates the radio industry, but is looking over its shoulder at satellite-delivered digital radio signals. AM has become a more specialized medium, concentrating more and more on news and talk. And the Internet is providing all broadcasters with a new distribution channel.

And everyone has had to cope with tighter budgets.

Those factors have changed our industry to the point where, in many markets, news departments no longer have the resources to devote to fully training their reporters, anchors and writers.

This new edition of the *Handbook* is intended to help close that training gap, by sharing with all news departments more detail about the skills needed to cover the news. We see this as another way in which The Associated Press can serve the industry that forms its membership.

Introduction

On the night of November 2, 1920, a transmitter atop the Westinghouse Electric factory in Pittsburgh crackled to life.

In the building below, people were busy on the telephone, taking down information from a newspaper office elsewhere in town. The information was run into the studio and read on the air — and radio station KDKA, reporting the results of the Harding-Cox presidential election, ushered in both commercial broadcasting and broadcast news.

The Associated Press participated in this birth of broadcast news. The election returns KDKA aired were gathered by AP and specially licensed for the station's use.

There were no rules back then, no basic tenets of on-air reporting, no guidelines for newcomers to the business. In fact, there was no "business" to speak of; KDKA improvised.

Since then, broadcast technology has grown up, branching into new audio and video fields. The programming and commercial aspects of broadcasting have become complex.

During these decades of growth, broadcast journalists have developed their own set of ground rules: basic, simple standards of good practice.

Many news organizations have, over the years, codified the basics. Among them is AP, which has the world's largest newsgathering operation and serves thousands of radio and television stations in the United States and around the world.

AP Broadcast division has established guidelines that work in newsrooms of three, 30 or 300 people. That's what this book is about.

Any stylebook serves two major functions: to give others the benefit of the organization's collective experience in the newsroom and to clear the air of basic stylistic questions, so more immediate and debatable matters can be tackled. After all, the main event in any newsroom isn't as much the style as the story.

PART 1

An Approach to Broadcast Style

CHAPTER 1

The Art of News Writing

There's nothing like a good story.

To be a journalist is to be a storyteller. Our job is to tell people what's going on — to tell them stories about events near and far, developments both earthshaking and merely amusing.

The six young men who reported for duty at AP headquarters on December 1, 1940, knew that. Their job was to set up a news wire written specifically for radio stations.

One of them was Mitchell Curtiss, who was later to write that the idea was to find a way "to string words together in such a way that they listened well."

That, in essence, is what broadcast news writing is all about.

Curtiss and his colleagues wouldn't recognize today's broadcast news industry. Newspeople are fascinated with the tools of today's trade. The skies are filled with our satellites, the world wired with our audio and video circuits. We're sending pictures on microscopically thin strands of fiber and routinely sending sound 44,000 miles through space (22,000 up and the same again down) in order to get it from one town to another.

Yet if you strip away the Betacams, digital audio editors, uplink trucks and all the rest, our business comes down to communicating facts — and how well we do that depends on what words we choose and how we relate them to the pictures and sounds we use.

And that means it all comes down to writing.

Your writing determines the order in which the facts are presented. It determines, in great part, the audience's "feel" for the story — its sense of the mood surrounding the event and of the importance of the developments you are recounting.

Most important, the way a story is written determines the degree to which the audience understands what happened. A well-written story will stay in the listener's mind for a long time. A poorly written one will never make it past the ears.

To an extent, our industry has denigrated the art of writing. The hardware has thrilled us to the point where the pictures and sounds often seem more important than the words we use to explain them.

It's understandable, since we spend so much time and money in the pursuit of sound and pictures. But the priority we have given that chase often obscures the importance of making the best possible use of the material once we have it in hand.

That won't do any good for the broadcast industry or, more importantly, the public. Once the newness of our news-gathering techniques wears off, we may be left with the realization that despite our achievement in getting the sound and the pictures, we've lost the art of making sense of them for the audience. That would mean our consumers, the public, will be less well-informed than before.

And so it is important that as we invent new methods of bringing the listener and viewer closer to the event, we put a new emphasis on the old-fashioned practice of marshaling the facts in explanation of the images.

The Science of Writing

Although writing is a subjective craft, it has its scientific aspects. These include the standard rules of good English composition: grammar, spelling and punctuation. Of course, broadcast news writing is a specialized form of composition, and its rules are tailored to its special needs.

Any writer who takes the business seriously must have a basic understanding of (and care a lot about) English grammar. Words are the implements of storytelling; grammar provides the guidelines for their proper use.

Even veteran writers come up against occasional grammatical questions, and a basic grammar primer is an indispensable tool for writers and editors alike. A book such as The Little, Brown Handbook or The Random House Handbook can help you figure out why a sentence simply doesn't sound right.

These texts also provide a basic grounding in punctuation. Proper punctuation is essential if the meaning of your copy is to come through to someone reading it "cold" — on the air without the benefit of previewing it.

In addition, this handbook provides details of the broadcast industry's specialized rules for commas, periods and the like — rules that provide the means of using these symbols to visually separate thoughts or to provide places for the anchor to take a breath.

A dictionary is another crucial reference book, both for word selection and for spelling. Even if you are writing for yourself and never expect anyone to edit or read your copy, proper spelling is an important aspect of good news writing. Broadcast copy may end up being seen by the public, the courts, or contest judges — and poor spelling can make a difference to all three. What's worse, a misspelled word is a stumble waiting to happen.

Finally, the science of writing includes some basic rules designed to ensure that your copy is comprehensible to your audience. These include guidelines on the placement of attribution, on methods for referring to newsmakers and of introducing tape. It is these rules, along with the aesthetics of news writing, that comprise the main focus of this handbook.

The Art of Writing

There's nothing easier to advocate but harder to do than to write well. Following the rules of grammar, punctuation and spelling is easy; capturing the essence of a story and imparting it to the audience isn't.

To speak to the public mind, one must know that mind, and have a feel for the textures and rhythms of everyday speech. People talk a certain way, and because they're listening to each other, it can be said that they listen a certain way, too. Good writing "talks" the way people want to listen.

An entire science is devoted to analyzing and cataloging our speech patterns, but when it comes to writing excellent copy, even a systematic understanding of American dialects is no substitute for a good ear.

Central to honing your writing skills is honing your listening skills. If you can't hear how people talk, you'll never be able to talk to them the same way — at least, not with any consistency. That's why it's important for everyone involved in news writing, including reporters, editors and producers, to think about how people express themselves.

For example, very few people would say (but more than a few newspeople might write), "The severity of the impact of the loss of position is directly proportional to the importance of the position." How much clearer to say, "The bigger they are, the harder they fall."

That's not to advocate the use of cliches. One of the primary challenges a writer faces is to use familiar, informal imagery without resorting to shopworn expressions which have lost value through overuse.

So how do the best writers do it? The best way to find out — and to tune up your ear — is to survey some examples.

One of the most challenging and dramatic stories of recent years was the war in the Falkland Islands in 1982. Britain sent a naval task force to the South Atlantic in response to Argentina's landings on the tiny islands. A small number of reporters accompanied the ships, but there was little audio and, in the early going, very few pictures.

Brian Hanrahan of the BBC thus found himself having to tell the story entirely in his own words. Here is how he described the first British air strikes on May 1, 1982:

> HMS Hermes, on its radar, tracked a Vulcan bomber in to shed its load of 21 thousand-pound bombs across Stanley airport. The night was an ideal one for surprise: dark and overcast, no moon, just an occasional star breaking through the clouds. As the big bomber turned back to base, we monitored its radio codeword: the mission was successful. A few hours after the Vulcan attack, it was Hermes' turn. ... At Stanley the planes went in low, in waves just seconds apart. They glimpsed the bomb craters left by the Vulcan and they left behind them more fire and destruction. The pilots said there had been smoke and dust everywhere, punctuated by the flash of explosions. They faced a barrage of return fire, heavy but apparently ineffective. I'm not allowed to say how many planes joined the raid, but I counted them all out, and I counted them all back.[1]

What makes this writing so good isn't any particular word or phrase: it is the way in which it paints a picture in your mind, giving you a clear, lasting sense of what happened.

It's easy to use war reporting to illustrate good writing: There's obvious drama in any clash of armies or navies. Here's an example of

---

[1] Brian Hanrahan and Robert Fox, *I Counted Them All Out and I Counted Them All Back: The Battle for the Falklands* (London: British Broadcasting Corporation, 1982), pp. 20-21.

There are many who will find it curious that the very first writing sample cited in this book is written in the past tense, particularly in light of subsequent pages' emphasis on the importance of using the present tense. War reports are generally delayed for hours (and sometimes days) for security or logistical reasons, so it is not unusual for accounts of battles to be written in the past tense.

In this case, the writing is so vivid that the reader will, I hope, excuse the tense.

something more common and closer to home: Edward R. Murrow's account of the flooding of the Missouri River in 1952:

> This is a business of men and machines against the river. It's rained all day. Over on the other side of the river about 600 blocks have been evacuated in Council Bluffs. There are no children in the playgrounds; the roller coaster stands like a monument to a past age. You can look straight through the houses. They even took the window curtains, as well as furniture, ice boxes and all the rest, when they moved out. There is no traffic except for an occasional official car. GIs with carbines huddle around fires built in garbage cans. They look like all the other soldiers you have seen trying to keep warm. They're there to prevent looting, and there has been very little of that. The garage doors stand open and the cars are gone. That part of Council Bluffs is a ghost town that hasn't had time to fall down. There is a sign outside one house saying, "I Shall Return!"[2]

You can write vividly about almost anything. If you're skeptical, take a look at this classic piece by Charles Kuralt, reporting from Niles, Illinois:

> The leaning tower of Pisa stands — leans — on Touhy Avenue. I've never known why, but there it is. It enriches the drive down Touhy Avenue. A little north, in Milwaukee, there's a Chinese pagoda gas station. In Florida there's a seashell shop that you enter by walking into the yawning concrete jaws of a giant alligator. These are relics.
>
> I like America's screwball architecture, but it's being

---

[2] Edward R. Murrow and Edward Bliss, *In Search of Light: The Broadcasts of Edward R. Murrow, 1938-1961*, Edited by Edward Bliss, Jr. (New York: Alfred A. Knopf, Inc., 1967), p. 211.

replaced everywhere by humorless glass and steel. This is a loss. The interstate highways have done in all those hamburger stands that were shaped like hamburgers; remember them? A historian named Peter H. Smith shares my view. After a few years of commercial archaeology, Mr. Smith says we ought to establish a museum of the American highway to preserve the alligator-jawed gift shops before they're all replaced by carbon-copy modular gas stations.[3]

You don't need a television screen to know what Kuralt was talking about. The words put the pictures in your mind's eye.

The best radio writing uses tape to engage the listener's imagination. Even the most routine topics — politics and the economy, for example — can be brought to life for the listener, as demonstrated in this campaign report by AP correspondent Bob Moon:

TAPE: (Music: "Happy days are here again ...")

The campaign themes of 1992 are small comfort in hard-hit New Hampshire:

TAPE: (Woman on street)

"People just can't afford to live. Y'know, I'm not talking Mercedes and stuff, I'm just talking a roof over their head and a decent car and something like that. The middle class people are hurting out there, and something's gotta give."

Throughout New England, the shakeout of computer and defense-related jobs has rippled throughout banking,

---

[3] Charles Kuralt, *Dateline America* (New York: Harcourt Brace Jovanovich, 1979), pp. 101-102.

retail, real estate and construction businesses.

TAPE: (fade up natural sound of street)

TAPE: (Buchanan)

"I walked up and down the streets of Concord and Manchester, and I think I must have met 50 to 75 people. ... "

(natural sound under)

Republican Pat Buchanan could speak for all of the presidential candidates:

TAPE: (Buchanan continues)

" ... I started after a while to ask them, 'Is there anything else on your mind but the economy?' They said no."

Buchanan does not exaggerate the point:

TAPE: (Montage of street interviews)

"What's the top issue in the primary, as far as you're concerned?"

"The economy."

"The economy."

"The economy, definitely."

"I think for New Hampshire there will be jobs and the economy."

"Keep waiting for that turnaround to come and it's just not happening."

"I think the economy right now. More jobs."

"Putting the economy back on track, getting people jobs."

"The economy. Just give us more jobs out there."

"Good paying jobs. Never mind this stuff with the service industry that is only minimum wage. Nobody can live on that.'

"I'd like to see some light at the end of the tunnel. And right now I think everybody around here is looking for the tunnel."

What a difference four years make. When New Hampshire voters went to the polls in their last presidential primary, the Granite State had a jobless rate of just two-point-seven percent — the lowest in the nation.

A final example shows that it doesn't take many words to bring the listener to the scene of the story. Knowing when to let the tape do the talking is an important skill:

Getting to shake the hand of a political candidate takes hard work, determination and, sometimes, the right approach. In the case of Democrat Bill Clinton and his Texas bus tour, it helps to have the favor of his wife, Hillary.

TAPE: (Watson)

"We've been here ever since before eleven o'clock."

TAPE: (Hillary Clinton)

"You're kidding."

Seventy-four-year-old Ruby Watson waited three hours in the East Texas sun to see the governor in front of the Dairy Queen in the crossroads town of Hubbard.

TAPE: (Watson)

"If I don't get to speak to your husband, I'll just die. You don't want me to die, do you?"

TAPE: (Hillary Clinton)

"No, no. I don't. And I'll get him right over here. I promise you."

Call it blackmail, if you will. But it works.

TAPE: (Watson. Opens with sound of a kiss.)

"Going to vote for you, thank you."

TAPE: (Bill Clinton)

"Thank you, bless you."

Mark Smith, AP Network News, with the Clinton campaign in Hubbard, Texas.

Each of these examples tells a story clearly and with great impact.

They do so by understanding how people talk and listen — and using that knowledge to guide their writing.

That is the goal you should aim for as, in the coming pages, we examine techniques for gathering and writing news for radio and television. For at the end of the day, our purpose as broadcast journalists is to do all we can to tell our audience what went on.

CHAPTER 2

Getting the Story: Field Reporting

There can be no higher law in journalism than to tell the truth and to shame the devil.

- Walter Lippmann [1]

The reporter's job is to observe events and to tell people about them.

We are watchers, not participants; our role is to stand in for the public to make it possible for everyone to stay abreast of the latest developments in government, the economy, education, science and society. Journalists, Harry Reasoner once said, "live a lot of things vicariously, and report them for other people who want to live vicariously."

Ours is a pluralistic society. We value differences of opinion. There are, to be sure, some widely accepted mainstream values, but they are subject to change as the national experience changes. Indeed, the fundamental theory of our political system is that everyone is entitled to an opinion, and only when the majority of people agrees on something does it get done.

By definition, the act of informing the members of such a society is the act of separating fact from opinion. People want to make up

---

[1] Barbara Rowes, *The Book of Quotes* (New York, E.P. Dutton, 1979), p. 119.

their own minds, and a reporter who seems to be trying to do it for them quickly loses credibility.

Walter Cronkite, who earned a reputation as America's most-trusted newsman, stressed the importance of this idea when he described reporting as the act of reflecting events to the public:

> Our job is only to hold up the mirror — to tell and show the public what has happened, and then it is the job of the people to decide whether they have faith in their leaders or government. We are faithful to our profession in telling the truth.[2]

This notion of objectivity is taken for granted by today's reporters, but it wasn't always the way journalists did business. When freedom of the press was enshrined in the First Amendment, newspapers were partisan instruments intended to support the various political factions of the day.

It was the formation of the New York Associated Press in 1848 that led to the introduction of journalistic objectivity. If it was to be credible to newspapers of all political views, the AP had no choice but to keep opinion out of its stories.

As AP Washington Correspondent Lawrence Gobright said a few years before the Civil War broke out, "My business is to communicate facts. My instructions do not allow me to make any comments upon the facts."

Not many years later, the AP's Washington bureau chief, Charles Boynton, issued instructions to his staff, warning them against the influence of lobbyists. If anyone tried to get an AP reporter to write a more favorable story, Boynton ordered, the reporter should "throw him out of the window and report the case to the coroner."[3]

Many have argued that it is impossible for anyone to be perfectly

---

[2] *ibid.*
[3] Oliver Gramling, *AP—The Story of News* (New York: Farrar and Rinehart, Incorporated, 1940), p. 192.

objective, that as reporters decide which facts to include in their stories, making judgments about what is newsworthy and what isn't, opinion inevitably must intrude.

There's no doubt that reporting and writing by definition involve making choices about which facts to use. Supremely important are the criteria used to make the selections.

If a reporter includes those facts that support a given viewpoint and leaves out those facts which support a competing viewpoint, that's bias. If, however, the story reports each relevant viewpoint (there may be more than two), giving each the weight it had in the event being covered, that's what newspeople call objective.

In both cases, judgments are made. But in the first example, a point of view is the yardstick against which each fact is measured. In the latter case, balance and accuracy are the criteria.

Perhaps the best illustration of the weight given to objective reporting comes from the Civil War. In 1861, when the State Department prohibited telegraphic dispatches from wartime Washington, the Associated Press was the only agency exempted from the order — because it devoted itself to straight reporting, without the luxury of opinion.

The same reasoning applies today. If newsmakers think a reporter is biased, they are less likely to want to talk to that reporter — for fear of their words being twisted (unless, of course, the reporter and the newsmaker share the same bias — limiting the reporter to a pretty small circle of sources!). Similarly, if listeners think a reporter is biased, they are less likely to believe what the reporter is saying.

How does a reporter select facts without injecting bias? By using accuracy as the main yardstick. That means every statement made in the story must be correct. But that isn't enough. It also means that the overall impression created by the selection and ordering of facts, the manner in which those facts are written and the way sound and video are presented must faithfully reflect what the reporter observed.

That is easier to say than it is to do, particularly because of the importance of brevity in radio and television reporting. We're supposed to tell stories in 30 or 35 seconds on the radio, in a minute or 90 seconds on television. That forces us to be ruthless in our selection of facts. There's so little time to say anything that many reporters are tempted to fall into a sort of shorthand, reporting their impressions of events rather than the facts.

That's where we get into trouble. Rather than saying, "Winds are blowing at 100 miles-an-hour and two inches of rain have fallen," we say, "There's a powerful storm out there." Often, as in that example, it's a safe conclusion to reach. But once you get in the habit of reaching conclusions, it's hard to break, and that can be dangerous.

Consider, for example, the many times in the late 1970s when Israeli jets flew at rooftop levels over Beirut. Often, these sorties would be accompanied by deafening booms and the shattering of windows.

It would be easy to conclude from these facts that the Israelis were bombing the Lebanese capital, particularly if you were on the ground in Beirut and shards of glass were falling all around you. But it would be the wrong conclusion. What the Israelis actually did was to create sonic booms to scare their adversaries on the ground.

Then there was the time that the pope was riding in a motorcade through the streets of Seoul. A man holding a gleaming metal object in his hands moved toward the popemobile. He crouched in the firing position and pulled the trigger. It was easy to believe that he had fired a shot at the pope — as one reporter believed. But it was wrong; he had fired a starter's pistol: There were no bullets.

The way to avoid such mistakes is to avoid writing any conclusions in any story. State facts; let your listeners decide what those facts mean to them.

A corollary to this rule is that, as a reporter, you should develop a fine sense of skepticism. You really should believe only what you see and hear and avoid jumping to conclusions.

Many things are not what they seem: handguns turn out to be starter pistols, the sound of bombs exploding turns out to be the sound of jet fighters surpassing Mach One.

Similarly, people don't always say what they mean. Lawyers, politicians and public officials are well-trained in the use of language to create impressions favorable to their causes. Former Secretary of State Henry Kissinger goes so far as to say that officials use reporters to serve "a partly governmental function":

> Officials seek him [the reporter] out to bring their pet projects to general attention, to settle scores, or to reverse a decision that went against them. Whatever the official's motive, it cannot be disinterested.[4]

Whether you're reporting on the activities of the local school board or the president of the United States, there is a subtext to almost every statement by almost every official. A big part of the reporter's job is to understand what that subtext is and to factor it into the story.

It's a touchy business, one that often leads to accusations that reporters have private agendas and are more interested in getting on the air than in listening to what people have to say. From the newsmaker's point of view, journalists are people who, having spent the day trying to get public figures to talk, don't believe a word that's said. So why trust newspeople at all — why talk to them?

This attitude is born of several factors, the principal of which is newsmakers' frustration over their inability to get reporters to tell the story the way they want it told.

Another reason newsmakers distrust reporters is because of their experience with those whose skepticism has hardened into cynicism.

---

[4] Henry Kissinger, *White House Years* (Boston: Little, Brown and Company, 1979), p. 21.

It is important to understand the difference between the two. Skeptics check the truthfulness of everything they hear; cynics believe everyone is motivated by selfishness alone. Skepticism makes you a good reporter. Cynicism means you've been working the beat too long.

In fact, while reporters must be skeptical, they also should have a healthy respect for the rights of the people they are covering.

Although it may seem obvious, every news source has a right to be accurately quoted. Everyone is entitled to have his or her words and deeds fairly and objectively reported.

People have a right to be treated courteously. They have a right to expect reporters to conduct themselves professionally.

In addition, the courts have, over the past century, established that people have a right of privacy. As Barbara Dill, a member of the legal staff of The New York Times, writes, privacy is taken in balance with the public's right to know certain information.

> For newspeople, the basic question is usually, "Is this interesting?" But when the issue of a person's privacy is at stake, the legal question becomes, "Is the publication of this material in the public interest and does the public interest in the material outweigh the private person's right to remain out of the public eye?"[5]

The rules for public figures are different from those for private figures. As we will see in Part 2, "The AP Libel Manual," the right of privacy is forfeited by people who become involved in news events — even if their participation was involuntary.

Yet factors such as the reporter's motives and procedures often come

---

[5] Barbara Dill, *The Journalist's Handbook on Libel and Privacy* (New York: Macmillan, The Free Press, 1986), pp. 135-6

into play when a court is judging whether a person's privacy has been invaded or his or her character injured. This is a very sensitive and complicated legal area — one that deserves your attention every time you cover a story.

Just as reporters must respect newsmakers' rights, public figures, and particularly officials, must respect their obligations to the public.

Our democracy is based on the idea that officials will be accountable to the electorate, and that only an informed electorate is able to make intelligent choices about candidates for office.

This places upon public officials the obligation to conduct the government's business in public and to share with the community the reasons behind public policy. Not every official is eager to fulfill this responsibility, but as a reporter, one of your most important jobs is to assist the audience in keeping officials accountable by obtaining and relaying information about the conduct of government.

The situation is different in other countries, where there are greater limitations on freedom of speech and where the notion of official accountability isn't very strongly held. Local laws and customs will dictate how far you can push.

Asking the Right Questions

Asking questions is an art, one every reporter must master, for asking the right question is central to getting the story.

Your approach to a newsmaker and the types of questions you ask are determined by the kind of story you are covering. Questions can be thought of as falling into three broad categories: those which are designed to elicit hard facts about a story, those which are intended to get a person to talk about how they think or feel about an event, and those which are intended to pin down an elusive newsmaker.

Eliciting Hard Facts. Often, the questions are obvious: if, for example, you are covering a fire, you want to know if anyone is still in the building, whether there are any casualties, whether the fire is under control, and so forth.

Or suppose you are staking out a closed meeting. When the participants emerge, the questions are simple and direct: What happened in there?

In addition to the usual *who, what, when, where* and *how,* make sure you ask about the *why* — and the *so what?*

That last one is aimed at understanding why the story is important to your audience. It is the question that ought to generate the lead of your story, since it is the question aimed at determining the impact of events on everyday people.

When you write the story, you are going to want to be able to give the listeners a sense of why the subject should interest them. In some cases, it's obvious: Taxes are going up. A street is being closed. Violent crime is rising.

Sometimes, though, the issues are more subtle.

Let's suppose you are covering a county board meeting, and the supervisors pass a new zoning ordinance that increases the amount of commercial development allowed.

You already have many of the key facts in the story — the number of votes for and against, the wording of the ordinance, the actual amount of development that will be allowed.

Now that the meeting is over, you have the opportunity to find out how various officials think the ordinance will affect homeowners and other taxpayers. Perhaps some of the debate suggested what the impact might be. Or, if you have a good idea of how zoning laws can affect real estate values, the tax base and other aspects of the local economy (as any reporter who covers county government should), your questions should be specific: Will this cause a drop in home property values? How much do you expect it will expand the tax base? What will be the combined effect of falling values and a rising tax base on the average county homeowner? On the tax bill for the average county resident?

There may be circumstances in which you don't know enough about the issue to ask such specific questions. If so, your approach should be to encourage the newsmakers to teach you.

In our example, you might find the official who drew up the ordinance — perhaps the planning commissioner — and ask for an explanation of the ways in which the ordinance could affect ordinary people. Make it clear that you want to be able to explain the importance of the story and want to make sure you fully understand all the ways in which taxpayers could be affected.

Most newsmakers will jump at the opportunity to give that sort of explanation. People respond to a non-confrontational approach that gives them time to say things their own way, that clearly indicates the value you place on what they have to say and that gives them a greater say in setting the terms of the conversation.

You need to be careful, though: Many newsmakers will use that sort of question to cast the issue in the terms most favorable to their point of view. That is why it is important that you listen closely to the explanation and follow it up with some intelligent questions. If the explanation makes some assumptions, question them.

For example, suppose the planning commissioner tells you one impact could be a small drop in residential property values, especially close to the commercial district. You might ask him to define "a small drop," or to explain how he arrived at the figure. You could also probe his confidence in the accuracy of the number or ask what factors could cause the drop to be greater.

Finally, take what you have learned and check it out with other newsmakers with differing views. For example, if you get your "tutorial" from the person who wrote the ordinance, see what an opponent has to say. By testing the proponent's assumptions on the opponent, you can get a sense for the range of possibilities. Be careful to report both points of view.

Finding Out How They Feel. Emotion can make a deep impact on people. We remember times when we have strong feelings, and we respond when we see strong feelings in others. If your story is to make an impression, you need to convey the emotions felt by the participants.

This can be.seen in sports reporting. There's a reason ABC used to talk about "the thrill of victory and the agony of defeat": Who can forget the image of victorious baseball players piling atop one another at the end of the World Series, or the football player joyously slamming the football to the ground after a touchdown? Such images make a much greater impact than the score alone.

In a way, sports reporters have it easy. Athletes often show their emotions in their actions. But most newsmakers express their emotions in words—and only when you ask the right way.

In such a case, your question is aimed at generating a sound bite. You're trying to get a sense, in the newsmaker's own words, of how the person thinks or feels. As we will discuss in Chapter 3, tape (audio actualities or video sound bites) is the most effective way to communicate the newsmaker's feelings: an audience gets a much better sense of the story if it hears a newsmaker being happy (or angry or sad or thoughtful) than if it hears a reporter saying "He was happy (or angry or sad or thoughtful)."

The key to getting this kind of tape is to ask open questions — ones that do not lend themselves to simple "yes" or "no" answers — and to know when to be quiet.

Sometimes, it's easy to find out how a person feels: you ask. This works when the person feels good. A basketball star who's just had a 50-point game will probably be happy to tell you he's happy. A politician who has just been elected will undoubtedly be eager to tell you she's ecstatic.

Interviews with angry people generally are easy, too, because people who are mad like to talk about it. Anger makes people blunt, and they respond to blunt questioning.

The hard interviews are those with people who are sad. The victims of tragedy, or those who witnessed a terrible event, sometimes are hesitant to speak. Some people need to express their sorrow; others need to be alone to deal with their grief.

A reporter must temper the need to get information with the need to treat people with respect. When dealing with tragedies, you need to be especially sensitive to the feelings of the victims.

If someone simply doesn't want to talk, don't force it. It isn't fair and it isn't of any use to you: you won't get good tape and you won't do journalism's reputation any good, either.

If your subject is willing to talk to you, choose your questions carefully. "How do you feel?" doesn't demonstrate the greatest sensitivity. Instead, ask such newsmakers how they are coping, what they remember about the event, whether they blame anyone for what happened.

The best reporters in these circumstances are gentle in their questions and aren't afraid of silence, because they know that silence means the newsmaker is thinking, and thought generally leads to speech. They also know that most human beings are uncomfortable with silence, and will, if you wait long enough, fill it.

Once people begin to share their feelings with you, *don't interrupt.* That may seem like a statement of the obvious, but most reporters are too impatient to give a newsmaker the time to be truly expressive. It takes most people a while to open up, and the more they talk, the more likely they are to give you a vivid description of how they feel. So be patient; the time invested usually is worth it.

Pinning Them Down. Reporters should save their toughest questioning for officials and would-be officials who are trying to avoid delivering bad news or admitting a mistake. Just as most officials know how to say one thing and mean another, many know how to talk a lot but say little. In both cases, part of your job is to cut through the words to the meaning.

There's a big difference between interviewing a public official and talking to someone who has been thrust into the public eye because of a chance association with an event.

Lawmakers, government executives and politicians have volunteered for public service. They have willingly taken on the responsibility for handling public affairs, and with it, the obligation to be accountable.

While your approach to an accident victim must take into account that person's right to say nothing, your approach to officials and candidates for public office should be based on the assumption that they are obliged to talk to the public — and you are one of the public's representatives.

If an official wants to avoid a subject, your goal should be to try to find a question the person is willing to answer. This usually involves asking about different aspects of the same general question, until the newsmaker hears something he or she can comfortably respond to — or can't avoid answering.

Often, it comes down to a test of wills between reporters and officials: Who will give up first, the people asking the questions or the person trying to duck them? This happens most frequently at news conferences, where officials make a show of being accessible but sometimes try to gloss over certain subjects.

Politicians are loath to say anything that puts them in a bad light. When, for example, the economy weakens, presidents don't like to say so. They especially dislike having to call it a recession. Yet one of your jobs as a correspondent is to find out how the president views the economy, so the country can compare its perceptions with the chief executive's.

There's no sure-fire way to elicit a firm characterization, since any newsmaker who really doesn't want to answer and is patient enough can simply dodge every question. But reporters can — and should — try.

Some reporters try the frontal approach, bluntly asking the president whether a recession is under way. The answer, almost invariably, is "no."

Others try a more open approach: "Mr. President, how would you characterize the current economic climate?" Their hope is that the president somehow will have to acknowledge that things have slowed down. This sometimes works, but allows lots of room to fudge the answer.

Still other reporters present a list of facts and then ask the president to agree to a characterization: "Mr. President, unemployment is up for the second month in a row, gross domestic product has been down for two months, housing starts are at record lows. Doesn't that mean, sir, that we are in a recession?" This works more often, although, again, there's still room for the president to answer "no." However, this type of question often brings newsmakers closer to making a characterization because they feel they must take into account the facts listed by the reporter.

One approach that has proven effective is to bracket the newsmaker by citing both sides of the question: "Mr. President, you have avoided using the term 'recession.' Yet, given the rise in unemployment and the fall in the economy's output, we clearly are not in an expansion. If it's not a recession and not an expansion, what is it?"

By casting the question this way, the reporter limits the newsmaker's room to fudge. The response probably will be an attempt to acknowledge that there's a downturn without using the term "recession," bringing you as close as you're going to get when questioning a determined official.

The key to this kind of questioning is to reduce the official's room to maneuver, so you get as straight an answer as possible. Remember, though, that your goal is to get the newsmaker to say something that casts light on his or her attitudes or policies. It should not be to get the newsmaker to fit your personal idea of what ought to be said.

A final pointer in this regard: Always be respectful in your questioning. Professionalism demands it. Besides, if you are disrespectful, you will provide the newsmaker with a convenient distraction from the point of your question, making it easier to duck.

In the Field

Radio and television reporters are increasingly expected to know the technical aspects of newsgathering. For decades, most radio reporters have handled their own tape recorders. Although most television reporters do not run their own cameras, reporters and producers are being pushed by technological advances and economic pressures to handle more of the mechanics of field news gathering.

Even at the network level, where, in some shops, there once was a strict division between those who handled words and those who handled equipment, barriers are falling, especially in radio.

There's a definite advantage to understanding the basic technology of broadcast news gathering. Your story relies heavily on audio or video: You have to write to it, and it has to be smoothly integrated into your piece if the story is to be effectively told. It is, therefore, in your interest as a reporter to do all you can to be sure you have the audio or video you need, and that it is properly recorded.

Beyond that, good mechanics in the field, including organized notetaking, good positioning for gathering sound and pictures and solid preparation for filing all will help you get a better story on the air

Reporter's Field Kit. Radio reporters still have to carry a lot more gear than television reporters (though in many places, correspondents often carry tripods and lights for their crews). Generally, the radio reporter must be self-sufficient when it comes to equipment. If you don't have the right gear, you won't be able to gather the sound you need.

You should always carry *two tape recorders*. There are several reasons, the most important of which is that, if one fails, you'll still be able to gather tape. In addition, you may need to produce a wrap in the field, or to leave one machine connected to a *mult* (an audio distribution box providing multiple feeds of a single sound source) while you are doing interviews using the second machine.

This doesn't mean you have to lug two large machines with you. Many reporters carry one larger machine and one pocket machine. The larger machine generally has more output power, and so can drive a telephone line more effectively for feeding spots and tape. That's the machine you would leave hooked up to the mult.

The smaller machine has the advantage of being lighter and less obtrusive, making it better suited to use in crowds and at times when you need to move quickly from one newsmaker to another. But don't use the built-in microphone to pick up sound. The quality won't be good enough. Use an external mike instead.

One caution: Don't use a micro-cassette machine. What you gain in convenience you lose in audio quality.

Use a microphone suited to the environment. If you are recording a speech and there is no mult available, a good *dynamic microphone* will do the job. Make sure you have a stand or clamp that will hold the mike firmly in place — one that the newsmaker won't be able to absent-mindedly slide around the table while trying to think of an answer!

If, on the other hand, you are staking out a newsmaker and the scene is very crowded, you will want to use a *shotgun mike* if one is available. A shotgun is a highly directional microphone that is used to pick one voice out of a crowd. If you use one, be sure to listen to your tape machine (if there's a *monitor switch*, make sure it is set to *source*) through your headphones, to be certain you have properly aimed the microphone.

To get the longest reach, attach the shotgun mike to an extension arm or *mike pole*. Make sure the microphone is *firmly* anchored to the pole; if it falls off in the middle of the event, you could miss some crucial tape.[6]

If a shotgun mike is not available, you can attach a *dynamic* or *condenser microphone* to the mike pole.

For this and many other essential purposes, you should always carry a roll of *gaffer's tape* or *duct tape*. This cloth tape, which usually has a gray metallic look, is strong, it doesn't cause reflections that would interfere with television shots, and it is easily removed after the event. Gaffer's tape is more expensive, has a better adhesive and has a paintable finish. Duct tape is more readily available — most hardware stores stock it — and works quite well for the purpose.

Another essential piece of gear is the *mult cord*. This is a piece of shielded cable with a female XLR connector on one end and a miniature phone plug on the other. The XLR connector is

---

Television Reporter's Field Kit

Although most video gear is handled by photographers, it's a good idea for television reporters to carry some personal newsgathering gear.

A pocket cassette recorder (preferably using a standard cassette) is an invaluable note-taking tool. If your video equipment doesn't use time code, it's essential that the audiotape recorder have a counter, so you can easily identify bites for editing purposes.

An accurate watch (if your equipment uses time code) or stopwatch will help you time sound bites, particularly if you have a prepared text to work from.

It's a good idea to bring a mult cord (XLR on one end, mini-phone plug on the other), so you can tape news conferences and speeches off the mult, for maximum sound quality.

Of course, if you will be doing a live shot, make sure you have an earpiece that fits comfortably. Don't count on someone else to bring it for you!

---

[6] One reporter was miking then-President Jimmy Carter one day when he accidentally bopped the president on the nose. Although Carter took it good-naturedly, the Secret Service did not, and jerked the mike and fish-pole away from the president. The mike stayed attached, though, and other than the noise of impact, nothing was amiss on the tape.

plugged into the audio mult at the scene of the event; the mini-phone plug goes into one of the input sockets on your tape recorder. This allows you to record audio directly off the distribution system.

Most mults are mike-level, so the mini-phone plug goes into the *microphone in* socket on your machine. Sometimes a line-level output is available; then, the mini-phone plug goes into your machine's *line in* or *aux* socket.

Many reporters carry an *audio pad* to help them deal with signals that are too hot. The pad plugs into the XLR end of the mult cord and has the effect of reducing the signal level. This can help eliminate distortion and make it possible to feed a line-level mult output into a microphone-level tape machine input.

In addition, you should carry one or more *mult extension cords*. These are long XLR-to-XLR cords that allow you to hook up to a mult across the room.

If you plan to produce wraps while in the field, a small battery-driven *mixer* is very helpful, especially if you will be working on a tight deadline. It is possible to make electronic edits — first recording the opening of the spot through the microphone, then dubbing the cut from a second tape machine, then recording the close — but the quality is much better, and the speed greater, if you use a mixer. Mixers are getting smaller and less expensive every year, and have become standard gear for many network reporters.

A small mixer is a necessity if you are doing live shots and plan to use tape. The output of the mixer clips into the telephone or audio circuit, while a microphone is plugged into one input, and a tape machine into the other.

Some stations and networks modify their cassette recorders to provide for mixing the mike channel with the tape playback channel. This eliminates the need for a mixer and reduces the weight of your kit bag.

In either case, it's also a good idea to carry an *isolation transformer* to help you cope with hum. This is a one-to-one transformer — that is, the level of the audio you feed in is the same as the level you get out. But the transformer, which works by magnetic induction rather than a direct wire-to-wire connection, isolates one piece of gear from another, reducing the chance of getting a hum.

Another important piece of gear for a live shot is a small battery-driven *headphone amplifier,* so you can hear your cues. The audio returning to you from the studio is usually IFB — *interruptible feedback* — which includes studio sound and a closed-circuit producer's channel.

If you're feeding on one phone and picking up IFB on another, use a set of clip-leads to connect the input of the amplifier across the ear-piece of the IFB phone. Plug your headphones into the output of the amplifier. Reporters who include sound in their live shots often carry headphones and a small *splitter box,* which provides IFB in one side of the phones and the output of the field mixer in the other. This allows them to hear their own tape.

If you are doing live shots using one telephone, feeding into a phone hybrid at the station, you can hear your cues by using *clip-leads* to connect your amplifier across the earpiece of the phone.

In either case, if you don't have an amplifier, you can use a tape recorder to amplify the cues. Clip the tape recorder's *line input* across the telephone earpiece and put the recorder in *record* and *pause.* If the tape recorder has a monitor switch, set it to *source.* You should be able to hear the telephone signal through the headphones.

Feeding the Story. We've made several references here to *clip-leads,* which may well be the most important cable you ever will carry. It consists of a mini-phone plug on one end and a pair of alligator clips on the other. They are essential for connecting tape recorders, mixers and amplifiers to the telephone.

Their most frequent use is to connect the output of a tape recorder across the mouthpiece of the telephone, for feeding spots.

On many older telephones, the mouthpiece can be opened by unscrewing the plastic cover. This allows the removal of the little microphone element. One alligator clip is attached to each prong in the handset, which feeds the audio directly into the telephone circuitry.

Most newer telephones, however, have a single piece covering both the mouthpiece and earpiece. Often, the housing is held together with plastic tabs and with screws hidden under the little clear plastic plate where the telephone number is printed.

You may find it difficult to get to the mouthpiece on this kind of phone. If so, you can open the main housing of the telephone, generally by removing the screws on the bottom of the unit. You can then clip across the mouthpiece leads where they emerge from the handset cord.

With the increasing popularity of this kind of telephone, it is becoming more important to carry a small screwdriver whenever you are in the field.

Another option for feeding audio into a telephone is to use an RJ-11 modular phone connector. It is possible to purchase or build a small box that plugs between the phone and its handset and provides sockets for the phone instrument, an audio input and an audio output.

Regardless of the electronics, it is best, when possible, to pre-record spots you are feeding from the field. It saves the newsroom time, saves you the frustration of multiple takes and most important, it allows you to better adjust the overall level of the signal you are feeding, since you can keep playing a portion of the tape and adjusting the volume until the level is optimal.

AP Style Guideline

AP Network News requires that all voicers, wraps and tape be fed through clip-leads, to obtain the best audio quality. Tape fed through the telephone microphone is not accepted for use on the network.

Where practical, dub your cuts to a work tape. That way, you can get the top and bottom of each cut cleanly. When it isn't possible to do so, make sure you provide the editor in the newsroom with verbatim in-cues as well as out-cues.

In addition, it is very helpful to have basic information about the material ready to give to the person taking in your feed. This includes the length of the spot, the name of the newsmaker used in the tape, the out-cue and a description of what the piece is about, including a suggested lead-in. Jot down the information *before* you call in, so you take up as little of the newsroom's time as possible.

> **AP Style Guideline**
>
> AP Network News provides its affiliates with complete descriptive material on all voicers, wraps and actualities on its closed-circuit feeds. Reporters filing material to the network need to provide the following information:
>
> - cut length
> - reporter and/or newsmaker name, including proper spelling
> - out-cue
> - description of cut
> - suggested lead-in
> - dateline where material was recorded.
>
> In addition, for payment purposes, stringers must provide their mailing address and Social Security number.

Remember, the folks back at the studio are handling many stories and need to be able to work efficiently.

News Conferences and Speeches. Of all the events a reporter can cover, news conferences and speeches provide the most comfortable, controllable environment. The event has a set start time, the location is prearranged, there is generally adequate power, a mult and easily available telephones.

Before the event starts, be sure to identify the location of the telephones available for filing. If possible, check to see if the mouthpiece is easily removable — in case you have to file from the scene.

As soon as you arrive, find out if there's a mult, and if there is, plug into it immediately. Many stories attract more reporters than there are mult outputs, and you don't want to be the one stuck with no audio.

If there is no mult, get your microphone into position as quickly as possible. People will fight for good mike positioning, and the early arrivals generally get the best spots. If possible, clamp or tape your microphone to the public address mike, so the newsmaker has to talk into it.

This is where the mult extension cord comes in handy. You want to have your tape recorder in your lap or on a chair next to you rather than at the front of the room, so you can start it without having to move around — and flip the cassette without disrupting the event. Once you've placed the mike, run the mult cord to your seat. If necessary, tape it to the floor so no one trips on it.

Whether you are a radio or television reporter, you should keep the tape recorder close at hand during the event so you can log the sound bites. You must have a convenient way to find the best bites on your tape.

In radio, you need to find the bites you will dub into your wrap. In television, you'll want to use your audio tape to conveniently find the in-cues and out-cues of the bites you want to write into your piece.

The widespread use of *timecode* (particularly in television) is making this easy. Timecode is a real-time clock pulse recorded on a separate track on the videotape; electronically attached to every frame is the precise time of day (hours, minutes, seconds, frame number) it was recorded. All the reporter has to do is note the clock time for each sound bite (and be sure your watch is reasonably well in sync with the clock in the camera's tape deck).

The newer radio tape decks, RDAT machines and digital audio recording terminals are using timecode; it may well become the standard in radio as well as television.

But most radio stations and some television operations do not have this convenience. In these shops, you can log your tape using the tape counter on your cassette machine. When you first put in the cassette, rewind it all the way to the beginning, and reset the counter to zero. That gives you a solid reference point in case your counter is accidentally reset later.

Whether you are using timecode or tape counter numbers, your notes should reflect the number when the bite starts, the in-cue and the out-cue. When the event is over, you will have a detailed list of actualities and their locations on the tape.

This is made even easier if you have a prepared text to work with. Before the speech begins, you can highlight those cuts you'll want to use, and then note the timecode or counter numbers as each bite comes up. Be prepared for some deviation from the text — and be ready to note the counter numbers.

Stakeouts. The opposite of the news conference is the stakeout. These can be tedious and uncomfortable ordeals that yield little. But they also can be very, very productive.

Stakeouts come in two forms: planned, prepared events, which occur most often when officials are meeting and some may wish to avail themselves of the opportunity to talk to reporters; and informal encampments of newspeople who hope to persuade their subject to say something about events.

The organized stakeout is a Washington tradition. For example, when congressional leaders meet with the president, a microphone stand is set up on the White House driveway so they can have a chance to talk.

In Britain, when the prime minister is meeting an important dignitary, there's often a planned stakeout on Downing Street, a few yards from the door of the prime minister's home at Number 10.

When the president travels, reporters are sometimes informed that he will say something "at the ropeline" — meaning the location along the president's route where a rope indicates where reporters may stand.

More common is the informal stakeout — the one in which the newsmaker's intention is unknown.

In Israel, for example, when the cabinet meets each Sunday, reporters are allowed to stake out the entrance to the prime minister's office, just in case a cabinet minister (or the prime minister) is willing to say something. There generally is no mike stand; everyone carries a fish-pole or a shotgun microphone. The results often are disappointing.

This kind of stakeout occurs across America every day, outside closed-door city council meetings, labor negotiations and other events not open to coverage.

It also happens when a person suddenly is thrust into the news. When Oliver North became a household name in the middle 1980s, his house was the subject of reporter stakeouts for weeks. Initially, reporters hoped for some comment from him. After a while, they were satisfied with video of him entering or leaving the property. They rarely got anything more.

Being at a stakeout is somewhat like sitting in the dentist's waiting room: It takes a long time, and no one is looking forward to what happens at the end.

Worse, stakeouts usually take place outside, often in the cold or rain. They can go on for hours, because it's never certain when the newsmakers will emerge. It is therefore important that you think of creature comforts when preparing to go to a stakeout.

One of the most important steps you can take is to protect yourself from the elements. Reporters covering Secretary of State George Shultz on a trip to Egypt once were made to wait in the courtyard of the presidential palace — on a blazing, 98-degree afternoon — for four hours. In that case, water, a hat and sun protection were called for. On the other hand, staking out the British prime minister in April — when it's chilly and rainy — requires bundling up and having plenty of hot coffee at hand.

Another top priority must be preparation to move quickly once the newsmaker is ready to talk. There are no mults at most stakeouts, and newsmakers often are coaxed to say something from a distance — so miking is crucial.

A shotgun mike is by far the best type of microphone to use in an informal stakeout. Keep the power off (to conserve batteries), but have the mike plugged into the tape machine and near at hand. Have your headphones ready, so you can easily monitor the signal to be sure you have the subject on-mike. Your goal is to be able to pick up the mike, turn it on and roll your tape before the newsmaker says anything.

Interviews. If you really want to control the questions asked of a newsmaker, nothing beats the one-on-one interview. These come in two flavors: the planned, formal sit-down, and the impromptu conversation at the scene of an event.

The latter is a staple of local news. Simply pulling a newsmaker aside as a meeting or news conference is breaking up is an effective way of posing your specific questions on tape. The newsmaker has been thinking about the subject for the entire event, so thoughts are organized. If evasion has been the official's strategy, his or her guard may be coming down as the event ends. In either case, the tape will be yours alone, and the questions will be tailored to your story's needs.

Whenever in this informal one-on-one situation, be certain to mike your questions as well as the answers. You never know when something revealing will be said in a fragmentary way — something that requires the question to be fully understood. You don't have to be on camera to pose the question (in fact, it's better to show the official's reaction as the question is asked), but whether it's radio or television, your voice must be heard.

In formal interviews, it's best to separately mike the reporter and newsmaker. Each mike goes into a mixer, and the output goes into the tape recorder. Some recorders have two mike inputs, in which case the mixer isn't needed. Often, newsmakers are most at ease with a tie-clip or *lavalier* mike, which is less obtrusive.

Not everyone has a mixer or good-quality lavalier mikes. If you're doing a one-mike interview for radio, try to sit close enough to the subject to mike your questions. If the setup won't permit that, you can use a small machine and a second mike to record your questions separately — so you can dub the audio in later.

Before going into any formal interview, be sure you have a strategy in mind. Ask yourself what you want to know from this newsmaker — and whether you are likely to encounter any difficulty in getting answers. Your approach to an evasive subject will be significantly different from your handling of other newsmakers.

Some people write out all of their questions, so they know exactly how they want to word them. Others prefer a more general list of subjects to be covered.

In either event, try to anticipate possible answers to your questions, or the subject's possible strategies for dealing with you. Not every interview is a confrontation, but every subject goes in with his or her own agenda — and you must have a strategy for making sure you run the interview.

Part of that strategy is to resist being distracted from the issues you want to explore. But another part is being ready to follow up on facts and opinions that emerge in the course of the interview. If you're trying to pin down an evasive subject, it's important to stick ruthlessly to your questions. But if the subject surprises you with a revealing comment, don't feel so tied to your prepared questions that you can't aggressively follow up on the new information.

Just as you log tape during news conferences and speeches, you should be noting timecode or counter numbers during interviews. This is particularly helpful if you come back to the same subject at various times during the interview, or if you are going to produce more than one story.

File — Fast! You can always tell the wire service and radio reporters at a news event: they're the people who bolt for the door as soon as news is made. We can add television reporters to the list, with the growth of 24-hour news channels.

Getting the story on the air quickly is a maxim of our business.

When Ronald Reagan was shot in 1981, ABC had videotape on the air within 10 minutes. AP Network News affiliates had the sound of the shots being fired in less time than that.

When war broke out in the Persian Gulf, AP reporter Edith Lederer was the very first to get the official word — she was the pool correspondent on the scene with U.S. commanders. She shared the information with her pool colleagues and then filed her story to the AP. Everyone had the information at the same time — yet her speed in filing enabled her to beat everyone else with the story.

CNN and ABC had correspondents in Baghdad as the bombing began that night — and their speed in filing gave them the very first accounts of action from the combat zone.

In each case, veteran correspondents or producers made it their business to find a way to get the story back to the newsroom immediately. They were able to do it on the big story because they had plenty of experience doing it on the smaller ones.

That's why it is important to scope out where the phones are when you first arrive at the scene of a story. You never know when you are going to have to file. Think about the reporters who went to cover a news conference by the Pennsylvania state treasurer in Harrisburg a few years ago. It was supposed to be a routine event.

Who knew the official would take out a gun and kill himself in front of all those reporters? The people who knew where the phones were got the story on the air first.

Once you have the newsroom on the phone, it's important that you clearly communicate the essence of the story before you actually file.

If you have something that needs to go on the air immediately, say so — and explain why. Remember, the person on the other end of the phone is starting from zero, with no idea of what story you have.

If you have tape to file, have it cued up before you call. If you're covering a fast-breaking story, you can cue it up while you are waiting for someone to put you on the air or take you in — but be ready as far in advance as possible. If you aren't quite ready, tell the desk so — don't put yourself on the air or onto tape if you're only going to blow it. Better to take an additional few seconds to be truly ready, so your story is well produced and makes sense when it does hit air.

The flip side, of course, is that you don't want to take too long to get ready: you want to get on the air quickly. Sometimes, it pays to go to air without tape first — when the story is important enough. Tell the audience what's going on, then take a break (even if the anchor in the studio stays on the air, you break away) to cue up your tape. Then you can go back on the air with a more complete report.

That is the thinking behind the AP wire policy of moving very short takes of bulletins or urgents when a story first breaks, and then following up with full-length stories (see chapter 3).

It also is the thinking behind the AP Network News bulletin — a short program, generally without tape, designed to get first word of a story on the air — which is followed by live special reports that include tape and additional details.

Your goal should be to find the most effective blend of speed and preparation. Let the urgency of the story and the complexities of production be your guides, and don't forget: People turn to the radio and television for first word of breaking news. They are counting on us.

CHAPTER 3

Getting the Story: In the Newsroom

There is a tendency in the news business to think of the person in the field as having all the fun. After all, field reporters get to go to the scene of events and get on the air a lot.

Yet it is the people who stay back in the newsroom who make those assignments and who have an important say in what actually gets on the air. And in-studio producers, writers, reporters and editors handle more news stories — and have a greater impact on what gets on the air — than anyone who works a beat.

It's easy to view tape-operations people in radio as audio editors rather than reporters. Yet they interview newsmakers, choose cuts and, in many newsrooms, do voicers and wraps. They make a very large and important contribution to the air product.

In television, it is the producer (in larger newsrooms) who selects the video and the editor who pieces it together into a coherent package. Together, those two people determine how the piece "feels" and how well it tells the story. In addition, the producers who select material from various news feeds have a big impact on what people see every night.

And, of course, there are the anchors, in radio and television, who participate in the selection, writing and ordering of newscasts, and who do the actual on-air presentation.

Each of these people makes news judgments every day, and although the setting lacks some of the excitement of being in the field, the decisions are every bit as important as those made by field reporters and producers. Your newsroom has a wide variety of resources available to it. Making the most of what's out there is crucial to airing the best possible newscast.

The Telephone

There is no more valuable tool for covering news than the telephone. This is most strikingly true in radio newsrooms, where an interview is only seven digits away. But in television, too, the phone is an indispensable tool in gathering the facts that will make up your stories.

Radio and television producers really are reporters — and they should think of themselves that way. The only difference between their work and that of the field reporter is that, instead of going to the scene, they operate over the telephone.

More radio news is gathered over the telephone than in person. That is not a result of budget cutbacks (although smaller news budgets have caused the proportion of stories covered in person to decline); it has been that way for decades.

Most of the information that airs on television newscasts is either gathered or confirmed over the telephone. Even beat reporters do much of their information-gathering in telephone conversations.

Yet the art of telephone reporting is probably the most under-appreciated skill in the business.

Yes, it is easy to get some officials to talk to you: Just call their offices. But it takes a special ability to find people who will give you compelling quotes or information over the telephone.

For example, suppose there's an explosion in a paint factory in the next town.

The easiest shot is calling the local police or fire department. They will tell you where to send your crew or reporter, but the tape they will give you will be dry, official pronouncements ("three companies have responded, and the fire is not yet contained").

What you really want is someone who saw the explosion or who can see the fire. Compare the sort of tape you're likely to get from the two phone calls:

Fire Department	**Eyewitness**
"Three companies are on the scene. Company one responded at 11:37 a.m., company two responded at 11:59 a.m. and company three responded at 12:17 p.m. The fire is not yet under control."	"There was this incredible boom and then a flash of light. I almost fell down, it was so sudden. And the fire's still burning — there's lots of smoke."

There's no doubt that the eyewitness reflects the feel of the story with much greater effectiveness. But it's also much harder to find people who saw the event and can express themselves that clearly.

The key, of course, is to know where to look. The best place to start is the telephone book or a travel guidebook.

In our paint factory example, once you know the address (that's why the fire department call is important), you can start looking for places located nearby — where someone might have seen the blast.

Coffee shops, convenience stores and hotels are excellent prospects. You can find these by using a CD-ROM phone directory, a Web phone directory, a cross directory or reverse telephone book — one that is organized by address rather than phone number — or by using a travel guide. Books that show the locations of hotels on city maps are especially useful.

Often, someone in the newsroom or elsewhere on the staff will have ties to the area where the story is developing. Be aware of each staffer's home town (if the staff is large enough, make a list and keep it at the news desk), so you can take advantage of any information your colleagues have about a particular town or county.

Of course, you should also have your own list of important phone numbers. Make a habit of jotting down the numbers of key locations

— including the numbers of pay phones at airports, important traffic intersections and arenas. If, in our paint factory example, you have the number of a pay phone across the street, you might be able to call directly to someone who is watching the fire.

If this seems wildly impractical to you, it should be noted that the best journalists are almost obsessive about collecting information on where to reach people. Notebooks and phone directories in newsrooms across the country are stuffed with smudged jottings of phone numbers of seemingly obscure people and places that might become important in the future. The reporter with the best Rolodex often gets the story first.

As a last resort, you can try asking the fire dispatcher,local police dispatcher or the local library's information desk what stores or hotels are nearby — and then start dialing.

If you can get through to anybody who is near the scene, you should be able to get some sort of description of what's going on. People like to share their impressions of events and are usually quite willing to help out.

In 1989, during an attempted coup in the Philippines, an AP Network News producer started dialing various homes in Manila. She got through to an English-speaking resident who described the shooting and flights of warplanes overhead — and then held the phone out the window, so the sounds could be recorded!

News Releases

The telephone is also an important tool in dealing with the ubiquitous news release. Just a few years ago, the capacity of the post office was the limiting factor in the delivery of the tons of news releases mailed out by politicians, lobbyists, corporations and others. The pipeline has been widened with the invention of the fax machine and data highways such as AP Express. The result is an amazing proliferation of these propaganda missives.

The news release has its place, but it usually isn't on the air.

Its primary usefulness is in tipping you to a development in a story: a new position by the local lawmaker, a new product by a local manufacturer or a statement by a utility. But always remember that a news release is a one-sided document designed to put its subject or author in the best possible light.

Rule No. 1: never, ever write a story based solely on a news release. There's often useful information in releases, but you must separate the facts from the spin put on them by the author.

For example, let's suppose a local utility is trying to get authorization to build a nuclear power plant, and some local environmental groups are opposed to it. As part of each party's attempt to make the case, news releases will be issued. They may well cite various studies or environmental impact statements.

The utility's release would likely lead with a statistic suggesting that the plant would be safe. The environmentalists' release would probably lead with statistics suggesting that the plant would be dangerous. To use either news release alone would be to miss half the story — and could seriously mislead your audience.

Too many broadcast stories start and end with one party's side of the story. Use the telephone or the in-person interview — and use your own research — to bring in all sides.

The Wires

General news wires are among the great untapped resources in American newsrooms.

In some shops, the wire printer sits off in a corner, on its own, clacking away (well, not clacking any more; today's printers tend to squeal), spilling paper onto the floor. Wading through all that paper seems a chore, and staffers skim right past the majority of items in their on-deadline search for the latest news, weather forecast or scores.

Yet the wire is a rich source of information, and newsrooms that learn to find and use that information have a tremendous edge over the competition.

One tool is the newsroom computer. It categorizes the wire, making it easier to target the information you need. But even then, there's a skill to getting the most out of the wire.

Why should that be so?

The answer lies in the nature of general news wires: they have to be all things to all people. This is particularly true of the Associated Press because of its cooperative nature — the members own the cooperative. The wire must serve the broad range of member needs, from the classic rock radio station's need for birthdays of rock stars to the major market television station's need to know when photo opportunities will take place. Radio needs news for drive time, packaged for radio's needs; television needs news for early-morning, afternoon and late night newscasts, packaged for television's needs.

And all-news radio and 24-hour cable news channels need as much information — fresh, up-to-the-minute information — as they can possibly get.

The AP alone moves six million words each day — and so many people have so many different ways of using the wire, and technology has allowed stations to receive so many different kinds of copy, that it's easy to get overwhelmed and to start ignoring the wire's possibilities.

It's a temptation you should try to avoid. The wires put a lot of information at your disposal — information you can use to make your stories, graphics, features and entertainment programming more timely and interesting.

Broadly speaking, AP wire copy falls into three categories:

> • source material intended to provide raw information to enable you to write a story;

• scripted stories, ready to read on the air;

• tabular material — lists and tables — with which you can ad-lib on the air and which can provide guidance when doing boards for graphics and packages.

Using Wires as Source Copy. The people who write air-ready scripts for the AP's wires, radio network and video services and the people in member newsrooms with services such as the APTV wire use AP wire copy for source information. They use stories written in newspaper style — stories with plenty of detail, including many quotes — to learn about events before writing their own scripts.

Although the wire is not always your only source of information, it often is the fastest and usually is the most complete source of facts available. Understanding how the copy is structured is important to getting the most out of each story.

Newspaper-style stories are written for specific cycles — for AMs, or morning papers, and PMs, or afternoon papers. The AMs cycle begins at noon each day, ending at about midnight, when the next morning's papers are put to bed; the PMs cycle begins at 11:30 p.m.

This means that each story leads with the angle most likely to be important when that cycle's newspapers are being

> Each cycle, APTV, NewsTalk and AP DataStream carry a digest of major stories AP will be covering – sort of a table of contents for the next 12 hours. Each story important enough to be on the digest is called a *budget* story and includes the abbreviation **Bjt** in its slug.

read. A story written Monday afternoon for Tuesday's AM papers will be written for people who will read it Tuesday morning.

While that might seem self-evident, its consequences are that the lead angle broadcasters care about — the event of the moment — may well be treated with little prominence in the newspaper story, since it will be of lesser importance tomorrow morning.

For example, if there have been floods in your state, and the governor is visiting the flood area today, he may be the lead — but his comments in one particular community, comments you might lead a newscast with because they are new, might end up in the fifth paragraph of a 10-paragraph story written in newspaper style.

As each new development comes in, the print story is rewritten, with the new information woven in where it will make sense to the overall story.

These rewritten versions of stories are called *leads*. The leads are numbered, and to call your attention to the new developments, the AP puts editor's notes at the top:

AM-Floods, 1st Ld-Writethru, a0403, 543

Governor Tours Flood Area
Eds: Includes three grafs Jones quotes in Jefferson Park

The lead is a retransmission of the entire story, with as much rewritten as is necessary to integrate the new information. That is why it is called a writethru.

The term *lead* can be confusing. A newspaper-style wire lead generally does not change the story's angle. The lead sentence is often left intact. What makes the copy a *lead* is that it brings new information into the story.

It takes a big development to change the actual lead of a newspaper-style story. That's because the story's perspective (the angle, not the facts) is usually pretty easy to predict 12 hours in advance.

In our flood story example, unless he says something quite surprising, it is likely that the fact that the governor toured the area will be the lead the next morning:

AM-Flood,Bjt,543

JEFFERSON PARK, Calif. (AP) — Gov. Joe Jones toured this flood-ravaged city
Monday and called for federal disaster relief.

This lead is likely to stand up all day, unless the aid is refused, his helicopter crashes or he sees something particularly dramatic. In the latter case, the lead could be rewritten:

AM-Flood,1st Ld,a0403,125

Eds: Leads with three grafs on Jones crying, demanding aid

JEFFERSON PARK, Calif. (AP) — Tears streamed down Gov. Joe Jones' face as
he toured this flood-ravaged city Monday and demanded immediate approval
for federal disaster relief.

"I've never seen anything so devastating in my life," Jones said as he watched
local residents sweep water from inside their shattered homes. "I demand that
the federal government act immediately to authorize disaster relief."

It's important to check thoroughly each version of a story for new information, which may be spread over several widely separated paragraphs. The copy contains important details, which will help you write the story, find people to interview, find local angles and make graphics. The story will, in its detail, tip you to good places to send crews.

This is particularly true because wire stories pull in a variety of angles and datelines and because wire services put reporters in so many places and have so many member radio and television stations and newspapers from which to draw information.

The flood story, for example, might contain a description of a particularly hard-hit home or neighborhood — one not necessarily on the governor's itinerary. The description might have come from a radio station in another part of the state or from a newspaper reporter. Seeing that description would tip you to a good video opportunity,

---

Decoding Print Copy Slugs

story number

priority code

cycle designator

editors note

category code

a0383

r a

keyword (slug)

version

AM-Floods,1st Ld,a0403,150

Governor Tours Flood Area

Eds: ADDS three grafs Jones arrival quotes

reference number

word count

summary line

resulting in a call to a nearby station or the dispatching of your own crew.

The greatest strength of AP's newspaper-style copy is its breadth and its capacity for detail. There is no other instant news source with access to so many reporters in so many places.

It's important to remember that your stories will be structured quite differently from the newspaper-style stories. The deadlines and priorities are different. The audience expectations are, too.

Many inexperienced broadcast writers fall into the trap of automatically following the newspaper story's lead. Their radio or television version becomes little more than a straight rewrite of the newspaper-style story, with the tense changed and the attribution moved from the back of the sentence to the front.

That's a big mistake, something the AP tells its own broadcast staff not to do. Newspaper-style copy is very important to broadcast newsrooms — but only as a collection of facts, not as a format for telling stories to our audiences.

As will be discussed in Chapter 4, the best way to handle this sort of source copy is to read it and put it aside while you write your story.

Complementary to the long newspaper-style stories are AP's NewsMinute scripts. These headline packages move on all AP broadcast wires just before the top of every hour for national stories and at key times throughout the day for state stories.

With the print-style stories for details and the *NewsMinute* as an indicator of the latest developments, the APTV wire and AP NewsPower Max are powerful packages of information.

NewsMinutes can help your television desk keep its story rundown fresh and keep current its priorities for national and state video and graphics. They also are an aid in writing stories, because they point you to the latest angles. As more television stations do hourly news updates, they are finding APTV's NewsMinutes invaluable.

Between NewsMinutes, in order to get breaking news to you immediately, all of the AP's news wires carry *bulletins* and *urgents*.

This copy is designed for speed, not comprehensiveness: A bulletin is usually only one line long, while an urgent is only a sentence or two. Both types of story provide you with the critical information you need to immediately update your story.

Bulletins and urgents generally are followed on the APTV, NewsPower Max and NewsPower+ wires with more detailed accounts, which give you the basis for a 30-second voicer or reader.

When these stories contain new information, they are called *tops*. It is not uncommon to see a story topped several times throughout the day.

In addition, the APTV wire, NewsPower Max and NewsPower+often carry tabular material to complement their scripts. A story about base closings, for example, might start with an urgent, be followed by a tops and then by a list of the bases affected. The list can be used in making graphics, in selecting places to seek audio or video and in ad-libbing reports on breaking stories.

Some stories lend themselves to tabular treatment all the time. For example, the wires carry a list of the Hollywood box office standings each Tuesday, and a list of record and CD sales for major music formats each Friday. There's a table of stock market activity every half-hour while the market is open and many tables of farm and commodity price activities each weekday. Every day, every AP broadcast wire carries detailed sports statistics, including standings, scores, league leaders and the upcoming day's schedule.

In addition, many of the wire's scripts can be used as source material. For example, when AP Network News feeds tape, there's always wire copy to go with it — copy that can be rewritten around the tape. The wire's various feature scripts, which are discussed in the box on the page 56, contain much valuable information which can be incorporated into your own consumer reports, talk shows and entertainment reports.

Using Wire Copy Directly on the Air. The cornerstone of the NewsPower+ service is the continuous flow of stories on breaking news. These items are written for the ear. They are called *separates* and are designed to be used as readers or radio voicers.

When a story breaks, it is put on the wire as quickly as possible. If a story continues to be the lead hour after hour, it is updated each hour. If nothing new has happened, a new angle is taken or a sidebar explored.

Every hour, the top stories are summarized in an *AP NewsMinute* — a capsule summary of the top five stories. In addition, the top separates on these and other stories are retransmitted in a single, convenient package called *AP News Agenda*.

The NewsMinute scripts and the News Agenda move on the wire in time to use at the top of the hour. They are written to be used in the hour in which they are transmitted. If something is scheduled to happen at 1 p.m., for example, the NewsMinute that moves just before 1:00 will say the event "is scheduled at this hour."

To make it easier to identify these newscast scripts, they are numbered — with the numbering corresponding to the hour of the day

AP's basic wire service for radio and television stations is **AP NewsPower+**.

This high-speed service provides a steady flow of the latest stories in air-ready form. Every hour, the top stories are summarized in a five-item NewsMinute, and the top separates are retransmitted in the AP News Agenda. **NewsPower+** also carries SportsWatches, SportsMinutes, BusinessWatches and BusinessMinutes and all of the urgents, bulletins, advisories and features described in these pages.

Newspower+ is available in morning drive, morning and afternoon drive, and 24 hours per day.

The APTV Wire, the service for television stations, also contains the newspaper-style stories described here. **AP NewsPower Max** is a similar service for radio stations with large news appetites.

AP's service for radio stations with smaller news appetites is **AP Headlines**, which provides NewsMinutes, SportsMinutes and BusinessMinutes as well as sports scores and weather forecasts.

All of these AP services provide state and zone weather forecasts around the clock. All provide 24-hour protection on bulletins and urgents, including weather watches and warnings, and a comprehensive morning prep package, including kickers, a look at the day in history, scores and the latest in entertainment news.

they are intended to be used (Eastern time, using the 24-hour clock). The *16th NewsMinute*, for example, is intended for use at 4 p.m. Eastern time. The *16th News Agenda* contains the top stories for inclusion in newscasts at 4 p.m. Eastern time.

The wires also carry regular sports news updates. *SportsMinute* and *SportsWatch* scripts follow the same formats as the general news scripts, although they move less frequently. *AP BusinessMinute* scripts are similar to NewsMinutes and SportsMinutes, but the *BusinessWatch* scripts emphasize tabular material (market prices, etc.).

Using the Wire to Plan for Tomorrow.

All AP wires contain some material about upcoming events. Advisories contain information about how the AP will cover an event or what a station needs to do to get credentials to provide its own coverage. For details on this kind of copy, see pages 63 and 217-218.

In addition, the APTV wire and AP NewsPower Max carry The Planner — a national guide to stories expected to break tomorrow and in the coming days and weeks. The Planner includes contact names and telephone numbers and is designed specifically to provide television and news-intensive radio stations with the logistical information they need to plan their day.

These wires also carry state daybooks, which provide similar, more localized information.

Finding the Copy You Need.

Wire services adhere to a series of practices designed to get copy to you quickly and in a form that is easy to use. These standards, which started in the Teletype era, have been evolving ever since: The introduction by the AP of newsroom computers in the 1970s and of satellite news delivery in the 1980s caused many changes in the way copy is handled. The growth of newsroom computer systems such as AP NewsDesk has accelerated this evolution.

All of the AP's radio and television wires carry feature material to aid in the preparation of morning programming. The AM Prep package has several features:

Today in History contains quick facts about what's happened on this date in the past and whose birthday it is.

Today in Entertainment History focuses on events in pop culture and birthdays of popular performers.

Segue covers the top general-interest entertainment stories of the morning.

Tonight's TV and *Today's Talks* list what's on television in the coming hours.

Scores and Skeds contains last night's sports scores and today's schedule of contests.

Kickers rounds up the funny and off-beat stories around the world.

Format Focus scripts include stories specific to country music, urban formats and rock formats.

Why should you care about the mechanics of wire copy? If you are a wire service staffer, the reason is obvious: You have to know how to get your copy to the right place at the right time. But why should the rest of us — the people who use the wires — care?

The answer lies in the tremendous growth in the amount of information that flows into newsrooms. When there were no satellites and wires clacked along at 66 words per minute, it wasn't too hard to keep up with the copy that came across. Today, though, there's so much information that there is an entire industry devoted to the sorting and storing of news copy. The more quickly your newsroom sees the copy it needs, the more quickly it can get stories on the air. So it is more important than ever that desk people, reporters and producers understand how copy moves around the newsroom.

Every piece of wire copy has a priority code, to determine how quickly it gets out, and a category code, to help member stations sort the copy. These codes have been standardized by the Radio-Television News Directors Association (RTNDA).

The priority code helps determine the order in which copy is sent. If two people in the AP system file stories at precisely the same time, the story with the higher priority will go out first.

Category codes are a bit more complicated. They are intended to provide newsroom computer systems with enough information to allow them to sort copy into various "bins" or "queues" — the way paper copy can be sorted by subject into various baskets.

Category codes help computers differentiate between state and national copy and among various broad subject areas such as domestic news, sports, financial copy and weather.

Some newsroom systems sort copy not only on the basis of coding, but through an examination of the actual contents of the copy. AP NewsDesk and AP NewsCenter, for example, can sort copy into user-created categories by searching for particular words. If, for example, you want to create a category about bulldogs, you could tell the software to set aside all stories that contain the word *bulldog*.

This is a very powerful feature, because it allows you to customize copy handling as your news priorities change.

Let's go back, for a moment, to that fictional flood in Jefferson Park, and suppose that, as an experienced NewsDesk user, you had created a custom "flood" category as soon as the story broke. All stories containing the words *flood* and *Jefferson Park* are stored in that special area, set off an alarm and automatically print out for you. When the story cools off, you might keep the category but take out the alarm and automatic printout. Days later, you might eliminate the category.

Of course, NewsDesk and NewsCenter come with several built-in categories. National and international news, for example, is kept in one place (and further subdivided into NewsMinute/News Agenda scripts, domestic separates and international separates), while state copy is kept in another. Sports has its own category, as does business copy.

One important feature in NewsDesk is the ability to decide whether stories that appear in your custom categories will also appear in the built-in categories. This is called story *duplication* and is controlled in the NewsDesk categories menu.

Do you want, for example, flood stories to show up in "state stories" as well as in the custom "flood" category?

The question is important because, if you have duplication turned off, you won't find stories about the flood in the state category — so if colleagues look there for the most current copy, they will be shocked to see no flood copy at all!

RTNDA Category Codes

a = domestic news
b = special events
c = features
d = national news summaries
e = entertainment news
f = business/financial news
g = state news summaries
h = national headlines
i = international news
j = state headlines, lottery
m= agriculture news
n = state news
o = weather forecasts and data
p = political copy and results
q = sports scores
r = radio network advisories
s = sports stories
t = television advisories
v = general advisories
w= Washington stories

That's why it's critical that everyone in the newsroom understand exactly how your computer's categories are set up and where to look for copy.

Category and priority coding standards are set by a committee of the Radio-Television News Directors Association and followed by wire services and computer vendors.

One of the great advantages of using these codes is that they allow the AP

RTNDA Priority Codes
f = flash
b = bulletin
u = urgent
r = rush
d = daily
a = advance
s = weekend advance

to put control of the wire in the hands of the local bureau. This means that people who work and live in your area make the news judgments about what copy moves when.

AP editors are very careful about what priority is given to every piece of copy. *Flash,* for example, is reserved for stories of transcendent importance; its most recent uses have been the *Challenger* explosion in 1986, the Nixon resignation in 1974 and the moon landing in 1969.

Often, a story's slug gives you a quick indication of what priority the story has. An f-priority story will certainly be a flash. B-coded items generally are *bulletins,* and u-coded items are *urgents.*

The slug is the wire service's way of telling you what the story is about. On a printer, the slug shows up at the top of the story — right after the story number, priority and category codes:

V11001alb—

u abx

^AP-Germany-Hijacking URGENT

> (New York) -- The Federal Aviation Administration says a hijacked German airliner has landed at John F. Kennedy International Airport in New York.

On NewsDesk and other newsroom computer systems, the slug shows up on a directory line:

AP v1100 ua 1alb- Germany-Hijacking URGENT	02-11	3:53p
AP v1097 ur apr— URGENT Network Advisory: Germany-Hijack	02-11	3:53p
AP v1098 ba 1alrt APNewsAlert,0014	02-11	3:53p

There are certain conventions about how some stories are slugged — conventions designed to be sure the wire has a consistent, predictable look so it is easier to use. The details are contained in Part 3, "The Specifics of Broadcast Style," under the specific type of story.

When a story first breaks, it may be covered in a bulletin or an urgent. The story is given a slug with *bulletin* or *urgent* at the end:

AP-California Quake URGENT

After the initial burst of copy, the details will be gathered together into a separate providing a more comprehensive version of the story:

AP-California Quake

When significant new information emerges, the story will be "topped":

AP-California Quake (Tops)

A *tops* slug indicates that there is a new development in a story that already has been covered on the wire. If the new information is urgent, the slug will say so:

AP-California Quake URGENT

You'll note that the "tops" designation is dropped for an urgent or bulletin, since either one obviously provides new information.

Sometimes, copy is too long to include in one computer file. This is particularly true of detailed, comprehensive reports on sports and business. In this case, the copy is divided into two or more files, called "takes." The first file's slug shows how many takes will be sent:

AP-Morning SportsWatch (Four Takes)

Subsequent takes are numbered:

AP-Morning SportsWatch, take 2

An urgent or a bulletin can run several takes, particularly if developments are coming in very quickly. And of course, it's impossible to indicate in the first take how many takes will follow. In the earthquake example used on the last page, the initial urgent might be followed with several takes:

AP-California Quake URGENT, take 2

Urgents and bulletins are intentionally kept quite short, in an effort to move the information into member hands as quickly as possible. It is therefore not unusual to have several short takes in a bulletin or urgent series.

Sometimes a story is so important and develops so quickly that the wire does a running account. The idea is to keep the members up to the minute. A running series is composed of many takes, each one containing a few sentences. Usually, the takes are slugged "Running." In this example, however, the running series started as a bulletin:

AP-Soviet-Major BULLETIN

>   **(London) — Britain's Prime Minister is confirming that there is fear of imminent conflict in Moscow.**

AP-Soviet-Major BULLETIN, take 2

>   **John Major says his information comes directly from Russian President Boris Yeltsin.**

>   **He says Yeltsin, speaking a short while ago from the Russian parliament, had told him that a column of Soviet tanks is headed for the building.**

AP-Soviet-Major BULLETIN, take 3

>   **He says Yeltsin doesn't believe he has much time left. And Major**

says he believes Yeltsin meant that the troops would storm the building.

AP-Soviet-Major BULLETIN, take 4

Major says Yeltsin asked the British and U-S governments to declare Mikhail Gorbachev the rightful president of the Soviet Union. The British leader says he assured Yeltsin that would be done.

He also offered Yeltsin the assurance that he will call for an international medical examination of Gorbachev to counter claims of coup leaders that he is in ill health.

AP-Soviet-Major BULLETIN, take 5

Major quotes Yeltsin as saying that Gorbachev remains unreachable at his detention point in the Crimea. And he says that as of August 19th, a doctor had seen Gorbachev and given him a nearly solid clean bill of health.

AP-Soviet-Major BULLETIN, take 6

Major also quotes Yeltsin as saying he hopes the West will continue to coordinate efforts against the coup and its leaders.

Major says he assured the Russian leader that Britain will continue to push for economic and democratic reforms.

The British leader says he and Yeltsin closed their call by saying they would try to keep in touch with each other in any way possible over the next few days.[1]

The wire has two other means of letting members know about new information: *updates* and *advisories.*

An *update* is is designed to keep member newsrooms on top of small but significant developments in the story. It contains important information about a story—information not worthy of treatment as an urgent or a separate story:

---

[1]This bulletin/running series ran from 12:01 p.m. to 12:10 p.m. Eastern time on August 20, 1991, and was written by AP world editor Phil Soucheray.

AP-Clinton Trip UPDATE

> President Clinton is wheels-down at Heathrow Airport in London.

Note that the copy is not intended for direct use on the air. Updates always have the same category code as the story they cover, which means they show up in the same category queue in newsroom computer systems.

An *advisory* tells member stations how the AP intends to cover various stories. Advisories do not advance the stories themselves; they inform the newsroom about what to expect on the wire:

AP-Clinton Trip ADVISORY

> President Clinton and the other participants in the seven-nation economic summit in London will release their joint communique at about 7 a.m. (eastern) tomorrow. We will carry the text of the communique on the wire as soon as it is available — probably about 7:10 a.m.

> **AP Broadcast News Center**

An advisory always has a **V** category code, meaning that all advisories show up in the advisories category queue in newsroom computer systems.

A *correction* fixes errors made in stories. Generally, a correction retransmits the entire story, indicating what has been changed:

AP-Clinton Treaty CORRECTION

> The following story replaces V1234, slugged Clinton-Treaty, which moved at 9:17 pm edt, to CORRECT by restoring the dropped word "abandon" in the third graf.

Corrections, like updates, are category-specific: The correction for a story will show up in the same queue as the original item. Chapter 6 contains specific guidelines on the filing of corrections, updates and advisories.

More serious errors may be subject to a *bulletin kill* or a *corrective*. They are covered in depth in Part 2, "The AP Libel Manual."

Part 3, "The Specifics of Broadcast Style," contains complete information on the details of wire formatting. Some of the entries you may want to consult include **abbreviations, acronyms, datelines, hyphen, numerals, pronouncers, quotation marks, time of day, times** and entries under the names of specific sports (for information on how scores are handled).

Radio Networks

Radio networks provide a great deal of source material for locally originated newscasts.

Networks are best known for their newscasts, which created network identities when radio was young. But since the 1970s, all networks have expanded their offerings. Some place more emphasis on programming, including music and talk, while others have put their resources into providing a broader range of building blocks for local newscasts.

AP Network News provides several types of tape in its closed-circuit news feeds, with a unique abbreviation for each type.

v = reporter voicer, maximum 35 seconds

w= reporter wrap, maximum 40 seconds

s = scener (reporter on scene), maximum 35 seconds

a = newsmaker actuality

r = raw (natural) sound

c = correspondent Q&A

All of the networks offer some form of *news call* — closed-circuit feeds of voicers, wraps and actualities, which can be embedded in local programs. These feeds cover news, sports, business and feature topics.

Some networks offer extensive live coverage—in anchored and unanchored form — of major events. Most also offer features on various lifestyle topics.

AP Network News billboards have a specific format designed to ensure that all important information is included. Here's a key to the elements in a typical billboard.

cut type   dateline

correspondent

cut number   length   lead-in line   person in tape, if wrap

123-w-38-Hollywood-(Michael Weinfeld with Kirk Douglas)-Kirk Douglas welcomes re-issue of "Spartacus."

124-a-12-(Kirk Douglas, in A-P interview)-"wonderful thing" -Douglas is delighted with audience response at premiere.

125-r-37-(sound of fans cheering as Douglas arrives at premiere)-Applause fades, for production purposes.

Note the lack of dateline in the second and third cuts, since they were recorded in the same place as the first.

Closed-circuit News Feeds. Although they vary in frequency and depth, most network news feeds are the same in basic concept and execution.

The feeds are intended to provide stations with correspondent reports and the sound of newsmakers and events, and with sufficient information to allow the user to write an introduction to the tape.

The material is fed down the network line in bulk form, with the station cherry-picking the tape it wants to use.

AP Network News has the most intensive schedule of feeds, with at least one every hour. In some hours, AP has two tape feeds: national news and sports or entertainment news.

These feeds are described on the wire in a rundown called a *billboard.* The AP sends its billboards on its news wires. Other networks use an AP service called AP Express, their own data links or fax services to deliver hard copy of the billboard — or they billboard the material verbally as the feed begins.

> AP Network News has special expanded feeds for morning drive. For East Coast stations, the 4:32 a.m. (Eastern) feed provides a comprehensive file of morning drive material. For West Coast stations, much of that material is repeated in the 4:32 a.m. Pacific time (7:32 a.m. Eastern) feed.

Written billboards are sent to the affiliates before the feed begins. The cuts are numbered, and when each cut is played, it is preceded by its number.

Although the formats vary, most networks include in their billboards the name of the reporter and/or newsmaker, the location where the tape was recorded, the out-cue, the length of the cut and a description of the contents.

When requesting a refeed, stations can identify the cut by its number. AP Network News feeds are usually at :32:30 past each hour (right after the newscast at the bottom of the hour), so the feed during the 2 o'clock hour would be the 2:32 p.m. feed.

Some networks provide audible signaling to allow stations to automate the recording of closed-circuit feeds. These signals include start and stop tones for each piece of tape.

AP Network News feeds provide an automated cut number announcement, followed by a cut-start tone, followed by one second of silence, followed by audio. The cut is then followed by a cut-end tone.

Some breaking news is so important that the network doesn't want to wait for the next feed to get material to its affiliates. The practice on AP Network News is to pre-feed such material: to play a few pieces of tape down the network line as soon as they are available, billboarding them verbally during the pre-feed and then following up with a wire billboard as quickly as possible. The same cuts are then included in the next scheduled feed.

Live Network Coverage. Some stations prefer to cut their own tape on major national stories, and to accommodate those needs, most networks provide live feeds of major national events. When they are important enough, these feeds are anchored, so stations can air them live. On lesser stories, the feeds are unanchored.

> AP Network News provides its affiliates with an audio channel devoted exclusively to the long-form coverage of important events. AP Hotline provides unanchored coverage of important speeches, briefings, hearings and news conferences, and anchored coverage of such major events as presidential news conferences, shuttle launches and political conventions.

Networks generally advise their stations that these feeds are coming up by making audio announcements on the network and sending written advisories on the wire.

These feeds can be used for strictly informational purposes—to keep tabs on important national stories— or as a rich source of actuality and natural sound.

Video News Services

The explosive growth of satellite services has made the handling of video news feeds one of the dominant activities in television newsrooms.

At the beginning of the 1980s, expensive landline video circuits were used in selected fixed locations, but that was of no help on breaking stories across the country and around the world. For most breaking stories, the only practical way to get video from one place to another was to hand-carry it or to use a microwave truck — and that was limited to locations in a direct line of sight to the microwave receiver.

By the end of the 1980s, stations with satellite trucks could transmit pictures from anyplace where there was a road and an unobstructed view of the sky.

This made it possible for stations to air live pictures they never could air before. It also provided opportunities for larger news organizations to gather and distribute video more economically than ever.

Video News Agencies. These video feeds can do a lot to enhance local newscasts, primarily because they put control of the coverage in the hands of the local staff, rather than a national newsroom. They provide the video building blocks for the coverage of major stories in local programs.

In 1994, AP launched APTV International, a video news service catering to the world-wide television market. APTV has its headquarter in London and provides feeds for every region of the world, including North America.

Most video news feeds consist of *rough-cuts* and *reporter packages*. Rough-cuts include natural sound and sound bites and are intended for use as voice-over material or as part of a locally produced package. Reporter packages include a voice track and, usually, a stand-up.

APTV concentrates on voice-over material and sound bites. Each item is accompanied by a suggested script transmitted on the wire.

Each video feed is accompanied by a text rundown of the contents. These rundowns are transmitted on the wire (for APTV) or over AP Express or an individual network's data feed.

Some stories are important enough to warrant coverage between feeds. Some services carry key presidential speeches, news conferences and congressional hearings live and unanchored. This allows affiliates to carry the event live (locally anchored) or to pull whatever sound bites or voice-over material they need directly as the event is taking place.

Such video can be a useful source of information as you write your story. Even if the material is never seen on the air, the detail you can glean from watching the video can provide depth and color to your script.

Another tool provided by major video services is the live shot. They can arrange live video interviews with major newsmakers or with correspondents. If, for example, you are working on a story about education, it is possible for a service to arrange a live interview with a top Education Department official. When you want to spend some time on a big national story, such services can arrange a live interact with a reporter. Usually, the interact is wrapped around a taped report (a *package*) the reporter has done that day.

Video News Releases. Just as the fax machine has given written news releases a new life, satellite news gathering has made it possible for companies to issue video news releases.

VNRs can be particularly seductive because all of the production already is done for you. They are problematic because you do not know where any of the video came from or whether it is being used in context.

The power of television's presentation is in its use of pictures, sound and words to reinforce one another. Journalists use that combination to give as vividly truthful an account of an event as possible. But the people who issue video news releases have a different agenda.

Like those who issue paper releases, their goal is to tell their side of the story, to their own advantage. This means that, by definition, a VNR is not a news story. It's a commercial packaged to look like a news story.

That's why you should never, ever put a video news release on the air in place of your own report.

What's more, you should never use video from a VNR without confirming where it came from and identifying the source on air. Suppose a company that has been charged with safety violations in a factory issues a VNR to rebut the charges. Was the factory video in the tape shot at the specific factory under investigation? Are the workers interviewed in the VNR in some sort of special position — or do they have their own agenda?

It's easy—and inexpensive—to lift a piece of video from a video news release for use in your own package. It's also dangerous. If that tape isn't what you assume it to be, your station's credibility will be damaged.

Graphics Services

Another area in which technology has made an important difference in the way news is presented is television graphics.

Paint systems are within the reach of most stations today. Most everyone is putting more graphics on the air to make stories more comprehensible and to give the newscast a visual identity.

It's only in the past few years that stations have had at their disposal daily feeds of news graphics. Wire services have been providing photos and color slides for decades, but the newer services provide immediate access to images on current stories, customized for television's needs.

Most of these services come in the form of satellite feeds of finished graphics. The networks include graphics in their affiliate news feeds, and a few companies provide daily feed services.

The newest type of graphics service is the on-line graphics archive. Introduced in 1991, AP GraphicsBank is a digital library of television graphic elements and finished graphics. Stations search for the image they want by typing a description into the GraphicsBank terminal, which in turn searches the AP's catalog of graphic images. Images can be previewed — for color content and composition — and only those that fit the station's needs are retrieved.

All graphics services can be important to the station's art department because they save time. Those which provide finished graphics can supplement the station's graphics and can provide ideas for locally produced images. Those which provide elements can save valuable time by eliminating the need to go searching for raw material. They also give stations valuable copyright protection.

Graphics services also can be important to reporters and producers. Locator maps make physical distances a lot easier to comprehend — making it easier to write your story. A picture of an object or location can help explain puzzling aspects of a story. A picture can communicate substantially more information than any script can — freeing the reporter to use that script to put the information in perspective.

In addition, when there isn't video available to illustrate an important element of a story, a graphic — static or animated — might become essential.

Many have argued that the availability of all this sound and video has bedazzled broadcast newsrooms to the point where they are more interested in the way their reports sound and look than they are in what the reports say.

It is true that having so much to choose from can obscure the importance of reporting the facts. It is the task of the reporter, producer and editor to make sure that doesn't happen. It is easy to mistake the means for the end: As broadcast journalists, clarity and accuracy should be our goal, and sound, pictures and graphics the tools for achieving it.

CHAPTER 4

Telling the Story: Structure

Before you write a word, you have to know why you are writing.

Whether you are a starting news writer or a veteran correspondent, your goal is to inform, using the strengths of our medium to accurately and objectively tell the story.

Accuracy means you have your facts straight. Objectivity means you have accurately reflected the various viewpoints about a story and left the audience to reach its own conclusions.[1]

To write effectively, you also must understand the medium for which you are writing.

The primary strengths of radio, for example, are its immediacy and its ability to give the listener a lasting mental image of the event through words and the actual sound from the scene.

Television stories fall into two broad categories: those meant to be used with video and those that stand alone as "readers." The latter are virtually identical to radio stories without actuality; the former must be written to provide the factual context for the video that will be shown.

There is an additional but critical complication: While most radio and television stations do news several times a day (or even once per hour), some do news all the time. The nature of the writing depends upon the nature of the programming.

Usually, radio copy is shorter than television copy. Both have to be written to the tape. Radio (and all-news television) copy generally stresses immediacy over depth. Television copy can afford to take a somewhat broader view.

---

[1] For a full treatment of accuracy and objectivity, see the beginning of Chapter 2.

In all cases, though, electronic journalism reports fewer facts and far fewer stories than print journalism. Radio and television are no substitute for newspapers. The media complement one another, with broadcasters giving the audience immediate, vivid and often experiential reports on breaking stories, and newspapers giving the audience details, background and perspective. Each medium requires its own special writing skills.

AP's Approach to Broadcast Writing

AP Broadcast style is based on the premise that all radio and television copy must be written for the ear, meaning that every story must be fully comprehended the first time it is heard.

The story must be structured simply. Each sentence must logically flow into the next. The way each thought follows the next should echo the way in which a person would think about the story as he or she saw it unfold.

Similarly, the sentences must be short. Each sentence should make one point. If the subject is complicated and the sentences must be longer than usual, they should be composed of easy-to-digest units.

Basic to AP's style is the use of images drawn from everyday experience. The idea is this: Everyone carries around a store of memories of things they've seen and felt. The most effective storytelling is that which uses those images to illustrate the essence of the event. The trick is to do it without using clichés.

Every writing style has a "feel," and AP's is conversational. This means that we use the idioms used in normal conversation. It does not mean we use slang (unless it is specifically called for) or bad grammar.

As part of our conversational style, we use common contractions such as *it's, they're* and *she's.* However, contractions are used only with personal pronouns. For example, while it is proper style to write *President Clinton says he's going to veto the bill,* it is not proper style to write *The Housing Act's in trouble.*

No matter how readable ("listenable") a style, it is of no use if the stories are not accurate. The central tenet of AP style is that we do not draw conclusions for the viewers and listeners: We present the facts and allow the audience to reach its own conclusions.

Thus, attribution is a key element of every story. Everything must be attributed unless the writer (or, by extension, the AP correspondent) has witnessed it personally.

Attribution should be high in the story and done conversationally. Hanging attribution at the end of a sentence, print-style, is the opposite of AP Broadcast style.

We write in the present tense, particularly in leads. Past perfect and future are preferable to past tense. After all, what we are reporting is what is happening, has happened or is about to happen. Our writing must reflect it.

John Doe is in Chicago is better than *John Doe has gone to Chicago*, which is still better than *John Doe went to Chicago*, even though all three are accurate.

Taken together, logical story and sentence structure, short sentences, the use of common images, the use of conversational idioms, the informal but direct attribution of facts and the use of the present tense add up to a bright, easy-to-understand writing style.

News Judgment: What's News?

A newscast is, in a sense, a conversation with your audience. Before you can start, you have to figure out what to talk about.

Choosing which stories to put into your newscast is at once the most basic exercise of news judgment and the most complex.

Story selection generally is taken for granted: If a person doesn't know what makes a story newsworthy, the logic goes, he has no business being in this business.

True enough. Certainly, some stories are obvious: major governmental actions, new developments clearly affecting war and peace, the death of a major figure.

But this has led to the widespread assumption that story selection is a purely intuitive process ("I know it when I see it"), that there is a mystical, shared knowledge of what makes something newsworthy — and that you either have that knowledge, or you're not qualified to be a journalist.

While news judgment is a subjective art, and there is plenty of room for individual differences, there are some basic criteria that apply to the selection of stories.

Nature of the Event. In a sense, stories fall into two categories: Those people want to talk about, and those people ought to talk about, because if they don't, six months from now they'll wonder why they were taken by surprise.

People want to talk about the big stories of the day: Events which are so dramatic or have such an influence on our lives that we would feel short-changed if we didn't know about them.

Among these "must-tell" stories are disasters, natural and man-made; wars and efforts to prevent (or start) them; important political stories, domestic and foreign; crime and punishment; stories about money; stories about the places we live, including everything from road-building to pollution; sci-

> ### AP Style Guideline
>
> While the "must-tell" stories come first, strive also to include those stories people ought to know about. Our wire separates and newscasts should include both types of stories. In all cases, our focus should be on telling stories that mean something to our listeners, including those which illuminate our society's condition, our economy, our leadership, our science and our popular culture.

entific stories, including health alerts and important discoveries; and major scandals.

People also want to talk about things that interest them, even if they aren't life-and-death issues. These are the stories people chat about around the coffee machine or water cooler. High on the list is news about major personalities, such as entertainers or sports figures, and stories about the funny or amazing things that happen to people.

The second category — stories people ought to talk about — is a bit harder to define. Generally, these are stories about things that will affect us at some point down the road: scientific breakthroughs, economic trends, emerging ethical issues and court cases that could set important precedents.

By definition, this kind of story doesn't have an obvious, immediate significance to your audience: You therefore must include in your account an explanation of why the event is important. The key in selecting these stories is to know the difference between those that are important enough to warrant such explanation and those which are so arcane they're boring.

When it Happened.   News is about change. Broadcast reporting is the art of telling people about change as quickly as you can.

The primary strength of radio and television is our immediacy. People tune in to find out what's going on now — not what happened yesterday or last week.

That's not to say there aren't times when it's appropriate to report something that happened a few days ago. But that's the exception. The rule is: the more recent (in terms of hours), the better.

In choosing stories and deciding what order to put them in, the two questions you must keep in mind are *what happened* and *when it happened.*

As a story about a major event gets older, it begins to fall lower in the newscast. When something new happens, it may be played higher than a weightier but older story. Your aim should be to balance the two factors.

Which Newscast? In addition to considering when the event happened, your story selection must take into account when the story will be told.

Newscasts fill different roles. The local morning television drop-in has different priorities from the hour-long program at 5 in the afternoon. Radio's morning drive newscasts — especially at 7 a.m. and 8 a.m. — require an approach quite different from a noon newscast.

If the newscast you're writing for is designed to give people a thorough summary of the day's events, you will want to give greater weight to the nature of the story and somewhat less weight to timeliness.

A good example is television's evening news program. The goal is to tell people what went on while they were at work — so a major story that broke at 11 a.m. may play higher than a less-important event which occurred at 4 p.m.

On the other hand, a radio newscast will always place more emphasis on immediacy.

Who Was Involved? Let's face it: Joe Six-Pack isn't Paul Newman. If Newman is robbed, it's a lot more interesting to people than if you or I are. The better-known the name, the more important the event.

On the other hand, don't overdo it. If Paul Newman locks his keys in the car, it isn't news — unless the car happens to be on a race course.

The involvement of a big name isn't enough to make a trivial event a major story. It is enough, though, to lower the threshold.

One word of caution: Many people try to promote their cause or product by becoming associated with a prominent personality. You must be alert to the possibility that someone will try to use a big name to draw reporters into giving them free promotion. Unless it has a natural, obvious news peg, any such story should be treated with great skepticism.

The Story's Context. Some stories break quickly and fade quickly, while others seem to last forever. Regardless of how long it goes on, as a story matures, its relative importance changes.

Age is, of course, an important factor: A new story is played much differently from an old one. The older a story, the more likely it is to succumb to what might be called *lead fatigue:* the feeling that "we've led with this story often enough."

But there are many other factors that affect a story's importance at any point in its life. Collectively, these can be thought of as the story's *context.*

Take, for example, the space shuttle story. The first shuttle launch was a lead story for a long time, while the launch prior to the *Challenger* explosion received very little attention. Compare that to the launch of *Discovery,* which restarted the shuttle program more than two years later!

In both cases, the event was the same: the launch of a shuttle. But the story's context had changed, so the event took on greater significance.

This is one reason why it is mandatory that everyone who writes, edits or reports the news keep up with developments in ongoing stories. You must know the story context to be able to intelligently judge where the latest development fits in.

Audience expectation is a very important factor in understanding a story's context. For example, if everyone expects the American and Russian presidents to reach agreement on a treaty, their failure to do so is an extraordinarily big story. If failure was expected, the story isn't quite as earthshaking.

The News Environment. If today's particular development must be viewed in the story's overall context, it follows that the story itself must be viewed in the day's overall news context.

The *news environment* includes the lineup of other active stories; the thematic relationships, if any, between this story and another working story (e.g., an oil import story and a balance-of-trade story); the schedule of news events later in the day; the ages of the various stories.

One of the most obvious ways in which news environment affects story selection is when a big story pulls a sidebar higher up in a newscast. For example, a story on a new type of airport metal detector would be played much higher than usual on a day when there's been a hijacking.

Your Audience. Although this category is the last on the list, its importance should have been clear in each of the preceding ones.

If the goal of a newscast is to inform the listener or viewer, it is logical that the people who produce the newscast must, to be effective, have a firm grasp of who the audience is.

In the case of the local newscast, the audience is broadly defined by the station's signal coverage area. It is more precisely defined in radio by the station's target demographic.

The audience served by a national newscast is less clearly defined. Most network radio newscasts serve stations of many formats (and therefore every target demographic), and network television newscasts, like their local counterparts, serve extremely broad audiences.

An important element in this discussion is recognition that the audience is not static: As the population ages and as viewing and listening habits change, the nature of the audience and its needs change. It is important to be aware of the changes that are taking place and to factor them into your news judgment.

Story Development

Every story starts with a lead. When you choose the lead, you do more than decide what words to use: You determine how the entire story will be structured. As the lead changes from hour to hour, the story's structure changes, too.

The way a story is written grows directly out of the way the story develops. Before we examine the details of strong writing, we must look at the interplay between the developing story and your lead.

To do this, we will use a hypothetical news story — one that is likely to happen in every local market. We'll use this example throughout this chapter and the one that follows to illustrate various elements of good writing technique. As we go along, we'll fill in the story's details and examine how they affect the copy.

Imagine that you are walking to work and you see a terrific fire eating away at a high-rise building. When you reach the office, the first thing you're likely to say is: "A big building's on fire downtown."

Someone else arrives and says the fire department is closing the street. She'll probably say something like this: "Traffic's a mess out there! They're closing Main Street down by Stafford."

"Because of the fire?" someone will ask.

"Uh-huh," comes the answer. "They're stringing hoses all over the place. Traffic's not moving at all."

Later, you may hear that seven people died in the fire. That's probably the first thing you'd mention to the next person you talked to: "I heard seven people died in that fire in the Stafford Building this afternoon."

"It must have been a big fire," your friend might reply. "I heard they had the street closed for hours."

"Yeah, traffic was awful all afternoon."

That's how you tell a story, in person and on the air. You lead with the newest and most important information, but you don't abandon the information that you mentioned earlier and that remains relevant. What stays in the story—and the order in which it is presented—depends on what you're leading with.

The Lead. One of the most important differences between broadcasting and print journalism is that radio and television reporters tell the story as it is unfolding. This has several implications, the most important of which is that the facts change in importance while we are still reporting the story. What was most important in last hour's newscast (or the last segment of our all-news program) may be eclipsed by something new in the next broadcast. In other words, when the story is developing on the air, the lead can change from hour to hour or minute to minute.

Another implication of our medium's immediacy is that our reports can have an effect on the outcome of the event — which places a tremendous responsibility on all radio and TV reporters and writers.

While it is our first job to report the story, it is also our responsibility to do so without causing panic, without unnecessarily drawing bystanders to the scene and without reporting unfounded rumors or speculation which may later turn out to be untrue.

This applies in national and world news as well as local coverage. Consider, for example, the live reporting of missile attacks during the Gulf War. Many military people, including some journalists, saw such reporting as having a potentially serious affect on the outcome of the attacks:

> Live reporting in the Gulf had the potential to be militarily
> damaging on a grand scale. In Israel, one network

immediately showed the impact of Iraqi-launched Scud missiles as they occurred. Only when the network's military analyst in Washington pointed out on national TV that the network was unwittingly serving Iraqi spotters did the network realize its error.[2]

This is not to suggest that there should be no live coverage of any breaking event. Rather, the reporter — and the editor and producer in the studio — must constantly be aware of the possible impact their reporting can have on the event they are covering.

A third consequence of broadcasting's immediacy is that the availability of sound and pictures from the scene plays an important role in the selection of the lead—and may prompt more frequent changes in story angle.

So when first word of the fire comes in, there are several considerations which will influence our reporting. How big is it? How many people are affected? What about traffic — remember, the radio audience is, to a great extent, an automotive one. Is it worth sending a reporter or a crew?

At every stage of the story's development, we must write what we know, and start gathering what we need to know.

Let's assume the story breaks just before 11 a.m. At first, we know little, and the lead of our 11 a.m. radio newscast is quite simple:

> We have word of a fire in the Stafford Building at Third Street downtown.

The body of the story will carry additional information, including who gave us word of the fire, but we'll get to that later. We are con-

---

[2] Renaldo R. Keene, "Dealing with the Media," U.S. Naval Institute Proceedings (August 1991): 69-70. Keene is a master gunnery sergeant, U.S. Marine Corps (retired) and former Vietnam combat correspondent.

cerning ourselves here with the lead, since it determines what's in the rest of the story.

As discussed in Chapter 3, the newsroom should be on the phone with the fire department by this time and might even be looking for eyewitnesses. Reports are that flames are visible, and the building is being evacuated. Our next story — in the noon radio and television newscast — leads with the latest known concrete development:

> The Stafford Building is being evacuated because of a two-alarm fire.

Note that in the lead we included the fact that there's a fire, but made it secondary to the fact that an evacuation is under way. The report about flames being visible is interesting, but not important enough to supersede the fact of an evacuation actually under way.

This fire isn't big enough to warrant special programming, so, once the midday television newscast is over, it's radio's story for several hours.

Now we have an eyewitness on the telephone, and he says he's heard a tremendous boom coming from the building. We cannot report his account without some further checking: If he's wrong, we could cause undue alarm, and possibly panic, at the scene. What's more, even if there *was* a boom, we cannot know whether it was in any way related to the fire.

So we call the fire department (or, if we have a reporter at the scene, try to get in touch with her). We are told that there was a loud, explosive sound in the building, but it is not known what caused it. Thus, our 1 p.m. lead:

> Flames and an ominous boom downtown this afternoon as the Stafford Building is evacuated.

Next comes some solid but somber news: Our reporter at the scene has seen three bodies being removed from the building, and has tape of the fire chief saying three people are dead, eight are injured and several are missing. That becomes the lead at 2 p.m.:

> Three people are dead in the fire at the Stafford Building.

Note that we did not have to attribute the deaths because our own reporter saw the bodies being taken out. Had we not seen the bodies for ourselves, we would have had to attribute the lead:

> Three people are dead in the fire at the Stafford Building.
> Fire Chief Edwin Wilcox says ...

As our next deadline approaches, there's been little change in the story: The fire remains out of control, the three bodies have been removed from the scene, the eight injured are at the hospital, and the search for the missing people continues. The choice of lead depends on the time of day, and since it's 3 p.m., the impact on rush-hour traffic might be of paramount importance. Another factor is the availability of audio. Here are a few possible 3 p.m. leads:

> Downtown traffic is at a standstill this rush hour because of the fire at the Stafford Building.

> Firefighters continue to search for several missing people in the Stafford Building, which is still burning.

> The Stafford Building continues to burn out of control — with several people still unaccounted for inside.

> The death toll remains at three in the Stafford Building fire.

Note that so far, none of these leads much resembles a print version of the story. All of them are written in the present tense, and it is very clear that the story is changing from hour to hour.

Next comes word of a dramatic rescue: Our reporter sees a firefighter emerge from an upper-story window and carry two people down the ladder to safety. Lacking any change in the death toll or word that the fire is under control, the drama takes over the lead at 4 p.m.:

> A firefighter walked through sheets of flame to rescue two people from the burning Stafford Building this afternoon.

You will note that this is the first past-tense lead we have run on the story. This sort of treatment is justified because of the narrative nature of the angle we chose: The story is in the amazing bravery the rescuer demonstrated. We could have used the present tense, but the flavor of the story would have been different:

> Two more people have been rescued from the burning Stafford Building.

> A daring rescue has saved two people trapped in the burning Stafford Building.

The timing of the rescue couldn't be better for television: By the time the 5 p.m. local news hour begins, the dramatic tape will be in house. The show might well begin with that footage and a lead similar to the one radio used at 4 p.m.:

> A firefighter walks through sheets of flame to rescue two people from the Stafford Building this afternoon.

Such a lead, combined with such powerful footage, sets up the drama of the story and provides the context in which the three deaths will be reported.

The next developments demand simple leads:

6 p.m.:　The fire in the Stafford Building is under control.

7 p.m.:　The fire that killed three people in the Stafford Building is out.

8 p.m.:　Four people are still missing in the Stafford Building.

9 p.m.:　Firefighters say they have found the bodies of the four people missing in the Stafford Building.

When the fire is out and the final casualty count is in, the story may begin to slip in importance. It will be treated from a variety of angles for the next several hours or days, starting with the cleanup and resumption of normal traffic and ending, perhaps, with the launch of an investigation into the cause of the fire:

10 p.m.:　Third Street has been reopened to traffic after this afternoon's fire in the Stafford Building.

11 p.m.　Fire Chief Edwin Wilcox says the sprinklers weren't working in the Stafford Building when fire broke out this morning.

This lead would work well in the late television news as well as an hourly newscast. It gives the story a new importance, because of the question of responsibility for the deaths, injuries and damage and because it may have an impact on the maintenance of fire safety systems in all of the city's buildings. By the next morning's drive-time and early television newscasts, reaction is leading the story:

6 a.m.:　City Council Chairwoman Marilyn Friedman is calling for an investigation to find out why the sprinklers didn't work during the Stafford Building fire.

7 a.m.　Grief — and anger—over the Stafford Building fire this morning: grief for the seven people who

> died, and anger over the broken sprinkler sys-
> tem that might have saved them.

Even though it has heard and seen our coverage of the fire, the audience will now turn to the newspaper to get the many details broadcast coverage inevitably has left out. The newspaper account will
take the long view:

> A faulty sprinkler system was blamed for seven
> deaths yesterday as fire swept through the Stafford
> Building, forcing an evacuation and bringing downtown
> traffic to a virtual standstill.
>
> "The sprinklers never came on," said a shaken
> Fire Chief Edwin Wilcox. "Those people didn't have to
> die."
>
> City Council Chairwoman Marilyn Friedman
> joined families of the victims in calling for an immediate
> investigation.
>
> The blaze began in a maintenance room on the
> top floor, Wilcox said, and quickly spread through the
> top half of the 30-story structure. Three of the dead were
> found on the 18th floor. The other four, found only after
> the fire had been extinguished, were in an office on the
> top floor.
>
> "They probably died instantly," coroner George
> Palmer said.
>
> The evacuation and the crowd of fire trucks
> forced officials to close Third Street, blocking traffic and
> causing one of the largest traffic jams in the city's history.

By now it should be clear that the selection of the lead depends upon
a series of interlocking factors, the dominant of which is the needs of
the audience.

If you are writing an hourly radio newscast, you are updating your listeners. While you must tell the essentials of the entire story, the emphasis should be on the latest angle. This varies only slightly when you are writing drive-time newscasts. Most commuters want quick recaps of the top stories at that hour, and the chances are that they haven't been in touch with the news for the previous eight hours or so. This means you must be sure to cover the important angles of each major story, while still emphasizing the latest wrinkle in each.

In television newscasts, there is a stronger assumption that viewers want the story from the top, so you should lead with the major development of the day, not the hour, and work your way along from there.

As all-news cable channels continue to develop, they tend more toward the radio model, freshening the lead each hour with the latest developments, but always coming back to the best available video.

Story Structure. The lead sets your story on its course. Your job as a writer is to make sure it follows that course in a way that makes sense to the listener.

No lead tells the whole story. Just the opposite is true: Your lead should set up the audience for the facts you are about to present.

Once you've chosen the lead, think of the most obvious question it raises. Imagine that, instead of writing a story, you're having a conversation — as we did at the beginning of this chapter. If the lead was the first thing you said in the conversation, what would your partner's likely response be?

Whatever it is, your story's second sentence should answer it. You should then be thinking about what question *that* sentence raises, and answer it. Your story must be a progression of facts that covers all of the major questions the listener might ask *in the order in which they might be asked.*

How this works will become clearer if we look at an example. Our noon radio newscast led with word that the building was being evacuated:

The Conversation	The Copy
YOU	
"What a mess out there! They're evacuating the Stafford Building."	The Stafford Building is being evacuated because of a two-alarm fire.
FRIEND	
"Why?"	
YOU	
"The building is on fire!"	
FRIEND	
"Anybody hurt?"	
YOU	
"They don't know yet.'	There's no word on injuries in the three-alarm blaze, which started more than an hour ago.
FRIEND	
"Well, is it serious — a bad fire?"	
YOU	
"Three alarms. You can see the flames coming out of the windows. There are so many fire trucks out there, they've had to close the street. They're stringing hoses all over the place."	Eyewitnesses say they can see flames shooting from windows on the top floor of the building at the corner of Main and Third streets. There are so many fire trucks, Third Street is being closed to traffic.

As you can see, a story can be thought of as your end of a conversation with your audience. The language is a bit more formal, but the flow from fact to fact is the same.

This is entirely different from the written word. When someone reads a newspaper or a magazine, her eyes can range over the entire page, rereading something that isn't quite clear, referring back to a previous sentence, or looking at charts or graphics that reinforce a point. If she is interrupted or loses her train of thought, she can pick up wherever in the story she wants.

Listening to or viewing the news is harder, in the sense that it is linear. The audience can't rehear a sentence or take another look at a picture. If the listener misses something, it's gone forever. If one sentence doesn't make sense, and the listener tries to figure it out, the next sentence goes unheard, and the whole story goes off the rails.

Because the audience hears the facts only once, and only in the order you choose, it is incumbent upon you to order and present the facts in the manner which is easiest to comprehend. You must do everything you can to help the listener to understand your story.

People do that every day in conversation, which is why we use the conversational model in structuring stories. In conversations, the speaker adjusts what he is saying, based on the reaction of the listener. That can't happen when you'Re writing a story, so the challenge is to imagine how the conversation would go and anticipate how the audience will react to your words. Try to imagine what question a sentence raises, and answer that question in the next sentence.

When a story is poorly structured, the results can be frightfully confusing.

> City Council Chairwoman Marilyn Friedman is calling for an investigation of the sprinkler system at the Stafford Building. Third Street was closed for five hours yesterday as firefighters tried to put out the blaze. There was a dramatic rescue when a firefighter walked through sheets of flame to save two people on the top floor. Fire Chief

Edwin Wilcox says the sprinklers in the building weren't working. It was a five-alarm fire. Seven people died, and 16 more were hurt.

Almost anyone can see that there's something wrong with this story. To analyze it, let's go back to the conversational model:

The Conversation	**The Copy**
YOU	
"The head of the city council wants to investigate the sprinkler system at the Stafford Building."	City Council Chairwoman Marilyn Friedman is calling for an investigation of the sprinkler system at the Stafford Building.
FRIEND	
"Why?"	
YOU	
"Well, they closed Third street—for five hours! They were trying to put out the fire."	Third Street was closed for five hours yesterday as firefighters tried to put out the blaze.
FRIEND	
"Huh? What's Third Street got to do with sprinklers?"	
YOU	
"See, there was this really dramatic rescue."	There was a dramatic rescue when a firefighter walked through sheets of flame to save two people on the top floor.
FRIEND	
"What are you talking about? What about the sprinklers?"	

The Conversation	**The Copy**
YOU	
"Oh, them. The fire chief says they weren't working."	Fire Chief Edwin Wilcox says the sprinklers in the building weren't working.
FRIEND	
"What an outrage! Did anyone die?"	
YOU	
"It was a five-alarmer."	It was a five-alarm fire.
FRIEND	
"Oh, that helps a lot. I asked, did anyone die?"	
YOU	
"Oh, yeah. Seven people died, and 16 others were hurt."	Seven people died, and 16 more were hurt.
FRIEND	
"Took you long enough to tell me. Traffic must have been awful."	
YOU	
"Yeah, it was. Third Street was closed. I already told you that."	

FRIEND

"You did? I don't remember that. And what about the investigation into the sprinklers? You never did tell me what that was all about.'

As you can see, that story didn't make for the best conversation, and the information about traffic conditions, while recovered through repetition in the conversation, was lost to the newscast audience through incomprehension. It would appear likely that your friend would go elsewhere for her news the next time something important happens.

So how can we fix this copy? Just answer the questions raised in the conversation:

The Conversation	The Copy
YOU	
"The head of the city council wants to investigate the sprinkler system at the Stafford Building."	City Council Chairwoman Marilyn Friedman is calling for an investigation of the sprinkler system at the Stafford Building.
FRIEND	
"Why?"	
YOU	
"Because they didn't work when the building burned down yesterday!"	The sprinkler failed to operate when the building caught fire yesterday.
FRIEND	
"Are you kidding? Anybody killed?"	

The Conversation	The Copy
YOU	
"Seven people. The fire chief says they wouldn't have died if the sprinklers had been working."	Seven people died in the blaze. Fire Chief Edwin Wilcox say they didn't have to die, but the sprinklers didn't come on.
FRIEND	
"Well, what are they going to do about it?"	
YOU	
"Friedman has called a council meeting for this afternoon to start an investigation."	Friedman has called a city council meeting for this afternoon, and she says she'll propose a formal investigation of the building's safety system.
FRIEND	
"It was a scary fire, wasn't it?"	
YOU	
"It was a big one: five alarms, and it went on for five hours or so. They had to close the street."	The fire burned for more than five hours. It took five companies to put it out. Third Street was closed the whole time, snarling last night's rush-hour traffic.

You won't find this kind of story structure in any newspaper or magazine. It is unique to broadcasting because ours is such an aural medium.

This can cause trouble for some writers, because so much of their source material is written in newspaper style. While drawing their facts from this copy, they sometimes draw their structure from it, too. That makes for bad broadcast writing.

When using print-style source copy, pull out the facts, weigh them and then hold that imaginary conversation in your head. Tell the story to yourself, then polish it up a bit and commit it to paper.

Tense and Time Element

The same considerations that drive your selection of a lead dictate the tense in which your story will be written. Just as you want to lead with the latest information, you should be writing in the present tense. Broadcasting is about what is happening now, and its writing style should reflect that role.

The present-tense rule is particularly important with regard to your lead. The choice of lead and choice of tense should be mutually supportive. When you sit down to write a story, the habit of thinking in the present tense should drive you to wonder whether you have the latest angle. Similarly, when you *do* get the newest information, that should keep you from slipping into the past tense.

Many times, you will quickly move from the present tense in the lead to the past tense in the body of the story. When

> ### AP Style Guideline
>
> As part of their training at the Broadcast News Center, new AP writers are given this technique for using print-style source copy:
>
> Take the copy from which you are writing and read it thoroughly. Try to gain a full understanding of the story.
>
> Once you know the story well, turn the copy over and put it aside. As you write your own story, don't refer to the source copy, unless you need to find a specific quote.
>
> You'll soon find that you are building your own structure. Rather than relying on the source copy's approach, you'll have to come up with one of your own. That's the single most important step you can take.

the video of the dramatic rescue in our fire story came into our television newsroom, we knew we would want to open the 5 p.m. news block with that footage. To explain the tape, we had to adopt the narrative approach, telling the story in chronological order. That requires use of the past tense.

> A firefighter walks through sheets of flame to rescue two people from the Stafford Building this afternoon. This dramatic rescue took place less than an hour ago, as volunteer fireman Bob Pascarelli saved a 42-year-old woman and her teenage daughter. Pascarelli says the fire was so hot, the

edges of his helmet were singed. That fire is still burning ...

Sometimes, the development you want to report cannot be properly understood unless it is set up with some background. This requires backing into the story, which also can mean using the past tense — even in the lead.

For example, let's suppose that the investigation launched regarding the maintenance of the sprinklers in the Stafford Building discovers that the building owner had bribed local inspectors to approve the building even though the sprinklers weren't hooked up. That's not a story that can easily be told without first reminding the audience of the fire and the related deaths.

> When the Stafford Building burned down last year, the sprinklers didn't work — and now there are charges that a city inspector was bribed to ignore the faulty system. The head of the city's investigation into the fire says building owner Eric Smith bribed city building inspector Fred Mayer. Investigator Claudia Colbert says Mayer was ready to close the building because the sprinklers didn't work, but decided not to when Smith offered him 50-thousand dollars. Mayer denies the charges and Smith won't comment. Last June's fire killed seven people and injured 16 others.

This sort of treatment should be reserved for the exceptional case, when the story so complex that a straightforward "This is happening" lead wouldn't be understood for lack of background.

In most cases, you should lead with the latest news, written in the present tense, and move to the past tense when you start giving background information.

Choosing a story, its lead, its structure and the verb tense you will use set all of the broad parameters for writing a news story. We will next examine the finer issues of writing graceful, clear and powerful news copy.

CHAPTER 5

Telling the Story: Style

Steffens, look at this cable: no fat, no adjectives, no adverbs — nothing but blood and bones and muscle. ... It's a new language.

— Ernest Hemingway to Lincoln Steffens[1]

To a great extent, the process of good broadcast writing is a subtractive one: Take away all the frills you planned to use, remove the stumbling blocks to easy reading, and you'll have a much better story.

In other words, say it simply.

Powerful broadcast copy uses the simple declarative sentence, follows popular speech patterns and uses common images to make its points. The copy is reinforced by the sound and pictures, words are carefully chosen and the writers know that their role is to inform, not dazzle.

All of this takes a certain amount of talent. But even the natural writer must follow certain practices to produce the best possible copy.

Attribution

Your story is only as good as your facts, and your facts are only as

---

[1] Jeffrey Meyers, *Hemingway: A Biography* (London, Harper, 1985), p. 94.

good as the people you got them from — so attribution is a critical element in all broadcast writing. The audience deserves to know who told us the things we are reporting, so it can judge for itself whether the information is credible.

Everything you report should be attributed. Every sentence should clearly indicate where its information came from. The only things that should be unattributed are things that you have seen for yourself.

There are those who will say that such a rule leads to overly stuffy, hard-to-read copy. It's true that having to attribute everything makes it harder to write graceful, flowing copy. Harder, but not impossible. That's a worthwhile trade-off for making your copy accurate and credible.

Just the Facts. The requirement for strong and clear attribution is a basic tenet of journalism. It's derived from our single most important rule: Report the facts — only what you know to be true. Don't guess. Don't draw conclusions. It's easy to make mistakes if you don't attribute carefully.

Take, for example, the muffled boom which an eyewitness told us he heard during the Stafford Building fire (see page 84). For a time, we had the eyewitness account ("There was a tremendous boom in the building"), with no confirmation from our own reporter or fire officials. If you weren't thinking carefully about attribution, you might have written the story this way:

> A large explosion has rocked the Stafford Building. The building already was on fire, and an evacuation was under way when the blast occurred.

This is a pretty dangerous way to treat the story, for several reasons.

First, your only source is a person with whom you spoke on the telephone, who says he heard an explosion coming from the building. You do not know for sure where he was when he heard the sound or whether the often-strange acoustics of central cities might not have made the boom *appear* to be coming from the burning building. The link between the boom and building is, at best, unproven.

Second, the fact that there was a boom, even if it did come from the building, doesn't mean there necessarily was an explosion. It could have been the sound of a large water pipe bursting. Perhaps one floor collapsed (a good story in itself, but surely no explosion). The point is, you don't know.

Third, you didn't attribute the account to anyone: You have stated that there was an explosion as a fact, as if you had seen it for yourself. Poor you, when it turns out that the boom was the sound of an air conditioning cooling tower falling over on top of the building: Will your audience believe you next time you report something?

The way to handle this story is to do a bit more checking and then to attribute everything:

> Flames and an ominous boom this afternoon as the Stafford Building is evacuated. The flames have been eating away at the 30-story building for more than two hours now. There's no word on casualties. An eyewitness says he heard a tremendous boom come from the building less than an hour ago. The fire department confirms the boom came from the building, but says firefighters don't know what caused it.

Note that we were careful to say only what we knew — someone heard a boom, the fire department says it came from the building — and to clearly indicate how we knew it.

There are, of course, some cases where attribution is not needed, or where information that once had to be attributed no longer has to be. When we first got word of the fire, we had to say where we heard it, since we didn't see it ourselves. Why? Because it's possible the fire department got the address wrong, and it is our only source for the information.

But once we've been to the building, or have it from enough different sources that there is indeed a fire, there's no need to attribute it. It becomes accepted fact.

Crime Stories. One area in which attribution is particularly important is criminal cases. If police report that a crime has been committed or an arrest has been made, and that report is the only source you have for the story, it is essential that you pin it all on the police. Of course, anything that is independently verifiable need not be attributed.

Remember that, in police cases, the victim and the accused both have rights. Both must be taken into account.[2]

Sometimes attribution isn't enough: You must handle all police statements carefully.

"We got him. We got the killer," a county sheriff once said after his men arrested a suspect. The man had not been formally charged — and never was. He was released a few days later and could well have proceeded to sue the sheriff and any news outlet that had carried the assertion.

Don't ever say that *John Doe has been arrested and will be charged with murder.* You don't know that he will be, and if, in the end, he isn't, you are in trouble.

Remember, too, that criminal law and procedures vary from state to state. When reading wire copy from another state, it is best not to make any changes in the wording of the section dealing with the sta-

---

[2] For a complete treatment of the legal issues surrounding a person's rights and reputation, see Part 2, "The AP Libel Manual."

tus of criminal charges, since the person who wrote that section presumably knows the exact laws in his state. You don't, and the laws in your state may be different.

This leads to the question of what to do with events reported by police, or in court, that are in legal doubt. You can't very well tack on the phrase *according to police* every time one of these questionable matters comes up.

The answer is a modifier such as *alleged* or *accused.* Such words must be used to make it clear that an unproved assertion is not being treated as fact.

Despite its specific meaning ("so declared, but without proof"), the term *alleged* is a word that often is thrown at any questionable situation. Be careful to apply the word only to those things that actually are unproved. When dealing with stories where there is a legal or factual issue, make sure you know just what that issue is — and make sure your copy reflects it.

In most criminal cases, the question is not whether a crime actually was committed, but whether the defendant is responsible for the crime.

It is important that you know just which one is at issue in a given case. For example, if Mr. X is on trial for murder in the dismemberment slaying of Mr. Y, it is pretty clear that Mr. Y was the victim of a crime, not an accident or suicide. So, we should not refer to an *alleged killing.*

However, whether Mr. X is the actual killer is in question. That is what the trial is all about. Therefore, Mr. X must be referred to as the *alleged killer, the defendant,* or *the man charged with killing Mr. Y.*

If Mr. Y is simply missing—disappeared without a trace—we have another situation entirely. We then have an *alleged killing* and a person charged with carrying out the *alleged crime.* The prosecution will first have to establish that a crime has occurred. Then it will try to pin it on Mr. X.

Remember that *alleged* has synonyms such as *accused, reputed, supposed* and *purported.* And remember, too, that you can turn the sentence around and express the same thought in another way: *The purported spy* can become *the man who is accused of spying,* which is how most people would say it.

Keep in mind also that *accused* and *charged* are not necessarily the same thing. Procedures vary widely from one state to another.

In some states, police may arrest someone and charge him with murder. In others, only the district attorney or a similar authority may file such a charge.

Terminology varies widely, too. In some states, the proper phrase is that someone is *being held for investigation* of the crime. Being *arrested* or *detained* is not the same thing as being formally charged. The charge must be filed in court, usually by the D.A. or by a grand jury. There is nearly always a hearing of some type in conjunction with the formal charge — sometimes a preliminary hearing, sometimes an arraignment. It is very important to know the difference.

Pickups. Another instance in which attribution is very important is when you pick up a report from another news organization. Suppose, for example, a station in the state capital has an exclusive story about a prominent state official. If you pick up the story, you must say that the originating station broke it—and you should cite the station's sourcing:

> A Sacramento television station is reporting that State Insurance Commissioner Joe Jones is being fired. WXXX-TV quotes sources in Governor Smith's office as saying Jones has been given 48 hours to submit his resignation. The station says its sources asked not to be named. Jones has been under fire...

Sources. One of the most difficult tests of accuracy and attribution is the use of anonymous sources. It is a practice to be resisted, but is sometimes unavoidable.

People don't want their names used for one of several reasons:

- they could face dangerous or unpleasant consequences if it were known they were revealing confidential information;

- they want the freedom to express their opinions without being held politically accountable for them;

- they want to influence public debate without it being known that they are the ones doing it.

The first reason is the best—and, to many, the only acceptable—reason for using a source's information without using his or her name. The latter two are manipulative of the media and the political process. They also are by far the most common motivation for anonymous sources:

> The [anonymous] news leak is a major weapon used by government for a variety of purposes: to mislead, to silence a political opponent, to test public or congressional reaction to a program under consideration, to signal the leaders of another nation, to marshal public support for a president, or a policy, to deny an embarrassing story, and, in various other ways, to influence and manipulate the news and the electorate.[3]

In Washington, it is everyday practice for top government officials to appear before reporters, express opinions and make predictions with the strict understanding that they are to be referred to not by name, but as *senior officials.*

---

[3] David Wise, *The Politics of Lying* (New Your, Random House, 1973), p. 412.

It is therefore quite important to handle anonymous sources with great care, committing to anonymity only when essential. When the ground rules are set, they should provide for the most specific possible identification of the source. It is crucial that you establish as firmly as possible who the source is and what his or her qualifications are.

For example, suppose a senator's administrative aide tells you that the senator is about to resign, but asks that you not divulge his role in reporting the story. You might report:

> A source says Senator John Smith is about to resign.

That doesn't give the listener any indication of the reliability of the report: who is the source and why should he or she be believed? Some might be tempted to firm up the sourcing by writing:

> A source who ought to know says Senator John Smith is about to resign.

But *ought to know* or *in a position to know* reflects a judgment on your part — and unfairly leaves the audience in the dark as to the facts of the case. That's a construction that should not be used. You must tell the listener *how* the source is in a position to know. To do this, turn to the facts:

> A source in Senator John Smith's office...

> A source close to Senator John Smith...

In both cases, you come as close as possible to telling the listener just why the source is believable. Your sourcing should be as specific as possible.

Polls. Another type of story that must be attributed carefully is public opinion polling. Always credit the polling organization with the results. In addition, your copy should indicate that the results are based on a particular sampling and reflect nothing more than a statistical projection of that sampling's responses. For example:

> The latest Gallup Poll gives President Jones a lower popularity rating than ever. The poll suggests that less than one-half of the country likes the job the president is doing. Gallup says 46 percent of those responding to this week's poll gave Jones a positive job rating. Last month, 52 percent approved of his work. The poll of a thousand Americans has a margin of error of plus or minus two percentage points.

Note that the story does not say that the president's *popularity* is down; it says that Gallup's *rating* of the president's popularity is down. And it does not say that the poll means that fewer people like the job Jones is doing; it says the poll *suggests* that conclusion. In each sentence, what we report is not where public opinion stands, but where the latest measure of public opinion stands.

Always be careful to prominently attribute poll results, to remind your audience that the numbers are based on a specific sampling (1,000 Americans) with a specific margin of error (plus or minus 2 points) and to say that the poll merely *suggests, predicts* or *estimates* the opinion of the nation as a whole.

Attribution Style. There are several different styles of attribution. The one most often encountered in print is "hanging" attribution:

> Seven people died and 16 were injured in a fire at the Stafford Building today, police said.

Of course, people don't talk that way, and there is usually a more conversational way of using attribution in broadcast copy. The most obvious is to put the attribution at the front of the sentence:

> Police say seven people are dead and 16 injured in a fire
> at the Stafford Building.

This is better than the "hanging" version, but don't get lazy and start
every story with someone saying something:

> Police say...
> The mayor says...
> The president says...

It is much better to work the attribution into the story in a natural
and more graceful way:

> The fire continues to burn in the 30-story Stafford
> Building, and police say seven people have died.
> Sixteen are reported injured.

Or:

> The death toll is now seven in the fire at the Stafford
> Building. Police issued the figure after four more bodies
> were found in the 30-story building. They say 16 people
> are injured.

There are as many ways to attribute a story as there are to tell it.
Don't fall into a rut.

Some writers resist attribution because it's so easy for long titles to
interrupt the flow of the copy. Here's an example from the days
before Boris Yeltsin was a well-known name:

> Boris Yeltsin, the new president of the Russian Republic, says
> food shortages in his country are reaching the critical level.

The key is to separate the title from the name:

> The new president of the Russian Republic says food
> shortages in his country are reaching the critical level.
> Boris Yeltsin told reporters...

Some titles are even longer. They are impossible to get around, but
at least their impact can be minimized:

> The head of the National Oceanic and Atmospheric
> Administration, John Smith, says it isn't true.

Try, instead,

> John Smith heads the National Oceanic and Atmospheric
> Administration, and he says it isn't true.

Or, back into the title:

> The head of the agency involved disagrees. And John
> Smith says the National Oceanic and Atmospheric
> Administration has the facts to back him up.

Quotes. In broadcast copy, the best quote is the one on tape. It generally is much clearer and more interesting to play a sound bite of a newsmaker talking than it is for the anchor to read the quote in the copy.

AP Style Guideline

The words within quotation marks in any AP copy must be the *precise* words used
by the newsmaker. Under no circumstances should different words be used. The
quotation marks are the visual signal that the enclosed words accurately reflect
exactly what the newsmaker said.

It is, however, AP policy to write such quotes in standard English, without reflecting
regional accents. If a newsmaker says "I pahked my cah in Hahvahd yahd," we
would write "I parked my car in Harvard yard," unless it was a story about regional accents. If a newsmaker says "It's playin' time," we would write, "It's playing
time."

There are, of course, instances where there's no tape available: Either the newsmaker wouldn't be recorded, or cameras and tape recorders weren't present when the words were uttered. In these cases, it may be more appropriate to paraphrase or summarize what was said rather than recounting the newsmaker's precise words.

The problem with quotes is the difficulty in signaling to the audience that the words the anchor is saying are someone else's. Stories peppered with quotes have a staccato sound to them, because the anchor frequently is stopping to indicate that the next words are the newsmaker's:

> A problem with the sprinkler system is said to have contributed to yesterday's tragedy in the Stafford Building downtown. Fire Chief Edwin Wilcox says, quote, "The sprinklers never came on." There were seven fatalities, and Wilcox says, quoting here, "Those people didn't have to die." A fire department spokesman says, quote, "The fire swept through the building's top floors within ten minutes." The victims, in the words of the city's coroner, George Palmer, "probably died instantly."

The Wilcox quotes would have made compelling tape, because they captured the sadness and frustration of the situation. The fire department spokesman and the coroner should have been paraphrased:

> Fire Chief Edwin Wilcox says the sprinklers weren't working in the Stafford Building when fire broke out this morning. Seven people died in the blaze, and Wilcox says the sprinklers are to blame:
>
> TAPE: The sprinklers never came on. Those people didn't have to die.
>
> The fire department says the flames swept through the

building's top floors within ten minutes. And City
Coroner George Palmer says the seven victims probably
died instantly.

But what if we didn't have Wilcox on tape? His remarks were
sufficiently important — and potentially controversial enough — to
quote directly:

> Fire Chief Edwin Wilcox says the sprinklers weren't work-
> ing in the Stafford Building when fire broke out this morn-
> ing. Seven people died in the blaze, and Wilcox says
> the sprinklers are to blame. He says the sprinklers never
> came on, and, in his words, "Those people didn't have
> to die." The fire department say the flames swept through
> the building's top floors within ten minutes. And City
> Coroner George Palmer says the seven victims probably
> died instantly.

Note how the use of the direct quote forces the pace of the story to
slow, calling attention to the most important, dramatic piece of information in the copy.

Another approach would be to lead with the tape or quote:

> "Those people didn't have to die": the words of Fire
> Chief Edwin Wilcox tonight, telling reporters that the
> sprinklers weren't working in the Stafford Building when
> fire broke out this morning. Seven people died in the
> blaze, and Wilcox says the sprinklers are to blame. He
> says the sprinklers never came on. The fire department
> says the flames swept through the building's top floors
> within ten minutes. And City Coroner George Palmer
> says it looks like the seven victims died instantly.

The sparing use of quotes can be quite effective. Don't divest yourself of that tool by using quotes too often. Let the tape do the talking.

Using Sound

One of the distinguishing characteristics of broadcast journalism is its ability to take the audience to the scene of the event. The ability to let listeners hear and, in television, see events for themselves is one of the medium's great strengths.

One of the most common criticisms of broadcast journalism is that we let tape drive our coverage: If there's good tape, the story will get more prominent play. By this argument, we are more driven by the story's ability to entertain than we are by its news value.

There undoubtedly have been stories, stations and situations in which this has been true. Tape does play an important role in telling news stories. But this perception about the news industry grows out of a misunderstanding about the relationship between tape, copy and news gathering.

It is critical that the news, not the sound, be the determining factor in how a story is handled. It is important that, whenever possible, your stories have sound — not for the sake of "bouncing the needle," but to make the story easier to comprehend and more interesting to listen to.

It is commonly accepted that television is such a powerful means of communication because pictures and sound combined make a deeper impression than they would individually. Sounds and pictures make things more concrete for the audience, assisting in comprehension. In radio, actuality plays the same role.

Our responsibility is to use words, sound and pictures to better tell our stories. That is why tape is so important.

Not surprisingly, the availability of tape has an influence on how copy is written, as we saw earlier in this chapter (see page 110). If the tape is to reinforce the main points of the copy, the two must be tailored for each other.

The Role of Sound Bites. Actualities are to radio and television what quotes are to newspapers and magazines. They are more powerful than words alone, because they carry so much information: In addition to the newsmaker's words, sound conveys the person's mood (through tone of voice, inflection, pacing) as well as a feel for the scene.

Seeing a quote such as "We're very pleased with this victory" is entirely less illuminating than hearing the newsmaker yell the words so she can be heard over a cheering crowd, or seeing the newsmaker jostled by that crowd as she speaks.

The actuality should speak to the main point of the story. The idea is to use the tape to give the listener the fullest possible sense of the emotion or feel of the event.

As in handling quotes, you must be especially careful to keep sound in context: If the mood was somber but there was one light moment, don't use that moment as if it represents the tone of the event. Make sure your sound typifies what went on.

Perhaps the easiest kind of sound to use is eyewitness tape. Let's go back to the noon newscast on the day of the Stafford Building fire. At that hour (see page 84, Chapter 4), we knew that an evacuation was under way and had reports of flames being visible from the building. We led our newscast with the evacuation. But what if an eyewitness account was available to us on tape?

We still would lead with the evacuation, because it's a concrete development affecting many people and clearly indicating the severity of the fire. But the tape would be used to give the audience a stronger sense of the scene:

The Stafford Building is being evacuated because of a two-alarm fire. One eyewitness says she can see the flames from two blocks away:

TAPE: They're shooting from windows all along the top two floors. The smoke is really dark and thick. It looks awful.

The fire department says the evacuation started a few minutes ago. The Stafford Building, at Third and Main downtown, is 30 stories tall. With all of the fire trucks in the area, traffic is being rerouted to Fourth Street.

This tape is so easy to use because its role is obvious and it's easy to write into: You simply say someone saw something and let the sound roll. In this example, by the way, note that the tape never used the word *flames:* We had to set it up in the lead-in.

Sometimes the scene is so dramatic, or the need to establish the severity of the situation is so great, that you will lead with the tape:

TAPE   The smoke is so thick, I couldn't see the car in front of me. It's scary out there!

Motorist Joan Martin on the gridlock that has frozen downtown traffic because of the fire in the Stafford Building. Smoke has blanketed a seven-block area ...

An important and more common use of tape is to report a news-maker's opinion:

Still trying to put allegations of adultery behind him, Clinton found his failure to serve in Vietnam an issue. An opponent of the war, Clinton signed up for R-O-T-C to avoid the draft, then quit R-O-T-C only to draw a high lottery number. He was furious when a letter he wrote at the time was leaked, apparently from his military file.

TAPE: My life is not going to be damaged by this. But the American political process is going to be undermined if at every turn in this process, which inevitably depends upon people being able to get their message out about what's going to happen tomorrow, a whole bunch of yesterdays start dropping in.

Clinton wasn't alone in bemoaning the process.

TAPE: Electability, as in what Clinton used to have until last week.

Jerry Brown continued to labor in relative obscurity, attracting small crowds and, perhaps more important, few TV cameras.

TAPE: Electability was the engine of this explosion of media coverage of Governor Clinton, and then poof, up it goes, and then poof, there it goes.[4]

As you can see, sound bites also can be used to help explain the meaning or impact of a story. This can be done without tape, but as the examples above show, newsmakers, speaking spontaneously, often say things more naturally and informally than a reporter or anchor can.

And when we actually record the sound of an event — whether it's the rat-tat-tat of gunfire, the U.S. Senate voting to confirm a Supreme Court nominee or the leader of the local teachers' union announcing a strike — how better to bring the audience to the scene than to play

---

[4] Excerpted form a report aired in the AP Network News public affairs program *Special Assignment*. The segment was written and filed by AP Network News Correspondent Mark Smith.

the tape?

Finally, a sound bite can give the audience a perspective on the news that an anchor never can. The need to be balanced, dispassionate and somewhat formal prevents the journalist from expressing wonder or sadness. But when a newsmaker expresses those emotions, the audience can share them:

> Looking over its shoulder as it races toward interstellar space, the "Voyager" spacecraft has provided the first-ever image of the solar system from beyond its boundaries. As NASA released the picture, astronomer Carl Sagan noted that the planet Earth shows up only as a small blue dot.
>
> TAPE: In the picture, you can see that it's slightly blue. And this is where we live — on a blue dot!
>
> The "family portrait" of the solar system is actually six separate images assembled by scientists. While Earth is visible, scattered sunlight washes out the images of three other planets. Scientists expect to continue receiving data from the two "Voyager" spacecraft for the next 25 years. [5]

Sound Bite Mechanics.   Different newsrooms have different rules about the length of audio cuts and sound bites. Tape length often is used as one means of defining a station's "sound" or "look." The shorter the bite, the faster-paced the newscast. Longer bites tend to yield a more relaxed feel as well as greater depth on each story (although there's a sacrifice in story count). As a rule of thumb, the sound shouldn't run so long that it loses its focus or starts to feel long-winded, and shouldn't be so short that the audience

---

[5] This piece was written and filed by AP Network News correspondent Dick Uliano.

doesn't have a chance to mentally establish who's talking and what he or she is talking about.

That broadly translates to actualities of at least 10 seconds and no more than 30 seconds, although many organizations, including the AP, have tighter time limits on tape.

For tape to be effective, the listener has to be able to understand what's being said, regardless of where he or she is. This is a bigger issue for radio than for television, because in the video world, the picture reinforces the sound and, as a last resort, captioning can be used to render the words more clearly.

Radio stations are listened to in a wide variety of acoustical environments, including, particularly, cars driving down noisy highways. Newsrooms must measure their audio by how it will sound in the most difficult circumstance: on an AM radio in a car with a small speaker in a noisy environment. If line noise, poor miking or other audio quality problems prevent the tape from being understood in that environment, better not to use it.

> ## AP Style Guideline
>
> AP Network News policy is that actualities run at least 10 seconds and no more than 20, with the ideal cut being 10-15 seconds in length.
>
> In extreme cases, slightly shorter or longer actualities will be used.

Remember: Incomprehensible tape will detract from the listener's ability to understand the entire story by derailing the train of thought. It's better to go with no sound than with bad sound.

The same rule applies to tape of a newsmaker with a heavy accent. If the tape will work in your audience's worst-case listening environment, use it. If not, don't.

It is possible to use foreign-language actuality, in cases where a translator is available and the tape is important enough to warrant such treatment. For example, during the attempted coup in the Soviet Union in 1991, networks were after any tape of anyone who could shed light on the status of the coup leaders, and translators were kept standing by to translate Moscow newscasts, official statements and man-on-the-street interviews.

When a translator is used, the bite should start with full audio of the actual speaker, which should then be faded down — but not out — so the translator can be heard clearly.

Natural Sound. Some of the most powerful tape has no voice in it at all: It is the sound (and pictures) of places. Natural sound is commonplace in television and has become more common in radio over the past few years.

What makes natural sound different from sound bites is that it's made to be used while the correspondent is talking, so it directly reinforces what is said. This makes it mandatory that the sound and the words match.

> ## AP Style Guideline
>
> Because it serves AM and FM stations of all formats, AP Network News faces a special challenge in judging the audio quality of actualities.
>
> Tape that wouldn't work on an AM station but will work on an FM outlet is generally considered acceptable for network feeds.
>
> This is done to protect FM affiliates, but occurs only when the actuality is particularly important and all efforts to improve audio quality have been exhausted.

If you are covering a flood, and you are using sound or pictures of the water rushing through the street, your copy must at that point be talking about the same thing. It would look pretty silly to be talking about the injured in the hospital while the audience hears or sees water rushing by.

This is what is meant by writing to the audio or video. Once you know what the story is about, and what sound is available, your job is to piece them together so one reinforces the other.

Let's return to the fire story and add some natural sound to our report.

VIDEO	COPY
Sprinkler pipes in burned-out ceiling of building.	Fire Chief Edwin Wilcox says the sprinklers weren't working in the Stafford Building when fire broke out this morning.
Ambulances taking victims from building yesterday. SOT: The sprinklers never came on. Those people didn't have to die. Super: Fire Chief Edwin Wilcox	Seven people died in the blaze, and Wilcox says the sprinklers are to blame:
Wide shot of building burning.	The fire department says the flames swept through the building's top floors within ten minutes.
Victims' bodies being brought out yesterday.	And City Coroner George Palmer says the seven victims probably died instantly.

Note how each sentence is specifically linked to a picture about the same thing.

There are fewer opportunities to use natural sound in the radio version of this story, because the time element would begin to get confused in listeners' minds. The sound of fire engines or even the roar of flames, playing under the reporter's voice as he talked about the flames sweeping through the building, would be confusing or, at best, sound contrived. While the fire was still burning, the story had better natural sound possibilities. Let's go back to 1 p.m., when we led with "flames and an ominous boom." We didn't get the boom on tape, but the flames are clearly audible:

AUDIO	COPY
Sound of flames burning (after two seconds, fade under, but not out.)	This is what it sounds like at the corner of Third and Main this afternoon,
Cross-fade to sound of people being evacuated.	as the burning Stafford Building is evacuated.
	And just a short while ago, there was an ominous boom. The fire department says it came from the building. Eyewitness Mike McCormick says he heard it.
Fade out evacuation sound.	
TAPE: It was this loud ka-boom, it sounded like a howitzer and echoed all over the place.	
	Firefighters say they don't know what caused the sound. There's no word on casualties in the fire, which has been burning for more than two hours.

When using natural sound, be sure to establish the audio or video for a few seconds before fading under for the voice-over. This gives the audience a moment to absorb the first image. Fading the audio too quickly can be confusing and detract from audience comprehension.

Similarly, once the voice-over has started, do not fade the audio all the way down. Leave it under the correspondent at a low but audible level.

Writing into Sound. As we've seen, the relationship between the copy and sound — bites or natural sound — is critical to making the best use of the tape. When writing into sound, you must be certain to set up the listener's ear without diluting the impact of the tape.

Here again, techniques for radio and television diverge. The use of supers (lettering superimposed along the bottom of the picture) in television reduces the importance of mentioning the newsmaker's name in the lead-in sentence. In radio, such a mention is a must, since it is the only way the listener will know who's talking.

Suppose we have tape of Chief Wilcox telling reporters about the first fatalities in the fire:

> "We found three people, all dead. We took them out from the top floor. We found eight more people, looks like they were suffering from smoke inhalation, but they should be all right."

The news here is that three people are dead and eight have been rescued. What bite do we use, and how do we get into it? We have several options.

The usual way of handling this tape is to open the piece with word of the fatalities and then go to the tape:

> The Stafford Building fire has claimed its first lives. Fire Chief Edwin Wilcox says firefighters have found three bodies:
>
> TAPE: We took them out from the top floor. We found eight more people, looks like they were suffering from smoke inhalation, but they should be all right.
>
> Wilcox says there are at least three more people still inside the burning office tower — everyone else has been evacuated. None of the victims has been identified. Five fire companies are battling the blaze in the 30-story building, and traffic in the entire downtown area is badly congested.

This approach works very well. Note how we advanced into the tape by one sentence, leaving the correspondent to include the number of deaths in the copy. If the lead-in hadn't included the number and made reference to fatalities, the bite would have made no sense.

Note, too, how we back-sold Wilcox after the cut. It's important to mention the newsmaker's name when the bite has finished so it is clear who was talking. Remember, people often tune in after the newscast has begun, so they may not have heard the lead-in line.

Another approach is to open the piece with tape, establish the deaths at the top of the story, and then come back to the rescues:

> TAPE: We found three people, all dead.

> Fire Chief Edwin Wilcox, announcing the first fatalities from the Stafford Building fire. Wilcox says the three victims were found on the top floor of the building:

> TAPE: We found eight more people, looks like they were suffering from smoke inhalation, but they should be all right.

> Wilcox says three people are still inside the burning office tower — everyone else has been evacuated. None of the victims has been identified. Five fire companies are battling the blaze in the 30-story building, and traffic in the entire downtown area is badly congested.

Note how our use of tape allows the fire chief to tell the most important news in his own words, while we fill in the supporting information. Where tape can tell the story better than a reporter or studio anchor can, use it. Where more concise exposition is needed, the reporter steps in.

This approach can be taken further by more closely interweaving sound and copy. It's a practice most commonly used in television: A correspondent will go into a sound bite with minimal setup, let the newsmaker talk for a moment, then dip the audio — keeping the same shot on the screen — while the person is identified. This "dip attribution" is useful when the sound lends itself to it — usually when there's a long pause between bites:

The expectations game is already being played, with the leading candidates on both sides insisting they'll do well, but being careful not to define just how well "well" is.

TAPE: I'm certainly going into this as a dog-eat-dog fight ...

(sound under, covering Bush saying "... and, uh, I'm pretty confident ...")

The president tells David Frost he's in it to win:

TAPE: (sound up) ... I think I'm going to be re-elected.

Incidentally, this example is from a radio documentary.[6] The dip attribution is a technique that works in either medium.

None of these approaches should be overused. If you have all of them at your disposal, you will be able to choose the one that best reflects the content of the story, the quality of the tape and the format you are working in.

All of these techniques make clear how closely the sound and the copy are tied. An important part of that link is that the copy shouldn't parrot what the sound says. Here's an extreme example:

The Stafford Building fire has claimed its first lives. Fire Chief Edwin Wilcox says firefighters have found three people, all of them dead:

TAPE: We found three people, all dead. We took them out from the top floor.

That sort of repetition sounds silly, yet it happens all the time. To avoid it, be certain you listen to the sound after you have written the lead-in.

---

[6] "Off and Running," a 1992 campaign preview, written and produced by AP Network News correspondent Bob Moon.

Clear Writing

Say it Simply. The task of the radio or television writer is to tell complicated stories using the simplest possible words, sentences and paragraphs.

As mentioned in the discussion of story structure in Chapter 4, because the audience only hears your words once, broadcast writing must be linear: Each fact must logically lead into the next. The point applies to every aspect of your story.

Just as your sentences must flow logically, so must the words within each sentence. The simpler the sentence, the greater the comprehension. And an important step in constructing simple sentences is choosing simple words.

Simple, direct words can be used in intelligent stories. In fact, they usually make any prose more understandable and powerful:

> Here is a sound rule: Use small, old words where you
> can. If a long word says just what you want to say, do
> not fear to use it. But know that our tongue is rich in
> crisp, brisk, swift, short words. Make them the spine and
> the heart of what you speak and write. Short words are
> like fast friends. They will not let you down. [7]

This paragraph is notable because it consists entirely of one-syllable words. Why use a big word when a little one will do? For example, why say *utilize* when you can say *use*? Why say *exacerbated* when you mean *made worse* or *worsened*? Why write *toxic substance* when you mean *poison*?

Similarly, try to avoid complicated or hard-to-pronounce names which are unfamiliar to the audience and don't add significantly to the story.

---

[7] Richard Leaderer, "The Case For Short Words," *RTNDA Communicator* (October 1991) p. 49. The article was excerpted from Leaderer's book, *The Miracle of Language.*

That's not to say you should talk down to the audience. But some writers use bigger, more formal-sounding words because they think such words make the newscast sound more authoritative. Avoid that temptation. Use simple words.

Whatever words you use, make sure you do a good job of stringing them together. Write simple sentences. The simpler the sentence, the better the listener's comprehension. One of the *25 Ingredients in Good Writing* cited by Canada's Broadcast News is brevity:

> Make every word count. Air time is a precious commodity, and each word you save can be used elsewhere to give the listener more news. [8]

As the AP's chief print writing watchdog, Rene J. Cappon, put it in *The Word*, "The aim is not simply to save words, but to improve writing. The shorter versions are invariably crisper."

In radio and television, the best sentences are simple and declarative. Some examples:

> The Stafford Building is on fire.
>
> Seven people are dead in the Stafford Building fire.
>
> There's been an explosion at the World Trade Center in New York.
>
> The last American hostage in Lebanon is free.

Each sentence contains one thought and expresses that thought as directly as possible.

This rule of thumb should apply to every sentence. Don't waste words. Make a point of searching your sentences for words that don't need to be there. Get to know the delete key on your computer.

---

[8] *Broadcast News Style Guide* (Toronto, Broadcast News Limited, 1988) p. 5.

Simplification Table

Here are a few examples of overblown words or bloated phrases and the plain-language words that should replace them in your copy.

waste disposal facility	trash dump	established conclusive evidence of	proved
correctional facility	jail		
utilize	use	held a meeting	met
determined the truth of	verified	prove of benefit to	benefited
		take into consideration	consider

Many of these examples originally appeared in "The Word."

Informality. One important reason to use short words and sentences is that people tend to think that way. People also think informally. The words they use — those of everyday life — are the words you should use to tell your stories. And the way people thread those words into sentences should be the phrasing you use in your stories.

Familiarity should be your guide. Use words and phrases the audience is comfortable with. Use common expressions to tell the essence of a story — the way your family and friends (the ones who aren't in the news business) do. Your stories will be easier to comprehend.

As an example, take the Iranian hostage story of the early 1980s, when militants in Tehran held American diplomats and embassy staffers prisoner for more than a year. Diplomatic efforts to end the crisis failed month after month, in part because of the divisions among various factions in the Iranian government. It was, to the American public, a frustrating time.

The individual developments in the story were hard to write about because they were so complicated. First one party said one thing, then another said something else, then a third contradicted the first.

It was easy to fall into a conventional, formal way of telling the story:

> The militants holding the American Embassy in Tehran say the only way they will release their 50 hostages is if the Shah returns to Iran. That contradicts Foreign Minister Sadegh Gotbzadeh, who earlier told...

That copy is not inaccurate. It is a bit confusing because it doesn't mention the contradiction — the new angle — until it describes what the militants have to say. And it captures nothing of the flavor of the story. One AP radio wire writer, though, tried a different approach:

> It's happened again. No sooner had Iran's foreign minister made a conciliatory statement about the hostage crisis than the militants occupying the U-S embassy contradicted him.

These sentences are phrased the way people think and talk. This copy mimics the way a conversation about the story might go, so it makes a deeper impression on the audience.

Reporters tend to stray from conversational writing as they become closer to a story or beat. Every subject has its jargon, and in the battle to keep sentences short, it may be tempting to reach for a bit of insider short-hand. The result is usually confusing copy.

One way to combat this tendency is to keep your focus on the story's impact on people. Reporters covering economics, for example, often find themselves caught up in the technicalities of markets, government agencies and banks — when the stories they write really need to be about how those institutions affect the audience. The Word cites a good example of this problem, with the original copy on the left and the "people" copy on the right: [9]

---

[9] Rene J. Cappon, *The Word* (New York, The Associated Press, 1982) p. 14. This book, written for newspaper writers, contains some excellent insights on the use of the language. In addition, the final section, "Bestiary: A compendium for the Careful and the Crotchety," is a delightful collection of usages Cappon considers beyond the pale. "In the matter of misuse of words," he writes, "I allow myself to overstate."

It is difficult to measure or quantify the impact of the energy crisis in terms of plant closings and job losses.	It's hard to say how many workers have lost their jobs and how many plants have closed because of the energy shortage.

Next to economics, government stories are the easiest to write in jargonese — and the most desperately in need of translation:

> President Carter says granting China most-favored-nation trade status could cause friction with the Soviet Union.

The sentence is too long and complicated, and doesn't use words most people use. This version does:

> President Carter says the Soviets might not like it if we grant better trade terms to China.

The story is easier to understand when it uses everyday language. Nobody says "It could cause friction," while sipping coffee at the breakfast table. But everyone has used the phrase, "They won't like it."

While you are composing the story, it feels like writing. But when the story is read on the air, it's just talking — and people like to be talked to in everyday words.

Proper Mechanics.   Let's exercise your imagination for a moment. You're about to go on the air when you knock over a cup of coffee — all over your script! The copy is sopping wet, unreadable, and the news sounder is about to go off. You have to get into the booth. What do you do?

If you're like most people, you'll grab the nearest, latest copy and run.

Now you're on the air, holding someone else's script in your hand,

and you start reading the first story. As you're talking, your eye is seeing all sorts of typos — combinations of letters that don't make sense to you — and sentences that don't read. And you are starting to stumble.

This nightmare — one that comes true in many newsrooms — is one important reason why your copy must be clean.

Following the standard rules of grammar, punctuation and capitalization is mandatory for people who write copy for others. Wire service writers, network news writers and writers who work at local stations all have to present their copy in a form that someone else can easily understand. And, because you never know when someone may have to read your copy in an emergency, even people who normally write just for themselves need to get into the habit of writing clean copy.

Even if you work in a one-person news department (in radio, a common occurrence these days), you should be writing clean copy today if you have aspirations toward working in a larger market. It's just good, professional practice.

You must start with the proper use of words. The person who cannot use words correctly is in trouble with the audience and will eventually be in trouble with the poor colleague who has to read the copy cold.

Some errors are easy to make on paper but hard to detect on the air. They include mixing up words such as *their* and *they're* or using the wrong form of *it's* and *its*. Fortunately — or maybe unfortunately — these words are *homonyms*: They sound the same on the air, even though they have different meanings. This saves many of us from sounding foolish, but makes it very difficult for anyone else to read our copy. In addition, this kind of imprecision tends to spill over into other aspects of word selection (see page 132). Once you get sloppy in one area, you tend to get sloppy in others.

Many of the entries in Part 3 deal with proper usage. The best way to be sure you are using a word properly is to check that section or, as a backup, the dictionary.

The same applies to spelling. There's an obvious reason for proper spelling on news wires. Good practice and readability for others argue for proper spelling in copy written for your own use.

Grammar is the body of rules about how words relate to one another to form sentences. Most

> ### AP Style Guideline
>
> For spelling, style and usage questions not covered in this handbook, consult Webster's New World Dictionary, Third College Edition, published by Macmillan, New York. For more specific guidelines, see the **dictionaries** entry in Part 3 of this handbook.
>
> If there is no listing in either this handbook or Webster's New World, the backup dictionary is Webster's Third New International Dictionary, published by G. &. C. Merriam Company of Springfield, Mass.

people are tempted to run away when someone starts talking about grammar, but in our line of work, it can be an important subject:

> Grammar describes how language works. Many people who write well would have difficulty explaining in grammatical terms how their sentences work. But when something goes wrong in a sentence, a knowledge of grammar helps in recognizing the problem and provides a language for discussing it. [10]

There are many textbooks on grammar. None provides leisure reading, but it is important to have one on the newsroom bookshelf for those times when sentences need help.

Proper punctuation is a function of good grammar, but the rules for broadcast writing are complicated by the need to provide visual clues about how copy should be read. Many of the entries in Part 3 deal with the AP's style for punctuation, including such items as ellipses (...) and double-dashes (--). For punctuation questions not covered

---

[10] H. Ramsey Fowler and Jane E. Aaron, *The Little, Brown Handbook* (Glenview, Ill.: Scott, Foresman and Company, 1989) p. 160.

in this handbook, refer to the dictionary.

With the more widespread use of newsroom computer systems, capitalization has become a more important issue for broadcasters. In the days of 66-word-per-minute news teleprinters, all broadcast copy was uppercase, and many broadcasters continue to write their own copy in capital letters.

But today's news wires are delivered with full upper- and lowercase characters, and many journalists don't want to see all-caps copy or improperly capitalized copy on their writing terminals.

AP Style Guideline

All AP broadcast copy follows full upper- and lowercase rules. This means, for example, that acronyms such as NATO, which once were transmitted with quotation marks around them ("NATO") to indicate that they were acronyms, are now transmitted all-caps only.

The AP has adopted full capitalization rules on all of its broadcast circuits. This edition of the handbook introduces capitalization entries in Part 3. There, you will see many entries that consist of only a single word — showing the word's proper spelling and capitalization.

One final issue on copy mechanics: Pronouncers. When your copy must include a name that is hard to say, provide a pronouncer. That will prevent you from mangling the name because you forgot how to say it. Part 3 includes pronouncers when appropriate, and the pronouncers entry includes a key to the AP's pronunciation guide system.

Graceful Writing

So far, in discussing writing techniques, we have concentrated on the things necessary to competently tell stories. As a cabinetmaker learns how to cut wood, make various types of joints and fasten one piece to another, we have learned to use short words, simple declarative sentences and logical story structure. None of these techniques is purely mechanical, but all can be learned, and all are necessary to the competent writing of broadcast news copy.

But to the reporter, the writer, the copy editor and the anchor, writing is about more than competence. As the primary factor in determining the quality of the journalist's work, it is a craft that requires more than mere proficiency. Truly great writing has grace and an individual style.

It takes a lot of talent to be a fine writer. That's something that cannot be learned from books. A text such as this can point out some of the issues to consider when trying to make your writing more graceful — but success depends upon the individual choices you make every time you sit down to write. The words you choose, the order in which you use them and the way you integrate them with sound collectively define your style.

The Right Word.   Everything in writing comes down to words. Choosing the right word is fundamental to writing clearly, accurately and gracefully. English is a language with a word — and often many words — for everything:

> The richness of the English vocabulary, and the wealth of available synonyms, means that English speakers can often draw shades of distinction unavailable to non-English speakers. The French, for instance, cannot distinguish between house and home, between mind and brain, between man and gentleman, between "I wrote" and "I have written." The Spanish cannot differentiate a chairman from a president, and the Italians have no equivalent of wishful thinking. [11]

Choosing the right word can be a challenge, but it is important if your writing is to be clear and objective.

---

[11] Bill Bryson, *The Mother Tongue* (New York, William Morrow and Company, 1990), p. 13

Some words shouldn't be used because they are judgmental. The best example is the simplest: The many variations on the word *say*. We write a lot about what people say, and we often look for synonyms to keep the copy from getting repetitious. But some of those synonyms put the wrong spin on the story.

Compare these sentences:

> Mayor Lee Turner says he doesn't know what happened to the 50-thousand dollars missing from the city treasury.

> Mayor Lee Turner claims he doesn't know what happened to the 50-thousand dollars missing from the city treasury.

> Mayor Lee Turner denies knowing what happened to the 50-thousand dollars missing from the city treasury.

> Mayor Lee Turner declares he doesn't know what happened to the 50-thousand dollars missing from the city treasury.

In each sentence, we've used a different verb to describe how the mayor expressed himself. The one-word difference changes the meaning of the entire sentence.

None of the four verbs — *say, claim, deny, declare* — is synonymous.

To *claim* is to state as fact something that might be called into question. The implication is that we have some reason to doubt the truth of the statement. *Claim* should be avoided.

A *denial* is a response to some charge or statement. If a reporter asked the mayor, "Do you know what happened to the $50,000?" and he said, "I have no idea," the word *deny* would be inaccurate. If another politician charged the mayor with embezzlement, and the mayor told reporters "That isn't true," *deny* would be accurate.

But what if the mayor, in response to the charge, said, "I don't know what happened to the money." That isn't a direct denial, although he did say he didn't know where the money went. But what if reporters pressed the point?

> Q: "Do you deny the charge?"
>
> A: "I don't know where the money went."
>
> Q: "But will you deny the charge?"
>
> A: "I've given you my answer."

In this case, it is accurate to say the mayor *refuses to deny* the charge but *says* he doesn't know where the money went.

To *declare* is to officially announce. It implies a more formal and forceful purpose behind the mayor's remarks and is appropriate only if he has made a formal statement, such as a speech or an opening statement at a news conference.

Says is the least judgmental of the verbs we've looked at. It means, simply, to express something. It does not imply that we particularly believe — or disbelieve — the statement. It is usually the most accurate choice.

Your selection of words matters. Make sure the words you use fit the facts and don't lead the audience to conclusions. Part 3 of this handbook, "The Specifics of Broadcast Style," deals with the use of hundreds of words. When in doubt, consult that section.

Powerful Writing. Every writer's goal is to make an impression, and the way to do that is through powerful sentences. To write powerfully, you must use active verbs, keep your sentences compact and use concrete language.

Your verbs should be active, not passive. Write that *Joe is demanding more money*, not that *More money is being demanded by Joe*. People think in terms of doing things, and you should write that way.

As we've already seen, your sentences should be lean. Extra words only slow things down. They drain the power from your sentences.

A sentence that is vague cannot be powerful. You should write about real things and real people, telling your audience what they are doing. William Strunk, Jr. advises us:

> If those who have studied the art of writing are in accord on any one point, it is on this: the surest way to arouse and hold the attention of the reader is by being specific, definite, and concrete. The greatest writers — Homer, Dante, Shakespeare — are effective largely because they deal in particulars and report the details that matter. Their words call up pictures. [12]

Use of Imagery. The mental pictures we all have in common are an important tool for every news writer. Even in television, where most stories have accompanying video and graphics, the ability to tap into the viewer's mental archive is important.

Most everyone has had experience with a stern parent, or a traffic jam, or a boring class in school or a playground fight. Many people know what it's like to be afraid of flying or heights or animals. Everyone has had that feeling that he or she might be coming down with a cold. Everyone knows what it's like to be a winner — and a loser.

In each of these examples, it took only a few words to evoke a

---

[12] William Strunk, Jr., and E. B. White, *The Elements of Style* (New York, Macmillan, 1959) p. 15-16.

detailed picture. That's the kind of leverage broadcast writers need in their copy.

When covering a story, look for details about how ordinary people are affected. What is it about the event you are witnessing that impresses you? Does it relate to some common human feeling or experience?

When writing a story from wire copy or information you have gathered over the telephone, look for the same sort of details. If, for example, you are working on our fire story, and you interview an eyewitness, listen (and ask) for details such as how that person is experiencing the fire. If he tells you he can feel the heat across the street, you have a human detail that will make people understand how big a fire it is.

Even matters with which people have no obvious experience can be handled in this way. Here is a story about a mundane experiment conducted in orbit around the Earth — a story made relevant by its references to common human fears:

> Imagine you're sealed inside a spaceship, 185 miles above the Earth — no way out — when suddenly a fire erupts, perhaps somewhere in the miles of electronic circuitry aboard. What happens to the flames in weightlessness? Will they spread faster? Will they be more difficult to extinguish?

> Today, the "Atlantis" crew plans to actually ignite a fire — safely inside a sealed chamber — and capture the flames on film with a high-speed camera.

> On Earth, natural convection pushes the flame upward because hot air weighs less and rises. The resulting air flow feeds the fire oxygen. But there's no "up" up there –

no gravity – and it's believed a flame spreads out, something like a ball.

The results of the test will be used in the development of safety systems for NASA's planned space station. [13]

Note how the lead keys into images we all carry around with us — the fears of fire and confinement. Just a few words (*you're sealed inside a spaceship...no way out...suddenly a fire erupts*) were needed to let the listener's imagination paint a detailed picture. This, in turn, made it obvious why the experiment was important.

The same technique can be applied to almost any story. Writing about the economic health of a local bank? Translate it into terms everyone can understand — how the individual's account might be affected, or how bank finances are similar to, or different from, personal finances.

Writing about national health care? Use a concrete example — someone who doesn't have health insurance or who can't afford coverage.

There are many ways to write a story as an uninteresting, abstract recitation of facts. But by tapping into the power of the audience's memory, you can make any story compelling without getting wordy.

Rhythm. Some words sound better together than others. Sentences, paragraphs and entire stories, much like music, have textures and rhythms. The words you choose will have an impact on the sound of your voice when you read the copy on the air — and on the impression the audience gets when it hears the story.

A series of short words, for example, may sound too staccato for the scene you are describing. On the other hand, you may want some rapid-fire wording to summarize a tense situation. Words such as

---

[13] This piece was written and filed by AP Network News correspondent Bob Moon.

sharp, crack and *burst* are immediately associated with violence. Using them, especially together, gives a story an entirely different feel than if you were to use *pointed, bang* and *break open.*

Listen mentally to the words you are using. If they don't fit the mood of your story, change them. Don't, for example, use words that sound or feel happy in a story about a tragedy.

The lengths of your sentences also contribute to the feel of the story:

> Seven people are dead in a fire downtown.
>
> The Stafford Building burned to the ground.
>
> Sixteen people were injured in the fire.
>
> The surrounding streets were closed to traffic.

The problem with this story is that the sentences are all the same length: The unfortunate soul who has to read this copy on the air will sound monotonous.

People tend to think — and talk — in short sentences. But some thoughts are longer than others, because of their complexity or because they contain more detail.

Short sentences have an abrupt, direct feel to them; longer sentences give the listener a sense of flow. The best copy contains an appropriate mix of the two. The faster you want your story to move along, the more short sentences you'll use.

The placement of long and short sentences within a story is important, too. As the story progresses, the copy, newscaster and listener all gain momentum. If a long and difficult phrase suddenly appears, that momentum will come to a crashing halt, the story will lose direction, and the audience will lose interest.

Complicated titles and other aspects of attribution are most often the reason for sudden loss of momentum in a story, and we have already looked at ways of handling that problem (see page 107). Another common cause is the clumsy handling of an abstract or complicated idea.

> NASA is vowing to go ahead with the countdown for the launch of the space shuttle "Atlantis," despite a lawsuit filed by citizens groups. The count began this morning. A federal judge in Washington will hear arguments tomorrow about the potential dangers of the nuclear-powered planetary probe in the shuttle's cargo bay. If the judge won't issue a restraining order, protesters are threatening to try to scrub Thursday's flight by sneaking into the launch area.

The third sentence really slows the story's momentum. In a case such as this, the best approach is to find a way to distribute the information more evenly throughout the story:

> There may be a lawsuit against it, but NASA is vowing to continue the countdown to the launch of the space shuttle "Atlantis." The count began this morning, even though the lawsuit won't go to court until tomorrow. Several citizens groups want the launch stopped because Atlantis is carrying a nuclear reactor. The reactor is part of a planetary probe, but the lawsuit says it's just too dangerous to be on board. If the judge won't issue a restraining order, protesters are threatening to try to scrub Thursday's flight by sneaking into the launch area.

Of course, there will be times when you will play with the momentum of a story to highlight a particular point. This usually takes the form of suddenly interrupting the flow with a short sentence, most often when you're reporting something ironic or surprising. After allowing the story's momentum to build, you suddenly drop in a very short sentence:

> Griffen was a technician at a hospital in Baltimore nine
> years ago, when he decided to try his hand at robbing
> banks. It was a whim, he says -- just one of those things.
> He pulled it off. Then he gave himself up.

The abrupt change in pacing reinforces the irony of the story and gives it a lot more impact. This technique is most frequently used in kickers.

Many factors contribute to good writing: A strong lead, a clear structure, careful word selection, use of short sentences, variety of sentence length, use of imagery and creative use of sound. An important thread, which runs through all of these attributes, is how the copy sounds.

Whether you are in radio or television, you are writing for the ear. The combination of words you choose must sound right. The sentences must flow not only logically, but aurally. You should guard against sentences that literally take your breath away because of their length. The texture of the copy must match the content of the story.

Broadcast writing is an aesthetic skill. Listen to what you write as you are writing it, for if it does not sound right to you, it surely won't to your audience.

CHAPTER 6

Editing and Producing the Story

In every newsroom, the desk sits in the center of the storm.

The role of the desk in broadcast newsrooms has changed in recent years. The importance of tape, the increasing use of satellites, the important role of graphics and the new economics of broadcasting all have contributed to this change.

The heyday of the radio news desk is over. Most stations don't have news departments large enough to staff a desk: With a staff of one or two people, everyone has to do everything. Gone is the experienced copy editor who tormented the rookie writer day after day, throwing back the copy until the newcomer got it right.

Producing a television newscast is a complicated enough business that a news desk is pretty much required. But that desk isn't very much like the radio desk of old. It's a fragmented operation, with assignments in one area, graphics in another and the actual copy-editing and story ordering somewhere else. The degree of specialization depends on market size — the bigger the market, the more fragmented the desk.

This makes it difficult to generalize about how a broadcast desk works. Our focus will be on the things these desks have in common: copy editing, setting newsroom priorities and constructing newscasts.

The Role of the Copy Editor

Someone in the newsroom has to decide how the copy will read. Whether it's a full copy desk, a story producer or the news director, someone edits the copy.

The editor usually lives in a state of tension with the writer. The best writers always look for new, creative ways to say things. Editors are in the business of making sure the copy is accurate and fits the station's style. There's plenty of potential for disagreement.

The role of the copy editor has changed in recent years because of the availability of audio and video news feeds. Editors today have access to a lot of information their reporters don't have. This is particularly true at the state and national level.

For example, suppose there is a fire in a national forest. A reporter on the scene has access to firefighters and eyewitnesses in that part of the forest, but the desk in the newsroom will be able to see the wire and video feeds from other parts of the fire and tape from officials in the state capital, the forest service regional office or Washington commenting on efforts to assist in the firefighting.

Before this kind of audio and video was available, the copy editor's role was limited to checking the reporter's copy for accuracy, clarity and objectivity, adding any information from the wires and deciding which stories were most important.

In essence, the editor was a traffic cop, making sure the right facts got into the right stories in the right order.

The editor still plays that role. But now, the flow of traffic is much greater. Today's news desk has more information than it can handle. Its role has evolved into that of sifter and prioritizer as well as editor.

Today's editors are virtual air traffic controllers, keeping tabs on the development of dozens of stories, sorting through all of the material their reporters, writers and producers give them each hour. They must try to keep up with the flow of copy from the wire, listen to their network feeds and keep an eye on the clock. They have dozens, perhaps hundreds of faxes to go through each day. And that's all in addition to actually editing the copy.

The editor is responsible for keeping the newsroom up to date. If the death toll in a story changes, he or she must make sure everyone knows about it, and make sure everyone's copy conforms. If a reporter calls in with a new development, the editor must be certain everyone is told.

The editor also must make sure breaking news is written and gets on the air as quickly as possible.

Editors are, of course, responsible for the accuracy, clarity and objectivity of the copy. Often, the editor sets the news priorities, including the rundown for the hour's newscast.

In addition, the editor is a teacher: As he makes changes in a person's copy, he teaches that person how to improve his or her writing. This is a very important aspect of the editor's work. The disappearance of strong editing in small-market radio has had a profound impact on the quality of writing and reporting in our industry.

All of these responsibilities are discharged under unyielding deadline pressure. In some newsrooms, there's a once-an-hour deadline. But at networks, at all-news radio stations and all-news cable channels, the deadline is *now*.

To make matters worse, most of these functions conflict with the others. It is the editor's lot to juggle the conflicting needs and desires adroitly so that the news report is turned out each day in good order while the staff and management remain relatively content.

In short, it is the editor who must say yes or no. Thus, editors are usually not popular people. But good editing is essential if the copy is to be accurate, objective and stylistically consistent.

Fundamentals of Copy Editing

The key to being a good editor is to know how to protect the accuracy and objectivity of the copy while preserving the writer's style. Editing must be a constructive effort, improving both the newscast and the writer's work.

A Light Touch. One of the advantages of computerized newsrooms is that it's easy for a writer to experiment with a lead. If it doesn't work, it's easy to change the copy. This makes it easier for the writer to be creative.

One of the disadvantages of newsroom computers is that it's easy for editors to substantially rewrite the copy they receive.

In the typewriter-and-blue-pencil days, it was harder to make major edits in the copy, so the desk tended to edit only what it really had to. There was a big difference between marking up the copy with the blue pencil and rolling a fresh piece of paper into the typewriter to do a complete rewrite. Many editors would hesitate to cross that line.

Today, the barrier is lower. It's easier to cut out a few sentences and drop in your own — and, in the process, take away the writer's identity. That's a temptation that many editors give in to.

It's unfortunate, because a writer learns a lot more from careful editing than from the wholesale rewriting of the story.

The editor should strive to balance the need to correct errors with the need to leave something of the writer in the copy. No editor wants to leave mistakes in the story. But neither should the editor want to make any more changes than are absolutely necessary.

Ideally, the editor should fix factual errors; remove any bias from the copy; make sure the copy is current; strengthen any weaknesses in the story's structure, sentence construction and word selection; fix any stylistic errors; and do so with a sensitivity to the writer's style. Achieving this mix of goals isn't easy.

Accuracy Check. The editor's first job is to make sure the copy is accurate. This means the editor must be inquisitive, skeptical and well-informed.

Suppose you're editing a story about the six-month investigation into the Stafford Building fire. If you're new to town, you may know nothing about the fire — and it will be awfully difficult to intelligently edit that story. Your first step will be to get some background.

Editors should keep themselves up to date on major stories in their coverage area. This means listening to the radio, watching television and reading the newspapers. In addition, an editor must ask questions. Something that doesn't sound right, that appears to contradict something else in the story or that seems to fly in the face of common sense should trigger a question.

The desk must also have an institutional memory: If we reported yesterday that the investigation has gone on for five months, and today we are reporting that it's lasted six, we have a problem.

Having asked the question, the editor must be stubborn about getting a precise answer. For example, imagine this copy coming across your desk:

> Mayor Lee Turner denies knowing what happened to the 50-thousand dollars missing from the city treasury. Turner was asked about the missing money in a City Hall news conference:
>
> TAPE:　I have no idea what happened to that money. It sure is a mystery that we are going to investigate quickly.
>
> Turner says he found out the money was missing when he checked this month's treasury bank statements.

Your eye should immediately be attracted to the word *denies*. As soon as you see it, you should be on the lookout for the charge he's denying and where it came from.

In this copy, though, there's nothing to indicate that there's anything for the mayor to deny. So it's time to ask the reporter, "why *deny?*"

If the reporter answers, "Well, he said he didn't know where the money went," you ought to ask whether anyone had accused the mayor of taking the money or of knowing where it was.

If the reporter doesn't know, insist that he or she find out. If in fact no one has made such an accusation, you should change *denies knowing* to *says he doesn't know.*

Some writers and reporters will react defensively to this kind of questioning and may accuse you of being picky. That's probably the best compliment they can pay an editor, so be sure to smile and say "Thank you" — and then insist on an answer to your question.

Conclusions and Objectivity. As we've discussed throughout this book, our job is to report what happens and what people say. Any conclusions about whether what happens is good or bad are left to the public. The editor is the newsroom's last line of defense against bias, accidental imbalance and inaccuracy through weak attribution or through jumping to a conclusion.

Reporters can form strong opinions about the stories they cover, and these opinions sometimes find their way into the copy. It is the editor's job to root them out.

Often, a single word can express a judgment about a story. The example on the previous page, in which the word *denies* was used instead of the more neutral *says he doesn't know,* is a case in point. As you read the copy, think about each word and whether it expresses a judgment. If you have any doubt, check the dictionary.

Editors must also watch for instances in which the writer has inadvertently taken an assertion as fact. As we've seen in our discussion of field reporting, official statements to reporters are often motivated by something other than an irresistible urge to tell the truth. Officials "position" issues by choosing which facts to reveal and the order in which to reveal them.

Just because a politician, for example, says he's getting more contributions than anyone else, doesn't make it so. What numbers are being compared? Do they provide an accurate measure?

Sometimes politicians and other public figures say things about their intentions in order to change the public's perception of them. To report those intentions as fact — *Jones plans no "attack ads"* — could prove embarrassingly inaccurate down the road.

From the editor's point of view, this means maintaining a constant vigilance against unattributed statements. Always ask, "How do we know this?" If the answer isn't, "We saw it ourselves" or "It's on the public record," find out who made the statement and insert the attribution.

Similarly, editors must be on the lookout for words and sentences that draw conclusions. This goes along with sticking to the facts. Frequently, a series of circumstances will seem to point to a certain conclusion, but be careful! It may not be so.

The editor generally can spot a conclusion by looking for unattributed statements and for "facts" that don't quite fit their context.

As we mentioned in Chapter 2, in 1984, Pope John Paul II was touring Korea when a man jumped out of the crowd and assumed the position a marksman might take when firing a pistol. There was a loud crack, after which the police subdued the man and took him away.

Was this an assassination attempt? It certainly appeared so to a reporter at the scene, who filed a story that shots had been fired at the pope's vehicle.

The man did indeed hold a pistol and did indeed pull the trigger —
but it was a starter's pistol, containing blanks. No shots were fired.

How could an editor know this?

The answer lies in what the story was missing. There was no word on
the "popemobile" swerving or hurrying from the scene. No one saw
anybody get hit, and no one saw any marks on the vehicle. Nobody
mentioned a hospital or a doctor. The pope simply continued on his
way. None of the things one would expect in these circumstances
materialized — but that one conclusion, that the pistol contained bullets, was fatal to the story.

You may be thinking that it's stretching a bit far to think that an editor could catch such a conclusion, given the circumstances. It certainly would take a keen eye, particularly under deadline pressure.
But consider this: Three years earlier, the same thing happened in
London. Someone fired a starter pistol at Queen Elizabeth II while
she was in a royal procession near Buckingham Palace. Any editor
who remembered that (hence the importance of being well back-
grounded) would be more likely to be suspicious of the pope story.
All it would have taken was a question or two.

The Latest Information. Because editors now have access to live
audio and video feeds, it is possible to keep on top of a story as it is
unfolding. More and more, editors are in a position to know whether
a story has changed since the copy was written.

This makes the monitoring of story development and the dissemina-
tion of information throughout the newsroom a crucial function of
the news desk. The copy editor and the assignment editor need to
work closely to make sure the copy about to go on the air isn't over-
taken by developments. In addition, fresh information, including
word on when things are expected to happen and when they actually
occur, must be distributed to all writers, anchors and those producers or reporters who are involved in covering the story.

Given the amount of information now available in real time, most newsrooms face the problem of managing the distribution of facts among the various members of the staff.

| **AP Style Guideline** |
| It is the responsibility of the world editor at the Broadcast News Center to send a computer "read me" message to all BNC terminals whenever a major development occurs in a story. |

Some newsrooms deal with this by having everyone work from the same pool of copy, either in the newsroom computer or through packets of printed copy. Others distribute word of developments to all of the players as soon as the information is available.

Making the Copy Read Well. As we've seen, an editor must be careful not to inadvertently stifle creativity in the name of consistency. It is not the editor's job to rewrite everything that crosses the desk just to fit some preconceived formula of what the story should say. But at the same time, the editor must ensure that the writer's words say what they are meant to say.

Copy may be factually correct, but if it doesn't read well it is wasted effort. If the copy is turgid and stale, it must be brought back to life.

When at all possible, copy should be given back to the writer with a clear explanation of what is wrong with it. This is the only way the writer will learn.

Often, time does not permit the writer to redo the copy. After the editor has made the changes, he or she should make sure the writer sees what edits were made, and has a chance to ask why they were necessary.

As a practical matter, the way to make copy more readable without rewriting it is to isolate the problem and work on only that aspect of the copy. Let's take a specific example:

> Representatives of U-S are to go before the World
> Court in the Netherlands this   morning — to argue that
> they have hard evidence that Libya was involved in the
> bombing of Pan Am Flight 103.   Yesterday — Libya
> denied this before the International Court of Justice —
> and asked for protection from attack or international
> sanctions.   The United Nations is discussing possible
> sanctions against Libya — and diplomats now beleive
> they could be approved by next week.

This story does not suffer from any fatal defect, but it could be
improved with the restoration of the dropped word *the* before U-S in
the lead and with some tightening.

The lead is too long. It could be substantially shortened by taking a
different approach — for example, splitting the "hard evidence" angle
from the calendar angle. You might make that suggestion if the
writer has time to redo the story.

But if there isn't time for a rewrite, there are some ways you can
shorten the lead without gutting it:

> Representatives of the U-S go before the World Court this
> morning to present hard evidence that Libya was involved
> in the bombing of Pan Am flight 103.

Note that we removed the location of the court and made the sentence more direct: *to present hard evidence* rather than *to argue that
they have hard evidence.*

It's possible to write such a direct lead only when the nature of the
evidence is well established, as was true in this case.

The second sentence has Libya denying something, but it is unclear
whether *denial* refers to the American claim of hard evidence or the
charge that Libya actually was involved in the bombing. Our goal is to
make that more specific without losing the nice connection to the lead:

> Yesterday, Libya denied involvement, and it asked for
> protection from attack or international sanctions.

We also took out the second reference to the court, both because it
was confusing (*International Court of Justice* is the formal name;
World Court is what most people call it) and because it needlessly
slowed down the sentence.

Finally, we need to strengthen the link between the second and third
sentences, to make clear that the court hearing and the Security
Council action are directly related:

> Those sanctions are being discussed by the U-N Security
> Council — and diplomats now beleive they could be
> approved by next week.

We also fixed the spelling error in *believe*.

The story is now shorter and sharper, but retains the flavor of the
original:

> Representatives of the U-S go before the World Court
> this morning to present hard evidence that Libya was
> involved in the bombing of Pan Am flight 103. Yesterday,
> Libya denied involvement, and it asked for protection
> from attack or international sanctions. Those sanctions
> are being discussed by the United Nations — and diplo-
> mats now believe they could be approved by next week.

Don't let the writer's pride keep you from pruning the copy. You're
making the writer look better, after all. No one is too good to be edited, and any sentence can be tightened up, including this one.

Be Prepared and Prepare Others. Editors are always hungry
for information. Whether it's the definition of a word or the time an
event is scheduled to take place, having the information close at

hand is critical for a desk working on deadline.

The editor's traditional reference book is the dictionary. The desk must always be mindful of spelling, punctuation, correct pronunciation and all of the other aspects of copy mechanics. In addition to the dictionary and this handbook it is a good idea to have a thesaurus and a gazetteer on hand for easy reference.

Factual references are important, too. Your own files, including the station's morgue and clippings from other sources, are invaluable. An almanac can be an important source of information, as can books listing sources for various types of information.

The Internet can be an invaluable source of information, but be very careful to verify what you find there. It's easy to create fake or misleading Web sites, and you don't want to put false information on the air because you were fooled by one.

In addition, your news department's daily coverage list and planning calendar are important: You don't want to be editing a story about an upcoming city council meeting only to find out it has already begun!

Finally, it is a good idea to keep a log of stories you are working on and to pass that log onto the next shift. In small-market radio where the staff is larger than one, this is generally done by posting the list on the bulletin board. Even if you are a one-person news department, it's important to share such information with the rest of the air staff, so everyone knows when important events, including sporting events, are taking place.

The Station Desk and the Wire Desk

Wire services maintain 24-hour national desk operations and keep their state bureaus open for most of the day (and often around the clock). The wires spend a lot of time advising stations what is being worked on and how it will affect the newsroom. If you're at a wire desk, you have to know how to keep stations informed of coverage plans, of changing information and of errors that need to be corrected. If you're at a station, understanding how a wire desk makes these decisions will help you use the wire more effectively.

Advisories. The simplest way for the wire desk to give its stations logistical and coverage information is through the *advisory*. These messages are intended for station information only: An advisory is never intended for use on the air.

Advisories are used to tell stations how the desk plans to handle a story, what features are coming up and who's on the desk at the state and national levels. Advisories also carry information about technical problems, state contests and style changes.

Most newsroom computer systems put advisories in a separate area. Advisories have a **v** category code.

Updates. An *update* pertains to developments in a story. It, too, is not intended for use directly on the air, although the information it contains can be used to update your own story.

Updates are used to keep the stations informed of minor story changes — developments that are not important enough to warrant a new version of the story.

For example, if the president is on a foreign trip, the departures and arrivals of Air Force One are not worth a new version of the story, but would be included in an update.

An update is given the same category code as the story it pertains to. An update to a domestic story, for example, would have an **a** category code.

To illustrate the role of advisories and updates, and the difference between them, let's look at the State of the Union message the president delivers each January. The wire would first issue an advisory:

ADVISORY

President Clinton will deliver his State of the Union address at 9 p.m. (Eastern) on January 28.

We will provide a running series on the speech's specific proposals.

AP Broadcast News Center

An update would be sent when the speech begins:

UPDATE

President Clinton has begun his State of the Union message.

AP Broadcast News Center

Once news is made, the story will be handled as outlined in the initial advisory. But when the speech is over — a development not worth a story on its own — an update will be sent.

NewsAlerts. Broadcasting is a real-time business, and it is important that stations get information from their wire service as quickly as possible. Sometimes they want the information before a full story can be written.

To accommodate this need, AP transmits a *NewsAlert* when an important story breaks.

A NewsAlert is a headline: *Earthquake strikes northern Japan.* It is intended to give stations the basic information they need to know when something significant has happened. A NewsAlert is followed by a story.

The NewsAlert does not replace the bulletin or urgent. A bulletin story doesn't need NewsAlert treatment, since the one sentence that would be in the NewsAlert is packaged as a bulletin instead.

Although NewsAlerts are not complete enough to be considered air-worthy, the information is solid, and they can be used for ad-libbing purposes.

Corrections. Nobody's perfect, and when you file millions of words each day, mistakes are bound to creep in. When a wire service makes a mistake, it has an obligation to correct the error as quickly as human-ly possible.

> **AP Style Guideline**
>
> The AP's broadcast wires have adopted the practice of repeating the entire story, in its corrected form, when an error is discovered.

Unless the mistake involves libel, it is fixed with the transmission of a *correction.*

Errors of a greater magnitude are subject to a *kill, withhold* or *elimi-nation.* For details, see Section 2, "The AP Libel Manual."

A correction is intended to clearly indicate the location and nature of the error and the way to fix it.

The correction starts with a paragraph indicating which story is being corrected and what is being fixed. The full story then follows:

U-S - Libya CORRECTION

News Directors: The following story replaces V1234, slugged U-S - Libya, to CORRECT the flight number in the first sentence to 103.

(The Hague, The Netherlands) — Representatives of the U-S go before the World Court this morning — to present hard evidence that Libya was involved in the bombing of Pan Am flight 103. Yesterday, Libya denied

involvement, and it asked for protection from attack or international sanctions.
Those sanctions are being discussed by the United Nations — and diplomats
now believe they could be approved by next week.

A correction is given the same category code as the story it pertains to. A correction to a domestic story, for example, would have an **a** category code. All corrections are transmitted with an urgent code or higher.

Corrections are used to fix mistakes made by the wire service. If the wire accurately reported an erroneous statement by someone else, that person's self-correction is reported as a news development.

For example, if police say three people have died in an accident, and the wire service quotes police as saying four people died, a correction will be issued.

But if police say three people have died, the wire service reports it accurately, and then police say, "We were wrong. It was two people who died," the story is topped with the new information (*Police have revised the death toll...*).

General Copy Flow. Generally, a news wire is a single pipeline through which all copy flows to the radio or television station. This imposes on the wire desk the task of making sure the right copy goes in the right order.

This task was once quite simple. Whatever the telegrapher at the wire service put on the wire, everyone got. When the national desk needed to file a story, an operator in New York pressed the keys and the copy flowed. When it was time for state copy, the wire "split," and each local bureau had control of its local wire.

This system had the strength of simplicity — but the weakness of inflexibility. It was hard for stories to cross state lines: If a story broke in California but involved a man from Tennessee, how could the copy filed locally in Los Angeles get to Memphis?

The advent of computers made it possible, and the introduction of satellite technology made it easy.

But those two developments also made managing the copy flow on the wire a very complicated business. Chapter 3 (see pages 56-59) contains details on the mechanics of wire coding and how it affects copy flow.

A primary function of the wire desk at the state and national level is making sure that information streams smoothly to the stations.

As we have seen, wire copy is a mix of air-ready copy, ad-lib material, source copy and advisories. As stories change, the information is relayed to stations as quickly as possible. How that information is packaged depends on the importance of the story and the news environment.

Generally, major stories are handled first with a NewsAlert, then a separate story (an *urgent* or *tops* if appropriate). The new information is then worked into the next *NewsMinute*. If called for, sidebars or tabular material will follow.

A bulletin is often followed by an urgent series, then, usually, by a tops. Again, the new information will be worked into the next *NewsMinute*. If called for, sidebars or tabular material will follow.

These separate stories are interspersed with the regularly scheduled scripts that run on the wires. The desk is required to keep those scripts updated with the latest information without significantly delaying their transmission.

News Emergencies. Sometimes, a story is so important that it requires the suspension of the wire format. This happens only in most extreme news emergencies (recent examples include the start of the 1991 Gulf War, the explosion of the space shuttle in 1986 and the attempt on President Reagan's life in 1981).

The wire format is suspended when the flow of critical information is so heavy that the wire must be devoted to nothing more than relaying breaking news.

In such circumstances, the wire desk provides running accounts of developments, periodically summarizing the story. All efforts are put into relaying new information, so stations are kept up to date.

Building a Newscast

Every newsroom's desk must ultimately think in terms of the newscast. How will each story get on the air? Which stories are most important? How do we give the audience the most accurate and engaging snapshot of the state of its world?

A newscast is the result of a series of decisions made by the desk or the anchor. All of these decisions must be made in light of a thorough understanding of the newscast's audience.

Most of today's radio stations appeal to much narrower audiences than television stations — or than the radio stations of a decade ago. Such demographic targeting makes a big difference in the way stories are selected and where they are played.

Some stories cut across demographic lines. Major disasters, stories that directly affect people's pocketbooks or health, and major crime and scandal stories are of interest to just about everyone.

But other stories are of interest to a narrower audience. Some people care more about fitness. Others about personal finance. Older listeners have a greater interest in foreign affairs and in government.

Knowing your audience will help you select the stories that matter most to the people listening to your station.

Although television stations tend to have broader audiences, knowing what the viewers care about is important. The station that reports most effectively on the issues its community cares about is the one that best serves it audience.

Another important element in your approach to building a newscast is the time of day. Stories that are important at 7 a.m. may not be important at 6 p.m. The 11 p.m. audience may be looking for still different stories.

An all-news radio station or cable channel that expects its audience to tune in for 40 minutes three times a day will write a different kind of newscast than would a classic rock station hoping to hold its audience for hours on end.

For most stations, though, mornings are set aside for reviewing what happened while the audience was asleep and previewing what will happen today. Midday is aimed at staying on top of breaking developments. Afternoons are intended to brief the audience on what happened while everyone was at work. Late-night newscasts recap the entire day.

Newscast Structure. A newscast is built from the top down. The selection of the lead story determines much of what happens for the rest of the show.

The choice of lead depends on the news environment, the target audience and the time of day in which the newscast will air. Generally, in radio, you lead with what's newest. Television tends to lead with what is biggest since the last newscast.

Stories within the newscast should be grouped logically. Two stories about taxes ought to be used together. If you're leading with a story about education, it should be followed by any other school stories you might have.

That's why the selection of the lead does so much to determine the structure of the newscast. Let's take a typical story lineup and see how choosing a different lead causes the newscast to change.

Suppose we have these stories to work with:

school budget cuts	police contract talks
hit-and-run accident	new Mideast peace talks
school anti-drug initiative	state gun control law passed
new federal deficit figures	big road project starts
aid to former Soviet Union	new unemployment figures
new mall to be built in town	local homeless ordinance

If the lead story is school budget cuts, you would want to group the related stories together, so the lineup might look like this:

school budget cuts
school anti-drug initiative
police contract talks
state gun control law passed
local homeless ordinance
new mall to be built in town
big road project starts
hit-and-run accident
new unemployment figures
new federal deficit figures
aid to former Soviet Union
new Mideast peace talks

On the other hand, leading with the new mall yields a different newscast, one built, perhaps, around the boost it will give the local economy:

new mall to be built in town
big road project starts
school budget cuts
local homeless ordinance
new unemployment figures
new federal deficit figures
police contract talks
state gun control law passed
school anti-drug initiative

hit-and-run accident
aid to former Soviet Union
new Mideast peace talks

In both cases, the stories are grouped so there is a natural transition from one to the next. In the second lineup, the overall lead might be that the local economy is expected to get hundreds of jobs because of construction of a new mall. The transition between the lead and the roads story might look like this:

> A project that's already produced more than a hundred jobs is now under way. Construction of highway 12 began this morning...

The transition to the school budget story can also be smooth:

> The creation of those new jobs comes too late to resolve this year's school budget problem....

Use such transitions only when the stories lend themselves to that sort of treatment. Don't force it.

Formats and Time Cues. When constructing the newscast lineup, keep in mind the program's format. Some people tune out after the top stories or the weather or the sports. Make sure you put in the most-listened-to section the stories you really want the audience to hear.

At the network level, radio newscasts are structured to allow stations to break away at designated points. Almost every newscast is built in sections to provide for spot breaks.

It's important that you time your stories, to be sure you can hit the spot breaks cleanly — and can keep related stories grouped together.

In some formats, it's also important to start each segment with a story that is worth teasing — so it can be promoted at the end of the previous segment.

Newscast Mechanics. Even if you are in radio, writing for yourself and running your own air board, it's important that you maintain good newscast mechanics.

Your copy should be clean. In television, this is important because other people depend on

> ### AP Style Guideline
>
> AP Network News hourly newscasts contain two breakaway time cues: at 2:00 into the program and at 3:00.
>
> These cues must be hit precisely, for stations cutting away through the use of a clock rather than a board operator.

your copy to tell them what has to happen at each moment in the show. In radio, it's important because someone else may read your copy — or because you may stumble if you come across indecipherable spelling or scribbling in your own handwriting. Clean copy prevents stumbles for everyone.

In radio, preview all of your carts before you get into the studio. You will never detect a faulty cart (such as one with a stop tone in the middle) if you don't listen first. You'll also hear an echoed lead if you listen to the cart.

Your carts should be clearly labeled and stacked in order. The cart number should be indicated in your copy, so if (when) you drop the carts, you can easily reorder them.

Be certain your copy contains the out-cue of all sound, so you know precisely when you should start speaking again.

These sound like commonsense guidelines, and they are. But many professional newscasters forget them and slip up as a result.

Here's another rule many people fail to follow: Be sure to get into the studio or onto the set with enough time to compose yourself before going on the air. No matter how sure you are of yourself, getting there only 30 seconds before air is asking for trouble.

Breaking Stories. The best broadcasting is coverage of breaking news. It can be crazy when it happens while you are on the air, but it's what the electronic media are all about.

If you're a one-person news department, try to have someone keeping an eye on the wire for you during newscasts — so that person can bring you any bulletins that come across. It would be awfully embarrassing to be on the air when a tremendous story breaks and not have it in your newscast because no one told you about it.

Larger operations have a variety of systems for getting breaking copy to the anchor. In radio, there's often an electronic link — a computer screen of some sort — that allows the desk to get copy into the studio. Television may use the prompter to do so. Of course, there's always the old-fashioned way: handing the anchor a piece of paper.

For the desk, the key is to be sure the copy you give the anchor is useable. A cryptic line is likely to lead to a stumble. A well-written sentence or two (speed counts, so keep it short) will give the anchor something to work with.

Sometimes, the breaking story is a development on something already covered in the program. In that case, a simple note (*crash death toll has risen to 12*) should be all the anchor needs to ad-lib an update.

In either case, though, the anchor should not be afraid to tell the audience that word is just coming in, that information is fragmentary (if it is) or that more information will be coming in soon. The audience likes to know it is being kept up to date, and if it knows that's what's going on, it will understand the rough edges that come with live coverage of breaking stories.

Sometimes you are lucky enough to have a reporter on the scene, ready for a story to break. Courtroom stories are good examples. There's advance warning that the jury is coming back, and if your reporter has staked out a phone, it's possible you'll get a call with the verdict while you are on the air. In that case, you can go straight to the reporter for a live update.

The desk should make sure the reporter knows when the newscast is scheduled to end. If it's possible for the anchor (or producer, in television) to talk to the reporter (say, during a spot break) beforehand, they can set up how long the reporter should go.

Regardless of whether it includes a field report, any breaking news reported in the newscast should be briefly recapped at the end of the program.

Live Coverage of Breaking News

Immediacy is the attribute that distinguishes the electronic media from newspapers and magazines. More and more, radio and television are using that strength to serve the audience by providing live coverage of breaking stories.

In its simplest form, live coverage consists of an anchor reading a bulletin on the air. Such a bulletin may run a minute or less, and contain no tape and no field report. The point of it is to get the basic information to the audience as quickly as possible.

The key factors in a bulletin are speed and brevity. There's nothing wrong with going on the air with two sentences, as long as the story is important enough to warrant it. There's also nothing wrong with repeating the information for emphasis.

Often, the story isn't important enough to warrant a bulletin, but is too important to wait for the next newscast. In that case, you may want to wait until you have sufficient information — or a field report or strong piece of tape — to sustain a 60- or 90-second program.

Such live special reports need to be more polished than a bulletin, because the format clearly signals to the audience that the report is important but not transcendent.

In either case, the sooner you can get a field report on the air, the better.

Live Continuous Coverage. Perhaps the most difficult live on-air situation is the one in which the story is of transcendent importance — but there's very little information available. You want to stay on the air, because people want to know what happened — but you cannot yet provide details.

In this case, the anchor must stitch together new information with background information, occasionally recapping what is known about the story.

It takes intense concentration, particularly because the story is apt to be dramatic. Not many people can carry it off, but it's an essential talent when anchoring stories such as the shuttle explosion. Here is how AP Network News correspondents Bob Moon and Dick Uliano handled it on January 28, 1986:

> *Mission Control: ...engines beginning throttling down now, at 94%. Normal throttles for most of the flight 104%.*

> Moon: Tremendous shock wave of sound on this one.

> *Mission Control: They'll be down to 65% shortly.*

> Uliano: And Bob, it's piercing a crystal blue sky, a 700-foot-long tail of flame and that long, long plume of white smoke.

> *Mission Control: ...engine throttling up, three engines now at 104%.*

> *Shuttle Communicator: "Challenger," go at throttle-up.*

> *Shuttle: Roger, go at throttle up.*

> Moon: A pillar of smoke and steam now, as the shuttle rises high in the sky.

> *Mission Control: A minute-15 seconds, velocity 2900 feet per second, altitude ...*

Moon: Something went wrong here, we've got a problem with a, what looks like a second plume of,
of smoke.

Uliano: We do have a problem, Bob. It looks — it looks
as if one of the solid — it may have lost a solid
rocket booster. It's hard to tell.

Moon: There are two separate plumes of smoke and the
uh, shuttle — we can't tell which one the shuttle
is now. They've separated.

Uliano: We should not have had solid rocket booster
separation for two and a-half minutes after it
leaves the pad. And at about a minute and a-
half —

*Mission Control: Flight controllers here looking
very carefully at the situation. Obviously a
major malfunction.*

Moon: The view from the ground is obscured by this pil-
lar of steam now.

Mission Control: We have no downlink.

Uliano: Something's gone terribly wrong.

Moon: If you're just joining us, the space shuttle
"Challenger" has just lifted off the pad, and
we've had a problem here, a major problem.
We're getting no telemetry, no data back from
the shuttle, according to what we're hearing
from mission control. It appeared that something separated, there may have been an
explosion.

Uliano: Bob, we see the long plume of smoke, twisted
up into the sky, and then strings of smoke, hanging down. Below —

> *Mission Control: We have a report from the flight dynamics officer that the vehicle has exploded. Flight director confirms that. We are out looking at checking with the recovery forces to see what can be done at this point.*

Moon: It, uh, would appear that the space shuttle "Challenger" has exploded, about, perhaps a minute, a minute and a-half into the launch. There is no radio communication back from the shuttle.

> *Mission Control: We'll report more as we have information available. Again, to repeat, we have a report relayed through the flight dynamics officer that the vehicle has exploded.*

At such moments, the audience wants the reassurance that the correspondent is there, keeping everyone up to date. It is the supreme test of the radio or television journalist, when skills in writing, reporting, editing and selecting sound all come together, and broadcasting becomes the link that can inform the entire world at once.

PART 2

The AP
Libel Manual

CHAPTER 7

AP Libel Manual

Associate Justice John Marshall Harlan once remarked that "the law of libel has changed substantially since the early days of the Republic."

And it has changed substantially since he made that observation more than two decades ago. Recent years have seen the Supreme Court of the United States decide several cases that made headlines and truly can be called landmarks.

But the working journalist remembers: The news stories which generate the most claims of injury to reputation—the basis of libel—are run-of-the-mill. Perhaps 95 of 100 libel suits are in that category and result from publication of charges of crime, immorality, incompetence or inefficiency.

A Harvard Nieman report makes the point: "The gee-whiz, slam-bang stories usually aren't the ones that generate libel, but the innocent-appearing, potentially treacherous minor yarns from police courts and traffic cases, from routine meetings and from business reports."

Most of these suits based on relatively minor stories result from factual error or inexact language—for example, getting the plea wrong or making it appear that all defendants in a case face identical charges.

Libel even lurks in such innocent-appearing stories as birth notices and engagements. The fact that some New York newspapers had to defend suits recently for such announcements illustrates the care and concern required in every editorial department.

Turner Catledge, retired managing editor of *The New York Times*, says in his book, *My Life and the Times*, that he learned over the years that newspapers must be extremely careful in checking engagement announcements. He noted that "sometimes people will call in the engagement of two people who hate each other, as a practical joke."

In short, there is no substitute for accuracy. But, of course, this does not mean that accurately reporting libelous assertions automatically absolves the journalist of culpability.

Accurate reporting will not prevent libel if there is no privilege, either the constitutional privilege or the fair report privilege.

A fair and impartial report of judicial, legislative and other public and official proceedings is privileged—that is, not actionable for libel. But it is important to know, for instance, what constitutes judicial action. In many states there is no privilege to report the filing of the summons and complaint in a civil suit until there has been some judicial action.

Many libel suits occur in the handling of court and police news, especially criminal courts. Problems can arise in stories about crime and in identifying a suspect where there has been no arrest or where no charge has been made.

Don't be deluded into thinking a safe approach is to eliminate the subject's name. If the description—physical or otherwise—readily identifies him to those in his immediate area, the story has, in effect, named him.

When accusations are made against a person, it is always well to try for balancing comment. The reply must have some relation to the original charges. Irrelevant countercharges can lead to problems with the person who made the first accusation.

The chief causes of libel suits are carelessness, misunderstanding of the law of libel, limitations of the defense of privilege (including the First Amendment privilege) and the extent to which developments may be reported in arrests. These are discussed in detail in this manual, which is "must" reading for every Associated Press staff member. It should be reviewed periodically.

Libel, Defenses and Privilege

Libel is injury to reputation.

Words, pictures or cartoons that expose a person to public hatred, shame, disgrace or ridicule, or induce an ill opinion of a person are libelous.

Actions for civil libel result mainly from news stories that allege crime, fraud, dishonesty, immoral or dishonorable conduct, or stories that defame the subject professionally, causing financial loss either personally or to a business.

There is only one complete and unconditional defense to a civil action for libel: that the facts stated are *provably true*. (Note well that word, *provably*.) Quoting someone correctly is not enough. The important thing is to be able to satisfy a jury that the libelous statement is substantially correct.

A second important defense is *privilege*. Privilege is one of two kinds — absolute and qualified.

Absolute privilege means that certain people in some circumstances can state, without fear of being sued for libel, material which may be false, malicious and damaging. These circumstances include judicial, legislative, public and official proceedings and the contents of most public records.

The doctrine of absolute privilege is founded on the fact that on certain occasions the public interest requires that some individuals be exempted from legal liability for what they say.

Remarks by a member of a legislative body in the discharge of official duties are not actionable. Similarly, libelous statements made in the course of legal proceedings by participants are also absolutely privileged, if they are relevant to the issue. Statements containing defamatory matter may be absolutely privileged if publication or broadcast is required by law.

The interests of society require that judicial, legislative and similar official proceedings be subject to public discussion. To that extent, the rights of the individual about whom damaging statements may be made are subordinated to what are deemed to be the interests of the community.

We have been talking about absolute privilege as it applies to participants in the types of proceedings described here.

As applied to the press, the courts generally have held that privilege is not absolute, but rather is qualified. That means that it can be lost or diluted by how the journalist handles the material.

Privilege can be lost if there are errors in the report of the hearing, or if the plaintiff can show malice on the part of the publication or broadcast outlet.

An exception: Broadcasters have absolute privilege to carry the broadcast statements of political candidates who are given air time under the "equal opportunity" rules.

The two key points are:

1. Does the material at issue come from a privileged circumstance or proceeding?

2. Is the report a fair and accurate summation?

Again, the absolute privilege legislators enjoy—they cannot be sued, for example, for anything said on the floor of the legislature—affords total protection.

The journalist's protection is not as tight. But it is important and substantial and enables the press to report freely on many items of public interest that otherwise would have to go unreported.

The press has a qualified privilege to report that John Doe has been arrested on a bank robbery charge. If the report is fair and accurate, there is no problem.

Statements made outside the court by police or a prosecutor or an attorney may not be privileged unless the circumstances indicate it is an official proceeding. However, some states do extend privilege to these statements if made by specified top officials.

Newspapers and broadcasters often carry accounts going beyond the narrow confines of what is stated in the official charges, taking the risk without malice because they feel the importance of the case and the public interest warrant doing so.

The source of such statements should be specified.

Sometimes there are traps.

In New York and some other states, court rules provide that the papers filed in matrimonial actions are sealed and thus not open to inspection by the general public.

But sometimes litigants or their lawyers may slip a copy of the papers to reporters. Publication of the material is dangerous because often the litigants come to terms outside of court and the case never goes to trial. So privilege may never attach to the accusations made in the court papers.

In one such case, the vice president of a company filed suit alleging that he was fired because the newspaper published his wife's charges of infidelity. The newspaper responded that its report was a true and fair account of court proceedings. The New York Court of Appeals rejected that argument on grounds that the law makes details of marital cases secret because spatting spouses frequently make unfounded charges. The newspaper appealed to the Supreme Court of the United States. But it lost.

Unless some other privilege applies, there is danger in carrying a report of court papers that are not available for public inspection by reason of a law, court rule or court order directing that such papers be sealed.

As stated earlier, a fair and accurate report of public and official proceedings is privileged.

There has never been an exact legal definition of what constitutes an official proceeding. Some cases are obvious—trials, legislative sessions and hearings, etc.

Strictly speaking, conventions of private organizations are not "public and official proceedings" even though they may be forums for discussions of public questions. Hence, statements made on the floor of convention sessions or from speakers' platforms may not be privileged.

Statements made by the president of the United States or a governor in the course of executive proceedings have absolute privilege for the speaker, even if false or defamatory. However, this absolute privilege may not apply to statements having no relation to executive proceedings.

President Kennedy once was asked at a news conference what he was going to do about "two well-known security risks" in the State Department. The reporter gave names when the president asked for them. This was not privileged and many newspapers and radio stations did not carry them. The Associated Press did because it seemed in the public interest to report the incident fully. No suits resulted.

After a civil rights march, George Wallace, then governor of Alabama, appeared on a television show and said some of the marchers were members of Communist and Communist-front organizations. He gave some names, which newspapers carried. Some libel suits resulted.

The courts have ruled that publishing that a person is a Communist is libelous on its face if he is not a Communist.

"The claimed charge that the plaintiff is a Nazi and a Communist is in the same category. ... The current effect of these statements is the decisive test. Whatever doubt there may have been in the past as to the opprobrious effect on the ordinary mind of such a charge ... recent events and legislation make it manifest that to label an attorney a Communist or a Nazi is to taint him with disrepute." (*Levy v. Gelber, 175 Misc. 746*)

The fact that news comes from official sources does not eliminate the concern. To say that *a high police official* said means that you are making the accusation. A statement that a crime has been committed and that the police are holding someone for questioning is reasonably safe, because it is provably true. However, there are times when the nature of the crime or the prominence of those involved requires broader treatment. Under those circumstances, the safest guide is whatever past experience has shown as to the responsibility of the source. The source must be trustworthy and certain to stand behind the information given.

Repetition of Libel. In reporting the filing of a libel suit, can we report the content of the charge? By so doing, do we compound the libel, even though we quote from the legal complaint?

Ordinarily, a fair and impartial report of the contents of legal papers in a libel action filed in the office of the clerk of the court is privileged. However, many states do not extend privilege to the filing of court actions; in such a case there is no privilege until the case comes to trial or until some other judicial action takes place.

But we have found that it is safe, generally speaking, to repeat the libel in a story based on the filing of a suit.

Fair Comment and Criticism. The publication of defamatory matter that consists of comment and opinion, as distinguished from fact, with reference to matters of public interest or importance, is covered by the defense of fair comment.

Of course, whatever facts are stated must be true.

The right of fair comment has been summarized as follows:

"Everyone has a right to comment on matters of public interest and concern, provided they do so fairly and with an honest purpose. Such comments or criticism are not libelous, however severe in their terms, unless they are written maliciously. Thus it has been held that books, prints, pictures and statuary publicly exhibited, and the architecture of public buildings, and actors and exhibitors are all the legitimate subjects of newspapers' criticism, and such criticism fairly and honestly made is not libelous, however strong the terms of censure may be." (*Hoeppner v. Dunkirk Pr.Co., 254 N.Y. 95*)

Criminal Libel. The publication of a libel may result in what is considered a breach of the peace. For that reason, it may constitute a criminal offense. It is unnecessary to review that phase of the law here because the fundamental elements of the crime do not differ substantially from those that give rise to a civil action for damages.

Libel of the Dead. In general, there can be no defamation of the dead. No one can sue on behalf of a deceased individual on the basis of false and defamatory statements made about the individual. Some states, however, permit an ongoing libel suit to continue after the death of the complaining person.

Public Officials, Public Figures, Public Issues

In a series of decisions commencing in 1964, the Supreme Court established important First Amendment protections for the press in the libel area.

But in more recent decisions, the tide in libel has been running against the press, particularly in the unrelenting narrowing of the definition of a public figure. This was the single most active area of libel law in the decade of the '70s.

While the full impact of the later decisions is not yet clear, a review of the rulings since the mid-1960s shows the trend.

Three basic cases established important precedents. They did so in a logical progression. The cases were:

— *New York Times v. Sullivan (1964)*

— *Associated Press v. Walker (1967)*

— *Gertz v. Robert Welch (1974)*

In *The New York Times* case, the Supreme Court ruled in March 1964 that public officials cannot recover damages for a report related to official duties unless they prove actual malice.

To establish actual malice, the official was required to prove that at the time of publication, those responsible for the story knew it was false or published it with reckless disregard of whether it was true or false.

The decision reversed a $500,000 libel verdict returned in Alabama against *The New York Times* and four black ministers. The court said:

"The constitutional guarantees (the First and 14th Amendments) require, we think, a federal rule that prohibits a public official from recovering damages for a defamatory falsehood relating to his official conduct unless he proves that the statement was made with 'actual malice' — that is, with knowledge that it was false or with reckless disregard of whether it was false or not."

This does not give newspapers absolute immunity against libel suits by officials who are criticized. But it does mean that when a newspaper publishes information about a public official and publishes it without actual malice, it should be spared a damage suit even though some of the information may be wrong.

The court said it considered the case "against the background of a profound national commitment to the principle that debate on public issues should be uninhibited, robust and wide-open, and that it may well include vehement, caustic and sometimes unpleasantly sharp attacks on government and public officials."

The ruling in *The New York Times* case with respect to public officials was extended by the Supreme Court in June 1967 to apply also to public figures.

In so holding, the court reversed a $500,000 libel judgment won by former Major General Edwin A. Walker in a Texas state court against The Associated Press.

The AP reported that Walker had "assumed command" of rioters at the University of Mississippi and "led a charge of students against federal marshals" when James H. Meredith was admitted to the university in September 1962. Walker alleged those statements to be false.

The court said: "Under any reasoning, Gen. Walker was a public man in whose public conduct society and the press had a legitimate and substantial interest."

The rulings in *The New York Times* and *The Associated Press* cases were constitutional landmark decisions for freedom of the press and speech. They offered safeguards not previously defined. But they did not confer license for defamatory statements or for reckless disregard of the truth.

The AP decision made an additional important distinction.

In the same opinion, the court upheld an award granted Wallace Butts, former athletic director of the University of Georgia, against Curtis Publishing Company. The suit was based on an article in the *Saturday Evening Post* accusing Butts of giving his football team's strategy secrets to an opposing coach prior to a game between the two schools.

The court found that Butts was a public figure, but said there was a substantial difference between the two cases. Justice Harlan said: "The evidence showed that the Butts story was in no sense 'hot news' and the editors of the magazine recognized the need for a thorough investigation of the serious charges. Elementary precautions were, nevertheless, ignored."

Chief Justice Warren, in a concurring opinion, referred to "slipshod and sketchy investigatory techniques employed to check the veracity of the source." He said the evidence disclosed "reckless disregard for the truth."

The differing rulings in The Associated Press and the *Saturday Evening Post* cases should be noted carefully. The AP-Walker case was "hot news"; the Post-Butts story was investigative reporting of which journalists are doing more and more.

Extension of the *Times* rule in one case was based on a column by Drew Pearson that characterized a candidate for the United States Senate as "a former small-time bootlegger." The jury held that the accusation related to the private sector of the candidate's life. Reversing this judgment, the Supreme Court said:

"We therefore hold as a matter of constitutional law that a charge of criminal conduct, no matter how remote in time or place, can never be irrelevant to an official's or a candidate's fitness for office for purposes of application of the 'knowing falsehood or reckless disregard' rule of *New York Times v. Sullivan.*"

Another case was brought by a Chicago captain of detectives against *Time* magazine, which had quoted from a report of the U.S. Civil Rights Commission without making clear that the charges of police brutality were those of the complainant whose home was raided and not the independent findings of the commission. The court described the commission's documents as "bristling with ambiguities" and said *Time* did not engage in a "falsification" sufficient to sustain a finding of actual malice.

The progression of *The New York Times* and AP cases was interrupted in June 1974 with the Supreme Court's decision in the case of *Gertz v. Robert Welch, Incorporated.*

Gertz, a lawyer of prominence in Chicago, had been attacked in a John Birch Society publication as a Communist. There were additional accusations as well.

Gertz sued and the Supreme Court upheld him, ruling that he was neither a public official nor a public figure.

The decision opened the door to giving courts somewhat wider lee-way in determining whether someone was a public person.

This also opened the way to giving state courts the right to assess what standard of liability should be used in testing whether a publi-cation about a private individual is actionable. It insisted, however, that some degree of fault, at least negligence, be shown.

For instance, some state courts have established a negligence stan-dard (whether a reasonable person would have done the same thing as the publisher under the circumstances). The New York courts fol-low a gross negligence test. Others still observe the actual malice test in suits by private individuals against the press.

Bear in mind that the significance of the *Gertz* decision still is being developed, as new cases arise and are adjudicated. But at a mini-mum it opened the way to judgments the earlier cases would seem to have barred.

More recently, in the case of *Time v. Firestone*, the Supreme Court again appears to have restricted the public figure and public issue standards.

The case stemmed from *Time* magazine's account of the divorce of Russell and Mary Alice Firestone. The magazine said she had been divorced on grounds of "extreme cruelty and adultery." The court made no finding of adultery. She sued.

She was a prominent social figure in Palm Beach, Fla., and held news conferences in the course of the divorce proceedings. Yet the Supreme Court said that she was not a public figure because "she did not assume any role of special prominence in the affairs of society, other than perhaps Palm Beach society, and she did not thrust herself to the forefront of any particular public controversy in order to influ-ence resolution of the issues involved in it."

As in the *Gertz* case, the decision opened the way to findings within the states involving negligence, a standard less severe than the actual malice standard that was the base of the earlier landmark cases.

Supreme Court decisions, starting with *Gertz* and extending through *Firestone* and more recent cases, have consistently narrowed the class of persons to be treated as public figures under the *Times-Sullivan* and *AP-Walker* standards.

Two 1979 rulings by the Supreme Court illustrate the narrowing of the protections that seemed so wide only a few years earlier:

Sen. William Proxmire of Wisconsin was sued for $8 million by Ronald Hutchinson, a research scientist who had received several public grants, including one for $50,000. Proxmire gave Hutchinson a "Golden Fleece" award, saying Hutchinson "has made a fortune from his monkeys and in the process made a monkey of the American taxpayer." Hutchinson sued. The Supreme Court found that, despite the receipt of substantial public funds, Hutchinson was not a public figure. The court also ruled that Proxmire's news release was not protected by congressional immunity.

Ilya Wolston pleaded guilty in 1957 to criminal contempt for failing to appear before a grand jury investigating espionage. A book published in 1974 referred to these events. Wolston alleged that he had been libeled. In ruling on *Wolston v. Reader's Digest*, the Supreme Court said he was not a public figure. The court said people convicted of crimes do not automatically become public figures. Wolston, the court said, was thrust into the public spotlight unwillingly.

In effect, the court extended the Firestone concept of unwilling notoriety to criminal as well as civil cases.

Thus the pattern through Gertz, Firestone, Proxmire and *Reader's Digest* is clear. The *Times* rule has been left standing, but it is tougher and tougher to get in under it.

The court is rejecting the notion that a person can be a public figure simply because of the events that led to the story at issue. The courts are saying that *public figure* means people who seek the lime-light, who inject themselves into public debate, etc. The courts are saying that involvement in a crime, even a newsworthy one, does not make one a public figure.

This means that the broad "public official" and "public figure" protections that came out of the *Times* and AP cases remain, but for shrinking numbers of people who are written about.

At the same time, the "reckless disregard of the truth" and "knowing falsity" standards of the *Times* decision also slip away, becoming applicable to fewer people as the public figure definition narrows.

And those standards are being replaced in state after state with simple negligence standards. In other words, the plaintiff, now adjudged to be a private citizen because of the recent rulings, must now prove only that the press was negligent, not reckless.

The difference is more than semantic. This development suggests that press lawyers will be relying more on some of the old standbys as defenses— plaintiff's inability to prove falsity, privilege, fair comment—and this puts the ball right back with editors and reporters.

The Supreme Court in 1986 held, however, in *Philadelphia Newspapers v. Hepps*, that, at least where a newspaper has published statements on a matter of public concern, a private figure plaintiff cannot prevail without showing the statements at issue are false. This case provides that the common law rule requiring a defendant to prove truth is supplanted by a constitutional requirement that the plaintiff demonstrate falsity when the statements involved are of public concern.

Another recent Supreme Court decision which provoked wide press controversy came in the case of *Herbert v. Lando*.

The court ruled in 1979 that retired Army Lieutenant Colonel Anthony Herbert, a Vietnam veteran, had the right to inquire into the editing process of a CBS "60 Minutes" segment, produced by Barry Lando, which provoked his suit. Herbert had claimed the right to do this so that he could establish actual malice.

The decision formalizes and calls attention to something that was at least implicit in the Times case, namely, that a plaintiff had the right to try to prove the press was reckless or even knew that what it was printing was a lie. How else could this be done except through inquiry about a reporter's or editor's state of mind?

So the ruling reminds plaintiffs' lawyers that they can do this and will, no doubt, be responsible for far more of this kind of inquiry than the press has had to face before.

A crucial test will be how far judges will let plaintiffs' lawyers range in their discovery efforts. Will they let the plaintiff widen the embrace of inquiry into stories other than the one at issue? Will they let the plaintiff rummage about the newsroom, probing unrelated news judgments, examining the handling of other unrelated stories, demanding to know why this investigative piece survived while that one died quietly on the kill hook?

That the questions are being prompted by the Herbert-Lando ruling is the best response to those who say that the decision didn't really mean very much.

The preliminary answer to these questions appears to be that there has been some widening of this sort of inquiry by plaintiffs newly alerted to this area by the Lando ruling.

The press should be certain that files include contemporaneous memorandums that will testify later to the care taken with the story and the conviction that it was true and fair.

There was a footnote in the Proxmire case that has had a marked effect on the way libel cases are litigated. Footnote nine questioned the practice of dismissing libel actions early in the course of litigation. The lower courts have paid serious attention to this footnote, with the result that more and more libel actions are being tried before a jury.

In a 1986 decision, *Anderson v. Liberty Lobby*, however, the Supreme Court held that summary judgment should be granted in libel actions against public officials and public figures unless the plaintiff can prove actual malice with "convincing clarity" or by "clear and convincing evidence." This rule should facilitate the early dismissal of unmeritorious claims without the expense and burden of proceeding to trial.

More recently, in *Malkovich v. Lorain Journal Company* (1990), the Supreme Court made clear that even statements of opinion may constitute libel if "sufficiently factual to be proven true or false." The *Milkovich* case therefore took away the opinion defense to libel that had been adopted by many lower courts. Although the decision did not alter the rules relating to public figures and events described above (e.g., the requirement of actual malice), the case may lead to more jury trials in libel suits, particularly where the person bringing suit is a private individual.

The huge jury verdicts that often result have caused much concern among legal commentators and the press. A number of remedies have been proposed, but it remains unclear at this point whether the Supreme Court will take any action to stem the tide of runaway million-dollar jury verdicts of recent years.

An indication that the Supreme Court is facing this problem appeared in its 1984 opinion in *Bose v. Consumers Union*. Bose Corporation sued Consumer Reports over its publication of disparaging comments concerning Bose's loudspeaker systems and obtained a damage judgment of about $211,000. The Court of Appeals, after a careful review of the record, reversed. The Supreme Court endorsed this process, underscoring the need for appellate courts in libel cases to make an independent review of the record—a standard of scrutiny that does not apply in most other appeals. For the foreseeable future, the press will continue to rely on the willingness of the appeals courts to overturn excessive jury verdicts.

Summary of First Amendment Rules
The gist of the principles established in the cases discussed above may be summarized as follows:

The Public Official Rule. The press enjoys a great protection when it covers the affairs of public officials. In order to successfully sue for libel, a public official must prove actual malice. This means the public official must prove that the editor or reporter had knowledge that the facts were false or acted with reckless disregard of the truth.

The Public Figure Rule. The rule is the same for public figures and public officials. That is, a public figure must prove actual malice. The problem is that it is very difficult in many cases to predict who will be classified as a public figure. In general, there are two types of public figures:

> **General Purpose Public Figure.** An individual who has assumed the role of special prominence in the affairs of society and occupies a position of persuasive power and influence. An example is the entertainer Johnny Carson.

> **Limited Purpose Public Figure.** A person who has thrust himself or herself into the vortex of public controversy in an attempt to influence the resolution of the controversy. An example would be a vocal scientist who has lectured and published articles in an attempt to influence a state legislature to ban the fluoridation of water.

The Private Figure Rule. A private figure is defined in the negative. It is someone who is not a public figure. The rule of law for libel suits brought by private figures varies from state to state. The variations fall into three general categories:

1. A number of states follow the same rules for private figures

and public figures. They require private figures to prove actual malice. Those states include Alaska, Colorado, Indiana and Michigan.

2. One state, New York, requires private figures to prove that the defendant acted in a "grossly irresponsible manner." To date, no other state has adopted this rule.

3. Most states require private figures to prove only negligence. Negligence is a term of art that is difficult to define. As a rule of thumb, a careless error on the part of the journalist will often be found to constitute negligence.

These distinctions become important after the story has moved on our wires when there is a challenge and we are preparing our legal defenses. These distinctions do not apply in our preparations of stories. We do not have a standard that lets us go easier with ourselves if the story concerns a public official/figure and be tougher on ourselves if it concerns a private figure.

The Right of Privacy

The right of privacy is a doctrine that has been developing in the past century. It is recognized by statute in only a few states, including New York, but courts increasingly are taking cognizance of it. It is clearly an area to be watched.

The doctrine is based on the idea that a person has the right to be let alone, to live a private life free from publicity.

In 1890, two Boston lawyers wrote in the *Harvard Law Review*:

"The press is overstepping in every direction the obvious bounds of propriety and decency."

It is of interest that one of those lawyers, who later became Justice Brandeis, said years later in one of his dissents:

"The makers of our Constitution undertook to secure conditions favorable to the pursuit of happiness. They recognized the signifi-cance of man's spiritual nature, of his feelings and of his intellect. They knew that only a part of the pain, pleasure and satisfactions of life are to be found in material things. They sought to protect Americans in their beliefs, their thoughts, their emotions and their sensations. They conferred, as against the government, the right to be let alone — the most comprehensive of rights and the right most valued by civilized men." (*Olmstead v. United States, 277 U.S. 438, 478*)

When a person becomes involved in a news event, voluntarily or involuntarily, he forfeits the right to privacy. Similarly a person somehow involved in a matter of legitimate public interest, even if not a bona fide spot news event, normally can be written about with safety.

However, this is different from use of a story or picture that dredges up the sordid details of a person's past and has no current newswor-thiness.

Paul P. Ashley, then president of the Washington State Bar Association, said in a talk on this subject at a meeting of The Associated Press Managing Editors Association:

"The essence of the wrong will be found in crudity, in ruthless exploitation of the woes or other personal affairs of private individu-als who have done nothing noteworthy and have not by design or misadventure been involved in an event which tosses them into an arena subject to public gaze."

Here are details of a few cases brought in the name of right of privacy:

— A leading case centering on publication of details of a person's past concerned a man who as a child prodigy in 1910 had attracted national attention. In 1937, *The New Yorker* magazine published a biographical sketch of the plaintiff. He alleged invasion of privacy.

The court said "he had cloaked himself in obscurity but his subse-quent history, containing as it did the answer to the question of whether or not he had fulfilled his early promise, was still a matter of public concern. The article ... sketched the life of an unusual personality, and it possessed considerable popular news interest."

The court said further:

"We express no comment on whether or not the newsworthiness of the matter printed will always constitute a complete defense. Revelations may be so intimate and so unwarranted in view of the victim's position as to outrage the community's notions of decency. But when focused upon public characters, truthful comments upon dress, speech, habits, and the ordinary aspects of personality will usually not transgress this line. Regrettably or not, the misfortunes and frailties of neighbors and 'public figures' are subjects of considerable interest and discussion to the rest of the population. And when such are the mores of the community, it would be unwise for a court to bar their expression in the newspapers, books, and magazines of the day."

— The unsavory incidents of the past of a former prostitute, who had been tried for murder, acquitted, married and lived a respectable life, were featured in a motion picture. The court ruled that the use of her name in the picture and the statement in advertisements that the story was taken from true incidents in her life violated her right to pursue and obtain happiness.

Some courts have ruled that a person who is recognizable in a picture of a crowd in a public place is not entitled to the right of privacy. But if a camera singled him out for no news-connected reason, then his privacy is invaded, some courts have ruled.

— Another example of spot news interest: A child was injured in an auto accident in Alabama. A newspaper took a picture of the scene before the child was removed and ran it. That was spot news. Twenty months later a magazine used the picture to illustrate an article. The magazine was sued and lost the case, the court ruling that 20 months after the accident the child was no longer "in the news."

— In another case, a newspaper photographer in search of a picture to illustrate a hot weather story took a picture of a woman sitting on her front porch. She wore a housedress, her hair in curlers, her feet in thong sandals. The picture was taken from a car parked across the street from the woman's home. She sued, charging invasion of privacy. A court, denying the newspaper's motion for dismissal of the suit, said the scene photographed "was not a particularly newsworthy incident," and the limits of decency were exceeded by "surreptitious" taking and publishing of pictures "in an embarrassing pose."

— A woman took her two children to the county fair and went with them into the funhouse. A newspaper photographer took her picture just as a jet of air blew up her dress. She sued, and the Supreme Court of Alabama upheld the damages.

The rules in New York state on the right of privacy that are applicable to unauthorized publication of photographs in a single issue of a newspaper may be summarized generally as follows:

1. The plaintiff may recover damages if the photograph is published in or as part of an advertisement, or for advertising purposes.

2. There is liability if the photograph is used in connection with an article of fiction in any part of a newspaper.

3. There may be no recovery under the statute for publication of a photograph in connection with an article of current news of immediate public interest.

4. Newspapers publish articles that are neither strictly news items nor strictly fictional in character. They are not the response to an event of peculiarly immediate interest, but, though based on fact, are used to satisfy an ever-present educational need. Such articles include, among others, travel stories, stories of distant places, tales of historical personages and events, the reproduction of past news and surveys of social conditions. These are articles educational and

informative in character. As a general rule, such cases are not within the purview of the statute. (*Lahiri v. Daily Mirror Inc., Misc. Reports, N.Y. 162, p780*)

The Supreme Court of the United States ruled in January 1967 that the constitutional guarantees of freedom of the press are applicable to invasion-of-privacy cases involving reports of newsworthy matters.

The ruling arose out of a reversal by the Supreme Court of a decision of a New York court that an article with photos in *Life* magazine reviewing a play, "The Desperate Hours," violated the privacy of a couple who had been held hostage in a real-life incident. In illustrating the article, *Life* posed the actors in the house where the real family had been held captive.

The family alleged violation of privacy, saying the article gave readers the impression that the play was a true account of their experiences. *Life* said the article was "basically truthful."

The court said:

"The line between the informing and the entertaining is too elusive for the protection of [freedom of the press]. Erroneous statement is no less inevitable in such case than in the case of comment upon public affairs, and in both, if innocent or merely negligent, it must be protected if the freedoms of expression are to have the 'breathing space' that they 'need to survive.'

"We create grave risk of serious impairment of the indispensable service of a free press in a free society if we saddle the press with the impossible burden of verifying to a certainty the facts associated in a news article with a person's name, picture or portrait, particularly as related to non-defamatory matter."

The court added, however, that these constitutional guarantees do not extend to "knowing or reckless falsehood." A newspaper still may be liable for invasion of privacy if the facts of a story are changed deliberately or recklessly, or "fictionalized." As with *The*

New York Times and *The Associated Press* decisions in the field of libel, the "Desperate Hours" case does not confer a license for defamatory statements or for reckless disregard of the truth.

Applying the Rules

We already have defined libel and explained the defenses available to the press. Let's now look at some applications.

In a society in which standards of right living are recognized by most people, any accusation that a member of society has violated such standards must be injurious. Members of a community establish in the minds of others an estimate of what they are believed to be. Injury to that reputation may mean business, professional or social ruin.

One court decision put the matter this way:

"The law of defamation is concerned only with injuries to one's reputation. ...

"Embarrassment and discomfort no doubt came to her from the publication, as they would to any decent woman under like circumstances. Her own reaction, however, has no bearing upon her reputation. That rests entirely upon the reactions of others. We are unable to find anything in this article which could appreciably injure plaintiff's reputation." (*Kimmerle v. New York Evening Journal Inc.*, *262 N.Y. 99*)

The traditional rule was that defamation was concerned only with injuries to one's reputation. That rule was altered in 1974 by the Gertz case, which held that emotional distress is also an element of damages in libel.

In order to be libelous, it is not necessary that a publication impute criminal activity. The following was held to be libelous:

Pauper's Grave For Poor Child

Unless financial aid is forthcoming immediately, the body of a 4-year-old boy who was run over Tuesday will be interred in Potter's Field, burying ground of the homeless, friendless and penniless, who die or are killed in New York City. The parents of this youngster are in dire financial straits, and at this writing have no alternative but to let their son go to his final rest in a pauper's grave.

The court said:

"It is reasonably clear, therefore that in some cases it may be a libel if the plaintiff has been written up as an object of pity. ... The reason is that in libel the matter is defamatory not only if it brings a party into hatred, ridicule or contempt by asserting some moral discredit upon his part, but also if it tends to make him be shunned or avoided, although it imputes no moral turpitude to him." (*Katapodis v. Brooklyn Spectator Inc., 287 N.Y. 17*)

A publication that does not discredit a person as an individual may nonetheless damage a person's professional status.

A story stated that after a youth's body had been taken from the water in which he had been swimming, he was pronounced dead by a doctor. Later, the youth was revived. The doctor sued because of the implication that he had been unable to determine whether a person was living or dead.

Similarly, a publication may affect a business.

Companies are naturally sensitive to news stories that reflect on their business prospects and practices. There have been many such news stories in the field of environmental and consumer protection. The issues are complicated, and the legal aspects not always clear. Formal charges and allegations should be reported precisely and fairly.

Likewise, there is no alternative to precision in reporting any criminal charge.

Not only what is written, but the instruments used in transmitting it, must be considered in handling news. It is safer to say *acquitted* or *innocent* rather than *not guilty* because of the danger that the negative may be dropped in transmission.

An essential element of an action for libel is that the complainant be identifiable to a third party. Nevertheless, the omission of names will not, in itself, provide a shield against a claim for libel. As was pointed out earlier, there may be enough details for the person to be recognizable.

A story may, by the use of a general description or name, make a libelous charge against an organized group. It is possible that any member of the group could bring an action on the story.

If the material is libelous and not privileged, then the question turns to proof.

Can the substance be established by documents, by testimony from trustworthy persons or by material from privileged sources? Hearsay evidence is not enough. It is not enough to show that somebody gave you the unprivileged information. The issue turns on proof.

Another libel pitfall is the mistaken identity case. There is no complete defense when a newspaper confuses a famous individual with a person bearing a similar name who gets into a scrape. Petty thieves running afoul of the law may give the names of famous people—often old-time athletes—in the hope of getting leniency from a judge.

A few years ago a man charged with a minor crime appeared in Magistrate's Court in New York and gave as his name that of a once-great baseball pitcher. The magistrate gave the prisoner a suspended sentence. The real baseball player was a prosperous auto salesman, who threatened multiple suits when he read the story in the newspapers.

Closed Courtrooms. In 1980, in Richmond Newspapers v. Virginia, the Supreme Court ruled that under the First Amendment, criminal trials are presumptively open to the public and the media and may be closed only when it is necessary to protect some interest which outweighs the interest in access. A trial judge must articulate findings, on the record, to support any closure. This decision marked the first time in the nation's history that the right to find out what a branch of government is doing had been afforded direct and specific constitutional protection.

In 1982, in Globe Newspapers vs. Superior Court, the Supreme Court recognized that the constitutional right of access to criminal trials applies even with respect to a sex-offense trial involving a minor victim. While it said that the states have a significant interest in protecting minor victims of sexual assault from the trauma of testifying in open court, the Supreme Court held that trial judges must determine on a case-by-case basis whether this interest outweighs the presumption of openness and stated that any closure order must be "narrowly tailored to protect that interest" without unduly infringing on First Amendment rights.

The Supreme Court further held in 1984 in Press-Enterprise v. Superior Court that the constitutional right of access to criminal trials encompasses the right to attend jury selection

In 1986, in a second case called Press-Enterprise v. Superior Court, the Supreme Court ruled that the First Amendment right to access attaches to preliminary hearings in a criminal case unless specific findings are made on the record to demonstrate that closure is essential to preserve higher values and is narrowly tailored to serve that interest. If the interest asserted is the defendant's right to a fair trial, the preliminary hearing may not be closed unless there is a "substantial probability" that the right to a fair trial will be prejudiced by publicity that closure would prevent and that reasonable alternatives to closure cannot adequately protect the right to a fair trial.

The Associated Press has distributed the following statement to be read in court by its reporters when confronted with an attempt to close a criminal proceeding.

The statement allows the reporter, when permitted to address the court, to state the basic press position and to seek time for counsel to appear to make the legal argument.

The following statement can be read verbatim, although if any parts are not applicable to a specific case they can be changed or omitted.

> May it please the Court, I am (name) of The Associated Press. I respectfully request the opportunity to register on the record an objection to the motion to close this proceeding to the public and to representative of the news media. The Associated Press requests a hearing at which its counsel may present to the court legal authority and arguments that closure in this case is improper.
>
> The United State Supreme Court has now firmly held that the press and the public have a constitutional right to attend criminal trials and pretrial proceedings and may not be excluded unless the court makes findings on the record that closure is required to preserve higher values and is narrowly tailored to serve that interest. There is, therefore, a presumption of openness which is firmly rooted in the Constitution and essential to proper function of the criminal justice system.
>
> The Associated Press takes the position that the defendant should be required to make the following showing in order to prevail on a motion to close this proceeding:
>
> — First, the defendant must demonstrate that by conducting this proceeding in public the defendant's right to a fair trial will be prejudiced by publicity which closure would prevent. The defendant must demonstrate therefore that disclosures made in this hearing will prejudice the case and that these disclosures would not otherwise be brought to the attention of potential jurors.

— Second, the defendant must demonstrate that none of the alternatives to an order closing this proceeding would effectively protect the right to a fair trial. Among the alternatives available to protect the defendant's rights are: a careful and searching voir dire, continuance, severance, change of venue, peremptory challenges, sequestration and admonition of the jury.

— Third, the defendant must demonstrate that closure will be effective in protecting the right to a fair trial. In the present case there has already been substantial publicity concerning the facts. The defendant must demonstrate that any prejudice to the right of a fair trial would result from publicity given to disclosures made in this proceeding, and not to previously published facts of allegations.

— Finally, the defendant must establish that reasonable alternatives to closure cannot adequately protect the defendant's free trial rights.

The Associated Press believes that there has been substantial public interest generated by this case. The public has a right to know how the court system is handling criminal matters, what kind of deals may be struck by prosecutors and defense lawyers, what kind of evidence may be kept from the jury, and what sort of police or prosecutorial acts or omissions have occurred. For these reasons, The Associated Press objects to the motion for closure and respectfully requests a hearing in which it can present full legal arguments and authority.

The Supreme Court has never addressed the question of whether there is a First Amendment right of access to civil trials and pretrial proceedings. Several federal appeals courts, employing the reasoning of the Supreme Court's criminal trial access decisions, have ruled that both civil trial and pretrial proceedings are presumptively open to the press and public.

Points to Remember

Obviously, the first question is whether it is libelous. That is, whether it is actionable on its face. If it is, can you prove it? Or is it privileged?

If the story is libelous or potentially libelous, if you can't prove it and if it is not privileged, don't move it. If it is already on the wire, KILL IT AT ONCE.

— Don't try to fix a possibly libelous story by elimination, correction, sub or new lead. If there is any unprivileged or unsafe material in the story, the dangerous portion MUST BE KILLED. That is the only way in which material definitely can be removed from the report.

— Remember that privilege does not remove the need for careful reporting and the use of editorial judgment. In many cases, courts have held that it is up to the jury to decide whether a particular publication was a fair and true report or whether there was "actual malice."

— If it is decided that a name should be withheld from a crime story, be certain that no potentially troublesome descriptive phrases are given. An elderly janitor of a nearby apartment house could lead to a suit from every elderly janitor in the neighborhood.

— The fact that police are questioning someone about a crime does not necessarily justify the label suspect. In most cases, a detective's telling you that someone is a suspect is not privileged. Again, the basic questions: Could you prove it, if it came to that? Or is it privileged?

— Picture and graphics captions must be as accurate and objective as a news story. You can commit libel in a picture caption as damagingly as in a story. The same is true of radio network billboards and APTV rundowns and shot lists.

— In writing about murder charges filed during a preliminary police investigation, it makes no difference legally whether you say John Doe is charged (a) with the murder of, (b) with murdering, or (c) with murder, in connection with the killing of Richard Roe.

AP counsel says:

"Each statement contains an accusation by The Associated Press that John Doe is guilty of murder. The accusation is made by implication in that the wording suggests that the charge was made by someone other than The Associated Press. That, however, does not relieve the AP of responsibility unless the publication is qualifiedly privileged.

"Thus a publication relating to a murder charge against John Doe in connection with the killing of Richard Roe must be either privileged (based on official proceedings), or provably true."

CHAPTER 8

Kills and Correctives

Prompt action must be taken when serious problems are found in a story that already has moved on the wire. This chapter summarizes procedures for dealing with stories when legal action and libel might be involved. Remember that if a legal problem develops with a story or if guidance is needed, the General Desk in New York must be consulted.

There are three ways to deal with problem stories: *withholds, kills* and *eliminations.*

* File a **withhold** when the accuracy of a story has been seriously challenged and the AP cannot quickly confirm the story. A withhold should be followed as soon as possible by a kill or an elimination if further checking makes either necessary. If the story turns out to be correct after further checking, file an advisory releasing it and lifting the withhold.

* Material that is libelous and unprivileged calls for a prompt **kill**. The kill is mandatory. It may also be necessary to file a corrective story, as explained below.

* An **elimination** is used when the story carries no threat of libel action but is objectionable for some other reason: error, poor taste, an old story inadvertently transmitted, etc.

Remember: Consult immediately with the General Desk.

Kills

Timing. Material considered libelous and unprivileged requires a prompt kill. The kill is mandatory.

The only exception: if the last version of the story moved more than 24 hours before the problem was discovered, it will probably be too late for a kill, but a corrective will be needed.

In cases where the problem is discovered several hours after the story moved, the kill and any corrective should be sent as soon as the problem is found. Also, an advisory telling news directors of the kill and the full text of the corrective should be sent the next day at about the same time as the erroneous story. This is intended to ensure that the material finds its way to the members who used the original story.

Form. The kill should say succinctly what was wrong with the original story — for example: *Smith was not arrested.*

It should not say the original was libelous. Just state the factual problem behind the kill.

Always use a **b** priority for the kill and the following advisory. Transmit the kill and advisory on the same circuits as the original story, with the same category code. This form should be followed exactly:

AP-ZYX BULLETIN KILL

**(New York) — KILL the ZYX company bankrupt story,
filed as v1234, which moved at 10:47 Eastern time.
The company is NOT bankrupt.**

AP Broadcast News Center

Follow the kill immediately with an advisory, stating whether a substitute story is planned:

AP-KILL Advisory

News Directors:

The New York story about the ZYX company being bankrupt, filed as V1234, has been killed. The company is **NOT** bankrupt.

A kill is mandatory.

Make certain the story is not aired.

A sub will be filed shortly. (Or: no sub will be filed.)

AP Broadcast News Center

Send an advisory the next day at roughly the same time as the original story:

AP-KILL Advisory

News Directors:

A New York story filed at 10:47 a-m Eastern time Monday under the slug ZYX-Bankrupt has been killed.

The ZYX company is **NOT** bankrupt.

A kill is mandatory.

A sub was filed Monday at 11:25 am, slugged ZYX-Petition.

AP Broadcast News Center

Circumstances will dictate whether a substitute story is required. (See the section on correctives, below.)

Report Requirements. For kills in the national broadcast report, a copy of the story killed and the kill itself should be given promptly to the managing editor, Broadcast Services, together with a letter telling who made the error and how it was made. This material will be relayed to New York.

For kills in state broadcast copy, the material should be given to the bureau chief, who will relay the material to New York.

If necessary, AP counsel will contact you for further information. This report will be forwarded to New York.

The file provided to the managing editor or bureau chief should include four things:

1. Wire copy of the erroneous story, the kill and the kill notes.

2. Wire copy of the substitute story or corrective.

3. A copy of any source material used by the writer or editor in preparation of the story, including source copy, member clip, audiotape, news releases, reporter's notes and the like.

4. A factual explanation from the staff member(s) who handled the story as to exactly how the error was made — what they did, where the information came from, etc.

The staff member's memorandum should be factual reports of what happened. The memorandum is not the place for extraneous comments about individuals or bureau procedures and definitely not for apologies.

Do not make any response to any letter or other communication in connection with any case where legal action seems possible without first consulting the managing editor or the General Desk.

Correctives

A kill may necessitate a corrective story. Or a corrective may be required for a story that contained an error but was not killed.

As with a kill, a corrective must be approved by the General Desk before it is filed by a bureau.

Do not feel you must be hasty in transmitting a corrective. When there is a factual error in the report, we want to correct it as quickly as possible. But remember that broadcast of a corrective does not safeguard us against legal action. You should be aware of any legal requirement in your state setting a time within which a corrective must appear.

The corrective story should identify the previous incorrect story by slug, transmission number, dateline, and the date. As follows:

AP-ZYX CORRECTIVE

> **News Directors:**
> **Members who used the March 15 story from New York, filed as V1234, slugged ZYX-Bankrupt are asked to use the following story.**

Remember that any story that has been on a broadcast circuit may well have been used before the kill moved.

Therefore, the corrective or substitute story should acknowledge the previous error and set the record straight.

While each case must be considered individually, the proper form for the corrective or sub will often be a straight assertion at the start that a previous AP account was in error.

Example:

> **The Associated Press erroneously reported on March 15th that ...**

In no instance should the story use any apologetic phrase such as *The Associated Press regrets the error.* The corrective is simply a factual account.

The corrective, with the same category code, should be filed on all circuits where the original was transmitted.

When a kill appears on any national or state general news wire, the national Broadcast Desk should check to determine whether the story was used on any of the broadcast circuits. If so, the kill and any subsequent correctives should be moved. If the story was not used on the broadcast wires, no further action is necessary—although the desk log should note that the matter has already been researched. This will save later shifts the trouble of checking through the files.

Report Requirements. If a corrective results from a kill, the corrective and all material relating to it must be gathered into a report as part of the procedures on kills. See page 206.

Again, do not make any response to any letter or other communication in connection with any case without first consulting the managing editor or the General Desk.

If a corrective to a story that was not killed is needed and has been approved by the General Desk supervisor, follow this procedure:

1. Mail to New York, to the attention of the managing editor, a letter explaining the need for the corrective. This letter should say what was wrong with the original story, when and how the error was made, when and how the error was discovered, and the names of the AP employees involved in the original error and the corrective.

2. Maintain a file in the bureau on the corrective that includes:

    — Wire copy of the erroneous story and wire copy of the substitute story or corrective.

    — A copy of any source material used by the writer or editor in preparation of the original story, including member clips, reporter's notes, actuality, news releases, etc.

    — A factual explanation from the staff member(s) who handled the story as to exactly how the error was made — what they did, where the information came from, etc.

The letter explaining the corrective must affirm that the above material has been retained in the bureau files.

If it is needed, the managing editor's office may request that this file be sent to New York later.

Withholds

A withhold is filed when the accuracy of a story has been seriously questioned and The Associated Press cannot quickly confirm the story. A withhold should be followed as soon as possible by a kill or an elimination if further checking makes either necessary.

If the information holds true after checking, file an advisory releasing the story.

The form for a withhold:

AP-Gold Find WITHHOLD

(Denver) — Withhold the Denver story slugged Gold Find, filed as V1234, which moved at 10:30 a-m Eastern time. Authorities say the miner's story has been questioned.

AP Broadcast News Center

The withhold should be filed on the same circuits, with the same category code, as the original copy.

Eliminations

An elimination is used for matter that carries no threat of libel action but is objectionable for some other reason: poor taste, error, an old story inadvertently transmitted, etc.

The form:

AP-Assassination Anniversary ELIMINATION

       (Dallas) — Eliminate the Assassination Anniversary story, filed as V1234, which moved at 8:15 a-m Eastern time. The story is old and was transmitted inadvertently.

AP Broadcast News Center

The elimination should be filed on the same circuits, with the same category code, as the original copy.

PART 3

The Specifics of Broadcast Style

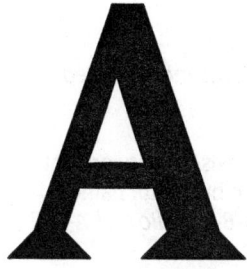

- **a, an** Use the article *a* before consonant sounds: *a one-year term* (sounds as if it begins with a *w*), *a united stand* (sounds like *you*).

  Use the article *an* before vowel sounds: *an energy crisis, an honorable man* (the *h* is silent), *an N-B-A record* (sounds like it begins with the letter *e*), *an 1890's celebration.*

- **a-** The rules in **prefixes** apply, but in general, no hyphen. Some examples:

atonal   atypical

- **A&P** Acceptable in all references to the *Great Atlantic and Pacific Tea Company, Incorporated.* Headquarters is in Montvale, N.J. Although the ampersand **(&)** is not generally acceptable in copy, it is used in this case because that is the way people are used to seeing *A&P.*

- **abbreviations** They should be avoided, except when they help the listener understand the story and help you keep wordiness to a minimum. Guidance on how a particular term should be handled is provided in the individual entries in this handbook.

  Some general principles:

  Familiarity: Use only those abbreviations that are so familiar to both broadcaster and listener that they do not form a stumbling block to the flow of copy. For example, most everyone knows what the *AFL-CIO* is, so you need not spell it out. But the term *A-P-I* does not immediately bring to mind the *American Petroleum Institute,* and so should not be used in any reference.

  Titles: The only titles that should be abbreviated are *Mr., Mrs. and Ms.* See **courtesy titles**.

  Junior and Senior: Do not abbreviate *junior* or *senior,* and do not set these words off with commas: *Martin Luther King Junior.*

  Time: Numeric clock references and periods in history should be abbreviated using a hyphen: *a-m, p-m, B-C, A-D.*

  Wrong: *Early this a-m; in the B-C era.* The abbreviations should be used only in connection with figures.

  Right: *In 450 B-C; at 9:30 a-m.*

  Right: *Early this morning; in the era before Christ was born.*

  It is always preferable to spell out these references (*9:30 this morning* rather than *9:30 a-m*) but when they are appropriate, the hyphenated abbreviation may be used. See **hyphen; time of day**.

    Do not abbreviate **state names**, or such terms as *company, incorporated* or *limited*. See **company names**.

- **A-B-C** Acceptable in all references to the radio and television networks of **ABC, Incorporated**. The corporation should be referred to by its full name. The network divisions can be referred to as *A-B-C News, A-B-C Radio* and *A-B-C T-V*.

- **A-B-C's**

- **able-bodied**

- **A-B-M, A-B-M's** Acceptable in second reference to *anti-ballistic missile(s)*. Avoid the redundant phrase *A-B-M missiles*.

- **A-bomb** Use *atomic bomb* unless a direct quotation is involved. See **Hiroshima**.

- **above-board**

- **absent-minded**

- **absent without leave** *AWOL (AY'-wawl)* is acceptable on second reference.

- **academic degrees** If mention of a degree is necessary to establish a person's credentials, avoid the abbreviation and use a phrase such as: *John Jones has a doctorate in psychology*.
  Use an apostrophe in *bachelor's degree, a master's*, etc. See **doctor**.

- **academic departments** Use lowercase except for words that are proper nouns or adjectives: *the department of history, the history department, the department of English, the English department*.

- **academic titles** Capitalize and spell out such formal titles as *professor, dean, president, chancellor* and *chairman* when they precede a name.
  Lowercase elsewhere: *Professor John Jones*, but *John Jones, a professor*.
  Modifiers such as *history* or *department* should be lowercase, as in *history Professor Oscar Handlin* or *department Chairman Jerome Wiesner*.

- **academy** See **military academies**.

- **Academy Awards** Presented annually by the *Academy of Motion Picture Arts and Sciences*. Also known as the *Oscars*, which is acceptable on first reference.
  Lowercase *the academy* and *the awards* whenever they stand alone.

- **accept, except** *Accept* means to receive. *Except* means to exclude.

- **accommodate**

- **accounts payable** The current liabilities or debts of a business that must be paid in the near future (within one year).

- **accounts receivable** Amounts due to a company for merchandise or services sold on credit. These are short-term assets.

- **accused** A person is accused *of*, not *with*, a crime. For guidelines on related words, see **allege**; **arrest** and **indict**.

- **Ace** A trademark for a brand of elastic bandage.

- **acknowledgment**

- **acquisitions** The process of buying or acquiring some asset. The term can refer to the purchase of a block of stock or, more often, to the acquisition of an entire company.

- **acre** Equal to 43,560 square feet, or 4,840 square yards. The metric equivalent is .4 (two-fifths) of a hectare or 4,047 square meters.
  To convert to hectares, multiply by .4 (5 acres times .4 = 2 hectares). See **hectare**.

- **acronyms** These are words that are formed from the first letters of a series of words. Use only those that are commonly known.
  Acronyms should be capitalized and should not be hyphenated: *NATO, CORE, the START treaty.*
  See individual entries for guidance on which acronyms may be used on first reference, and which are too obscure to be used. See **abbreviations.**

- **act** Legislation that has been passed into law. Such legislation is a *bill* prior to passage, and an *act* thereafter.
  Capitalize when part of the name of a law: *the Taft-Hartley Act, the act.*

- **acting** Always lowercase, but capitalize any formal title that may follow before a name: *acting Mayor Peter Barry.* See **titles**.

- **act numbers** Follow the rules for **numerals**. Capitalize *act* and the number: *Act One; Act One, Scene Two.* But: *the first act, the third scene.*

- **actor** (male) **actress** (female)

- **Actors' Equity Association** Headquarters is in New York.
  Actors' Equity or *Equity* is acceptable on second reference.

- **actuality** Audiotape of a newsmaker talking. Generally, radio actuality should be 10 to 20 seconds long.

  Don't use an actuality for the sake of using it. Often, the anchor can tell the story better than a piece of tape can. An actuality should contribute something to the story, such as the point of view of the newsmaker or the unique way the newsmaker said or did something. See the entries for **natural sound; Q&A; scener; voicer** and **wrap**.

- **A-D** Acceptable in all references for *anno Domini*: In the year of the Lord.

  Generally, the term is unnecessary: Any date or century number is presumed to be *A-D*. Thus, *the fourth century* is assumed to be different from *the fourth century B-C*.

  When specifying a year where there might be confusion, use *A-D* after the year number: *96 A-D*.

  In print contexts, *A-D* precedes the year number, since, if spelled out, the full phrase would be *in the year of the Lord 96*. But the construction in which *A-D* follows the number has gained such widespread acceptance in speech that it is more appropriate in broadcast scripts. See **B-C**.

- **-added** Follow this form in sports copy: *The 50-thousand-dollar-added sweepstakes.*

- **addresses** Spell out all terms such as *street, road* or *drive*. Follow the rules for **numerals**.

  Street addresses should be put in copy only when they are specifically relevant to the story. They should not be put in parentheses.

  If you want to make the use of the address optional, put the address in a separate advisory or at the bottom of the story. See **highway designations; ZIP codes**.

- **adjectives** The abbreviation *adj.* is used in this handbook to identify the spelling of the adjectival forms of words that frequently are misspelled.

  The **comma** entry provides guidance on punctuating a series of adjectives.

  The **hyphen** entry provides guidance on handling compound modifiers used before a noun.

- **ad-lib** (n., v., adj.)

- **administration** Lowercase: *the administration, the president's administration, the Clinton administration.*

  See the **government, junta, regime** entry for distinctions that apply in using these terms and *administration*.

- **administrative law judge** This is the federal title for the position formerly known as *hearing examiner*. Capitalize it when used as a formal title before a name.

  To avoid the long title, seek a construction that puts the title in a separate sentence: *The case is being heard by Administrative Law Judge John Williams. He disagrees with Jones' contention.*

- **administrator** Never abbreviate. Capitalize when used as a formal title before a name. See **titles**.

- **admiral** See **military titles**.

- **admissible**

- **admits, admitted** These words may in some contexts give the erroneous connotation of wrongdoing or imply that the subject is responding to an accusation. A person who announces that he is a homosexual, for example, may be *acknowledging* it to the world, not *admitting* it. *Says* usually is sufficient.

- **ad nauseam**

- **adopt, adapt** To *adopt* is to accept or approve. *The resolution was adopted. The child was adopted.*
  To *adapt* is to change. *He had to adapt to the circumstances.*

- **adopt, approve, enact, pass** Amendments, ordinances, resolutions and rules are *adopted* or *approved*.
  Bills are *passed*.
  Laws are *enacted*.

- **Adrenalin** A trademark for the synthetic or chemically extracted forms of epinephrine (eh-pin-EH'-frin), a substance produced by the adrenal gland. The non-proprietary terms are *epinephrine hydrochloride* or *adrenalin* (note lower case).

- **Adventist** See **Seventh-Day Adventist Church.**

- **adverbs** The abbreviation *adv.* is used in this handbook to identify the spelling of adverbial forms of words frequently misspelled.
  See the **hyphen** entry for guidelines on when an adverb should be followed by a hyphen in constructing a compound modifier.

- **adverse, averse** *Adverse* means unfavorable. *He predicted adverse weather.*
  Averse means reluctant or opposed: *She is averse to change.*

- **adviser** Not *advisor*.

- **advisory** Not *advisery*.
  An advisory is intended to pass on information about how a story will be covered or to impart purely logistical developments within a story.

Advisories are not intended to be read on the air. The form:

Clinton Speech ADVISORY

>   **The start of President Clinton's speech has been delayed
by ten minutes.**

AP Broadcast News Center

See **newsalert; updates.**

• **Aer Lingus** (ayr LIN'-guhs) The headquarters of the airline is in Dublin,
Ireland.

• **Aeroflot** (AYR'-oh-flaht) The headquarters of this airline is in Moscow.

• **Aeromexico** This airline formerly was known as Aeronaves de Mexico.
Headquarters is in Mexico City.

• **aesthetic**

• **affect, effect** *Affect,* as a verb, means to influence. *The game will affect
the standings.*
  Affect, as a noun, is best avoided. It occasionally is used in psychology to
describe an emotion, but it is rarely used in everyday language.
  Effect, as a verb, means to cause. *He will effect many changes in the
company.*
  Effect, as a noun, means result: *The effect was overwhelming. He
miscalculated the effect of his actions. It was a law of little effect.*

• **Afghan** (adj.) *Afghani* is the Afghan unit of currency.

• **AFL-CIO** Acceptable in all references for the *American Federation of Labor
and Congress of Industrial Organizations.* This is an exception to the normal rules
of hyphenation, since the term is so familiar and the fully hyphenated version
would be more difficult to read.
  The *AFL-CIO* is not a union. It is a federation of many unions.

• **A-frame**

• **African** Of or pertaining to Africa, or any of its peoples or languages. Do
not use the word as a synonym for *black* or *Negro.*
  In some countries of Africa, *colored* is used to describe those of mixed white
and black ancestry. In other societies *colored* is considered a derogatory word.
  Because of the ambiguity, avoid the term in favor of a phrase such as *mixed
racial ancestry.* If the word cannot be avoided, place it in quotation marks and
provide its meaning. See **colored** and **black.**

- **AFSCME** (AF'-smee) Acceptable on second reference to the *American Federation of State, County and Municipal Employees*. But be certain to use the full name on first reference to prevent confusion with other unions that represent government workers. Headquarters is in Washington.

- **after-** For readability, use a hyphen after this prefix when it is used to form a noun or a compound modifier:

after-effect	after-dinner drink	after-thought	after-theater snack

   See **hyphen.**

- **afterward** Not *afterwards*.

- **AFTRA** Acceptable on second reference to *American Federation of Television and Radio Artists*. Headquarters is in New York.

- **Agency for International Development** The abbreviation *A-I-D* is acceptable on second reference.

- **agenda** A list. It takes singular verbs and pronouns: *The agenda has run its course.* The plural is *agendas*.

- **agent** Lowercase unless it is a formal title used before a name.
   In the FBI, the formal title is *special agent*. Use *Special Agent William Smith* if necessary to distinguish among different types of agents. Otherwise, the preferred form is *agent William Smith* or *F-B-I agent William Smith*. See **titles.**

- **ages** Follow the rules for **numerals** in expressing the ages of persons or objects.
   Hyphenate the age when it is used as an adjective before a noun: *the five-year-old agreement,* but *it was five years old.* Similarly, hyphenate when the age is used in place of a noun: a youngster is *five years old* or *a five-year-old.*
   Do not use the common print-style construction in which the age is placed immediately after a name and offset with commas.
   Wrong: *The woman, 26, has a daughter two months old.*
   Right: *The woman is 26. She has a two-month-old daughter.*
   A person's age should be used only when it is directly relevant to the story.
   Avoid redundancies in expressing ages. It is enough to say someone is a *boy* or *girl* without saying he or she is *young.* See **boy; girl; infant** and **youth.**

- **ages of history** See the **historical periods and events** entry.

- **agnostic, atheist** An *agnostic* is a person who believes it is impossible to know whether there is a God.
   An *atheist* is a person who believes there is no God.

- **agricultural parity** The relationship between a farmer's purchasing power today and that of a base period representative of a time when farm incomes were considered equivalent to income standards in the rest of the economy. Farm purchasing power is a function of the ratio between the prices a farmer pays for supplies and the prices the farmer receives for crops.

  In the United States, when parity falls below 100 (that is, equivalence with the base period) for certain commodities, the farmer receives price support from the government, in the form of a percentage of the actual parity figure.

- **aid, aide** *Aid* is assistance.

  An *aide* is a person who serves as an assistant.

- **aide-de-camp, aides-de-camp** A military officer who serves as an assistant and confidential secretary to a superior.

- **AIDS** Acronym for *acquired immune deficiency syndrome*. *AIDS* is acceptable on all references.

  AIDS is an affliction in which a virus has weakened the body's immune system and cancer or serious infections have occurred.

  AIDS is most often transmitted through sexual contact; the sharing of contaminated hypodermic needles or syringes, generally by drug abusers; transfusions of infected blood or blood products; and from pregnant women to their offspring.

  The scientific name for the virus is *human immunodeficiency virus,* or *H-I-V.* The most common strain of the virus is often designated *H-I-V - One* to distinguish it from another type called *H-I-V - Two.*

  National *AIDS* statistics are updated monthly and are available from the federal government's Centers for Disease Control in Atlanta.

  A note about *AIDS* tests: Routine *AIDS* tests look for the presence of antibodies the body has made to defend against the *AIDS* virus. A positive antibody test is evidence of an infection with the *AIDS* virus. It does not mean the person has *AIDS.* People who test positive are often described as being *H-I-V-positive.*

  AIDS antibody tests should be distinguished from tests for the *AIDS* virus itself. The presence of the *AIDS* virus can be confirmed by laboratory cultures or by the much more sensitive polymerase (puh-LIM'-uhr-ays) chain reaction, or PCR, test.

  Many people infected with the virus remain apparently healthy for years. Only if an infected person develops serious symptoms is he or she said to have *AIDS.*

- **ain't** A dialectical or substandard contraction. Use it only in quoted matter or special contexts.

- **air base** Two words. Follow the practice of the U.S. Air Force, which uses *Air Force Base* as part of the proper name for its bases in the United States, and *Air Base* for installations abroad: *Lackland Air Force Base, Texas,* but *Rhein-Main Air Base, Germany.*

  On second reference, *the Air Force base, the air base, the base.*

  Do not abbreviate, even in datelines.

- **Air Canada**   Headquarters is in Montreal.

- **air-condition, air-conditioned** (v. and adj.) Note hyphens. The nouns are: *air conditioner, air conditioning.*

- **aircraft names**   Strive for readability. When the name includes numbers and letters, follow rules for numerals and hyphenate: *D-C-ten, L-ten-eleven, B-A-C one-eleven, F-four-C, MiG-21, C-five-A, Phantom-Two.*
  If the aircraft has only a model number, with no letters, it is not necessary to spell out the numbers: *707, 727, 737, 747, 757,* etc.
  Wide-body jets—or jumbo jets—include the *D-C-ten, L-ten-eleven,* and *747.*
  When referring to more than one aircraft, follow the guidelines in **plurals**: *three 747's, four D-C-tens, more than a dozen 747-B's.*
  Commercial aircraft are generally referred to as *airliners* or *jetliners.*
  Do not use quotation marks for aircraft with familiar, easily recognizable names which are in common use: *Air Force One, the Concorde.*
  Use quotation marks for the individual name of a particular aircraft: *the "Spirit of St. Louis." Air Force One* is excepted from this rule because the term applies to any airplane in which the president rides. See **Air Force One**.

- **aircraft terms**   Use *engine,* not *motor: a twin-engine plane* (not *twin-engined*). Use *jet plane* or *jetliner* only to describe those aircraft driven solely by jet engines. Use *turboprop* to describe an aircraft on which the jet engine is geared to a propeller. Turboprops are sometimes called *propjets.* See the **engine, motor** entry.

- **air force**   Capitalize when referring to U.S. forces: *the U-S Air Force, the Air Force, Air Force regulations.* Do not use the abbreviation *U-S-A-F.*
  Use lowercase for the forces of other nations: *the Israeli air force.*
  This approach has been adopted for consistency, because many foreign nations do not use *air force* as the proper name. See the **military academies** and **military titles** entries.

- **air force base**   See **air base**.

- **Air Force One**   The Air Force applies this name to any aircraft the president of the United States may be using. But in ordinary usage, *Air Force One* is the name for the particular jet that is normally reserved for the president's use. This is a Boeing 747, which was put into service in 1990.

- **Air France**   Headquarters is in Paris.

- **Air-India**   The hyphen is part of the formal name. Headquarters is in Bombay, India.

- **Air Jamaica**   Headquarters is in Kingston, Jamaica.

- **airline, airlines** Capitalize *airlines, air lines* and *airways* when used as part of a proper airline name. Major airlines are listed in this book separately by name. Companies that use *airlines* in their names include Alitalia, American, Continental, Hawaiian, Northwest, Trans World, United and Western.
  Companies that use *air lines* include Delta, Japan and Ozark.
  Companies that use *airways* include British and Qantas (KWAN'-tuhs).
  Companies that use none of these include Aer Lingus, Aeromexico, Air Canada, Air France, Air-India, Air Jamaica, Iberia, KLM and Western Alaska.
  On second reference, use just the proper name — as in *Delta* — or, if applicable, an abbreviation, such as *T-W-A*. Also acceptable are *the airline* or *the carrier*.
  The generic term is *airline*. Use *airlines* when referring to more than one.

- **airmail**

- **airman** See **military titles**.

- **Air National Guard**

- **airport** Capitalize as part of a proper name: *LaGuardia Airport, Newark International Airport*.
  The first name of an individual and the word *international* may be deleted from the formal name of an airport in all references: *John F. Kennedy International Airport, Kennedy Airport*. Note that the remainder of the name is capitalized. Use whichever construction is most familiar to the audience.
  But do not make up airport names. Instead, opt for more conversational constructions, such as the possessive. *Logan Airport* in Boston may be called *Boston's airport*, but it should not be called *Boston Airport*.

- **air-tight**

- **air traffic controller** Note: no hyphen.

- **airways** The system of routes that the federal government has established for airplane traffic. See the **airline, airlines** entry for the word's use in carriers' names.

- **Alabama** See **state names**.

- **a la carte**

- **a la king, a la mode**

- **Alaska** It contains the largest land area of the 50 states: 586,432 square miles. See **state names**.

- **Alaska-Hawaii Standard Time** The time zone used in Hawaii and most of Alaska. There is an *Alaska Daylight Time*, but there is no daylight time in Hawaii.

Bering time applies in some far western sections of Alaska. *Yukon time* is used in a small section south of the Yukon border. *Pacific time* applies in most of the area that borders British Columbia, including the city of Juneau. See **time zones**.

• **Alberta** A province of western Canada. See **datelines**.

• **albino, albinos**

• **Alcoa** The acronym is acceptable in all references to the *Aluminum Company of America*. The company has dropped the all-capitalized acronym *ALCOA* and made *Alcoa* the acceptable acronym for the company name.

Alcoa also is a city in Tennessee.

• **alcoholic** Use *recovering*, not *reformed*, in referring to those afflicted with the disease of alcoholism. Do not use *former*.

• **alderman** See **legislative titles**.

• **alert** See **weather terms**.

• **Al Fatah** (al fah-TAH′) A Palestinian guerrilla organization. Drop the article *Al* if preceded by an English article: *The Fatah statement, a Fatah leader.*

• **align**

• **Alitalia** (ahl-ih-TAHL′-yah) **Airlines** Headquarters is in Rome.

• **all-** Use a hyphen:

all-around (not all-round)   all-clear   all-out   all-star

See **all right** and the **all time, all-time** entry.

• **All-America, All-American** The Associated Press recognizes only one All-America football and basketball team each year. In football, only Walter Camp's selection through 1924, and AP selections after that, are recognized. Do not call anyone an *All-America* selection unless listed on either the Camp or AP roster.

Similarly, do not call anyone an *All-America basketball player* unless an AP selection. The first All-America basketball team was chosen in 1948.

Use *All-American* when referring specifically to an individual: *He is an All-American*, or *All-American Pat Ewing.*

Use *All-America* when referring to the team: *All-America team* or *He is an All-America player.*

- **allege** The word must be used with great care. Avoid any suggestion that the anchor or reporter is making an allegation.

  Some guidelines:

  Source: Specify the source of an allegation. In a criminal case, it should be an arrest record, an indictment or the statement of a public official connected with the case.

  Unproved action: Use *alleged bribe* or similar phrase when necessary to make it clear that an unproved action is not being treated as fact. Be sure that the source of the charge is specified in the story.

  Redundancy: Avoid redundant uses of *alleged*. It is proper to say: *The district attorney alleged that she took a bribe.* Or: *The district attorney accused her of taking a bribe.* But not: *The district attorney accused her of allegedly taking a bribe.*

  What is being alleged: Be careful about the placement of *alleged* in reference to an event that is known to have occurred when the dispute is over who participated in it. Do not say: *He attended the alleged meeting* when what you mean is: *He allegedly attended the meeting.*

  Synonyms: Do not use *alleged* as a routine qualifier. Instead, where appropriate, use words such as *apparent, reputed, suspected, reported* or *accused.*

  For guidelines on related words, see **accused**; **arrest**; and **indict**.

- **Allegheny Mountains** Or simply: *the Alleghenies.*

- **alley** See **addresses**.

- **allies, allied** Capitalize *allies* or *allied* only when referring to the combination of the United States and its Allies during World War I or World War II: *The Allies defeated Germany. He was in the Allied invasion of France.* But: *The United States and Britain are allies in NATO;* the NATO allies.

- **allot, allotted, allotting**

- **all right** (adv.) Never *alright.* Hyphenate only if used colloquially as a compound modifier: *He is an all-right guy.*

- **all time, all-time** An *all-time high,* but *the greatest runner of all time.* Avoid the redundant phrase *all-time record.*

- **allude, refer** To *allude* to something is to speak of it without specifically mentioning it.

  To *refer* is to mention it directly.

- **allusion, illusion** *Allusion* means an indirect reference: *The allusion was to his opponent's war record.*

  Illusion means an unreal or false impression: *The scenic director created the illusion of choppy seas.*

- **alma mater**

- **almost never** Don't use. Instead use *seldom* or *hardly ever.*

- **also-ran** (n.)

- **altar, alter** An *altar* is a table-like platform used in a church service. To *alter* is to change.

- **Aluminum Company of America** *Alcoa* is acceptable in all references. Headquarters is in Pittsburgh.

- **alumnus, alumni, alumna, alumnae** Use *alumnus* (*alumni* in the plural) when referring to a man who has attended a school.
  Use *alumna* (*alumnae* in the plural) for similar references to a woman.
  Use *alumni* when referring to a group of men and women.

- **Alzheimer's disease** Note the apostrophe. *Alzheimer's* is acceptable on second reference.
  This is a progressive, irreversible neurological disorder. Most victims are older than 65, but Alzheimer's can strike in the 40s or 50s. Symptoms include gradual memory loss, impairment of judgment, disorientation, personality change, difficulty in learning and loss of language skills. The cause is unknown, and no cure is yet available.

- **A-M** Acceptable in all references for the amplitude modulation system of radio transmission and the band of frequencies associated with it: *an A-M radio station.*

- **a-m, p-m** Lowercase, and note the hyphen. Avoid the redundant *10 a-m in the morning.* See **midnight** and the various **time** entries.

- **Amalgamated Clothing and Textile Workers Union of America** The shortened forms *Amalgamated Clothing Workers* and *clothing workers union* are acceptable in all references. Headquarters is in New York.

- **Amalgamated Transit Union** Use this full name in the first reference. Do not use the abbreviation *A-T-U* in any reference. Instead, use *the union.* Headquarters is in Washington.

- **ambassador**
  Use for both men and women. Capitalize as a formal title before a name. See **titles**.

- **amendments to the Constitution** Follow the guidelines in **numerals**, and capitalize: *the First Amendment, the 22nd Amendment.*
  Colloquial references to the Fifth Amendment's protection against self-

incrimination are best avoided, but where appropriate: *He took the Fifth seven times.*

• **American** An acceptable description of a resident of the United States. Do not use it to mean any resident or citizen of nations in North or South America.

• **American Airlines** Headquarters is in Forth Worth, Texas.

• **American Automobile Association** *Triple-A* is acceptable in all references, as is *the automobile association*. Do not use the abbreviation *A-A-A*.
    Triple-A is a national organization of local automobile clubs, each of which sets its own policies. Headquarters is in Heathrow, Fla.

• **American Baptist Association** See **Baptist churches**.

• **American Baptist Churches in the U-S-A** See **Baptist churches**.

• **American Bar Association** *A-B-A* is also acceptable, as is *the bar association*. Headquarters is in Chicago.

• **American Civil Liberties Union** *A-C-L-U* is acceptable on first reference, but the name must be spelled out somewhere in the story. Headquarters is in New York.

• **American Federation of Government Employees** Use this full name on first reference to prevent confusion with other unions that represent government workers. Do not abbreviate. Headquarters is in Washington.

• **American Federation of Labor and Congress of Industrial Organizations** *AFL-CIO* is acceptable in all references. Note the lack of hyphens between the individual letters; this is because the abbreviation is so familiar. Headquarters is in Washington.

• **American Federation of Musicians** Use this full name on first reference. The shortened form *musicians union* is acceptable on second reference. Note the lack of an apostrophe. Headquarters is in New York.

• **American Federation of State, County and Municipal Employees** Use this full name on first reference to prevent confusion with other unions that represent government workers. Headquarters is in Washington.
    The acronym *AFSCME (AF'-smee)* may be used on second reference.

• **American Federation of Teachers** Use this full name on first reference to prevent confusion with other unions that represent teachers. *A-F-T* is acceptable on second reference. Headquarters is in Washington.

- **American Federation of Television and Radio Artists** *AFTRA* is acceptable on second reference. Headquarters is in New York.

- **American Hospital Association** Do not abbreviate. Use *the hospital association* or *the association* on second reference. Headquarters is in Chicago.

- **Americanisms** Words and phrases that have become part of the English language as spoken in the United States are listed in Webster's New World Dictionary with a star *.
  Most Americanisms are acceptable in news stories, but let the context be the guide. See **word selection**.

- **American Legion** Capitalize *the Legion* in second reference.
  Members are *Legionnaires*, just as members of the Lions Club are *Lions*.
  Legion and *Legionnaires* are capitalized because they are not being used in their common-noun sense. A *legion* (lowercase) is a large group of soldiers or, by derivation, a large number of items: *His friends are legion.* A *legionnaire* (lowercase) is a member of such a legion. It is best to avoid this usage if any confusion with the American Legion could result. See the **fraternal organizations and service clubs** entry.

- **American Medical Association** *A-M-A* is acceptable on first reference, but the name must be spelled out somewhere in the story. Headquarters is in Chicago.

- **American Motors Corporation** *A-M-C* is acceptable on second reference. Headquarters is in Southfield, Mich.

- **American Newspaper Publishers Association** See **Newspaper Association of America**.

- **American Petroleum Institute** An industry promotional group. Do not use the abbreviation *A-P-I*. Headquarters is in Washington.

- **American Postal Workers Union** This union represents clerks and similar employees who work inside post offices.
  Use the full name on first reference to prevent confusion with the **National Association of Letter Carriers**. The shortened form *Postal Workers union* is acceptable on second reference. Do not abbreviate. Headquarters is in Washington.

- **American Press Institute** Do not use the abbreviation *A-P-I*. Headquarters is in Reston, Va.

- **American Society for the Prevention of Cruelty to Animals** This organization is limited to the five boroughs of New York City. *A-S-P-C-A* is acceptable on second reference. See **Society for the Prevention of Cruelty to Animals**.

- **American Society of Composers, Authors and Publishers**
ASCAP is acceptable on first reference, but the full name, or a reference to *the music licensing organization* must appear somewhere in the story. Headquarters is in New York.

- **American Stock Exchange** *Amex* is acceptable on the first reference, but the name must be spelled out somewhere in the story.

- **American Telephone and Telegraph Company** *A-T-and-T* is acceptable on all references. Headquarters is in New York.

- **American Veterans of World War Two, Korea and Vietnam**
AMVETS is acceptable in second reference. Headquarters is in Washington.

- **Americas Cup** (golf)

- **America's Cup** (yachting)

- **Amex** (A'-mex) See **American Stock Exchange**.

- **amid** Not *amidst*.

- **amidships**

- **ammunition** See **weapons**.

- **amnesty** See the entry that reads **pardon, parole, probation**.

- **amok** Not *amuck*.

- **among, between** The maxim that *between* introduces two items and *among* introduces more than two covers most questions about how to use these words: *The funds were divided among Ford, Carter and McCarthy.* However, *between* is the correct word when expressing the relationships of three or more items considered one pair at a time: *Negotiations on a debate format are under way between the network and the Ford, Carter and McCarthy committees.*
  As with all prepositions, any pronouns that follow these words must be in the objective case: *among us, between him and her, between you and me.*

- **ampersand (&)** It is hardly ever used in wire copy. See **punctuation** and individual entries (such as **A&P**) for specific usage rules.

- **amplitude modulation** Don't use it; use *A-M* instead.

- **Amtrak** This is the marketing name used by the *National Railroad Passenger Corporation*, and may be used in all references. The name originally was derived from the words *American travel by track*.

The corporation was established by Congress in 1970 to take over inter-city passenger operations from railroads that wanted to drop passenger service. Amtrak contracts with railroads for the use of their tracks and of certain other operating equipment and crews. Amtrak is subsidized in part by federal funds appropriated yearly by Congress and administered through the Department of Transportation.

Amtrak should not be confused with **Conrail** (see separate entry). However, the legislation that established Conrail provided for Amtrak to gradually take over ownership of certain trackage in the Boston-Washington corridor and from Philadelphia to Harrisburg, Pa. Amtrak headquarters is in Washington.

- **AMVETS** Acceptable on second reference for *American Veterans of World War Two, Korea and Vietnam.*

- **anchor** (v., n.) Acceptable in all references as a verb describing the act of anchoring a newscast: *Peter Jennings will anchor A-B-C's coverage.*
  Acceptable on second reference to an anchorman or anchorwoman.

- **anchorman, anchorwoman** *Anchor* or *co-anchor* is acceptable on second reference.

- **anemia, anemic**

- **anesthetic**

- **Anglican Communion** This is the name for the worldwide association of the 22 separate national Anglican churches. Each national church is independent. A special position of honor is accorded to the archbishop of Canterbury, as the pre-eminent officer in the original Anglican body, the Church of England.
  The test of membership in the Anglican Communion traditionally has been whether a church is in communion with the See of Canterbury. No legislative or juridical ties exist, however.
  Beliefs: Anglicans believe in the Trinity, the humanity and divinity of Christ, the virginity of Mary, salvation through Christ, and everlasting heaven and hell. Baptism and the Lord's Supper are recognized as sacraments, although belief in the degree to which Christ is present in the Eucharist may vary. Together with Scripture, the Book of Common Prayer serves as the principal guide to belief and practice.
  A principal difference between Roman Catholics and Anglicans is still the dispute that led to the formation of the Church of England—refusal to acknowledge that the pope, as bishop of Rome, has ruling authority over other bishops.
  The communion also contends that its clergy have a direct link to Christ's apostles that is traceable through an unbroken series of ceremonies in which authority was passed down by a laying-on of hands. The Roman Catholic Church, which claims the same type of historic succession for its clergy, has held that 16th century Anglican practice broke the continuity of apostolic succession among its clergy.
  Among individual Anglican (or *Episcopal* in the United States) parishes, practices fall into one of three categories—high, broad or low. A high parish

stresses the sacraments and extensive ritual in worship. A low parish favors simpler services and emphasizes the preaching of the Gospel. A broad parish embraces portions of high and low worship practices while tending to be activist on social questions and flexible in matters of church government. The term *Anglo-Catholic* occasionally is used to describe high Anglican practice. See **catholic, catholicism**.

Anglican Churches: Members of the Anglican Communion, in addition to the Church of England, include the Scottish Episcopal Church, the Anglican Church of Canada and, in the United States, the Protestant Episcopal Church. See **Episcopal Church**.

• **Anglo-** Always capitalized. Hyphenate in cases where the word that follows is capitalized:

Anglo-American   Anglo-Catholic   Anglo-Indian   Anglo-Saxon

Otherwise, no hyphen.

Anglo is used in some parts of the country to refer to a white person and can be regarded by some as derogatory. It should be used only in a direct quotation.

• **angry** *At* someone or *with* someone.

• **animals** Do not apply a personal pronoun to an animal unless its gender has been established or the animal has a name: *The dog was scared; it barked. Rover was scared; he barked. The cat, which was scared, ran to its basket. Susie the cat, who was scared, ran to her basket. The bull tosses his horns.*

Capitalize the name of a specific animal and spell out the numbers to show sequence: *Bowser, Whirlaway Two.*

For breed names, follow the spelling and capitalization in Webster's New World Dictionary. For breeds not listed in the dictionary, capitalize words derived from proper nouns; use lowercase elsewhere: *basset hound, Boston terrier.*

• **anno Domini** See **A-D**.

• **annual** An event cannot be described as *annual* until it has been held in at least two successive years. For that reason, do not use the term *first annual.* Instead, use *first* and note that sponsors plan to hold an event annually.

• **annual meeting** Lowercase in all uses.

• **anoint**

• **another** *Another* is not a synonym for *additional*; it refers to an element that somehow duplicates a previously stated quantity.
Right: *Ten women passed, another ten failed.*
Wrong: *Ten women passed, another six failed.*
Right: *Ten women passed, six others failed.*

- **antarctic, Antarctica, Antarctic Ocean** They refer to the area near the South Pole.

- **ante** (AN'-tee) A colloquialism derived from poker and meaning the amount one must pay as his or her share to enter the game, as in: *He upped the ante.* Don't overuse.

- **ante-** It means before or in front of. The rules in **prefixes** apply, but in general, no hyphen. Some examples:

antebellum   antedate

- **anthems** See **composition titles**. Lowercase the term *national anthem*.

- **anti-** Hyphenate all except the following words, which have specific meanings of their own:

antibiotic	antigen	antipasto	antiserum
antibody	antiknock	antiperspirant	antithesis
anticlimax	antimatter	antiphon	antitoxin
antidote	antimony	antiphony	antitrust
antifreeze	antiparticle*	antiseptic	antitussive
antihistamine			

*And similar terms in physics such as *antiproton.*
This approach has been adopted in the interests of readability and easily remembered consistency.
Hyphenated words, many of them exceptions to Webster's New World, include:

anti-aircraft	anti-inflation	anti-labor	anti-social
anti-bias	anti-intellectual	anti-slavery	anti-war

See **Antichrist, anti-Christ**.

- **Antichrist, anti-Christ** *Antichrist* is the proper name of the individual the Bible says will challenge Jesus Christ.
The adjective *anti-Christ* refers to anyone or anything opposed to Christ.

- **anticipate, expect** To *anticipate* means to expect and prepare for something; *expecting* something does not include the notion of preparation:
They expected a record crowd.
They have anticipated it by adding more seats to the auditorium.

- **Antiochian** (an-tee-OH'-kee-uhn) **Orthodox Christian Archdiocese of North America** Formed in 1975 by the merger of the Antiochian Orthodox Christian Archdiocese of New York and all North America and the Antiochian Orthodox Archdiocese of Toledo, Ohio and Dependencies in North America. It is under the jurisdiction of the patriarch of Antioch. See **Eastern Orthodox churches**.

- **antitrust** Any law or policy designed to encourage competition by curtailing monopolistic power and unfair business practices.

- **anybody, any body, anyone, any one** One word for an indefinite reference: *Anyone can do it.*
  Use two words when the emphasis is on singling out one element of a group: *Any one of them may speak up.*

- **A-P** Acceptable on second reference to *The Associated Press.* Hyphenated only when included in a story to be read on the air. Otherwise, as, for example, in an advisory, *AP.* Do not capitalize *the* when it precedes *A-P.* Headquarters is in New York. See **Associated Press.**

- **A-P Broadcast News Center** Headquarters of the electronic media operations of The Associated Press.
  On second reference, *the center.* Do not use the abbreviation *B-N-C.*
  Located at the Broadcast News Center are the desks producing the AP's broadcast wires, radio network, graphics and North American video services. The address is 1825 K Street N.W., Washington, D.C, 20006.

- **A-P Network News** A radio network service provided by The Associated Press. Do not use the abbreviation *A-P-N-N.* Use *the network* on second reference. Headquarters is at the Broadcast News Center in Washington.

- **apostolic delegate, papal nuncio** An *apostolic delegate* is a Roman Catholic diplomat chosen by the pope to be his envoy to the church in a nation that does not have formal diplomatic relations with the Vatican.
  A *papal nuncio* is the pope's envoy to a nation with which the Vatican has diplomatic relations.

- **apostrophe (')** The apostrophe is used to indicate the possessive, a contraction or the omission of letters or figures. In using it, strive for readability. Some guidelines:
  Possessives: see the **possessives** entry.
  Contractions: see the **contractions** entry.
  Omitted Letters: Use an apostrophe to indicate omitted letters: *rock 'n' roll, 'tis the season.*
  Omitted Figures: When indicating a specific year, use an apostrophe: *the class of '62.* But when indicating a decade, no apostrophe is needed before the figure: *the roaring 20's.*
  Plurals: When adding an *s* to letters or figures: *He got three B's on his report card. There were five 747's in a row on the runway.*
  Pronouncers: Use the apostrophe to indicate the stressed syllable. See the **pronouncers** entry.

- **Appalachia** (a-puh-LAYCH'-yuh) In the broadest sense, the word applies to the entire region along the Appalachian Mountains, which extend from

Maine into northern Alabama.

The word also is used in a sense that suggests economic depression and poverty. In that case, the reference is to sections of eastern Tennessee, eastern Kentucky, southeastern Ohio and the western portion of West Virginia.

The Appalachian Regional Commission, established by federal law in 1965, has a mandate to foster development in 397 counties in 13 states—all of West Virginia and contiguous parts of Alabama, Georgia, Kentucky, Maryland, Mississippi, New York, North Carolina, Ohio, Pennsylvania, South Carolina, Tennessee and Virginia.

When the word *Appalachia* is used, specify the extent of the area in question.

• **Appalachian Mountains** Or simply: *the Appalachians.*

• **appeals court** See **U-S Court of Appeals** and **judicial branch.**

• **apposition** When two terms appear next to each other in a sentence, and one is used to explain the other: *Joe, the tallest person in town, had to use a ladder to rescue the cat.* Avoid using this construction. Break the sentence into two: *Joe is the tallest person in town. But he had to use a latter to rescue the cat.*
See the **essential phrases, non-essential phrases** entry for examples.

• **appreciation** An increase in the value of property. A decrease would be *depreciation.*

• **approve** See the **adopt, approve, enact, pass** entry.

• **April** See **months.**

• **April Fools' Day**

• **Aqua-Lung** A trademark for an underwater breathing apparatus. See **scuba.**

• **Arabian American Oil Company** Now known as **Saudi Arabian Oil Company.** See that entry.

• **Arabic names** In general, use an English spelling that approximates the way a name sounds in Arabic. And use a pronouncer in any case.

If an individual has a preferred spelling and pronunciation in English, use it. Otherwise, use the spelling established in common usage.

Problems in transliteration of Arabic names often are traceable to pronunciations that vary from region to region. The *g*, for example, is pronounced like the *g* of *go* in North Africa, but like the *j* of *joy* in the Arab Peninsula. Thus it is *Gamal* in Egypt but *Jamal* in nations on the peninsula. Follow local practice in deciding which letter to use and how to write the pronouncer.

Arabs commonly are known by two names (*Fuad Butros*) or by three (*Ahmed*

Zaki Yamani). Follow the individual's preference on the first reference, and use only the final name in the sequence in subsequent references.

Use the prefix *al* or *el* on first reference only if it is the individual's preference. Do not carry *al* or *el* through to subsequent references.

The Arabic word for son (*ibn* or *bin*, depending upon personal preference and the nation) is sometimes part of a name (*Rashid bin Humaid).* On second reference, use only the final word in the name: *Humaid.*

The word *abu*, meaning *father of*, occasionally is used as a last name (*Abdul Mohsen Abu Maizer).* Capitalize and repeat it on second reference: *Abu Maizer.*

The titles *king, emir, sheik* and *imam* are used, but *prince* usually replaces *emir.* Some Arabs are known only by the title and a given name on first reference (*King Hussein).* Others are known by a complete name (*Sheik Sabah Salem Sabah).* Follow the common usage on the first reference.

On second reference, drop the title, using only the given name if it stood alone (*Hussein)* or the final name in the sequence if more than one was used on first reference (*Sabah).* Make an exception to this procedure for second reference if an individual commonly is known by some other one of the names used on first reference.

The *al*, when found in front of many newspaper names, means *the.* It should be capitalized.

- **Arabic numerals** The numerical figures 1, 2, 3, 4, 5, 6, 7, 8, 9, 0. Generally, they are not used in broadcast writing. In this handbook, they are referred to as Arabic numerals or figures. See **numerals**.

- **arbitrage** Buying currency, commercial bills or securities in one market and selling them at the same time in another. The objective is to make a profit on the price discrepancy.

- **arbitrate, mediate** Both terms are used in reports about labor negotiations, but they should not be interchanged.

One who *arbitrates* hears evidence from all persons concerned, then hands down a decision.

One who *mediates* listens to arguments of both parties and tries by the exercise of reason or persuasion to bring them to an agreement.

- **arch-** It is best to use a hyphen after this prefix to ease readability, as in:

arch-conservative   arch-rival   arch-enemy   arch-Republican

But in cases where a hyphen is not commonly used, as in *archbishop*, don't use one.

- **archbishop** See **Episcopal Church; Roman Catholic Church**; and **religious titles**.

- **archbishop of Canterbury** In general, lowercase *archbishop* unless it is used before the name of the individual who holds the office.

Capitalize *Archbishop of Canterbury* standing alone only when it is used in a story that also refers to members of Britain's nobility. See the **nobility** entry for the relevant guidelines. See **Anglican Communion**.

- **archdiocese** Capitalize as part of a proper name: *the Archdiocese of Chicago, the Chicago Archdiocese.* Lowercase when it stands alone. See the entry for the particular denomination in question.

- **arctic, Arctic Circle, Arctic Ocean** They refer to the area near the North Pole.

- **arctic fox**

- **are** (ayr) (n.) A unit of surface measure in the metric system equal to 100 square meters. An *are* is equal to about 1076.4 square feet, or 119.6 square yards. See **hectare** and **metric system**.

- **area codes** See **telephone numbers**.

- **Arizona** See **state names**.

- **Arkansas** See **state names**.

- **Armenian Church of America** The term encompasses two independent dioceses that cooperate in some activities: The Eastern Diocese of the Armenian Church of America, covering areas outside California, and that state's Western Diocese of the Armenian Church of America, which serves California. See **Eastern Orthodox churches**.

- **Armistice Day** Originally a celebration of the armistice that ended World War I. See **Veterans Day**.

- **army** Capitalize when referring to American forces: *the U-S Army, the Army, Army regulations.* Do not use the abbreviation *U-S-A.*
  Use lowercase for the forces of other nations: *the French army.*
  This approach has been adopted for consistency, because many foreign nations do not use *army* as the proper name. See **military academies** and **military titles**.

- **arrest** To avoid any suggestion that someone is being judged before a trial, do not use a phrase such as *arrested for murder.* Instead, use *arrested in connection with the killing* or *arrested at the scene of the killing,* or similar phrases. For guidelines on related words, see **accused; allege** and **indict**.

- **arrive** It requires the preposition *at.* Do not omit, as airline dispatchers often do, as in: *He will arrive LaGuardia.*

- **artifact**

- **artificial intelligence** Ideally, computers that think like humans. Currently, computers can only crudely apply experience, logic and prediction to problem-solving—based entirely upon the programmer's predictions about the problems the machine will face.

- **artillery** See **weapons**.

- **artworks** See **composition titles**.

- **as** See **like, as**.

- **ASCII** (AS'-kee) An acronym for *American Standard for Computer Information Interchange*. A standard computer code for the easy exchange of information among various types of data processing and data communications equipment. *ASCII* represents as numbers every letter in the alphabet, Arabic numerals and standard symbols such as punctuation marks.

- **ash can, ash tray**

- **Ash Wednesday** The first day of Lent, 46 days before Easter. See **Easter** and **Lent**.

- **Asian, Asiatic** Use *Asian* or *Asians* when referring to people. Some Asians regard *Asiatic* as offensive when applied to people.

- **Asian flu**

- **Asian subcontinent** In popular usage the term applies to Bangladesh, Bhutan, India, Nepal, Sikkim and the island nation of Sri Lanka (formerly Ceylon) at the southeastern tip of India. For definitions of terms that apply to other parts of Asia, see **Far East; Middle East** and **Southeast Asia**.

- **as if** The preferred form, but *as though* is acceptable.

- **assassin, killer, murderer** An *assassin* is a politically motivated killer. A *killer* is anyone who kills with a motive of any kind. A *murderer* is one who is convicted of murder in a court of law. See **execute** and the **homicide, murder, manslaughter** entry.

- **assassination, date of** A prominent person is shot one day and dies the next. Which day was he assassinated? The day he was attacked.

- **assault, battery** Popularly, *assault* almost always implies physical contact and sudden, intense violence. Legally, however, *assault* means simply to threaten violence, as in pointing a pistol at an individual without firing it.

Assault and battery is the legal term when the victim was touched by the assaulter or something the assaulter put in motion.

• **assembly** Capitalize when part of the proper name for the lower house of a legislature: *the California Assembly.* Retain capitalization if the state name is dropped but the reference is specific:

(Sacramento) -- The state Assembly ...

If a legislature is known as a general assembly: *the Missouri General Assembly, the General Assembly, the assembly.* In such cases, *legislature* may also be used as the proper name. See **legislature**.

Lowercase all plural uses: *the California and New York assemblies.*

• **assemblyman, assemblywoman** See **legislative titles**.

• **assets** Everything a company or individual owns or is owed. Assets may be categorized further as:

Current Assets: Cash, investments, money due to a corporation, unused raw materials and inventories of finished but unsold products.

Fixed Assets: Buildings, equipment, land, long-term investments—assets that cannot be readily turned to cash without disturbing the operation of the business.

Intangible Assets: Patents and good will.

• **assistant** Do not abbreviate. Capitalize only when part of a formal title before a name: *Assistant Secretary of State George Ball.* When practical, break up the title: *George Ball is assistant secretary of state.* See **titles**.

• **associate** (n.) Do not abbreviate. Apply the same capitalization rules as in **assistant**. See **titles**.

• **Associated Press, The** A news gathering cooperative dating from 1848. Use *The Associated Press* on first reference. The capitalized article is part of the formal name.

Use *the A-P* on subsequent references. Note that the article is lowercase unless the name is spelled out.

The address is 50 Rockefeller Plaza, New York, N.Y. 10020. The telephone number is (212) 621-1500.

The following are service names used most frequently by the AP:

AP Alert Wires	AP Fax Services	AP PhotoExpress
AP All News Radio	AP Full DataStream	AP PhotoStream
AP Audiotex	AP GraphicsBank	AP Race Wire
AP Business News Wire	AP Headlines	AP Spanish-language wires
AP BusinessStream	AP International News Wires	AP SportsStats
AP BusinessWatch	AP MegaStream	AP Sports Wire
AP DriveTime	AP Network News	APTV (video)

AP Election Wires	AP NewsCenter	APTV Wire
AP Express NewsLink	AP NewsDesk	AP Washington Report
AP Express Newspaper Network	AP NewsPower	AP Worldstream
AP Express ProgramLink	AP NewsTalk	Canadian News
AP Express PromotionLink	AP Online	PromotionLink

See **A-P; A-P Broadcast News Center** and **A-P Network News**.

- **Association** Do not abbreviate. Capitalize when part of a proper name: *the American Medical Association.*

- **astronaut** It is not a formal title. Do not capitalize when used before a name: *astronaut John Glenn.*
  The term applies to men and women.

- **AstroTurf** A trademark for a type of artificial grass. *Artificial grass* or *artificial surface* are preferred when referring to the generic type.

- **Atchison, Topeka and Santa Fe Railway** A subsidiary of Santa Fe Industries. Headquarters is in Chicago.

- **atheist** See **agnostic, atheist.**

- **athlete's foot, athlete's heart** Note apostrophes.

- **athletic club** Do not abbreviate.

- **athletic teams** Capitalize team names, association names and recognized nicknames: *the Red Sox, the Big Ten, the A's, the Colts.*

- **Atlanta** The city in Georgia stands alone in datelines.

- **Atlantic Coast Conference** The college sports conference that includes Clemson, Duke, Maryland, North Carolina, North Carolina State, Virginia, Wake Forest.

- **Atlantic Ocean**

- **Atlantic Richfield Company** *Arco* is acceptable on second reference. Note that this acronym is not all-caps, an exception to the rule. Headquarters is in Los Angeles.

- **Atlantic Standard Time, Atlantic Daylight Time** Used in the Maritime Provinces of Canada and in Puerto Rico. See **time zones.**

- **at large** Usually two words for an individual representing more than a single district: *congressman at large, councilman at large.*

But it is *ambassador-at-large*, for an ambassador assigned to no particular country.

- **Atomic Age** Began on Dec. 2,1942, at the University of Chicago, with the creation of the first self-sustaining nuclear chain reaction.

- **Atomic Energy Commission** No longer exists. See **Nuclear Regulatory Commission**.

- **attache** (a-ta-SHAY′) It is not a formal title. Always lowercase.

- **attorney, lawyer** In common usage the words are interchangeable.
  Technically, however, an *attorney* is someone (usually, but not necessarily, a lawyer) empowered to act for another. Such an individual occasionally is called an *attorney-in-fact*.
  A *lawyer* is a person admitted to practice in a court system. Such an individual occasionally is called an *attorney-at-law*.
  Do not abbreviate. Do not capitalize unless it is an officeholder's title: *defense attorney Perry Mason, attorney Perry Mason, District Attorney Hamilton Burger*. See **lawyer.**

- **attorney general, attorneys general** Never abbreviate.

- **augur** A transitive verb meaning foretell. It should not be followed with the preposition *for: The tea leaves augur a time of joy*. Preferred terms are *foretell, predict, suggest* and *forecast*.

- **August** See **months.**

- **author** As a noun, it is used for both men and women. Do not use it as a verb; use *write* instead.

- **automaker, automakers** No hyphen.

- **automatic** See the **pistol** and **weapons** entries.

- **automobiles** Capitalize brand names: *Buick, Ford, Mustang, M-G, Honda.* Lowercase generic terms: *a Volkswagen van, a Mack truck.*

- **auto racing** In covering major events in short separate items, report the order of the top finishers as well as the winner's speed.

- **Auto-Train Corporation** Note hyphen. A private company that hauls passengers and their cars, leasing rails and equipment owned by other companies. Headquarters is in Washington.

- **autoworker, autoworkers** One word when used generically. But *Auto*

Worker when referring specifically to the membership and the activities of the *U-A-W*—the United Automobile, Aerospace and Agricultural Implement Workers of America.

- **autumn** See **seasons**.

- **avenue** Do not abbreviate. See **addresses**.

- **average, mean, median, norm** *Average* refers to the result obtained by dividing a sum by the number of quantities added together: *The average of seven, nine, and 17 is eleven: Their sum divided by three — the number of factors. The average is eleven.*
  Mean commonly designates a figure intermediate between two extremes: *The mean temperature of the day with a high of 56 and a low of 34 is 45.*
  Median is the middle number of points in a series arranged in order of size: *The median grade in the group of 50, 55, 85, 88, 92 is 85. The average is 74.*
  Norm implies a standard of average performance for a given group: *The child was below the norm for his age in reading comprehension.*

- **average of** The phrase takes a plural verb in a construction such as: *An average of 100 new jobs are created daily.*

- **averse** See **adverse, averse.**

- **Avianca** (ah-vee-AHN′-kah) The headquarters of this airline is in Bogota, Colombia.

- **aviator** Use for both men and women.

- **awards and decorations** Capitalize them: *Bronze Star, Medal of Honor,* etc. See **Nobel Prizes** and **Pulitzer Prizes.**

- **awe-struck**

- **awhile, a while** *He plans to stay awhile. He plans to say for a while.*

- **AWOL** (AY′-wawl) Acceptable on second reference to *absent without leave.*

- **ax** Not *axe*. The verb forms: *ax, axed, axing.*

- **Axis** The alliance of Germany, Italy and Japan during World War II.

- **Baby Bells** A collective description of the regional telephone companies formed out of the breakup of the Bell System of AT&T. The term is not generally known and should be avoided except in quotes.

- **baby boomer** Lower case, no hyphen. Generally considered to be a person born during the years immediately following World War II.

- **baby-sit, baby-sitting, babysitter**

- **baccalaureate**

- **bachelor of arts, bachelor of science** A *bachelor's degree* or *bachelor's* is acceptable in any reference. See **academic degrees**.

- **backboard, backcourt, backfield, backhand, backspin, backstop, backstretch, backstroke** Some are exceptions to Webster's New World, made for consistency in handling sports stories.

- **back up** (v.)

- **backup** (n. and adj.)

- **backward** Not backwards.

- **back yard** (n.)

- **backyard** (adj.)

- **B-A-C One-eleven** The less cumbersome *Tristar Jet* is preferable.

- **bad, badly** *Bad* should not be used as an adverb. It does not lose its status as an adjective, however, in a sentence such as *I feel bad.* Such a statement is the idiomatic equivalent of *I am in bad health.* An alternative, *I feel badly,* could be interpreted as meaning that your sense of touch was bad. See the **good, well** entry.

- **Bahamas** In datelines, give the name of the city or town followed by *the Bahamas*:

(Nassau, the Bahamas) --

In stories, use *Bahamas, the Bahamas* or *the Bahama Islands* as the construction of a sentence dictates. Identify a specific island in the copy if relevant.

- **bail** *Bail* is money or property that will be forfeited to the court if an accused individual fails to appear for trial. It may be posted as follows:
  - The accused may deposit with the court the full amount or its equivalent in collateral such as a deed to property.
  - A friend or relative may make such a deposit with the court.
  - The accused may pay a professional bail bondsman a percentage of the total figure. The bondsman, in turn, guarantees the court that it will receive the full amount in the event the individual fails to appear for trial.

It is correct in all cases to say that an accused *posted bail* or posted a *bail bond* (the money held by the court is a form of bond). When a distinction is desired, say that the individual *posted bail*, that *bail was posted by a friend or relative*, or that *bail was obtained through a bondsman*.

- **Bakelite** A trademark for a type of plastic resin.

- **baker's dozen** It means 13.

- **Bakery and Confectionery Workers' International Union of America** The shortened form *Bakery Workers union* is acceptable in all references. Headquarters is in Washington.

- **balance of payments, balance of trade** The *balance of payments* is the difference between the amount of money that leaves a nation and the amount that enters it during a period of time.

The *balance of payments* is determined by computing the amount of money a nation and its citizens send abroad for all purposes—including goods and services purchased, travel, loans and foreign aid—and subtracting from it the amount that foreign nations send into the nation for similar purposes.

The *balance of trade* is the difference between the monetary value of the goods a nation imports and the goods it exports.

An example illustrating the difference between the two:

The United States and its citizens might send 10 billion dollars—5 billion for goods, 3 for loans and foreign aid, 1 for services and 1 for tourism and other purposes. Other nations might send 9 billion into the United States—6 billion for goods, 2 for services and 1 for tourism. The United States would then have a *balance-of-payments deficit of one billion dollars*, but a *balance-of-trade surplus of one billion*.

- **balance sheet** A listing of assets, liabilities and net worth showing the financial position of a company at a specific time. A bank's balance sheet generally is referred to as a *statement of condition.*

- **ball carrier**

- **ballclub, ballpark, ballplayer**

- **balloon mortgage** A mortgage in which the amortization schedule will not extinguish the debt by the end of the mortgage term. This leaves a large payment (called the *balloon payment*) of the remaining principal to be made at the end of the term.

- **ball-point pen**

- **ballroom**

- **baloney** Foolish or exaggerated talk. Use this word only in quotes and special contexts.
The sausage or luncheon meat is *bologna.*

- **Baltimore** The city in Maryland stands alone in datelines.

- **Band-Aid** A trademark for a type of adhesive bandage.

- **Bank of America** Acceptable in all references to *Bank of America National Trust and Savings Association.* The parent company is Bank America Corporation of San Francisco.

- **bankruptcy** The process by which an individual or organization, acting voluntarily or by court order, liquidates its assets and distributes the proceeds to creditors. The action may be involuntary, as the result of a suit by creditors, or it may be a voluntary effort to deal with bills that cannot be paid.
Often a company with financial problems announces that it is seeking to *reorganize under federal bankruptcy laws.* In such a case, it is incorrect to describe the company as *bankrupt.*
A story that announces such a filing should specify the chapter of the Federal Bankruptcy Act under which the reorganization is sought and describe the basic provisions. Here are some of the filings under the U.S. Bankruptcy Code:
Chapter Seven: Sometimes referred to as *straight bankruptcy,* this filing usually leads to liquidation of the company. A firm in Chapter Seven proceedings is able to continue to operate under the direction of a court trustee until the matter is settled. If the company can resolve its problems and settle with creditors in the interim, it may not have to be liquidated.
Chapter Eleven: This is the most common filing. Under it, a company obtains a federal court order that frees it from the threat of creditors' lawsuits until it can develop a plan to put its finances in order. Unless the court rules otherwise, the

debtor remains in control of the business and its assets. The ultimate reorganization plan must be accepted by a majority of the creditors. It may involve various options, including a full or partial payment of debts.

Chapter 12: This is an extension of Chapter Eleven, designed to help debt-burdened family farms. It allows family farmers to operate under bankruptcy court protection while paying off creditors.

Chapter 13: Called the "wage earner" bankruptcy, this is available to individuals who promise to repay as many debtors as possible from available income.

- **baptism** See **sacraments**.

- **baptist, Baptist** A person who baptizes is called a *baptist* (lowercase).
  A *Baptist* (uppercase) is a person who is a member of the Protestant denomination described in the next entry.

- **Baptist churches** It is incorrect to apply the term *church* to any Baptist unit except the local church.
  The ultimate governing power rests with members of the local congregation. Majority rule prevails. This emphasis on the authority of the individual churches helps account for the existence of more than 20 Baptist bodies in the United States. The largest, the Southern Baptist Convention, has more than 12 million members, most of them in the South, although it has churches in 50 states. The largest Northern body is American Baptist Churches in the U.S.A, with about 1.5 million members. Blacks predominate in three other large Baptist bodies, the National Baptist Convention of America, the National Baptist Convention U.S.A. Incorporated and the Progressive National Baptist Convention Incorporated.
  The roster of Baptist bodies in the United States also includes the Baptist General Conference, the Conservative Baptist Association of America, the General Association of Regular Baptist Churches, the General Association of General Baptists, and the North American Baptist General Conference.
  The Baptist World Alliance, a voluntary association of Baptist bodies throughout the world, organizes the Baptist World Congress meetings generally held every five years. Headquarters is in Washington.
  Beliefs: Baptists are free to interpret Scripture as their consciences dictate. In general, however, Baptists believe that no one can be validly baptized without first giving a personal confession of faith in Christ as the savior. They also believe that the baptism should be by immersion.
  In addition to belief in original sin and the need for redemption, Baptists generally believe in the Trinity, the humanity and divinity of Christ, salvation through Christ, and everlasting heaven and hell.
  Clergy: All members of the Baptist clergy may be referred to as *ministers*. *Pastor* applies if a minister leads a congregation.
  On first reference, use *the Reverend* before the name of a man or woman. On second reference, use only the last name, following the rules in **courtesy titles**.
  See **religious titles**. See **religious movements** for definitions of some descriptive terms that often apply to Baptists but are not limited to them.

- **barbecue** Not *barbeque* or *Bar-B-Q.*

- **barbiturate**

- **barmaid** Do not use, except in quotes.

- **bar mitzvah** The Jewish religious ritual and family celebration that marks a boy's 13th birthday. Judaism regards the age of 13 as the benchmark of religious maturity. *Bar mitzvah* translates as "one who is responsible for the Commandments."
  Conservative congregations have instituted the *bas mitzvah* or *bat mitzvah,* a similar ceremony for girls.

- **baron, baroness** See **nobility.**

- **barrel** A standard barrel in American measure contains 31.5 gallons. A standard barrel in British and Canadian measure contains 36 imperial gallons. In international dealings with crude oil, a standard barrel contains 42 American gallons or 35 imperial gallons.
  See the **oil** entry for guidelines on computing the volume and weight of petroleum products.

- **barrel, barreled, barreling**

- **barrel-chested, barrelhouse** Also: *double-barreled shotgun.*

- **barrister** See **lawyer.**

- **barroom**

- **baseball** The spellings for some frequently used words and phrases:

backstop	foul ball	pinch hit (v., n)	shoestring catch
ballclub	foul line	pinchhit (adj.)	shortstop
ballpark	foul tip	pinch hitter (n.)	shut out (v.)
ballplayer	ground-rule double	pitch out	shutout (n., adj.)
base line	home plate	play off (v.)	slugger
bullpen	home run	playoff (n., adj.)	squeeze play
center field	left-hander	put out (v.)	strike
center fielder	line drive	put out (n.)	strike zone
designated hitter	line up (v.)	r-b-i, r-b-i's	Texas-leaguer
double header	lineup (n.)	rundown (n.)	triple play
double play	major league(s) (n.)	sacrifice	twi-night double header
fair ball	major-league (adj.)	sacrifice fly	wild pitch
fastball	major leaguer (n.)	sacrifice hit	outfielder
first baseman	passed ball		

Numbers: Follow the rules for **numerals,** except in tabular material and in reporting scores in the body of a story. In reporting scores, use figures, hyphens, and *to*: *The Reds won 2-to-1. The Giants posted a 5-to-4 victory over the Cardinals.*

Leagues: Use *American League, National League, American League West, National League East,* etc. On second reference, *the league, the pennant in the West, the league's West Division,* etc.

Scores: A full scorecard is sent every half-hour while games are being played. Cover all games, using final and partial scores as appropriate and indicating pitching changes and home runs:

Here is the latest from the ballparks:

> **National League**
> Final St. Louis 7 Atlanta   4
> Final N-Y Mets 3 Los Angeles 2, first game
>
> N-Y Mets 2 Los Angeles 1 (Top 2nd, second game)
>
> Houston 2 Philadelphia 1 (Bot 7th)
> Donne Wall ptg, Houston 6th
> HR: Lenny Dykstra, Philadelphia 6th, none on, his 14th
>
> **American League**
> Final Texas 4 Anaheim 3, 10 innings
> Cleveland at Seattle postponed, rain

Final scores are sent on a spot basis, using this form:

> **NL Final: S-F 1 Pit 0**
>
> Final   **San Francisco Giants 1 Pittsburgh Pirates 0**

They are followed by final linescores, using this form:

> **AP-NL: Mets/Padres**
> ```
>                     R  H E
> New York  022 301 000 - 8 14 0
> San Diego 010 001 100 - 3  6 2
> ```
> **S. Fernandez, Innis (9)**
> **Ashby, Worrell (6), Smith (8)**
> **WP - S. Fernandez (4-4)**
> **LP - Ashby (5-2)**
> **Save - Innis (10)**
> **HR - Mets: L. Johnson (12)**
> **Padres: Gwynn (3), C. Jones 2 (14)**

The visiting team is always listed first, the home team second.
Use the first game designation only if it is the first game of a doubleheader.
In linescores, the visiting team's pitchers are listed first under the scores, with

the inning of change indicated in parentheses. The home team's pitchers follow on the next line.

In the listing of winning and losing pitchers, the pitcher's updated record follows his name in parentheses.

League Standings: The form:

NATIONAL LEAGUE
East Division

	W	L	PCT.	GB
ATLANTA	23	16	.590	-
FLORIDA	23	17	.575	1/2
NEW YORK	23	19	.548	1 1/2

- **BASIC** An acronym for *Beginners' All-Purpose Symbolic Instruction Code*, a computer programming language. Use of the acronym is acceptable on first reference if it is identified as a programming language. For example: *Most personal computers can run the BASIC language.*

- **basis point** The movement of interest rates or yields, expressed in hundredths of a percent.

- **basketball** The spellings of some frequently used words and phrases:

backboard	foul shot	half-court pass	man-to-man
backcourt	free throw	halftime	midcourt
backcourtman	free-throw line	hook shot	pivotman
baseline	frontcourt	jump ball	play off (v.)
field goal	full-court press	jump shot	playoff (n., adj.)
foul line	goaltending	layup	

Numbers: Follow the rules for **numerals** except in reporting scores in the body of the story. In those cases use figures, hyphens and *to*: *the '76ers posted a 95-to-93 victory over the Lakers. It was the Knicks 102, the Nets 100.*

League: *National Basketball Association* or *N-B-A.* For subdivisions: *The Atlantic Division of the Eastern Conference,* etc. On second reference: *the division, the conference,* etc.

Scores: A full scorecard is sent every half-hour while games are being played. Cover all games, using final and period scores as appropriate:

Here is the latest from the N-B-A:

> **Final Cleveland 107 Chicago 81**
> **First New York 30 Detroit   14**

Final scores are sent on a spot basis, using this form:

> **NBA Final: Cle 107 Chi 81**
> **Final: Cleveland Cavaliers 107 Chicago Bulls 81**

Standings: The format:

```
        NBA
Eastern Conference
Atlantic Division
               W    L   PCT.  GB
Boston        43   22  .662   -
Philadelphia  40   30  .571  5 1/2
```

• **battalion** Capitalize when used with a number or figure to form a name: *The Third Battalion, the 12th Battalion.*

• **battlefield** Also: *battlefront, battleground, battleship.* But *battle station.*

• **baud** (bawd) A unit for measuring the speed of data transmission by computer.

• **Bavarian cream**

• **bay** Capitalize as an integral part of a proper name: *Hudson Bay, San Francisco Bay.* But: *the bay* on second reference.
An exception to this is the *San Francisco Bay area* or *the Bay area* as the popular name for the nine-county region that has San Francisco as its focal point.

• **bazaar** A fair. *Bizarre* means unusual.

• **B-B-C** Acceptable in all references to the **British Broadcasting Corporation**. See that entry.

• **B-C** Acceptable in all references to a calendar year in the period *before Christ*. Because the full phrase would be *in the year 43 before Christ*, the abbreviation *BC* is placed after the figure for year: *43 B-C.* See **A-D**.

• **bear market** A period of generally declining stock prices.

• **bearer bond** A bond for which the owner's name is not registered on the books of the issuing company. Interest and principal are thus payable to the bond holder.

• **bearer stock** Stock certificates that are not registered in any name. They are negotiable without endorsement and transferable by delivery.

• **because, since** Use *because* to denote a specific cause-effect relationship: *He went because he was told.*
Since is acceptable in a causal sense when the first event in a sequence led logically to the second but was not its direct cause: *He went to the game, since he had been given the tickets.*

- **before Christ** See **B-C.**

- **Beijing** (bay-ZHING´) The city in China (formerly Peking) stands alone in datelines.

- **Belize** (bay-LEEZ´) The former British Honduras.

- **Bell System** See **American Telephone and Telegraph Company.**

- **bellwether**

- **benefit, benefited, benefiting**

- **Benelux** (BEH´-neh-luhks) Belgium, the Netherlands and Luxembourg. The term is no longer in common use and should be avoided if possible. If *Benelux* is used, explain that it is an inclusive word for these three nations.

- **Ben-Gurion International Airport** Located in Lod (lohd), Israel, about 10 miles south of Tel Aviv.

- **Benzedrine** (BEN´-zuh-dreen) A trademark for a type of pep pill or stimulant.

- **Bering Standard Time, Bering Daylight Time** Used in the far western section of Alaska, including Nome. See **time zones.**

- **Berlin** The capital of Germany. Stands alone in datelines.

- **Berlin Wall** On second reference, lowercase: *the wall.*

- **Bermuda collar, Bermuda grass, Bermuda shorts** But: *Bermuda Triangle.*

- **beside, besides** *Beside* means at the side of. *Besides* means in addition to.

- **besiege**

- **best-seller** (n.)

- **betting odds** Use figures, a hyphen, and the word *to*: *3-to-2 odds, odds of 3-to-2, the odds were 3-to-2.*
  But at the beginning of a sentence, spell out the figures: *Three-to-two were the odds on Beetlebaum today.*

- **bettor** A person who bets.

- **between** See the **among, between** entry.

- **bi-** The rules in **prefixes** apply, but in general, no hyphen. Some examples:

  bifocal   bilateral   bilingual   bimonthly   bipartisan

- **biannual, biennial** *Biannual* means twice a year and is a synonym for the word *semi-annual.*
  Biennial means once every two years.
  Both terms lead to confusion, and ought to be avoided. Instead, use such phrases as *twice a year* or *every two years.*

- **Bible** Capitalize, without quotation marks, when referring to the Scriptures in the Old Testament or the New Testament. Capitalize also related terms such as *the Gospels, the Gospel of Saint Mark, the Scriptures, the Holy Scriptures.*
  Lowercase *biblical* in all uses.
  Lowercase *bible* as a non-religious term: *My dictionary is my bible.*
  The books of the Old Testament, in order, are: Genesis, Exodus, Leviticus, Numbers, Deuteronomy, Joshua, Judges, Ruth, the first book of Samuel, the second book of Samuel, the first book of Kings, the second book of Kings, the first book of Chronicles, the second book of Chronicles, Ezra, Nehemiah, Esther, Job, Psalms, Proverbs, Ecclesiastes, Song of Solomon, Isaiah, Jeremiah, Lamentations, Ezekiel, Daniel, Hosea, Joel, Amos, Obadiah, Jonah, Micah, Nahum, Habakkuk, Zephaniah, Haggai, Zechariah, Malachi. The books of the New Testament, in order, are: Matthew, Mark, Luke, John, Acts, Romans, the first book of Corinthians, the second book of Corinthians, Galatians, Ephesians, Philippians, Colossians, the first book of Thessalonians, the second book of Thessalonians, the first book of Timothy, the second book of Timothy, Titus, Philemon, Hebrews, Epistles of James, first book of Peter, the second book of Peter, the first book of John, the second book of John, the third book of John, Jude, Revelation.
  Citations listing the number of chapter and verse use this form: *Matthew, chapter three, verse 16. Luke, chapter 21, verses one through 13.*

- **Bible Belt** Those sections of the United States, especially in the South and Middle West, where fundamentalist religious beliefs prevail. Use with care, because in certain contexts it can give offense. See **religious movements.**

- **bicycle**

- **big-bang theory** The theory that the universe began with the explosion of a superdense primeval atom and has been expanding ever since.
  The **oscillating theory**, another hypothesis, maintains that expansion eventually will stop and be followed by contraction to a superdense atom, which would be followed by another big bang.
  The **steady-state theory**, an alternate hypothesis, maintains that the universe always has existed and that matter constantly is being created to replace matter that constantly is being destroyed.

- **Big Board** Acceptable on second reference for the *New York Stock Exchange.*

- **big brother** One's older brother is a *big brother*. *Big Brother* (capitalized) is used to describe the watchful eye of big government, a term coined by George Orwell in his novel, "1984."

  Capitalize also in references to members of Big Brothers-Big Sisters of America, Incorporated. Headquarters is in Philadelphia.

- **Big Eight Conference** The college sports conference that includes Colorado, Iowa State, Kansas, Kansas State, Missouri, Nebraska, Oklahoma, Oklahoma State.

  On second reference: *the conference, the Big Eight.*

- **Big Ten Conference** The college sports conference that includes Illinois, Indiana, Iowa, Michigan, Michigan State, Minnesota, Northwestern, Ohio State, Purdue, Wisconsin.

  On second reference: *the conference, the Big Ten.*

- **Big Three automakers** General Motors, Ford, Chrysler. The *Big Four*: *The Big Three* plus American Motors.

- **bigwig**

- **(b) billion** A thousand million. It should always be spelled out. See **(m) millions, (b) billions**.

- **Bill of Rights** The first 10 amendments to the Constitution.

- **bimonthly** It means every other month. *Semi-monthly* means twice a month.

  Try to avoid using either. Instead, spell out your meaning in phrases such as: *The magazine is published twice each month.*

- **birthday** Capitalize as part of the name for a holiday: *Washington's Birthday*. Lowercase in other uses.

- **bishop** See **religious titles** and the entry for the denomination in question.

- **bit, byte** *Bit (bit)* is acceptable in all references as an abbreviated form of *binary digit*. Data transmission takes the form of electrical impulses, which can be thought of as being *on* or *off* – which is interpreted at *zero* or *one*. Each pulse is one *bit*.

  A *byte (byt)* is a collection of *bits*. Generally, a byte contains eight bits.

- **biweekly** Means every other week. *Semi-weekly* means twice a week.

  Try to avoid using either. Say instead: *The newspaper is published twice weekly.*

- **bizarre** Unusual. A fair is a *bazaar*.

- **black**   Preferred usage for those of the Negro race. *African-American* also is acceptable in all references. Use *Negro* only in names of organizations or in quotes. Do not use *colored* as a synonym. See the **colored** and **African** entries.

- **Black Muslims**   See **Muslim.**

- **blackout, brownout**   A *blackout* is a total power failure over a large area or the concealing of lights that might be visible to enemy raiders. The term *rotating blackout* is used by electric companies to describe a situation in which electric power to some sections temporarily is cut off on a rotating basis to ensure that voltage will meet minimum standards in other sections.
  A *brownout* is a small, temporary voltage reduction, usually from 2 to 8 percent, implemented to conserve electric power.

- **blast off** (v.) **blastoff** (n. and adj.)   *Launch* is preferable in references to manned space missions. See **space shuttle** and related entries.

- **Blessed Sacrament, Blessed Virgin**

- **blizzard**   See **weather terms.**

- **bloc, block**   A *bloc* is a coalition of people, groups or nations with the same purpose or goals.
  Block has more than a dozen definitions, but a political alliance is not one of them.

- **blond, blonde**   *Blond* is an adjective describing a hair color. As a noun, it applies to males.
  Blonde is the noun meaning a female with blond hair. Don't use either noun except in special contexts or quotes.

- **bloodhound**

- **Bloody Mary**   A drink made of vodka and tomato juice. The name is derived from the nickname for Queen Mary I of Britain, who reigned from 1553 to 1558.

- **blue-chip stock**   Stock in a company known for its long-established record of making money and paying dividends.

- **B'nai B'rith** (buh-NAY' brith)   A Jewish fraternal and service organization.

- **board**   Capitalize only when an integral part of a proper name. See **capitalization**.

- **board of aldermen**   See **city council.**

- **board of directors, board of trustees** Always lowercase. See the **organizations and institutions** entry.

- **board of supervisors** See **city council.**

- **boat, ship** A *boat* is a watercraft of any size, but generally is used to indicate a small craft. A *ship* is a large, seagoing vessel.
  The term *boat* is, however, used in some phrases that apply to larger craft: *ferryboat, P-T boat, gunboat.*
  The names of boats and ships should be put in quotation marks. Follow the rules for **quotation marks; numerals** and **hyphen.** Some examples: The *"Queen Elizabeth Two," the "Q-E-Two," the U-S-S "Enterprise."*
  The reference for military ships is **Jane's Fighting Ships;** for non-military ships, **Lloyd's Register of Shipping.**

- **Boeing Company** Formerly Boeing Aircraft Company. Headquarters is in Seattle.

- **bologna** The sausage. *Baloney* is foolish or exaggerated talk.

- **bona fide** (BOH'-nuh fyd) Genuine.

- **bond ratings** The two most popular are prepared by Moody's Investors Service and Standard and Poor's Corporation.
  Moody's uses nine ratings. The range, from the designation for top quality issues to the one for those judged the greatest risk: *Triple-A, Double-A, A, B-Double-A, B-A, B, C-Double-A, C-A,* and *C.*
  Standard and Poor's uses seven basic grades. The range, from top to bottom: Triple-A, Double-A, A, Triple-B, Double-B, B, and D. Sometimes it adds a plus or minus sign on grades Double-A through Double-B: *A-plus, Double-A-minus.*

- **bonds** See **loan terminology.**

- **B-one bomber**

- **Books on Tape** A trademark for a brand of pre-recorded audiotape in which a book is read out loud.

- **book titles** See **composition titles.**

- **book value** The difference between a company's assets and liabilities. The *book value* per share of common stock is the figure obtained by dividing the total number of common shares outstanding into the *book value* of the company as a whole. The *book value* of a stock may have little or no significant relationship to the selling price.

- **borscht** (bawrsht) Beet soup.

- **Bosporus** (BAHS'-puhr-uhs), **the** Not the *Bosporus Strait.* It is the strait between the Black Sea and the Sea of Marmara in Turkey.

- **Boston** The city in Massachusetts stands alone in datelines.

- **Boston brown bread, Boston cream pie, Boston terrier**

- **boulevard** See **addresses**.

- **boundary**

- **bow-legged**

- **boxing** Some frequently used terms and their definitions:
  The Weight Classes:
  Flyweight: A boxer weighing no more than 112 pounds.
  Bantamweight: 113 to 118 pounds.
  Featherweight: 119 to 126 pounds.
  Lightweight: 127 to 135 pounds.
  Welterweight: 136 to 147 pounds.
  Middleweight: 148 to 160 pounds.
  Light heavyweight: 161 to 175 pounds.
  Heavyweight: 176 or more pounds.
  Some Other Terms:
  Kidney punch: A punch to an opponent's kidney when the puncher has only one hand free. An illegal punch. If the puncher has both hands free, a punch to the opponent's kidney is legal.
  Knock out (v.) Knockout (n. and adj.): A fighter is knocked out if he takes a 10 count.
  If a match ends early because one fighter is unable to continue, say that the winner *stopped* the loser. In most boxing jurisdictions there is no such thing as a *technical knockout.*
  Outpointed: Not *outdecisioned.*
  Rabbit Punch: A punch behind an opponent's neck. It is illegal.

- **box office** (n.) **box-office** (adj.)

- **boy** Applicable until his 18th birthday is reached. Use *man* or *young man* afterward. Avoid redundancy in reference to boys; do not write *young boy,* for example. To convey his relative youth, note his age.

- **boycott, embargo** A *boycott* is an organized refusal to buy a particular product or service, or to deal with a particular merchant or group of merchants.
  An *embargo* is a legal restriction against trade. It usually prohibits goods from entering or leaving a country.

- **boyfriend, girlfriend**

- **Boy Scouts**
The full name of the national organization is *Boy Scouts of America.*
Headquarters is in Irving, Texas.
Cub Scouting is for boys 8 through 10. Members are *Cub Scouts* or *Cubs.*
Boy Scouting is for boys 11 through 17. Members are *Boy Scouts* or *Scouts.*
Exploring is a separate program open to boys and girls from high school age
through 20. Members are *Explorers,* not *Explorer Scouts.* Some units stress
nautical programs; members are *Sea Explorers.* See **Girl Scouts** for programs
that a separate organization runs for girls.

- **bra** Acceptable in all references for *brassiere.*

- **brackets [ ]** They cannot be transmitted over news wires. See
parentheses.

- **Brahman, Brahmin** *Brahman* applies to the priestly Hindu caste. It also
is the name of a breed of cattle.
Brahmin applies to the aristocracy in general, as in *Boston Brahmin.* It is a
judgmental term that should be used only with great care.

- **brand names** *Brand names* normally should be used only if they are
essential to a story. When they are used, capitalize them.
Sometimes, however, the use of a brand name may not be essential but is
acceptable because it more vividly sketches the mood of the story: *His Cadillac
was destroyed* says much more than *His luxury car was destroyed.*
Brand name is a non-legal term for **service mark** or **trademark**. See entries
under those words.

- **brand-new** (adj.)

- **break in** (v.) **break-in** (n. and adj.)

- **break up** (v.) **break-up** (n. and adj.)

- **Bricklayers, Masons and Plasterers International Union of
America** The shortened form *Bricklayers union* is acceptable in all references.
Headquarters is in Washington.

- **bride, bridegroom, bridesmaid** *Bride* (or *groom)* is appropriate in
wedding stories, but use *wife* (or *husband)* or *spouse* in other circumstances.

- **brigadier** See **military titles**.

- **Bright's disease** After Dr. Richard Bright, the London physician who first
diagnosed this form of kidney disease.

- **Brill's disease** It is a form of epidemic typhus fever in which the disease recurs years after the original infection. It is named after Nathan Brill, an American physician.

● **Britain** Acceptable in all references to *Great Britain*, which consists of England, Scotland and Wales. See **United Kingdom**.

● **British, Britons** The people of Great Britain: the English, the Scottish and the Welsh.

● **British Airways** The successor to British European Airways and British Overseas Airways Corporation. Headquarters is in Hounslow (HOWNS'-low), England.

● **British Broadcasting Corporation** *B-B-C* is acceptable on all references. Headquarters is in London.
    The BBC is composed of several divisions, including the *World Service*, which broadcasts internationally, and the *Home Service*, which broadcasts within the United Kingdom. The BBC is supported through government funding and is non-commercial.

● **British Columbia** The Canadian province bounded on the west by the Pacific Ocean. Do not abbreviate. See **datelines**.

● **British Commonwealth** See **Commonwealth, the**.

● **British Petroleum Company, Limited** *British Petroleum* is acceptable in all references. *B-P* is acceptable on second reference. Headquarters is in London.

● **British thermal unit** The amount of heat required to increase the temperature of one pound of water one degree Fahrenheit.
    B-T-U or *B-T-U's* is acceptable on the second reference.

● **British ton** See **ton.**

● **British Virgin Islands** Use with a community name in datelines on stories from these islands. Specify an individual island in the text if relevant. See **datelines.**

● **broadcast** The past tense also is *broadcast*, not *broadcasted.*

● **broadcast media** Radio and television. When referring to all non-print media (including cable as well as broadcast organizations), use *electronic media*.

● **Broadway, off-Broadway, off-off-Broadway** When applied to stage productions, these terms refer to distinctions made by union contracts, not to the location of a theater.

Actors' Equity Association and unions representing craft workers have one set of pay scales for *Broadway* productions (generally those in New York City theaters of 300 or more seats) and a lower scale for smaller theaters, classified as *off-Broadway* houses.

The term *off-off-Broadway* refers to workshop productions that may use Equity members for a limited time at substandard pay. Other unions maintain a hands-off policy, agreeing with the Equity attitude that actors should have an opportunity to whet their talents in offbeat roles without losing their Equity memberships.

- **broccoli**

- **Bromo Seltzer** A trademark for a brand of bicarbonate of soda.

- **Bronze Age** The age characterized by the development of bronze tools and weapons, from 3500 to 1000 B.C. Regarded as coming between the Stone Age and the Iron Age.

- **brother** See **Roman Catholic Church**.

- **Brotherhood of Locomotive Engineers** Do not use the abbreviation *B-L-E* in any reference. Headquarters is in Cleveland.

- **Brotherhood of Railway, Airline and Steamship Clerks, Freight Handlers, Express and Station Employees** See **Transportation Communications International Union**.

- **brothers** Capitalize but do not abbreviate in formal company names: *Warner Brothers.*

- **brownout** See the **blackout, brownout** entry.

- **brunet, brunette** *Brunet* is an adjective describing a hair color. As a noun, it refers to males with that hair color.
  Brunette is a noun meaning females with brunet hair.
  Don't use either noun except in special contexts or quotes.

- **brussels sprouts**

- **B-T-U, B-T-U's** See **British thermal unit**.

- **Bucharest** The capital of Romania. In datelines, follow it with *Romania.* Do not confuse it with Budapest, which is the capital of Hungary.

- **buck** Do not use as a synonym for *dollar* except in quoted matter.

- **Budapest** The capital of Hungary. In datelines, follow it with *Hungary.* Do not confuse it with Bucharest, which is the capital of Romania.

- **Buddha, Buddhism** A major religion founded in India about 500 B.C. by Gautama Siddhartha. He was given the name Buddha, which means "enlightened one," by his followers.

  Buddhism has about 250 million followers, mostly in India, Tibet, China, Japan, Korea and Southeast Asia. About 250,000 people practice Buddhism in North America.

  Buddhists believe that correct thinking and self-denial will enable the soul to reach nirvana, a state of release into ultimate enlightenment and peace. Until nirvana is reached, believers cannot be freed from the cycle of death and rebirth.

  There are four major groups within Buddhism.

  Hinayana or Theravada: Followers stress monastic discipline and attainment of nirvana by the individual through meditation. It is dominant among Buddhists in Myanmar, Cambodia, Laos, Thailand and Sri Lanka.

  Mahayana: Followers emphasize idealism. The ideal life is that of virtue and wisdom. The sect is found mostly in Japan, Korea and eastern China.

  Mantrayana: Major centers for this group are in the Himalayas, Mongolia and Japan. It is similar to Mahayana but also has a structure of spiritual leaders and disciples, believes in various evil spirits and deities, uses magic and has secret rituals.

  Zen: Followers seek enlightenment through introspection and intuition. The doctrines are again similar to Mahayana, and like Mantrayana there is a loose structure of leaders and disciples. This group is found mostly in Japan.

- **Bufferin** A trademark for a form of buffered aspirin.

- **bug, tap** A concealed listening device designed to pick up sounds in a room, an automobile and so on, is a *bug*.

  A *tap* is a device attached to a telephone circuit to pick up conversations on the line.

- **building** Never abbreviate. Capitalize the proper names of buildings, including the word *building* if it is an integral part of the proper name: *the Empire State Building*.

- **build up** (v.) **buildup** (n. and adj.)

- **bullet** See weapons.

- **bulletin** A one-sentence story of an extremely urgent nature. It is not merely a very important story. It should be an item of special interest and immediate urgency.

  A *bulletin* is air-ready. It may be followed by several more one- or two-sentence takes (making it a *bulletin series*) if the flow of information lends itself to such treatment.

  Generally, a *bulletin* series should be followed by an *urgent*. The form:

  Soviet-Major BULLETIN

      (Moscow) — Britain's Prime Minister says there is fear of imminent conflict in Moscow.

Soviet-Major BULLETIN, take 2

John Major says his information comes directly from Russian President Boris Yeltsin.

Soviet-Major BULLETIN, take 3

He says Yeltsin, speaking a short while ago from the Russian parliament, told him that a column of Soviet tanks is headed for the building.

Note the space between the slug and *BULLETIN* and the comma before the take number.

- **bullfight, bullfighter, bullfighting**

- **bullpen**   One word, for the place where baseball pitchers warm up, and for a pen that holds cattle.

- **bull's-eye**

- **bureau**   Capitalize when part of the formal name of an organization or agency: *the Bureau of Labor Statistics, the Radio Advertising Bureau.*
  Lowercase when used alone or to designate a corporate subdivision: *the Washington bureau of The Associated Press.*

- **bureaucrat, bureaucracy**

- **burglary, larceny, robbery, theft**   Legal definitions of *burglary* vary, but in general a *burglary* involves entering a building (not necessarily by breaking in) and remaining unlawfully with the intention of committing a crime.
  Larceny is the legal term for the wrongful taking of property. Its non-legal equivalents are *stealing* or *theft.*
  Robbery in the legal sense involves the use of violence or threat in committing *larceny.* In a wider sense it means to plunder or rifle, and may thus be used even if a person was not present: *His house was robbed while he was away.*
  Theft describes a *larceny* that did not involve threat, violence or plundering.
  Usage Note: You *rob* a person, bank, house, etc., but you *steal* the money or the jewels.

- **Burma**   See **Myanmar**.

- **bus, buses**   Transportation vehicles. The verb forms: *bus, bused, busing.* See **buss**.

- **bushel**   A unit of dry measure equal to four pecks or 32 dry quarts. It is the principal unit of measure used by farmers. The metric equivalent is approximately 35.2 liters.
  To convert bushels to liters, multiply by 35.2 (five bushels times 35.2 equals 176 liters).

In stories involving farm exports, always convert the tonnage figure (usually given in metric tons) into bushels. The conversion factor varies. There are 39.4 bushels to every metric ton of corn. To convert to bushels, multiply the number of metric tons by 39.4. There are 36.7 bushels of wheat to every metric ton. To convert to bushels, multiply the number of metric tons by 36.7.

- **buss, busses** Kisses, which is the preferred term. The verb forms: *buss, bussed, bussing.* See **bus.**

- **by-** The rules in **prefixes** apply, but in general, no hyphen. Some examples:

  byline   bypass   byproduct   bystreet

- **by-election** A special election held between regularly scheduled elections. The term most often is associated with special elections to the British House of Commons.

- **bylaw**

- **bylines** Used in broadcast wire copy to indicate the writer of a story, script or news summary. Generally, the *byline* is placed at the bottom of the copy. See **lockouts.**

- **byte** (byt) A computer "word," most commonly made up of eight bits. See the **bit, byte** entry.

- **cabinet** Capitalize references to a specific body of advisers heading executive departments for a president, king, governor, etc.: *The president-elect says he has not made his Cabinet selections.*

  Each member of the U.S. president's cabinet heads a department within the executive branch. See **Departments of** for a listing of all U.S. Cabinet departments.

- **Cabinet titles** Capitalize the full title when used before a name; lowercase in other uses: *Secretary of State Henry Kissinger,* but *Henry Kissinger, who is secretary of state.*

  To avoid stumbling blocks in the copy, informalize titles whenever possible: *Agriculture Secretary Bob Bergland, Housing Secretary Patricia Harris.* Note the capitalization. But always use the first name of the official in the first reference. See **titles.**

- **cactus, cactuses**

- **cadet** See **military academies.**

- **Caesarean section**

- **caliber** The form: *38-caliber pistol.* Follow the rules in **numerals.** See **weapons.**

- **California** See **state names.**

- **call letters** Use all-caps. Use hyphens to separate the letters of a broadcast station: W-A-B-C, W-B-Z, K-N-X. But do not use a hyphen between the call letters and the type of station: W-N-B-C T-V, K-C-B-S Radio, K-F-R-C- A-M.

  Avoid the use of long strings of letters and numbers in stories referring to citizens band licenses or amateur radio. See **channel, citizens band, radio station** and **television station.**

- **call up** (v.) **call-up** (n. and adj.)

- **Cambodia** Use this name rather than *Kampuchea (kam-poo-CHEE'-uh)* in datelines, since the country continues to be most widely known by this name.

When the context demands the use of *Kampuchea* in the story, it should be identified as the formal name of the nation.

- **Cameroon** (kam-uh-ROON′) Not *Camerouns* or *Cameroun.* See **geographic names**.

- **Camp Fire** The full name of the national organization is *Camp Fire, Incorporated.* It was founded in 1910 as Camp Fire Girls. The name was changed in 1979 to reflect the inclusion of boys. Headquarters is in Kansas City, Mo.
  Both girls and boys are included in all levels of the organization. Boys and girls 6 through 8 are called *Camp Fire Blue Birds.* Children 9 through 11 are *Camp Fire Adventure* members, or *Adventurers.* Children 12 and 13 are *Camp Fire Discovery* members. Youths 14 through 17 are *Camp Fire Horizon* members.

- **campaign manager** Do not treat as a formal title. Always lowercase. See **titles**.

- **Canada** Montreal, Ottawa, Quebec and Toronto stand alone in datelines. For all other datelines, use the city name and spell out the name of the province or territory.
  The 10 provinces of Canada are Alberta, British Columbia, Manitoba, New Brunswick, Newfoundland (includes Labrador), Nova Scotia, Ontario, Prince Edward Island, Quebec and Saskatchewan. The two territories are the Yukon and the Northwest Territories.
  The provinces have substantial autonomy from the federal government. The territories are administered by the federal government, although residents of the territories do elect their own legislators and representatives to Parliament. See **datelines**.

- **Canada goose** Not *Canadian goose.*

- **Canadian Broadcasting Corporation** *C-B-C* is acceptable on second reference. Headquarters is in Ottawa.

- **canal** Capitalize as an integral part of a proper name: *the Suez Canal.*

- **Canal Zone** Do not abbreviate. No longer used except when referring to the Panama Canal area during the time it was controlled by the United States, 1904-1979.

- **cancel, canceled, canceling, cancellation**

- **cannon, canon** A *cannon* is a weapon. See the **weapons** entry.
  A *canon* is a law or rule, particularly of a church.

- **cannot** One word. *Can't* is better.

- **cant** The distinctive stock words and phrases used by a particular sect or class. See **dialect**.

- **can't hardly** A double negative is implied. Use *can hardly* instead.

- **Canuck** (can-UK') It means a French Canadian, and often is considered a derogatory racial label. Avoid the word except in formal names (*the Vancouver Canucks*, a professional hockey team) or in quoted matter. See the **nationalities and races** entry.

- **canvas, canvass** *Canvas* is heavy cloth.
Canvass is a noun and verb denoting a survey.

- **cape** Capitalize as part of a proper name: *Cape Cod, Cape Hatteras*. Lowercase when it stands alone.
Although local practice may call for capitalizing *the Cape* when the rest of the name is clearly understood, always use the full name on first reference. On second reference, *the cape* should be lowercase.

- **Cape Canaveral, Florida** Formerly Cape Kennedy. It is the name of the cape on which the Kennedy Space Center is located. See **John F. Kennedy Space Center** and **Lyndon B. Johnson Space Center**.

- **capital** The city where a seat of government is located. Do not capitalize. See **capitol**.
When used in a financial sense, *capital* describes money, equipment or property used in a business by a person or corporation.

- **capital gain, capital loss** The difference between the cost of a capital asset and the price when it is sold.

- **capital investment** The process of using money to buy goods, tools, equipment or real estate: Major investments that are paid off over a period of time.

- **capitalization** The introduction of newsroom computer systems and improvements in data transmission technology have eroded the practice of printing broadcast copy in an all-uppercase format. All AP broadcast copy is now transmitted with upper- and lowercase characters.
In general, avoid unnecessary capitals. Use a capital letter only if you can justify it by one of the principles listed here.
Many words and phrases, including special cases, are listed separately in this book. Entries that are capitalized without further comment should be capitalized in all uses.
If there is no relevant listing in this book for a particular word or phrase, consult Webster's New World Dictionary. Use lowercase if the dictionary lists it as an acceptable form for the sense in which the word is being used.

As used in this book, *capitalize* means to use uppercase for the first letter of a word. If additional letters of the word should be capitalized, the entry will indicate so with an example or a phrase such as *use all-caps.*

Some basic principles:

Proper nouns: Capitalize nouns that constitute the unique identification for a specific person, place or thing: *John, Mary, America, Boston, England.*

Some words, such as the examples just given, are always proper nouns. Some common nouns receive proper noun status when they are used as the name of a particular entity: *General Electric, Gulf Oil.*

Proper names: Capitalize common nouns such as *party, river, street* and *west* when they are an integral part of the full name of a person, place or thing: *Democratic Party, Mississippi River, Fleet Street, West Virginia.*

Lowercase these common nouns when they stand alone in subsequent references: *the party, the river, the street.*

Lowercase the common noun elements of names in all plural uses: *the Democratic and Republican parties, Maine and State streets, lakes Erie and Ontario.*

Among entries that provide additional guidelines are:

animals	**historical periods and events**
brand names	**holidays and holy days**
buildings	**legislature**
committee	**months**
congress	**monuments**
datelines	**nationalities and race**
days of the week	**nicknames**
directions and regions	**organizations and institutions**
family names	**plants**
food	**planets**
foreign governmental bodies	**police department**
foreign legislative bodies	**religious references**
geographic names	**seasons**
governmental bodies	**trademarks**
heavenly bodies	**unions**

Popular names: Some places and events lack officially designated proper names but have popular names that are the effective equivalent: *the Combat Zone* (a section of downtown Boston), *the Main Line* (a group of Philadelphia suburbs), *the South Side* (of Chicago), *the Badlands* (of North Dakota), *the Street* (the financial community in the Wall Street area of New York).

The principle applies also to shortened versions of the proper names of one-of-a-kind events: *the Series* (for the World Series), *the Derby* (for the Kentucky Derby). This practice should not, however, be interpreted as a license to ignore the general practice of lowercasing the common noun elements of a name when they stand alone.

Derivatives: Capitalize words that are derived from a proper noun and still depend on that noun for their meaning: *American, Christian, Christianity, English, French, Marxist, Shakespearean.*

Lowercase words which are derived from a proper noun but no longer depend upon that noun for their meaning: *french fries, herculean, manhattan cocktail, malapropism, pasteurize, quixotic, venetian blind.*

Sentences: Capitalize the first word in a statement that stands as a sentence. See **sentences** and **parentheses**.

In poetry, capital letters are used for the first words of some phrases that would not be capitalized in prose. See **poetry**.

Compositions: Capitalize the principal words in the names of books, movies, operas, plays, poems, radio and television programs, songs, works of art, etc. See **composition titles; magazine names;** and **newspaper names**.

Titles: Capitalize formal titles when used immediately before a name. Lowercase formal titles when used alone or in constructions that set them off from a name by commas: *President Bill Clinton,* but *Bill Clinton, the president.* See **academic titles; courtesy titles; legislative titles; military titles; nobility; religious titles** and **titles**.

Abbreviations: Some abbreviations should be capitalized. See **abbreviations**.

Acronyms: They are almost always capitalized. See **acronyms**.

Pronouncers: The syllable that is stressed in a pronouncer is all-caps. Everything else is lowercase. See **pronouncers**.

Call letters: They always are all-caps. See **call letters**.

- **capitol** The building in Washington: *The meeting was held on Capitol Hill, in the west wing of the Capitol Building.* It can also refer to the building that houses state governments: *The Virginia Capitol,* as opposed to *Albany is the capital of New York.* See **capital.**

- **captain** See **military titles** for military and police usage. Lowercase in such uses as *team captain Carl Yastrzemski.*

- **carat, caret, karat** The weight of precious stones, especially diamonds, is expressed in *carats.* A carat is equal to 200 milligrams or about three grains. A *caret* is a writer's and proofreader's mark. The proportion of pure gold used with an alloy is expressed in *karats.*

- **carbine** See **weapons.**

- **cardinal** See **Roman Catholic Church.**

- **CARE** Acceptable in all references to *Cooperative for American Relief Everywhere, Incorporated.* Headquarters is in New York.

- **carefree**

- **caretaker**

- **Caribbean** (kuh-RIB'-ee-uhn) See **Western Hemisphere.**

- **carmaker, carmakers**

- **car pool**

- **carry-over** (n. and adj.)

- **cash on delivery** *C-O-D* is preferred in all references.

- **caster, castor** *Caster* is a roller.
  Castor is the spelling for the oil and the bean from which it is derived.

- **catalog, cataloged, cataloger, cataloging, catalogist**

- **Caterpillar** A trademark for a brand of crawler tractor.
  Use lowercase for the worm-like larva of various insects.

- **catholic, catholicism** Use *Roman Catholic Church, Roman Catholic* or
  Roman Catholicism in first references to those who believe that the pope, as
  bishop of Rome, has the ultimate authority in administering an earthly
  organization founded by Jesus Christ.
  Most subsequent references may be condensed to *Catholic Church, Catholic* or
  Catholicism. Roman Catholic should continue to be used, however, if the context
  requires a distinction between Roman Catholics and members of other
  denominations who often describe themselves as Catholic. They include some
  high church Episcopalians (who often call themselves *Anglo-Catholics*), members
  of Eastern Orthodox churches, and members of some national Catholic churches
  that have broken with Rome. Among churches in this last category are the Polish
  National Catholic Church and the Lithuanian National Catholic Church.
  The word *catholic* (lowercase) means universal, and should be avoided
  because of the possibility of confusion with the religious term.
  Those who use *Catholic* in a religious sense are indicating their belief that they
  are members of a universal church that Jesus Christ left on Earth.

- **Caucasian**

- **cave in** (v.) **cave-in** (n. and adj.)

- **C-B** See **citizens band**.

- **C-B-S** Acceptable in all references for *C-B-S, Incorporated*, the former
  Columbia Broadcasting System. Divisions include *C-B-S News, C-B-S Radio* and
  C-B-S T-V. Headquarters is in New York.

- **C-D** Acceptable in all references for *compact disc.*
  Be careful in contexts in which *C-D* could be taken to mean *certificate of
  deposit*, an investment instrument. In such cases, spell out *compact disc* on first
  reference. See **compact disc**.

- **C-D-ROM** Note hyphenation. Acceptable in all references to *compact disc read-only memory.* Make sure the story explains what a *C-D-ROM* is.

- **cease-fire, cease-fires** (n. and adj.) The verb form is *cease fire.*

- **celebrant, celebrator** Reserve *celebrant* for someone who conducts a religious rite: *He was the celebrant of the Mass.*
  Use *celebrator* for someone having a good time: *The celebrators kept the party going until 3 a-m.*

- **cellophane** Formerly a trademark, now a generic term.

- **Celsius** (SEL'-see-uhs) Use this term rather than *centigrade* for the temperature scale that is part of the metric system. Always uppercase.
  The Celsius scale is named for Anders Celsius, a Swedish astronomer who designed it. In it, zero represents the freezing point of water, and 100 degrees is the boiling point (at sea level).
  To convert to *Fahrenheit,* multiply a Celsius temperature by nine, divide the result by five, and add 32 (25 degrees celsius times nine equals 225, divided by five equals 45, plus 32 equals 77 degrees Fahrenheit).
  When giving a Celsius temperature, use this form: *40 degrees Celsius.* Do not abbreviate. See **Fahrenheit** and **metric system.**

- **cement** *Cement* is the powder mixed with water and sand or gravel to make concrete. The proper term is *concrete* (not cement) *pavement, blocks* and *driveways.*

- **censer, censor, censure** A *censer* is a container in which incense is burned.
  To *censor* is to prohibit or restrict the use of something.
  To *censure* is to condemn.

- **Centers for Disease Control and Prevention** The centers, located in Atlanta, form the U.S. Public Health Service's national agency for control of infectious and other preventable diseases. They work with state health departments to provide specialized services that the states are unable to maintain on an everyday basis.
  The normal form for first reference is the *national Centers for Disease Control.* *C-D-C* is acceptable on the second reference.

- **centi-** A prefix denoting one-hundredth of a unit: *A centimeter is one-hundredth of a meter.* To convert to the basic unit, move the decimal point two places to the left: *155-point-six centimeters equals one-point-55 meters.*
- **centigrade** See **Celsius.**

- **centimeter** One-hundredth of a meter. There are 10 millimeters in a centimeter. A centimeter is approximately the width of a large paper clip.

To convert to inches, multiply by four-tenths. For example, *five centimeters times four-tenths equals two inches.* See **meter; metric system** and **inch.**

• **Central America** See **Western Hemisphere.**

• **central bank** A bank having responsibility for controlling a country's monetary policy. In the United States, the central bank is the *Federal Reserve.*

• **Central Conference of American Rabbis** See **Jewish congregations.**

• **Central Intelligence Agency** *C-I-A* is acceptable in all references. The formal title for the individual who heads the agency is *Director of Central Intelligence. C-I-A Director* is acceptable in all references.

• **Central Standard Time (c-s-t), Central Daylight Time (c-d-t)**
See **time zones.**

• **cents** Follow the rules for **numerals** and lowercase *cents.* See **monetary figures.**

• **century** Lowercase. Follow the rules in **numerals.**
   For proper names, follow the organization's practice: *20th Century Fox, Twentieth Century Fund.*

• **Ceylon** (say-LAHN′) It is now *Sri Lanka (shree LAHN′-kuh),* which should be used in datelines and other references to the nation. The people may be referred to as *Ceylonese* (n. or adj.) or *Sri Lankans.* The language is *Sinhalese (sin-huh-LEEZ′).*

• **Chagas' disease** After Charles Chagas, a Brazilian physician who identified the chronic wasting disease caused by a parasite carried by insects.

• **chain saw** Two words.

• **chairman, chairwoman** Do not use the more cumbersome *chairperson* unless it is an organization's formal title for an office.
   Capitalize as a formal title before a name: *company Chairman Henry Ford, committee Chairwoman Margaret Chase Smith.*
   Do not capitalize as a casual, temporary position: *meeting chairman Robert Jones.* See **titles.**

• **chamber of deputies** See **foreign legislative bodies.**

• **chancellor** The translation to English for the first minister in the governments of Germany and Austria. Capitalize as a formal title when used before a name: *Chancellor Helmut Kohl. Kohl, the chancellor of Germany.* See the **premier, prime minister** entry and **titles.**

- **changeable**

- **changeover**

- **change up** (v.) **change-up** (n. and adj.)

- **channel** Capitalize and follow the rules in **numerals** when identifying a specific television channel: *The F-C-C has authorized the use of Channel One. The game will be on Channel Four.*
  Otherwise, lowercase: *The game isn't on any channel.* Also: *the English Channel* but *the channel* on second reference.

- **chapters** Capitalize *chapter* and follow the rules in **numerals** when referring to a specific one: *Chapter Three contains details of his decision to go to war.* Otherwise, lowercase.

- **character, reputation** *Character* refers to moral qualities. *Reputation* refers to the way a person is regarded by others.

- **charge off** A loan that no longer is expected to be repaid and which is therefore written off as a bad debt.

- **charismatic groups** See **religious movements.**

- **Charleston, Charlestown, Charles Town** *Charleston* is the name of the capital of West Virginia and of a port city in South Carolina.
  Charlestown is a section of Boston.
  Charles Town is the name of a small city in West Virginia.

- **chauffeur**

- **chauvinism** (SHOH'-van-ism), **chauvinist** It means unreasoning devotion to a characteristic or thing, such as one's race, gender or country, with contempt for other races, genders or countries. The terms come from *Nicolas Chauvin,* a soldier of Napoleon I, who was famous for his devotion to the lost cause.

- **check up** (v.), **checkup** (n.)

- **Chemical Mace** A trademark, usually shortened to *Mace,* for a brand of tear gas that is packaged in an aerosol canister and temporarily stuns its victims.

- **Chevy** Not *Chevie* or *Chevvy.*

- **Chicago** The city in Illinois stands alone in datelines.

• **Chicago Board of Trade** The largest commodity trading market in the United States. On second reference, *the Board of Trade.*

• **Chicago Board of Options Exchange** An exchange set up by the Chicago Board of Trade to trade stock options. Do not use the abbreviation *C-B-O-E.* On second reference, *the exchange.*

• **Chicano** (chee-KAHN'-oh) Although not always derogatory, *Chicano* should be avoided as a routine description for American citizens or residents of Mexican descent. *Mexican Americans* is preferred.
Some say *Chicano* resulted from Indian attempts to pronounce *Mexicano.* Others say its origin is a derisive description that Mexicans used for what they regarded as the chicanery of bureaucrats during the French rule of Mexico.
Chicano has been adopted by some social activists of Mexican descent, and may be used when activists use it to describe themselves. To apply it to all Spanish-surnamed citizens would be roughly the same as calling all blacks Muslims. See **nationalities and races**.

• **chief** Capitalize as a formal title before a name: *He spoke to Police Chief Michael Codd. He spoke to Chief Michael Codd of the New York police.*
Lowercase when it is not a formal title: *union chief Walter Reuther.*

• **chief justice** Capitalize only as a formal title before a name: *Chief Justice William Rehnquist.* The office-holder is the *chief justice of the United States*, not of the Supreme Court.
The other justices are *associate justices*, but may be called simply *justices* in all references. See **judge.**

• **chief petty officer** See **military titles.**

• **chief warrant officer** See **military titles.**

• **Chile** The nation.

• **chili, chilies** The peppers.

• **chilly** Moderately cold.

• **China** When used alone, it refers to the mainland nation. Use it in datelines and other routine references. Use *People's Republic of China, Communist China* or *Mainland China* only in direct quotations or when needed to distinguish the mainland and its government from Taiwan.
For datelines on stories from the island of Taiwan, use the name of a community and *Taiwan.* In the body of a story, use *Nationalist China* or *Taiwan* for references to the government based on the island. Use the formal name of the government, the *Republic of China,* when required for legal precision.

- **Chinaman** A patronizing term. Confine it to quoted matter.

- **Chinese names** Always use a pronouncer. For most Chinese place names and personal names, use the official Chinese spelling system known as Pinyin: *Senior leader Deng Xiaoping* or *Zhejiang province.*
  Note that the Chinese give the family name first (*Deng*) followed by the given name (*Xiaoping*). Second reference should be the family name only: *Deng.*
  The Pinyin spelling system eliminates the hyphen and/or apostrophe previously used in many given names. There are some exceptions to the use of the Pinyin spelling. Use the traditional American spelling in these cases:
  - the place names *Canton, China, Inner Mongolia, Shanghai, Tibet.*
  - well-known deceased people such as *Chou En-lai, Mao Tse-tung, Sun Yat-sen.*
  Follow local spellings in stories dealing with Hong Kong and Taiwan.
  Some Chinese have westernized their names, putting their given names or the initials for them first: *P.Y. Chen, Jack Wang.* In general, follow an individual's preferred spelling.
  Normally, Chinese women do not take their husbands' surnames. Use a courtesy title only when specifically requested by the individual. Never use *Madame* unless in quoted matter.

- **chip** Acceptable on second reference for a *computer chip*, an integrated circuit used in computers.

- **Christian Church (Disciples of Christ)** The parentheses and the words they surround are part of the formal name. The body owes its origins to an early 19th century frontier movement to unify Christians. The Disciples, led by Alexander Campbell in western Pennsylvania, and the Christians, led by Barton Stone in Kentucky, merged in 1832. The local church is the basic organizational unit. National policies are developed by the General Assembly, made up of representatives chosen by local churches and regional organizations. The church lists more than 1 million members.
  Beliefs: The church allows for varied opinions and stresses freedom of interpretation, based on the historic conviction that there is no creed but Christ and no saving doctrines except those of the New Testament.
  Clergy: All members of the clergy may be referred to as *ministers. Pastor* applies if a minister leads a congregation. On first reference, use *the Reverend* before the name of a man or woman.
  On second reference, follow the rules in **courtesy titles**. See **religious titles.**

- **Christian Methodist Episcopal Church** See **Methodist churches.**

- **Christian Science Church** See **Church of Christ, Scientist.**

- **Christmas, Christmas Day** Dec. 25. The federal legal holiday is observed on Friday if Dec. 25 falls on a Saturday, on Monday if it falls on a Sunday. Never abbreviate *Christmas* to *Xmas* or any other form.

- **Chrysler Corporation** Headquarters is in Highland Park, Mich.

- **church** Capitalize as part of the formal name of a building, congregation or denomination; lowercase in other uses: *Saint Mary's Church, the Roman Catholic Church, the Catholic and Episcopal churches, a Roman Catholic church, a church.*
  Lowercase in phrases where the term church is used in an institutional sense: *He believes in the separation of church and state. The pope says the church opposes abortion.* See **religious titles** and the entry for the denomination in question.

- **Churches of Christ** Approximately 18,000 independent congregations, with a total American membership of more than 2 million, cooperate under this name. They sponsor numerous educational activities, primarily radio and television programs.
  Each local church is autonomous and operates under a governing board of elders. The minister is an evangelist, addressed by members as *Brother*. The ministers do not use clergy titles. Do not precede their names by a title.
  The churches do not regard themselves as a denomination. Rather, they stress a non-denominational effort to preach what they consider basic Bible teachings. The churches also teach that baptism is an essential part of the salvation process. See **religious movements.**

- **church-goer**

- **Church of Christ, Scientist** This denomination was founded in 1879 by Mary Baker Eddy, who attributed her recovery from an illness to insights she gained from reading Scripture.
  The Mother Church in Boston is the international headquarters. Its board of directors guides all the approximately 3,200 churches throughout the world.
  A branch church, governed by its own democratically chosen board, is named First Church of Christ, Scientist, or Second Church, according to the order of its establishment in a community.
  The term *Christian Science Church* is acceptable in all references.
  Beliefs: Christian Science describes God as the source of all real being, so that nothing except what he has created can ultimately be real. Death, disease and sin are regarded as having no real existence because they are not created by God. Scripture is cited as evidence that a true understanding of God heals sickness as well as sin.
  The principal beliefs are contained in "Science and Health With Key to the Scriptures," the denominational textbook written by Mrs. Eddy.
  The word *Christian* is used because New Testament writings are an integral element of the denomination's teachings. The word *science* denotes the concept that reality can be understood and proved in Christian experience.
  A distinction is made between Christ, regarded as the divine nature or godliness of Jesus, and Jesus, regarded as the human Wayshower and Exemplar of man's sonship with God.
  Clergy: The church is composed entirely of lay members and does not have

clergy in the usual sense. Either men or women may hold the three principal
offices: *reader, practitioner* or *lecturer.*
Readers are elected from congregations to conduct worship services.
Practitioners devote full time to the public healing ministry of the church.
Lecturers, appointed by the directors of the Mother Church, give public lectures
on Christian Science.
When using these titles, be certain to explain their meaning. The preferred
form is to set the title off from the name in a separate sentence and immediately
explain it: *John Jones is a reader in the church. In that role, he conducts church
services.*
The terms *pastor* and *minister* are not applicable. Do not use *the Reverend* in
any reference. See **religious titles.**

• **Church of England** See **Anglican Communion.**

• **Church of Jesus Christ of Latter-day Saints** Note the
punctuation and capitalization in Latter-day. *Mormon Church* is acceptable in all
references.
The church is based on revelations that Joseph Smith said were brought to him
in the 1820s by heavenly messengers. After Smith's death in 1844, his followers
split into factions, the largest of them the Church of Jesus Christ of Latter-day
Saints. Led west by Brigham Young, they founded Salt Lake City, Utah in 1847.
Today, the church headquarters there directs more than 12,000 congregations
with more than 6 million members worldwide.
Church hierarchy is composed of men known as general authorities.
Among them, the policy-making body is the First Presidency, made up of a
president and two or more counselors. It has final authority in all spiritual and
worldly matters.
The Council of the Twelve Apostles, primarily an advisory body, helps the First
Presidency direct church activities. When the church president dies, the First
Presidency is dissolved and the Council of the Twelve Apostles selects a new
president, traditionally the man who is the senior apostle in the council. He then
chooses his counselors.
Other general authorities include the church patriarch, a spiritual adviser; a
three-member Presiding Bishopric, which administers temporal affairs; and the
First Quorum of Seventy, in charge of missionary work. Women may not become
general authorities.
The church's basic geographical units are called *stakes.* They are governed by
a stake presidency, made up of a president and two counselors, and a stake high
council. Individual congregations within a stake are called wards. Missions,
which oversee members where there are no stakes, are headed by a president and
may include one or more congregations known as branches.
Beliefs: Mormons believe that Jesus Christ established one church on earth,
that it was taken away upon his death and not restored until the revelations to
Smith. They believe that Jesus came to America after his Resurrection, visiting its
people, who had immigrated to the continent in ancient times.
Among the revelations were directions to gold plates that Smith said he found

on Hill Cumorah, near Palmyra, N.Y. He taught that the plates, left by a prophet who lived some time after Jesus, contained the records of the people Jesus had visited in America and the true word of God.

The "Book of Mormon," written by Smith, contains what members believe are his translation of the hieroglyphics on the plates. The plates were later returned to Moroni, the heavenly messenger who led Smith to them. Smith also wrote the "Book of Doctrine and Covenants" and the "Pearl of Great Price." These three books and the Bible are the key church documents, although revelation is considered to continue today through members of the First Presidency.

Clergy: All faithful male members over the age of 11 are members of the priesthood and may attain positions of leadership in the all-lay clergy. Younger members go through a series of ranks from deacon to teacher to priest before becoming elders sometime after their 18th birthdays. They may later become seventies or high priests. A high priest may become a bishop or one of two bishop's counselors, who lead local congregations.

The only formal titles are *president* (for the head of the First Presidency), *bishop* (for members of the Presiding Bishopric and for local bishops) and *elder* (for other general authorities and church missionaries). Capitalize these formal titles before a name on first reference; use only the last name on second reference.

The terms *minister* or *the Reverend* are not used. See **religious titles.**

Splinter Groups: The term *Mormon* is not properly applied to the other Latter Day Saints churches that resulted from the split after Smith's death.

The largest is the Reorganized Church of Jesus Christ of Latter Day Saints (note the lack of a hyphen and the capitalized *Day*), with headquarters in Independence, Mo. It was founded by Smith's son Joseph III, and claims to be the continuation of the original church. It has about 1,000 churches and 150,000 members.

- **C-I-A** Acceptable in all references for Central Intelligence Agency.

- **cigarette**

- **Cincinnati** The city in Ohio stands alone in datelines.

- **Citibank** The former First National City Bank. The parent holding company is Citicorp of New York. It is the second-largest bank in the nation.

- **cities and towns** Capitalize them in all uses.
See **datelines** for guidelines and when they should be followed by a state or country name.

Capitalize the names of such separate political entities as *East Saint Louis, Illinois* or *West Palm Beach, Florida.*

The preferred form for a section of a city is lowercase: *the west end, northern Los Angeles.* But capitalize widely recognized names for the section of a city: *Lower East Side of New York, South Side of Chicago, London's West End.*

Spell out the names of cities except in quotes and special contexts: *They went to Los Angeles* but in their words, *"We loved L-A."*

There are legal, political and legislative differences between cities, towns and villages. When in doubt, refer to the "National Geographic Atlas of the World." See **city**.

- **citizen, resident, subject, national, native** A *citizen* is a person who has acquired the full civil rights of a nation either by birth or naturalization. Cities and states in the United States do not confer citizenship. To avoid confusion, use *resident*, not citizen, in referring to inhabitants of states and cities.

  Subject is the term used when the government is headed by a monarch or other sovereign.

  National is applied to a person residing away from the nation of which he or she is a citizen, or to a person under the protection of a specified nation.

  Native is the term denoting that an individual was born in a given location.

- **citizens band** No apostrophe after the *s*. This is an exception to Webster's New World based on widespread practice.

  C-B is acceptable on second reference.

  The term describes a group of frequencies set aside by the Federal Communications Commission for local use at low power by individuals or businesses.

  Do not use C-B call letters unless central to the story. In such cases, use the rules for **numerals**.

- **city** Capitalize *city* as part of a proper name: *Kansas City, New York City, Oklahoma City, Jefferson City*.

  Lowercase elsewhere: *a Texas city; the city government; the city Board of Education;* and all *city of* phrases: *the city of New Orleans*.

  Capitalize when part of a formal title before a name: *City Manager Francis McGrath*. Lowercase when not part of the formal title: *city Health Commissioner Frank Smith*. See **city council** and **governmental bodies**.

- **city commission** See the next entry.

- **city council** Generally, the basic governing body of a city.

  Capitalize when part of a proper name: *the Boston City Council*. Retain capitalization if the reference is to a specific council but the context does not require the city name:

  (Boston) — The City Council says ...

  Lowercase in other uses: *the council, the Boston and New York city councils, a city council*.

  Use the proper name if the body is not known as the city council: *the Miami City Commission, the City Commission, the commission; the Louisville Board of Aldermen, the Board of Aldermen, the board*.

  Use city council in the generic sense for plural references: *the city councils of Boston, Miami and Louisville*.

• **city hall** Capitalize with the name of a city, or without the name if the reference is specific: *Boston City Hall, City Hall.*
Lowercase plural uses: *the Boston and New York city halls.*
Lowercase generic uses: *You can't fight city hall.*

• **city-wide**

• **Civil Aeronautics Board** *C-A-B* is acceptable on second reference. See **Federal Aviation Administration.**

• **civil cases, criminal cases** A *civil case* is one in which an individual, business or agency of government seeks damages or relief from another individual, business or agency of government. Civil actions generally involve a charge that a contract has been breached or that someone has been wronged or injured.
A *criminal case* is one that a state or the federal government brings against an individual charged with committing a crime.

• **Civil War** Capitalize in reference to the U.S. Civil War. Lowercase otherwise.

• **clean up** (v.) **cleanup** (n. and adj.)

• **clear-cut** (adj.)

• **clerical titles** See **religious titles.**

• **Cleveland** The city in Ohio stands alone in datelines.

• **clientele**

• **cloak-and-dagger**

• **Clorox** A trademark for a brand of bleach.

• **closed shop** A *closed shop* is an agreement between a union and an employer that requires workers to be members of the union before they may be employed.
A *union shop* requires workers to join the union within a specified period after they are employed.
An *agency shop* requires that the workers who do not want to join the union pay the union a fee instead of union dues.
A *guild shop*, a term often used when the union is The Newspaper Guild, is the same as a *union shop.*
See the **right-to-work** entry for an explanation of how some states prohibit contracts that require workers to join unions. See **union; union names.**

• **closely held corporation** A corporation in which stock shares and voting control are concentrated in the hands of a small number of investors, but for which some shares are available and traded on the market.

• **close-up** (n. and adj.)

• **cloture** The parliamentary procedure for closing debate. Not *closure.* Whenever practical, use a phrase such as *closing debate* or *ending debate* instead of the technical term.

• **co-** Retain the hyphen when forming nouns, adjectives and verbs that indicate occupation or status:

co-author	co-host	co-partner	co-signer
co-chairman	co-owner	co-pilot	co-star
co-defendant (in a divorce suit)		co-respondent	co-worker

Several of these are exceptions to Webster's New World in the interest of consistency. Use no hyphen in other combinations:

coeducational	coexist	cooperate	coordinate
coequal	coexistence	cooperative	coordination

Cooperate, coordinate and related words are exceptions to the rule that a hyphen is used if a prefix ends in a vowel and the word that follows begins with the same vowel.

• **coach** Capitalize only when used without a qualifying term before the name of the person who directs an athletic team: *Coach John Jones signed a new contract.*
If *coach* is preceded by a qualifying word, make it lowercase: *third base coach Frank Crosetti, defensive coach George Perles.*
Lowercase *coach* when it stands alone or is set off from the name by commas: *Jack Smith, the Bulls' coach, was charged with a technical.* But avoid this construction.

• **coastal waters** See **weather terms.**

• **coast guard** Capitalize when referring to the American force: *the U-S Coast Guard, the Coast Guard, the Guard, Coast Guard policy.* Do not use the abbreviation *U-S-C-G.*
Use lowercase for similar forces of other nations. This approach has been adopted for consistency, because many foreign nations do not use *coast guard* as the proper name. See **military academies.**

• **Coast Guardsman** Note spelling. Avoid if possible; use *member of the coast guard.*

Capitalize as a proper noun when referring to an individual in a U-S Coast Guard unit: *She is a Coast Guardsman.*
Lowercase *guardsman* when it stands alone. See **military titles**.

- **coastline**

- **coattails**

- **COBOL** (KOH'-bawl) A computer programming language. An acronym for *Common Business-Oriented Language.*

- **Coca-Cola, Coke** Trademarks for a brand of cola drink.

- **cocaine** The slang term *coke* should appear only in quoted matter.
Cocaine is *taken, inhaled or used.*
Crack is a refined cocaine in crystalline rock form. Do not use the redundant *crack cocaine.*

- **C-O-D** Preferred in all references for *cash on delivery* or *collect on delivery.*

- **Cold War** Capitalize when referring specifically to the rivalry between the United States and the Soviet Union. The Cold War began in the years immediately after World War II and ended with the breakup of the Soviet Union in 1991.

- **collateral** Stock or other property that a borrower is obliged to turn over to a lender if unable to repay a loan. See **loan terminology.**

- **collective nouns** Nouns that denote a unit take singular verbs and pronouns: *class, committee, crowd, family, group, herd, jury, orchestra, team.*
Some usage examples: *The committee is meeting to set its agenda. The jury reached its verdict. A herd of cattle was sold.*
Some words that are plural in form become collective nouns and take singular verbs when the group or quantity is regarded as a unit.
Right: *A thousand bushels is a good yield.* (A unit.)
Right: *A thousand bushels were created.* (Individual items.)
Right: *The data is sound.* (A unit.)
Right: *The data have been carefully collected.* (Individual items.)

- **collectors' item**

- **college** A *university* consists of several *colleges.* But the term *college* can be used in the generic sense to refer to higher education: *More people are going to college this year than last.*
Consult special sections of Webster's New World for lists of junior colleges, colleges and universities in the United States and Canadian colleges and universities.
Capitalize *college* when part of a proper name: *Dartmouth College.* See **organizations and institutions.**

- **College of Cardinals** See **Roman Catholic Church.**

- **collide, collision** Two objects must be in motion before they can *collide*. An automobile cannot *collide* with a utility pole, for example; it simply *hits* it.

- **colloquialisms** Because of the conversational tone of most broadcast writing, many colloquialisms are acceptable. The tone and subject of the story should be the ultimate guide—the lighter the story, the more acceptable colloquialisms will be.
  The term itself describes the informal use of language. Webster's New World lists some colloquialisms as substandard; these should not be used.
  Sometimes, colloquialisms are particularly useful in the lead of a story, to catch the mood or essence of the event. In such cases, the lead must be supported by a full exposition of the event. See the **dialect** and **word selection** entries.

- **colon (:)** A colon is used at the end of a phrase or sentence to introduce material that is directly related. The most frequent use of the colon is to introduce lists, texts and quotations.
  Emphasis: The colon can be effective in giving emphasis: *He had only one hobby: eating.*
  Introducing Quotations: Use a comma to introduce a direct quotation of one sentence that remains within a paragraph. Use a colon to introduce longer quotations within a paragraph and to end all paragraphs that introduce a paragraph of quoted material. These constructions should only be rarely used.
  Placement with Quotation Marks: Colons go outside quotation marks unless they are part of the quotation itself.
  Times: Use colons in direct clock readings: *1:30 this morning.* See the **times** entry.
  Miscellaneous: Do not combine a dash and a colon or a double dash and a colon.

- **colonel** See **military titles.**

- **colonial** Capitalize *Colonial* as a proper adjective for all references to the *Colonies.* See the next entry.

- **colonies** Capitalize only for the British dependencies that declared their independence in 1776, now known as the United States.

- **Colorado** See **state names.**

- **color-blind** The hyphen is for readability.

- **colored** In some societies, including the United States, the word is considered derogatory and should not be used.
  In some countries of Africa, it is used to denote individuals of mixed racial

ancestry. Whenever the word is used, place it in quotation marks and provide an explanation of its meaning. See **African.**

- **colt** A male horse from 2 to 5 years old.

- **Columbus Day** October 12. The federal legal holiday is the second Monday in October.

- **combat, combated, combating**

- **comedian** Use for both men and women.

- **comma** The following guidelines treat some of the most frequent questions about the use of commas. Additional guidelines on specialized uses are provided in separate entries such as **months.** For more detailed guidance, consult the punctuation section in the back of Webster's New World Dictionary.
  In a series: Use commas to separate element in a series, but do not put a comma before the conjunction in a simple series: *The flag is red, white and blue. He would nominate Tom, Dick or Harry.*
  Put a comma before the concluding conjunction in a series, however, if an integral element of the series requires a conjunction: *I had orange juice, toast, and ham and eggs for breakfast.*
  Use a comma also before the concluding conjunction in a complex series of phrases: *The main points to consider are whether the athletes are skillful enough to compete, whether they have the stamina to endure the training, and whether they have the proper mental attitude.* See the **double dash** and **semicolon** entries for cases when elements of a series contain internal commas.
  With equal adjectives: Use commas to separate a series of adjectives equal in rank. If the commas could be replaced by the word *and* without changing the sense, the adjectives are equal: *a thoughtful, precise manner; a dark, dangerous street.*
  Use no comma when the last adjective before a noun outranks its predecessors because it is an integral element of a noun phrase, which is the equivalent of a single noun: *a cheap fur coat* (the noun phrase is *fur coat*); *the old oaken bucket; a new, blue spring bonnet.*
  With non-essential clauses: A non-essential clause must be set off by commas. An essential clause must not be set off from the rest of the sentence by commas. See the **essential clauses, non-ssential clauses** entry.
  With non-essential phrases: A non-essential phrase must be set off by commas. An essential phrase must not be set off from the rest of the sentence by commas. See the **essential phrases, nonessential phrases** entry.
  With introductory clauses and phrases: A comma normally is used to separate an introductory clause or phrase from a main clause: *When he had tired of the mad pace of New York, he moved to Dubuque.* Although technically the comma may be omitted after short introductory phrases if no ambiguity would result, it is best to leave it in for the sake of anchors who may read the copy cold.
  With conjunctions: When a conjunction such as *and, but* or *for* links two

clauses that could stand alone as separate sentences, use a comma before the conjunction in most cases: *She was glad she had looked, for a man was approaching the house.*

As a rule of thumb, use a comma if the subject of each clause is expressly stated: *We are visiting Washington, and we also plan a side trip to Williamsburg. We visited Washington, and our senator greeted us personally.* But no comma when the subject of the two clauses is the same and is not repeated in the second: *We are visiting Washington and plan to see the White House.* The comma may be dropped if two clauses with expressly stated subjects are short. In general, however, favor use of a comma unless a particular literary effect is desired or if using a comma would distort the sense of a sentence.

Introducing direct quotes: The use of direct quotes is discouraged: Paraphrase or use tape instead. In those cases where a quote is central to the story, use a comma to introduce a complete, one-sentence quotation within a paragraph: *In the president's words, "He can run, but he can't hide."*

Do not use a comma at the start of an indirect or partial quotation: *He said his victory put him "firmly on the road to a first-ballot nomination."*

With hometowns and ages: Do not use commas to set off ages or hometowns. Instead, use the words *who is* or *of.*

Wrong: *Mary Richards, 48, was there.*
Right: *Mary Richards is 48. She was there.*
Wrong: *Mary Richards, New York, was there.*
Right: *Mary Richards of New York was there.*
Better: *Mary Richards is from New York. She was there.*

Names of states and nations used with city names: *His journey will take him from Dublin, Ireland, to Fargo, North Dakota, and back. The Selma, Alabama, group saw the governor.*

With yes and no: *Yes, I will be there.*

In direct address: *Baseball fans, the season is about to begin. No sir, we have no bananas.*

Separating similar words: in those rare instances when duplicate words occur next to each other, use a comma to separate them: *The question is, is there life on Mars?* These constructions are, however, best avoided.

Placement with quotes: Commas always go inside quotation marks. See **semicolon; academic degrees; company names** and **party affiliation.**

• **commander** See **military titles.**

• **commander-in-chief** Note hyphens, which are included to indicate to the anchor that the words form one title. Capitalize only if used as a formal title before a name.

• **commercial paper** One of the various types of short-term negotiable instruments whereby industrial or finance companies obtain cash after agreeing to pay a specific amount of money on the date due.

• **commissioner** Capitalize when used as a formal title. See **titles.**

- **commitment**

- **committee**   Capitalize when part of a formal name: *the House Appropriations Committee.*
  Do not capitalize when used in shortened versions of long committee names: *the Special Senate Select Committee to Investigate Improper Labor-Management Practices,* for example, became *the rackets committee.* See **subcommittee.**

- **commodities futures contract**   A contract to purchase or sell a specific amount of a given commodity at a specified future date. Traders buy and sell such contracts hoping to make a profit on the difference between the contractual price and the commodity's actual price on the specified date.

- **commodity**   When used in a financial sense, the word describes the products of mining and agriculture before they have undergone extensive processing.

- **Common Market**   See **European Union.**

- **common stock, preferred stock**   An ownership interest in a corporation.
  If other classes of stock are outstanding, the holders of *common stock* are the last to receive dividends and the last to receive payments if a corporation is dissolved. The company may raise or lower common stock dividends as its earnings rise or fall.
  When *preferred stock* is outstanding and company earnings are sufficient, a fixed dividend is paid. If a company is liquidated, holders of preferred stock receive payments up to a set amount before any money is distributed to holders of common stock.

- **commonwealth**   A group of people united by their common interests. See **state.**

- **Commonwealth, the**   Formerly, the British Commonwealth. The members of this free association of sovereign states recognize the British sovereign as head of the Commonwealth. Some also recognize the sovereign as head of their state; others do not.
  The members are: Australia, Bahamas, Bangladesh, Barbados, Botswana, Canada, Cyprus, Fiji, Gambia, Ghana, Grenada, Guyana, India, Jamaica, Kenya, Lesotho, Malawi, Malaysia, Malta, Mauritius, New Zealand, Nigeria, Papua New Guinea, St. Lucia, Seychelles, Sierra Leone, Singapore, Sri Lanka, Swaziland, Tanzania, Tonga, Trinidad and Tobago, Uganda, United Kingdom, Western Samoa and Zambia. Nauru, a special member, participates in activities but not in meetings of government heads.

- **Communicable Disease Center**   The former name of the *Centers for Disease Control.* See entry under that name.

- **Communications Satellite Corporation** *Comsat* is acceptable on all references. Note that the lack of full capitalization is an exception to the rule for acronyms.

  Comsat is a consortium of firms from the United States and other countries. It was set up to own international satellite capacity which it leases to its customers. Headquarters is in Washington.

- **Communications Workers of America** The shortened form *Communications Workers union* is acceptable in all references. The abbreviation *C-W-A* is acceptable on second reference. Headquarters is in Washington.

- **communism, communist** Lowercase *communism*. Capitalize *communist* only when referring to the activities of the Communist Party or to individuals who are members of it: *The Communists won the election. She ran on the Communist ticket.* See the **political parties and philosophies** entry.

- **commutation** See the **pardon, parole, probation** entry.

- **compact disc** A plastic disc used to store digital data, usually music. *C-D* is acceptable in all references, but in contexts in which it can be confused with a certificate of deposit, spell out *compact disc* on first reference.

  Compact discs also are used to store computer information (text, sound and pictures). That type of compact disc is referred to as a **C-D-ROM**.

- **company** Never abbreviate. Capitalize when part of the formal name of a theatrical organization: *the Martha Graham Dance Company.*

  In military usage, capitalize only when part of a name: *Company B*, but *he met up with his company.*

  For business applications, see the next entry.

- **company names** Whenever possible, use informal constructions that do not require the use of the full formal name of the company or corporation. For example, use *Ford* rather than *Ford Motor Company* unless the context demands the more formal name. Consult the company or "Standard and Poor's Register of Corporations" if in doubt about a formal name.

  Use a comma before *incorporated* or *limited*. Do not abbreviate those terms or *company* or *corporation*.

  Do not use all capital letter names unless the letters are individually pronounced—in which case, follow the rules for **hyphen**. Others should be uppercase and lowercase. See the **organizations and institutions** entry.

- **compared to, compared with** Use *compared to* when the intent is to assert, without the need for elaboration, that two or more items are similar: *She compared her work for women's rights to Susan B. Anthony's campaign for women's suffrage.*

  Use *compared with* when juxtaposing two or more items to illustrate similarities and/or differences: *His time was two hours, eleven minutes and ten seconds, compared with two hours, 14 minutes for his closest competitor.*

- **compatible**

- **complacent, complaisant** *Complacent* means self-satisfied. *Complaisant* means eager to please. Don't use it.

- **complement, compliment** *Complement* is a noun and verb denoting completeness or the process of supplementing something: *The ship has a complement of 200 sailors and 20 officers. The tie complements his suit.* A *compliment* is a noun or verb that denotes praise or the expression of courtesy: *The captain complimented the sailors. He was flattered by the compliments on his suit.*

- **complementary, complimentary** *The husband and wife have complementary careers. She received complimentary tickets to the show.*

- **compose, comprise, constitute** *Compose* means to create or put together. It commonly is used in both the active and passive voices: *He composed a song. The United States is composed of 50 states. The zoo is composed of many animals.*
  Comprise means to contain, to include all or to embrace. It is best used only in the active voice, followed by a direct object: *The United States comprises 50 states. The jury comprises five men and seven women. The zoo comprises many animals.*
  Constitute, in the sense of *form* or *make up*, may be the best word if neither *compose* nor *comprise* seems to fit: *Fifty states constitute the United States. Five men and seven women constitute the jury. A collection of animals can constitute a zoo.*
  Use *include* when what follows is only part of the total: *The price includes breakfast. The zoo includes lions and tigers.*

- **composition titles** Apply the guidelines listed here to the titles of books, movies, operas, plays, poems, songs and television programs, and the titles of lectures, speeches and works of art.
  The guidelines, followed by a block of examples:
  Principal words: Capitalize the principal words, including prepositions and conjunctions of four or more letters.
  Article: Capitalize an article—*the, a, an*—or a word of fewer than four letters if it is the first or last word in the title.
  Use quotation marks: Put quotation marks around the names of all such works except the Bible and the names of books that are primarily catalogs or reference material. In addition to catalogs, such works include almanacs, dictionaries, directories, encyclopedias, gazetteers, handbooks and similar publications.
  Foreign title: Translate a foreign title into English unless the work is widely known in the United States under its foreign name.

Examples: *"War and Peace," "For Whom the Bell Tolls."* But: *Webster's New World Dictionary, the Congressional Record. "The Star-Spangled Banner," "Gone With The Wind," "The C-B-S Evening News," The N-B-C "Today" Program, Rousseau's "War,"* not *Rousseau's "La Guerre."* But: *da Vinci's "Mona Lisa."* See **television program titles; music; musical performers; reference works**.

- **compound adjectives** See the **hyphen** entry.

- **comptroller, controller** *Comptroller* generally is the accurate word for government financial officers.
  The U.S. comptroller of the currency is an appointed official in the Treasury Department who is responsible for the chartering, supervising and liquidation of banks organized under the federal government's National Bank Act.
  Controller generally is the proper word for financial officers of businesses and for other positions such as *aircraft controller.*
  There is no difference in pronunciation.
  Capitalize *comptroller* and *controller* when used as formal titles for financial officers. Use lowercase for *air traffic controller* and similar applications of the word.

- **computer chip** On second reference, *chip.* An integrated circuit used in computers.

- **conclave** A private or secret meeting. In the Roman Catholic Church, it describes the private meeting of cardinals to elect a pope.

- **concrete** See **cement.**

- **Confederate States of America** The formal name for the states that seceded during the Civil War. The shortened form *the Confederacy* is acceptable in all references.

- **confess, confessed** In some contexts the words may be erroneous. Use extreme caution. See **admits, admitted.**

- **confirmation** See **sacraments.**

- **conglomerate** A corporation that has diversified its operations, usually by acquiring enterprises in widely varied industries.

- **Congo** Formerly Zaire. In datelines, give the name of the city followed by *Congo:*

  (Kinshasa, Congo) --

  But in the body of the story, make it *the Congo.* Do not confuse with the Republic of Congo, a different country.

- **Congo River** Not *Zaire River.*

- **Congregationalist churches** The word *Congregational* still is used by some individual congregations. The principal national body that used the term dropped it in 1961 when the Evangelical and Reformed Church merged with the Congregational Christian Churches to form the United Church of Christ. It has some 1.8 million members.

The word *church* is correctly applied only to an individual local church. Each such church is responsible for the doctrine, ministry and ritual of its congregation. The local churches also appoint delegates to associations. Their functions include recognizing local churches; promoting cooperation among the churches; and the licensing, ordination, installation and dismissal of ministers.

Conferences, generally organized along state lines, recognize associations and specialize in missionary and educational work. A general synod, made up of delegates elected by associations and conferences, is designed primarily to discuss questions of concern to all the churches and to handle communications with other denominations.

A small body of churches that did not enter the United Church of Christ is known as the National Association of Congregational Churches. Churches in the association have more than 100,000 members.

Beliefs: Jesus is regarded as man's savior, but no subscription to a set creed is required for membership. Emphasis is placed on the value of having persons band together for common worship and to help each other lead religious lives.

Clergy: Members of the clergy are known as *ministers. Pastor* applies if a minister leads a congregation. On first reference, use *the Reverend* before the name of a man or woman. Do not carry the title through on subsequent references. See **religious titles**.

- **congress** Capitalize *U-S Congress* and *Congress* when referring to the U.S. Senate and House of Representatives. Although *Congress* sometimes is used as a substitute for the House, it properly is reserved for reference to both the Senate and House. However, *congressman* or *congresswoman* is acceptable for members of the House. See that entry.

Capitalize *Congress* also if referring to a foreign body that uses the term, or its equivalent in a foreign language, as part of its formal name: *the Argentine Congress, the Congress.* See **foreign legislative bodies**.

Lowercase when used as a synonym for *convention* or in second reference to an organization that uses the term as part of its formal name: *the Congress of Racial Equality, the congress.*

- **congressional** Lowercase unless part of a proper name: *congressional hearings, the "Congressional Quarterly," the "Congressional Record."*

- **"Congressional Directory"** Use this as the reference source for questions about the federal government that are not covered in this handbook.

- **congressional districts** Follow the rules in **numerals** and capitalize the

numeral and *District* when referring to a specific district: *the First Congressional District, New York's 28th District.*
Otherwise, lowercase.

- **"Congressional Record"** A daily publication of the proceedings of Congress including a complete stenographic report of all remarks and debates.

- **congressman, congresswoman** Use only in references to members of the U.S. House of Representatives. See **legislative titles.**

- **Congress of Racial Equality** *CORE* is acceptable on second reference. Headquarters is in New York.

- **Connecticut** See **state names.**

- **connote, denote** *Connote* means to suggest or imply something beyond the explicit meaning: *To some persons, the word "marriage" connotes too much restriction.*
  Denote means to be explicit about the meaning: *The word "demolish" denotes destruction.*

- **Conrail** This acronym is acceptable in all references to *Consolidated Rail Corporation.* Note that the lack of all uppercase treatment is an exception to the rule for acronyms.
  Conrail is a private, for-profit corporation. It was set up by Congress in 1976 to reorganize and consolidate six bankrupt Northeast railroads—the Penn Central, Erie Lackawanna, Reading, Central of New Jersey, Lehigh Valley, and Lehigh and Hudson River.
  The legislation provided for a $2 billion federal loan to the corporation and set a phased schedule of repayments. A total of 25 million shares of common stock were created, but the shares were not made available for public trading. Instead, the shares were issued in the names of voting trustees chosen to represent the individuals designated as the ultimate recipients after the settlement of litigation over the value of the property that Conrail took over.
  Do not confuse *Conrail* with *Amtrak* (see separate entry). However, the legislation that set up Conrail also provided for Amtrak gradually to acquire from Conrail some of the property that had been owned by the bankrupt railroads. Headquarters is in Philadelphia.

- **consensus**

- **conservative** See the **political parties and philosophies** entry.

- **Conservative Judaism** See **Jewish congregations.**

- **constable** Capitalize when used as a formal title before a name. See **titles.**

• **constitute**   See the **compose, comprise, constitute** entry.

• **constitution**   Capitalize references to the U.S. Constitution, with or without the *U-S* modifier: *The president says he supports the Constitution.*
    When referring to the constitutions of other nations or of states, capitalize only with the name of the nation or state: *the French Constitution, the Massachusetts Constitution, the country's constitution, the state constitution.*
    Lowercase in other uses: *the organization's constitution.*
    Lowercase *constitutional* in all uses.

• **consul, consul general, consuls general**   Capitalize when used as a formal title before a name. See **titles**.

• **consulate**   A *consulate* is the residence of a consul in a foreign city. It handles the commercial affairs and personal needs of citizens of the appointing country.
    Capitalize with the name of a nation; lowercase without it: *the French Consulate, the U-S Consulate, the consulate.* See **embassy** for the distinction between a consulate and an embassy.

• **consumer credit**   Loans extended to individuals or small businesses, usually on an unsecured basis and providing for monthly repayment. Also referred to as *installment credit* or *personal loans.*

• **consumer price index**   A measurement of changes in the retail prices of a constant marketbasket of goods and services. It is computed by comparing the cost of the marketbasket at a fixed time with its cost at subsequent or prior intervals.
    The *U-S Consumer Price Index* is issued monthly by the Bureau of Labor Statistics, an agency of the Labor Department. It should not be referred to as a *cost-of-living index*, since it does not include the impact of taxes or the changes in buying patterns that result from inflation. It is, however, the basis for computing cost-of-living raises in many union contracts.
    Use *the index* on second reference; avoid using the abbreviation *C-P-I.*

• **Consumer Product Safety Commission**   Do not use the abbreviation C-P-S-C.
• **Contac**   A trademark for a brand of decongestant.

• **contagious**

• **contemptible**

• **continent**   The seven continents, in order of their land size: Asia, Africa, North America, South America, Europe, Antarctica and Australia.
    Capitalize *the Continent* and *Continental* only when referring to Europe or things European. Lowercase in other uses such as: *the continent of Europe, the European continent, the African and Asian continents.*

- **Continental Airlines** Use this spelling of *Airlines*, which Continental has adopted for its public identity. Only its incorporation papers still read *Air Lines*. Headquarters is in Houston.

- **Continental Divide** The ridge along the Rocky Mountains that separates rivers flowing east from those that flow west.

- **continental shelf, continental slope** Lowercase. The *shelf* is the part of a continent that is submerged in relatively shallow sea at gradually increasing depths, generally up to about 600 feet below sea level.

  The *continental slope* begins at the point where the descent to the ocean bottom becomes very steep.

- **continual, continuous** *Continual* means a steady repetition, over and over again: *The merger has been the source of continual litigation.*

  Continuous means uninterrupted, steady, unbroken: *All she saw ahead of her was a continuous stretch of desert.*

- **Contra, Contras** Uppercase when used to describe the Nicaraguan rebel groups.

- **contractions** Contractions reflect informal speech and writing and therefore are appropriate to most broadcast stories, depending upon the subject and tone.

  The most commonly used contractions are *isn't, aren't* and those formed with the words *is* and *not*: *He's going to school, they won't stop him.*

  The best rule of thumb is: Use contractions in circumstances where they reflect the way a phrase commonly occurs in speech.

  Do not, however, use contractions that are ambiguous—particularly those which may be read either as a contraction or the possessive case. For example, do not use contractions involving someone's name. Such a construction could easily be misread as a possessive, causing the anchor to stumble.

  Wrong: *President-elect Clinton's moving to Washington.*

  Right: *President-elect Clinton is moving to Washington.*

  Right: *It's moving day for President-elect Clinton. He's moving to Washington.*

  See **Americanisms; colloquialisms; quotations in the news** and **word selection.**

- **contrasted to, contrasted with** Use *contrasted to* when the intent is to assert, without the need for elaboration, that two items have opposite characteristics: *He contrasted the appearance of the house today to its ramshackle look last year.*

  Use *contrasted with* when juxtaposing two or more items to illustrate similarities and/or differences: *He contrasted the Republican platform with the Democratic platform.*

  Memory Aid: See the **compared to, compared with** entry. The same principle applies here.

- **control, controlled, controlling**

- **controller**   See the **comptroller, controller** entry.

- **controversial**   An overused word; avoid it. See **non-controversial.**

- **convention**   Capitalize as part of the name of a specific national or state political convention: *the Democratic National Convention, the Republican State Convention.*
  Lowercase in other uses: *the national convention, the state convention, the convention, the annual convention of the American Medical Association.*

- **convertible bond**   See **loan terminology.**

- **convict** (v.)   Follow with the preposition *of*, not *for. He was convicted of murder.*

- **convince, persuade**   You may be *convinced that* something or *of* something. You must be *persuaded to do* something.
  Wrong: *The robbers convinced him to open the vault.*
  Right: *The robbers persuaded him to open the vault.*
  Wrong: *The robbers persuaded him that it was the right thing to do.*
  Right: *The robbers convinced him that it was the right thing to do.*

- **cookie, cookies**

- **cooperate, cooperative**   But *co-op* as a short form of cooperative, to distinguish it from *coop*, a cage for animals.

- **Cooperative for American Relief Everywhere, Incorporated**   See **CARE.**

- **coordinate, coordination**

- **cop**   Often a derogatory term for police officer. Confine it to quoted matter.

- **copter**   Acceptable shortening of *helicopter.* But use it only as a noun or adjective. It is not a verb.

- **copyright** (n., v. and adj.)   *The disclosure was made in a copyright story.*
  Use *copyrighted* only as the past tense of the verb: *He copyrighted the article.*
  See the **Copyright Guidelines** section at the end of this book for information on the application of copyright regulations in connection with news copy and the production of radio and television pieces.

- **co-respondent**   In a divorce suit.

- **Corn Belt**   The region in the north central Midwest where much corn and corn-fed livestock are raised. It extends from western Ohio to eastern Nebraska and northeastern Kansas.

- **corporal** See **military titles**.

- **corporate names** See **company names**.

- **corporation** An entity that is treated as a person in the eyes of the law. It is able to own property, incur debts, sue and be sued.
 Do not use the abbreviation *corp.* in any context.

- **corps** The possessive form is corps' for both singular and plural: *one corps' location, two corps' assignments.*
 Capitalize when used with a word or figure to form a proper name: *the Marine Corps, the Signal Corps.* When using numbers, follow the rules for **numerals**: *the Ninth Corps.*
 Capitalize when standing alone only if it is a shorthand reference to the *U-S Marine Corps.*

- **corral, corralled, corralling**

- **(correct)** Do not use this construction to indicate that an unlikely looking piece of information is correct. Instead, put an advisory at the bottom of the copy, enclosed in parentheses:

 (News directors: the passenger count of two in graf three is correct.)

- **correction** The function of a wire correction is to enable the broadcaster to easily identify the offending story and fix the error involved.
 All wire corrections must move with great speed. Highspeed wires allow for the retransmission of the entire story.
 The correction should contain the same slug and category code as the story and should begin with a paragraph giving the story number and indicating the error that is being fixed. The proper form:

 Clinton CORRECTION

 The following story replaces V1234, slugged Clinton, to CORRECT by restoring the dropped word "abandon" in the third sentence.

- **correctional institution** See the **prison, jail** entry.

- **Corsica** (KAWR'-sih-kuh) Use instead of *France* in datelines on stories from communities on this island.

- **Cortes** (KAWR'-tez) The Spanish parliament. See **foreign legislative bodies.**

- **cosmonaut** An astronaut from one of the countries of the former Soviet Union. Always lowercase. See **titles**.

- **co-star**

- **cost of living** The amount of money needed to pay taxes and to buy the goods and services deemed necessary to make up a given standard of living, taking into account changes that may occur in tastes and buying patterns.

  The term often is treated incorrectly as a synonym for the *U-S Consumer Price Index*, which does not take taxes into account and measures only price changes, keeping the quantities constant over time.

  Hyphenate when used as a compound modifier: *The cost of living went up, but he did not receive a cost-of-living raise.* See the **consumer price index** and **inflation** entries.

- **cost-plus**

- **Cotton Belt** The region in the South and Southeastern sections of the United States where much cotton is grown.

- **council, councilor, councilman, councilwoman** A deliberative body and those who are members of it. See the **counsel** entry and **legislative titles.**

- **Council of Economic Advisers** A group of advisers who help the president prepare the administration's annual economic report to Congress and who recommend economic measures throughout the year.

- **counsel, counseled, counseling, counselor, counselor-at-law** To *counsel* is to advise. A *counselor* is one who advises.

  A *counselor-at-law* is a lawyer. See **lawyer.**

- **count, countess** See **nobility**.

- **counter-** The rules in prefixes apply, but in general, use a hyphen if necessary for readability. Some examples:

counteract	countercharge	counter-proposal	counter-culture

- **countryside**

- **county** Capitalize when an integral part of a proper name: *Dade County.*
  Capitalize the full names of county governmental units: *the Dade County Commission, the Orange County Department of Social Services, the Suffolk County Legislature.*

Retain capitalization for the name of a county body if the proper noun is not needed in the context; lowercase the word *county* if it is used to distinguish an agency from its state or federal counterparts: *the Board of Supervisors, the county Board of Supervisors; the Department of Social Services, the county Department of Social Services.* Lowercase *the board, the department,* etc., whenever they stand alone.

Capitalize *county* if it is an integral part of a specific body's name even without the proper noun: *the County Commission, the County Legislature.* Lowercase *the commission, the legislature,* etc., when not preceded by the word *county.*

Capitalize as part of a formal title before a name: *County Commissioner Mary Jones.* Lowercase when it is not part of the formal title: *county Health Commissioner John Smith.*

Avoid *county of* phrases where possible, but when necessary, always lowercase: *the county of Westchester.* Apply the same rules to similar political terms such as *parish.* See **governmental bodies.**

- **county court** In some states, it is not a court, but the administrative body of a county. In most cases, the *court* is presided over by a *county judge,* who is not really a judge in the traditional sense, but is instead the chief administrative officer of the county. The terms should be explained if they are not clear in the context.

Capitalize all references to a specific *county court,* and capitalize *county judge* when used as a formal title before a name.

Do not use *judge* alone before a name except in direct quotations when an administrative rather than judicial official is involved.

- **coup d'etat** (koo-day-TAH') The word *coup* usually is sufficient for the forcible overthrow of a government.

- **couple** In the sense of a single unit, use a singular verb: *Each couple was asked to give ten dollars.*

Constructions that use *couple* in the sense of two people are awkward and best avoided. Here's why: In those cases, the word takes plural verbs and pronouns: *The couple were married Saturday and left Sunday on their honeymoon. They will return in two weeks.* Better would be *Dick and Jane were married Saturday.*

- **couple of** The *of* is necessary. Never use *a couple tomatoes* or a similar phrase.

The phrase takes a plural verb in constructions such as: *A couple of tomatoes were stolen.*

- **course numbers** Follow the rules in **numerals**: *History 101.*

- **court decisions** Follow the rules for **numerals** and use hyphens and the word *to*: *The Supreme Court ruled five-to-four that schools be desegregated.*

- **court districts** See **court names.**

- **courtesy titles** The rule is readability: Use whichever construction is clearest. In general, do not use the courtesy titles *Miss, Mr., Mrs.* or *Ms.* in the first reference. Instead, use the first and last names of the person: *Hillary Rodham Clinton, Jimmy Carter.*
  Do not use courtesy titles in other references unless needed to distinguish among people with the same last name.
  If a woman's courtesy titles is used, follow the person's expressed preference: *Miss, Mrs., Ms.*

- **courthouse** One word, except in the proper names of some communities: *Appomattox Court House, Virginia.*
  Capitalize with the name of a jurisdiction: *the Cook County Courthouse, the U-S Courthouse.*
  Lowercase in other uses: *the county courthouse, the courthouse, the federal courthouse.*

- **court-martial, court-martialed, courts-martial.**

- **court names** Capitalize the full proper names of courts at all levels.
  Retain capitalization if *U-S* or a state name is dropped: *the U-S Supreme Court, the Supreme Court; the state Superior Court, the Superior Court, Superior Court.*
  For courts identified with a numeral, follow the rules in **numerals** and capitalize: *the Eighth U-S Court of Appeals, Second District Court.*
  For additional details on federal courts, see **judicial branch** and separate listings under **U-S** and the court name. See **judge** for guidelines on titles before the names of judges.

- **Court of St. James's** Note the *'s.* The formal name for the royal court of the British sovereign. Derived from St. James's Palace, the former scene of royal receptions.

- **courtroom**

- **cover up** (v.) **cover-up** (n. and adj.) *He tried to cover up the scandal. He was prosecuted for the cover-up.*

- **crack** Not *crack cocaine.* See **cocaine**.

- **crack up** (v.) **crack-up** (n. and adj.)

- **crawfish** Not *crayfish.* An exception to Webster's New World based on the dominant spelling in Louisiana, where it is a popular delicacy.

- **criminal cases** See the **civil cases, criminal cases** entry.

- **Crisco** A trademark for a brand of vegetable shortening.

- **crisis, crises**

- **criss-cross**

- **criterion, criteria**

- **cross country** No hyphen, an exception to Webster's New World based on the practices of American and international governing bodies for this sport.

- **cross-examine, cross-examination**

- **cross-eye** (n.) **cross-eyed** (adj.)

- **cross-fire**

- **crossover** (n. and adj.)

- **cross section** (n.) **cross-section** (v.)

- **C-R-T** Abbreviation for *cathode ray tube.* Do not use. *Monitor* or *display* are among the preferred terms.

- **C-T scan** *Computerized tomography,* a method of making multiple X-ray images of the body or part of the body and using a computer to construct, from those images, cross-sectional views. Formerly known as the *CAT scan.*

- **Cub Scouts** See **Boy Scouts.**

- **cuckoo clock**

- **cup** Equal to eight fluid ounces. The approximate metric equivalents are 240 milliliters or .24 of a liter.
  To convert to liters, multiply the number of cups by .24 (14 cups times .24 equals 3.36 liters). See **liter.**

- **cupful, cupfuls** Not *cupsful.*

- **curate** See **religious titles**.

- **cure-all**

- **Curia** See **Roman Catholic Church.**

- **currency depreciation, currency devaluation** A nation's money *depreciates* when its value falls in relation to the currencies of other nations or in relation to its own prior value.
  A nation's money is *devalued* when the government deliberately reduces its

value in relation to the currency of other nations.

When a nation devalues its currency, the goods it imports tend to become more expensive. Its exports tend to become less expensive in other nations and thus more competitive.

- **curtain-raiser**

- **customs** Capitalize *U-S Customs Service,* or simply *the Customs Service.*
  Lowercase elsewhere: *a customs official; a customs ruling; British customs checked his bag; she went through customs.*

- **cut back** (v.) **cutback** (n. and adj.) *He cut back spending. The cutback will require frugality.*

- **cut off** (v.) **cutoff** (n. and adj.) *He cut off his son's allowance. The cutoff date for applications is Monday.*

- **cyclone** See **weather terms.**

- **Cyclone** A trademark for a brand of chain-link fence.

- **cynic, skeptic** A *cynic* is a disbeliever.
  A *skeptic* is a doubter.

- **czar** Not *tsar.* It was a formal title only for the ruler of Russia and some other Slavic nations.
  Lowercase in all other uses.

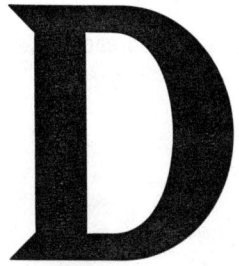

- **Dacron** A trademark for a brand of polyester fiber.

- **dalai lama** (DAH'-lee LAH'-mah) The traditional high priest of Lamaism, a form of Buddhism practiced in Tibet and Mongolia. *Dalai lama* is a title rather than a name, but it is all that is used when referring to that person.
   Capitalize *Dalai Lama* when referring to the holder of the title, in keeping with the principles outlined in the **nobility** entry.

- **Dallas** The city in Texas stands alone in datelines.

- **Dalles, The** A city in Oregon.

- **dam** Capitalize when part of a proper name: *Hoover Dam.*

- **damage, damages** *Damage* is destruction: *Officials say damage from the storm will total more than a (b) billion dollars.*
   Damages are awarded by a court as the compensation for injury or loss: *The woman received 25-thousand dollars in damages.*

- **damn it** Use instead of *dammit,* but like other profanity it should be avoided unless there is a compelling reason. See the **obscenities, profanities, vulgarities** entry for guidelines on usage and flagging.

- **dangling modifiers** Avoid modifiers that do not refer clearly and logically to some word in the sentence.
   Dangling: *Taking our seats, the game started.* (*Taking* does not refer to the subject, *game*, nor to any other word in the sentence.)
   Correct: *Taking our seats, we watched the opening of the game.* (*Taking* refers to *we*, the subject of the sentence.)

- **Danish pastry**

- **Dardanelles, the** Not *the Dardanelles Strait.* Note that *the* is not capitalized.

- **Dark Ages** The period beginning with the sack of Rome in 476 and ending at about the end of the 10th century. The term is derived from the idea that this period in Europe was characterized by intellectual stagnation, widespread ignorance and poverty.

- **Dark Continent** Don't use it. Say *Africa* instead.

- **dark horse**

- **dash (-dash-)** No longer in use.
It once was a frequently used means of indicating the place where a story could be wrapped up without the loss of any essential information.
For the punctuation mark (- -), see **double dash.**

- **data** A plural noun, it normally takes plural verbs and pronouns.
See the **collective nouns** entry, however, for an example of when nouns such as *data* may take singular verbs and pronouns.

- **database** The collection of all data used and produced by a computer program.

- **data processing** (n. and adj.) Do not hyphenate the adjective.

- **date line** Two words for the imaginary line that separates one day from another. See the **international date line** entry.

- **datelines** Every wire story, including items within longer scripts, takes a dateline.
The presence of the dateline does not eliminate the need to mention the story's dateline in the body of the copy. All stories should be written assuming that the dateline will not be read on the air:

(New Orleans) - - There's been an explosion aboard an oil-drilling platform in the Gulf of Mexico, about 60 miles south of New Orleans.

In most cases, a dateline should contain a city name, followed by the name of the country, state, county or territory in which the city is located. A dateline follows normal capitalization rules, is in parentheses and is followed by a double dash.
Domestic datelines: A list of domestic cities that stand alone in datelines follows. The norms that influenced the selection were the population of the city, the population of its metropolitan region, the frequency of the city's appearance in the news, the uniqueness of its name, and experience that has shown the name to be almost synonymous with the state where it is located.
No state with the following:

Atlanta	Detroit	Minneapolis	St. Louis
Baltimore	Honolulu	New Orleans	Salt Lake City
Boston	Houston	New York	San Antonio

Chicago	Indianapolis	Oklahoma City	San Diego
Cincinnati	Las Vegas	Philadelphia	San Francisco
Cleveland	Los Angeles	Phoenix	Seattle
Dallas	Miami	Pittsburgh	Washington
Denver	Milwaukee		

Also *Hollywood*, when used instead of *Los Angeles* on stories about films and the film industry.

In addition, the following special datelines stand alone:

Capitol Hill	Pentagon	White House	United Nations
Kennedy Space Center	Supreme Court		

Stories from all other American cities should have both the city and the state name in the dateline.

Regional circuits: On state wires, it is generally assumed that a city which stands alone is in the state in question.

(Springfield) - - Governor Jim Thompson has signed a bill giving state troopers the right to retire after 20 years of service.

However, the availability of each state's copy to members in adjacent states raises the possibility of confusion when a dateline is common to two states. Kansas City is the best-known example. Names such as Springfield, Quincy, Columbia, Washington and Lincoln are extremely common. Use the state name in addition to the city name whenever there's a substantial chance of confusion.

Foreign cities: These foreign locations stand alone in datelines:

Beijing	Jerusalem	Montreal	Rome
Berlin	Kuwait	Moscow	San Marino
Geneva	London	Ottawa	Singapore
Gibraltar	Luxembourg	Panama City	Tokyo
Guatemala City	Macao	Paris	Toronto
Havana	Mexico City	Quebec	Vatican City
Hong Kong	Monaco		

In addition, use *United Nations* alone, and without *New York*, in stories from U.N. headquarters.

Canadian datelines: Datelines on stories from Canadian cities other than Montreal, Ottawa, Quebec and Toronto should contain the name of the city followed by the name of the province. Do not abbreviate the province or territory name.

Datelines from former Soviet Union: Use the city name, followed by the republic:

(Alma-Ata, Kazakstan) - -

Do not use the designation *Commonwealth of Independent States* in a dateline.

Other foreign nations: Stories from other foreign cities that do not stand alone in datelines should contain the name of the country or territory (see the next section) spelled out.

Island nations and territories: When reporting from nations and territories that are made up primarily of islands but commonly are linked under one name, use the city name and the general name in the dateline. Identify an individual island, if needed, in the body of the story.

Examples:

British Virgin Islands   Netherlands Antilles   Indonesia   Philippines

Overseas territories: Some overseas territories, colonies and other areas that are not independent nations commonly have accepted separate identities based on their geographic character or special status under treaties. In these cases, use the commonly accepted territory name after a city name in a dateline.

Examples:

Bermuda	Grenada	Martinique	Sicily
Corsica	Guadeloupe	Puerto Rico	Sikkim
Faeroe Islands	Guam	Sardinia	Tibet
Greenland			

Pronouncers: Do not use pronouncers in datelines. Use them in the body of the story, when the location's name is first used.

Spelling and choice of names: In most cases, the name of the nation in a dateline is the conventionally accepted short form of its official name: *Argentina*, for example, rather than *Republic of Argentina*.

If in doubt, look for an entry in this book. If none is found, follow Webster's New World Dictionary.

Note these special cases:
- Instead of *United Kingdom*, use *England, Northern Ireland, Scotland* or *Wales*.
- For divided nations, use the commonly accepted names based on geographic distinctions: *North Korea, South Korea*.
- Use an article only with *El Salvador*. For all others, use just a country name— *Gambia, Netherlands, Philippines*.

See **geographic names** for guidelines on spelling the names of foreign cities and nations not listed here or in separate entries.

Undated stories: A story that has no dateline — a roundup, for example — should have an *Undated* dateline:

(Undated) · ·

This is for visual consistency on the wire.

Within stories: In citing other cities within the body of a story:
- Generally, no further information is necessary if a city is in the same state

as the datelined city in domestic stories, or if it is in the same nation as the datelined city in foreign stories. But include the state or country name if failure to do so would result in confusion.

- Follow the city name with further identification in most cases where it is not in the same state or nation as the datelined city. The additional identification may be omitted, however, if no confusion would result. There is no need, for example, to refer to *Boston, Massachusetts* in a story datelined *New York.*
- Provide a state or nation identification for the city if the story is undated. However, cities that stand alone in datelines may be used alone in undated stories if no confusion would result.
- Regardless of the style for the dateline, use an article with the name of the location in the body of the copy if that is how people identify the nation in normal speech. Example:

(Amsterdam, Netherlands) — Tourism in the Netherlands is ...

- **dateline selection** A radio or television piece should be datelined in the location where the reporter spoke the words. If the reporter covers an event in New Jersey but records the piece in New York, the dateline must be New York. The audience must never be misled about the reporter's actual location.

On the wires, a dateline should indicate the city in which the basic information for the story was gathered. For example, a story filed by the Washington bureau takes a Washington dateline. But if a local radio station in Chicago carries a report by its Washington correspondent, the story should carry a Washington dateline when it is picked up by the AP.

A few specific locations are so familiar and so frequently used that they warrant their own datelines: Capitol Hill, Kennedy Space Center, Pentagon, Supreme Court, White House, and United Nations.

Any story contributed by a broadcast member should carry the dateline of the city where the member gathered the story, if the reporter was physically present there. For example, if a station in Springfield, Mo., contributes a Joplin story which it covered by phone, the story takes a Springfield dateline. If the Springfield station sent a reporter to Joplin, the story takes a Joplin dateline.

A foreign dateline should be used only if the information in a story was obtained by a full- or part-time correspondent who was physically present in the datelined community.

If a foreign radio broadcast monitored in another city was the source of information, use the dateline of the city where the monitoring took place and mention that fact in the story.

When a story has been assembled from sources in widely separated areas, it should be undated. For example, if the Atlanta bureau does a round-up of storm damage in the South, it should be undated. See **datelines**.

When a datelined story contains supplementary information obtained in another location, make the point clear in the copy.

- **dates** The guidelines are similar to those for **numerals**:

- For the first through the eleventh of the month, spell out the date.
- For the 12th through the 31st, use Arabic figures and the appropriate suffix. See **months** for examples and punctuation guidelines.

- **daughter-in-law, daughters-in-law**

- **Daughters of the American Revolution** *D-A-R* is acceptable on the second reference. Headquarters is in Washington.

- **daylight-saving time** Not *savings*. Note the hyphen. When linking the term with the name of a time zone, use only the word *daylight*: *Eastern Daylight Time, Pacific Daylight Time*.
  Lowercase *daylight-saving time* in all uses and *daylight time* when it stands alone.
  A federal law, administered by the Transportation Department, specifies that daylight time applies from 2 a.m. on the first Sunday of April to 2 a.m. on the last Sunday of October in areas that do not specifically exempt themselves. See **time zones**.

- **day-long**

- **days of the week** Capitalize them. Do not abbreviate. See **time element**.

- **daytime**

- **day to day, day-to-day** Hyphenate when used as a compound modifier: *they have extended the contract on a day-to-day basis.*

- **D-C-Ten**

- **D-Day** June 6, 1944, the day the Allies invaded Europe in World War II.

- **D-D-T** Preferred in all references to the insecticide *dichlorodiphenyl-trichloroethane (dy-KLAW'-roh-dy-FEE'-nil-try-KLAW'-roh-EH'-thayn).*

- **de-** See **foreign particles**.

- **deacon** See the entry for the individual's denomination.

- **dead center**

- **dead end** (n.) **dead-end** (adj.) *She reached a dead end. He has a dead-end job.*

- **Dead Sea Scrolls**

- **deaf-mute** This term may be used, but the preferred form is to say that an individual cannot hear or speak. A *mute* person may be deaf or may be able to hear.
Do not use *deaf and dumb.* Do not use *hearing-impaired.* If the person has a reduced ability to hear but is not deaf, say so.

- **dean** Capitalize when used as a formal title before a name: *Dean John Jones, Deans John Jones and Susan Smith.*
Lowercase in other uses: *John Jones is dean of the college; the dean.*

- **dean's list** Lowercase in all uses: *He is on the dean's list. She is a dean's list student.* Note no hyphen in the second example.

- **deathbed** (n. and adj.)

- **debenture** See **loan terminology.**

- **debt service** The outlay necessary to meet all interest and principal payments during a given period.

- **decades** Use Arabic figures to indicate decades of history. For the 20th century, only the decade itself is needed.
Do not use an apostrophe to the left of the figures, but do use one to the right—along with an *s: The Roaring 20's, the 50's.*
For all previous centuries, use the century as well as the decade number: *The 1890's, the 1760's.*
In special references, which are widely known, the century may be dropped, as in *the Gay 90's.* See **historical periods and events** and **century.**

- **December** See **months.**

- **deci-** A prefix denoting one-tenth of a unit. Move the decimal point one place to the left in converting to the basic unit: 15.5 decigrams equals 1.55 grams.

- **decimal units** All decimal amounts should be spelled out, following the guidelines in **numerals.**
Spell out the word *point* and use a hyphen to connect it to numerals: *five-point-three, point-two, point-oh-one.*
Use decimal values only when directly relevant to the story. Round off when possible. Informalize when possible: *Three-point-five* is best expressed as *three and a-half. Three-point-seven* can, in many contexts, be expressed as *almost three and three-quarters.*
Decimalization should not exceed one place unless there are special circumstances.
For clarity, decimals also can be expressed in terms of tenths: *three-point-two equals three and two-tenths.* In these cases, hyphenate the number of tenths: *two-tenths of an inch, four and a-tenth percent.* See **fractions; monetary figures** and **percentages.**

- **Declaration of Independence** Lowercase *the declaration* when it stands alone.

- **decorations** See the **awards and decorations** entry.

- **Deepfreeze** A trademark for a brand of home freezer.
  If something is being postponed indefinitely, use two words, lowercase: *The project is in the deep freezer.*

- **deep-sea** (adj.)

- **Deep South** The region consists of Alabama, Georgia, Louisiana, Mississippi and South Carolina.

- **deep water** (n.) **deep-water** (adj.) *The creature swam in deep water. The ship needs a deep-water port.*

- **default** The failure to meet a financial obligation, the failure to make payments either of principal or of interest due, or a breach or non-performance of the terms of a note or mortgage. See **loan terminology.**

- **defendant**

- **defense** Do not use it as a verb.

- **defense attorney** Always lowercase; never abbreviate. See **attorney, lawyer** and **titles.**

- **defense spending** *Military spending* usually is the more precise term.

- **definitely** Overused as a vague intensifier. Avoid it.

- **deflation** A decrease in the general price level, which results from a decrease in total spending relative to the supply of available goods on the market. Deflation's immediate effect is to increase purchasing power.

- **degree-day** See **weather terms.**

- **degrees** See **academic degrees.**

- **dek-, deka-** A prefix denoting 10 units of a measure. Use *dek-* before words starting with a vowel and *deka-* before words starting with a consonant.
  Move a decimal point one place to the right to convert to the basic unit: 15.6 dekameters equals 156 meters.

- **Delaware** Has a land area of 2,057 square miles. Only Rhode Island is smaller in area, with 1,049 square miles. See **state names.**

- **delegate** The formal title for members of the lower houses of some legislatures. Capitalize only when used before a name. See **legislative titles.**
Always lowercase in other uses: *convention delegate Richard Henry Lee.*

- **Delta Air Lines** Headquarters is in Atlanta.

- **demagogue, demagoguery** Not *demagog.*

- **democrat, democratic, Democratic Party** See the **political parties and philosophies** entry.

- **Democratic Governors' Conference** Note the apostrophe.

- **Democratic National Committee** On second reference: *the national committee, the committee.*
Similarly: *Democratic State Committee, Democratic County Committee, Democratic City Committee, the state committee, the city committee, the committee.*

- **demolish, destroy** Both mean to do away with something completely. Something cannot be *partially demolished* or *destroyed.* It is redundant to say *totally demolished* or *totally destroyed.*

- **denote** See the **connote, denote** entry.

- **Denver** The city in Colorado stands alone in datelines.

- **depart** *Leave* is better. When you must use *depart,* follow it with a preposition: *He will depart from LaGuardia. She will depart at 11:30 a.m.*
Do not drop the preposition as some airline dispatchers do.

- **Departments of: Agriculture, Commerce, Defense, Education, Energy, Health and Human Services, Housing and Urban Development, the Interior, Justice, Labor, State, Transportation, the Treasury** The basic governmental departments in the executive branch. Each one is headed by a Cabinet secretary.
Informalize the names on all references: *the Agriculture Department, the Housing Department.*
Note that capitalization is retained in these informal constructions. Shorthand references to the departments also retain capitalization: *In the president's words, "State and Justice must resolve their differences."*
Lowercase *department* in plural uses, but retain capitalization of the proper name element: *the State and Justice departments.* Also lowercase *department* when it stands alone.
Do not abbreviate any department names except Housing and Urban Development: the acronym *HUD* is acceptable as an adjective: *The HUD grants will total 50 (m) million dollars.* See **Cabinet titles.**

- **dependent** (n. and adj.) Not *dependant.*

- **depreciation** The reduction in the value of capital goods due to wear and tear or obsolescence.
  Estimated depreciation may be deducted from income each year as one of the costs of doing business.

- **depression** A severe decline in economic conditions, generally characterized by extremely high unemployment and a fall off in business activity.
  The *Great Depression* refers to the worldwide economic hard times generally regarded as having begun with the stock market collapse of October 28 and 29, 1929.
  Capitalize *Great Depression* and *Depression* when referring to that period. Lowercase *depression* in other uses.

- **deputy** Capitalize when used as a title before a name. See **titles**.

- **derogatory terms** Do not use derogatory terms such as *krauts* or *niggers* except in direct quotes, and then only when their use is an integral, essential part of the story. See the **obscenities, profanities, vulgarities** entry and **word selection**.

- **-designate** Hyphenate: *chairman-designate, secretary-designate.* Capitalize only the first word when used as a title before a name.
  Avoid this usage whenever possible. Instead, use a phrase such as *the man expected to be named chairman, the president's choice for secretary of state.* See **titles**.

- **destroy** See the **demolish, destroy** entry.

- **detective** Do not abbreviate. Capitalize before a name only if it is a formal rank: *police Detective Frank Serpico* but *private detective Richard Diamond.* See **titles**.

- **detente** (day-TAHNT')

- **detention center** See the **prison, jail** entry.

- **Detroit** The city in Michigan stands alone in datelines.

- **devaluation** See the **currency depreciation, currency devaluation** entry.

- **devil** But capitalize *Satan.*

- **Dexedrine** (DEKS'-uh-dreen) A trademark for a brand of appetite suppressant. Its chemical name is *dextroamphetamine (DEKS'-troh-am-FEH'-tuh-meen) sulfate.*

- **dialect** The form of language peculiar to a region or a group, usually in matters of pronunciation or syntax.
  Dialect should be avoided, even in quoted matter, unless it is central to the story.
  Remember: Everyone has an accent. Do not make gratuitous references to a person's way of speaking unless it is absolutely necessary to the story: *Atlanta police say the ransom demand came from a caller with a New England accent.*
  See **Americanisms; colloquialisms; quotations in the news; word selection.**

- **dialogue** (n.) Never use it as a verb.

- **diarrhea**

- **Dictaphone** A trademark for a brand of dictation recorder.
  Dictation machine is the generic term.

- **dictionaries** For spelling, style and usage questions not covered in this handbook, consult Webster's New World Dictionary, Third College Edition, published by Macmillan, a division of Simon and Schuster.
  Use the first spelling listed in Webster's New World unless a specific exception is listed in this handbook. Most of the exceptions listed here are tailored for the requirements of radio and television copy.
  If Webster's provides different spellings in separate entries, use the spelling that is followed by a full definition.
  If Webster's New World provides definitions under two different spellings for the same sense of a word, either use is acceptable. For example, *although* and *though.*
  If there is no listing in either this book or Webster's New World, the backup dictionary, with more listings, is Webster's Third New International Dictionary, published by G. & C. Merriam Company.
  Webster's New World also is the first reference for geographic names not covered in the handbook. See **geographic names.**

- **die-hard** (n. and adj.)

- **Diet** The Japanese parliament. See **foreign legislative bodies.**

- **dietitian** Not *dietician.*

- **different** Takes the preposition *from,* not *than.*

- **differ from, differ with** To *differ from* means to be unlike.
  To *differ with* means to disagree.

- **dilemma** It means more than a problem. It implies a choice between two unattractive alternatives.

- **dimensions** Spell out such measurements as inches, feet, yards, meters and millimeters to indicate depth, height, length and width. Follow the rules for **numerals**, and hyphenate only the adjectival forms before nouns. Use commas to separate units. Examples:
  He is five feet, six inches tall. The five-foot-six man. The new center is a seven-footer.
  The storm left five inches of snow. It was a five-inch snowfall. We took a 150-mile trip.

- **Diners Club** No apostrophe, in keeping with the practice the company has adopted for its public identity. Only its incorporation papers still read *Diner's Club.* Headquarters is in New York.

- **diocese** Capitalize as part of a proper name: *the Diocese of Rochester, the Rochester Diocese, the diocese.* See **Episcopal church** and **Roman Catholic Church**.

- **directions and regions** In general, lowercase *north, south, northeast, northern,* etc., when they indicate compass direction; capitalize these words when they designate regions. Some examples:
  Compass directions: *He drove west. The cold front is moving east.*
  Regions: *A storm system that developed in the Midwest is moving eastward. It will bring showers to the East Coast by morning and to the entire Northeast by late in the day. The Western states will be sunny.*
  The North won the Civil War. The South will rise again. She has a Southern accent.
  With names of nations: Lowercase unless part of a proper name or used to designate a politically divided nation: *northern France, eastern Canada, the western United States (but, as above, the Western states).*
  But: *Northern Ireland, South Korea.*
  With states and cities: The preferred form is to lowercase compass points only when they describe a section of a state or city: *western Texas, southern Atlanta.*
  Capitalize compass points when used with state and city names in these cases:
  When part of a proper name: *North Dakota, West Virginia.*
  When used in denoting widely known sections: *Southern California, the South Side of Chicago, the South Bronx.* If in doubt, use lowercase.
  In forming proper names: Uppercase when combining with another common noun to form a region or location: *the North Woods, the South Pole, the Far East, the Middle East, the West Coast* (the entire region, not the coastline itself).

- **director** The formal title for the individuals who head the Federal Bureau of Investigation and the Central Intelligence Agency. Capitalize when used directly before their names or those of others for whom *director* is a formal title: *F-B-I Director J. Edgar Hoover.*
  Most uses of *director,* however, involve an occupational description not capitalized in any use: *company director Joseph Warren.* See **titles**.

- **dis-** The rules in **prefixes** apply, but in general, no hyphen. Some examples:

  dismember   dissemble   disservice   dissuade

- **disc** Use this spelling for references to flat audio and video storage media such as *compact disc, laserdisc* and *videodisc.* For computer-related references, see **disk.**

- **disc jockey** This term has fallen into disrepute in some circles. Many performers who host music programs prefer to be called *air personalities* or just *announcers.*

  Never use it to refer to broadcast journalists. Call them *newsmen* or *newswomen*, or just *reporters.*

  Most wire advisories should be directed to the *news director*, who is generally the person in charge of the station's news department.

  The person in charge of the station is usually the *general manager.*

  The *program director* is in charge of programming, sometimes including news, sometimes specifically excluding news.

- **discount rate** The rate of interest charged by the Federal Reserve on loans it makes to member banks. This rate has an influence on the rates banks then charge their customers.

- **discreet, discrete** *Discreet* means prudent, circumspect: *The president told reporters he was trying to be discreet.*

  Discrete means detached, separate: *There are two discrete sounds from a stereo system.*

- **discus** The disk thrown in track and field events.

- **diseases** Generally, do not capitalize: *arthritis, emphysema, leukemia, migraine, pneumonia,* etc.

  When a disease is known by the name of a person identified with it, capitalize only the individual's name: *Bright's disease, Parkinson's disease,* etc.

- **disinterested, uninterested** *Disinterested* means impartial, which is usually the better word to use.

  Uninterested means that someone lacks interest.

- **disk** Use this spelling for any round, flat object.

  It also is the spelling for computer storage media: *hard disk, floppy disk.* See **disc.**

- **dispel, dispelled, dispelling**

- **disposable personal income** The income that a person retains after deductions for income taxes, Social Security taxes, property taxes and for other payments such as fines and penalties to various levels of government.

- **Disposall** A trademark for a type of mechanical garbage disposal.

- **dissociate** Not *disassociate*.

- **distances** Follow the rules in **numerals**. See **dimensions.**

- **Distant Early Warning Line** Now known as **North Warning System**. See that entry.

- **district** Follow the rules for **numerals** and capitalize *District* when forming a proper name: *the Second District, the 12th District.*

- **district attorney** The prosecutor in many jurisdictions. Sometimes called the *county attorney* or *state's attorney.*
    Capitalize when used as a title before a person's name: *District Attorney Hamilton Burger.*
    D-A is acceptable on second reference. See **titles.**

- **district court** See **court names** and **U-S District Courts**.

- **District of Columbia** Abbreviate as *D-C* when the context requires that it be used in conjunction with *Washington.* In such cases, it does not take a comma: *Washington D-C.*
    The term should be spelled out when it is used alone: *the District of Columbia has a unique form of government.*
    In both cases, *the district,* rather than *D-C,* should be used in subsequent references.

- **dive, dived, diving** Not *dove* for the past tense.

- **divided nations** See **datelines** and entries under the names of nations such as South Korea.

- **dividend** In a financial sense, the word describes the payment per share that a corporation distributes to its stockholders as their return on the money they have invested in its stock. See **profit terminology.**

- **division** See the **organizations and institutions** entry; **military units; political divisions**.

- **divorcee** (dih-vawr-SAY') The fact that a woman has been divorced should be mentioned only if a similar story about a man would mention his marital status.
    When the woman's marital status is relevant, it seldom belongs in the lead. Avoid stories that begin: *A 35-year-old divorcee...* The preferred form is to say in the body of the story that a woman is divorced.

- **Dixie Cup** A trademark for a type of paper drinking cup.

- **doctor** Do not abbreviate.
Always use the term on the first reference to a person who holds a doctor of medicine degree. It is a formal title and should be capitalized when used before a name.
If appropriate to the context, it may also be used on the first reference to an individual who holds another type of doctoral degree. But because the public frequently associates the title doctor with physicians, care should be taken to make sure that the individual's specialty is stated close to the reference. Do not use *doctor* in subsequent references.
Do not use *doctor* before the names of people with honorary doctorates. See **academic degrees; courtesy titles** and **religious titles.**

- **dollars** Always spell out, lowercase and follow the guidelines in **monetary figures**.
For specified amounts, the word takes a singular verb: *He said 500-thousand dollars is what they want.*

- **domino, dominoes**

- **door to door, door-to-door** Hyphenate when used as a compound modifier: *He is a door-to-door salesman.*
But: *He went from door to door.*

- **DOS** An acronym for *disk operating system.* The most popular version is *M-S-DOS*, manufactured by Microsoft.
DOS is acceptable on all references.

- **double dash (- -)** Single hyphens are used to connect two or more letters or words. Double dashes are used to imply an abrupt change in thought, and as a visual symbol to set off datelines. Follow these guidelines:
Abrupt changes: Use a double dash to denote an abrupt change in thought in a sentence. It gives the broadcaster the visual clue that an emphatic pause is called for: *We will fly to Paris in June -- if I get a raise. Smith offered a plan -- an unprecedented one -- to raise revenues.*
Series within a phrase: When a phrase that otherwise would be set off with commas contains a series of words that themselves must be separated by commas, use double dashes to set off the full phrase: *She listed the qualities -- speed, storage capacity, light weight -- that she wanted in a computer.*
In lists: Double dashes should be used to introduce individual sections of a list. Each of the sections must contain a full sentence. Example:
Jones gave the following reasons:
-- He never ordered the package.
-- If he did, it didn't come.
-- If it did, he sent it back.

Use spaces: Put a space on both sides of a double dash in all uses except at the start of a paragraph.

In datelines: A dateline is placed in parentheses and always followed by a double dash:

(New York) --

Location on keyboard: On most word processors and typewriters, the double dash is indicated by typing two hyphens (--). Do not use uppercase version of this key, which generates an underscore (_) on most newsroom computer systems and printers.

- **doughnut** Not *donut*.

- **Dow Jones and Company** The company publishes the "Wall Street Journal" and "Barron's National Business and Financial Weekly." It also operates the Dow Jones News Service. For stock market watchers, it provides the Dow Jones industrial average, the Dow Jones transportation average, the Dow Jones utility average, and the Dow Jones composite average. Headquarters is in New York.

- **down-** The rules in **prefixes** apply, but in general, no hyphen. Some examples:

downgrade   downtown

- **-down** Follow Webster's New World. Some examples, all nouns and/or adjectives:

breakdown   countdown   rundown   sit-down

All are two words when used as verbs.

- **Down East** Use only in reference to Maine.

- **downside risk** A measurement of the chance that the price of an investment will fall.

- **downstate** Lowercase unless part of a proper name: *downstate Illinois*. But: *The Downstate Medical Center*.

- **Down syndrome** Not *Down's*. It is the name for the genetic chromosomal disorder first reported in 1866 by Dr. J. Langdon Down.

- **Down Under** Australia, New Zealand and environs.

- **Dr.** Do not use this abbreviation. See **doctor**.

- **draft beer** Not *draught beer.*

- **drama** See **composition titles**.

- **Dramamine** (DRAM'-uh-meen) A trademark for a brand of motion sickness remedy.

- **Drambuie** (dram-BOO'-ee) A trademark for a brand of Scottish liqueur.

- **dressing room**

- **drive-in** (n.)

- **drop out** (v.) **dropout** (n.)

- **drought**

- **drowned, was drowned** If a person suffocates in water or other fluid, the proper statement is that the individual *drowned.* To say that someone *was drowned* implies that another person caused the death by holding the victim's head under the water.

- **Dr Pepper** Note the lack of a period after the *Dr.* This is a trademark for a brand of soft drink. Headquarters is in Dallas.

- **drugs** Because the word *drugs* has come to be used as a synonym for narcotics in recent years, *medicine* is frequently the better word to specify that an individual is taking medication.

- **drunk, drunken** *Drunk* is the spelling of the adjective used after a form of the verb *to be*: *He was drunk.*
  Drunken is the spelling of the adjective used before nouns: *a drunken driver, drunken driving.*

- **drunkenness**

- **duel** A contest between two people. Three people cannot duel.

- **duffel** Not *duffle.*

- **duke, duchess** See **nobility**.

- **dumping** The selling of a product in a foreign market at a price lower than the domestic price. It usually is done by a monopoly when it has such a large output that selling entirely in the domestic market would substantially reduce the price.

- **Dumpster** A trademark for a large metal trash bin. Use *trash bin* or *trash container* instead.

- **Dunkirk** Use this spelling rather than *Dunkerque*, in keeping with widespread practice.

- **du Pont, E.I.** Note that the second name of the French-born American industrialist is two words. The company named after him is *E.I. du Pont de Nemours and Company* of Wilmington, Del. The shortened reference *Du Pont* (note the capitalized *Du*, which is in keeping with company practice) is acceptable on all references. See **foreign particles**.

- **durable goods** Long-lasting products, such as appliances, which are bought by consumers. Durable goods represent a larger investment for the consumer than other goods.

- **dust storm** See **weather terms**.

- **dyed-in-the-wool** (adj.)

- **dyeing, dying** *Dyeing* refers to changing colors. *Dying* refers to death.

- **each** Takes a singular verb.

- **each other, one another** Two persons look at *each other*. More than two look at *one another*.
    Either phrase may be used when the number is indefinite: *We help each other. We help one another.*

- **earl, countess** See **nobility**.

- **earmark**

- **earnings per share** See **profit terminology**.

- **earth** Generally lowercase; capitalize when used as the proper name of the planet. *She is down to earth. How does the pattern apply to Mars, Jupiter, Earth, the sun and the moon? He says he'll move heaven and earth.* See **planets**.

- **earthquakes** Hundreds of earthquakes occur each year. Most are so small they cannot be felt.
    The best source for information on major earthquakes is the National Earthquake Information Service operated by the U.S. Geological Survey in Golden, Colo.
    Measuring earthquakes: Earthquake magnitudes are measures of earthquake size calculated from ground motion recorded on seismographs. The Richter scale, named for Dr. Charles F. Richter, is no longer widely used.
    Magnitudes are usually reported simply as *magnitude six-point-seven*, for example, without specifying the scale being used. The various scales differ only slightly from one another.
    In the first hours after a quake, earthquake size should be reported as a *preliminary magnitude of six-point-seven*, for example. Early estimates are often revised, and it can be several days before seismologists calculate a final figure.
    Magnitudes are measured on several different scales. The most commonly used measure is the *moment magnitude*, related to the area of the fault on which an earthquake occurs, and the amount the ground slips.
    The magnitude scale being used should be specified only when necessary. An example would be when two centers are reporting different magnitudes because they are using different scales.
    With each scale, every increase of one number, say from 5.5 to 6.5, means that

the quake's magnitude is 10 times as great. Theoretically, there is no upper limit to the scales.

A quake of magnitude 2.5 to 3 is the smallest generally felt by people.
- Magnitude 3.5 can cause slight damage.
- Magnitude 4 can cause moderate damage.
- Magnitude 5 can cause considerable damage.
- Magnitude 6 can cause severe damage.
- Magnitude 7: a major earthquake, capable of widespread and heavy damage.
- Magnitude 8: a "great" earthquake, capable of causing tremendous damage.

Notable quakes: Earthquakes noted for both their magnitude and the amount of damage they caused include:
- Shensi province of China, January 1556: killed 830,000 people, the largest number of fatalities on record from an earthquake.
- Tokyo and Yokohama, Japan, September 1923: highest Richter reading was later computed at 8.3. The quake and subsequent fires destroyed most of both cities, killing an estimated 200,000 people. Until the China quake of 1976, this was the highest death toll in the 20th century.
- San Francisco, April 1906: highest Richter reading later computed at 8.3. The quake and fires were blamed for an estimated 700 deaths.
- Alaska, March 1964: Highest Richter reading 8.5. Killed 114 people.
- Guatemala, February 1976: Highest Richter reading was 7.5. Officials reported more than 23,000 deaths.
- Hopeh province of northern China, July 28, 1976: Highest Richter reading 8.3. A government document later said 655,237 people were killed, and 779,000 were injured. The fatality toll was second only to that of the Shensi quake of 1556.

Other terms: The word *temblor*—not *tremblor*—is a synonym for *earthquake*. The word *epicenter* refers to the point on the earth's surface directly above the underground center, or focus, of the earthquake.

An earthquake is always followed by a series of *aftershocks*. These can be quite strong, sometimes approaching the magnitude of the original event. On occasion, earthquake scientists have difficulty in immediately determining whether an event is an aftershock of a previous quake or a new earthquake. In that case, explain the confusion in your copy: *It isn't yet known whether this was an aftershock from last week's quake -- or a new earthquake that could set off aftershocks of its own.*

- **east, eastern** See the **directions and regions** entry.

- **Easter** In the computation used by the Latin Rite of the Roman Catholic Church and by Protestant churches, it falls on the first Sunday after the first full moon that occurs on or after March 21. If the full moon falls on a Sunday, Easter is the next Sunday.

  Easter may fall, therefore, between March 22 and April 25 inclusive.

- **Eastern Europe** No longer a separate political region. Use only in the historical sense. The same applies to *Western Europe.*

- **Eastern Hemisphere** The half of the earth made up primarily of Africa, Asia, Australia and Europe.

- **Eastern Orthodox churches** The term applies to a group of churches that have roots in the earliest days of Christianity and do not recognize papal authority over their activities.

Churches in this tradition were part of the undivided Christendom that existed until the Great Schism of 1054. At that time, many of the churches in the western half of the old Roman Empire accorded the bishop of Rome supremacy over other bishops. The result was a split between eastern and western churches.

The autonomous churches that constitute Eastern Orthodoxy are organized along mostly national lines. They recognize the patriarch of Constantinople (modern-day Istanbul) as their leader. He convenes councils, but his authority is otherwise that of a "first among equals."

Eastern Orthodox Churches today count about 200 million members. They include the Greek Orthodox Church and the Russian Orthodox Church.

In the United States, organizational lines are based on the national backgrounds of various ethnic groups. The largest is the Greek Orthodox Archdiocese of North and South America, with about 2 million members. Next is the Orthodox Church in America, with about 1 million members, including people of Bulgarian, Romanian, Russian and Syrian descent.

Beliefs: The term *orthodox* (literally "right believing") derives from the adherence of these churches to the teachings of only the seven ecumenical councils held before the Great Schism. The schism was caused, in part, by a Rome-approved change in wording that the Council of Nicea had used in defining the doctrine of the Holy Spirit.

Aside from the question of papal supremacy, beliefs are generally the same as those described in the **Roman Catholic Church** entry.

Liturgies reflect cultural heritages. The principal worship service is called the Divine Liturgy.

The churches have their own disciplines on matters such as married clergy—a married man may be ordained, but a priest may not marry after ordination.

Clergy: Some of these churches call the archbishop who leads them a *metropolitan*, others use the term *patriarch*. He normally heads the principal archdiocese within a nation. Working with him are other archbishops, bishops, priests and deacons.

Archbishops and bishops frequently follow a monastic tradition in which they are known only by a first name. When no last name is used, repeat the title before the sole name in subsequent references.

Some forms: *Metropolitan Ireney, Archbishop of New York and Metropolitan of America and Canada.* On second reference: *Metropolitan Ireney. Archbishop* may be replaced by *the Most Reverend* on the first reference. *Bishop* may be replaced by *the Right Reverend* on the first reference.

Use *the Reverend* before the name of a priest on the first reference. See **religious titles.**

- **Eastern Rite churches**   The term applies to a group of Roman Catholic churches that are organized along ethnic lines traceable to the churches established during the earliest days of Christianity.

  These churches accept the authority of the pope, but they have considerable autonomy in ritual and questions of discipline such as married clergy—a married man may be ordained, but marriage is not permitted after ordination.

  Worldwide membership totals more than 10 million.

  Among the largest Eastern Rite churches are the Antiochean-Maronite, Armenian Catholic, Byzantine-Byelorussian, Byzantine-Russian, Byzantine-Ruthenian, Byzantine-Ukrainian and Chaldean Catholic.   See **Roman Catholic Church**.

- **Eastern Shore**   A region on the east side of Chesapeake Bay, including parts of Maryland and Virginia.   *Eastern Shore* is not a synonym for *East Coast.*

- **Eastern Standard Time (e-s-t), Eastern Daylight Time (e-d-t)**   See **time zones**.

- **East Germany**   It no longer exists as a political entity.   See **Berlin** and **Germany**.

- **easy-going**

- **ecology**   The study of the relationship between organisms and their surroundings.   It is not synonymous with *environment.*

  Wrong: *Even so simple an undertaking as maintaining a lawn affects ecology.* (Use *environment* instead.)

  Right: *The laboratory is studying the ecology of man and the desert.*

  An *ecologist* is a scientist who studies the interactions among plants, animals and their environments.   An *environmentalist* is a person who advocates a program focusing on the protection of humans' surroundings.

  To be called an *ecologist*, one must have studied interrelated disciplines including biology, zoology and botany.

- **editor**   Capitalize *editor* before a name only when it is an official corporate or organizational title.   Do not capitalize as a job description.   See **titles**.

- **editorial, news**   In references to radio and television stations, reserve *news* for the news department, its employees and the programs they air.

  Use *editorial* in reference to the programs that express the opinion of the station's management.

  Similarly, in references to a newspaper, reserve *news* for the news department, its employees and news articles.   Reserve *editorial* for the department that prepares the editorial page, its employees, and the articles that appear on the editorial page.

- **editor-in-chief**   The hyphens are for readability.   Capitalize when used as a formal title before a name: *Editor-in-Chief Horace Greeley.*   See **titles**.

- **effect** See the **affect, effect** entry.

- **Eglin** (EG'-lin) **Air Force Base, Florida** Not *Elgin.*

- **either** Use it to mean one or the other, not both.
Wrong: *There were lions on either side of the door.*
Right: *She said to use either door.*
Right: *There were lions on each side of the door. There were lions on both sides of the door.*

- **either ... or, neither ... nor** The nouns that follow these words do not constitute a compound subject; they are alternate subjects and require a verb that agrees with the nearer subject: *Neither they nor he is going. Neither he nor they are going.*

- **El Al Israel Airlines** An *El Al airliner* is acceptable in any reference. Headquarters is in Tel Aviv.

- **elder** For its use in religious contexts, see the entry for an individual's denomination.

- **elderly** Use this word carefully and sparingly.
It is appropriate in generic phrases that do not refer to specific individuals: *concern for the elderly, a home for the elderly,* etc.
If the intent is to show that an individual's physical or mental faculties have deteriorated as a direct result of age, cite a graphic example and attribute it.
Apply the same principle to terms such as *senior citizen.*

- **-elect** Always hyphenate and lowercase: *President-elect Clinton.*

- **Election Day** The first Tuesday after the first Monday in November.

- **election returns** Handled differently in stories than in tables.
Election tables carry the exact number of votes, using Arabic numerals:

Here are the latest nationwide election returns in the race for president with 62 percent of the nation's precincts reporting:

Clinton 28,317,285 — 44 percent
Has won 27 states and the District of Columbia with 342 e.v.
Leads in 5 states with 38 e.v.

Bush 25,158,879 — 39 percent
Has won 10 states with 74 e.v.
Leads in 7 states with 81 e.v.

Perot 11,508,423 — 18 percent
Has won 0 states with 0 e.v.
Leads in 0 states with 0 e.v.

But in stories, the numbers are used only sparingly, to explain the trend that is developing:

With almost two-thirds of the nation's precincts reporting, Clinton already has won 342 electoral votes — more than enough to make him the 42nd president. He's leading Bush 44-to-39 percent in the popular vote. Ross Perot is at 18 percent.

Always try to simplify.

Wrong: *Jimmy Carter defeated Gerald Ford 40 (m) million, 827 thousand, 292 to 39 (m) million, 146 thousand, 157 in 1976.*

Right: *Jimmy Carter defeated Gerald Ford by nearly one-point-seven (m) million votes, out of a total of almost 41 (m) million votes cast in the 1976 election.*

- **Electoral College** But *electoral votes.*

- **electrocardiogram**   *E-K-G* is acceptable on second reference.

- **ellipsis (...)** One of the most overused forms of punctuation in broadcast writing and one that should be used sparingly.

Technically, the ellipsis indicates that words have been deleted. Keep in mind, however, that when a statement is condensed for broadcast, the listener cannot see the ellipsis, as can a newspaper or magazine reader. It is therefore a practice that should almost always be avoided. Example:

"I said that I would not do it, and I meant that I would not do it and I did not want anyone to misunderstand me when I said I would not do it, which is why I said I think I would not do it in the clearest possible way I could think of, and in fact I did not do it, just as I said I would not," the sheriff said.

Condensed for broadcast, this might read: *The sheriff put it this way: "I said that I would not do it, and I meant that I would not do it ... and in fact I did not do it."*

The editing of the quote took away the flavor of the original statement, and did so in such a way that the listener will never know what was missed. The best alternative is to use tape, but if there isn't any, avoid the use of ellipses whenever possible.

Many broadcast writers let themselves fall into the trap of using the ellipsis as a substitute for the comma and other standard punctuation marks. Example:

The City Council took action on a number of matters ... including sewers ... the new city budget ... three zoning protests ... including one involving a new shopping center proposed for Third and Main ... the firing of the police chief ... remodeling of City Hall ... as recommended by a consultant ... and the closing of Fourth Street for a parade on Thanksgiving.

Such careless use of the ellipsis is not only confusing, but also paves the way to very long sentences and generally sloppy writing.

It is not AP style to substitute the ellipsis for a comma, semicolon, colon or any other appropriate punctuation mark.

The ellipsis can occasionally be used to indicate hesitation, although the double dash is usually better: *The president said he would definitely go to Rome ... unless the pope asks him not to.*

Preferred: *The president said he will definitely go to Rome -- unless the pope asks him not to.*

The double dash is a better signal to the announcer to use a rising inflection to indicate that there is more to come.

The one case in which the ellipsis works well is as a signal to the announcer to let the voice trail off. Example:

Are the hostages coming home? The answer could be yes -- but it could also be no ... See **double dash.**

• **El Salvador** The use of the article in the name of this nation helps to distinguish it from its capital, *San Salvador.*

Use *Salvadoran(s)* in references to citizens of the nation.

• **embargo** See the **boycott, embargo entry.**

• **embargo times** See **release times.**

• **embarrass, embarrassing, embarrassed, embarrassment**

• **embassy** An *embassy* is the official residence of an ambassador in a foreign country and the office that handles the political relations of one nation with another.

A *consulate*, the residence of a consul in a foreign city, handles the commercial affairs and personal needs of citizens of the appointing country.

Capitalize with the name of a nation; lowercase without it: *the French Embassy, the American Embassy, the embassy.* See **consulate.**

• **emcee, emceed, emceeing**

• **emeritus** This word often is added to formal titles to denote that individuals who have retired retain their rank or title.

When used, place *emeritus* after the formal title, in keeping with the general practice of academic institutions: *Professor Emeritus Samuel Eliot Morison, Dean Emeritus Cortney Brown, Publisher Emeritus Barnard Colby.*

Lowercase when not used before a name: *Samuel Eliot Morison is professor emeritus of history.*

• **emigrate, immigrate** One who leaves a country *emigrates* from it.
One who comes into a country *immigrates* to it.
The same principle holds for *emigrant* and *immigrant.*

• **Emmy, Emmys** The annual awards by the National Academy of Television Arts and Sciences.

• **Empirin** (EM'-pir-in) A trademark for a brand of aspirin compound.

- **employee**   Not *employe.*

- **empty-handed**

- **enact**   See the **adopt, approve, enact, pass** entry.

- **encyclopedia**   But follow the spelling of formal names: *Encyclopaedia Britannica.*

- **Energy Research and Development Administration**   In 1977, this offshoot of the Atomic Energy Commission was absorbed into the new federal Department of Energy.

- **enforce**   But *reinforce.*

- **engine, motor**   An *engine* develops its own power, usually through internal combustion or the pressure of air, steam or water passing over vanes attached to a wheel: *an airplane engine, an automobile engine, a jet engine, a missile engine, a steam engine, a turbine engine.*
  A *motor* receives power from an outside source: *an electric motor, a hydraulic motor.*

- **England**   *London* stands alone in datelines. Use *England* after the names of other English communities in datelines.
  England is one of the nations in the *United Kingdom* and is not synonymous with it. See **datelines** and **United Kingdom**.

- **English muffin, English setter, English sparrow**

- **Enovid**   (EN'oh-vid)   A trademark for a brand of birth control pill. The chemical name is *norethynodrel with mestranol.*

- **enquire, enquiry**   The preferred words are *inquire* and *inquiry.*

- **enroll, enrolled, enrolling**

- **en route**   Always two words.

- **ensign**   See **military titles**.

- **ensure, insure**   Use *ensure* to mean guarantee: *Steps were taken to ensure accuracy.*
  Use *insure* for references to insurance: *The policy insures his life.*

- **entitled**   Use it to mean a right to do or have something. Do not use it to mean titled.
  Wrong: *The book was entitled "Gone with the Wind."*

Right: *She was entitled to the refund.*
Right: *The book was titled "Gone With the Wind."*

- **enumerations** See examples in the **double dash** and **periods** entries.

- **envelop** Other verb forms: *enveloping, enveloped.* But: *envelope* (n.).

- **environment** See **ecology.**

- **Environmental Protection Agency** *E-P-A* is acceptable on second reference.

- **envoy** Not a formal title. Lowercase. See **titles.**

- **epicenter** The point on the earth's surface directly above the underground center, or focus, of an earthquake. See **earthquakes.**

- **epidemiology** (eh-pih-dee-mee-AH'- loh-jee)

- **Episcopal, Episcopalian** *Episcopal* is the adjective form; use *Episcopalian* only as a noun referring to a member of the Episcopal Church: *She is an Episcopalian.* But: *She is an Episcopal priest.*
Capitalize *Episcopal* when referring to the *Episcopal Church.* Use lowercase when the reference simply is to a body governed by bishops.

- **Episcopal Church** Acceptable in all references for the *Protestant Episcopal Church in the United States of America,* the U.S. national church that is a member of the Anglican Communion.
The church is governed nationally by two bodies—the permanent National Council and the General Convention, which meets every three years. After the council, the principal organizational units are, in descending order of size: provinces, dioceses or missionary districts, local parishes and local missions.
The National Council is composed of bishops, priests, laymen and laywomen. One bishop is designated the leader and holds the formal title of *presiding bishop.* The council is responsible for furthering the missionary, educational and social work of the church.
The General Convention has final authority in matters of policy and doctrine. All acts must pass both of its houses—the House of Bishops and the House of Deputies. The latter is composed of an equal number of clergy and lay delegates from each diocese.
A province is composed of several dioceses. Each has a provincial synod made up of a house of bishops and a house of deputies. The synod's primary duty is to coordinate the work of the church in its area.
Within a diocese, a bishop is the principal official. He is helped by the Diocesan Convention, which consists of all the clergy in the diocese and lay representatives from each parish. The convention adopts a budget, elects a bishop in the case of a vacancy, and elects delegates to the General Convention

The parish or local church is governed by a vestry, composed of the pastor and lay members elected by the congregation.

Beliefs: See **Anglican Communion**.

Clergy: The clergy consists of bishops, priests, deacons and brothers. A priest who heads a parish is described as a *rector* rather than a pastor. The term *minister* seldom is used.

For first reference to bishops, use *Bishop* before the individual's name: *Bishop John M. Allin*. An acceptable alternative in referring to American bishops is *the Right Reverend*. The designation *the Most Reverend* is used only before the name of the Archbishops of Canterbury and York.

For first references to men, use *the Reverend* before the name of a priest, *Deacon* before the name of a deacon, and *Brother* before the name of a brother.

For first references to women, use *the Reverend* before the name of a priest, *Deacon* before the name of a deacon.

Do not carry the title through to the second reference. See **religious titles**.

- **epoch** See **historical periods and events**.

- **equal** An adjective without comparative forms.
When people speak of a *more equal* distribution of wealth, what is meant is *more equitable*.

- **equal, equaled, equaling**

- **Equal Employment Opportunity Commission** Do not use the cumbersome abbreviation *E-E-O-C*. *The commission* is preferable on the second reference.

- **equally as** Do not use the words together; one is sufficient.
Omit the *equally* shown here in parentheses: *The deficit is (equally) as large as last year.*
Omit the *as* shown here in parentheses: *The 1992 deficit and 1993 deficit are equally (as) large.*

- **Equal Rights Amendment** *E-R-A* is acceptable on second reference.
It failed to win approval of enough states. Ratification required approval of three-quarters of the 50 states—38—by June 30, 1982. The original deadline—March 22, 1979—was extended by Congress in October of 1978.
The Text:
Section One: Equality of rights under the law shall not be denied or abridged by the United States or by any state on account of sex.
Section Two: The Congress shall have the power to enforce, by appropriate legislation, the provisions of this article.
Section Three: This amendment shall take effect two years after the date of ratification.

- **equal time, fairness doctrine** Both are contained in the Communication Act of 1934.

    Equal time applies to the Federal Communications Commission regulation that requires a radio or television station to provide a candidate for political office with air time equal to any time that an opponent receives beyond the coverage of news events.

    If a station broadcasts material that takes a stand on a controversial issue, the *fairness doctrine* may require the station to give advocates of a different position an opportunity to respond.

    Enforcement of the *fairness doctrine* was considerably weakened by the F.C.C. in the 1980s.

- **equator** Always lowercase.

- **equitable** See **equal**.

- **equity** When used in a financial sense, *equity* means the value of property beyond the amount that is owed on it.

    A *stockholder's equity* in a corporation is the value of the shares he or she holds.

    A *homeowner's equity* is the difference between the value of the house and the amount of the unpaid mortgage.

- **E-R-A** Acceptable in all references to baseball's *earned run average*. Follow the rules for numerals and hyphens.

    Acceptable on second reference for the *Equal Rights Amendment*.

- **eras** See the **historical periods and events** entry.

- **escalator** Formerly a trademark, now a generic term.

- **escalator clause** A clause in a contract providing for increases or decreases in wages or prices based on fluctuations in the cost of living, production or expenses.

- **escapee** The preferred words are *escaped convict* or *fugitive*.

- **Eskimo, Eskimos** Some, especially in Canada, prefer the term *Inuit (IN'-oo-it)* for these native peoples of northern America.

- **espresso** The coffee is *espresso*, not *expresso*.

- **essential clauses, non-essential clauses** These terms are used in this handbook instead of *restrictive clause* and *nonrestrictive clause* to convey the distinction between the two in a more easily remembered manner.

    Both types of clauses provide additional information about a word or phrase in the sentence.

The difference between them is that the *essential clause* cannot be eliminated without changing the meaning of the sentence—it so "restricts" the meaning of the word or phrase that its absence would lead to a substantially different interpretation of what the author meant.

The *non-essential* clause, however, can be eliminated without altering the basic meaning of the sentence—it does not "restrict" the meaning so significantly that its absence would radically alter the author's thought. Non-essential clauses should be avoided. Write a separate sentence instead.

Punctuation: An essential clause must not be set off from the rest of a sentence by commas. A non-essential clause must be set off by commas.

The presence or absence of commas provides the newscaster with critical information about the writer's intended meaning. Note the following examples:

- *Reporters who do not read the stylebook should not criticize their editors.* (The writer is saying that only one class of reporters, those who do not read the stylebook, should not criticize their editors. If the *who ... stylebook* phrase were deleted, the meaning of the sentence would be changed substantially.)
- *Reporters, who do not read the stylebook, should not criticize their editors.* (The writer is saying that all reporters fail to read the stylebook and should not criticize their editors. If the *who ... stylebook* phrase were deleted, this meaning would not be changed.)

Use of who, that, which: When an essential or non-essential clause refers to a human being or an animal with a name, it should be introduced by *who* or *whom.* (See the **who, whom** entry. This would be better written: Reporters don't read the Stylebook, so they shouldn't criticize their editors.)

Do not use commas if the clause is essential to the meaning; use them if it is not.

That is the preferred pronoun to introduce essential clauses that refer to an inanimate object or an animal without a name. *Which* is the only acceptable pronoun to introduce a non-essential clause that refers to an inanimate object or an animal without a name.

The pronoun *which* occasionally may be substituted for *that* in the introduction of an essential clause that refers to an inanimate object or an animal without a name. In general, this use of *which* should appear only when *that* is used as a conjunction to introduce another clause in the same sentence: *He said Monday that the part of the army which suffered severe casualties needs reinforcement.* See **that (conjunction)** for guidelines on the use of **that** as a conjunction.

• essential phrases, non-essential phrases These terms are used in this handbook instead of *restrictive phrase* and *non-restrictive phrase* to convey the distinction between the two in a more easily remembered manner. The underlying concept is the one that also applies to clauses:

An *essential phrase* is a word or group of words critical to the listener's understanding of what you have in mind.

A *non-essential phrase* provides additional information about something. Although the information may be helpful to the audience's comprehension, the listener would not be misled if the information were not there.

Punctuation: Do not set an essential phrase off from the rest of the sentence with commas:

There was a 50th-anniversary showing of the classic cartoon "Snow White and the Seven Dwarfs" last night. (No comma, because many movies are considered classics, and without the name of the movie the audience would not know which movie was meant.)

There was a 50th-anniversary showing of the first animated feature film, "Snow White and the Seven Dwarfs," last night. (Only one movie was the first animated feature film. The name is informative, but even without the name no other movie could be meant.)

President Bush ate dinner with his son Jeb last night. (The inclusion of the name is critical because Bush has more than one son.)

President Bush ate dinner with his eldest son, Jeb, last night. (Bush has only one eldest son. Without the commas, the sentence would suggest that he had more than one eldest son.)

The company chairman, Henry Ford the second, spoke. (In the context, only one person could be meant.)

Indian corn, or maize, was harvested. (*Maize* provides the audience with the name of the corn, but its absence would not change the meaning of the sentence.)

Descriptive words: Do not confuse punctuation rules for non-essential clauses with the correct punctuation when a non-essential word is used as a descriptive adjective. The distinguishing clue often is the lack of an article or pronoun:

Right: *Julie and husband David went shopping. Julie and her husband, David, went shopping.*

Right: *Company Chairman Henry Ford the second made the announcement. The company chairman, Henry Ford the second, made the announcement.*

- **Eurasian** Of European and Asian descent.

- **Eurodollar** A dollar on deposit in a European bank, including foreign branches of American banks.

- **European Community** See **European Union**.

- **European Union** Do not abbreviate. The *European Union,* based in Brussels, Belgium, was created by the Treaty on European Union signed in February 1992 and took effect Nov. 1, 1993. Its six founding members are France, Germany, Italy, Netherlands, Belgium, and Luxembourg. Other members are Denmark, Greece, Ireland, Portugal, Spain and the United Kingdom, with Austria, Sweden and Finland joining as of Jan. 1, 1995.

- **evangelical** See **religious movements**.

- **Evangelical Friends Alliance** See **Quakers**.

- **evangelism** See **religious movements**.

- **evangelist** Capitalize only in reference to the men credited with writing

the Gospels: *The four Evangelists were Matthew, Mark, Luke and John.*
In lowercase, it mean a preacher who makes a profession of seeking conversions.

● **eve** Capitalize when used after the name of a holiday: *New Year's Eve, Christmas Eve.* But: *the eve of Christmas, the eve of the Gulf War.*

● **even-steven** Not *even-stephen.*

● **every day** (adv.) **every-day** (adj.) *He goes to work every day. She wears every-day shoes.*

● **every one, everyone** Two words when it means each individual item: *Every one of the clues was worthless.*
One word when used as a pronoun meaning all persons: *Everyone wants life to be happy.* (Note that *everyone* takes singular verbs and pronouns.)

● **ex-** Use no hyphen for words that use *ex-* in the sense of *out of*:

excommunicate   expropriate

Hyphenate—but do not capitalize— when using *ex-* in the sense of *former*:

ex-convict   ex-president

The prefix modifies the entire term: *ex-New York Mayor Ed Koch*—not *New York ex-Mayor Ed Koch.*
Usually *former* is better.

● **exaggerate**

● **Excedrin** A trademark for a brand of aspirin compound.

● **except** See the **accept, except** entry.

● **exclamation point** Exclamation points generally should be avoided in broadcast writing.

● **execute** To *execute* a person is to kill him in compliance with a military order or judicial decision.
An *execution-style killing* is one that appears to have characteristics of an execution, including a specific order to carry out the killing. Be careful in using this term. See the **assassin, killer, murderer** entry and the **homicide, murder, manslaughter** entry.

● **executive branch** Always lowercase.

● **executive director** Often the chief operational officer of an organization—and so a far better source than the often ceremonial president or chairman.

Capitalize before a name only if it is a formal corporate or organizational title. See **titles**.

- **Executive Mansion** Capitalize only when referring to the White House.

- **Executive Protective Service** It is now the *Secret Service Uniformed Division*. See **Secret Service**.

- **executor** Used for both men and women. Not a formal title. Always lowercase. See **titles**.

- **exorcise, exorcism** Not *exorcize*.

- **Explorers** See **Boy Scouts**.

- **Export-Import Bank of the United States** *Export-Import Bank* is acceptable in all references. Do not use the shorthand *Ex-Im Bank*. Headquarters is in Washington.

- **extol, extolled, extolling**

- **extra-** Do not use a hyphen when *extra* means *outside of* unless the prefix is followed by a word beginning with *a* or a capitalized word:

extralegal   extramarital   extraterrestrial

But:

extra-alimentary   extra-Britannic

Follow *extra* with a hyphen when it is part of a compound modifier describing a condition beyond the usual size, extent or degree:

extra-base hit   extra-large book   extra-dry drink   extra-mild taste

- **extraordinary loss, extraordinary income** See **profit terminology**.

- **extrasensory perception** *E-S-P* is acceptable in all references.

- **extreme unction** See **sacraments**.

- **Exxon Corporation** Formerly Standard Oil Company—the one in New Jersey. Headquarters is in New York.

- **eye, eyed, eyeing**

- **eyestrain**

- **eye to eye, eye-to-eye**   Hyphenate when used as a compound modifier: *an eye-to-eye confrontation.*

- **eyewitness**

F

- **facade** (fuh-SAHD')

- **face-to-face** When a story says two people meet for discussions, talks or debate,it is unnecessary to say they met *face-to-face*.
  For example, *face-to-face* is redundant in this sentence: *It was the first face-to-face meeting between Clinton and Bush since the election.*

- **fact-finding** (adj.) **fact-finder** (n.)

- **factor** A financial organization whose primary business is purchasing the accounts receivable of other firms, at a discount, and taking the risk and responsibilities of making collection.

- **fade out** (v.) **fade-out** (n.)

- **Faeroe** (FEHR'-oh) **Islands** Use in datelines after a community name in stories from this group of Danish islands in the northern Atlantic Ocean between Iceland and the Shetland Islands.

- **Fahrenheit** The temperature scale commonly used in the United States. Always uppercase.
  The scale is named for Gabriel Daniel Fahrenheit, a German physicist who designed it. In it, the freezing point of water is 32 degrees and the boiling point is 212 degrees.
  To convert to Celsius, subtract 32 from the Fahrenheit figure, multiply by five and divide by nine. For example, 77 minus 32 equals 45, times five equals 225, divided by nine equals 25 degrees

F	C	F	C	F	C
-26	-32	19	-7	64	18
-24	-31	21	-6	66	19
-22	-30	23	-5	68	20
-20	-29	25	-4	70	21
-18	-28	27	-3	72	22
-17	-27	28	-2	73	23
-15	-26	30	-1	75	24
-13	-25	32	0	77	25
-11	-24	34	1	79	26
-9	-23	36	2	81	27
-8	-22	37	3	82	28
-6	-21	39	4	84	29
-4	-20	41	5	86	30
-2	-19	43	6	88	31
0	-18	45	7	90	32
1	-17	46	8	91	33
3	-16	48	9	93	34
5	-15	50	10	95	35
7	-14	52	11	97	36
9	-13	54	12	99	37
10	-12	55	13	100	38
12	-11	57	14	102	39
14	-10	59	15	104	40
16	-9	61	16	106	41
18	-8	63	17	108	42

In cases that require mention of the scale, use this form: *86 degrees Fahrenheit.* Do not abbreviate. See **Celsius** and **Kelvin scale.**

For guidelines on when Celsius temperatures should be used, see the **metric system** entry.

Temperature conversions: For the conversion table on the preceding page, Celsius temperatures have been rounded to the nearest whole number.

- **fairness doctrine** See **equal time, fairness doctrine.**

- **fall** See **seasons.**

- **fallout** (n.)

- **family names** Capitalize words denoting family relationships only when they precede the name of a person or when they stand unmodified as a substitute for a person's name: *I wrote to Grandfather Smith. I wrote Mother a letter.* But: *I wrote my mother a letter.*

- **Fannie Mae** See **Federal National Mortgage Association.**

- **Fannie May** A trademark for a brand of candy.

- **Far East** The easternmost portions of the continent of Asia: China, Japan, North and South Korea, Taiwan, Hong Kong and the eastern republics of what used to be the Soviet Union.

  Confine *Far East* to this restricted sense. Use *the Far East and Southeast Asia* when referring to a wider portion of eastern Asia. See the **Asian subcontinent** and **Southeast Asia** entries.

- **far-flung** (adj.)

- **Farm Credit System** The federally chartered cooperative banking system that provides most of the nation's agricultural loans. The system is cooperatively owned by its farm borrowers and is made up of the regional banks that issue operating and mortgage loans through local land bank associations and production credit associations.

- **far-off** (adj.)

- **far-ranging** (adj.)

- **farsighted** When used in a medical sense, it means that a person can see objects at a distance but has difficulty seeing things at close range.

- **farther, further** *Farther* refers to physical distance: *He walked farther into the woods.*

Further refers to an extension of time or degree: *She will look further into the mystery.*

• **Far West** Capitalize when referring to the region west of the Rocky Mountains.

• **fascism, fascist** See the **political parties and philosophies** entry.

• **father** Use *the Reverend* in first reference before the names of Episcopal, Orthodox and Roman Catholic priests. Use *Father* before a name only in direct quotations. See **religious titles**.

• **father-in-law, fathers-in-law**

• **Father's Day** The third Sunday in June.

• **Father Time**

• **fax** Acceptable as a short version of facsimile: *She sent a fax. He used a fax machine. The statement was faxed to reporters.*

• **faze, phase** *Faze* means to embarrass or disturb: *The snub did not faze her. Phase* denotes an aspect or stage: *They will phase in a new system.*

• **F-B-I** Acceptable in all references for *Federal Bureau of Investigation.* See **Federal Bureau of Investigation**.

• **feather bedding, featherbedding** *Feather bedding* is a mattress stuffed with feathers.
Featherbedding is the practice of requiring an employer to hire more workers than needed to handle a job.

• **features** Although they are not exempt from normal style rules, those with specialized audiences qualify as **special contexts** in which some style rules are waived. See that entry for details.

• **February** See **months**.

• **federal** Use a capital letter for the architectural style and for corporate or governmental bodies that use the word as part of their formal names: *Federal Express, the Federal Trade Commission.* See also separate entries for the various governmental agencies.
Lowercase when used as an adjective to distinguish something from state, county, city, town or private entities: *federal assistance, federal court, the federal government, a federal judge.*
Also: *federal District Court* (but *U-S District Court* is preferred) and *federal Judge John Jones* (but *U-S District Judge John Jones* is preferred).

- **Federal Aviation Administration** F-A-A is acceptable on second reference.
The FAA is responsible for policing the manufacture, operation and maintenance of aircraft as well as the rating and certification of pilots and airports. Its function is to make sure all of these are safe.
The Civil Aeronautics Board polices the air carriers, authorizing them to engage in interstate commerce.
The National Transportation Safety Board is responsible for investigating transportation safety and recommending improvements to agencies such as the FAA.

- **Federal Bureau of Investigation** F-B-I is acceptable in all references. When necessary to avoid alphabet soup, use *the bureau.*

- **Federal Communications Commission** F-C-C is acceptable on second reference.

- **federal court** Always lowercase.
For clarity, it is best to use the proper name of the court in one reference in the story. See entries under **U-S** and the court name.
For readability, names can be informalized in other references. But be careful not to invent court names such as *Manhattan Federal Court.* Instead, use *a federal court in Manhattan.* See **judicial branch**.

- **Federal Crop Insurance Corporation** Do not abbreviate.

- **Federal Deposit Insurance Corporation** F-D-I-C is acceptable on second reference.

- **Federal Emergency Management Agency** FEMA (FEE'-muh) is acceptable on second reference, although *the agency* is preferred.

- **Federal Energy Regulatory Commission** This agency replaced the Federal Power Commission in 1977. It regulates interstate natural gas and electricity transactions.
Do not use the abbreviation *F-E-R-C.* Use *the commission* on second reference.

- **Federal Farm Credit Board** Do not abbreviate.

- **federal funds, federal funds rate** Money in excess of what the Federal Reserve says a bank must have on hand to back up deposits.
The excess can be lent overnight to banks that need more cash on hand to meet their reserve requirements. The interest rate of these loans is the *federal funds rate.*

- **Federal Highway Administration** Do not abbreviate. The abbreviation *F-H-A* is reserved for the Federal Housing Administration.

- **Federal Home Loan Bank Board** Do not abbreviate.

- **Federal Home Mortgage Corporation** The nickname for this agency is *Freddie Mac.* While that is acceptable on the second reference in business copy, it is not to be used in general news copy.
  Similarly, the association's bonds may be referred to as *Freddie Macs* in business copy only.
  The association is a government-chartered organization formed to help provide money for home mortgages by buying mortgages from lenders such as banks and repackaging them as investment securities.
  It is owned by savings institutions across the country. See **Federal National Mortgage Association**.

- **Federal Housing Administration** *F-H-A* is acceptable on second reference.

- **federal legal holidays** See the **holidays and holy days** entry.

- **Federal Maritime Commission** Do not abbreviate.

- **Federal Mediation and Conciliation Service** Do not abbreviate. Use *the service* on second reference.

- **Federal National Mortgage Association** The nickname for this agency is *Fannie Mae.* While that is acceptable on the second reference in business copy, it is not to be used in general news copy.
  Similarly, the association's bonds may be referred to as *Fannie Maes* in business copy only.
  The association is a publicly held, government-chartered organization formed to help provide money for home mortgages by buying mortgages from lenders such as banks and repackaging them as investment securities.
  The association mostly packages Federal Housing Administration mortgages. See **Federal Home Mortgage Corporation**.

- **Federal Power Commission** It no longer exists. See **Federal Energy Regulatory Commission**.

- **Federal Register** This publication, issued every workday, is the legal medium for recording and communicating the rules and regulations established by the executive branch of the federal government.
  Individuals or corporations cannot be held legally responsible for compliance with a regulation unless it has been published in the Register.
  In addition, executive agencies are required to publish in advance some types of proposed regulations, particularly when they would impose restrictions on a citizen (require seat belts in cars, for example) or institute a penalty for non-compliance. The advance publication is designed to provide the public with an opportunity to comment.

- **Federal Reserve System, Federal Reserve Board**
On second reference, use *the Federal Reserve, the Fed, the system* or *the board.*
For the individual banks that are members of the system, capitalize: *the Federal Reserve Bank of New York.* On second reference: *the bank.*

- **Federal Trade Commission** *F-T-C* is acceptable on second reference.

- **felony, misdemeanor** A *felony* is a serious crime. A *misdemeanor* is a minor offense against the law. A fuller definition of what constitutes a felony or misdemeanor depends on the governmental jurisdiction involved.
At the federal level, a *misdemeanor* is a crime that carries a potential penalty of no more than a year in jail. A *felony* is a crime that carries a potential penalty of more than a year in prison. Often, however, a statute gives a judge options such as imposing a fine or probation in addition to or instead of a jail or prison sentence.
A *felon* is a person who has been convicted of a felony, regardless of whether the individual actually spends time in confinement or is given probation or a fine instead. See the **prison, jail** entry.

- **Ferris wheel**

- **ferryboat**

- **fertility rate** As calculated by the federal government, it is the number of live births per 1,000 females age 15 to 44.

- **fewer, less** In general, use *fewer* for individual items and *less* for bulk or quantity.
Wrong: *The trend is toward more machines and less people.* (*People* in this sense refers to individuals.)
Wrong: *She was fewer than 60 years old.* (*Years* in this sense refers to a period of time, not individual years.)
Right: *Fewer than ten applicants called.* (Individuals.)
Right: *I have less than 50 dollars in my pocket.* (An amount). But: *I have fewer than 50 dollar-bills.* (Individual items.)

- **F-Four** See aircraft names.

- **fiance** (man) **fiancee** (woman) In common usage, both are pronounced (fee-ahn-SAY').

- **Fiberglas** Note the single *s*. A trademark for fiberglass or glass fiber.

- **figuratively, literally** *Figuratively* means in an analogous sense, but not in the exact sense: *He bled them white.*
Literally means in an exact sense; do not use it to mean *figuratively.*

Wrong: *He literally bled them white.* (Unless he actually drained blood from their bodies.)

• **figure** The symbol for a number. See **numerals**.

• **filibuster** To *filibuster* is to make long speeches to obstruct the passage of legislation.
A legislator who uses such methods also is a *filibuster*, not a *filibusterer*. See **cloture**.

• **Filipinos** The people of the Philippines.

• **filly** A female horse 2-5 years old.

• **film ratings** See **movie ratings**.

• **firearms** See **weapons**.

• **firefighter, fireman** *Firefighter* is the preferred term. Avoid such slang references as *smokeater*.
The term *fireman* also can mean a person who tends fires in a furnace.

• **firm** A business partnership is correctly referred to as a *firm*: *He joined a law firm.*
Do not use *firm* in reference to an incorporated business entity. Use *the company* or *the corporation* instead.

• **first degree, first-degree** Hyphenate when used as a compound modifier: *It was murder in the first degree. He was convicted of first-degree murder.*

• **first family** Always lowercase.

• **first lady** Not a formal title. Do not capitalize, even when used directly before the name of a chief of state's wife: *first lady Hillary Clinton.*

• **first quarter, first-quarter** Hyphenate when used as a compound modifier: *He scored in the first quarter. The team took the lead on his first-quarter goal.*

• **fiscal, monetary** *Fiscal* applies to budgetary matters. *Monetary* applies to the money supply.

• **fiscal year** The 12-month period that a corporation or governmental body uses for bookkeeping purposes. The federal government's fiscal year starts three months ahead of the calendar year—fiscal 1999, for example, runs from Oct. 1, 1999, to September 30, 2000.

- **fitful**   It means restless, not a condition of being fit.

- **flack, flak**   *Flack* is slang for publicity agent.
Flak is a type of anti-aircraft fire, hence figuratively a barrage of criticism: *Never take flak from a flack.*

- **flagpole, flagship**

- **flail, flay**   To *flail* is to swing the arms widely.
To *flay* is, literally, to strip off the skin by whipping. Figuratively, to *flay* means to tongue-lash a person.

- **flair, flare**   *Flair* is conspicuous talent.
Flare is a verb meaning to blaze with sudden, bright light or to burst out in anger. It also is a noun meaning a flame.

- **flare up** (v.) **flare-up** (n.)   See the **flair, flare** entry.

- **flash**   In wire-service terminology a *flash* is the highest possible story classification. It is reserved for presidential assassinations, atomic confrontations and other transcendent events.
A *flash* often consists of just a few words:

   Flash
   Man on moon.

   Flash
   Roosevelt dead.

   If in any doubt, do not send a *flash*.

- **flash flood**   See **weather terms**.

- **flaunt, flout**   To *flaunt* is to make an ostentatious or defiant display: *The rebels flaunted their power.*
To *flout* is to show contempt for: *The rebels flouted the law.*

- **flautist**   The preferred word is *flutist*. It is someone who plays the flute.

- **fleet**   Follow the rules in **numerals** and capitalize when forming a proper name: *the Sixth Fleet.*
Lowercase *fleet* when it stands alone.

- **flier, flyer**   *Flier* is the preferred term for an aviator or a handbill.
Flyer is the proper name of some trains and buses: *"The Western Flyer."*

- **flim-flam, flim-flammed** The hyphen is for readability. Use only in direct quotes.

- **flip-flop**

- **float** Money that has been committed but not yet credited to an account—such as a check that has been written but not yet cleared.

- **floods, flood stage** See **weather terms**.

- **floodwaters**

- **floor leader** Do not use when a formal title such as *majority leader, minority leader* or *whip* would be the accurate description. When you do use it, treat it as a job description, lowercased, rather than a formal title: *Republican floor leader John Smith*. See the **legislative titles** and **titles** entries.

- **floppy disk** Do not use *diskette*. See **disc** and **disk**.

- **Florida** See **state names**.

- **Florida Keys** A chain of small islands extending southwest from the southern tip of mainland Florida. Cities, or islands themselves, are followed by *Florida* in the dateline:

    (Key West, Florida) - -

- **flounder, founder** A *flounder* is a fish; to *flounder* is to move clumsily or jerkily, to flop about: *The fish floundered on land.*
    To *founder* is to bog down, become disabled or sink: *The ship floundered in the heavy seas for hours, then foundered.*

- **flout** See the **flaunt, flout** entry.

- **flowers** See **plants**.

- **fluid ounce** A *fluid ounce* is equal to 1.8 cubic inches, two tablespoons or six teaspoons. The metric equivalent is about 30 milliliters.
    To convert to milliliters, multiply by 30: *three ounces times 30 equals 90 milliliters.* See **liter**.

- **fluorescent**

- **flush** To become red in the face. See **livid**.
    To *flush out* something is to force it into the open.
    To *flesh out* something is to describe it in greater detail.

- **flutist** The preferred term for someone who plays the flute. Don't use *flautist*.

- **flyer** See the **flier, flyer** entry.

- **F-M** Acceptable on all references to the *frequency modulation* system of radio transmission.

- **f-o-b** Do not use as an abbreviation for *free on board*.
  F-O-B was also used as a slang term for *Friends of Bill*, a reference to the friends of Bill Clinton when he was president-elect. Do not use in any context.

- **-fold** For readability, use a hyphen:

  two-fold   four-fold

- **folk singer, folk song**

- **following** The word usually is a noun, verb or adjective: *He has a large following. He is following his conscience. The following statement was made.*
  Although Webster's New World records its use as a preposition, the preferred word is after: *He spoke after dinner.* Not: *He spoke following dinner.*

- **follow up** (v.) **follow-up** (n. and adj.) *The president says he will follow up on the matter. Congress says the follow-up was insufficient. The committee will hold follow-up hearings.*

- **food** Most food names are lowercase: *apples, cheese, peanut butter.*
  Capitalize brand names and trademarks: *Roquefort cheese, Tabasco sauce.*
  Most proper nouns or adjectives are capitalized when they occur in a food name: *Boston brown bread, Russian dressing, Swiss cheese, Waldorf salad.*
  Lowercase is used, however, when the food does not depend on the proper noun or adjective for its meaning: *french fries, graham crackers, manhattan cocktail.*
  If a question arises, check the separate entries in this book. If there is no entry, follow Webster's New World. Use lowercase if the dictionary lists it as an acceptable form for the sense in which the word is used.

- **Food and Agriculture Organization** Not *Agricultural*. Do not abbreviate the name of this United Nations agency.

- **Food and Drug Administration** *F-D-A* is acceptable on second reference.

- **foot** The basic unit of length in the measuring system that is in use in the United States. Its origin was a calculation that this was the length of the average human foot.
  The metric equivalent is exactly 30.48 centimeters, which may be rounded to

30 centimeters for most comparisons. Therefore, for most conversions to centimeters, simply multiply by 30: 5 feet times 30 equals 150 centimeters. For more precise figures, multiply by 30-point-48: *five feet times 30.48 equals 152.4 centimeters.* Similarly, to convert from feet to meters, multiply by .3: 5 feet times .3 equals 1.5 meters. See **centimeter, meter** and **dimensions.**

- **foot-and-mouth disease**

- **football** The spellings of some frequently used words and phrases:

ball carrier	goal line	lineman	quarterback
ballclub	goal-line stand	line of scrimmage	runback (n.)
blitz (n.,v.)	halfback	out of bounds (adv.)	running back
end line	halftime	out-of-bounds (adj.)	split end
end zone	handoff	pitchout (n.)	tailback
fair catch	kick off (v.)	placekick	tight end
field goal	kickoff (adj.)	placekicker	touchback
fourth-and-one (adj.)	left guard	play off (v.)	touchdown
fullback	linebacker	playoff (n., adj.)	wide receiver

Numbers: Follow the rules for **numerals** except when reporting scores in the text of a story and in tabular material. When reporting scores in scripted material, use figures, hyphens, and *to: The Bills beat the Giants 24-to-nothing. It was a 54-to-12 defeat. The Cowboys won 7-to-3.*

Scores: NFL quarter-scores are sent on a spot basis, as are finals. College scores are sent at half-time and at the end of each game. All scores take this format:

NFL
first Green Bay 7 N.Y. Jets 3

Finals take the same format, but with *final* in place of the period number.

Standings: The form for professional standings:

American Conference
East

	W	L	T	PCT.	PF	PA
Washington	10	4	0	.714	395	269
N.Y. Jets	9	5	0	.643	387	275
Etc.						

- **forbid, forbade, forbidding**

- **force majeure** (muh-ZHUR') Literally an overpowering force. In business terms it means a condition that permits a company to depart from the strict terms of a contract because of an event or effect that reasonably cannot be controlled.

It is a technical term that should be used only when central to the story—and should be fully explained.

- **forcible rape** A redundancy that usually should be avoided. It may be used, however, in stories dealing with both rape and statutory rape, which does not necessarily involve the use of force.

- **Ford Motor Company** Use *Ford*, not *F-M-C*, on the second reference. Headquarters is in Dearborn, Mich.

- **fore-** The rules in **prefixes** apply, but in general, no hyphen. Some examples:

forebrain	forefather	foregoing	foretooth

There are three nautical exceptions based on long-standing practice:

fore-topgallant	fore-topsail	fore-topmast

- **forecast** Use *forecast* also for the past tense, not *forecasted*. See **weather terms**.

- **forego, forgo** To *forego* means to go before, as in *foregone conclusion*. To *forgo* means to abstain from.

- **foreign governmental bodies** Capitalize the names of specific foreign governmental agencies and departments, either with the name of the nation or without it if clear in the context: *the French Foreign Ministry, the Foreign Ministry*. Lowercase *the ministry* or a similar term when it stands alone.

- **foreign legislative bodies** In general, capitalize the proper names of a specific legislative body abroad, whether using the name in a foreign language or the English equivalent.
  The most frequent names in use are *congress, national assembly* and *parliament*.
  Generic uses: *Parliament* is the appropriate generic descriptive for the *Diet* in Japan, the *Cortes* in Spain and the *Knesset* in Israel.
  Lowercase *parliament* only when used generically along with the foreign name: *The Diet is Japan's parliament*.
  Uppercase when it is used instead of the foreign name: *Demonstrators have disrupted a meeting of Japan's Parliament*.
  Plurals: Lowercase parliament and similar terms in plural constructions: *the French and British parliaments*.
  Individual houses: The principle applies also to individual houses of the nation's legislature, just as *Senate* and *House* are capitalized in the United States:

  (Rome) - - New leaders have taken control of Italy's Chamber of Deputies.

  Parliaments: Nations in which *parliament* is the name include: Australia, Canada, Denmark, Finland, France, India, Ireland, Italy, New Zealand, Norway, Poland and the United Kingdom.

National Assemblies: Nations in which *national assembly* is the name include: Bulgaria, Czechoslovakia, Egypt, Hungary, Nepal, Pakistan, Portugal, Tunisia, Uganda, Zaire and Zambia.

Lowercase *assembly* when used as a shortened reference to *national assembly*. In many countries *national assembly* is the name of a unicameral legislative body. In some, such as France, it is the name for the lower house of a legislative body known by some other name such as *parliament.*

• **foreign money** Generally, amounts of foreign money mentioned in news stories should be converted to dollars. If it is necessary to mention the amount, put it into context by explaining the dollar equivalent or by giving an example of the purchasing power of the amount of money.

The basic monetary units of nations are listed in Webster's New World Dictionary under "Monetary Units of All Nations." Do not use the exchange rates listed in the dictionary. Instead, use, as appropriate, the official exchange rates, which change from day to day on the world's markets.

• **foreign names** Use foreign names only when they are central to the story. The unnecessary inclusion of a foreign name usually causes the anchor to stumble and distracts the audience.

For foreign place names, use the primary spelling in Webster's New World Dictionary.

For personal names, follow the individual's preference for an English spelling if it can be determined.

Otherwise:

- Use the nearest phonetic equivalent in English if one exists: *Alexander Solzhenitsyn,* for example, rather than *Aleksandr,* the spelling that would result from a transliteration of the Russian letters into the English alphabet.
- If a name has no close phonetic equivalent in English, express it with an English spelling that approximates the sound in the original language: *Anwar Sadat.*

Always use a pronouncer. For additional guidelines, see **Arabic names; Chinese names; Russian names** and **Spanish and Portuguese names.**

• **foreign particles** They are part of the last name but precede it, with a space in between: *Charles de Gaulle, Baron Manfred von Richthofen.*

On the second reference: *de Gaulle, von Richthofen.*

Capitalize the particles only when the last name starts a sentence: *De Gaulle spoke to von Richthofen.*

• **foreign words** Some foreign words have been accepted universally into the English language: *bon voyage, versus, et cetera.* They may be used without explanation if they are clear in the context.

Many foreign words are not understood universally, although they may be used in special applications such as medical or legal terminology. Such words are marked in Webster's New World by a double dagger. If such a word or phrase is critical to a story, place it in quotation marks and provide an explanation: *"ad astra per aspera"* is a Latin phrase meaning *"to the stars through difficulty."* Unless the foreign word is universally familiar, use a pronouncer.

* **foreman, forewoman** Seldom a formal title.

* **formal titles** See **titles**.

* **former** Always lowercase. But retain capitalization of the formal title used immediately before the name: *former President George Bush.*

* **Formica** A trademark for a brand of laminated plastic.

* **Formosa** See **Taiwan**.

* **Formosa Strait** Not *the straits of Taiwan.*

* **formula, formulas** Avoid the use of mathematical formulas in copy. When it is essential to the story, follow the rules in **numerals**.

* **forsake, forsook, forsaken**

* **fort** Do not abbreviate, for cities or for military installations.
  In datelines for cities:

  (Fort Lauderdale, Florida) --

  In datelines for military installations:

  (Fort Bragg, North Carolina) --

* **fortnight** Say *two weeks* instead.

* **FORTRAN** An acronym for the computer programming language *Formula Translation*. The acronym is acceptable in all references, but be certain to identify it as a programming language.

* **fortune-teller, fortune-telling**

* **forward** Not *forwards.*

* **foul, fowl** *Foul* means offensive, out of line, or, in sports, out of bounds.
  A *fowl* is a bird, especially the larger domestic birds used as food: *chickens, ducks, turkeys.*

* **founder** See the **flounder, founder** entry.

* **Four-H Club** Members are *Four-H'ers.*

- **four-star general**

- **Fourth Estate** Capitalize. A collective name for journalism and journalists. The description is attributed to Edmund Burke, who is reported to have called the reporters' gallery in Parliament a "Fourth Estate." The three estates of early English society were the Lords Spiritual (the clergy), the Lords Temporal (the nobility) and the Commons (the bourgeoisie).
  The broadcasting industry occasionally is referred to as the *Fifth Estate.*

- **Fourth of July, July Fourth** Also: *Independence Day.* The federal legal holiday is observed on Friday if July 4 falls on a Saturday—on Monday if it falls on a Sunday.

- **fractions** Spell them out, using hyphens between units and numerals: *three and a-half, six and two-thirds, one-half of one percent.*
  Informalize fractions wherever possible: instead of *one-half of a dollar,* use *a half-dollar.* Note placement of hyphen. See **numerals; decimal units** and **percentages.**

- **fragment, fragmentary** *Fragment* describes a piece or pieces broken from the whole: *She sang a fragment of the song.*
  Fragmentary describes disconnected and incomplete parts: *Early returns were fragmentary.*

- **frame up** (v.) **frame-up** (n.)

- **frankfurters** They first were called *hot dogs* in 1906 when a cartoonist, T.A. "Tad" Dorgan, showed a dachshund inside an elongated bun.

- **fraternal organizations and service clubs** Capitalize the proper names: *American Legion, Lions Club, Independent Order of Odd Fellows, Rotary Club.*
  Capitalize also words describing membership: *He is a Legionnaire, a Lion, an Odd Fellow, an Optimist and a Rotarian.* See **American Legion** for the reasons for *Legionnaire.*
  Capitalize the formal titles of officeholders when used before a name. See **titles.**

- **free-for-all** (n. and adj.)

- **free-lance** (v. and adj.) The noun: *free-lancer.*

- **freely floating** Describes an exchange rate that is allowed to fluctuate in response to supply and demand in the foreign markets.

- **free on board** An arrangement under which the seller of a good agrees to put an item on a truck, ship or other means of transportation at no charge, but the transportation costs must be paid by the buyer.

A technical term that should be used only if central to the story—and then fully explained.

Do not use the abbreviation *F-O-B.*

- **freewheeling**

- **Free World**   An imprecise description, particularly since the end of the Cold War. Use only in quoted matter.

- **freeze-dry, freeze-dried, freeze-drying**

- **freezing drizzle, freezing rain**   See **weather terms**.

- **French Canadian, French Canadians**   Without a hyphen. An exception to the normal practice in describing a dual ethnic heritage.

- **French Foreign Legion**   Retain capitalization if shortened to *the Foreign Legion.*
   Lowercase *the legion* and *legionnaires.*
   Unlike the American Legion's members, members of the French Foreign Legion are active soldiers.

- **french fries**   See **capitalization** and **food**.

- **frequency modulation**   *F-M* is acceptable in all references.

- **Friends General Conference, Friends United Meeting**   See **Quakers**.

- **Frigidaire**   A trademark for a brand of refrigerator.

- **Frisbee**   A trademark for a plastic disk thrown as a toy or in an outdoor sport.

- **front line** (n.) **front-line** (adj.)

- **front page** (n.) **front-page** (adj.)

- **front-runner**

- **frost**   See **weather terms**.

- **fulfill, fulfilled, fulfilling**

- **full-** Hyphenate when used to form compound modifiers:

full-dress   full-length   full-page   full-scale
full-fledged

See the listings that follow and Webster's New World Dictionary for the spelling of other combinations.

- **full faith and credit bond** See **loan terminology**.

- **full house** (poker)

- **full time, full-time** Hyphenate when used as a compound modifier: *He works full time. She has a full-time job.*

- **fulsome** It means disgustingly excessive. Do not use it to mean lavish or profuse.

- **fundamentalist** See **religious movements**.

- **fund raising, fund-raising, fund-raiser** *Fund raising is difficult. They planned a fund-raising campaign. A fund-raiser was hired.*

- **funnel cloud** See **weather terms**.

- **furlough**

- **further** See the **farther, further** entry.

- **fuselage**

- **fusillade**

- **futures contracts** A *futures contract* is an agreement to deliver or take delivery of a commodity at a fixed price at a fixed future date. The amount, quality, and other terms of the contract are fixed in the futures agreement — and generally are standardized at major futures trading centers.

Futures options, which also are widely traded on the nation's commodities exchanges, give buyers the right but not the obligation to buy or sell a commodity at a certain price within a specified period.

The purpose of the futures exchanges is to transfer the risk of price fluctuations from people who don't want the risk—such as farmers or metals processors —to speculators who are willing to take a gamble of making big profits. They buy and sell futures contracts hoping to make a profit on the difference between the price fixed in the contract and the price of the commodity as the contract maturity date approaches.

Major American commodities exchanges are the Chicago Board of Trade, Chicago Mercantile Exchange, the New York Commodity Exchange, the New York Cotton Exchange and the Coffee, Sugar and Cocoa Exchange.

• **F.W. Woolworth Company**   *Woolworth's* is acceptable in all references. Headquarters is in New York.

- **G** The *general audience* rating. See **movie ratings**.

- **gage, gauge** A *gage* is a security or a pledge. Either of those words is preferred.
  A *gauge* is a device to measure something. *Gauge* is also a term used to designate the size of shotguns. See **weapons.**

- **gaiety**

- **gale** See **weather terms**.

- **gallon** Equal to 128 fluid ounces. The metric equivalent is roughly 3.8 liters.
  To convert to liters, multiply by 3.8: 3 gallons times 3.8 equals 11.4 liters. See **imperial gallon; liter; metric system**.

- **Gallup Poll** Prepared by The American Institute of Public Opinion in Princeton, N.J. See **polls and surveys**.

- **game plan**

- **gamut, gantlet, gauntlet** A *gamut* is a complete range of musical notes or, more generally, a term meaning the entire range or extent.
  A *gantlet* is a flogging ordeal, literally or figuratively.
  A *gauntlet* is a glove. To *throw down the gauntlet* means to issue a challenge. To *take up the gauntlet* means to accept a challenge.

- **gamy, gamier, gamiest**

- **garnish, garnishee** *Garnish* means to adorn or decorate.
  As a verb, *garnishee (garnisheed, garnisheeing)* means to attach a debtor's property or wages to satisfy a debt. As a noun, it identifies the individual whose property was attached.

- **gauge** See the **gage, gauge** entry.

- **gay** Acceptable as a synonym for *homosexual* (n. and adj.).

- **general, general of the air force, general of the army** See **military titles**.

- **General Accounting Office** This federal agency, the non-partisan investigative arm of Congress, may be referred to as the *G-A-O* on second reference.

- **general assembly** See **legislature** for the treatment of *general assembly* as the name of a state's legislative body.
  Capitalize when it is the formal name for the ruling or consultative body of an organization: *the General Assembly of the World Council of Churches.*

- **General Assembly** Always identify as the *United Nations* or *U-N General Assembly* in at least one reference.
  Use *the assembly* on second reference.

- **general court** Part of the official proper name for the legislatures in Massachusetts and New Hampshire. Capitalize specific references with or without the state name: *the Massachusetts General Court, the General Court.*
  But in keeping with accepted practice, *Legislature* may be used in all references and treated as a proper name. See **legislature**.
  Lowercase *legislature* in generic references: *The General Court is the legislature in Massachusetts.*

- **General Electric Company** *G-E* is acceptable on second reference. Headquarters is in Fairfield, Conn.

- **general manager** Capitalize only as a formal title before a name. See **titles**.

- **General Motors Corporation** *G-M* is acceptable on second reference. Headquarters is in Detroit.

- **general obligation bond** See **loan terminology**.

- **General Services Administration** *G-S-A* is acceptable on the second reference for this federal housekeeping and office supply agency.

- **genie** Not *jinni*, the spelling under which Webster's New World gives the definition.

- **gentile** Generally, any person not a Jew; often, specifically a Christian. But to Mormons it is anyone not a Mormon.

- **gentleman** Do not use as a synonym for man. See **lady**.

- **geographic names** The basic guidelines:

Domestic: The authority for spelling place names in the 50 United States and territories is The U.S. Postal Service Directory of Post Offices, although there are two exceptions:

* Do not use the postal abbreviations.
* *Saint* may be abbreviated *St.* and *Sainte*, as in *Sault Sainte Marie*, may be abbreviated *Ste.*

Foreign: The first source for the spelling of all foreign place names is Webster's New World Dictionary as follows:

Use the first-listed spelling if an entry gives more than one. If the dictionary provides different spellings in separate entries, use the spelling that is followed by a full description of the location. There are three exceptions:

* Use *Cameroon*, not *Cameroons* or *Cameroun*.
* Use *Sri Lanka*, not *Ceylon*.
* Use *Maldives*, not *Maldive Islands*.

These exceptions conform with the United Nations and U.S. Board of Geographic Names.

If the dictionary does not have an entry for the name in question, consult the first-listed spelling in The National Geographic Atlas of the World.

New names: Follow the styles adopted by the United Nations and the U.S. Board of Geographic Names on new cities, new independent nations and nations that change their names.

Datelines: see the **datelines** section.

Capitalization: Capitalize common nouns when they form an integral part of a proper name, but lowercase them when they stand alone: *Pennsylvania Avenue, the avenue; the Philippine Islands, the islands; the Mississippi River, the river.*

Lowercase common nouns that are not a part of a specific name: *the Pacific islands, the Swiss mountains, Chekiang province.*

For additional guidelines, see **addresses; capitalization; directions and regions; island.**

* **Georgia** See **state names.**

* **German measles** Also known as *rubella.*

* **Germany** East Germany and West Germany were reunited on Oct. 3, 1990. *Berlin* stands alone in datelines.

* **getaway** (n.)

* **get-together** (n.)

* **ghetto, ghettos** Do not use indiscriminately as a synonym for the sections of cities inhabited by minorities or the poor. *Ghetto* has a connotation that government decree has forced people to live in a certain area.

In most cases, *section, district, slum, area* or *quarter* is the more accurate word. Sometimes a place name alone has connotations that make it best: *Harlem, Watts.*

- **G-I, G-I's**   *Soldier* is preferred unless the story contains the term in quoted matter or involves a subject such as the *G-I Bill of Rights.*

- **gibe, jibe** (jyb)   To *gibe* means to taunt or sneer: *They gibed him about his mistakes.*
   Jibe means to shift direction or, colloquially, to agree: *They jibed their ship across the wind. Their stories didn't jibe.*
   Do not confuse *jibe* with *jive*, which describes a kind of slang.

- **Gibraltar, Strait of**   Not *Straits*. The entrance to the Mediterranean from the Atlantic Ocean.
   The British colony on the peninsula that juts into the strait, Gibraltar, stands alone in datelines.

- **giga-** (GIG'-uh)   A prefix denoting 1 billion units of a measure. It is best avoided.
   Move a decimal point nine places to the right, adding zeros if necessary, to convert to the basic unit: *five-point-five gigatons equals five (b) billion, 500 (m) million tons.*

- **girl**   Applicable until 18th birthday is reached. Use *woman* or *young woman* afterward. *Young girl* or *little girl* is redundant; simply use her age.

- **girlfriend, boyfriend**

- **Girl Scouts**   The full name of the organization is the *Girl Scouts of the United States of America.* Headquarters is in New York.
   Girls aged 6 through 8 are *Brownie Girl Scouts* or *Brownies.*
   Girls 9 through 11 are *Junior Girl Scouts* or *Juniors.*
   Girls 12 though 14 are *Cadette Girl Scouts* or *Cadettes.*
   Those aged 15 through 17 are *Senior Girl Scouts* or *Seniors.* See **Boy Scouts** for programs run by that separate organization.

- **gizmo**   Not *gismo.*

- **glamour**   One of the few *our* endings still used in American writing. But the adjective is *glamorous.*

- **globe-trotter, globe-trotting**   But the proper name of the basketball team is the *Harlem Globetrotters.*

- **G-M-T**   Acceptable in all references to *Greenwich Mean Time.* See that entry, as well as **time zones**.

- **gobbledygook**   Avoid it.

- **go-between** (n.)

- **godchild, goddaughter** Also: *godfather, godliness, godmother, godsend, godson, godspeed.* Always lowercase.

- **gods and goddesses** Capitalize *God* in references to the deity of all monotheistic religions. Capitalize all noun references to the deity: *God the Father, Holy Ghost, Holy Spirit,* etc. Lowercase personal pronouns: *he, him, thee, thou.*
    Lowercase *gods* and *goddesses* in references to the deities of polytheistic religions.
    Lowercase *god, gods* and *goddesses* in references to figurative gods: *He made money his god.* See **religious references**.

- **go-go**

- **golf** Some frequently used terms and some definitions:
Americas Cup: No possessive.
Birdie, Birdies: One stroke under par.
Bogey, Bogeys: One stroke over par. The past tense is *bogeyed.*
Eagle: Two strokes under par.
Fairway: One word.
Masters Tournament: No possessive. *The Masters* is acceptable in all references.
Tee, Tee Off: no hyphen.
U.S. Open Championship: Use *the U-S Open* or *the Open* on second reference.
Numbers: Follow the rules for **numerals** and **hyphens** except when reporting scores in text or tabular material: *He has a three handicap; she has a three-stroke lead.*
    When reporting scores, use figures and hyphens: *He shot a 7-under-par 64.* But: *He shot a par five to finish two up for the round.*
    Some other examples: *It is a par-five hole. She used a five-iron. The first hole; the tenth hole; the back nine; the final 18; the third round.*
Associations: *P-G-A* is acceptable in all references to the *Professional Golfers' Association* (note apostrophe). The same principle applies to the *Ladies Professional Golf Association* (no apostrophe, in keeping with *L-P-G-A* practice).

- **good, well** *Good* is an adjective that means something is as it should be or is better than average.
    When used as an adjective, *well* means suitable, proper, healthy. When used as an adverb, *well* means in a satisfactory manner or skillfully.
    Good should not be used as an adverb. It does not lose its status as an adjective in a sentence such as *I feel good.* Such a statement is the idiomatic equivalent of *I am in good health.* An alternative, *I feel well,* could be interpreted as meaning that your sense of touch was good. See **bad, badly** entry and **well**.

- **goodbye** Not *goodby.*

- **Good Conduct Medal**

- **Good Friday** The Friday before Easter.

- **good will** (n.) **goodwill** (adj.)

- **G-O-P** See **Grand Old Party.**

- **Gospels, gospel** Capitalize when referring to any or all of the first four books of the New Testament: *the Gospel of Saint John, the Gospels.* Lowercase in other references: *She is a famous gospel singer.*

- **gourmand, gourmet** A *gourmand* is a person who likes good food and tends to eat to excess; a glutton.
  A *gourmet* is a person who likes fine food and is an excellent judge of food and drink.

- **government** Always lowercase, never abbreviate: *the federal government, the state government, the U-S government.*

- **government, junta, regime** A *government* is an established system of political administration: *the U-S government.*
  A *junta* is a group or council that often rules after a coup: *A military junta controls the nation.*
  A *junta* becomes a *government* after it establishes a system of political administration.
  The word *regime* is a synonym for political system: *a democratic regime, an authoritarian regime.* Do not use *regime* to mean *government* or *junta.* For example, use *the Franco government* in referring to the government of Spain under Francisco Franco, not *the Franco regime.* But: *The Franco government was an authoritarian regime.*
  An *administration* consists of officials who make up the executive branch of a government: *the Clinton administration.*

- **governmental bodies** Always refer to a governmental body by the name that is most familiar to the audience. Most names are treated informally for readability. Often, a generic version will be clearer and less cumbersome.
  Follow these guidelines:
  Full name: Capitalize the full proper names of governmental agencies, departments and offices: *The U-S Department of State, the Georgia Department of Human Resources, the Boston City Council, the Chicago Fire Department.*
  Informal version of name: Generally, it is preferable to use the informal version of a body's name, to keep sentences simpler. In most stories, the full formal name of the department will not be used. The informal version of a name usually is derived by flip-flopping the formal name to delete the word *of.*

Capitalization is retained: *the State Department, the Georgia Human Resources Department.*

Without jurisdiction: Retain capitalization in referring to a specific body if the context makes the name of the nation, state, county or city unnecessary: *the state Human Resources Department, the Fire Department, the City Council.*

If the name is further condensed, use lowercase: *the department, the council.*

For additional, specific guidance, see **assembly; city council; committee; congress; legislature; house of representatives; senate; Supreme Court of the United States** and **supreme courts of the states.**

Generic equivalents: If a generic term has become the equivalent of a proper name in popular use, treat it as a proper name: *Walpole State Prison,* for example, even though the proper name is the *Massachusetts Correctional Institution-Walpole.* For additional examples, see **legislature; police department** and the **prison, jail** entry.

Plurals, non-specific references: All words that are capitalized when part of a proper name (except proper nouns) should be lowercased when they are used in the plural or do not refer to a specific, existing body. Some examples:

All states except Nebraska have a state senate. The town does not have a fire department. The bill requires city councils to provide matching funds. The president will address the lower houses of the New York and New Jersey legislatures.

Foreign bodies: The same principles apply. See **foreign governmental bodies** and **foreign legislative bodies.**

- **governor** Capitalize when used as a formal title before a name (or names): *Governor Bill Clinton, Governors George Pataki and William Weld.*

  Lowercase in all other uses: *the Arkansas governor, New York's governor, the governors of New York and Massachusetts.*

  Never abbreviate.

  On first reference to the governor of the audience's home state, use last name only: *Governor Weld.* On first reference to the governor of another state, use first and last name and identify the state in the same or an adjacent sentence: *Governor George Pataki of New York, New York Governor George Pataki, New York's Governor says ... George Pataki told.* See the next entry and **titles.**

- **governor general, governors general** The formal title for the British sovereign's representatives in Canada and elsewhere.

  Do not abbreviate in any use.

- **grade, grader** Follow the rules for **numerals** and hyphenate both the noun forms (*first-grader, second-grader, tenth-grader*) and the adjective forms (*a fourth-grade pupil, a 12th-grade pupil*).

- **graduate** (v.) *Graduate* is correctly used in the active voice: *She graduated from the university.* It is correct, but unnecessary, to use the passive voice: *He was graduated from the university.*

  Do not, however, drop *from: John Adams graduated from Harvard.* Not: *John Adams graduated Harvard.*

- **graham, graham crackers** The crackers are made from a finely ground whole-wheat flour named for Sylvester Graham, a U.S. dietary reformer.

- **grain** The smallest unit in the system of weights that is in use in the United States. It originally was defined as the weight of one grain of wheat.

  It takes 437.5 grains to make an ounce. There are about 7,000 grains in a pound. See **ounce (weight)** and **pound (weight)** .

- **gram** The basic unit of weight in the metric system. It is the weight of one cubic centimeter of water at 4 degrees Celsius.

  A *gram* is roughly equivalent to the weight of a paper clip—1/28 of an ounce.

  To convert to ounces, multiply by .035: 86 grams times .035 equals 3 ounces. See **metric system**.

- **grammar**

- **granddad, granddaughter** Also: *grandfather, grandmother, grandson.*

- **grand jury** Always lowercase: *A Los Angeles County grand jury, the grand jury.* This style has been adopted because, unlike the case with *city council* and similar governmental units, a jurisdiction frequently has more than one grand jury in session.

- **Grand Old Party** *G-O-P* is acceptable as a second-reference synonym for *Republican Party* without spelling out *Grand Old Party.*

- **grant-in-aid, grants-in-aid**

- **gray** Not *grey.* But: *Greyhound* for the bus company and *greyhound* for the type of dog.

- **great-** Hyphenate: *Great-grandfather, great-great-grandmother.*
  Use *great grandfather* only if the intended meaning is that the grandfather was a great man.

- **Great Atlantic and Pacific Tea Company, Incorporated** *A&P* is acceptable in all references. Headquarters is in Montvale, New Jersey. See **A&P.**

- **Great Britain** It consists of England, Scotland and Wales, but not Northern Ireland.
  Britain is acceptable in all references; *England* is not. See **United Kingdom**.

- **Great Depression** See **depression.**

- **greater** Capitalize when used to define a community and its surrounding region: *Greater Boston.*

- **Great Lakes** The five, from the largest to the smallest: Lake Superior, Lake Huron, Lake Michigan, Lake Erie, Lake Ontario.

- **Great Plains** Capitalize when used in reference to the prairie lands that extend from North Dakota to Texas and from the Missouri River to the Rocky Mountains. Also: *the Plains.*
  Use *northern Plains, southwestern Plains* and the like when referring to a portion of the region.

- **Greek Orthodox Archdiocese of North and South America** See **Eastern Orthodox churches.**

- **Greek Orthodox Church** See **Eastern Orthodox churches.**

- **Green Revolution** The substantial increase in agricultural yields that resulted from the development of new varieties of grains. Don't use it

- **Greens** Some European environmental movements took on the formal name *Greens* or *Green Party* in the mid-80s as they became more politically active. Capitalize when used as a formal party name.
  The term gained widespread use as an informal reference to all environmental activists in parts of Europe. Avoid using it except when it is a formal name. See the **political parties and philosophies** entry.

- **Greenwich Mean Time** The abbreviation *G-M-T* is acceptable in all references. *G-M-T* is five hours ahead of Eastern Standard Time and four hours ahead of Eastern Daylight Time. See **time zones** and **meridians.**

- **gringo** See the **nationalities and races** entry.

- **grisly, grizzly** *Grisly* is horrifying, repugnant.
  Grizzly means grayish or is a short form for *grizzly bear.*

- **grits** Ground hominy. The word normally takes plural verbs and pronouns: *Grits are to country ham what Yorkshire pudding is to roast beef.*

- **gross domestic product** The total value at retail prices of all the goods and services produced by a nation's economy in a given time period.
  G-D-P is acceptable on second reference.
  Lowercase *gross domestic product* in all uses.
  This economic figure used to be known in the United States as the *gross national product.* As calculated quarterly by the Department of Commerce, the *gross domestic product* of the United States is considered the broadest available measure of the nation's economic activity.

The *G-D-P* is used to determine whether the nation is in a period of economic decline. Both **recession** and **depression** are defined by periods of declining *G-D-P.*

- **gross national product** The term formerly used to describe *gross domestic product.* See that entry.

- **gross profit, gross revenue** See **profit terminology**.

- **Groundhog Day** Feb. 2.

- **groundskeeper**

- **groundswell**

- **group** Takes singular verbs and pronouns: *The group is reviewing its position.*

- **grown-up** (n. and adj.)

- **Grumman Corporation** See **Northrop Grumman**.

- **G-string**

- **Guadalupe** (gwah-dah-LOOP'-ay) (Mexico)

- **Guadaloupe** (gwah-dah-LOOP') (West Indies)

- **Guam** Use in datelines after the name of a community. See **datelines**.

- **guarantee** Preferred to *guaranty,* except in proper names.

- **guard** Usually a job description, not a formal title. See **titles**.

- **guardsman** See **national guard** and **Coast Guardsman**.

- **Guatemala City** Stands alone in datelines.

- **gubernatorial**

- **guerrilla** Unorthodox soldiers and their tactics.

- **guest** Do not use as a verb except in quoted matter. (An exception to a use recorded by Webster's New World.)

- **Gulf Coast** Capitalize when referring to the region of the United States lying along the Gulf of Mexico.

- **Gulf Oil Corporation**   Headquarters is in Pittsburgh.

- **Gulf Stream**   But the racetrack is *Gulfstream Park.*

- **gunbattle, gunboat, gunfight, gunfire, gunpoint, gunpowder**

- **gung-ho**   A colloquialism to be used sparingly.

- **guns**   See **weapons**.

- **guru**

- **gypsy, gypsies**   Capitalize references to the wandering Caucasoid people found throughout the world.
    Lowercase when used generically to mean one who is constantly on the move: *I plan to become a gypsy. She hailed a gypsy cab.*

- **gypsy moth**

- **habeas corpus** (HAY'-bee-uhs KAWR'-puhs) A writ or form of petition filed to seek the prompt release of someone in custody. It places the burden of proof on those detaining the person to justify the detention. Literally, *habeus corpus* means "produce the body," and such a writ orders that a person in custody be brought before the court.
  When *habeas corpus* is used in a story, define it.

- **Hades** But lowercase *hell*.

- **Hague** (hayg), **The** Use the article *The* in datelines and all references to the capital of the Netherlands. In datelines:

  (The Hague, Netherlands) - -

  In text: *The capital of the Netherlands is The Hague.* Note the capital *T*.

- **half** It is not necessary to use the preposition *of*: *half the time* is correct, but *half of the time* is not wrong.

- **half-** Follow Webster's New World Dictionary. Hyphenate if not listed there. Some frequently used words without a hyphen:

  halfback   halfhearted   halftone   halftrack

  Also: *halftime*, an exception to the dictionary in keeping with widespread practice in sports copy.
  Some frequently used combinations that include a hyphen:

  half-baked   half-cocked   half-life   half-truth
  half-blood   half-hour   half-moon

- **half-mast, half-staff** On ships and at naval stations ashore, flags are flown at *half-mast*.
  Elsewhere ashore, flags are flown at *half-staff*.

- **hallelujah**

- **Halley's comet** After Edmund Halley, an English astronomer who predicted the comet's appearance once every 75 years, last seen in 1985-86.

- **Halloween**

- **halo, halos**

- **handicapped, disabled, impaired** In general, do not describe an individual as *disabled* or *handicapped* unless it clearly is pertinent to the story. If such a description must be used, make it clear what the handicap is and how much the person's physical or mental performance is affected.
  Some terms include:
  Disabled: a general term used for a condition that interferes with an individual's ability to do something independently.
  Handicap: It should be avoided in describing a disability.
  Blind: describes a person with complete loss of sight. For others, use a term such as *partially blind.*
  Deaf: describes a person with total hearing loss. For others, use *partial hearing loss.*
  Mute: describes a person who physically cannot speak. Others with speaking difficulties are *speech impaired.*
  Wheelchair-bound: Do not use this term or any variations on it. A person may use a wheelchair occasionally or may have to use it for mobility. If a wheelchair is needed, say why.

- **handicaps** Follow the rules for **numerals**, hyphenating adjectival forms before a noun: *He has a three handicap, he is a three-handicap golfer.*

- **handmade**

- **hand-picked**

- **hands off, hands-off** Hyphenate when used as a compound modifier: *He kept his hands off the matter. He follows a hands-off policy.*

- **hand to hand, hand-to-hand, hand to mouth, hand-to-mouth** Hyphenate when used as compound modifiers: *The cup was passed from hand to hand. They live a hand-to-mouth existence.*

- **hang, hanged, hung** One *hangs* a picture, a criminal or oneself.
  For past tense or the passive, use *hanged* when referring to executions or suicides, *hung* for other actions.

- **hangar, hanger** A *hangar* is a building.
  A *hanger* is used for clothes.

- **hangover**

- **hanky-panky**

- **Hanukkah** (HAH'-noo-kuh) The Jewish Festival of Lights, an eight-day commemoration of the re-dedication of the Temple by the Macabees after their victory over the Syrians. Usually occurs in December but sometimes falls in late November.

- **harass, harassment**

- **harebrained** Use only in quoted matter.

- **harelip** Avoid. Use *cleft palate* instead.

- **Harris Survey** Prepared by Louis Harris and Associates of New York.

- **Havana** The city in Cuba stands alone in datelines.

- **Hawaii** Residents are *Hawaiians*, technically natives of Polynesian descent. The state is comprised of 132 islands, about 2,400 miles southwest of San Francisco. Collectively, they are the *Hawaiian Islands*. The largest island in terms of land area is Hawaii. Honolulu and Pearl Harbor are on Oahu (oh-AH'-hoo), where more than 80 percent of the state's residents live.
  Honolulu stands alone in datelines. Use *Hawaii* after all other cities in datelines. If need be, specify the island in the body of the story. See **datelines** and **state names**.

- **Hawaiian Airlines** Headquarters is in Honolulu.

- **H-bomb** Use *hydrogen bomb* unless a direct quotation is involved.

- **he, him, his, thee, thou** Personal pronouns referring to the deity are lowercase.

- **headlong**

- **head-on** (adj. and adv.)

- **headquarters** May take a singular or a plural verb. Do not use *headquarter* as a verb.

- **health care** Two words.

- **hearing examiner** See **administrative law judge**.

- **hearsay**

- **heaven**

- **heavenly bodies** Capitalize the proper names of planets, stars, constellations, etc.: *Mars, Arcturus, the Big Dipper, Aries.* See **earth**.

  For comets, capitalize only the proper noun element of the name: *Halley's comet.*

  Lowercase *sun* and *moon*, but capitalize their Greek or Latin names: *Helios, Luna.*

  Lowercase nouns and adjectives derived from the proper names of planets and other heavenly bodies: *jovian moons, lunar probe, solar system, venusian atmosphere.* In such cases, however, it generally is clearer to use a construction which preserves the proper name: *the moons of Jupiter* or *Jupiter's moons* rather than *jovian moons.*

- **hect-** (before a vowel) **hecto-** (before a consonant) A prefix denoting 100 units of a measure.

  Move a decimal point two places to the right, adding zeros if necessary, to convert to the basic unit: 5.5 hectometers equals 550 meters.

- **hectare** A unit of surface measure in the metric system equal to 100 ares or 10,000 square meters. A hectare equals 2.47 acres, 107,639.1 square feet, or 11,959.9 square yards.

  To convert to acres, multiply by 2.47: 5 hectares times 2.47 equals 12.35 acres. See **acre** and **metric system**.

- **hedging** A business term referring to a method of selling for future delivery. *Hedging* is a device dealers use to protect themselves from falling prices between the time they buy a product and the time they resell or process it.

  A miller, for example, who buys wheat to convert into flour will sell a similar quantity of wheat he doesn't own at near the price at which he bought his own. He will agree to deliver it at the same time his flour is ready for market. If at that time the price of wheat—and therefore flour— has fallen, he will lose on the flour but he can buy the wheat at a low price and deliver it at a profit. If prices have risen, he will make an extra profit on his flour, which he will have to sacrifice to buy the wheat for delivery. But either way, he has protected his originally planned profit.

- **heights** See **dimensions**.

- **heliport**

- **helter-skelter**

- **hemisphere** Capitalize *Northern Hemisphere, Western Hemisphere*, etc.

  Lowercase *hemisphere* in other uses: *the Eastern and Western hemispheres, the hemisphere.*

- **hemorrhage**

- **hemorrhoid**

- **her** Do not use this pronoun in reference to nations, ships or tropical weather systems.
  Use *it* instead.

- **here** Do not use in reference to the story's dateline unless you actually are speaking from that location.
  In wire copy, do not use *here* to indicate the location of the story. Use the name of the dateline's community. Wrong:

  (Homestead, Florida) - - Hurricane "Andrew" has come ashore here ...

  Right:

  (Homestead, Florida) - - Hurricane "Andrew" has come ashore in Homestead, Florida...

  In voicers and wraps, use *here* only if you actually are in the location when taping the report.

  (natural sound of storm winds)

  Hurricane "Andrew" has made its landfall here. The winds are tearing up trees ...

- **Her Majesty** Capitalize when it appears in quotations or is appropriate before a name as the long form of a formal title.
  For other purposes, use the woman's name or *the queen.* See **nobility**.

- **heroin** The narcotic, originally a trademark.

- **hertz** This term, the same in singular or plural, has been adopted as the international unit of frequency equal to one cycle per second. In contexts where it would not be understood by most listeners, it should be explained. Follow the rules for **numerals**. Do not abbreviate.

- **hideaway**

- **hi-fi**

- **high-tech**

- **highway designations** Follow the rules for **abbreviations; numerals** and **hyphen**.
  Interstate highways should be identified as such on the first reference: *Interstate Route 495* or *Interstate 495.* But on the second reference, the more familiar *I-495* may be used.
  Capitalize words such as *Route* and *Highway* when used as part of a road's full

name. Lowercase, as in *the highway*, on second reference. Some examples: *U-S Highway One, U-S Route One, U-S One, state Route 34.*

When a letter is appended to a number, capitalize it and hyphenate: *Route One-A.*

• **highway patrol** Capitalize if used in the formal name of a police agency: *the Kansas Highway Patrol, the Highway Patrol.*

Lowercase *highway patrolman* in all uses. See **state police**.

• **Hinduism** The dominant religion of India. It has about 470 million followers, making it the world's third-largest religion after Christianity and Islam. There are more than 300,000 followers in North America.

Beliefs: The basic teaching is that the soul never dies, but is reborn each time the body dies. The soul may be reborn in either human or animal form.

The rule of *karma* states that no matter how small the action or thought of an individual, it will affect how the soul will be reborn in the next generation. The cycle of death and rebirth continues until the soul reaches spiritual perfection. At that point, the soul is united in total enlightenment and peace with the supreme being and the cycle is ended.

There are many gods and goddesses, all of whom are different focuses of the one supreme being. The primary gods are Brahma; Vishnu, called the preserver; and Siva, called the destroyer. Hindus believe that Vishnu has had important human incarnations as Krishna and Rama. The primary goddess is Devi, who also is known as Durga, Kali, Sarasvati, Lakshimi and other names. She represents in her forms either destruction or motherhood and good fortune.

There are thousands of other deities and saints who also may receive prayers and offerings. Hindus also believe that animals have souls and many are worshiped as gods.

Clergy: There is no formal clergy. There are thousands of sects and organization runs from virtually none to very strict, depending on the group.

• **Hiroshima** On Aug. 6, 1945, the Japanese city and military base were the targets of the first atomic bomb dropped as a weapon. The explosion had the force of 13,000 tons—13 kilotons—of TNT. It destroyed more than four square miles and killed or injured 160,000 people.

• **his, her** Do not presume maleness in constructing a sentence, and try to avoid indefinite antecedents, which may be male or female:

Wrong: *A reporter attempts to protect his sources.* (Forces you to choose *his* or *her* as second reference to *reporter.*)

Right: *Reporters attempt to protect their sources.* (The plural form eliminates the need to be gender-specific.)

• **His Majesty** Capitalize when it appears in quotations or is appropriate before a name as the long form of a formal title.

For other purposes, use the man's name or *the king.* See **nobility**.

- **Hispaniola** The island shared by the Dominican Republic and Haiti. See **Western Hemisphere**.

- **historic, historical** A *historic* event is an important occurrence, one that stands out in history. Any occurrence in the past is a *historical* event.
Use the article *a* before both these words.

- **historical periods and events** Capitalize the names of widely recognized epochs in anthropology, archaeology, geology and history: *the Bronze Age, the Dark Ages, the Middle Ages, the Pliocene Epoch.*
Capitalize also widely recognized popular names for periods and events: *the Atomic Age, the Boston Tea Party, the Civil War, the Exodus* (of the Israelites from Egypt), *the Great Depression, Prohibition.*
However, *ice age* is always lowercase, since it denotes not a single period but any of a series of periods.
Lowercase *century: the 18th century.*
Capitalize only proper nouns or adjectives in general descriptions of a period: *The Victorian age, ancient Greece, classical Rome, the fall of the Roman Empire.*
For additional guidance, see separate entries in this handbook for many epochs, events and historical periods. If this book has no entry, follow the capitalization in Webster's New World, using lowercase if the dictionary lists it as an acceptable form for the sense in which the word is used.

- **history** Avoid the redundant *past history.*

- **hit and run** (v.) **hit-and-run** (n. and adj.) *The coach told him to hit and run.*
He scored on a hit-and-run. She was struck by a hit-and-run driver.

- **hitchhike, hitchhiker**

- **hockey** The spellings of some frequently used words:

blue line	goal line	play off (v.)	red line
crease	goal post	playoff (n., adj.)	short-handed
face off (v.)	goaltender	power play	slap shot
faceoff(n., adj.)	penalty box	power-play goal	two-on-one break
goalie			

The term *hat trick* applies when a player has scored three goals in a game. Use it sparingly, however.
Numbers: Follow the rules in **numerals** except when reporting scores in the text of a story or in tabular material. When reporting scores in scripts, use figures, hyphens and *to: The Islanders beat the Capitals 3-to-2. They won by a one-goal margin.*
Scores: Period scores and final scores are moved on a spot basis, using this format:

NHL
First Boston 2 NY Rangers 1

Final scores would substitute *final* for the period number.
Standings: The form:

Campbell Conference
Patrick Division

	W	L	T	Pts	Gf	Ga
Philadelphia	47	10	14	108	314	184
NY Islanders	45	17	9	99	310	192

- **hocus-pocus**

- **hodgepodge**

- **Hodgkin's disease** After Dr. Thomas Hodgkin, the English physician who first described the disease of the lymph nodes.

- **ho-hum**

- **holding company** A company whose principal assets are the securities it owns in companies that actually provide goods or services. The usual reason for forming a holding company is to enable one corporation and its directors to control several companies by holding a majority of their stock.

- **hold up** (v.) **holdup** (n. and adj.)

- **holidays and holy days** Capitalize them: *New Year's Eve, New Year's Day, Groundhog Day, Easter, Hanukkah,* etc.
  The legal holidays in federal law are New Year's, Martin Luther King Jr. Day, Washington's Birthday, Memorial Day, Independence Day, Labor Day, Columbus Day, Veterans Day, Thanksgiving and Christmas. See individual entries for the official dates and when they are observed if they fall on a weekend.
  The designation of a day as a federal legal holiday means that federal employees receive the day off or are paid overtime it they must work. Other requirements that may apply to holidays generally are left to the states. Many follow the federal lead in designating holidays, but they are not required to do so.

- **Hollywood** Stands alone in datelines when used instead of *Los Angeles* on stories about films and the film industry.

- **Holocaine** A trademark for a type of local anesthetic.

- **Holy Communion** See **sacraments**.

• **Holy Father**   The preferred form is to use *the pope* or *the pontiff,* or to give the individual's name.
Use *Holy Father* in direct quotations or special contexts where a particular literary effect is desired.

• **holy orders**   See **sacraments**.

• **Holy See**   The headquarters of the Roman Catholic Church in Vatican City.

• **Holy Spirit**   Now preferred over *Holy Ghost* in most usage.

• **Holy Week**   The week before Easter.

• **home-made**

• **hometown** (n. and adj.)   See **comma** for guidelines on how to list a hometown after an individual's name.

• **homicide, murder, manslaughter**   *Homicide* is a legal term for slaying or killing.
Murder is malicious, premeditated homicide. Some states arbitrarily define certain homicides as murder if the killing occurs on the course of armed robbery, rape, and so on.
Manslaughter is homicide without malice or premeditation.
A person should not be described as a *murderer* until convicted of the charge.
Unless authorities say premeditation was obvious, do not say that a victim *was murdered* until someone has been convicted of murder in court. Instead, say that a victim was *killed.* See **execute, assassin, killer,** and **murderer**.

• **Hong Kong**   Stands alone in datelines.

• **honky**   A term of abuse directed toward whites by blacks. Use it only in quoted matter. See **nationalities and races** entry.

• **Honolulu**   The city in Hawaii stands alone in datelines. It is on the island of Oahu (oh-AH'-hoo). See **Hawaii**.

• **honorary degrees**   All references to honorary degrees should specify that the degree was honorary.
Do not use *doctor* before the name of an individual whose only doctorate is honorary.

• **hoof-and-mouth disease**   Use *foot-and-mouth disease.*

• **hooky**   Not *hookey.*

• **hopefully**   It means *in a hopeful manner.* Do not use it to mean *it is hoped,* *let us hope* or *we hope.*

Wrong as a way to express the thought in the following two sentences: *Hopefully, we will complete our work in June.*

Right: *It is hoped that we will complete our work in June.*

Right: *We hope that we will complete our work in June.*

- **horsepower**

- **horse races** Capitalize their formal names: *Kentucky Derby, Preakness, Belmont Stakes,* etc.

- **horse racing** Some frequently used terms and their definitions:

   Colt: a male horse from two to five years old.

   Horse: a male horse five years or older.

   Gelding: A castrated male horse.

   Filly: A female horse two to five years old.

   Mare: A female horse five years or older.

   Stallion: A male horse used for breeding.

   Broodmare: A female horse used for breeding.

   Furlong: One-eighth of a mile. Race distances are given in *furlongs* up through seven furlongs. After that, they are expressed in miles and fractions of a mile, as in *one and a-16th miles.*

   Entry: Two or more horses owned by the same owner running as a single betting interest. In some states two or more horses trained by the same person but having different owners also are coupled in betting.

   Mutuel field: Two or more horses, long shots, that have different owners and trainers. They are coupled as a single betting interest to give the field not more than 12 wagering interests.

   There cannot be more than 12 betting interests in a race. The bettor wins if either horse finishes in the money.

   Half-mile pole: The pole on a race track that marks one-half mile from the finish. All distances are measured from the finish line, meaning that when a horse reaches the quarter pole, he is one-quarter mile from the finish.

   Bug boy: An apprentice jockey, so called because of the asterisk beside the individual's name in a program. It means that the jockey's mount gets a five-pound weight allowance.

- **horses' names** Capitalize and place in quote marks on first reference. See **animals**.

- **hotel** Capitalize as part of the proper name for a specific hotel: *the Waldorf-Astoria Hotel.*

   Lowercase when standing alone or used in an indefinite reference to one hotel in a chain: *The city has a Sheraton hotel.*

- **Hotel and Restaurant Employees and Bartenders International Union** The shortened forms *Hotel and Restaurant Employees*

Union and *Bartenders Union* are acceptable in all references. Headquarters is in Cincinnati.

- **hot line** The circuit linking the United States and the Soviet Union. Lowercase.

- **household, housing unit** In the sense used by the Census Bureau, a *household* is made up of people who occupy a house, room, group of rooms or an apartment that constitutes a *housing unit*. A *household* may contain more than one family or may be used by one person.

  A *housing unit*, as defined by the bureau, is a group of rooms or a single room occupied by people who do not live and eat with any other persons in the structure. It must have either direct access from the outside or through a common hall, or have a kitchen or cooking equipment for the exclusive use of the occupants.

- **House of Commons, House of Lords** The two houses of the British Parliament. The House of Commons is elected. The House of Lords is made up of the British nobility and certain representatives of the Anglican Church.

  On second reference: *Commons* or *the Commons, Lords* or *the Lords.*

- **house of delegates** See the next entry.

- **house of representatives** Capitalize when referring to a specific governmental body: *the U-S House of Representatives, the Massachusetts House of Representatives.*

  Capitalize shortened references that delete the words *of Representatives: the U-S House, the Massachusetts House.*

  Retain capitalization if *U-S* or the name of the state is dropped but the reference is to a specific body:

  > **(Capitol Hill) — The House has voted overwhelmingly to ...**

  Lowercase plural uses: *the Massachusetts and Rhode Island houses.*

  Apply the same principle to similar legislative bodies such as *the Virginia House of Delegates.*

  See the **organizations and institutions** entry for guidelines on how to handle the term when it is used by a non-governmental body.

- **Houston** The city in Texas stands alone in datelines.

- **Hovercraft** A trademark for a vehicle that travels on a cushion of air.

- **however** *But* is better.

- **howitzer** See **weapons**.

* **Hughes Airwest** Headquarters is in San Mateo, Calif.

* **human, human being** *Human* is preferred, but either is acceptable.

* **hurly-burly**

* **hurricanes** Capitalize *hurricane* when it is part of the name that weather forecasters assign to a storm: *Hurricane Andrew.*
Use *it* and *its* in pronoun references to hurricanes.
Weather forecasters assign both masculine and feminine names to the storms. Do not use the presence of a woman's name as an excuse for the use of sexist images in describing the storm's course. Avoid, for example, such sentences as: *The fickle Hazel teased the Louisiana coast.* See **weather terms.**

* **husband, widower** Use *husband*, not *widower*, in referring to the spouse of a woman who dies.

* **hush-hush**

* **Hyannis Port, Massachusetts**

* **hydro-** The rules in **prefixes** apply, but in general, no hyphen. Some examples:

    hydroelectric   hydrophobia

* **hyper-** The rules in **prefixes** apply, but in general, no hyphen. Some examples:

    hyperactive   hypercritical

* **hyphen** Hyphens are joiners. They are used to avoid ambiguity as well as to form a single idea from two or more words.
They are also used in broadcast writing to guide the announcer through unusual constructions, long rows of numbers and unusual combinations of letters.
In general, writers are urged to avoid unnecessary hyphenation. But in broadcast writing, it is far better to use an extra hyphen now and then if it makes the copy easier to read aloud.
Some general guidelines:
Avoid ambiguity: Use a hyphen whenever the thought would be unclear without it. *He is a small-business representative* sounds the same on the air as: *He is a small business representative.* But the announcer knows upon seeing the hyphen that the person in question is a representative of small businesses, not a small person who represents business.
Compound modifiers: A compound modifier, two or more words expressing a single concept, should be tied together with hyphens when followed by a noun:

A first-quarter touchdown, a bluish-green dress, a full-time job, a know-it-all attitude.

But it is not necessary to use hyphens to connect the adverb very or any adverb ending in *ly*: *A very good time, an easily remembered rule.*

Two-thought compounds: *Socio-economic, serio-comic.* Use when necessary; avoid when possible.

Compound proper nouns and adjectives: *Italian-American, Mexican-American.*

Prefixes and suffixes: See the **prefixes** and **suffixes** entries for the most frequently used forms.

Break up duplicated vowels, tripled consonants: *anti-intellectual, pre-empt, shell-like.*

Numerals: Use a hyphen to link numerals and the word *to* in odds, scores and ratios: *He beat him two-to-one; It was a 7-to-5 loss.* Also to link compound numerals: *ten-thousand, 500 dollars.*

Fractions: Use hyphens to link units and numerals: *six-tenths, one-half, two-thirds, four and a-quarter.*

Large numbers: Do not use hyphens with millions and billions.

Wrong: *ten-(m)-million dollars.*

Right: *ten (m) million dollars.*

But: *ten-point-five (m) million dollars.*

With abbreviations: Use hyphens with abbreviations that should be pronounced letter-by-letter: *U-N, C-B-S, A-B-C, N-B-C, AFL-CIO* (an exception to the rule because of its familiarity).

Don't use hyphens in acronyms — abbreviations that should be pronounced as a word: *UNESCO, WATS.* See **numerals; abbreviations; acronyms; fractions; double dash**.

- **Iberia Air Lines of Spain** An *Iberia airliner* is acceptable in any reference. Headquarters is in Madrid.

- **I-B-M** Acceptable in all references to *International Business Machines*. Headquarters is in Armonk, N.Y.

- **I-C-B-M, I-C-B-M's** Acceptable on first reference to *intercontinental ballistic missile*, but the term should be defined in the body of the story.
  Avoid the redundant *I-C-B-M missiles*.

- **ice age** Lowercase. Denotes not a single period, but any of a series of cold periods marked by glaciation alternating with periods of relative warmth.
  Capitalize the proper nouns in the names of individual ice ages, such as the *Wisconsin ice age*.
  Together, the ice ages, which began about 600,000 years ago, make up glacial epochs. During the first, called the *Pleistocene* (PLY'-stoh-seen), glaciers covered much of North America and Northwestern Europe.
  The present epoch, the *Helocene* (HEEL'-oh-seen) or *Recent*, began about 12,000 years ago, with glaciers restricted to Antarctica and Greenland.

- **Icelandair** Headquarters is in Reykjavik (RAY'-kyuh-vik), Iceland.

- **ice storm** See **weather terms**.

- **Idaho** See **state names**.

- **illegal** Use *illegal* only to mean a violation of the law. Be especially careful in labor-management disputes, where one side often calls an action by the other side *illegal*. Usually it is a charge that a contract or rule, not a law, has been violated.

- **Illinois** See **state names**.

- **illusion** See the **allusion, illusion** entry.

- **imam** The leader of a prayer in a Moslem mosque. Lowercase.
  Capitalize before a name when used as the formal title for a Moslem leader or ruler. See **religious titles**.

- **immigrate** See **emigrate, immigrate** entry.

- **impact** Do not use as a verb.

- **impassable, impassible, impassive** *Impassable* means that passage is impossible: *The bridge was impassable.*
  Impassible and *impassive* describe a lack of sensitivity to pain or suffering. Webster's New World notes, however, that *impassible* suggests an inability to be affected, while *impassive* implies only that no reaction was noticeable: *They were impassive throughout the ordeal.*

- **impeachment** The constitutional process accusing an elected official of a crime in an attempt to remove the official from office. Do not use as a synonym for *convicted* or *removed from office.*
  The only U.S. president to be impeached was Andrew Johnson. He was, however, acquitted in the U.S. Senate. Richard Nixon resigned before pending impeachment articles were approved by the U.S. House of Representatives.

- **impel, impelled, impelling**

- **imperial gallon** The standard British gallon, equal to 277.42 cubic inches or about 1.2 U.S. gallons.
  The metric equivalent is about 4.5 liters. See **liter.**

- **imperial quart** One-fourth of an imperial gallon.

- **implausible**

- **imply, infer** Writers or speakers *imply* in the words they use.
  A listener or reader *infers* something from the words.

- **impostor** Not *imposter.*

- **impromptu** It means without preparation or advance thought.

- **in, into** *In* indicates location: *He was in the room.*
  Into indicates motion: *She walked into the room.*

- **"in"** When employed to indicate that something is in vogue, use quotation marks: *It was the "in" thing to do. Racoon coats are "in" again.*

- **in-** No hyphen when it means *not*:

  inaccurate   insufferable

  Often solid in other cases:

inbound	infighting
indoor	infield (n., adj.)

A few combinations take a hyphen, however:

in-depth	in-group	in-house	in-law
in-patient			

Follow Webster's New World when in doubt.

- **-in** Precede with a hyphen:

break-in	cave-in	walk-in	write-in

- **Inauguration Day** Capitalize only when referring to the total collection of events that include inauguration of a U.S. president; lowercase in other uses: *Inauguration Day is January 20th. The inauguration day for the change has not been set.*

- **Inc.** Do not use this abbreviation for **incorporated**. See that entry.

- **inch** One-12th of a foot.
  The metric equivalent is exactly 2.54 centimeters.
  To convert to centimeters, multiply by 2.54: 6 inches times 2.54 equals 15.24 centimeters. See **centimeter; foot** and **dimensions**.

- **inches-per-second** A rating used for the speed of tape recorders.
  Follow the rules for numerals. Do not use the abbreviation *i-p-s* except in special contexts such as a show about home entertainment.

- **include** Use *include* to introduce a series when the items that follow are only part of the total: *The price includes breakfast. The zoo includes lions and tigers.*
  Use *comprise* when the full list of individual elements is given: *The zoo comprises 100 types of animals, including lions and tigers.* See the **compose, comprise, constitute** entry.

- **income** See **profit terminology**.

- **incorporated** Do not abbreviate. Generally, it should be used only when referring to the formal title of a corporation: *J.C. Penney Company, Incorporated.* In those cases, capitalize.
  But in most contexts, informalize the name: *J.C. Penney says it is opening a new store.* See **company names**.

- **incredible, incredulous** *Incredible* means unbelievable. *Incredulous* means skeptical.

- **incur, incurred, incurring**

- **Independence Day** *July Fourth* or *Fourth of July* also are acceptable.
The federal legal holiday is observed on Friday if July 4 falls on a Saturday, and on Monday if it falls on a Sunday.

- **index, indexes**

- **Index of Leading Economic Indicators** A composite of 12 economic measurements that was developed to help forecast likely shifts in the economy as a whole. It is compiled by the Commerce Department.

- **Indiana** See **state names.**

- **Indianapolis** The city in Indiana stands alone in datelines.

- **Indian Ocean** See **oceans.**

- **Indians** In news stories about American Indians, such words as *wampum, warpath, powwow, tepee, brave* and *squaw* are disparaging and offensive. Avoid them.
American Indian is the preferred term for those in the United States. Where possible, be precise and use the name of the tribe: *He is a Navajo commissioner. Native American* is acceptable in quotations and names of organizations.

- **indict** Use *indict* only in connection with the legal process of bringing charges against an individual or corporation.
Indictments are *handed up.*
To avoid any suggestion that someone is being judged before a trial, do not use phrases such as *indicted for killing* or *indicted for bribery.* Instead, use *indicted on a charge of killing, indicted on a bribery charge.*
For guidelines on related words, see the entries under **accused; allege; arrest.**

- **indiscreet, indiscrete** *Indiscreet* means lacking prudence. Its noun form is *indiscretion.*
Indiscrete means not separated into distinct parts, and is best avoided. Its noun form is *indiscreteness.*

- **indiscriminate, indiscriminately**

- **indispensable**

- **indo-** Usually hyphenated and capitalized:

Indo-Aryan	Indo-German	Indo-Hittite	Indo-Iranian

But: *Indochina.*

• **Indochina** Formerly French Indochina, now divided into Cambodia, Laos and Vietnam.

• **Indochinese peninsula** Located here are the nations of Cambodia, Laos, Myanmar (also known as Burma), Thailand and Vietnam.

• **Indonesia** Use after the name of a community in datelines on stories from this nation. Specify an individual island, if needed, in the body of the script.

• **indoor** (adj.) **indoors** (adv.) *He plays indoor tennis. He went indoors.*

• **infant** Applicable to children through 12 months old.

• **infantile paralysis** The preferred term is *polio.*

• **inflation** A sustained increase in prices. The result is a decrease in the purchasing power of money.
   Inflation may increase or decrease, but it always means rising prices.
   There are two basic types of inflation:
   · *Cost-push inflation* occurs when rising costs are the chief reason for the increased prices.
   · *Demand-pull inflation* occurs when the amount of money available exceeds the amount of goods and services available for sale.

• **infra-** The rules in **prefixes** apply, but in general, no hyphen. Some examples:

infrared   infrastructure

• **infrastructure** An economy's capital in the form of roads, railways, water supplies, educational facilities, health services, etc., without which investment in factories could not be fully productive.

• **initials** Avoid whenever possible. See **middle initials**.
   Some people prefer to use their initials instead of a first name. In that case, use periods and no space; this ensures that the two initials run on the same line when sent on the wire: *H.L. Mencken.*
   Do not use only an initial for a first name unless it is the individual's preference or the first name cannot be learned: *Police identified the victim only as J. Jones.*

• **injuries** They are *suffered* or *sustained*, not *received.*

• **in-law**

• **Inner Light** See **Quakers**.

• **innocent** Use *innocent*, rather than *not guilty*, in describing a defendant's plea or a jury's verdict, to guard against the word *not* being dropped inadvertently.

It is impossible to be too careful when reporting criminal pleas and verdicts. Always check carefully before sending or airing the story.

- **innocuous**

- **innuendo**

- **inoculate**

- **input** Do not use as a verb in describing the feeding of data into a computer.

- **inquire, inquiry** Not *enquire, enquiry.*

- **insignia** Singular and plural.

- **in spite of** *Despite* means the same thing and is shorter.

- **intelligence quotient** Lowercase. *I-Q* is acceptable in all references.

- **inter-** The rules in **prefixes** apply, but in general, no hyphen. Some examples:

inter-American   interracial   interstate

- **Intercollegiate Association of Amateur Athletes of America** Spell it out on the first reference. After that, use *the association.*

- **intercontinental ballistic missile** See **I-C-B-M, I-C-B-M's**.

- **Internal Revenue Service** *I-R-S* is acceptable in all references. Capitalize also *Internal Revenue*, but lowercase *the revenue service.*

- **International Association of Machinists and Aerospace Workers** The shortened form *Machinists union* is acceptable in all references. Headquarters is in Washington.

- **International Bank for Reconstruction and Development** *World Bank* is acceptable in all references. Headquarters is in Washington.

- **International Brotherhood of Electrical Workers** Use the full name on the first reference to avoid confusion with the United Electrical, Radio and Machine Workers of America.

The abbreviation *I-B-E-W* is acceptable on second reference. Headquarters is in Washington.

- **International Brotherhood of Painters and Allied Trades of the United States and Canada** The shortened form *Painters union* is acceptable in all references. Headquarters is in Washington.

- **International Brotherhood of Teamsters, Chauffeurs, Warehousemen and Helpers of America** The shortened form *Teamsters union* – no apostrophe – is acceptable in all references.
  Capitalize *Teamsters* and *the Teamsters* in references to the union or its members.
  Lowercase *teamster* when no specific reference to the union is intended. Headquarters is in Washington.

- **International Business Machines** I-B-M is acceptable in all references. Headquarters is in Armonk, N.Y.

- **International Court of Justice** The principal judicial organ of the United Nations, established at The Hague in 1945.
  World Court is accepted in all reference. The court is not open to individuals. It has jurisdiction over all matters specifically provided for either in the U.N. charter or in treaties and conventions in force. It also has jurisdiction over cases referred to it by U.N. members and by non-members such as Switzerland that subscribe to the court statute.
  The court serves as the successor to the Permanent Court of International Justice of the League of Nations, which also was known as the World Court.
  On second reference use *international court* or the *court*, always lowercase. Do not abbreviate.

- **International Criminal Police Organization** *Interpol* is acceptable in all references. Headquarters is in Paris.

- **international date line** Three words. It is the imaginary line drawn north and south through the Pacific Ocean, largely along the 180th meridian. By international agreement, when it is 12:01 a.m. Sunday just west of the line, it is 12:01 a.m. Saturday just east of it. See **time zones**.

- **International Labor Organization** *I-L-O* is acceptable on second reference. Headquarters is in Geneva.

- **International Ladies' Garment Workers Union** The shortened forms *Ladies' Garment Workers* and *Ladies' Garment Workers union* are acceptable in all references. Do not abbreviate.
  Lowercase *garment workers* when no specific reference to the union is intended. Headquarters is in New York.

- **International Longshore and Warehouse Union** Do not abbreviate. On second reference, *the union*. Headquarters is in San Francisco.

- **International Longshoremen's Association** Do not abbreviate. On second reference, *the union* or *the association*. Headquarters is in New York.

- **International Monetary Fund** *I-M-F* is acceptable on second reference, as is *the fund*.
  The IMF is a supply of money supported by subscriptions of member nations, for the purpose of stabilizing international exchange and promoting orderly and balanced trade. Member nations may obtain foreign currency needed, making it possible to correct temporary maladjustments in their balance of payments without currency depreciation. Headquarters is in Washington.

- **International Telecommunications Satellite Organization** *Intelsat* is acceptable on first reference, but the body of the story should identify it as the shortened form of the full name.
  The original name was International Telecommunications Satellite Consortium. Headquarters is in Washington.

- **International Telephone and Telegraph Corporation** *I-T-T* is acceptable in all references. Headquarters is in New York.

- **International Union, United Automobile, Aerospace and Agricultural Implement Workers of America** This is the full, formal name for the union known more commonly as the *United Auto Workers*. See the entry that begins **United Automobile**.

- **Interpol** Acceptable in all references for *International Criminal Police Organization*.

- **intra-** The rules in **prefixes** apply, but in general, no hyphen. Some examples:

  intramural   intrastate

  It means within, as opposed to *inter*, which means between or among. Thus, *intrastate commerce* is commerce within a single state, while *interstate commerce* occurs between two or more states.

- **intra-uterine device** *I-U-D* is acceptable in all reference.

- **I-O-U, I-O-U's**

- **Iowa** See **state names**.

- **i-p-s** See **inches-per-second**.

- **I-Q** Acceptable in all references to *intelligence quotient*.

• **Iran** The nation formerly called Persia. It is not an Arab country. The people are *Iranians*, not *Persians* or *Irani*. For the language, use *Persian*, the word widely accepted outside Iran. Inside Iran, the language is called *Farsi*.

• **Iraq** The Arab nation coinciding roughly with ancient Mesopotamia. Its people are *Iraqis*. The dialect of Arabic is *Iraqi*.

• **Ireland** Acceptable in most references to the independent nation known formally as the Irish Republic.
Use *Irish Republic* when a distinction must be made between this nation and Northern Ireland, a part of the United Kingdom.

• **Irish International Airlines** The preferred name is *Aer Lingus*. Headquarters is in Dublin, Ireland.

• **Irish Republican Army** A group that fights to wrest Northern Ireland from British rule and unite it with the Irish Republic.
I-R-A is acceptable on second reference.

• **Iron Curtain**

• **irregardless** A double negative. *Regardless* is correct.

• **Islam** Followers are called *Muslims*. The adjective is *Islamic*.
It is the religion of about 850 million people. Although Arabic is the language of the Koran and Muslim prayers, not all Arabs are Muslims and not all Muslims are Arabs.
Most of the world's Muslims live in a wide belt that stretches halfway around the world, across West Africa and North Africa, through the Arab countries of the Middle East and on to Turkey, Iran, Afghanistan, Pakistan and other Asian countries, parts of the former Soviet Union and western China to Indonesia and southern Philippines.
Beliefs: The holy book is the Koran, which according to Islamic belief was revealed by Allah (God) to the prophet Mohammed in the seventh century in Mecca and Medina.
There are two major divisions in Islam, stemming from a dispute over Mohammed's successors as caliph, the spiritual and temporal leader of Muslims.
• Sunni (SOO'-nee): The biggest single sect in Islam, comprising about 85 percent of all Muslims. Nations with Sunni majorities include Egypt, Saudi Arabia and most other Arab nations, as well as non-Arab Turkey and Afghanistan. Most Palestinian Muslims and most West African Muslims are Sunnis. The Saudis sometimes are referred to as Wahhabi Muslims. This is a sub-group within the Sunni branch of Islam.

- Shiite (SHEE'-eyt): The second-largest sect, after the Sunni. Iran, home of militant Islamic fundamentalism, is the only nation with an overwhelming Shiite majority. Iraq, Lebanon and Bahrain have large Shiite communities, in proportion to their overall populations. The schism between Sunni and Shiite stems from the very early days of Islam. The Shiites wanted the caliphate to descend through Ali, Mohammed's son-in-law. Ali eventually became the fourth caliph, but he was murdered. His son al-Hussein was massacred with his fighters, at Karbala, in what is now Iraq. Shiites considered the later caliphs to be usurpers. The Sunnis no longer have a caliph.

Clergy: Titles vary from sect to sect and from country to country. The most common:
  - Grand Mufti: the highest authority in Koranic law and interpretation, a title used mostly by Sunnis.
  - Sheik: Used by most clergymen in the same manner as *the Reverend* is used as a Christian clerical title, especially common among Sunnis. Not all *sheiks* are clergymen. *Sheik* can also be a secular title of respect or nobility.
  - Ayatollah: used by Shiites, especially in Iran, to denote senior clergymen, such as *Ayatollah Ruhollah Khomeini.*
  - Hojatoleslam: a rank below *Ayatollah.*
  - Mullah: lower-level clergy.
  - Imam: Used by some sects as a title for the prayer leader at a mosque. Among the Shiites, it usually has a more exalted connotation.

The place of worship is the *mosque* and the weekly holy day, equivalent to the sabbath, begins at sunset Friday and ends at sunset Saturday. See **Muslim.**

- **island** Capitalize *island* or *islands* as part of a proper name: *Prince Edward Island, the Hawaiian Islands.*
Lowercase *island* and *islands* when they stand alone or when the reference is to the islands in a given area: *the Pacific islands.*
Lowercase all *island of* constructions: *the island of Nantucket.*
Some guidelines:
  - In Domestic Datelines: For communities on islands within the United States, use the community and state names:

    (Edgartown, Massachusetts) --

Honolulu, however, stands alone.
  - In Foreign Datelines: If an island has an identity of its own — for example, Bermuda, Puerto Rico, or Taiwan — use it in the dateline:

    (Hamilton, Bermuda) --

Havana, Hong Kong, Macao and Singapore stand alone, however.
If the island is part of a chain, use the chain's name:

    (Manila, the Philippines) --

If necessary, identify the name of the island in the copy: *Manila is on the island of Luzon.*

For additional guidelines, see **datelines**.

● **it** Use this pronoun, rather than *she*, in references to nations, ships and tropical weather systems.

● **it's, its** *It's* is a contraction for *it is* or *it has*: *It's up to you. It's been a long time.*

Its is the possessive form of the neuter pronoun: *The company lost its assets.*

● **I-U-D** Acceptable on all references to *intra-uterine device.*

● **Ivy League** Brown University, Columbia University, Cornell University, Dartmouth College, Harvard University, Princeton University, the University of Pennsylvania and Yale University.

- **jail** Not interchangeable with *prison*. See the **prison, jail** entry.

- **"Jane's All the World's Aircraft," "Jane's Fighting Ships"**
The reference sources for questions about aircraft and military ships not covered in this book.
The reference for non-military ships is "Lloyd's Register of Shipping."

- **January** See **months**.

- **Japan Air Lines** *J-A-L* is acceptable on second reference. Headquarters is in Tokyo.

- **Japan Current** A warm current flowing from the Philippine Sea east of Taiwan and northeast past Japan.

- **jargon** The special vocabulary and idioms of a particular class or occupational group. In general, avoid jargon. When it is appropriate in a special context, include an explanation of any words likely to be unfamiliar to the audience. See **dialect** and **word selection**.

- **Jaycees** Members of the U.S. Junior Chamber of Commerce, which is affiliated with the worldwide body, the Junior Chamber International. U.S. headquarters is in Tulsa, Okla. International headquarters is in Coral Gables, Fla. See **fraternal organizations and service clubs**.

- **J.C. Penney Company, Incorporated** *J.C. Penney* or *Penney's* is acceptable on all references. Headquarters is in Dallas.

- **jeep, Jeep** Lowercase the military vehicle.
Capitalize if referring to the civilian vehicle which bears this trademark.

- **Jehovah's Witnesses** The denomination was founded in Pittsburgh in 1872 by Charles Taze Russell, a former Congregationalist layman.
Witnesses do most of their work through three legal corporations: the Watch

Tower and Tract Society of Pennsylvania; the Watchtower Bible and Tract Society of New York, Incorporated; and, in England, the International Bible Students Association. The principal officers of the corporation elect a director, who becomes the international head of the Jehovah's Witnesses.

American membership is listed at more than 500,000.

Beliefs: Witnesses believe that they adhere to the oldest religion on earth, the worship of Almighty God revealed in the Bible as Jehovah.

They regard civil authority as necessary and obey it "as long as its laws do not contradict God's law." Witnesses refuse to bear arms, salute the flag or participate in secular government.

They refuse blood transfusions as being against the Bible, citing the section of Leviticus that reads: "Whatsoever man ... eats any manner of blood, I will cut him off from among his people."

Clergy: Witnesses consider themselves a society of ministers. A public ceremony of water immersion sets an individual apart as a minister of Jehovah.

There are no formal titles, but there are four levels of ministry: *publishers* (part-time workers expected to devote 60 hours a month to distributing literature), *general pioneers* and *special pioneers* (terms for part-time workers who devote more than 60 hours a month to activities) and *pioneers* (full-time workers).

- **Jell-O** A trademark for a brand of gelatin dessert.

- **Jerusalem** Stands alone in datelines.

- **Jesus** The central figure of Christianity, he also may be called *Jesus Christ*. Personal pronouns referring to him are lowercase.

- **jet, jetliner, jet plane** See **aircraft terms**.

- **Jew** Use for men and women. Do not use *Jewess*.

- **Jewish congregations** A Jewish congregation is autonomous. No synods, assemblies or hierarchies control the activities of an individual synagogue.

  In the United States, there are three major expressions of Judaism:

  Orthodox Judaism: Most of its congregations are represented nationally by the Union of Orthodox Jewish Congregations of America. Most of its rabbis are members of the Rabbinical Council of America.

  Conservative Judaism: its national representatives are the United Synagogue of America and the Rabbinical Assembly.

  Reform Judaism: its national representatives are the Union of American Hebrew Congregations and the Central Conference of American Rabbis.

  These six groups make up the New York-based Synagogue Council of America. It is the vehicle for consultation among the three expressions and coordinates joint activities.

  The council estimates that its members represent about three million synagogue-affiliated American Jews, divided about equally among the three major groupings. The council also estimates that one million American Jews, most of them Orthodox, are members of congregations not represented in the council.

Beliefs: Jews generally believe that a divine kingdom will be established on earth, opening a messianic era that will be marked by peace and bliss. They also believe that they have a mandate from God to work toward this kingdom.

The key to beliefs is the Torah, or Law of Moses, which consists of the first five books of the Bible. Jewish Scripture also includes the other books of the Old Testament. Additional elements of Jewish belief are contained in the Talmud, a detailed interpretation of the written and oral law of the faith. Orthodox Jews expect the coming of the Messiah, who is to be a descendant of King David. They are strict adherents of the biblical dietary laws, ritual forms and traditional holy days.

Reform Jews regard dietary laws and ritual forms as concessions to the customs of ancient times that may be adapted to the modern needs.

Conservative Jews take a middle position, generally adhering to traditional customs of diet and ritual but stressing that faith is not static and should adapt to the needs of contemporary culture.

Clergy: The only formal titles in use are rabbi, for the spiritual leader of a congregation, and cantor, for the individual who leads the congregation in prayer. Capitalize these titles before an individual's full name on first reference. Do not carry the title through to subsequent references. See **religious titles** and **Zionism.**

• **Jewish holy days** See separate listings for **Hanukkah; Passover; Purim; Rosh Hashana; Shavuot; Sukkot** and **Yom Kippur.** The *High Holy Days* are Rosh Hashana (Rohsh hah-SHAH'-nah) and Yom Kippur (Yohm kee-POOR').

• **jibe** See the **gibe, jibe** entry.

• **job descriptions** Always lowercase a word or words that describe a job but do not constitute a formal title. See **titles.**

• **John F. Kennedy Space Center** Located in Cape Canaveral, Fla., it is NASA's principal launch site for manned spacecraft. It also has been increasingly used as the main landing site for the space shuttle.

Kennedy Space Center is acceptable on all references. For datelines on launch stories:

(Cape Canaveral, Florida) --

See **Cape Canaveral, Florida** and **on B. Johnson Space Center.**

• **Johns Hopkins University** No apostrophes.

• **Joint Chiefs of Staff** Also: *the Joint Chiefs.* But lowercase *the chiefs* or *the chiefs of staff.*

The Joint Chiefs is a committee of the chiefs of staff of the various armed services. The chairman is nominated by the president and approved by the Senate.

- **Jr.** Do not use this abbreviation. See **junior, senior**.

- **judge** Capitalize before a name when it is the formal title for an individual who presides in a court of law. Do not carry through the title after the first reference.

  Do not use *court* as part of the title unless confusion would result without it:

  No court in the title: *U-S District Judge John Sirica, District Judge John Sirica, federal Judge John Sirica, Judge John Sirica, U-S Circuit Judge Homer Thornberry, appellate Judge John Blair.*

  Court needed in the title: *Juvenile Court Judge John Jones, Criminal Court Judge John Jones, Superior Court Judge Robert Harrison, state Supreme Court Judge William Cushing.*

  When the formal title *chief judge* is used, put the court name after the judge's name: *Chief Judge John Sirica of U-S District Court in Washington, Chief Judge Clement Haynesworth of the Fourth Circuit Court of Appeals.* In such cases, it is often best to break the title in two, using *chief judge* in reference to the person's name in one sentence, and the full court name in another.

  Do not pile up long court names before the name of a judge. Make it *Judge John Smith of Allegheny County Common Pleas Court,* not *Allegheny County Common Pleas Court Judge John Smith.* See **administrative law judge; court names; judicial branch; justice**.

- **judge advocate** The plural: *judge advocates.* Also: *judge advocate general, judge advocates general.*

  Capitalize as a formal title before a name. See **titles**.

- **judgment** Not *judgement.*

- **judicial branch** Always lowercase.

  The federal court system that exists today as the outgrowth of Article III of the Constitution is composed of the Supreme Court of the United States, the U.S. Court of Appeals, U.S. District Courts, the U.S. Court of Claims, the U.S. Court of Customs and Patent Appeals, and the U.S. Customs Court. There are also four district judges for U-S territories.

  The U.S. Tax Court and U.S. Court of Military Appeals are not part of the judicial branch.

  For more detail on federal courts, see separate entries under the names listed above.

- **Judicial Conference of the United States** This rule-making body for the courts of the judicial branch meets twice a year. Its 25 members are the Chief Justice of the United States, the chief judges of the II circuit courts, one district judge from each of the circuits, and the chief judges of the U.S. Court of Claims and the U.S. Court of Customs and Patent Appeals.

  Day-to-day functions are handled by the Administrative Office of U.S. Courts.

- **jukebox**

- **July** See **months**.

- **jumbo jet** Any very large jet plane, including the *Boeing 747*, the *D-C Ten*, the *L-Ten-Eleven* and the *C-Five-A*.

- **June** See **months**.

- **junior, senior** Do not abbreviate, and do not precede by a comma: *Joseph Kennedy Junior.*
  The notation *the second* may be used if it is the person's preference. But note that *the second* is not necessarily the equivalent of *junior*; it often is used by a nephew or grandson. If necessary to distinguish between father and son on the second reference, use phrases such as *the elder Smith* or *the younger Smith.* See **names.**

- **Junior Chamber of Commerce** See **Jaycees**.

- **junta** (HOON'-tuh) See the **government, junta, regime** entry.

- **jury** The word takes singular verbs and pronouns: *The jury has been sequestered until it reaches a verdict.*
  Do not use awkward phrases such as *seven-man, five-woman jury.* Make it: *jury of seven men and five women.*
  Do not capitalize: *a U-S District Court jury, a federal jury, a Massachusetts Superior Court jury, a Los Angeles County grand jury.* See **grand jury**.

- **justice** Capitalize before a name when it is the formal title.
  It is the formal title for members of the Supreme Court and for jurists on some state courts. In such cases, do not use *judge* in first or subsequent references. See **judge; Supreme Court of the United States** and **titles.**

- **justice of the peace** Capitalize as a formal title before a name. Do not abbreviate. See **titles.**

- **juvenile delinquent** Juveniles may be declared delinquents in many states for anti-social behavior or for breaking the law. In some states, laws prohibit publishing or broadcasting the names of juvenile delinquents.
  Follow the local practice unless there is a compelling reason to the contrary. Consult with the General Desk if you believe such an exception is warranted.

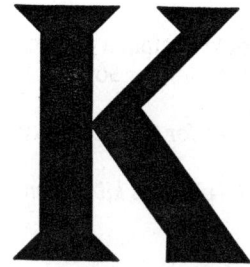

- **K** (or k) Abbreviation for *kilobyte*. Don't use; say *kilobytes* instead. See **kilobyte**.

- **Kansas** See **state names**.

- **Kansas City** Use the state name to avoid confusion between Kansas City, Kan., and Kansas City, Mo.

- **karat** See the **carat, caret, karat** entry.

- **Kelvin scale** A scale of temperatures based on, but different from, the Celsius scale. It is used primarily in science to record very high and very low temperatures. The Kelvin scale starts at zero and indicates the total absence of heat (absolute zero).
  Zero on the Kelvin scale is equal to minus 273.15 degrees Celsius, or minus 460 degrees Fahrenheit.
  The freezing point of water is 273.16 degrees Kelvin. The boiling point of water is 373.16 degrees Kelvin.
  To convert from Celsius to Kelvin, add 273.15 to the Celsius temperature. See **Celsius** and **Fahrenheit**.

- **Kennedy Space Center** See **John F. Kennedy Space Center**.

- **Kentucky** Legally a commonwealth, not a state. See **state** and **state names**.

- **Kentucky Derby** On second reference, *the Derby* — an exception to normal second-reference capitalization practice.

- **kerosene** Formerly a trademark, now a generic term.

- **ketchup** Not *catchup* or *catsup*.

- **keynote address** Also: *keynote speech*.

- **Keystone Kops** Be careful not to make a reference to this silent comedy group in a manner that is judgmental about a person's or group's competence.

- **K-G-B** Acceptable on first reference, but the story should contain a phrase identifying it as the secret police and intelligence agency of the former Soviet Union.
  The initials stand for the Russian words meaning *Committee for State Security*.

- **kibbutz** (kih-BUTS') An Israeli collective settlement. The plural is *kibbutzim* (kih-but-SEEM').

- **kidnap, kidnapped, kidnapping, kidnapper**

- **killer** See the **assassin, killer, murderer** entry.

- **kilo-** A prefix denoting 1,000 of a unit. Move a decimal point three places to the right, adding zeroes if necessary, to convert to the basic unit: 10.5 kilograms equals 10,500 grams. See the next entry for an important exception to this definition.

- **kilobyte** (KIL'-oh-byt) An exception to the definition of the prefix *kilo*, this measurement of computer memory means 1,024 bytes. Similarly, *64 kilobytes* means 64 times 1,024, or 65,536 bytes. See **bit, byte**.

- **kilocycles** The new term is **kilohertz**. See that entry.

- **kilogram** The metric term for 1,000 grams.
  A kilogram is equal to about 2.2 pounds, or 35 ounces.
  To convert to pounds, multiply a kilogram measurement by 2.2: 9 kilograms times 2.2 equals 19.8 pounds. See **gram; metric system; pound (weight)**.

- **kilohertz** (KIL'-oh-hurts) 1,000 cycles per second. The term replaces *kilocycles* as the correct term in applications such as broadcast frequencies.
  Do not abbreviate.

- **kilometer** (kil-AH'-mih-tur) The metric term for 1,000 meters.
  A kilometer is equal to about 3,281 feet — five-eighths of a mile.
  To convert a kilometer measurement to miles, multiply by .62: 5 kilometers times .62 equals 3.1 miles. See **meter; metric system; mile**.

- **kiloton, kilotonnage** The unit used to measure the power of nuclear explosions. One kiloton has the explosive force of 1,000 tons of TNT.
  The atomic bomb dropped on Aug. 6, 1945, on the Japanese city of Hiroshima, had an explosive force of 13 kilotons.
  A *megaton* has the force of 1 million tons of TNT.
  A *gigaton* has the force of 1 billion tons of TNT.

- **kilowatt-hour** The amount of electricity consumed when one-thousand watts are used for one hour.
  Do not abbreviate.

- **kindergarten**

- **king** Capitalize only when used before the name of royalty: *King George the Sixth.* Continue in subsequent references that use the king's given name: *King George,* not *George.*
  Lowercase *king* when it stands alone. Capitalize in plural uses before names: *Kings George and Edward.*
  Lowercase in phrases such as *chess king Bobby Fischer.* See **nobility** and **titles.**

- **Kitty Litter** A brand of absorbent material used in cat litter boxes. Use a generic term such as *cat box litter.*

- **Klan in America** See **Ku Klux Klan.**

- **Kleenex** A trademark for a brand of facial tissue.

- **K-L-M Royal Dutch Airlines** A *K-L-M airliner* is acceptable in any reference. Headquarters is in Amsterdam, the Netherlands.

- **K-mart** Lowercase *m.* This is an exception to the company's preference (which is *Kmart*), for readability. Headquarters is in Troy, Mich.

- **Knesset** (kuh-NES'-et) The Israeli parliament. See **foreign legislative bodies.**

- **knick-knack** The hyphen is for readability.

- **knight** See **nobility.**

- **Knights of Columbus** Use *the Knights* on second reference. See the **fraternal organizations and service clubs** entry.

- **knot** One nautical mile — 6,076.10 feet — per hour. It is a rate of travel; it is therefore redundant to say *knots-per-hour.*
  A knot is computed as the length of one minute of a meridian. To convert knots to approximate statute miles per hour, multiply knots by 1.15. See **nautical mile.**

- **know-how**

- **Kodak** A trademark for cameras and other photographic products made by Eastman Kodak Co. of Rochester, N.Y.

- **Koran** (koh-RAN') The sacred book of Muslims, who believe that it contains the words of Allah dictated to the Prophet Mohammed through the Angel Gabriel. See **Islam.**

- **Korean War** But lowercase *Korean conflict.*

- **kosher** Always lowercase.

- **kowtow**

- **Kriss Kringle** Not *Kris.*

- **kudos** It means credit or praise for an achievement.
  The singular is *kudos* and the word takes singular verbs: *Kudos goes to John Jones.*

- **Ku Klux Klan** Not *Klu.*
  There are 42 separate organizations known as the *Klan in America.*
  Some of them do not use the full name *Ku Klux Klan,* but each may be called that, and the *K-K-K* initials may be used for any of them on second reference.
  The two largest Klan organizations are the National Knights of the Ku Klux Klan, based in Stone Mountain, Ga., and the United Klans of America, based in Tuscaloosa, Ala. An Imperial Board, composed of leaders from the various groups, meets occasionally to coordinate activities.
  Capitalize the formal titles before a name: *Imperial Wizard James Venable, Grand Dragon Dale Reusch.*
  Members are *Klansmen.*

- **Kuomintang** (GWOH′-min-tahng) The Chinese Nationalist political party. Do not follow with the word *party; tang* means party.

- **Kuril** (KOO′-ril) **Islands** Use in datelines after a community name in stories from these islands. Name an individual island, if needed, in the copy.
  Explain in your story that the islands are claimed by Japan but were occupied by the Soviet Union at the end of World War II and remain occupied by Russia.

- **Kuwait** (koo-WAYT′) Stands alone in datelines.

- **la** See **foreign particles**.

- **Labor Day** The first Monday in September.

- **Laborers' International Union of North America** The shortened form *Laborers' union* is acceptable in all references. Headquarters is in Washington.

- **Labor Party** Not *Labour*, even if British.

- **Labrador** The mainland portion of the Canadian province of Newfoundland.
   Use *Newfoundland* in datelines after the name of a community. Specify in the story that the location is in Labrador.

- **lacrosse** Scoring is in goals, each worth one point.
   The playing field is 110 yards long. The goals are 80 yards apart, with 15 yards of playing area behind each goal.
   A match consists of four 15-minute periods. Overtime may be played to break a tie.

- **Ladies' Home Journal**

- **Ladies Professional Golf Association** No apostrophe after *Ladies*. In news copy, spell out on first reference. A phrase such as *L-P-G-A tournament* may be used on first reference to avoid a cumbersome lead. In sports copy, L-P-G-A is acceptable in all references.

- **lady** Do not use as a synonym for *woman*. *Lady* may be used when it is a courtesy title or when a specific reference to fine manners is appropriate. See **nobility**.

- **Laetrile** (LAY'-uh-tril) A trademark for a substance derived from the chemical amygdalin (uh-MIG'-duh-lin), found naturally in the pits of apricots and peaches and in bitter almonds.
   It is believed by some to be an effective cancer treatment. The U.S. Food and Drug Administration has said that the substance has not been proved safe and

effective as an anti-cancer agent and has banned its interstate transportation. Marketed in some areas under the names Bee-Seventeen or Aprikern.

- **lager** (LAH'-guhr) (beer)

- **lake** Capitalize as part of a proper name: *Lake Erie, Canandaigua Lake, the Finger Lakes.*
Lowercase in plural uses: *lakes Erie and Ontario; Canandaigua and Seneca lakes.*

- **lamebrain**

- **lame duck** (n.) **lame-duck** (adj.)

- **Land-Rover** With a hyphen. A trademark for a brand of all-terrain vehicle.

- **languages** Capitalize the proper names of languages and dialects: *Aramaic, Cajun, English, Galluh, Persian, Serbo-Croatian, Yiddish.*

- **lanolin** Formerly a trademark, now a generic term.

- **larceny** See the **burglary, larceny, robbery, theft** entry.

- **last** Avoid the use of *last* as a synonym for *latest* if it might imply finality. *The last time it rained, I forgot my umbrella,* is acceptable. But: *The last announcement was made at noon today* may leave the newscaster and listener wondering whether the announcement was the final announcement or whether others are to follow.
The word *last* is not necessary to convey the notion of *most recent* when the name of a month or day is used:
Preferred: *It happened Wednesday. It happened in April.*
Correct, but redundant: *It happened last Wednesday.*
But: *It happened last week. It happened last month.*

- **Lastex** A trademark for a type of elastic yarn.

- **Last Supper**

- **late** Do not use it to describe someone's actions while alive.
Wrong: *Only the late senator opposed this bill.* (He was not dead at that time.)

- **latex** (LAY'-tex) A resin-based substance used in making elastic materials and paints.

- **Latin America** See **Western Hemisphere**.

- **Latin Rite** See **Roman Catholic Church.**

- **latitude and longitude** *Latitude*, the distance north or south of the equator, is designated by parallels. *Longitude*, the distance east or west of Greenwich, England, is designated by meridians.

  Generally speaking, locations should be identified by latitude and longitude only when central to the story, as when a border or demarcation line is defined in these terms.

  Following the rules for **numerals**, use these forms to express degrees of latitude or longitude: *New York City lies at 40 degrees, 45 minutes north latitude and 74 degrees, zero minutes west longitude. New York City is south of the 41st parallel north, and along the 74th meridian west.*

- **Latter Day Saints, Latter-day Saints** See **Church of Jesus Christ of Latter-day Saints.**

- **Laundromat** A trademark for a coin-operated laundry.

- **Law Enforcement Assistance Administration** *L-E-A-A* is acceptable on second reference.

- **laws** Capitalize legislative acts but not bills: *the Taft-Hartley Act, the Kennedy bill.*

- **lawsuit**

- **lawyer** A generic term for all members of the bar.

  An *attorney* is someone legally appointed or empowered to act for another, usually, but not always, a *lawyer*. An *attorney-at-law* is a lawyer.

  A *barrister* is a British lawyer who is specially trained and appears exclusively as a trial lawyer in higher courts. He is retained by a *solicitor*, not directly by the client. There is no equivalent term in the United States.

  Counselor, when used in a legal sense, means a person who conducts a case in court, usually, but not always, a lawyer. A *counselor-at-law* is a lawyer. *Counsel* frequently is used collectively for a group of counselors.

  A *solicitor* in Britain is a lawyer who performs legal services for the public. A solicitor appears in lower courts but does not have the right to appear in higher courts, which are reserved for barristers.

  A *solicitor* in the United States is a lawyer employed by a governmental body. *Solicitor* is generally a job description, but in some agencies it is a formal title.

  Solicitor general is the formal title for a chief law officer (where there is no attorney general) or for the chief assistant to the law officer (when there is an attorney general). Capitalize when used before a name.

  The *Solicitor General of the United States* is the lawyer who represents the American government in court.

  Do not use *lawyer* as a formal title. See the **attorney, lawyer** entry and **titles.**

- **lay, lie** The action word is *lay*. It takes a direct object. *Laid* is the form for its past tense and its past participle. Its present participle is *laying*.
  Lie indicates a state of reclining along a horizontal plane. It does not take a direct object. Its past tense is *lay*. Its past participle is *lain*. Its present participle is *lying*.
  When *lie* means to make an untrue statement, the verb forms are *lie, lied, lying*. Some examples:
  Present or Future Tenses: Wrong: *He lays on the beach all day. I will lay down.*
  Right: *He lies on the beach all day. I will lie down.*
  Right: *I will lay the book on the table. The prosecutor tried to lay the blame on him.*
  Past Tense: Right: *I laid the book on the table. The prosecutor has laid the blame on him.*
  Right: *He lay on the beach all day. He has lain on the beach all day. I lay down. I have lain down.*
  With the Present Participle: Right: *I am laying the book on the table. The prosecutor is laying the blame on him.*
  Right: *He is lying on the beach. I am lying down.*

- **Leaning Tower of Pisa**

- **leatherneck** Lowercase this nickname for a member of the U.S. Marine Corps. It is derived from the leather lining that was formerly part of the collar of the Marine uniform.

- **lectern, podium, pulpit, rostrum** A speaker stands *behind* a *lectern*, *on* a *podium* or *rostrum*, or *in* the *pulpit*.

- **lecturer** A formal title in the Christian Science Church, so uppercase before a name. A job description in other uses, so lowercase.

- **lectures** Capitalize and use quotation marks for their formal titles, as described in the **composition titles** entry.

- **left hand** (n.) **left-handed** (adj.) **left-hander** (n.) *Leftie* is acceptable in all references to *left-hander*.
  Use *southpaw* only in sports contexts.

- **leftist, ultra-leftist** In general, avoid these terms in favor of a more precise description of an individual's political philosophy.
  As popularly used today, particularly abroad, *leftist* often applies to someone who is merely liberal or believes in a form of democratic socialism.
  Ultra-leftist suggests an individual who subscribes to a communist view or one holding that liberal or socialist change cannot come within the present form of government. See **radical** and the **rightist, ultra-rightist** entry.

- **left wing** (n.) But: *left-wing* (adj.), *left-winger* (n.).

- **legal holiday** See the **holidays and holy days** entry.

- **legion, legionnaire** See **American Legion; French Foreign Legion**.

- **Legionnaires' disease** It takes its name from the outbreak at the Pennsylvania American Legion convention held at the Bellevue-Stratford Hotel in Philadelphia in July 1976. Thirty-four people died – 29 Legionnaires or family members and five other people who had been near the hotel. The disease was diagnosed for the first time after 221 people contracted the illness in Philadelphia.

    The bacterium believed to be responsible is found in soil and grows in water and environments such as air-conditioning ducts, storage tanks and rivers.

    The Centers for Disease Control in Atlanta estimates that 25,000 people get the disease each year in the United States. The pneumonia-like symptoms begin two or three days after exposure.

- **legislative titles** Don't abbreviate them. Use them as formal titles, uppercase, before a name on first reference.

    A member of the Senate is a *Senator*. A member of the House is a *Representative, Congressman* or *Congresswoman*.

    It is not necessary to add *U-S* or *State* before *Senator* or *Representative* unless failure to do so would result in confusion: *U-S Senator Nancy Kassebaum met with state Senator Hugh Carter*.

    Other titles commonly encountered include *assemblyman, assemblywoman, city councilman, city councilwoman, alderman* and *delegate*. All should be capitalized when used as a formal title before a name, and lowercased when they stand alone.

    Second Reference: Do not use legislative titles before a name on second reference. *Senator Nancy Kassebaum* on first reference; *Kassebaum* or *the senator* or *the Kansas senator* on subsequent references.

    Clutter: Don't try to cram all of the titles and affiliations into the first sentence: *Arizona Republican Senator Barry Goldwater today ...*

    Instead, try: *Barry Goldwater says President Reagan is doing an "outstanding job." The Arizona senator said he and all other Republicans are proud of Reagan.*

    With a well-known politician, the title can be worked into the story later.

    Organizational Titles: Capitalize these formal titles of the federal legislative leaders when used before the individuals' names:

Senate Majority Leader	Senate Minority Leader
Senate Democratic Whip	Senate Republican Whip
President Pro Tem	
Speaker of the House	House Majority Leader
House Minority Leader	House Majority Whip
House Minority Whip	

Capitalize these terms as formal titles before a name even without the name of the chamber: *Speaker Newt Gingrich, Majority Leader George Mitchell.*

Capitalize *chairman* when used as part of a formal title before a name: *Intelligence Committee Chairman David Boren.* See **party affiliation; titles.**

- **legislature** Capitalize when preceded by the name of a state: *the Kansas Legislature.*

Retain capitalization when the state name is dropped but the reference is specifically to that state's legislature:

(Topeka, Kansas) - - Both houses of the Legislature adjourned today. ...

Capitalize *legislature* in subsequent specific references and in such constructions as *the state Legislature, the 100th Legislature.*

Although the word *legislature* is not part of the formal, proper name for the lawmaking body in many states, it commonly is used that way and should be treated as such in any story that does not use the formal name.

If a given context or local practice calls for the use of a formal name such as *Missouri General Assembly*, retain the capital letter if the name of the state can be dropped, but lowercase the word *assembly* if it stands alone. Lowercase *legislature* if a story uses it in a subsequent reference to a body identified as a *general assembly.*

Lowercase *legislature* when used generically: *No legislature has approved the amendment.*

Use *legislature* in lowercase for all plural references: *The Arkansas and Colorado legislatures are considering the amendment.*

In 49 states, the separate bodies are the state *senate* and the state *assembly* or *house.*

The exception is the *Nebraska Legislature*, which is a unicameral body. See **assembly; governmental bodies; general assembly; house of representatives** and **senate.**

- **Lent** The period from Ash Wednesday through Holy Saturday, the day before Easter. The 40-day Lenten period for penance, suggested by Christ's 40 days in the desert, does not include the six Sundays between Ash Wednesday and Easter. See **Easter** for the method of computing when Easter occurs.

- **lesbian, lesbianism** Lowercase in references to homosexual women, except in the names of organizations. See **gay.**

- **less** See the **fewer, less** entry.

- **-less** No hyphen before this suffix:

childless	tailless	regardless

- **let up** (v.) **letup** (n. and adj.)

- **leverage** The use of borrowed assets by a business to enhance the return of the owner's equity. The expectation is that the interest rate charged will be lower than the earnings made on the money, so the borrower makes a profit.

- **leveraged buyout** A corporate acquisition in which the bulk of the purchase price is paid with borrowed money. The debt is then repaid with the acquired company's cash flow, with money raised by the sale of its assets or by the later sale of the entire company.

- **Levi's** A trademark for a brand of jeans.

- **liabilities** When used in a financial sense, the word means all the claims against a corporation. They include accounts payable; wages and salaries due but not paid; dividends declared payable; taxes payable; and fixed or long-term obligations such as bonds, debentures and bank loans. See **assets**.

- **liaison** (lee-AY'-zahn)

- **liberal, liberalism** See the **political parties and philosophies** entry.

- **lie** See the **lay, lie** entry.

- **lie in state** Only people who are entitled to a state funeral may formally *lie in state*. In the United States, this occurs in the rotunda of the Capitol.
  Those entitled to a state funeral are the president, former presidents, a president-elect or any other person designated by the president.
  Members of Congress may lie in state, and a number have done so. The decision is either house's to make, although the formal process normally begins with a request from the president.
  Those entitled to an official funeral, but not to lie in state, are the vice president, the chief justice, Cabinet members and other government officials when designated by the president.

- **lieutenant** See **military titles**.

- **lieutenant governor** Do not abbreviate.
  Capitalize when used as a formal title before a name. Lowercase in all other uses. See **titles**.

- **Life Saver, Live Savers** Trademarks for a brand of hard candy.

- **life-size**

- **lifestyle**

- **lifetime** (n., adj.)

- **light, lighted, lighting** *Lit* is acceptable for the past tense form.

- **lightning** The electrical discharge.

- **light-year** The distance that light travels in one year. The speed of light is 186,282 miles per second.
 One light-year works out to almost 6 trillion miles (5,878,612,800,000 miles).

- **likable** Not *likeable*.

- **like, as** Use *like* as a preposition to compare nouns and pronouns. It requires an object: *Jim blocks like a pro.*
 The conjunction *as* is the correct word to introduce clauses: *Jim blocks the linebacker as he should.*

- **like-** Follow with a hyphen when used as a prefix meaning similar to:

like-minded   like-natured

 No hyphen in words that have meanings of their own:

likelihood   likeness   likewise

- **-like** Do not precede this suffix by a hyphen unless the letter *l* would be tripled:

bill-like   businesslike   lifelike   shell-like

- **limited** Do not abbreviate. When used as part of a formal corporate name, capitalize and precede with a comma: *the Smith Corporation, Limited.* See **company names**.

- **limousine**

- **linage** (LYN'-ij), **lineage** (LIN'-ee-ij) *Linage* is the number of lines. *Lineage* is ancestry or descent.

- **Lincoln's Birthday** Capitalize *Birthday* in reference to the holiday.
 It is February 12. While it is widely celebrated, it is not a federal legal holiday. See **holidays**.

- **linoleum** Formerly a trademark, now a generic term.

- **lion's share** The term comes from an Aesop fable in which the lion took all the spoils of a joint hunt.
 Use it to mean the whole of something, or the best and biggest portion. Do not use it to mean *majority*.

- **liquefied** Not *liquified.*

- **liquidation** When used in a financial sense, the word means the process of converting stock or other assets into cash.
  When a company is *liquidated*, the cash obtained is first used to pay debts and obligations to holders of bonds and preferred stock. Whatever cash remains is distributed on a per-share basis to the holders of common stock.

- **liquidity** The ease with which assets can be converted to cash without loss in value.

- **liter** The basic unit of volume in the metric system. It is defined as the volume occupied by one kilogram of water at 4 degrees Celsius. It works out to a total of 1,000 cubic centimeters (one cubic decimeter).
  It takes 1,000 milliliters to make a liter.
  A liter is equal to about 34 fluid ounces or 1.06 liquid quarts. It also works out to just over nine-tenths (.91) dry quarts. The metric system makes no distinction between wet and dry volume.
  To convert to liquid quarts, multiply by 1.06: 4 liters times 1.06 equals 4.24 liquid quarts. To convert to dry quarts, multiply by .91: 4 liters times .91 equals 3.64 dry quarts. To convert to liquid gallons, multiply by .26: 8 liters times .26 equals 2.08 gallons. See **gallon; kilogram; metric system; quart (dry); quart (liquid)**.

- **literally** See the **figuratively, literally** entry.

- **literature** See **composition titles**.

- **livable** Not *liveable.*

- **livid** It is not a synonym for *fiery, bright, crimson, red* or *flaming.* When people turn livid with rage, their faces become ashen or pale. It can mean *blue, bluish gray, gray, dull white, dull purple* or *grayish black.*

- **Lloyds Bank International, Limited** No apostrophe. A prominent bank with headquarters in London.

- **Lloyd's of London** A prominent group of insurance companies with headquarters in London.

- **"Lloyd's Register of Shipping"** The reference source for questions about non-military ships not covered in this handbook. It is published by Lloyd's Register of Shipping Trust Corp., Ltd., in London.

- **loan terminology** Note the meanings of these terms in describing loans by governments and corporations:
  Bond: A certificate issued by a corporation or government stating the amount

of a loan, the interest to be paid, the time for repayment and the collateral pledged if payment cannot be made. Repayment generally is not due for a long period, usually seven years or more.

Collateral: Stock or other property that a borrower is obligated to turn over to a lender if unable to repay a loan.

Commercial paper: A document describing the details of a short-term loan between corporations.

Convertible bond: A bond carrying the stipulation that it may be exchanged for a specific amount of stock in the company that issued it.

Coupon: A slip of paper attached to a bond that the bondholder clips at specified times and returns to the issuer for payment of the interest due.

Default: A person, corporation or government is in default if it fails to meet the terms for repayment.

Debenture: A certificate stating the amount of a loan, the interest to be paid and the time for repayment, but not providing collateral. It is backed only by the corporation's reputation and promise to pay.

Full faith and credit bond: An alternate term for a *general obligation bond*, often used to contrast such a bond with a *moral obligation bond.*

General obligation bond: A bond that has had the formal approval of either the voters or their legislature. The government's promise to repay the principal and pay the interest is constitutionally guaranteed on the strength of its ability to tax the population.

Maturity: The date on which a bond, debenture or note must be repaid.

Moral obligation bond: A government bond that has not had the formal approval of either the voters or their legislature. It is backed only by the government's moral obligation to repay the principal and interest on time.

Municipal bond: A general obligation bond issued by a state, county, city, town, village, possession or territory, or a bond issued by an agency or authority set up by one of these governmental units. In general, interest paid on municipal bonds is exempt from federal income taxes. It also usually is exempt from state and local income taxes if held by someone living within the state of issue.

Note: A certificate issued by a corporation or government stating the amount of a loan, the interest to be paid and the collateral pledged in the event payment cannot be made. The date for repayment is generally more than a year after issue but not more than seven or eight years. The shorter interval for repayment is the principal difference between a *note* and a *bond.*

Revenue bond: A bond backed only by the revenue of the airport, turnpike or other facility that was built with the money it raised.

Treasury borrowing: A *Treasury bill* is a certificate representing a loan to the federal government that matures in three, six or 12 months. A *Treasury note* may mature in one to 10 years or more. A *Treasury bond* matures in seven years or more.

- **local** Avoid the irrelevant use of the word.
  Irrelevant: *The injured were taken to a local hospital.*
  Better: *The injured were taken to a hospital.*

- **local** (union) Follow the rules for **numerals** and capitalize when giving the name of a union subdivision: *Local 222 of The Newspaper Guild. U-A-W Local Three.*

  Lowercase *local* when it stands alone or in plural uses: *The local will vote tomorrow. He will address locals two, ten and 112.*

- **locker room**

- **Lockheed Martin Corporation** Headquarters is in Bethesda, Md.

- **lockouts** The reporter's sign-off at the end of a live or recorded piece, it contains the reporter's name and location.

  The lockout must reflect the actual location of the reporter when the words are spoken. If you gather information or tape at the scene but record your report in the studio, the lockout should indicate the community in which the studio is located, or contain no dateline at all.

  AP Network News staffers use these forms: *Thelma LeBrecht, Capitol Hill; Warren Levinson, New York; I'm Mark Smith* (undated spot).

  Stringers use this form: *John Smith, New York.* Stringers do not do undated spots.

- **lodges** See the **fraternal organizations and service clubs** entry.

- **London** The city in England stands alone in datelines.

- **long distance, long-distance** Always a hyphen in reference to telephone calls: *We keep in touch by long-distance. He called long-distance. She took the long-distance call. Long-distance rates are down.*

  In other uses, hyphenate only when used as a compound modifier: *She traveled a long distance. She made a long-distance trip.*

- **longitude** See the **latitude and longitude** entry.

- **longshoreman** Capitalize *longshoreman* only if the intended meaning is that the individual is a member of the International Longshoremen's and Warehousemen's Union or the International Longshoremen's Association.

- **long term, long-term** Hyphenate when used as a compound modifier: *We will win in the long term. He has a long-term assignment.*

- **long time, long-time** *They have known each other a long time. They are long-time partners.* The hyphen, an exception to Webster's, is for readability.

- **long ton** Also known as a *British ton.* Equal to 2,240 pounds. See **ton.**

- **Lord's Supper** See **sacraments.**

- **Los Angeles** The city in California stands alone in datelines. *L-A* is acceptable on second reference.

- **LOT** (laht) **Polish Airlines** Note that *LOT* is all-caps but is not an abbreviation. Headquarters is in Warsaw, Poland.

- **Louisiana** See **state names**.

- **Low Countries** Belgium, Luxembourg and the Netherlands.

- **lowercase** One word (n., v., adj.) when referring to the absence of capital letters. An exception to Webster's New World in keeping with printers' practice.

- **L-S-D** Acceptable in all references for *lysergic acid diethylamide*.

- **L-Ten-Eleven** *Tristar jet* also is acceptable.

- **Lt. Gov.** Do not use this abbreviation for **lieutenant governor**. See that entry.

- **Lucite** A trademark for acrylic plastic.

- **Lufthansa** (luf-TAHN'-suh) **German Airlines** A *Lufthansa airliner* is acceptable in any reference. Headquarters is in Cologne (kuh-LOHN'), Germany.

- **Lutheran churches** The basic unit of government in Lutheran practice is the congregation. It normally is administered by a council, headed either by the senior pastor or a layperson elected from the membership of the council. The council customarily consists of a congregation's clergy and elected laypersons.
  National church bodies are made up of congregations and governed by conventions. Congregations are grouped into territorial *districts* or *synods* whose functions vary. The term *synod* also is used in the names of some national bodies.
  The three major Lutheran bodies in the United States merged on Jan.1, 1988, into a new organization, the Evangelical Lutheran Church in America, with about 5.3 million members in more than 11,000 congregations.
  The Lutheran Church in America was the largest of three major Lutheran bodies in the United States. Of the three, it takes the least rigid or literalistic stand on doctrine and Bible interpretation. It was formed in 1962 from a merger of four bodies with Danish, Finnish, German and Swedish backgrounds. It merged with the American Lutheran Church, a mostly Midwestern group formed in 1960 through a merger of four bodies with Danish, German and Norwegian backgrounds, and the relatively small west-central Association of Evangelical Lutheran Churches.
  The Lutheran Church-Missouri Synod, with about 2.6 million members, is a separate and distinct body. It was formed in 1847 and its background is predominantly German.

Beliefs: Lutheran teachings go back to Martin Luther, a 16th-century Roman Catholic priest whose objections to elements of Roman Catholic practice began the movement known as the Protestant Reformation.

Lutherans believe in the Trinity and emphasize both the divinity and humanity of Christ. There are two sacraments, baptism and the Lord's Supper.

In recent years, the question of Bible interpretation has divided Lutherans into "moderate" and "conservative" camps. Conservatives argue for a literal interpretation of passages others consider symbolic. Moderates argue that some truths in the Bible are expressed in allegories.

Clergy: Members of the clergy are known as ministers. Pastor applies if a minister leads a congregation.

On first reference, use *the Reverend* before the name of a man or woman. Do not carry the title through on subsequent references.

Lay members of a church council frequently are designated *elders, deacons* or *trustees.* Do not use as formal titles. See **religious titles**.

● **Luxembourg** Stands alone in datelines.

● **-ly** Do not use a hyphen between adverbs ending in *ly* and adjectives they modify: *an easily remembered rule, a badly damaged island, a fully informed woman.* See the compound modifiers section of the **hyphen** entry.

● **Lyndon B. Johnson Space Center** Formerly the *Manned Spacecraft Center.* Located in Houston, it is the National Aeronautics and Space Administration's principal control and training center for manned spaceflight.

During a space shuttle launch, *launch control,* located at the Kennedy Space Center in Florida, runs the countdown and all flight activities until the spacecraft clears the launch tower. At that point, *mission control,* located at the Johnson Space Center, takes over control of the craft.

Johnson Space Center is acceptable in all references.

In datelines:

(Johnson Space Center, Houston) —

See **John F. Kennedy Space Center.**

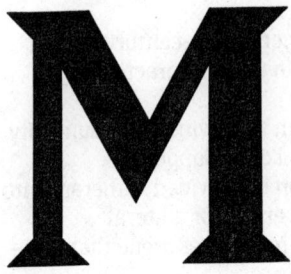

- **Macao** Stands alone in datelines.

- **Mace** A trademark, shortened from *Chemical Mace,* for a brand of tear gas that is packaged in an aerosol canister and temporarily stuns its victims.

- **machine gun** (n.) But: *machine-gun (v.* and adj.), *machine-gunner.* See **weapons**.

- **Mach** (mahk) **number** Follow the rules for **numerals** and capitalize *Mach* when reporting speed measurements using this scale.
  Named for Ernst Mach, an Austrian physicist, the figure represents the ratio of the speed of an object to the speed of sound in the surrounding medium, such as air.
  A rule of thumb for the speed of sound is that it is roughly 750 miles-per-hour at sea level, and about 660 miles-per-hour at 30,000 feet.
  A body traveling at Mach one would be traveling at the speed of sound, while one traveling at Mach two would be traveling twice as fast.

- **Mafia, Mafiosi** The secret society of criminals and its members. Do not use as a synonym for *organized crime* or *the underworld.*

- **magazine names** Capitalize the name but do not place it in quotes. Lowercase *magazine* unless it is part of the publication's formal title: *Harper's Magazine, Newsweek magazine, Time magazine.* Check the masthead if in doubt.

- **magistrate** Capitalized when used as a formal title before a name. See **titles**.

- **Magna Carta** (KAHR'-tuh) Not Magna Charta.
  The charter the English barons forced King John of England to grant at Runnymede in June 1215. It guaranteed certain civil and political liberties.

- **Mailgram** A trademark for a telegram sent to a post office near the recipient's address and delivered to the address by letter carrier.

- **mailman**

- **Maine** See **state names**.

- **mainland China** See **China**.

- **major** See **military titles**.

- **Majorca** (mah-YAWR'-kah) Use instead of *Spain* in datelines on stories from communities on this island.

- **majority, plurality** *Majority* means more than half. *Plurality* means more than the next highest number.

  Computing a majority: To describe how large a majority is, take the winning figure and subtract everything else from it: if 100,000 votes were cast, and one candidate received 60,000 while the rest, combined, received 40,000, the winner would have a *majority* of 20,000 votes.

  Computing a plurality: To describe how large a plurality is, take the highest number and subtract it from the next highest number: if, in the example cited above, the second-place finisher had 25,000 votes, the winner's *plurality* would have been 35,000 votes.

  Suppose, however, that no candidate in this example had a majority. If the first-place finisher had 40,000 votes and the second-place finisher had 30,000 for example, the leader's *plurality* would be 10,000 votes.

  Usage: When *majority* and *plurality* are used alone, they take singular verbs and pronouns: *The majority has made its decision.*

  If a plural word follows an *of* construction, the decision on whether to use a singular or plural verb depends on the sense of the sentence: *A majority of two votes is not adequate to control the committee. The majority of the houses on the block were destroyed.*

- **majority leader, minority leader** Capitalize when used as a formal title before a name: *Senate Majority Leader Trent Lott.* Lowercase in all other uses.

  These congressional—and state—legislative leaders are usually selected by caucuses of their parties in their legislative chambers. See **legislative titles**.

- **make up** (v.) **makeup** (n. and adj.)

- **malarkey** Not *malarky*.

- **Maldives** (MAL'-dyvz) Use this official name with a community name in a dateline. The body of the story should note that the nation frequently is called the *Maldive Islands*. See **datelines**.

- **man, mankind** Either may be used when both men and women are involved and no other term is appropriate. In these cases, do not use duplicate phrases such as *a man or a woman* or *mankind and womankind*.

  Usually the best choice is a substitute term such as *humanity, a person* or *an individual.* See **women**.

- **manageable**

- **manager** Capitalize when used as a formal title before a name: *Manager Casey Stengel, General Manager Dick O'Connell.*
  Do not capitalize in job descriptions such as *equipment manager John Smith* or *plant manager Joe Jones.* See **titles.**

- **Manitoba** A province of central Canada. Do not abbreviate. See **datelines.**

- **manslaughter** See the **homicide, murder, manslaughter** entry.

- **mantel, mantle** A *mantel* is a shelf.
  A *mantle* is a cloak.

- **Maoism (maoist)** The communist philosophy and policies of Mao Zedong. See the **political parties and philosophies** entry.

- **March** See **months.**

- **Mardi Gras** Literally "fat Tuesday," the term describes a day of merrymaking on the Tuesday before Ash Wednesday.
  In New Orleans and many Roman Catholic countries, the Tuesday celebration is preceded by a week or more of parades and parties.

- **mare** A female horse five years or older.

- **margin** The practice of purchasing securities in part with borrowed money, using the purchased securities as collateral in anticipation of an advance in the market price. If the advance occurs, the purchaser may be able to repay the loan and make a profit. If the price declines, the stock may have to be sold to settle the loan.
  The *margin* is the difference between the amount of the loan and the value of the securities used as collateral.

- **marijuana** Not *marihuana.*

- **Marines** Capitalize when referring to U.S. forces: *the U-S Marines, the Marine Corps, Marine regulations.* Do not use the abbreviation *U-S-M-C.*
  Capitalize *Marine* when referring to an individual in a Marine Corps unit: *He is a Marine.*

- **Maritime Provinces** The Canadian provinces of Nova Scotia, New Brunswick and Prince Edward Island.

- **marketbasket, marketplace**

- **marquess** (MAHR'-kwis), **marchioness** (mahr-shun-ES'), **marquis** (mahr-KEE'), **marquise** (mahr-KEZ') See **nobility.**

- **marshal, marshaled, marshaling, Marshall** *Marshal* is the spelling for both the verb and the noun: *Marilyn will marshal her forces. Erwin Rommel was a field marshal.*

  Marshall is used in proper names: *George Marshall, John Marshall, the Marshall Islands.*

- **Marshall Islands** Named for John Marshall, a British explorer.

  In datelines, give the name of a city and *Marshall Islands.* List the name of an individual island in the copy if it's important to the story.

- **Martin Luther King Junior Day** The federal holiday honoring Martin Luther King Jr., who was born Jan. 15, 1929, is on the third Monday in January. It was first celebrated in 1986.

- **Marxism** (Marxist) The system of thought developed by Karl Marx and Friedrich Engels. See the **political parties and philosophies** entry.

- **Maryland** See **state names.**

- **Mason-Dixon Line** The boundary line between Pennsylvania and Maryland, generally regarded as separating the North from the South.

- **Masonite** A trademark for a brand of hardboard.

- **Mass** It is *celebrated* not *said.* Always capitalize when referring to the ceremony, but lowercase any preceding adjectives: *high Mass, low Mass, requiem Mass.*

  In Eastern Orthodox churches the correct term is *Divine Liturgy.* See **Roman Catholic Church.**

- **Massachusetts** Legally a commonwealth, not a state. See **state** and **state names.**

- **master of arts, master of science** A *master's degree* or a *master's* is acceptable in any reference. Do not abbreviate. See **academic degrees.**

- **matrimony** See **sacraments.**

- **maturity** In a financial sense, the date on which a bond, debenture or note must be repaid. See **loan terminology.**

- **May** See **months.**

- **May Day, mayday** *May Day* is May 1, often observed as a festive or political holiday.

  Mayday is the international distress signal, from the French *m'aidez,* which means "help me."

- **mayors' conference** See **U-S Conference of Mayors**.

- **M-C** Do not use this abbreviation for *Master of Ceremonies*. Use **emcee**— and see that entry.

- **McDonnell Douglas Corporation** Headquarters is in St. Louis.

- **M-D** Do not use when you mean *doctor* or *physician* or *surgeon*. See **doctor** and **academic titles**.

- **meager**

- **mean** See the **average, mean, median, norm** entry.

- **Medal of Freedom** It is now the *Presidential Medal of Freedom*. See entry under that name.

- **Medal of Honor** The nation's highest military honor, given by Congress for risk of life beyond the call of duty in combat.
  There is no *Congressional Medal of Honor*.

- **Medfly** The Mediterranean fruit fly. The capital *M* is an exception to Websters.

- **media** In the sense of mass communication, such as magazines, newspapers, the news services, radio and television, the word is plural: *The news media are resisting attempts to limit their freedom.*

- **median** See the **average, mean, median, norm** entry.

- **mediate** See the **arbitrate, mediate** entry.

- **Medicaid** A federal-state program that helps pay for health care for the needy, aged, blind and disabled, and for low-income families with children. A state determines eligibility and which health services are covered. The federal government reimburses a percentage of the state's expenditures.

- **Medicare** The federal health care insurance program for people aged 65 and over, and for the disabled. Eligibility is based mainly on eligibility for Social Security.
  Medicare helps pay charges for hospitalization, for stays in skilled nursing facilities, for physician's charges and for some associated health costs. There are limitations on the length of stay and type of care.
  In Canada, *Medicare* refers to the nation's national health insurance program.

- **medicine** See the **drugs, medicine** entry.

- **medieval**

- **mega-** A prefix denoting 1 million units of a measure. Move the decimal point six places to the right, adding zeroes if necessary, to convert to the basic unit: 5.5 megatons equals 5,500,000 tons.

- **Melchite** (MEL'-kit) **Church** See **Eastern Rite churches.**

- **melee** (MAY'-lay)

- **memento, mementos**

- **memo, memos**

- **memorandum, memorandums**

- **Memorial Day** Formerly May 30. The federal legal holiday is the last Monday in May.

- **menage a trois** (men-AZH' ah twah)

- **menswear** Not *men's wear.*

- **Mercalli scale** See **earthquakes.**

- **Mercurochrome** A trademark for a brand of antiseptic for wounds.

- **meridians** Follow the rules for **numerals** when identifying the imaginary locator lines that ring the globe from north to south through the poles.
  They are measured in units of zero to 180 degrees east and west of the prime meridian, which runs through Greenwich, England. Examples: *the first meridian west, the 100th meridian east, the 33rd meridian.* Note in the final example that the east or west designation is not necessary if the location east or west of Greenwich is obvious. See **latitude and longitude.**

- **merry-go-round**

- **messiah** Capitalize in religious uses. Lowercase when used generically to mean a liberator.

- **meter** The basic unit of length in the metric system. It is defined as being equal to 1,650,763.73 wavelengths of the orange-red radiation of an isotope of krypton. That's for reference only. There's no context in which it should be so precisely defined.

It is equal to about 39.37 inches, which may be rounded off to 39.5 inches in most comparisons.

It takes 100 centimeters to make a meter.

It takes 1,000 meters to make a kilometer.

To convert to inches, multiply the meter measurement by 39.37: 5 meters times 39.37 equals 196.85 inches.

To convert to yards, multiply by 1.1: 5 meters times 1.1 equals 5.5 yards. See **inch; metric system; yard**.

- **Methodist churches** The term *Methodist* originated as a nickname applied to a group of 18th century Oxford University students known for their methodical application to Scripture study and prayer.

The principal Methodist body in the United States is the United Methodist Church, which also has some member conferences outside the United States. It was formed in 1968 by the merger of the Methodist Church and the Evangelical United Brethren Church. It has about 10 million members.

The government of the United Methodist Church follows a stratified pattern from the General Conference through several intermediate conferences down to the local congregation. The General Conference, which meets every four years, has final authority in all matters. Its members, half lay and half clergy, are elected by the annual conferences. Jurisdictional conferences covering major sections of the nation are composed of ministers and lay delegates. Their principal function is to elect bishops. Annual conferences, generally organized along state lines, elect delegates to higher conferences and make official appointments within their areas.

A Methodist bishop presides over a "church area," which may embrace one or more annual conferences. Bishops have extensive administrative powers, including the authority to place, transfer and remove local church pastors, usually in consultation with district superintendents.

Districts in each conference are responsible for promotion of mission work, support of colleges, hospitals and publications, and examination of candidates for the ministry.

Members of a congregation form a "charge conference." It elects officers to a board that assists the pastor.

Methodism in the United States also includes three major black denominations: The African Methodist Episcopal Church, the African Methodist Episcopal Zion Church and the Christian Methodist Episcopal Church.

Beliefs: Methodist teachings emphasize that the Holy Scriptures contain all the knowledge necessary for salvation. Tradition is not acknowledged as a valid source of revelation, although the writings of John Wesley, a leader of the Oxford University group, are regarded as sound interpretations of the Scriptures.

Methodists believe in the Trinity and the humanity and divinity of Christ. There are two sacraments, baptism and the Lord's Supper.

Clergy: Ordained individuals are known as *bishops* and *ministers. Pastor* applies if a minister leads a congregation.

For first references to bishops, use the word: *Bishop Kenneth Goodson of Richmond, Virginia.*

For first references to ministers, use *the Reverend.* Do not use the title on subsequent references. See **religious titles**.

• metric system

Metric terms should be used only when they are central to the story.

In all cases, the rule is clarity: When a metric term will only confuse the newscaster or audience, convert to the more familiar form of measurement. When the metric term is relevant and clear, use it.

Never mix forms of measurement in a story, unless you are trying to clarify quoted matter or tape:

METRIC CONVERSION TABLE

INTO METRIC			OUT OF METRIC		
If you know:	Multiply by:	To get:	If you know:	Multiply by:	To get:
Length			**Length**		
inches	2.54	centimeters	millimeters	0.04	inches
feet	30.	centimeters	centimeters	0.4	inches
yards	0.91	meters	meters	3.3	feet
miles	1.6	kilometers	kilometers	0.62	miles
Area			**Area**		
sq. inches	6.5	sq.	sq. centimeters	0.16	sq. inches
centimeters			sq. meters	1.2	sq. yards
sq. feet	0.09	sq. meters	sq. kilometers	0.4	sq. miles
sq. yards	0.8	sq. meters	hectares	2.47	acres
sq. miles	2.6	sq. kilometers			
acres	0.4	hectares			
Mass (Weight)			**Mass (Weight)**		
ounces	28.	grams	grams	0.035	ounces
pounds	0.45	kilograms	kilograms	2.2	pounds
short tons	0.9	metric tons	metric tons	1.1	short tons
Volume			**Volume**		
teaspoons	5.	milliliters	milliliters	0.03	fluid ounces
tablespoons	15.	milliliters	liters		
fluid ounces	30.	milliliters	liters	2.1	pints
cups	0.24	liters	liters	1.06	quarts
pints	0.47	liters	liters	0.26	gallons
quarts	0.95	liters	cubic meters	35.	cubic feet
gallons	3.8	liters	cubic meters	1.3	cubic yards
cubic feet	0.03	cubic meters			
cubic yards	0.76	cubic meters			
Temperature			**Temperature**		
Fahrenheit	subtract 32, then multiply by 0.556	Celsius	Celsius	multiply by 1.8 then add 32	Fahrenheit

Dr. John Smith says it was a close call:

TAPE: The bullet missed his heart by no more than two millimeters.

Two millimeters is less than an inch.

An even better way to write it: *The doctor says the bullet stopped less than an inch from his heart.*

Don't provide metric or American equivalents in parentheses; that will confuse the newscaster reading the story cold. If an equivalency must be given, do it conversationally:

Officials say it happened about a kilometer away. That's just over half a mile.

In any case, avoid using too many measurements. Use figures only when they serve to clarify the story or make the scene more vivid. But in all cases, stay with what's most familiar so the story is easy to understand.

Conversion formulas: A conversion table for frequently used metric terms appears on the previous page.

In addition, the separate entries for **gram, meter, liter, Celsius** and other frequently used metric units define them and give examples of how to convert them to equivalents in the terminology that has been used in the United States.

Similarly, entries for **pound (weight), inch, quart, Fahrenheit** contain examples of how to convert these terms to metric forms.

Prefixes: To avoid the need for long strings of figures, prefixes are added to the metric units to denote fractional elements or large multiples.

The prefixes are: *pico-* (PEYE'-koh) for one-trillionth, *nano-* for one-billionth, *micro-* for one-millionth, *milli-* for one-thousandth, *centi-* for one-hundredth, *deci-* for one-tenth, *deka-* for ten times, *hecto-* for 100 times, *kilo-* for 1,000 times, *mega-* for one million times, *giga-* for one billion times, and *tera-* for one trillion times.

Entries for each prefix show how to convert a unit preceded by the prefix to the basic unit.

Abbreviations: Do not abbreviate any units. For reference, in the event abbreviations are used by a source, here are the principal abbreviations: *g* (gram), *kg* (kilogram), *t* (metric ton), *m* (meter), *cm* (centimeter), *km* (kilometer), *mm* (millimeter), *L* (liter, capitalized to avoid confusion with the figure *1*), and *mL* (milliliter).

- **metric ton**   A unit of measure equal to 2,204.62 pounds. In agricultural stories, metric tonnages should be converted to **bushels**; see that entry. See **ton**.

- **Metro-Goldwyn-Mayer, Incorporated**   *M-G-M* is acceptable in all references. Headquarters is in Culver City, California.

- **Mexico City**   The city in Mexico stands alone in datelines.

- **Miami**   The city in Florida stands alone in datelines.

- **Michigan** See **state names**.

- **micro-** A prefix denoting one millionth of a unit.
Move the decimal point six places to the left in converting to the basic unit: *2,000,000 microseconds equals two seconds.*

- **mid-** No hyphen unless a proper noun follows:

mid-America   mid-Atlantic   midsemester   midterm

But use a hyphen when *mid-* precedes a figure: *mid-30's.*

- **Middle Ages** 476 *A-D* to 1450 *A-D*.

- **Middle Atlantic States** As defined by the Census Bureau, they are New Jersey, New York and Pennsylvania. Less formal references often consider Delaware part of the group. See **Northeast region.**

- **middle class, middle-class** *He is a member of the middle class. He promised a middle-class tax cut.*

- **Middle East** The term applies to southwest Asia west of Pakistan (Afghanistan, Iran, Iraq, Israel, Kuwait, Jordan, Lebanon, Oman, Qatar, Saudi Arabia, South Yemen, Syria, Turkey, the United Arab Emirates and Yemen), northeastern Africa (Egypt and Sudan), and the island of Cyprus.
Popular usage once distinguished between the *Near East* (the westerly nations in the listing) and the *Middle East* (the easterly nations), but the two terms now overlap, with current practice favoring *Middle East* for both areas.
Use *Middle East* unless *Near East* is used by a source in a story.
Mideast is also acceptable for the adjectival form: *In the Middle East at this hour ...* but *the Mideast peace talks have resumed.*

- **middle initials** Avoid them whenever possible. The middle initial should be used, however, when it is integral to the way a person is normally identified: *John Q. Public.* In addition, use middle initials in casualty lists, stories about criminal proceedings and other cases where exact identification is important.
When the middle initial is used, follow it with a period and a space: *John Y. Brown.* See **names.**

- **middleman**

- **Middle West** *Midwest* is acceptable in all uses. Definitions vary, but the term generally applies to the 12 states that the Census Bureau includes in the North-Central region. See **North-Central region.**
The forms for adjectives are *Middle Western* or *Midwestern,* which is preferred. See **directions and regions.**

- **midnight** Do not put a *12* in front of it.
It is part of the day that is ending, not the one that is beginning.
To avoid confusion, when there is, for example, a midnight Sunday deadline, write *early Monday morning* or *at 12:01 a-m Monday.*

- **Midwest, Midwestern** See the **directions and regions** and **Middle West** entries.

- **MiG** Note that *MiG* is an acronym. The *i* is lowercase because it stands for the Russian word *and.* The *M* and *G* stand for the names of the designers of this type of Soviet fighter, Arten Mikoyan (mih-KOY'-an) and Mikhail Gurevich (GUR'-eh-vich).
The forms: *MiG-19, MiG-21's.* See **aircraft names.**

- **mile** Also called a *statute mile*, it equals 5,280 feet.
The metric equivalent is about 1.6 kilometers.
To convert to kilometers, multiply the mileage figure by 1.6: 5 miles times 1.6 equals 8 kilometers. See **foot; kilometer; knot; nautical mile.**

- **miles-per-gallon** Note hyphens. The abbreviation *M-P-G* is acceptable on second reference.

- **miles-per-hour** Note hyphens. Do not use the abbreviation *M-P-H. Miles-an-hour* is acceptable in all references.

- **military academies** While the formal titles include the designation *U-S*, it is not needed in any reference except to distinguish the American academy from foreign institutions.
The U-S Air Force Academy, for example, may simply be referred to as *the Air Force Academy.*
Capitalize the names of American military academies, with or without the *U-S: Air Force Academy, Coast Guard Academy, Military Academy, Naval Academy.*
Lowercase *academy* when it stands alone.
Cadet is the proper title on first reference for men and women enrolled at the Army, Air Force and Coast Guard academies. *Midshipman* is the proper title for men and women enrolled at the Naval Academy.
The title should be used on the first reference only.

- **military titles** Spell them out. On first reference, use the appropriate title before the full name of a member of the military.
In subsequent references, do not continue using the title before a name.
Capitalize the person's military rank when it is used as a formal title before the name. Lowercase the title when it is used as a substitute for the name:

General John Pershing has arrived. An aide says the general will review the troops.

MILITARY TITLES

ARMY

Commissioned Officers

General	Lieutenant Colonel
Lieutenant General	Major
Major General	Captain
Brigadier General	First Lieutenant
Colonel	Second Lieutenant

Warrant Officers

Chief Warrant Officer	Warrant Officer

Enlisted Personnel

Sergeant Major of the Army	Staff Sergeant
Command Sergeant Major	Sergeant
Sergeant Major	Corporal
First Sergeant	Specialist
Master Sergeant	Private First Class
Sergeant First Class	Private

NAVY, COAST GUARD

Commissioned Officers

Admiral	Lieutenant Commander
Vice Admiral	Lieutenant
Rear Admiral	Lieutenant J-G
Captain	(junior grade)
Commander	Ensign

Warrant Officers

Chief Warrant Officer	Warrant Officer

Enlisted Personnel

Master Chief

Petty Officer	Petty Officer Third Class
Senior Chief Petty Officer	Seaman
Chief Petty Officer	Seaman Apprentice
Petty Officer First Class	Seaman Recruit
Petty Officer Second Class	

MARINE CORPS

Ranks for commissioned officers are the same as those in the Army. Warrant officer ratings follow the same system used in the Navy. There are no specialist ratings.

Others

Sergeant Major	Sergeant
Master Gunnery Sergeant	Corporal
Master Sergeant	Lance Corporal
First Sergeant	Private First Class
Gunnery Sergeant	Private
Staff Sergeant	

AIR FORCE

Ranks for commissioned officers are the same as those in the Army.

Enlisted Designations

Chief Master

Sergeant of the Air Force	Sergeant
Senior Master Sergeant	Senior Airman
Master Sergeant	Airman First Class
Technical Sergeant	Airman
Staff Sergeant	Airman Basic

In some cases, it may be necessary to explain the significance of a title:

John Jones, retired as a sargeant major. That's the Army's highest rank for enlisted men.

In addition to the ranks listed here, each service has ratings such as *machinist, radarman* and *torpedoman* that are job descriptions. Do not use any of these designations as a title on first reference—no capitalization.

Plurals: Add *s* to the principal element in the title: *Majors John Jones and Robert Smith; Major Generals John Jones and Robert Smith.*

Retired Officers: A military rank may be used in first reference before the name of an officer who has retired if it is relevant to a story.

Use *retired* just as *former* would be used before the title of a civilian: *They invited retired Army General John Smith.*

Fire and police officers: The same general guidelines apply when using military-style titles for civilian firefighters or police officers. Add *police* or *fire,* lowercase, before the title when needed for clarity: *police Sergeant John Jones, fire Captain William Smith.*

- **military units** Follow the rules for numerals and capitalize the numbers and key words in referring to military units: *the First Infantry Division, the Third Division, the Fifth Battalion, the Sixth Army, 395th Field Artillery.*
But: *the division, the battalion, the artillery, the fleet.*

- **milli-** A prefix denoting one-thousandth of a unit. Move the decimal point three places to the left to convert to the basic unit: 1,000 millimeters equals 1 meter.

- **milliliter** One-thousandth of a liter. Equal to about one-fifth of a teaspoon. Thirty milliliters equal one fluid ounce.
To convert to teaspoons, multiply by .2: 5 milliliters times .2 equals 1 teaspoon.

- **millimeter** One-thousandth of a meter.
It takes 10 millimeters to make a centimeter.
A millimeter is roughly equal to the thickness of a paper clip.
To convert to inches, multiply by .04: 5 millimeters times .04 equals .2 of an inch.
Do not abbreviate. See **meter; metric system; inch**.

- **(m) millions, (b) billions**
Should always be spelled out and preceded by the identifying letter in parentheses. This confirms the unit, reducing the chance of typographical error. Similarly, *(t) trillions.*
Follow the rules for **numerals**. In general, when dealing with *(b) billions* and fractions of *(m) millions,* spell out both units: *seven (b) billion, 100 (m) million dollars* is preferable to *seven-point-one (b) billion dollars.* Round off when possible: *more than seven (b) billion dollars.*

Note that a hyphen is not used to join the figure and the unit, even in this type of phrase: *The president submitted a 300 (b) billion dollar budget.* This is an exception to the rules in **hyphen**.

- **milquetoast** Not *milk toast* when referring to a shrinking, apologetic person. Such references should be in quoted matter only.
  Derived from Caspar Milquetoast, a character in a comic strip by H.T. Webster.

- **Milwaukee** The city in Wisconsin stands alone in datelines.

- **mimeograph** Formerly a trademark, now a generic term.

- **mini-** The rules in prefixes apply, but in general, no hyphen. Some examples:

minibus   miniskirt   miniseries

- **minister** It is not a formal title. Do not use it before the name of a member of the clergy. See **religious titles** and the entry for an individual's denomination.

- **ministry** See **foreign governmental bodies**.

- **Minneapolis** The city in Minnesota stands alone in datelines.

- **Minnesota** See **state names**.

- **Minnesota Mining and Manufacturing** Its products are known under the names *3-M* (the hyphen is for readability) and *Scotch*. The company also is popularly known as *3-M*. Headquarters is in St. Paul, Minn.

- **minority leader** Treat the same as **majority leader**. See that entry and **legislative titles**.

- **minuscule** Not *miniscule*.

- **minus sign** Don't use it. Use *minus* or *below zero*, as appropriate.

- **mips** An acronym for *million instructions per second*, a measurement of the computational speed of a computer.
  Don't use it; spell out the term instead.

- **MIRV, MIRVs** Acceptable on first reference for *multiple independently targetable re-entry vehicle(s)*. Explain in the text that a MIRV is an intercontinental ballistic missile with several warheads, each of which can be directed to a different target.

- **misdemeanor** See the **felony, misdemeanor** entry.

- **mishap**   A minor misfortune. People are not killed in *mishaps*.

- **Miss**   See **courtesy titles**.

- **missile names**   Follow the rules for **numerals** and capitalize the proper name, including the number, but not the word *missile*: *a Pershing-Two missile*. See **aircraft names; A-B-M; I-C-B-M; MIRV;** and **SAM**.

- **Mississippi**   See **state names**.

- **Missouri**   See **state names**.

- **mix up** (v.) **mix-up** (n. and adj.)

- **Mobil Corporation**   Headquarters is in New York. Mobil Oil Corporation is a subsidiary.

- **mock-up** (n.)

- **model numbers**   Don't use them unless they are central to the story. See **serial numbers**.

- **modem**   A computer term referring to a modulator/demodulator—a device that allows for the transmission and reception of data over long-distance connections such as telephones.

- **Mohammed**   The preferred spelling for the founder of the Islamic religion.

- **Monaco**   After the Vatican, the world's smallest state.
  The *Monaco* section stands alone in datelines. The other two sections, *La Condamine* and *Monte Carlo*, are followed by Monaco:

    (Monte Carlo, Monaco) —

- **Monday**   See **days of the week**.

- **Monday morning quarterback**   One who second-guesses.

- **M-One, M-14**   Note capitalization of numeral. See **weapons**.

- **monetary**   See the **fiscal, monetary** entry.

- **monetary figures**   Follow the rules in **numerals**. All monetary units should be spelled out. Use a comma to separate units, as in *five dollars, ten cents* or *135-thousand, 400 dollars*.
  Follow the rules in **hyphen** to link figures with *thousand* or *hundred*: *four-thousand dollars, 14-hundred dollars*.

The preferred style, particularly when dealing with large amounts, is to truncate the amount and use a *more than* or *almost* construction: *almost six (b) billion dollars* instead of *five-point-nine (b) billion dollars*; *more than 15-hundred dollars* instead of *one-thousand, 538 dollars*.

Informalize monetary figures where appropriate: *two dollars, 50 cents* can be expressed as *two and a-half dollars* or *two-50*.

Decimal expressions of (*m*) *millions* and (*b*) *billions* of dollars should be avoided: *three-point-two (b) billion is better expressed as three (b) billion, 200 (m) million dollars*, although the former is acceptable if necessary for brevity. Similarly, *five-point-one (m) million dollars* is usually more comprehensible when expressed as *five (m) million, 100-thousand dollars*.

When possible, find ways to explain large dollar amounts in terms people can relate to practical experience. Often, a ratio (dollars per person, dollars spent per dollar of revenue, etc.) is easier to understand than a number with six or nine zeroes attached to it. See **foreign money**.

- **monetary units** See **cents; dollar;** and **pound**.

- **moneymaker**

- **money market** The market for various money market instruments.

- **monsignor** See **Roman Catholic Church**.

- **Montana** See **state names**.

- **Montessori method** After Maria Montessori. A system of training young children, it emphasizes training of the senses and guidance to encourage self-education.

- **month-long** The hyphen is for readability.

- **months** Never abbreviate. Capitalize the names of months in all uses.
  When a phrase lists only a month and a year, do not separate the year with commas: *April 1979 was a pleasant month.*
  When the month, day and year are included, set off the year with commas: *November 22nd, 1963, is a day we will always remember.*
  Follow the rules in **numerals**: *December First, April 14th, August 30th*. See also **dates; years**.

- **Montreal** The city in Canada stands alone in datelines.

- **monuments** Capitalize the popular names of monuments and similar public attractions: *the Lincoln Memorial, Statue of Liberty, Washington Monument, Leaning Tower of Pisa.*

- **moon** Lowercase. See **heavenly bodies**.

- **mo-ped**

- **mop up** (v.) **mop-up** (n. and adj.)
- **Moral Majority**   Not *the* Moral Majority.

- **moral obligation bond**   See **loan terminology.**

- **more than**   See **over.**

- **Mormon Church**   Acceptable in all references for *Church of Jesus Christ of Latter-day Saints,* but always include the full name in a story dealing primarily with church activities. See the entry under the formal name.

- **Moscow**   The city in Russia stands alone in datelines.

- **Moslem**   See **Muslim..**

- **mosquito, mosquitoes**

- **mother-in-law, mothers-in-law**

- **Mother Nature**   Do not use in sexist terms.

- **Mother's Day**   The second Sunday in May.

- **motor**   See the **engine, motor** entry.

- **mount**   Spell out in all uses, including the names of communities and of mountains: *Mount Clemens, Michigan; Mount Everest.*

- **mountains**   Capitalize as part of a proper name: *Appalachian Mountains, Ozark Mountains, Rocky Mountains.* Or simply: *the Appalachians, the Ozarks, the Rockies.*

- **Mountain Standard Time (m-s-t), Mountain Daylight Time (m-d-t)**   See **time zones.**

- **Mountain States**   As defined by the Census Bureau, the eight are Arizona, Colorado, Idaho, Montana, Nevada, New Mexico, Utah and Wyoming.

- **movie ratings**   The categories used by the Motion Picture Association of America, Incorporated, are:
  G: For general audiences. All ages admitted.
  P-G: Parental guidance suggested. Some material may not be suitable for children.
  P-G-13: Special parental guidance strongly suggested for children under 13. Some material may be inappropriate for them.

R: Restricted. People under 17 must be accompanied by a parent or adult guardian.

N-C-17: No one under 17 admitted. When the ratings are used in news stories or reviews, use these forms as appropriate: *the movie has an R rating, an R-rated movie, the movie is R-rated.*

The *P-G-13* and *N-C-17* ratings do not lend themselves to use as compound modifiers: *an N-C-17-rated movie* is too cumbersome. Say *the movie is rated N-C-17* instead.

- **movie titles** See **composition titles**.

- **m-p-h** Don't use it. Use *miles-per-hour* or *miles-an-hour* instead.

- **Mr., Mrs.** These abbreviations are acceptable in all references, including direct quotations. See **courtesy titles**.
  Avoid constructions that call for the use of the plurals of *Mr.* or *Mrs.*

- **Ms.** (miz) This is the spelling and punctuation for all uses of the courtesy title, including direct quotations.
  Avoid constructions which call for the use of the plural of *Ms.* (there isn't one). See **courtesy titles** for guidelines on when to use *Ms.*

- **Muhammad** The preferred spelling is *Mohammed*.

- **multi-** The rules in prefixes apply, but in general, no hyphen. Some examples:

multicolored	multilateral	multimillion	multimillionaire

- **Multigraph** A trademark for a brand of dictation machine.

- **Multilith** A trademark for a brand of duplicating machine.

- **municipal bond** See **loan terminology**.

- **murder** See the **homicide, murder, manslaughter** entry.

- **murderer** See the **assassin, killer, murderer** entry.

- **Murphy's Law** The law is: If something can go wrong, it will.

- **music** The basic guidelines for capitalization and the use of quotation marks on the titles of musical works are listed in **composition titles**.
  The names of all popular songs, videos, CDs and albums are capitalized and placed in quotation marks: *Eric Clapton's new album "Unplugged"; The single "Up to My Ears in Tears" from Alan Jackson's album, "A Lot About Livin'."*
  Capitalize, but do not use quotation marks, on descriptive titles for orchestral

works: *Bach's Suite Number One for Orchestra; Beethoven's Serenade for Flute, Violin and Viola.* If the instrumentation is not part of the title but is added for explanatory purposes, the names of the instruments are lowercased: *Mozart's Sinfonia Concertante in E flat major* (the common title) *for violin and viola.* If in doubt, lowercase the names of the instruments.

Use quotation marks for non-musical terms in a title: *Beethoven's "Eroica" Symphony.* If the work has a special full title, all of it is quoted: "Symphonie Fantastique," "Rhapsody in Blue."

In subsequent references, lowercase *symphony, rhapsody, concerto,* etc.

- **musical performers** Capitalize the names of performing groups, do not put them in quotes: *Pink Floyd, Led Zeppelin.* Capitalize informal versions of the name as well: *the Rolling Stones, the Stones.*

  Use the spelling and capitalization the individual or performer prefers: *Boyz II Men.*

- **musket** See **weapons**.

- **Muslim** The preferred term for describing adherents of Islam.

  A *Black Muslim* is a member of a predominantly black Islamic sect in the United States. However, the term is considered derogatory by members of the sect, who call themselves *Muslims*. See **Islam**.

- **Mutual News** *Mutual Radio* is acceptable in all references. On second reference, *Mutual*. Headquarters is in Arlington, Va.

  The network is now owned, along with N-B-C Radio, by the Westwood One Companies, Incorporated, which is owned by CBS.

- **Muzak** (MYOO'-zak) A trademark for a type of recorded background music.

- **Myanmar** The Southeast Asian nation formerly known as *Burma.* The capital is *Yangon,* formerly Rangoon. *Myanmar* should also be used as an adjective: *the Myanmar currency, Myanmar officials.*

- **n.** See **nouns**.

- **naive**

- **names** In general, people are entitled to be known however they want to be known, as long as their identities are clear.

When a person elects to change the name by which he or she has been known, such as Cassius Clay's transition to Muhammad Ali, provide both names in stories until the new name is known by the public. After that, use only the new name unless there is a specific reason for including the earlier identification.

Except when referring to the president or vice president and, in state copy, the governor, always use a person's first name as well as the last name on first reference.

First references to the governor of another state should include first and last name. See the **junior, senior** entry and the entries under **middle initials, nicknames;** and **sex changes**.

- **nano-** A prefix denoting one billionth of a unit.

Move the decimal point nine places to the left when converting to the basic unit: *two (b) billion nano-seconds equals two seconds.*

- **naphtha** (NAP'-thuh) See **oil**.

- **narrow-minded**

- **NASA** Acceptable in all references for the *National Aeronautics and Space Administration.*

- **Nasdaq** (NAZ'-dak) **Stock Market, The** This is the formal name of the computerized trading network that used to be known as the *National Association of Securities Dealers Automated Quotations system*—which yielded the acronym *NASDAQ.* The name was changed from the acronym in 1990.

Nasdaq does not operate from a single trading floor, but is a computer network of dealers operated by the National Association of Securities Dealers. Headquarters is in Washington. See **stock markets**.

- **national** See the **citizen, resident, subject, national, native** entry.

- **National Aeronautics and Space Administration** *NASA* and *the space agency* are acceptable on all references.

- **national anthem** Lowercase. But: *"The Star-Spangled Banner."*

- **national assembly** See **foreign legislative bodies**.

- **National Association for Stock Car Auto Racing** *NASCAR* is acceptable in all references in sports stories.
   In general news stories, spell out the name someplace in the story.

- **National Association for the Advancement of Colored People** *N-Double-A-C-P* is acceptable in all references. Headquarters is in Baltimore.

- **National Association of Letter Carriers** The shortened form *Letter Carriers union* (no apostrophe) is acceptable in all references. Headquarters is in Washington.

- **National Association of Securities Dealers** Do not abbreviate. The association operates The Nasdaq (NAZ'-dak) Stock Market. Headquarters is in Washington. See **Nasdaq Stock Market, The**.

- **National Baptist Convention of America** See **Baptist churches**.

- **National Baptist Convention, U-S-A, Incorporated** See **Baptist churches**.

- **National Broadcasting Company** See **N-B-C**.

- **national chairman** Capitalize when used as a formal title before the name of an individual who heads a political party: *Democratic National Chairman Ron Brown.*

- **National Collegiate Athletic Association** *N-C-A-A* is acceptable on all references.

- **National Conference of Catholic Bishops** See **Roman Catholic Church**.

- **National Council of the Churches of Christ in the U-S-A** This interdenominational, cooperative body includes most major Protestant and Eastern Orthodox denominations in the United States.
   The shortened form *National Council of Churches* is acceptable in all references. Headquarters is in New York. See **World Council of Churches.**

- **National Education Association** *N-E-A* is acceptable on second reference. Headquarters is in Washington.

- **National Governors' Conference** Note the apostrophe. Represents the governors of the 50 states and four territories. Its office is in Washington.

- **national guard** Capitalize when referring to national or state-level forces: *the National Guard, the Iowa National Guard, the Guard, Iowa's National Guard, National Guard troops.*
  Use lowercase for the forces of other nations.

- **National Guardsman** Not *guardman.* Capitalize as a proper noun when referring to an individual in a federal or state National Guard unit: *He is a National Guardsman.*
  Lowercase *guardsman* when it stands alone. See **military titles.**

- **National Hurricane Center** See **weather terms.**

- **National Institutes of Health** This agency within the Department of Health and Human Services is the principal biomedical research arm of the federal government. It consists of the National Library of Medicine, 12 separate institutes and various divisions that provide centralized support services for the individual institutes.
  The 12 institutes are: National Cancer Institute; National Eye Institute; National Heart, Lung, and Blood Institute; National Institute of Allergy and Infectious Diseases; National Institute of Arthritis, Metabolism, and Digestive Diseases; National Institute of Child Health and Human Development; National Institute of Dental Research; National Institute of Diabetes and Digestive and Kidney Diseases; National Institute of Environmental Health Sciences; National Institute of General Medical Sciences; National Institute of Neurological and Communicative Disorders and Stroke; National Institute on Aging.

- **nationalist** Generally, this term is descriptive of a person's political philosophy, rather than a specific party affiliation.
  Lowercase when referring to the partisan of a country.
  Capitalize only when referring to alignment with a political party for which *nationalist* is part of the proper name. See **political parties and philosophies.**

- **Nationalist China** See **China.**

- **nationalities and races** See **race** for guidelines on when racial identification is pertinent to a story.
  Derogatory racial references should be avoided unless in quoted matter that is central the story. If such references are used, flag the story. See **obscenities, profanities, vulgarities.**
  Capitalize the proper names of nationalities, peoples, races and tribes: *Arab, Arabic, African, African-American, American, Caucasian, Cherokee, Chinese* (both singular and plural), *French Canadian, Gypsy, Jew, Jewish, Latin, Oriental, Sioux,* etc.
  Lowercase *black, white, mulatto,* etc., in both noun and adjectival forms. See **colored.**

- **National Labor Relations Board** *N-L-R-B* is acceptable on second reference.

- **National League of Cities** Its members are the governments of cities and towns and some state municipal leagues.

  It is separate from the *U-S Conference of Mayors,* which has a membership limited to mayors of cities with 30,000 or more residents. The organizations often engage in joint projects, however. The office is in Washington.

- **National Organization for Women** Not *of. NOW* is acceptable on second reference. Headquarters is in Washington.

- **National Rifle Association** *N-R-A* is acceptable in second reference. Headquarters is in Washington.

- **National Weather Service** It is no longer formally called the *U-S Weather Bureau.* But *the weather service* or *the weather bureau,* lowercase, may be used in any reference. See **weather terms**.

- **nationwide**

- **native** See the **citizen, resident, subject, national, native** entry.

- **NATO** Acceptable in all references for *the North Atlantic Treaty Organization,* but use a descriptive phrase such as *the Western alliance* in the story, too.

- **natural sound** The nonverbal sound of an event.

  Natural sound can include the ambient sound of a scene (trucks rumbling down a street with cheers in the background) or be dominated by one particular sound (a band playing, a chainsaw cutting up debris from a storm).

  Natural sound should run 30 to 40 seconds, with a fade at the start and at the end. Generally, the fade at the start is fast and the fade at the end is slower.

  In writing natural sound into a story, be sure to leave enough time to establish the sound, at full volume, before fading under, so the audience recognizes it. See the entries for **actuality; q&a; scener; voicer** and **wrap**.

- **Naugahyde** A trademark for a brand of simulated leather.

- **nautical mile** It equals one minute of arc of a great circle (a circle drawn on the surface of the earth), or 6,076.12 feet — 1,852 meters.

  To convert to approximate statute miles — 5,280 feet — multiply the number of nautical miles by 1.5. See **knot**.

- **naval, navel** *Naval* pertains to a navy.

  A *navel* is a bellybutton.

  A *navel orange* is a seedless orange, so named because it has a small depression, like a *navel.*

- **naval station** Capitalize only as part of a proper name: *Norfolk Naval Station.*

- **navy** Capitalize when referring to U.S. forces: *the U-S Navy, the Navy, Navy policy.* Do not use the abbreviation *U-S-N.*
  Lowercase when referring to the naval forces of other nations: *the British navy.*
  This approach has been adopted for consistency, because many foreign nations do not use *navy* as the proper name. See **military academies** and **military titles**.

- **Nazi, Nazism** Derived from the German words for National Socialist German Workers' Party, the fascist political party founded in 1919 and abolished in 1945. Under Adolf Hitler, it seized control of Germany in 1933. See the **political parties and philosophies** entry.

- **N-B-C** Acceptable in all references for the National Broadcasting Company, a subsidiary of General Electric Company. Divisions are N-B-C News and N-B-C Television. Headquarters is in New York.
  The NBC Radio Network is now owned by Westwood One Companies, now owned by CBS.

- **N-C-R Corporation** Formerly National Cash Register Company. Headquarters is in Dayton, Ohio.

- **N-C-17** The movie rating that denotes individuals under 17 are not permitted. Previously known as the *X rating.*

- **Near East** There is no longer a substantial distinction between this term and *Middle East.* See the **Middle East** entry.

- **nearsighted** When used in a medical sense, it means an individual can see well at close range but has difficulty seeing objects at a distance.

- **Nebraska** See **state names**.

- **negligee**

- **negro, negroes** See **black; nationalities and races** and **race**.

- **neither ... nor** See the **either ... or, neither ... nor** entry.

- **Netherlands** In the body of the story, refer to it as it is commonly referred to: *the Netherlands.* But in datelines, drop *the*:

  (Amsterdam, Netherlands) — The Netherlands has announced ...

  Note also that *the Netherlands* is treated in the singular.

- **Netherlands Antilles** (an-TIL'-eez) In datelines, give the name of the community followed by *Netherlands Antilles*. Identify the individual island, if needed, in the body of the copy.

- **net income, net profit** See **profit terminology**.

- **neutron bomb** There isn't one. See the next entry.

- **neutron weapon** A small warhead designed to be mounted on a Lance missile or fired from an 8-inch gun. It produces twice the deadly radiation of older tactical nuclear weapons, but less than one-tenth the explosive power, heat and fallout. This means that the warhead can kill people without causing extensive damage to buildings and other structures.
  It is not a *bomb*. It is a *weapon* or *warhead*. The formal title for the weapon is *enhanced radiation weapon*.
  If the term *neutron bomb* is used in a direct quote, explain that it is actually a warhead that would be fired on a missile or from artillery—and not dropped, like a bomb, from a plane.

- **Nevada** See **state names**.

- **New Brunswick** One of the three Maritime Provinces of Canada. Do not abbreviate. See **datelines**.

- **New England** Connecticut, Maine, Massachusetts, New Hampshire, Rhode Island and Vermont.

- **Newfoundland** (new-fund-LAND') This Canadian province comprises the island of Newfoundland and the mainland section known as Labrador. Do not abbreviate.
  In datelines, use *Newfoundland* after the names of all cities and towns. Specify in the text whether the community is on the island or in Labrador. See **datelines**.

- **New Hampshire** See **state names**.

- **New Jersey** See **state names**.

- **New Mexico** See **state names**.

- **New Orleans** The city in Louisiana stands alone in datelines.

- **New South** The era that began in the South in the 1960s with a thriving economy and the election of officials who advocated the abolition of racial segregation.
  Old South applies to the South before the Civil War.

- **Newspaper Association of America** Formerly called American Newspaper Publishers Association. Headquarters in Reston, Va.

- **Newspaper Guild, The** Formerly the American Newspaper Guild, it is a union for newspaper and news service employees, generally those in the news and business departments.

  On second reference, *the Guild.* Headquarters is in Washington.

- **newspaper names** Capitalize the name but do not put in quotation marks.

  Capitalize *the* if that is the way the publication prefers to be known.

  Lowercase *the* if the story mentions several newspapers, some of which use *the* as part of the name and some of which do not.

  If the location is not clear from the paper's name, explain it in the copy.

- **newsstand**

- **New Testament** See **Bible**.

- **New World** The Western Hemisphere.

- **New Year's, New Year's Day, New Year's Eve** The federal legal holiday is observed on Friday if Jan. 1 falls on a Saturday, and on Monday if the Jan. 1 falls on a Sunday.

- **New York** In national copy, use *New York state* when a distinction must be made between state and city. See **state names.**

- **New York City** Use *New York* in datelines, not the name of an individual community or borough such as *Flushing* or *Queens.* Identify the borough in the body of the story if pertinent.

- **New York Stock Exchange** *NYSE (NY'-zee)* is acceptable on second reference as an adjective. Use *the stock exchange* or *the exchange* for other second references.

  The nickname *Big Board* also is acceptable. See **stock markets.**

- **nicknames** A nickname should be used in place of a person's given name in news stories only when it is the way the individual prefers to be known: *Jimmy Carter.*

  Try to avoid constructions in which a nickname is inserted into the identification of an individual: *Senator Henry Jackson* is preferable to *Senator Henry "Scoop" Jackson.* But when it is necessary to insert the nickname, put it in quotation marks. Also: *Jackson is known as "Scoop."*

  When using tape in which the person is referred to by his or her nickname, make sure the identification is clear.

  In sports stories and sports columns, commonly used nicknames may be substituted for a first name without the use of quotation marks: *Woody Hayes, Bear Bryant, Catfish Hunter, Bubba Smith,* etc. But in sports stories where the given name is used: *Paul "Bear" Bryant.*

Capitalize without quotation marks such terms as *Sunshine State, the Old Dominion, Motown, the Magic City, Old Hickory* and *Old Glory*. See **names**.

- **nightclub**

- **nighttime**

- **nit-picking**

- **nitty-gritty**

- **No.** Do not use the abbreviation *no.* for the word *number.*

- **Nobel Prizes** The five established under terms of the will of Alfred Nobel are: Nobel Peace Prize, Nobel Prize in chemistry, Nobel Prize in literature, Nobel Prize in physics, Nobel Prize in physiology or medicine. Note the capitalization styles.

The Nobel Memorial Prize in Economic Science is not a *Nobel Prize* in the same sense. The Central Bank of Sweden established it in 1968 as a memorial to Alfred Nobel. References to this prize should include the word Memorial to help make this distinction. Explain the status of the prize in the story when appropriate.

Nobel Prize award ceremonies are held on Dec. 10, the anniversary of Alfred Nobel's death in 1896. The award ceremony for peace is in Oslo and the other ceremonies are in Stockholm.

Capitalize *prize* in references that contain the word *Nobel* but do not mention the category: *He is a Nobel Prize winner. She is a Nobel Prize-winning scientist.*

Lowercase *prize* when not linked with the word *Nobel*: *The peace prize is being awarded this morning.*

- **nobility** References to members of the nobility in nations that have a system of rank present special problems because nobles frequently are known by their titles rather than their given or family names. Their titles, in effect, become their names.

The guidelines here relate to Britain's nobility. Adapt them as appropriate to members of the nobility in other nations.

Orders of rank among British nobility begin with the royal family. The term *royalty* is reserved for the families of living and deceased sovereigns.

Next, in descending order, are dukes, marquesses (also called marquises), earls, viscounts and barons. Many hold inherited titles; others have been raised to the nobility by the sovereign for their lifetimes. Occasionally the sovereign raises an individual to the nobility and makes the title inheritable by the person's heirs, but the practice is increasingly rare.

Sovereigns also confer honorary titles, which do not make an individual a member of the nobility. The principal designations, in descending order, are baronet and knight.

In general, the guidelines in **courtesy titles** and **titles** apply. However, honorary titles and titles of nobility are capitalized when they serve as an alternate name.

Some guidelines and examples:

Royalty: Capitalize *king, queen, prince* and *princess* when they are used directly before one or more names. Lowercase when they stand alone: *Queen Elizabeth the Second, the queen, Kings George and Edward, Queen Mother Elizabeth, the queen mother.* Also capitalize a longer form of the sovereign's title when its use is necessary: *Her Majesty Queen Elizabeth.* But as a general rule, keep the title as short as possible.

Use *Prince* or *Princess* before the names of a sovereign's children: *Princess Anne, the princess.*

The male heir to the throne normally is designated *Prince of Wales*, and the title becomes, in common usage, an alternate name: *The queen invested her eldest son as Prince of Wales. Prince Charles is now the Prince of Wales. The prince is a bachelor. Charles, Prince of Wales, has separated from his wife. Diana remains the Princess of Wales.*

Duke: The full title—*Duke of Wellington*, for example—is an alternative name, capitalized in all uses. Lowercase *duke* when it stands alone.

The designation *Arthur, Duke of Wellington*, is correct but generally should be avoided. Never use *Duke Arthur* or *Lord Arthur.*

On second reference, the British often refer to nobility by the proper name of the title: *The Duke of Wellington* on first reference, *Wellington* on the second. Avoid this construction. On second reference, use *the duke.*

The wife of a *duke* is a *duchess* (note: no *t*): *the Duchess of Wellington, the duchess,* but never *Duchess Diana* or *Lady Diana.*

A duke normally also has a lesser title. It commonly is used for his eldest son, if he has one. Use the courtesy title *Lord* or *Lady* before the first names of a duke's child. Some examples:

Lady Jane Wellesley, only daughter of the eighth Duke of Wellington, has been linked romantically with Prince Charles, heir to the British throne. One of Lady Jane's four brothers is Arthur Charles, the Marquess Douro. The Wellingtons, whose family name is Wellesley, are not of royal blood. But they rank among the nation's most famous aristocrats thanks to the first duke, who was the victor over Napoleon at Waterloo.

Marquess (MAHR'-kwis), marquis (mahr-KEE'), earl, viscount, baron: The full titles serve as alternate names and should be capitalized. Frequently, however, the holder of such a title is identified as a lord: *the Marquess of Bath*, for example, is more commonly known as *Lord Bath.*

Use *Lady* before the name of a woman married to a man who holds one of these titles. The wife of a marquess is a marchioness (mahr-shun-ES'), the wife of a marquis is a marquise (mahr-KEZ'), the wife of an earl is a countess (earl is the British equivalent of count), the wife of a viscount is a viscountess, and the wife of a baron is a baroness.

Use *Lord* or *Lady* before the first names of children of a marquess.

Use *Lady* before the first name of the daughter of an earl.

The Honorable often appears before the names of sons of earls, viscounts and barons who do not have titles. Their names should stand alone in news stories, however.

The Honorable also appears frequently before the names of unmarried daughters of viscounts and barons. Their names should stand alone in news stories, however. Some examples:

Queen Elizabeth gave her sister's husband the title Earl of Snowdon. Their son, David, is the Viscount Linley. They also have a daughter, Lady Sarah Armstrong-Jones. Lord Snowdon, who is a photographer, was known as Anthony Armstrong-Jones before he received his title.

Baronet, knight: Use *Sir* before a name if appropriate in the context; otherwise, follow routine practice for names: *Sir Harold Wilson* on first reference, *Sir Harold*—not *Sir Wilson*—on second. Or *Prime Minister Harold Wilson* on first reference, *Wilson* on second.

Do not use both an honorary title and a title of authority such as *prime minister* before a name.

Use *Lady* before the name of the wife of a baronet or a knight.

For a woman who has received an honor in her own right, use *Dame* before her name if it is the way she is known or if it is appropriate to the context: *Dame Margot Fonteyn* on first reference, *Dame Margot* on second.

- **nobody**

- **noisome, noisy** *Noisome* means offensive or noxious. Don't use it. *Noisy* refers to something that makes a lot of noise.

- **nolo contendere** (NOH'-lo kohn-TEN'-duh-reh) The literal meaning is, "I do not wish to contend." Terms such as *no contest* or *no-contest plea* are acceptable in all references.

When defendants in a criminal case enter this plea, it means they are not admitting guilt and are stating that they will offer no defense. The person is then subject to being judged guilty and punished as if a guilty plea had been entered or a conviction won. The principal difference is that the defendant retains the option of denying the same charge in another legal proceeding.

- **no man's land**

- **non-** Hyphenate all except the following words, which have specific meanings of their own:

nonchalance	nondescript	nonsense	nonsensical
nonchalant			

This rule is an exception to general usage and is for readability.

- **non-aligned nations** A political rather than economic or geographic term. The term has lost much of its relevance with the dissolution of the Warsaw Pact: There no longer are two dominant, competing blocs of nations.

Non-aligned nations do not profess to be neutral, like Switzerland. Rather, they present themselves as activist alternatives.

Do not confuse *non-aligned* with *Third World*, although many Third World nations belong to the non-aligned group. See the **Third World** entry.

- **non-controversial** All issues are controversial.
A *non-controversial issue* is impossible. A *controversial issue* is redundant.

- **none** It usually means *no single one*. When used in this sense, it always takes singular verbs and pronouns: *None of the seats was in its right place.*
Use a plural verb only if the sense is *no two* or *no amount: None of the consultants agree on the same approach. None of the taxes have been paid.*

- **non-restrictive clauses** See the **essential clauses, non-essential clauses** entry.

- **noon** Do not put a *12* in front of it. See **midnight** and **times**.

- **no one**

- **norm** A standard, model or pattern for a group. See the **average, mean, median, norm** entry.

- **north, northeast, northern, northwest** See the **directions and regions** entry.

- **North America** See **Western Hemisphere**.

- **North Atlantic Treaty Organization** *NATO* is acceptable in all references, but use somewhere in the copy a term such as *the alliance* or *the Western alliance*.

- **North Carolina** See **state names**.

- **North-Central Region** As defined by the Census Bureau, the 12-state region is broken into eastern and western divisions.
The five *East North-Central* states are Illinois, Indiana, Michigan, Ohio and Wisconsin.
The seven *West North-Central* states are Iowa, Kansas, Minnesota, Missouri, Nebraska, North Dakota and South Dakota. See **Northeast region; South;** and **West** for the bureau's other regional breakdowns.

- **North Dakota** See **state names**.

- **Northeast region** As defined by the Census Bureau, the nine-state region is broken into two divisions—he *New England* states and the *Middle Atlantic* states.
Connecticut, Maine, Massachusetts, New Hampshire, Rhode Island and

Vermont are the *New England* states.

New Jersey, New York and Pennsylvania are classified as the *Middle Atlantic* states. See **North-Central region; South** and **West** for the bureau's other regional breakdowns.

- **Northern Ireland** It is a British province located on the same island as the Republic of Ireland. Use *Northern Ireland* after the names of all communities in datelines. See **datelines** and **United Kingdom**.

- **Northrop Grumman Corporation** Headquarters is in Los Angeles.

- **North Slope** The portion of Alaska north of Brooks Range, a string of mountains extending across the northern part of the state.

- **Northwest Orient Airlines** *Northwest Airlines* is acceptable in all references. Headquarters is in St. Paul, Minn.

- **North Warning System** A series of radar stations near the 70th parallel in North America. Formerly known as the Distant Early Warning Line.

- **Northwest Territories** A territorial section of Canada. Do not abbreviate. Use in datelines after the names of all cities and towns in the territory.

  If necessary, specify in the copy whether the community is in one of the three territorial subdivisions: *Franklin, Keewatin* and *Mackenzie*. See **Canada**.

- **note** For use in a financial sense, see **loan terminology**.

- **nouns** The abbreviation *n.* is used in this book to identify the spelling of the noun forms of words frequently misspelled.

- **Nova Scotia** One of the three Maritime Provinces of Canada. Do not abbreviate. See **datelines**.

- **November** See **months**.

- **Novocain** A trademark for a drug used as a local anesthetic. It also may be called *procaine*.

- **nowadays** Not *nowdays*. In any case, avoid it except in quoted matter.

- **Nuclear Regulatory Commission** This commission has taken over the regulatory functions previously performed by the Atomic Energy Commission.

  N-R-C is acceptable on second reference, but *the agency* or *the commission* is preferred.

- **nuclear terminology** In reporting on nuclear energy, include the definitions of appropriate terms, especially those related to radiation.

Core: The part of a nuclear reactor that contains its fissionable fuel. In a *reactor core*, atoms of fuel, such as uranium, are split. This releases energy in the form of heat which, in turn, is used to boil water for steam. The steam powers a turbine, and the turbine drives a generator to produce electricity.

Fission: The splitting of the nucleus of an atom, releasing energy.

Meltdown: The worst possible nuclear accident, in which the reactor core overheats to such a degree that the fuel melts. If the fuel penetrates its protective housing, radioactive materials will be released into the environment.

Rad: The standard unit of measurement for absorbed radiation. A *millirad* is a thousandth of a rad. There is considerable debate among scientists as to whether there is any safe level of absorption.

Radiation: Invisible particles or waves given off by radioactive material, such as uranium. Radiation can damage or kill body cells, resulting in latent cancers, genetic damage or death.

Rem: The standard unit of measurement of absorbed radiation in living tissue, adjusted for different kinds of radiation so that one rem of any radiation will produce the same biological effect. A *millirem* is a thousandth of a rem.

A diagnostic chest X-ray involves between 20 millirems and 30 millirems of radiation. Each American, on average, receives 100 millirems to 200 millirems of radiation a year from natural background sources, such as cosmic rays, and man-made sources, such as diagnostic X-rays. There is considerable debate among scientists over the safety of repeated low doses of radiation.

Roentgen (RENT'-gen): The standard measure of X-ray exposure.

Uranium: A metallic, radioactive element used as fuel in nuclear reactors.

- **numerals** A numeral is a figure, letter, word or group of words expressing a number.

The goal is to write so that an announcer reading the copy cold can do so easily and correctly. Follow these guidelines:
- Spell out the numbers one through eleven.
- Use Arabic numerals—the figures *1,2,3,4,5,6,7,8,9* and *0*—for the numbers 12 through 999.

Numerals such as *one, two, ten, 101,* etc., are called *cardinal numbers.* The term *ordinal numbers* refers to *first, second, tenth* and *101st.*

Large numbers: Use words to express *thousands, (m) millions, (b) billions* and *(t) trillions.* Numerals above 1,000 and below 10,000 are normally expressed using *thousand,* but can be expressed using *hundreds* if it is more conversational: *two-thousand dollars,* but *12-hundred dollars.*

Use a hyphen to combine numbers and the word *hundreds* or *thousands: It will cost 45-thousand dollars. He spent 15-hundred dollars.*

Hyphens are not needed to connect numbers with *(m) millions, (b) billions* and *(t) trillions: The comet will travel seven (m) million miles. It will be a seven (m) million mile journey.*

To guard against typos, *(m) millions, (b) billions* and *(t) trillions* should be preceded by the word's first letter in parentheses: *45 (m) million; 118 (b) billion; two (t) trillion.*

Start of sentence: Spell out any numeral that starts a sentence: *Thirty-seven people have been nominated for governor. Twelve-hundred petitions have been*

Exception: do not spell out a year at the start of a sentence: *1992 was a good year for the Democrats.*

Roman numerals: Don't use them. Convert them to regular numerals and follow the rules elsewhere in this entry: *World War Two, Native Dancer the Second, King George the Sixth, Pope John the 23rd.*

Ordinals: Follow the same pattern, with one through eleven spelled out: *First, fifth, eleventh,* etc.

Use figures to express ordinals 12 through 999: *12th, 14th, 234th, 819th.*

Fractions: Should be spelled out, using the appropriate combination of words: *two-tenths; three-fifths; eight-hundredths.* See **fractions**.

Decimals: Always spell them out. Use hyphens, and the word *point*: *five-point-three, point-two, point-oh-one, 137 point-seven.*

Decimalization should exceed two places only when crucial to the story. A number that appears *.005* on the printed page needs to be translated for broadcast. It should be treated as a fraction rather than a decimal: *He won by five-thousandths of a second.* See **decimal units**.

Proper names: use words or figures and capitalize according to an organization's practice: *20th Century Fox, Twentieth Century Fund, Big Ten.*

Performing groups and album names: use words or figures and capitalize according to the group's practice: *U-2, Boyz II Men.*

Similarly, write the name of albums and CDs as they appear on the work itself: *The album "2Pocalypse Now."* See **music; musical performers; composition titles**.

In addition, these separate entries contain information relevant to the use of numerals:

act numbers	**highway designations**
addresses	**lattitude and longitude**
ages	**(m) millions, (b) billions**
aircraft names	**monetary figures**
amendments to the Constitution	**page numbers**
betting odds	**parallels**
channel	**percentages**
chapters	**political divisions**
congressional districts	**proportions**
court decisions	**ratios**
court names	**room numbers**
dates	**route numbers**
decades	**scene numbers**
dimensions	**scores**
district	**serial numbers**
earthquakes	**spacecraft designations**
election returns	**speeds**
fleet	**telephone numbers**
handicaps	**temperatures**

See also **apostrophe; hyphen** and entries for individual sports.

- **nuns** See **sister**.

- **Nuremberg** Use this spelling for the city in Germany, instead of *Nuernberg*, in keeping with widespread practice.

- **nylon** Not a trademark.

- **oasis, oases**

- **obscenities, profanities, vulgarities** Do not use them in stories unless they are part of direct quotations and there is a compelling reason for them.

Do not use a profanity, obscenity or vulgarity in a live program without the prior approval of the supervisor or, whenever possible, an assistant managing editor. If such use is approved, advise the members in an advisory. Be certain that you include the potentially offensive words in the advisory, so each station can make an informed choice whether to carry the program:

Please note that the xxx story contains the word xxxx.

When a profanity, obscenity or vulgarity must be used on the wire, flag the story at the top:

(News directors: portions of the following may be offensive to some listeners. Note word xxx in xx paragraph.)

When a profanity, obscenity or vulgarity must be used in a spot or pre-recorded program on the radio network, flag the item before and after its billboard:

(News directors: the following cut contains the word xxxx.)

(News directors: the preceding cut contains the word xxxx.)

These guidelines apply also to stories in which the subject matter may be considered offensive even though the story does not contain profanity.

Be guided by the principal that the member, who is the broadcast licensee, must always be given the opportunity to choose whether to air a program, piece or script that might be offensive to its audience. This is particularly important because the taste standards that apply in some radio formats clearly do not apply in others.

In reporting profanity that normally would use the words *damn* or *god*, lowercase *god* and use the following forms: *damn, damn it, goddamn it.* Do not change the offending words to euphemisms. Do not, for example, change *damn it* to *darn it.*

For guidelines on racial and ethnic slurs, see the **nationalities and races** entry.

• **Occident, Occidental** Capitalize when referring to Europe, the Western Hemisphere or an inhabitant of these regions. Whenever possible, use a more conversational term.

• **Occidental Petroleum Corporation** Headquarters is in Los Angeles.

• **Occupational Safety and Health Administration** *OSHA* is acceptable on second reference.

• **occupational titles** They always are lowercased. See **titles**.

• **occur, occurred, occurring** Also: *occurrence.*

• **ocean-going**

• **oceans** The five, from the largest to the smallest: Pacific Ocean, Atlantic Ocean, Indian Ocean, Antarctic Ocean, Arctic Ocean.
  Lowercase *ocean* when it stands alone or in plural uses: *the ocean, the Atlantic and Pacific oceans.*

• **October** See **months**.

• **odd-** Follow with a hyphen:

odd-looking   odd-numbered

• **odds** See **betting odds**.

• **oddsmaker**

• **off-, -off** Follow Webster's New World Dictionary. Hyphenate if not listed there. Some commonly used combinations with a hyphen:

off-color   off-season   send-off   stop-off
off-peak   off-white

Some combinations without a hyphen:

blastoff   offshore   offstage   standoff
cutoff   offside   playoff   takeoff
offhand   offset

• **off-Broadway, off-off-Broadway** See the **Broadway, off-Broadway, off-off-Broadway** entry.

- **office** Capitalize *office* when it is part of an agency's formal name: *Office of Management and Budget.*
  Lowercase all other uses, including phrases such as: *the office of the attorney general, the U-S attorney's office.* See **Oval Office.**

- **officeholder**

- **off of** The *of* is unnecessary: *He fell off the bed.* Not: *He fell off of the bed.*

- **Ohio** See **state names.**

- **oil** In shipping, oil and oil products normally are measured by the ton. For news stories, convert these tonnage figures to gallons.
  In international oil transactions, there are 42 gallons to each barrel of oil. The number of barrels per ton varies, depending on the type of oil product.
  To convert tonnage to gallons:
  - Determine the type of oil.
  - Consult the table which follows to find out how many barrels per ton for that type of oil.
  - Multiply the number of tons by the number of barrels per ton. The result is the number of barrels in the shipment.
  - Multiply the number of barrels by 42. The result is the number of gallons.
  Example: A tanker spills 20,000 metric tons of foreign crude. The table shows

OIL EQUIVALENCY TABLE

Type of Product	Barrels Per Short Ton (2,000 lbs.)	Barrels per Metric Ton (2,204.6 lbs.)	Barrels per Long Ton (2,240 lbs.)
crude oil, foreign	6.349	6.998	7.111
crude oil, domestic	6.770	7.463	7.582
gasoline and naphtha	7.721	8.511	8.648
kerosene	7.053	7.775	7.900
distillate fuel oil	6.580	7.253	7.369
residual fuel oil	6.041	6.660	6.766
lubricating oil	6.349	6.998	7.111
lubricating grease	6.665	7.346	7.464
wax	7.134	7.864	7.990
asphalt	5.540	6.106	6.205
coke	4.990	5.500	5.589
road oil	5.900	6.503	6.608
jelly and petrolatum	6.665	7.346	7.464
liquefied pet. gas	10.526	11.603	11.789
Gilsonite	5.515	6.080	6.177

- Table: The table above is based on figures supplied by the American Petroleum

6.998 barrels of foreign crude per metric ton. 6.998 times 20,000 equals 139,960 barrels, times 42 gallons per barrel equals 5,878,320 gallons.

- **Oil, Chemical and Atomic Workers International Union** The shortened forms *Oil Workers union, Chemical Workers union* and *Atomic Workers union* are acceptable in all references. Headquarters is in Denver.

- **O-K, O-K'd, O-K'ing, O-K's** Do not use *okay.*

- **Oklahoma** See **state names.**

- **Oklahoma City** Stands alone in datelines.

- **Old City of Jerusalem** The walled part of the city.

- **Old South** The South before the Civil War. See **New South.**

- **Old Testament** See **Bible.**

- **old-time, old-timer, old times**

- **Old West** The American West as it was being settled in the 19th century.

- **Old World** The Eastern Hemisphere: Asia, Europe, Africa. The term also may be used in referring to European culture and customs.

- **Olympic Airways** Headquarters is in Athens, Greece.

- **olympics** Capitalize all references to the international athletic contests held every two years: *the Olympics, the Winter Olympics, the Olympic Games, the Games, an Olympic-sized pool.*
  An Olympic-sized pool is 50 meters long by 25 meters wide.
  Lowercase all other uses: *a beer-drinking olympics.*

- **on** Do not use *on* before a date or day of the week when its absence would not lead to confusion: *The meeting will be held Monday. He will be inaugurated January 20th.*
  Use *on* to avoid an awkward juxtaposition of a date and a proper name: *John met Mary on Monday. He told Carter on Thursday that the bill was doomed.*
  If you find yourself needing to use *on* to avoid any suggestion that a date is the object of a transitive verb—*The House killed on Tuesday a bid to raise taxes*—rewrite the sentence to put the date first: *On Tuesday, the House killed a bid to raise taxes.*

- **one-** Hyphenate when used in writing fractions:

    one-half   one-third

Constructions such as *a-half* or *a-third* are equally acceptable and often make the copy more conversational. See **fractions**.

- **one another** See the **each other, one another** entry.

- **one man, one vote** The adjective form: *one-man, one-vote*. Some examples: *He supports the principle of one man, one vote. The one-man, one-vote rule.*

- **one-sided**

- **one time, one-time** *He did it one time. He is a one-time winner.*

- **Ontario** This Canadian province is the nation's first in total population and second to Quebec in area. Do not abbreviate. See **datelines**.

- **operas** See **composition titles**.

- **opinion polls** See the **polls and surveys** entry.

- **opossum** The only North American marsupial. No apostrophe is needed to indicate missing letters in a phrase such as *playing possum*.

- **option** In a financial sense, the word means an agreement that allows a person or a corporation to buy or sell something, such as shares of stock, within a stipulated time and for a certain price.
  A *put option* gives the holder the right to sell blocks of 100 shares of stock within a specified time at an agreed-upon price.
  A *call option* gives the holder the right to buy blocks of 100 shares of stock within a specified time at an agreed-upon price.

- **oral, verbal, written** Use *oral* to refer to spoken words: *He gave an oral promise.*
  Use *verbal* to compare words with some other form of communications: *His tears revealed the sentiments that his poor verbal skills could not express.*
  Use *written* to refer to words committed to paper: *We had a written agreement.*

- **ordinal numbers** See **numerals**.

- **Oregon** See **state names**.

- **Oreo** A trademark for a brand of chocolate sandwich cookie held together by a white filling.
  The use of the term by blacks indicates belief that a person is "black outside but white inside." Do not use the word in this sense except in quoted matter.

- **Organization of American States** *O-A-S* is acceptable on second reference. Headquarters is in Washington.

- **Organization of Petroleum Exporting Countries** *OPEC* is acceptable in all references, but be sure to further identify it somewhere in the copy with a term such as *the oil cartel.*
  The 13 *OPEC* members: *Algeria, Ecuador, Gabon, Indonesia, Iran, Iraq, Kuwait, Libya, Nigeria, Qatar, Saudi Arabia, United Arab Emirates, Venezuela.* Headquarters is in Vienna, Austria.

- **organizations and institutions** They are best referred to by their most recognizable names. For example, the *National Aeronautics and Space Administration* is most commonly called *NASA* or *the space agency,* and can be referred to in those ways in all references.
  Capitalize the full names of organizations and institutions: *the American Medical Association, First Presbyterian Church, General Motors Corporation, Harvard University, Harvard University Medical School, the Procrastinators Club, the Society of Professional Journalists, Sigma Delta Chi.*
  Retain capitalization if *company, corporation* or a similar word is dropped from the proper name: *General Motors Corporation, General Motors.* See **company; corporation** and **incorporated**.
  Some further guidelines:
  Internal elements: Use lowercase for internal elements of an organization when they have names that are widely used generic terms: *the board of directors of General Motors, the Columbia University board of trustees, the history department at Harvard University.*
  Capitalize internal elements of an organization when they have names that are not widely used generic terms: *the General Assembly of the World Council of Churches, the House of Delegates of the American Medical Association, the House of Bishops and House of Deputies of the Episcopal Church.*
  Informalized names: The names of organizations and institutions should be informalized whenever possible. As a general principle, use the most familiar, least cumbersome form of a name. OPEC, for example, is formally called *the Organization of Petroleum Exporting Countries,* but is most commonly called by its acronym or *the oil cartel.*
  Do not informalize names when the formal version is better-known: *Massachusetts Institute of Technology* or *M-I-T* is better than *the technology institute.*
  Flip-flopped names: Perhaps the most-used method of informalizing a name is to flip the words to delete the word *of.* In such a case, retain capitalization: *College of the Holy Cross, Holy Cross College; Department of State, State Department; Harvard School of Dental Medicine, Harvard Dental School.*
  In those cases where the *of* construction is better-known— *Massachusetts Institute of Technology*—don't use the flipped construction.
  Subsidiaries: Capitalize the names of major subdivisions: *The Pontiac Motor Division of General Motors, Pontiac.*
  Abbreviations and acronyms: Many organizations are widely known by an

abbreviation: *Alcoa, G-O-P, N-Double-A-C-P, N-C-A-A*. Others are best-known by an acronym: *NATO, NASA*. The general rule is to use the construction which is most familiar, but for specific guidelines, see an organization's individual listing or **abbreviations; acronyms** and **second reference**.

• **Orient, Oriental** Capitalize when referring to the Far East nations of Asia and the nearby islands. Asian is the preferred term for an inhabitant of these regions. Also **Oriental rug.**

• **Orlon** A trademark for a form of acrylic fiber similar to nylon.

• **orthodox** Capitalize when referring to membership in or the activities of an Eastern Orthodox church. See **Eastern Orthodox churches**.

Capitalize also in reference to the Orthodox expression of Judaism: *Orthodox Judaism* or *Orthodox Jew*. See **Jewish congregations**.

Do not describe a member of an Eastern Orthodox church as a *Protestant*. Use a phrase such as *Orthodox Christian* instead.

Lowercase *orthodox* in nonreligious uses: *an orthodox procedure.*

• **Orthodox Church in America** See **Eastern Orthodox churches**.

• **Oscar, Oscars** Acceptable on first reference to the **Academy Awards**. See that entry.

• **oscillating theory** See **big-bang theory**.

• **Ottawa** The capital of Canada stands alone in datelines.

• **Ouija** (WEE'-juh) A trademark for a board used in spiritual seances.

• **ounce** (dry) Units of dry volume are not customarily carried to this level. See **pint (dry)**.

• **ounce** (liquid) See **fluid ounce**.

• **ounce** (weight) It is defined as 437.5 grains. The metric equivalent is about 28 grams.

To convert to grams, multiply by 28: 5 ounces times 28 equals 140 grams. See **grain; gram**.

• **out-** Follow Webster's New World. Hyphenate if not listed there. Some frequently used words:

outargue	outfield	outpost	outscore
outbox (adj.)	outfox	output	outstrip
outdated	outpatient (n., adj.)		

• **-out** Follow Webster's New World. Hyphenate nouns and adjectives not listed there. Some frequently used words (all nouns):

cop-out	fallout	hide-out	walkout
fade-out	flameout	pullout	washout

Two words for verbs:

fade out	pull out	walk out	wash out
hide out			

• **Outer Banks** The sandy islands along the North Carolina coast.

• **out of bounds** But as a modifier: *out-of-bounds. The ball went out of bounds. He took an out-of-bounds pass.*

• **out of court, out-of-court** *They settled out of court. He accepted an out-of-court settlement.*

• **Oval Office** The White House office of the president.

• **over** It generally refers to spatial relationships: *The plane flew over the city.* It can, at times, be used with numerals: *She is over 30. I paid over $200 for this suit.* But *more than* may be better: *Their salaries went up more than $20 a week.* Let your ear be your guide.

• **over-** Follow Webster's New World. A hyphen is seldom used. Some frequently used words:

overbuy	overexert	overrate	override

See the **overall** entry.

• **-over** Follow Webster's New World. Hyphenate if not listed there.
Some frequently used words (all are nouns; some also are used as adjectives):

carry-over	stopover	takeover	walkover
holdover			

Use two words when any of these occurs as a verb. See **suffixes**.

• **overall** A single word in adjectival and adverbial use: *Overall, the Democrats succeeded. Overall policy.*
The word for the garment is *overalls.*

• **over the counter** A term for the method of trading in which securities are not listed on a recognized securities exchange with a trading floor. Over-the-counter transactions take place on **The Nasdaq Stock Market**. See that entry

- **owner** Not a formal title. Always lowercase: *Atlanta Braves owner Ted Turner.*

- **Oyez** (OH′-yes) Not *oyes*. The cry of court and public officials to command silence.

- **Ozark Mountains** Or simply: *the Ozarks.*

- **Pablum** A trademark for a soft, bland food for infants.
The word *pabulum* (note the additional *u*) means any oversimplified or bland writing or idea.

- **pabulum** See the previous entry.

- **pacemaker** Formerly a trademark, now a generic term for a device that electronically helps a person's heart maintain a steady beat.

- **Pacific Ocean** See **oceans**.

- **Pacific Standard time (p-s-t), Pacific Daylight Time (p-d-t)**
See **time zones**.

- **Pacific Ten Conference** Arizona, Arizona State, California, Oregon, Oregon State, Southern Cal, Stanford, UCLA , Washington, Washington State.
Pac-Ten is acceptable on second reference.

- **paddy wagon** Don't use except in quoted matter.

- **page numbers** Follow the rules for **numerals** and capitalize: *Page One, Page 12.*
When a letter is appended to the numeral, capitalize and use a hyphen: *Page One-A, Page 12-A.*

- **paintings** See **composition titles**.

- **palate, palette, pallet** *Palate* is the roof of the mouth and also can refer to culinary taste.
A *palette* is an artist's paint board.
A *pallet* is a bed.

- **Palestine Liberation Organization** Not *Palestinian*. *P-L-O* is acceptable on second reference. Headquarters is in Gaza City.

- **pan-** A suffix meaning "all." It takes no hyphen when combined with a common noun:

panchromatic   pantheism

Most combinations with *pan* are proper nouns, however, and they are hyphenated:

pan-African   pan-Asiatic
pan-American

- **Panama City** Use *Panama City, Florida,* or *Panama City, Panama,* in datelines to avoid confusion between the two.

- **pantsuit** Not *pants suit.*

- **pantyhose**

- **papal nuncio** Do not confuse with an *apostolic delegate.* See the **apostolic delegate, papal nuncio** entry.

- **Pap test, Pap smear** After George Papanicolaou, the American anatomist who developed this test for cervical and uterine cancer.

- **parallel, paralleled, paralleling**

- **parallels** Follow the rules for **numerals** and lowercase when referring to the imaginary locater lines that ring the globe from east to west. They are measured in units of zero to 90 degrees north or south of the equator.
  Note that they are rarely used in routine copy; only when a parallel is used as a specific marker (as in *the 38th parallel* in Korea) should it be referred to in a story. Examples: *the fourth parallel north, the 89th parallel south.* If, as in the Korean example, the location north or south of the equator is obvious: *the 38th parallel.* See **latitude and longitude.**

- **Paramount Communications, Incorporated** Headquarters is in New York.

- **pardon, parole, probation** The terms often are confused, but each has a specific meaning. Do not use them interchangeably.
  A *pardon* forgives and releases a person from further punishment. It is granted by a chief of state or a governor. By itself, it does not expunge a record of conviction, if one exists, and it does not by itself restore civil rights.
  A *general pardon,* usually for political offenses, is called *amnesty.*
  Parole is the release of a prisoner before the sentence has expired, on condition of good behavior. It is granted by a parole board, part of the executive branch of government, and can be revoked only by the board.
  Probation is the suspension of sentence for a person convicted, but not yet imprisoned, on condition of good behavior. It is imposed and revoked only by a judge.

• **parentheses ( )** Use them sparingly. Parentheses on the broadcast wires are used primarily to set off material that should not be read on the air.

Some guidelines:

Datelines: Always enclose datelines in parentheses. See **datelines**.

Pronouncers: Phonetic guides to pronunciation should be enclosed in parentheses. See **pronouncers**.

Parenthetical phrases: Do not enclose them in parentheses. If something is important enough to include in the story, even parenthetically, then write it in such a way that the parenthetical nature of the material is clear.

Wrong: *Mrs. Schroeder (who was first elected to Congress in 1972) has never lost a statewide election.*

Right: *Mrs. Schroeder was first elected to Congress in 1972. She has never lost a statewide election.*

(Correct): Do not use this construction to indicate than an unlikely looking piece of information is correct. Instead, put an advisory at the bottom of the copy and enclose it in parentheses as indicated in the next section.

Advisories: Use parentheses to set off advisory information from the rest of a story. Use this construction when flagging a story for possibly offensive content, when including an address or telephone number that is not appropriate for inclusion in the script itself, or when indicating that a piece of information that looks unlikely actually is correct.

Some examples:

(News directors: The passenger count of "two" in graf three is correct.)

(The toll-free telephone number is xxxxx.)

(The news conference is scheduled to begin at 2 p.m.)

See **obscenities, profanities, vulgarities;** and the entries for **addresses** and **telephone numbers**.

Party affiliation: Do not use parentheses to set off a person's political party affiliation. Work the information into the sentence where relevant. See **party affiliation**.

Punctuation: Place commas, periods and other punctuation marks outside and after the parentheses: *the unlikely grouping of Peres (PEH'-rehs), Smith, Jones and Shamir (shah-MEER').*

• **parent-teacher association** Note the hyphen. *P-T-A* is acceptable in all references.

Capitalize when part of a proper name: *the Franklin School Parent-Teacher Association* or *the Franklin School P-T-A.*

• **pari-mutuel**

• **Paris** The city in France stands alone in datelines.

- **parish** Capitalize as part of the formal name of a church congregation or a governmental jurisdiction: *St. John's Parish, Jefferson Parish.*
  Lowercase when standing alone or in plural combinations: *the parish, St. John's and St. Mary's parishes, Jefferson and Plaquemines parishes.* See **county** for additional guidelines on governmental jurisdictions.

- **parishioner**

- **Parkinson's disease** After James Parkinson, the English physician who described this degenerative disease of later life.

- **Parkinson's law** After C. Northcote Parkinson, the British economist who came to the satirical conclusion that work expands to fill the time allotted to it.

- **parliament** See **foreign legislative bodies**.

- **parliamentary** Lowercase unless part of a proper name.

- **parole** See the **pardon, parole, probation** entry.

- **partial quotes** See **quotation marks** and **quotations in the news.**

- **particles** See **foreign particles**.

- **part time, part-time** Hyphenate when used as a compound modifier: *She works part time. She has a part-time job.*

- **party** See the following entry and the one called **political parties and philosophies.**

- **party affiliation** Let relevance be the guide in determining whether to include a political figure's party affiliation in a story.
  Party affiliation is pointless in some stories, such as an account of a governor accepting a button from a poster child.
  It will occur naturally in many political stories.
  For stories between these extremes, include party affiliation if the audience needs it for understanding or is likely to be curious about what it is.
  Party affiliations should not be abbreviated. The following forms are acceptable: *Democratic Senator George McGovern of South Dakota; Senator George McGovern, the South Dakota Democrat; Senator George McGovern disagreed. The South Dakota Democrat said...*
  In stories about party meetings, such as a report on a political convention, no specific reference to party affiliation is needed unless the individual in question is not a member of the party in question. See **legislative titles**.

- **pass** See the **adopt, approve, enact, pass** entry.

- **passenger lists** When providing a list of victims in a disaster, arrange names alphabetically according to last name, include street address if available, and use a paragraph for each name:
  Jones, Joseph, 260 Town Street, Sample, New York.
  Williams, Susan, 780 Main Street, Example, New Jersey.

- **passenger-mile** One passenger carried one mile, or its equivalent, such as two passengers carried one-half mile.

- **passer-by, passers-by**

- **Passover** The week-long Jewish commemoration of the deliverance of the ancient Hebrews from slavery in Egypt. Occurs in March or April.

- **pasteurize**

- **pastor** See **religious titles** and the entry for the individual's denomination.

- **patriarch** Lowercase when describing someone of great age and dignity.
  Capitalize as a formal title before a name in some relgious uses. See **Eastern Orthodox churches; religious titles** and **Roman Catholic Church**.

- **patrol, patrolled, patrolling**

- **patrolman, patrolwoman, policeman, policewoman** Or *police officer.* But not *cop.*
  Capitalize before a name only if the word is a formal title. See **titles**.

- **payload**

- **peacekeeping** No hyphen.

- **peacemaker, peacemaking**

- **peace offering**

- **peacetime**

- **peacock** It applies only to the male. The female is a *peahen (PEE' -hen).* Both are *peafowl.*

- **peck** A unit of dry measure equal to eight dry quarts or one-quarter of a bushel.
  The metric equivalent is about 8.8 liters.
  To convert to liters, multiply the peck measurement by 8.8: 5 pecks times 8.8 equals 44 liters. See **liter**.

- **pedal, peddle**   When riding a bicycle or similar vehicle, you *pedal* it. When selling something, you may *peddle* it.

- **peddler**

- **Peking**   See **Beijing**.

- **pell-mell**

- **penance**   See **sacraments**.

- **peninsula**   Capitalize as part of a proper name: *the Florida Peninsula, the Upper Peninsula of Michigan.*

- **penitentiary**   See the **prison, jail** entry.

- **Pennsylvania**   Legally a commonwealth, not a state. See **state** and **state names**.

- **Pennsylvania Dutch**   The individuals are of German descent. The word *Dutch* is a corruption of *Deutsch*, the German word for "German."

- **penny-wise**   See **-wise**.
  Also: *pound-foolish.*

- **Pentecost**   The seventh Sunday after Easter.

- **Pentecostalism**   See **religious movements**.

- **people, persons**   Use them as they are used in conversation.
  Person is used when referring to an individual: *One person is waiting for the bus.*
  People is used in plural references: *Thousands of people were there. Five people were hurt.*
  People also is a collective noun that takes a plural verb when used to refer to a single race or nation: *The American people are united.* In this sense, the plural is *peoples*, as in *freedom-loving peoples everywhere speak the same language.*

- **people's**   Use this possessive form when the word occurs in the formal name of a nation: *the People's Republic of Albania.*
  Use this form also in such phrases as *the people's desire for freedom.*

- **Pepsi, Pepsi Cola**   Trademarks for a brand of cola soft drink.

- **Pepsico, Incorporated**   Formerly the Pepsi Cola Company. Headquarters is in Purchase, N.Y.

- **percent** One word. It takes a singular verb when standing alone or when a singular word follows an *of* construction: *The teacher said 60 percent was a failing grade. He said 50 percent of the membership was there.*
  It takes a plural verb when a plural word follows an *of* construction: *He said 50 percent of the members were there.*

- **percentages** Follow the rules for **numerals; decimal units** and **fractions**.
  Examples: *one percent, three-tenths of one percent, seven and a-half percent.*
  While it is preferable to repeat the word *percent* with each figure, don't if the construction would be too cumbersome: *The turnout is between ten percent and 30 percent,* but *he says ten to 30 percent of the electorate may not vote.*

- **performing artists** See **musical performers**.

- **performing groups** See **musical performers**.

- **periods (.)** Follow these guidelines:
  Abbreviations: Use hyphens, not periods. See **abbreviations** or individual entries.
  End of declarative sentence: *The stylebook is finished.*
  End of a mildly imperative sentence: *Shut the door.* Use an exclamation point if greater emphasis is desired: *Be careful!*
  End of some rhetorical questions: A period is preferable if a statement is more a suggestion than a question: *Why don't we go.*
  End of an indirect question: *He asked what the score was.*
  Initials: *John F. Kennedy, T.S. Eliot.* (No space between *T.* and *S.*, to prevent them from being placed on two lines.)
  Ellipsis: See **ellipsis**.
  Placement with quotation marks: Periods go inside quotation marks. See **quotation marks**.

- **perk** A shortened form of *perquisite*, often used by legislators to describe fringe benefits.
  In the state of New York, legislators also use the word *lulu* to describe the benefits they receive *in lieu of pay.*
  When either word is used, define it.

- **permissible**

- **Persian Gulf** Use this long-established name for the body of water off the southern coast of Iran.
  The Iranian government calls it the *Gulf of Iran.* Some Arab nations call it the *Arabian Gulf.*
  Use either name only in direct quotes or tape, and explain in the copy that the body of water is more generally known as the *Persian Gulf.*

- **personifications** Capitalize them: *the Grim Reaper, John Barleycorn, Mother Nature, Old Man Winter,* and so forth.

- **persons** See the **people, persons** entry.

- **-persons** Do not use coined words such as *chairperson* or *spokesperson.* Instead, use a neutral word such as *leader* or *representative* whenever possible.
  If the copy cannot be rewritten to use a netural term, use *chairman* or *spokesman* if referring to a man or the office in general. Use *chairwoman* or *spokeswoman* if referring to a woman.
  Use *chairperson* or similar coinage only in direct quotations or when it is the formal description for an office.

- **persuade** See the **convince, persuade** entry.

- **Peter Principle** It is: Each employee is promoted until he reaches his or her level of incompetence. From the book by Laurence J. Peter.

- **petty officer** See **military titles.**

- **P-G, P-G-13** The *parental guidance* ratings. See **movie ratings.**

- **phase** See the **faze, phase** entry.

- **P-H-D, P-H-D's** The preferred form is to say a person *holds a doctorate* and name the individual's area of specialty. See **academic degrees; doctor.**

- **phenomenon, phenomena**

- **Philadelphia** The city in Pennsylvania stands alone in datelines.

- **Philippines** In datelines, give the name of the city or town followed by *Philippines*:

  (Manila, Philippines) —

  But in the copy itself, use *the* as well:

  (Manila, Philippines) — The last American forces have left the Philippines. ...

  If needed, the name of the individual island can be identified in the story. The people are *Filipinos* and the institutions are *Philippine: The Philippine government says Filipinos will make more money next year.*

- **Photostat** A trademark for a type of photocopy.

- **piano, pianos**

- **picket, pickets, picketed, picket line** *Picket* is both the verb and the noun. Do not use *picketer.*

- **picnic, picnicked, picnicking, picnicker**

- **pico-** A prefix denoting one-trillionth of a unit.
Move a decimal point 12 places to the left in converting to the basic unit.

- **pigeon**

- **pigeon-hole** (n. and v.) The hyphen is for readability.

- **Pikes Peak** No apostrophe. After Zebulon Mongomery Pike, an American general and explorer.
The 14,110 foot peak is in the Rockies of central Colorado.

- **pile up** (v.) **pile-up** (n. adj.)

- **pill** Do not capitalize in reference to oral contraceptives. Use *birth control pill* on first reference if necessary for clarity, though *the pill* often is clear enough.

- **pilot** Not a formal title. Do not capitalize before a name. See **titles.**

- **pingpong** A synonym for *table tennis.* The trademark name is *Ping-Pong.*

- **pint** (dry) Equal to 33.6 cubic inches, or one-half of a dry quart.
The metric equivalent is about .55 liters—just over one-half liter.
To convert pints to liters, multiply by .55: 5 dry pints times .55 equals 2.75—two and three-quarters—liters. See **liter; quart (dry).**

- **pint** (liquid) Equal to 16 fluid ounces, or two cups. The rough metric equivalents are 470 milliliters or .47 liters—just under a half-liter.
To convert liquid pints to liters, multiply by .47: 4 pints times .47 equals 1.88 liters. See **liter.**

- **Pinyin** The official Chinese spelling system. See **Chinese names.**

- **pipeline**

- **pistol** A *pistol* can be either an automatic or a revolver, but *automatic* and *revolver* are not synonymous.
A *revolver* has a revolving cylinder that holds the cartridges; an *automatic* does not. See **weapons.**

- **Pittsburgh** The city in Pennsylvania stands alone in datelines.

The spelling is *Pittsburg* (no *h*) for communities in California, Illinois, Kansas, New Hampshire, Oklahoma and Texas.

- **plains** See **Great Plains**.

- **planets** They are, in order of closeness to the sun: *Mercury, Venus, Earth, Mars, Jupiter, Saturn, Uranus, Neptune, Pluto.* Capitalize their proper names.
  Capitalize *earth* when used as the proper name of our planet: *the astronauts have returned to Earth.*
  Lowercase nouns and adjectives derived from the proper names of planets and other heavenly bodies: *martian, jovian, lunar, solar, venusian.* See **earth** and **heavenly bodies**.

- **planning** Avoid the redundant *future planning.*

- **plants** In general, lowercase the names of plants, but capitalize proper nouns or adjectives that occur in a name.
  Some examples: *tree, fir, white fir, Douglas fir, Scotch pine; clover, white clover, white Dutch clover.*
  Avoid botanical names; they are meaningless to most people.

- **Plastic Wood** A trademark for a brand of wood-filler compound.

- **platform tennis** See **tennis**.

- **play off** (v.) **playoff, playoffs** (n. and adj.)

- **play titles** See **composition titles**.

- **plead, pleaded, pleading** Do not use the colloquial past tense form, *pled.*

- **Plexiglas** Note the single *s.* A trademark for a plastic glass.

- **plow** Not *plough.*

- **plurality** See the **majority, plurality** entry.

- **plurals** Follow these guidelines in forming and using plural words:
  Most words: Add *s: boys, girls, ships, villages.*
  - Words ending in *ch, s, sh, ss, x* and *z:* Add *es: Churches, lenses, parishes, glasses, boxes, buzzes.* (*Monarchs* is an exception.)
  - Words ending in *is:* Change *is* to *es: oases, parentheses, theses.*
  - Words ending in *y:* If *y* is preceded by a consonant or *qu,* change *y* to *i* and add *es: armies, cities, navies, soliloquies.* See the section on proper names in this entry for an exception.
  Otherwise, add *s: donkeys, monkeys.*

- Words ending in *o*: If *o* is preceded by a consonant, most plurals require *es*: *buffaloes, dominoes, echoes, heroes, potatoes.*
But there are exceptions: *pianos.* See individual entries in this book for many of these exceptions.
  - Words ending in *f*: Change *f* to *v* and add *es*: *leaves, selves.*

Latin endings: For Latin-root words ending in *us*, change *us* to *i*: *alumnus, alumni.*

For most which end in *a*, change *a* to *ae*: *alumna, alumnae. Formula, formulas* is an exception.

Those ending in *on* change to *a*: *phenomenon, phenomena.*

Most ending in *um* add *s*: *memorandums, referendums, stadiums.* Among those that still use the Latin ending: *addenda, curricula, media.*

Use the plural that Webster's New World lists as most common for a particular sense of a word.

Form change: *Man, men; child, children; foot, feet; mouse, mice;* etc.

Caution: When *s* is used with any of these words it indicates possession and must be preceded by an apostrophe: *men's, children's,* etc.

Words the same in singular and plural: *corps, chassis, deer, moose, sheep,* etc.

The sense in a particular sentence is conveyed by the use of a singular or plural verb.

Words plural in form, singular in meaning: Some take singular verbs: *measles, mumps, news.* Others take plural verbs: *grits, scissors.*

Compound words: Those written solid take an *s* at the end: *cupfuls, handfuls, tablespoonfuls.*

For those that involve separate words or words linked by a hyphen, make the most significant word plural.

When the significant word is first: *adjutants general, aides-de-camp, attorneys general, courts-martial, daughters-in-law, passersby, postmasters general, presidents-elect, secretaries general, sergeants major.*

When the significant word is in the middle: *assistant attorneys general, deputy chiefs of staff.*

When the significant word is last: *assistant attorneys, assistant corporation counsels, deputy sheriffs, lieutenant colonels, major generals.*

Words as words: Do not use *'s*: *His speech had too many ifs, ands and buts.* (An exception to Webster's New World.) See **words as words**.

Proper names: Most ending in *es* or *z* add *es*: *Charleses, Joneses, Gonzalezes.*

Most ending in *y*, add *s* even if preceded by a consonant: *the Duffys, the Kennedys, the two Germanys, the two Kansas Citys.* Exceptions include *Alleghenies* and *Rockies.*

For others, add *s*: *the Carters, the McCoys, the Reagans.*

Figures: Add *'s*: *The custom began in the 1920's. The airline has two 727's. Temperatures will be in the low 20's.*

Single Letters: Use *'s*: *Mind your p's and q's. He learned the three R's and brought home a report card with four A's and two B's. The Oakland A's won the pennant.*

Multiple Letters: Add *'s*: *She knows her A-B-C's. I gave him five I-O-U's. Four V-I-P's were there.*

Problems, doubts: Separate entries in this book give plurals for troublesome words and guidance on whether certain words should be used with singular or plural verbs and pronouns. See also **collective nouns** and **possessives**.

For questions not covered by this book, use the plural that Webster's New World lists as most common for a particular sense of a word.

Note also the guidelines that the dictionary provides under its "plural" entry.

- **p-m, a-m** Lowercase, with hyphens, not periods. Avoid the redundant *ten p-m tonight.*

- **pocket veto** Occurs only when Congress has adjourned.

If Congress is in session, a bill that remains on the president's desk for 10 days becomes law without his signature. But if Congress adjourns, a bill that fails to get his signature within 10 days is automatically vetoed.

Many states have similar rules.

- **podium** See the **lectern, podium, pulpit, rostrum** entry.

- **poetic license** It is valid for poetry—not news or feature stories. See **colloquialisms** and **special contexts**.

- **poetry** See **composition titles** for guidelines on the names of poems.

- **poinsettia** Note the *ia.*

- **point** Do not abbreviate. Capitalize as part of a proper name: *Point Pleasant.*

- **point-blank**

- **Polaroid** A trademark for Polaroid Land instant-picture cameras and for transparent material containing embedded crystals capable of polarizing light.

- **police department** In communities where this is the formal name, capitalize *police department* with or without the name of the community: *the Los Angeles Police Department, the Police Department.*

If a police agency has some other formal name, such as *Division of Police*, use that name if that is the way the department is known to the public. If the story uses *police department* as a generic term for such an agency, put *police department* in lowercase.

If a police agency with an unusual formal name is known to the public as a *police department*, treat *police department* as the name, capitalizing it with or without the name of the community. Use the formal name only if there is a special reason in the story.

Lowercase *police department* in plural uses: *the Los Angeles and San Francisco police departments.*

Lowercase *the department* whenever it stands alone.

- **police titles** See **military titles** and **titles**.

- **policy-maker** (n.) **policy-making** (n. and adj.)

- **polio** The preferred term for *poliomyelitis* and *infantile paralysis*.

- **Politburo** Acceptable in all references for the *Political Bureau of the Communist Party*. Under the Soviet system, it was the chief policy-making body in the Soviet Union and other Communist nations.

- **political divisions** Follow the rules for **numerals** and capitalize when giving the names of political districts, wards, etc.: *the First Ward, the 12th Precinct, the 28th District, the ward, the precinct, the district*. See **congressional districts**.

- **political parties and philosophies** Capitalize both the name of the party and the word *party* if it is customarily used as part of the organization's proper name: *the Democratic Party, the Republican Party*.
  Capitalize *Communist, Conservative, Democrat, Liberal, Republican, Socialist*, etc. when they refer to the activities of a specific party or to individuals who are members of it. Lowercase these words when they refer to political philosophies.
  Lowercase the name of a philosophy in its noun and adjective forms unless it is derivative of a proper name: *communism, communist; fascism, fascist;* but *Marxism, Marxist; Nazism, Nazi*.
  Some examples:
  John Adams was a Federalist, but a man who subscribed to his philosophy today would be described as a federalist, since the party no longer exists. The liberal Republican senator and his Conservative Party colleague say they believe that democracy and communism are incompatible. But the Communist says he's basically a socialist who has reservations about Marxism. See **convention** and **party affiliation**.

- **politicking**

- **politics** Usually it takes a plural verb: *My politics are my own business.*
  As a study or science, it takes a singular verb: *Politics is a demanding profession.*

- **polls and surveys** Stories based on public opinion polls must include enough information so the audience can make an intelligent evaluation of the results. Such stories must be carefully worded to avoid exaggerating the meaning of the numbers.
  The idea behind public opinion polls is that the responses of a truly random sample of the population can be mathematically projected across the country's entire population. If the process is scientifically controlled to prevent bias, the results can be accurate within a specified margin of error. Anything that biases the selection of the sample population (i.e., that makes the sample *not* random) or that biases the questions will make the poll less accurate.

Information that should be in every poll story includes the answers to these questions:

Who did the poll? The place to start is the polling firm, political campaign or other group that conducted the poll.

Who paid for the poll? Be wary of polls paid for by candidates or interest groups. The release of poll results is often a campaign tactic or publicity ploy. Any reporting of such polls must highlight the poll's sponsor and the potential for bias from such sponsorship.

How many people were interviewed? How were they selected? Only polls based on a scientific sample of a population can be used as a reliable and accurate measure of that population's opinions. Polls based on interviews on street corners, or respondents to a 900 telephone number, or those who mailed in coupons, may be good entertainment, but such polls have no statistical validity and should be avoided. In such unscientific psuedo-polls, the opinions come from people who select themselves to participate, so the sample, by definition, is not random. If such a poll is reported for entertainment value, it is essential that the story clearly indicate that the poll was not a scientific, random sample and the results cannot be used as an indicator of public opinion. To prevent such stories from being misleading, the failings in the poll's methodology must be highlighted in the copy.

Who was interviewed? A valid poll reflects only the opinion of the population that was sampled. A poll of business executives can only represent the views of business executives, not of all adults. Many political polls are based on interviews with registered voters, since registration usually is required for voting. Close to the election, polls may be based on "likely voters." In that case, ask the pollster how "likely voter" is defined.

How was the poll conducted? Was it by telephone, in people's homes or in some other forum?

When was the poll taken? Opinions can change quickly, especially in response to events and at the very end of a political campaign.

What are the sampling error margins for the poll and for subgroups mentioned in the story? Sampling error margins should be supplied by the polling organization. The error margins vary inversely with the sample size: the fewer people interviewed, the larger the sampling error. If the opinions of a subgroup—women, for example—are important to the story, the sampling error for that sub-group should be included. The subgroup error margins are by definition larger than the error margins for the entire poll.

What questions were asked and in what order? Small differences in question wording can cause big differences in results. The exact texts of questions need not be in every story unless it is crucial or controversial.

When writing and editing poll stories, here are areas for close attention:

Perspective: Do not exaggerate poll results. A difficult situation arises with pre-election polls in deciding when to write that the poll says one candidate is leading another.

The rules are:

• If the margin between the candidates is more than twice the sampling error margin, then the poll suggests one candidate is leading.

- If the margin is less than the sampling error margin, the poll suggests that the race is close, that the candidates are *about even* or in *a statistical dead heat.*
- If the margin is more than the sampling error, but less than twice the sampling error, then one candidate can be said to be *apparently leading* or *slightly ahead* in the poll.

Context: Comparisons with previous polls often are newsworthy but must be made with great care. Comparisons can demonstrate changes in public opinion. But when comparing polls, make sure the techniques, including the question wording, sample size and type of interview (telephone or in person) are the same.

Sources of Error: Sampling error is not the only source of error in a poll, but it is the one that can be quantified. Question wording, interviewer skill, computing processes and method of sample selection are all sources of errors in surveys.

Role of Polls: No matter how good the poll, no matter how wide the margin, the poll does NOT say which candidate will win the election. Polls can be wrong, circumstances can change and voters can change their minds before they cast their ballots.

Make sure all poll stories are written in such a way that these uncertainties are clear. When referring to the poll's conclusions about public opinion, say that the poll *suggests, estimates* or *concludes.*

You can write in more certain terms about the poll's sample population: *the respondents said, favored, approved.*

Some examples:

Wrong: *Bill Clinton will beat Bob Dole next Tuesday. That's the finding of several nationwide polls made public today.*

Right: *A new round of polls suggests that Bill Clinton continues to lead Bob Dole less than a week before the election.*

Wrong: *The poll says Clinton is leading Dole nationwide, 37 percent to 30 percent.*

Right: *Thirty-seven percent of those polled favor Clinton. Thirty percent favor Dole.*

- **pom-pom, pompon** *Pom-pom* is sometimes used to describe a rapid-firing automatic weapon. Define the word if it must be used.

A *pompon* is a large ball of crepe paper or fluffed cloth, often waved by cheerleaders or used atop a hat. It is also a flower that appears on some varieties of chrysanthemums.

- **pontiff** Not a formal title. Always lowercase.

- **pooh-pooh**

- **pope** Capitalize when used as a formal title before a name. Lowercase in all other uses: *Pope Paul spoke to the crowd. At the close of his address, the pope gave his blessing.* See **Roman Catholic Church** and **titles.**

- **Pope John Paul the Second**

- **pop music** See **music** and **musical performers**.

- **Popsicle** A trademark for a brand of flavored ice on a stick.

- **popular names** See **capitalization**.

- **pore, pour** The verb *pore* means to gaze intently or steadily: *She pored over her books.*
  The verb *pour* means to flow in a continuous stream: *It poured rain. He poured the coffee.*

- **port, starboard** Nautical for left and right (when facing forward, toward the bow). *Port* is left. *Starboard* is right. Use the more common terms except in quotes.

- **Portuguese names** See the **Spanish and Portuguese names** entry.

- **possessives** Follow these guidelines:
  Plural nouns not ending in *s*: Add *'s: the alumni's contributions, women's rights.*
  Plural nouns ending in *s*: Add only an apostrophe: *the churches' needs, the girls' toys, the horses' food, the ships' wake, states' rights.*
  Nouns plural in form, singular in meaning: Add only an apostrophe: *mathematics' rules, measles' effects.* (But see the section on inanimate objects later in this entry.)
  Apply the same principle when a plural word occurs in the formal name of a singular entity: *General Motors' profits, the United States' wealth.*
  Nouns the same in singular and plural: Treat them the same as plurals, even if the meaning is singular: *one corps' location, the two deer's tracks, the lone moose's antlers.*
  Singular nouns not ending in *s*: Add *'s: the church's needs, the girl's toys, the horse's food, the ship's route, the V-I-P's seat.*
  Some style guides say that singular nouns ending in *s* sounds such as *ce, x,* and *z* may take either the apostrophe alone or *'s.* See the section on special expressions below, but otherwise, for consistency and ease in remembering a rule, always use *'s* if the word does not end in the letter *s: Butz's policies, the fox's den, the justice's verdict, Marx's theories, the prince's life, Xerox's profits.*
  Singular common nouns ending in *s*: Add *'s* unless the next word begins with *s: the hostess's invitation, the hostess' seat; the witness's answer, the witness' story.*
  Singular proper names ending in *s*: Use only an apostrophe: *Achilles' heel, Agnes' book, Ceres' rites, Descartes' theories, Dickens' novels, Euripides' dramas, Hercules' labors, Jesus' life, Jules' seat, Kansas' schools, Moses' law, Socrates' life, Tennessee Williams' plays, Xerxes' armies.*
  Special expressions: The following exceptions to the general rule for words not ending in *s* apply to words that end in an *s* sound and are followed by a word that begins with *s: for appearance' sake, for conscience' sake, for goodness' sake.*

Use *'s* otherwise: *the appearance's cost, my conscience's voice.*

Pronouns: Personal, interrogative and relative pronouns have separate forms for the possessive. None involves an apostrophe: *mine, ours, your, yours, his, hers, its, theirs, whose.*

Caution: If you are using an apostrophe with a pronoun, always doublecheck to be sure that the meaning calls for a contraction: *you're, it's, there's, who's.* Do not use contractions that can be mistaken for possessives. See **contractions**.

Follow the rules listed above in forming the possessives of other pronouns: *another's idea, others' plans, someone's guess.*

Compound words: Applying the rules above, add an apostrophe or *'s* to the word closest to the object possessed: *the major general's decision, the major generals' decisions, the attorney general's request, the attorneys general's request.* See **plurals** for guidelines on forming the plurals of these words.

Also: *anyone else's attitude, Benjamin Franklin of Pennsylvania's motion.* Whenever possible, recast the phrase to avoid ambiguity: *the motion by Benjamin Franklin of Pennsylvania.*

Joint possession, individual possession: Use a possessive form after only the last word if ownership is joint: *Fred and Sylvia's apartment, Fred and Sylvia's stocks.*

Use a possessive form after both words if the objects are individually owned: *Fred's and Sylvia's books.*

Descriptive phrases: Do not add an apostrophe to a word ending in *s* when it is used primarily in a descriptive sense: *citizens band radio, a Cincinnati Reds infielder, a teachers college, a Teamsters request, a writers guide.*

Memory aid: The apostrophe usually is not used if *for* or *by* rather than *of* would be appropriate in the longer form: *a radio band for citizens, a college for teachers, a guide for writers, a request by the Teamsters.*

An *'s* is required, however, when a term involves a plural word that does not end in *s*: *a children's hospital, a people's republic, the Young Men's Christian Association.*

Descriptive names: Some governmental, corporate and institutional organizations with a descriptive word in their names use an apostrophe; some do not. Follow the user's practice: *Actors Equity, Diners Club, the Ladies' Home Journal, the National Governors' Conference, the Veterans Administration.* See separate entries for these and similar names frequently in the news.

Quasi-possessives: Follow the rules above in composing the possessive form of words that occur in such phrases as *a day's pay, two weeks' vacation, three days' work, your money's worth.*

Frequently, however, a hyphenated form is clearer: *a two-week vacation, a three-day job.*

Double possessive: Two conditions must apply for a double possessive—a phrase such as *a friend of John's*—to occur: The word after *of* must refer to an animate object and the word before *of* must involve only a portion of the animate object's possessions.

Otherwise, do not use the possessive form on the word after *of: The friends of John Adams mourned his death.* (All the friends were involved.) *He is a friend of the college.* (Not *college's,* because *college* is inanimate).

Memory aid: This construction occurs most often, and quite naturally, with the possessive forms of personal pronouns: *He is a friend of mine.*

Inanimate objects: There is no blanket rule against creating a possessive form for an inanimate object, particularly if the object is treated in a personified sense. See some of the earlier examples, and note these: *death's call, the wind's murmur.*

In general, however, avoid excessive personalization of inanimate objects, and give preference to an *of* construction when it fits the makeup of the sentence. For example, the earlier references to mathematics' rules and measles' effects would better be phrased: *the rules of mathematics, the effects of measles.*

- **post-** Follow Webster's New World. Hyphenate if not listed there. Some words without a hyphen:

postdoctoral	postelection	postnuptial	postscript
postdate	postgraduate	postoperative	postwar

Some words that use a hyphen:

post-bellum	post-mortem

Often, though, it's best to use a different construction: *after the election,* instead of *postelection.*

- **post office** It may be used but it is no longer capitalized because the agency is now the *U-S Postal Service.*
  Lowercase, too, when referring to an individual location: *I went to the post office.*

- **post-season, pre-season**

- **pot** Acceptable on second reference for *marijuana.*

- **potato, potatoes**

- **pot-hole**

- **pound** (monetary) The British pound sign is not used. Spell out the word instead. Convert the figures to dollars in most cases. Follow the rules for **numerals** and **monetary figures**.

- **pound** (weight) Equal to 16 ounces.
  The metric equivalent is about 454 grams, or point-45 kilograms—just under half a kilogram.
  To convert pounds to kilograms, multiply by .45: *20 pounds times .45 equals 9 kilograms.* See **gram; kilogram**.

- **poverty level** An income level judged to be the minimum required to provide a family or individual with the essentials of life. The figure for the United States is adjusted regularly to reflect changes in the Consumer Price Index.

• **P-O-W** Acceptable on second reference to *prisoner of war.* See the following entry.

• **POW-MIA** An exception to the rules in **abbreviations**, for readability when referring to issues which affect both *prisoners of war* and members of the military who are *missing in action.*
But: *P-O-W* and *M-I-A* when they stand alone.

• **practitioner** See **Church of Christ, Scientist**.

• **pre-** The rules in **prefixes** apply. The following examples of exceptions to first-listed spellings in Webster's New World are based on the general rule that a hyphen is used if a prefix ends in a vowel and the word that follows begins with the same vowel:

pre-election	pre-empt	pre-establish	pre-exist
pre-eminent			

Otherwise, follow Webster's New World, hyphenating if not listed there. Some examples:

prearrange	predispose	pre-ignition	preseason
precondition	pre-flight	prejudge	pre-tax
pre-cook	pre-heat	premarital	pre-test
predate	prehistoric	prenatal	pre-war
predecease			

Some hyphenated coinages, not listed in the dictionary:

pre-convention   pre-dawn

• **preacher** A job description, not a formal religious title. Do not capitalize. See **titles** and **religious titles**.

• **precincts** See **political divisions**.

• **predominant, predominantly** Use these primary spellings listed in Webster's New World for the adjectival and adverbial forms. Do not use the alternates it records, *predominate* and *predominately.*
The verb form, however, is *predominate.*

• **preferred stock** See the **common stock, preferred stock** entry.

• **prefixes** See separate listings for commonly used prefixes.
If in doubt, hyphenate for readability.
Three rules are constant, although they yield some exceptions to first listed spellings in Webster's New World Dictionary.

- Except for *cooperate* and *coordinate*, use a hyphen if the prefex ends in a vowel and the word that follows begins with the same vowel.
- Use a hyphen if the word that follows is a proper noun.
- Use a hyphen to join doubled prefixes: *sub-subunits.*

● **premier, prime minister**   These two titles often are used interchangeably in translating to English the title of an individual who is the first minister in a national government that has a council of ministers.

Prime minister is the correct title throughout the Commonwealth, formerly the British Commonwealth. See **Commonwealth** for a list of members.

Prime minister is the best or traditional translation from most other languages. For consistency, use it throughout the rest of the world with these exceptions:

- Use *premier* for France and its former colonies.
- Use *chancellor* in Austria and Germany.
- Follow the practice of a nation if there is a specific preference that varies from this general practice.

Premier is also the correct title for the individuals who lead the provincial governments in Canada and Australia. See **titles**.

● **premiere**   A first performance.

● **Presbyterian churches**   There are four levels of authority in Presbyterian practice—individual congregations, presbyteries, synods and a general assembly.

Congregations are led by a *pastor*, who provides guidance in spiritual matters, and by a *session*, composed of ruling elders chosen by the congregation to represent the members in matters of government and discipline.

A *presbytery* is composed of all the ministers and an equal number of ruling elders, including at least one from each congregation, in a given district. Although the next two levels are technically higher, the presbytery has the authority to rule on many types of material and spiritual questions.

Presbyteries unite to form a *synod*, whose members are elected by the presbyteries. A synod generally meets once a year to decide matters such as the creation of new presbyteries and to pass judgment on appeals and complaints that do not affect the doctrine or constitution of the church.

A *general assembly*, composed of delegations of pastors and ruling elders from each presbytery, meets yearly to decide issues of doctrine and discipline within a Presbyterian body. It also may create new synods, divide old ones and correspond with general assemblies of other Presbyterian bodies.

The assembly also chooses the *stated clerk* and the *moderator* for a denomination. The stated clerk, the chief administrative officer, normally serves for an extended period. The moderator, the presiding officer, serves for a year.

The Northern and Southern branches of Presbyterianism merged in 1983 to become the Presbyterian Church U.S.A. Its membership totals 3 million people.

Formerly, Presbyterianism in the United States was concentrated in two bodies. The principal body in the North was the United Presbyterian Church in the United States of America. The Presbyterian Church in the United States was the principal Southern body.

Beliefs: The characteristic teachings rely heavily on the writings of John Calvin, a 16th-century French lawyer turned theologian who emphasized the "sovereignty of God." He taught that church government is a purely human organization, quasi-democratic in nature. Christ, rather than any human individual, is the only real head of the church.

Presbyterians believe in the Trinity and the humanity and divinity of Christ. Baptism, which may be administered to children, and the Lord's Supper are the only sacraments. The basic doctrinal standard is the Westminster Confession of Faith, a document drawn up by an assembly of leaders who met from 1643 to 1648 in England.

Clergy: All Presbyterian clergymen may be described as *ministers. Pastor* applies if a minister leads a congregation.

On first reference, use *the Reverend* before the name of a man or woman. Do not carry the title through to subsequent references.

Other officials: The preferred form for elected officials such as *elders* or *deacons* is to work the title into the sentences as a job description rather than a formal title.

- **presently** Use it to mean *in a little while* or *shortly*, but not to mean *now.*

- **presidency** Always lowercase.

- **president** The formal title of the chief executive of the United States. Capitalize before one or more names: *President Clinton, Presidents Reagan and Bush.*

   Lowercase in all other uses: *The president will speak today. He is running for president. Lincoln was president during the Civil War.*

   In most cases, the first name of a current or former president is not necessary on the first reference. But use it if confusion might otherwise result: *President Andrew Johnson, President Lyndon Johnson.*

   The President of the United States is both chief of state and head of government.

   President also is the formal title of national leaders in some other countries. In many countries, the *president* is chief of state—a largely ceremonial role— while the *prime minister* or *premier* is head of government.

   For presidents of other nations and of organizations and institutions, use the full name on first reference and capitalize the word *president* as a formal title before the name. Do not carry the title through on subsequent references.

- **presidential** Lowercase unless part of a proper name.

- **Presidential Medal of Freedom** This is the nation's highest civilian honor. It is given by the president, on the recommendation of the Distinguished Civilian Service Board, for "exceptionally meritorious contribution to the security of the United States or other significant public or private endeavors."

   Until 1963 it was known as the Medal of Freedom.

- **Presidents Day** This name has not been adopted by the federal government as the official name of the Washington's Birthday holiday, but some federal agencies and state and local governments use it. See **Washington's Birthday**.

- **presiding officer** Always lowercase.

- **press conference** *News conference* is preferred.

- **press secretary** *News secretary* or *presidential spokesman* or *spokeswoman* is preferred for the White House official.
Press secretary seldom is a formal title. For consistency, always use lowercase, even when used before an individual's name.
The formal title is *assistant to the president for press relations*.
In other cases, *spokesman* or *spokeswoman* is preferred: *a spokesman for Chrysler Corporation, the Chrysler spokeswoman*. See **titles**.

- **pretense, pretext** A *pretext* is something that is put forward to conceal a truth: *He was discharged for tardiness, but the reason given was only a pretext for general incompetence.*
A *pretense* is a false show, a more overt act intended to conceal a truth: *My profuse compliments were all pretense.*

- **price-earnings ratio** The price of a share of stock divided by earnings per share for a 12-month period. In Associated Press stock tables, the ratios reflect earnings for the most recent 12 months. For example, a stock selling for $60 per share and earning $6 per share would be selling at a price-earnings ratio of 10-to-one. See **profit terminology**.

- **priest** A vocational description, not a formal title. Do not capitalize. See **religious titles** and the entries for **Roman Catholic Church** and **Episcopal Church**.

- **prima-facie** (PRY'-muh FAY'-shuh)

- **primary** Do not capitalize: *the New Hampshire primary, the Republican primary, the primary.*

- **primary day** Use lowercase for any of the days set aside for balloting in a primary.
- **prime meridian** See **meridians**.

- **prime minister** See the **premier, prime minister** entry.

- **prime rate** A benchmark rate used by banks to set interest charges on a variety of corporate and consumer loans, including some adjustable-rate mortgages, revolving credit cards and business loans.

The prime is the interest rate that commercial banks charge on loans to their borrowers with the best credit ratings. Banks set the rate based on their borrowing costs, as reflected by the interest on short-term Treasury securities in the bond market.

- **prince, princess** Capitalize when used as a royal title before a name; lowercase when used alone: *Prince Charles, the prince.* See **nobility**.

- **Prince Edward Island** One of the three **Maritime Provinces** of Canada. Do not abbreviate. See **datelines**.

- **principal, principle** *Principal* is a noun and adjective meaning someone or something first in rank, authority, importance or degree: *She is the school principal. He was the principal player in the trade. Inflation is the principal problem.*
  Principle is a noun that means a fundamental truth, law, doctrine or motivating force: *They fought for the principle of self-determination.*

- **prior to** *Before* is less stilted for most uses. *Prior to* is appropriate, however, when a notion of requirement is involved: *The fee must be paid prior to the examination.*

- **prison, jail** Do not use the two words interchangeably.
  Definitions: *Prison* is a generic term that may be applied to the maximum security institutions often known as *penitentiaries* and to the medium security facilities often called *correctional institutions* or *reformatories.* All such facilities confine persons serving sentences for felonies.
  A *jail* is a facility normally used to confine people serving sentences for misdemeanors, people awaiting trial or sentencing on either felony or misdemeanor charges, and people confined for civil matters such as failure to pay alimony and other types of contempt of court. See the **felony, misdemeanor** entry.
  Prisons: Many states have given elaborate formal names to their prisons. They should be capitalized when used, but commonly accepted substitutes should also be capitalized as if they were proper names. For example, use either *Massachusetts Correctional Institute-Walpole* or *Walpole State Prison* for the maximum-security institution in Massachusetts.
  Do not construct a substitute when the formal name is commonly accepted: It is *the Colorado State Penitentiary,* for example, not *Colorado State Prison.*
  On second reference, any of the following may be used, all in lowercase: *the state prison, the prison, the state penitentiary, the penitentiary.*
  Jails: Capitalize *jail* when linked with the name of a jurisdiction: *Los Angeles County Jail.* Lowercase *county jail, city jail* and *jail* when they stand alone.
  Federal institutions: Maximum security institutions are known as *penitentiaries:* the *U-S Penitentiary at Lewisburg* or *Lewisburg Penitentiary* on first reference; *the federal penitentiary* or *the penitentiary* on second reference.

Medium security institutions include the word *federal* as part of their formal names: *the Federal Correctional Institution in Danbury, Conn.* On second reference: *the correctional institution, the federal prison, the prison.*

Most federal facilities that are used to house persons awaiting trial or serving sentences of a year or less have the proper name *Federal Detention Center.* The term *Metropolitan Correctional Center* is being adopted for some new installations. On second reference: *the detention center, the correctional center, the center.*

- **prisoner of war**   *P-O-W* is acceptable on second reference.
As a compound modifier: *a prisoner-of-war trial or a P-O-W trial.* See **POW-MIA**.

- **private** See **military titles**.

- **privilege, privileged**

- **pro-** Use a hyphen when coining words that denote support for something. Some examples:

pro-business   pro-labor   pro-war

No hyphen when *pro* is used in other senses: *produce, profile, pronoun,* etc.

- **probation** See the **pardon, parole, probation** entry.

- **Procter and Gamble Company** Do not use the abbreviation *P-and-G*. Headquarters is in Cincinnati.

- **producer price index** A measurement of the changes in the average prices that businesses pay for a selected group of industrial commodities, farm products, processed foods and feed for animals.
The U-S index is issued monthly by the Bureau of Labor Statistics, an agency of the Labor Department.

- **profanity** See the **obscenities, profanities, vulgarities** entry.

- **Professional Golfers' Association** Note the apostrophe. The abbreviation *P-G-A* is acceptable in all references in sports copy.

- **professor** Never abbreviate. Capitalize when used as a formal title before a name. Do not carry through the title on subsequent references. See **academic titles** and **titles**.

- **profit-sharing** (n. and adj.) The hyphen for the noun is an exception to Webster's New World.

- **profit-taking** (n. and adj.) Avoid this term.
It means selling a security after a recent rapid rise in price. It is inaccurate if the seller bought the security at a higher price, watched it fall, and then sold it after a recent rise but for less than he paid for it. In such a case, the seller would be cutting his losses, not taking his profit.

- **profit terminology** Note the meanings of the following terms in reporting a company's financial status. Always be careful to specify whether the figures given apply to quarterly or annual results.
The terms, listed in the order in which they might occur in analyzing a company's financial condition:
Revenue: The amount of money a company took in, including interest earned and receipts from sales, services provided, rents and royalties.
The figure also may include excise taxes and sales taxes collected for the government. If it does, the fact should be noted in any report on revenue.
Sales: The money a company received for the goods and services it sold.
In some cases the figure includes receipts from rents and royalties. In others, particularly when rents and royalties make up a large portion of a company's income, figures for these activities are listed separately.
Gross profit: The difference between the sales price of an item or service and the expenses directly attributed to it, such as the cost of raw materials, labor and overhead linked to the production effort.
Income before taxes: Gross profits minus companywide expenses not directly attributed to specific products or services. These expenses typically include interest costs, advertising and sales costs, and general administrative overhead.
Net income, profit, earnings: The amount left after taxes have been paid.
A portion may be committed to pay preferred dividends. Some of what remains may be paid in dividends to holders of common stocks. The rest may be invested to obtain interest revenue or may be spent to acquire new buildings or equipment to increase the company's ability to make future profits.
To avoid confusion, do not use the word *income* alone—always specify whether the figure is *income before taxes* or *net income*.
The terms *profit* and *earnings* commonly are interpreted as meaning the amount left after taxes. The terms *net profit* and *net earnings* are acceptable synonyms.
Earnings per share (or *loss per share* for companies posting a net loss): The figure obtained by dividing the number of outstanding shares of common stock into the amount left after dividends have been paid on any preferred stock.
Dividend: The amount paid per share per year to holders of common stock. Payments generally are made in quarterly installments.
The *dividend* usually is a portion of the earnings per share. However, if a company shows no profit during a given period, it may be able to use earnings retained from profitable periods to pay its dividend on schedule.
Return on investment: A percentage figure obtained by dividing the company's assets into its net income.
Extraordinary loss, extraordinary income: An expense or source of income that does not occur on a regular basis, such as a loss due to a major fire

or the revenue from the sale of a subsidiary. Extraordinary items should be identified in any report on the company's financial status to avoid creating the false impression that its overall profit trend has suddenly plunged or soared.

• **Prohibition**   The period that began when the 18th amendment to the Constitution was put into law, prohibiting the manufacture, sale or transportation of alcoholic liquors.
Capitalize when referring to that period.
The amendment was declared ratified on Jan. 29, 1919, and took effect Jan. 16, 1920. It was repealed by the 21st Amendment, which took effect on Dec. 5, 1933, the day it was declared ratified.

• **pronouncers**   Always try to provide a pronouncer for words that are unusual or which the broadcaster is unlikely to recognize.
The pronouncer should be in parentheses and immediately follow the word in question. Make the syllable that should be stressed all-caps with an apostrophe (for those stations which print their copy all-caps): *Police in Tucson are trying to regain control of the Pima (PEE'-muh) County Jail. A spokesman for Ayatollah Khomeini (hoh-MAY'-nee) says the religious leader is ill.*
In general, provide pronouncers for proper nouns, technical terms and obscure words which are not in general usage.
Try to err on the side of caution. If you know the pronunciation of a potentially puzzling word, by all means use it—but first ask yourself if you should be using the word at all. If it's so unusual that no one will know how to pronounce it, it is probable that no one will know what it means, either.
When handling foreign copy, try to eliminate as many non-essential names as possible. See **foreign names**.
If you are using a technical term, try to find a simpler, generic term that will work just as well.
Be careful about providing pronouncers for private citizens' names unless you have spoken to the person in question. Stations often want pronouncers for the names of accident victims, criminal defendants, etc. But if you have obtained the name from a police officer, the prosecutor or some other third party, remember that the third party might be guessing about how the person pronounces the name.
In other words, don't guess. If you don't know, don't use it.
The most serious obstacle to providing proper pronunciation guides is that newsroom computers and printers do not have nearly enough characters to reproduce the standard phonetic alphabet used by dictionaries and other linguistic guides. Instead, standard letters must be used to provide an approximation of what the word sounds like.

Here are the basic sounds represented by AP phonetic symbols:

Vowels	Consonants
a — bat, apple	g — got, beg
ah — father, arm	j — job, gem
aw — raw, board	k — keep, cap
ay — fate, ace	ch — chair, butcher
e, eh — bed	sh — shut, fashion
ee — feel, tea	zh — vision, mirage
i, ih — pin, middle	th — thin, math
oh — go, oval	kh — gutteral k
oo — food, two	
ow — scout, crowd	
oy — boy, join	
u — curl, foot	
uh — puff	
y, eye — ice, time, guide	
yoo — fume, few	

- **propeller**

- **proper nouns**   See **capitalization**.

- **prophecy** (n.) **prophesy** (v.)

- **proportions**   Follow the rules for **numerals** when expressing proportions: *It's a mix of two parts powder to six parts water.* See **ratios**.

- **proposition**   Do not abbreviate. Capitalize and follow the rules for **numerals** when describing a ballot question: *He is uncommitted on Proposition Five. She opposes Proposition 15.*

- **prosecutor**   Capitalize before a name when it is the formal title. In most cases, however, the formal title is a term such as *attorney general, state's attorney* or *U-S attorney.* If so, use the formal title on first reference. See **titles**.

- **prostate gland**   Not *prostrate*.

- **protective tariff**   A duty high enough to assure domestic producers against any effective competition from foreign producers.

- **Protestant, Protestantism**   They refer to denominations formed as a result of the break from the Roman Catholic Church in the 16th century and to the members of these denominations.
  Church groups covered by the term include Anglican, Baptist, Congregational, Methodist, Lutheran, Presbyterian and Quaker denominations. See separate entries for each.

Protestant is not generally applied to Christian Scientists, Jehovah's Witnesses or Mormons.

Do not use *Protestant* to describe a member of an Eastern Orthodox church. Use a phrase such as *Orthodox Christian* instead. See **religious movements**.

- **Protestant Episcopal Church** See **Episcopal Church**.

- **protester** Not *protestor*.

- **prove, proved, proving** Use *proven* only as an adjective: *a proven remedy*.

- **provinces** Names of provinces are set off from community names just as state names are set off from community names. Thus: *Halifax, Nova Scotia*.

Do not capitalize *province*: *They visited the province of Nova Scotia. The earthquake struck Shensi province*. See **datelines**.

- **proviso, provisos**

- **provost marshal** The plural is *provost marshals*.

- **P-T-A** See **parent-teacher association**.

- **P-T boat** It stands for *patrol torpedo* boat.

- **Public Broadcasting Service** It is not a network, but an association of public television stations organized to buy and distribute programs selected by a vote of the members.

P-B-S is acceptable on all references.

- **public schools** Follow the rules for **numerals** and capitalize *public school*: *Public School Three, Public School 24*. Also: *P-S-23, P-S-Three*. If a school has a commemorative name: *Benjamin Franklin School*.

- **Pulitzer Prizes** These annual awards for outstanding work in journalism and the arts were endowed by the late Joseph Pulitzer, publisher of the New York World, and first given in 1917. They are awarded by the trustees of Columbia University on recommendation of an advisory board.

Capitalize *Pulitzer Prize*, but lowercase the categories: *Pulitzer Prize for public service, Pulitzer Prize for fiction*. Also: *She is a Pulitzer prize winner. He is a Pulitzer Prize-winning author*.

- **pull back** (v.) **pullback** (n.)

- **pull out** (v.) **pullout** (n.)

- **pulpit** See the **lectern, podium, pulpit, rostrum** entry.

- **punctuation** Think of it as a service to the newscasters, designed to help them understand a story.

  Inevitably, a mandate of this scope involves gray areas. For this reason, punctuation entries in the handbook refer to guidelines rather than rules. See separate entries under: **colon; comma; dash; double dash; ellipsis; exclamation mark; hyphen; parentheses; period; question mark; quotation mark** and **semicolon**.

- **pupil, student** Use *pupil* for children in kindergarten through eighth grade. *Student* or *pupil* is acceptable for grades nine through 12. Use *student* for college and beyond.

- **Purim** The Jewish Feast of Lots, commemorating Esther's deliverance of the Jews in Persia from a massacre plotted by Haman. Occurs in February or March.

- **push-button** (n., adj.)

- **push up** (v.) **push-up** (n., adj.)

- **put out** (v.) **putout** (n.)

- **pygmy**

- **Pyrex** A trademark for a brand of oven glassware.

- **q&a** An actuality of a correspondent taken from a question-and-answer session. Q&A cuts run from 10 to 20 seconds and provide the reporter with a format in which a brief aspect of a story is reported.

  A Q&A cut is not a forum in which a reporter should express views or draw conclusions about the story. The rules of balance, objectivity and attribution all apply.

  There is no lockout. The reporter is identified by the anchor in the lead-in. See the entries under **actuality; natural sound; scener; voicer;** and **wrap**.

- **Qantas** (KWAHN'-tuhs) **Airways** Headquarters is in Sydney, Australia.

- **"Q-E-Two"** Acceptable on second reference to the ocean liner *Queen Elizabeth Two*.

- **Q-tips** A trademark for a brand of cotton swabs.

- **Quaalude** (KWAY'-lood) A trade name for a drug containing methaqualone. Not synonymous with illegal drugs containing methaqualone.

- **Quakers** This informal name may be used in all references to members of the *Religious Society of Friends*.

  The denomination originated with George Fox, an Englishman who objected to Anglican emphasis on ceremony. In the 1640s, he said he heard a voice that opened the way for him to develop a personal relationship with Christ, described as the Inner Light, a term based on the Gospel description of Christ as the "true light." Brought to court for opposing the established church, Fox tangled with a judge who derided him as a "quaker" in a reference to his agitation over religious matters.

  The basic unit of Quaker organization is the weekly meeting, which corresponds to the congregation in other churches. A monthly meeting receives and records members, extends spiritual care and, if necessary, material aid for members of one or more weekly meetings.

  A quarterly meeting consists of representatives from several monthly meetings. Quarterly meetings unite into larger groups called yearly meetings, which are the rough equivalent of conventions, conferences, synods or dioceses in other faiths.

  Various yearly meetings form larger associations that assemble at intervals of a year or more. The largest is the Friends United Meeting. Its 15 yearly meeting members represent about half the Friends in the world.

Others include the Evangelical Friends Alliance and the Friends General Conference. Members of the conference include some yearly meetings that also are affiliated with the Friends United Meeting.

Overall, Friends count about 120,000 members in the United States and Canada, and a total of 200,000 world-wide.

Beliefs: Fox taught that the Inner Light emancipates a person from adherence to any creed, ecclesiastical authority or ritual forms. Many weekly meetings of worship involve silent meditation, in which any participant may speak when spiritually moved to do so. In others, there is a service of prayer and preaching.

Clergy: There is no recognized ranking of clergy over lay people. However, there are meeting officers, called *elders* or *ministers*. But they do not go through an ordination ceremony. Many Quaker ministers, particularly in the Midwest and West, use *the Reverend* before their names and describe themselves as *pastors*.

Capitalize *elder, minister* or *pastor* when used as a formal title before a name. Use *the Reverend* before a name on the first reference if it is a minister's practice. Do not carry the title through to subsequent references. See **religious titles**.

- **quart** (dry) Equal in volume to 67.2 cubic inches. The metric equivalent is about 1.1 liters.

   To convert to liters, multiply by 1.1: 5 dry quarts times 1.1 equals 5.5 liters. See **liter**.

- **quart** (liquid) Equal in volume to 57.75 cubic inches. It also equals 32 fluid ounces.

   The approximate metric equivalents are 950 milliliters or .95 liters.

   To convert to liters, multiply by .95: 4 quarts times .95 equals 3.8 liters. See **liter**.

- **quasar** (KWAY'-zahr) Acceptable in all references for a *quasi-stellar astronomical object*, often a radio source. Most astronomers consider quasars the most distant objects observable in the heavens.

- **Quebec** This city in Canada stands alone in datelines.

   Use *Quebec City* in the body of a story if the city must be distinguished from the province.

   Do not abbreviate any reference to the province of Quebec, Canada's largest in area and second-largest in population. See **datelines**.

- **queen** Capitalize only when used before the name of royalty: *Queen Elizabeth the Second*. Carry through in subsequent references that use the queen's given name: *Queen Elizabeth*.

   Lowercase when *queen* stands alone.

   Capitalize in plural uses: *Queens Elizabeth and Victoria*. See **nobility** and **titles**.

- **Queen Elizabeth the Second**   But the ocean liner is the *Queen Elizabeth Two.*

- **queen mother**   The mother of a reigning monarch. See **nobility.**

- **question mark (?)**   Sentences constructed as questions can be difficult for a news anchor to handle, and so should be used with great care.

  This is particularly true in connection with quotes, which are awkward in the first place. A quote that ends in a question mark is likely to cause a stumble or awkward inflection, so use it only when central to the story.

  When you do use questions in your copy, follow these guidelines for use of the question mark:

  End of a direct question: *Who started the riot?*

  Did he ask who started the riot? (The sentence as a whole is a direct question despite the indirect question at the end.)

  You started the riot? (A question in the form of a declarative statement.)

  Interpolated question: *You told me — Did I hear you correctly? — that you started the riot.* This is a construction used only very rarely in broadcast contexts.

  Multiple questions: Use a single question mark at the end of the full sentence:

  Did you hear him say, "What right have you to ask about the riot?"

  Did he plan the riot, employ assistants, and give the signal to begin?   Or, to cause full stops and throw emphasis on each element, break into separate sentences: *Did he plan the riot? Employ assistants? Give the signal to begin?*

  Caution: Do not use question marks to indicate the end of indirect questions:

  He asked who started the riot. To ask why the riot started is unnecessary. I want to know what the cause of the riot was. How foolish it is to ask what caused the riot.

  Placement with quotation marks: Inside or outside, depending on the meaning: *Who wrote "Gone With the Wind"? He asked, "How long will it take?"*

  Miscellaneous: The question mark supersedes the comma that normally is used when supplying attribution for a quotation: *"Who is there?" she asked.*

- **questionnaire**

- **quick-witted**

- **quotation marks**   This entry describes the mechanics of using quotation marks. For guidelines on when to use quotations in your copy, see **quotations in the news**.

  Quotation marks serve as the visual cue to the broadcaster that the words which follow are *precisely* the words said by the newsmaker. Never alter quotations.

  Quotation marks also tell the anchor or reporter that the words which follow need special treatment: They are direct quotes, proper names or unusual terms.

  But remember: Only the anchor sees them. They are invisible to the listeners and viewers. They must therefore be used with great care.

Some guidelines on the mechanics:

Direct quotations: It is especially important to avoid the first-person pronoun whenever possible.

Awkward: *The sheriff told reporters, "I am outraged by the order and I will not obey it."*

Better: *The sheriff said he is "outraged" by the order and will not obey it.*

Leading into quotations: It is often best to include in the copy words which reinforce the fact that you are reading a quote. This includes such phrases as *in his words, as he put it,* or even *quoting here.*

Example: *The sheriff called the attorney general — in his words — "a damned liar," and said he would not believe anything the attorney general said.*

There are many phrases which can be used to emphasize that the next few words are those of the person being quoted, not those of the newscaster. Even though these phrases may slow the flow of the copy, they should still be used whenever there is any danger of misinterpretation.

Some examples:

The attorney general said that the sheriff — as he put it — "has never had a reputation for excessive honesty."

The sheriff has denounced the attorney general again. He called him — quote — "a damned liar."

The attorney general used two words to describe the sheriff. Those two words were: "damned fool."

The sheriff accused the attorney general of dishonesty. He called him — and these are his exact words — "a crook."

In all of these cases, tape would have been better, but lacking it, the quote was essential.

Running quotations: Never carry a quotation beyond the end of a sentence.

Abbreviations: Do not use quotation marks around abbreviations. See **abbreviations**.

Acronyms: Do not use quotation marks around acronyms. See **acronyms**.

Composition titles: See the **composition titles** entry for guidelines on the use of quotation marks in book titles, movie titles, etc. See **music** for guidelines on using quotation marks in connection with the names of albums, CDs and individual songs.

In general, quotation marks go around the names of most compositions. However, the following types of books do not get quotation marks around the names: the Bible, dictionaries, encyclopedias, almanacs, gazetteers and other similar publications.

Irony: Put quotation marks around a word or words used in an ironical sense. But be certain the copy reinforces the sense of irony so the anchor isn't confused.

Awkward: *The "debate" turned into a free-for-all.*

Better: *Organizers called it a "debate," but it turned into a free-for-all.*

Nicknames: See the **nicknames** entry.

Quotes within quotes: Avoid them. They don't work in broadcast copy.

Proper names: Use quotation marks around the proper names of ships, airplanes and other craft: *the U-S-S "Enterprise," the space shuttle "Discovery," the "Queen Elizabeth Two."* See **aircraft names**.

Do not use quotation marks around the names of performing groups. See
musical performers.

Special emphasis: Any words needing special emphasis in a sentence can be put
in quotation marks: *The word "silly" has a negative connotation to many people. The
word "crook" was used today in the sheriff's trial.* See **words as words**.

Unfamiliar terms: Words or phrases that are likely to be new to the
broadcaster and hence to the audience should be in quotation marks so they are
read with special emphasis: *Broadcast frequencies are now being measured in a
unit called "kilohertz."*

Punctuation: The placement of punctuation marks relative to the quotation
marks depends on the nature of the sentence. Dashes, semicolons, questions
marks and exclamation points go inside the quotation marks when they apply to
the quoted matter only. Otherwise, they go outside. Periods and commas always
go inside quotation marks. See **comma**.

- **quotations in the news** Quotations are hard to handle on the air: The
anchor or reporter must change inflection to telegraph that the words were said
by someone else.

Whenever possible, use tape. A quotation is a poor substitute for the sound of
the person saying the words. If tape isn't available, paraphrase the quote if at all
possible.

Use a direct quote only if it is central to the story and tape is not available.

When using quotes, keep them as short as possible. A sentence-long quote is
almost impossible for the anchor to handle. By the end of it, the listener is
uncertain of whether the words are the anchor's or the newsmaker's. For details,
see the section on quotes in Chapter 5, "Telling the Story: Style," page 109.

Never alter quotations, even to correct minor grammatical errors or word
usage. Casual minor tongue slips can be removed using ellipses, but even that
should be done with extreme caution. If there is a question about a quote, either
don't use it or ask the speaker to clarify.

If a person is unavailable for comment, detail your attempts to reach that
person. For example, *Smith was out of the country on business; Jones did not
return phone calls to his office.*

Do not routinely use abnormal spellings such as *gonna* in attempts to convey
regional dialects or mispronunciations. Such spellings are appropriate, however,
when relevant to the story or in special contexts in which the atmosphere is
important. See **dialect**.

Full vs. partial quotes: In general, avoid full-sentence quotes. As noted
above, it is difficult for a listener to distinguish between the words of the anchor
and the words of the newsmaker if the quote goes on for too long.

The use of one or two quoted words often helps make clear the nature of a
newsmaker's comments. In each of the following examples, the newsmaker
replied in the negative, but to say *he said no* doesn't tell the whole story: *Smith
said "no". Smith said "no way." Smith said "absolutely not — under no
circumstances." Smith said, "Are you crazy?"*

Context: Remember that you can misquote someone by giving a startling
remark without its modifying passage or qualifiers. The manner of delivery

sometimes is part of the context, which is why tape always is preferable. Reporting a smile or deprecatory gesture may be as important as conveying the words themselves.

Offensive language: There are instances in which the use of possibly offensive language is central to the story. For guidelines, see the **obscenities, profanities, vulgarities** entry.

Punctuation: See the **quotation marks** entry.

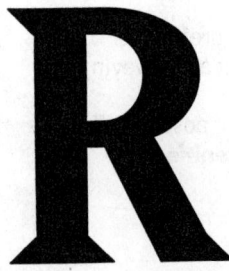

- **R** The *restricted* rating. See **movie ratings**.

- **rabbi** See **Jewish congregations**.

- **Rabbinical Assembly** See **Jewish congregations**.

- **Rabbinical Council of America** See **Jewish congregations**.

- **raccoon**

- **race** Identification by race is pertinent:
  - In biographical and announcement stories, particularly when they involve a feat or appointment that has not routinely been associated with members of a particular race.
  - When it provides the audience with a substantial insight into conflicting emotions known or likely to be involved in a demonstration or similar event.
  - When describing a person sought in a manhunt.

  In some stories that involve a conflict, it is equally important to specify that an issue cuts across racial lines. If, for example, a substantial number of whites are involved in a demonstration by supporters of busing to achieve racial balance in schools, that fact should be noted.

  Do not use racially derogatory terms unless they are part of a quotation that is essential to the story. See the **obscenities, profanities, vulgarities** entry and the **nationalities and races** entry.

- **rack, wrack** The noun *rack* applies to various types of framework; the verb *rack* means to arrange on a rack, to torture, trouble or torment: *He was placed in the rack. She racked her brain.*

  The noun *wrack* means ruin or destruction, and generally is confined to the phrase *wrack and ruin*.

  The verb *wrack* has substantially the same meaning as the verb *rack*, which is preferred.

- **racket** Not *racquet,* for the light bat used in tennis and badminton.

- **radar** A lowercase acronym for *radio detection and ranging.*

- **radical** In general, avoid this description in favor of a more precise definition of an individual's political views.

  When used, it suggests that an individual believes change must be made by tearing up the roots or foundation of the present order.

  Although *radical* often is applied to individuals who hold strong socialist or communist views, it also is applied at times to individuals who believe an existing form of government must be replaced by a more authoritarian or militaristic one. See the **leftist, ultra-leftist** and **rightist, ultra-rightist** entries.

- **radio** Capitalize and use before a name to indicate an official voice of government: *Radio Moscow.*

  When the term is used lowercase after the city name, as in *Havana radio,* it refers merely to broadcasts on stations located in that city.

- **radio station** The call letters alone are frequently adequate, but when needed to differentiate from a television station, use these constructions, lowercase: *radio station W-H-E-C* or *W-H-E-C radio.* See **call letters.**

- **railroads** Capitalize when part of a formal name: *the Illinois Central Gulf Railroad.*

  Railroad companies vary the spellings of their names, using *Railroad, Rail Road, Railway* and other combinations. Consult the "Official Railway Guide-Freight Service" and the "Official Railway Guide-Passenger Service" for official spellings.

  Use *the railroad* on second reference.

  Use *railroads* in lowercase for all plurals: *the Penn Central and Santa Fe railroads.* See **Amtrak** and **Conrail.**

- **rainstorm** See **weather terms.**

- **raised, reared** Only humans may be *reared.*
  Any living thing, including humans, may be *raised.*

- **RAM** Acronym for *random-access memory,* the "working memory" of a computer into which programs are introduced and then executed.

  RAM is acceptable on second reference in a computer feature program, but in every context, *memory* is the preferable term.

- **ranges** Strive for informality, but be careful to avoid confusion when dealing with ranges of numbers. For example, the phrase *12 to 14 (m) million dollars* is preferable to *12 (m) million to 14 (m) million dollars* — unless the context makes it confusing.

  You need not state the units on the first reference in a range unless failure to do so would leave the broadcaster and listeners confused. See **numerals.**

- **rank and file** (n.) The adjective form: *rank-and-file.*

• **rarely** It means *seldom*. *Rarely ever* is redundant, but *rarely if ever* is often the appropriate phrase.

• **ratios** Use hyphens and the word *to* and follow the rules for **numerals** when describing a ratio: *It was a 75-to-one shot; He beat the president two-to-one; He beat the president by a two-to-one margin.*
Use the term *ratio* or *margin* if there might be confusion between the ratio and the actual figures.

• **ravage, ravish** To *ravage* is to wreak great destruction or devastation: *Union troops ravaged Atlanta.*
To *ravish* is to abduct, rape or carry away with emotion: *Soldiers ravished the women.*
Although both words connote an element of violence, they are not interchangeable. Buildings and towns cannot be *ravished*.

• **rayon** Not a trademark.

• **R-C-A Corporation** Formerly Radio Corporation of America. The abbreviation *R-C-A* is acceptable on all references. *R-C-A* is now owned by the General Electric Company. Headquarters is in New York.

• **re-** The rules in **prefixes** apply. The following examples of exceptions to first-listed spellings in Webster's New World are based on the general rule that a hyphen is used if a prefix ends in a vowel and the word that follows begins with the same vowel:

re-elect	re-employ	re-equip	re-enlist
re-election	re-enact	re-establish	re-enter
re-emerge	re-engage	re-examine	re-entry

For many other words, the sense is the governing factor:

recover (regain)	reform (improve)	resign (quit)
re-cover (cover again)	re-form (form again)	re-sign (sign again)

Otherwise, follow Webster's New World. Use a hyphen for words not listed there unless the hyphen would distort the sense.

• **reader** See **Church of Christ, Scientist**.

• **Realtor** The term *real estate agent* is preferred. Use *Realtor* only if there is a reason to indicate that the individual is a member of the National Association of Realtors. See **service mark**.

• **reared** See the **raised, reared** entry.

- **rebut, refute** *Rebut* means to argue to the contrary: *He rebutted his opponent's statement.*
  Refute connotes success in argument and almost always implies an editorial judgment. Instead, use *deny, dispute, rebut* or *respond to.*

- **receivership** A legal action in which a court appoints a *receiver* to manage a business while the court tries to resolve problems such as insolvency which could ruin the business.
  Receivership is often used in federal bankruptcy court proceedings. But it also can be used for non-financial troubles, such as an ownership dispute. In bankruptcy proceedings, the court appoints a trustee called a *receiver* who attempts to settle the financial difficulties of the company while under protection from creditors.

- **recession** A falling-off of economic activity that may be a temporary phenomenon or could continue into a depression. Although definitions vary, economics generally consider the economy to be in recession if the gross domestic product has declined for two consecutive quarters.

- **recision** The preferred spelling is *rescission.*

- **reconnaissance**

- **Reconstruction** The process of reorganizing the Southern states after the Civil War.

- **record** Avoid the redundant *new record.*

- **record-holder**

- **rector** See **religious titles.**

- **recur, recurred, recurring** Not *reoccur.*

- **Red** Capitalize when used as a political, geographic or military term: *the Red army.*

- **Red China** See **China.**

- **red-haired, redhead, redheaded** All are acceptable for a person with red hair.
  Redhead also is used colloquially to describe a type of North American diving duck.

- **red-handed** (adj. and adv.)

- **red-hot**

• **redneck** From the characteristic sunburned neck acquired in the fields by farm laborers. It refers to poor, white rural residents of the South and often is a derogatory term. Do not use except in quoted matter.

• **re-elect, re-election**

• **refer** See the **allude, refer** entry.

• **referable**

• **reference works** Capitalize their proper names.
Do not use quotation marks around the names of books that are primarily catalogs of reference material. In addition to catalogs, this category includes almanacs, dictionaries, directories, encyclopedias, gazetteers, handbooks and similar publications.
Examples: *Congressional Directory, Webster's New World Dictionary, the AP Stylebook, the AP Broadcast News Handbook.* But: "The Careful Writer" and "Modern American Usage."

• **referendum, referendums**

• **reformatory** See the **prison, jail** entry.

• **Reform Judaism** See **Jewish congregations**.

• **refute** See the **rebut, refute** entry.

• **regime** See the **government, junta, regime** entry.

• **regions** See the **directions and regions** entry.

• **reign, rein** *Reign* is the period a ruler is on the throne: *The king began his reign.*
The leather strap for a horse is a *rein*, hence figuratively: *seize the reins, give free rein to.*

• **release times** Material is sometimes provided by a source on the condition that it not be broadcast or published until a specific time.
Government agencies often provide complex reports, studies or speeches with the understanding that they will not be broadcast or published until after the news conference at which they are explained. Without such agreements, members would receive the material much later than is now the case.
Members should note that their membership agreements specifically require them to observe release times.
If the source does not specify a particular time but says the material is for release in morning papers, the automatic release time for broadcast and print is 6:30 p.m. Eastern time.

If the source says only that material is for release in afternoon papers, the automatic release time for broadcast and print is 6:30 a.m. Eastern time.

Such stories should be slugged to indicate the release time:

(Following advance for use at 6:30 p-m E-S-T)

If the material is to be held until the beginning of a news conference or until the beginning of a speech, it should be slugged:

(Hold for release on delivery, expected at 10:30 a-m)

When the material is released, an advisory should be sent to that effect:

Clinton Speech ADVISORY

Inaugural speech released. The president has begun speaking. His prepared text may now be released.

• **religious affiliations** Capitalize the names and the related terms applied to members of the order: *He is a member of the Society of Jesus. He is a Jesuit.*

• **religious movements** The terms that follow have been grouped under a single entry because they are related and frequently cross denominational lines.

Evangelical: Historically, *evangelical* was used as an adjective describing dedication to conveying the message of Christ. Today it also is used as a noun, referring to a category of doctrinally conservative Christians. They emphasize the need for a definite, adult commitment or conversion to faith in Christ and the duty of all believers to persuade others to accept Christ.

Evangelicals make up some conservative denominations and are numerous in broader denominations. Evangelicals stress both doctrinal absolutes and vigorous efforts to win others to belief.

The National Association of Evangelicals is an interdenominational, cooperative body of relatively small, conservative Protestant denominations. It has a total of about 2.5 million members, and has headquarters in Wheaton, Ill.

Evangelism: The word refers to activity directed outside the church fold to influence others to commit themselves to faith in Christ, to his work of serving others and to infuse his principles into society's conduct.

Styles of evangelism vary from direct preaching appeals at large public meetings to practical deeds of caring in the name of Christ, indirectly conveying the same call to allegiance to him.

The word *evangelism* is derived from the Greek *evangelion*, which means the gospel or good news of Christ's saving action on behalf of humanity.

Fundamentalist: The word gained usage in an early 20th century fundamentalist-modernist controversy within Protestantism. In recent years, however, *fundamentalist* has to a large extent taken on pejorative connotations except when applied to groups that stress strict, literal interpretations of Scripture and separation from other Christians.

In general, do not use *fundamentalist* unless a group applies the word to itself.

Liberal: In general, avoid this word as a descriptive classification in religion. It has objectionable implications to many believers.

Acceptable alternate descriptions include *activist, more flexible* and *broad view.*

Moderate is appropriate when used by the contending parties, as is the case in the conflict between the moderate or more flexible wing of the Lutheran Church-Missouri Synod and conservatives, who argue for literal interpretations of biblical passages others consider symbolic.

Do not use the term *Bible-believing* to distinguish one faction from another, because all Christians believe the Bible. The differences are over interpretations.

Neo-Pentecostal, charismatic: These terms apply to a movement that has developed within mainline Protestant and Roman Catholic denominations since the mid-20th century. It is distinguished by its emotional expressiveness, spontaneity in worship, speaking or praying in "unknown tongues" and healing. Participants often characterize themselves as "spirit-filled" Christians.

Unlike the earlier Pentecostal movement, which led to separate denominations, this movement has swelled within major churches.

Pentecostalism: A movement that arose in the early 20th century and separated from historic Protestant denominations. It is distinguished by belief in tangible manifestations of the Holy Spirit, often in demonstrative, emotional ways such as speaking in "unknown tongues" and healing.

Pentecostal denominations include the Assemblies of God, the Pentecostal Holiness Church, the United Pentecostal Church, Incorporated and the International Church of the Foursquare Gospel founded by Aimee Semple McPherson.

- **religious references** The basic guidelines:

Deities: Capitalize the proper names of monotheistic deities: *God, Allah, the Father, the Son, Jesus Christ, the Son of God, the Redeemer, the Holy Spirit,* etc.

Lowercase pronouns referring to the deity: *he, him, his, thee, thou,* etc.

Lowercase *gods* in referring to the deities of polytheistic religions.

Capitalize the proper names of pagan and mythological gods and goddesses: *Neptune, Thor, Venus,* etc.

Lowercase such words as *god-awful, goddamn, god-like, godliness, godsend.*

Life of Christ: Capitalize the names of major events in the life of Jesus Christ in references that do not use his name: *The doctrines of the Last Supper, the Crucifixion, the Resurrection and the Ascension are central to Christian belief.*

But use lowercase when the words are used with his name: *According to Christian belief, the ascension of Jesus into heaven took place 40 days after his resurrection from the dead.*

Apply the principle also to events in the life of his mother: *He cited the doctrines of the Immaculate Conception and the Assumption.* But: *She referred to the assumption of Mary into heaven.*

Rites: Capitalize proper names for rites that commemorate the Last Supper or signify a belief in Christ's presence: *the Lord's Supper, Holy Communion, Holy Eucharist.*

Lowercase the names of other sacraments. See the **sacraments** entry. Capitalize *Benediction* and *Mass*. But: *a high Mass, a low Mass, a requiem Mass*.

Holy days: Capitalize the name of holy days. See the **holidays and holy days** entry and separate entries for major Christian and Jewish feasts.

Other words: Lowercase *heaven, hell, devil, angel, cherub, an apostle, a priest*, etc.

Capitalize *Hades* and *Satan*.

For additional details, see **Bible**, entries for frequently used religious terms, the entries for major denominations, **religious movements** and **religious titles**.

- **Religious Society of Friends** See **Quakers**.

- **religious titles** The first reference to a clergyman, clergywoman or nun should include a capitalized formal title before the individual's name.

In many cases, *the Reverend* is the designation that applies. Use *the Reverend Doctor* only if the individual has earned a doctoral degree—Doctor of Divinity degrees frequently are honorary—and the reference to the degree is relevant.

On second references, do not carry the title through unless the individual is best known with it: *the Reverend Billy Graham*, but *Graham* on the second reference. But: *Pope John Paul II, the pope* (not *John Paul*); *Metropolitan Ireney, the metropolitan*.

Detailed guidance on specific titles and descriptive words such as *priest* and *minister* are provided in the entries for the major denominations. In general:

Cardinals, archbishops, bishops: The preferred form for first reference is to use *Cardinal, Archbishop* or *Bishop* before the individual's name: *Cardinal Timothy Manning, the archbishop of Los Angeles*. On second reference, *Manning* or *the cardinal*.

Substitute *the Most Reverend* if applicable and appropriate in the context: *He spoke to the Most Reverend Joseph Bernardin, archbishop of Cincinnati*. On second reference, *Bernardin* or *the archbishop*.

Entries for individual denominations tell when *the Most Reverend, the Very Reverend*, etc. are applicable.

Ministers and priests: Use *the Reverend* before a name on first reference.

Substitute *Monsignor* before the name of a Roman Catholic priest who has received this honor.

Do not routinely use *curate, father, pastor* or similar words before an individual's name. If they appear before a name in a quotation, capitalize them.

Rabbis: Use *Rabbi* before a name on first reference. Do not carry the title to subsequent references.

Nuns: Always use *Sister*, or *Mother* if applicable, before a name: *Sister Agnes Rita* in all references if the nun uses only a religious name; *Sister Clare Regina Torpy* on first reference if she uses a surname, *Sister Torpy* on second—or no title, as she prefers.

Officeholders: The preferred first-reference form for people who hold church office but are not ordained clergy in the usual sense is to use a construction that explains the title without using it directly before the name. If it must be used directly before the name, capitalize it.

- **reluctant, reticent** *Reluctant* means unwilling to act: *He is reluctant to enter the primary.*
  Reticent means unwilling to speak: *The candidate's husband is reticent.*

- **Reorganized Church of Jesus Christ of Latter Day Saints** Not properly described as a *Mormon church.* See the explanation under **Church of Jesus Christ of Latter-day Saints.**

- **representative** Do not use the abbreviation *Rep.* See **legislative titles** and **party affiliation.**

- **republic** Capitalize *republic* when used as part of a nation's formal name: *the Republic of Argentina.* See **datelines.**

- **Republican, Republican Party** *G-O-P* may be used on second reference. See the **political parties and philosophies** entry.

- **Republican Governors Association** No apostrophe.

- **Republican National Committee** On second reference: *the national committee, the committee.*
  Similarly: *Republican State Committee, Republican County Committee, Republican City Committee, the state committee, the county committee, the city committee, the committee.*

- **reputation** See **character, reputation.**

- **rescission** Not *recision.*

- **Reserve** Capitalize when referring to U.S. armed forces, as in *Army Reserve.* Lowercase in reference to members of these backup forces: *reserves,* or *reservists.*

- **Reserve Officers' Training Corps** The *s'* is military practice. *R-O-T-C* is acceptable in all references.
  When the service is specified, use it before the *R-O-T-C* reference: *Army R-O-T-C, Navy R-O-T-C, Air Force R-O-T-C.* But not *A-R-O-T-C* or *N-R-O-T-C.*

- **resident** See the **citizen, resident, subject, national, native** entry.

- **resistible**

- **restaurateur** No *n.* Not *restauranteur.*

- **restrictive clauses** See the **essential clauses, non-essential clauses** entry.

- **restrictive phrases** See the **essential phrases, non-essential phrases** entry.

- **Retail Clerks International Association** See **United Food and Commercial Workers International Union**.

- **retail sales** The sales by retail stores, including merchandise sold and receipts for repairs and similar services.
    A business is considered a *retail store* if it is engaged primarily in selling merchandise for personal, household or farm consumption.

- **return on investment** See **profit terminology**.

- **Reuters** (ROY'-tuhrs) A private British news agency, named for Baron Paul Julius von Reuter, the founder.
    The official name is *Reuters, Limited.* It is referred to as *Reuters.* When it is used as an adjective, the *s* is dropped: *a Reuter correspondent, a Reuter story.*

- **revenue** See **profit terminology**.

- **revenue bond** See **loan terminology**.

- **Reverend** Do not use the abbreviation *Rev.*
    When this description is used before a name, precede it with the word *the* because, unlike the case with *Mr.* and *Mrs.*, it is not a noun.
    If an individual has a secular title, use whichever title is appropriate to the context, but not both. See **religious titles**.

- **revolution** Capitalize when part of a name for a specific historical event: *the American Revolution, the Russian Revolution, the French Revolution.*
    The Revolution, capitalized, also may be used as a shorthand reference to the *American Revolution.* Also: *the Revolutionary War.*
    Lowercase in other uses: *a revolution, the revolution, the American and French revolutions.*

- **revolutions per minute** The abbreviation *R-P-M* is acceptable on first reference in specialized contexts such as an auto feature or home entertainment feature. Otherwise, do not use it until second reference.

- **revolver** See **pistol** and **weapons**.

- **revolving credit** Describes an account on which a limited amount of credit may be accessed repeatedly, the payment is any amount less than the total balance, and the remaining balance carried forward is subject to finance charges.

- **R-H factor**   Also: *R-H negative, R-H positive.*

- **Rhode Island**   It is the smallest of the 50 states in terms of total land area: 1,049 square miles. See **state names.**

- **Richter scale**   See **earthquakes.**

- **RICO** (REE'-koh) An acronym for *Racketeer Influenced and Corrupt Organizations Act.* Do not use except in quoted matter or tape—and in those cases, be certain to make clear that *RICO* means *the anti-racketeering law* or *the anti-corruption law.*

- **riff-raff**

- **rifle**   See **weapons.**

- **rifle, riffle**   To *rifle* is to plunder or steal.
To *riffle* is to leaf rapidly through a book or pile of papers.

- **right hand** (n.) **right-handed** (adj.) **right-hander** (n.)

- **rightist, ultra-rightist**   In general, avoid these terms in favor of more precise descriptions of an individual's political philosophy.
As popularly used today, particularly abroad, *rightist* often applies to someone who is conservative or opposed to socialism. It also often indicates an individual who supports an authoritarian government that is militantly anti-communist or anti-socialist.
Ultra-rightist suggests an individual who subscribes to rigid interpretations of a conservative doctrine or to forms of fascism that stress authoritarian, often militaristic views. See **radical** and the **leftist, ultra-leftist** entry.

- **right of way, rights of way**

- **right-to-work** (adj.)   A *right-to-work* law prohibits a company and a union from signing a contract that would require the affected workers to be union members.
Federal labor laws generally permit such contracts. There is no federal right-to-work law, but Section 14-B of the Taft-Hartley Act allows states to pass such laws if they wish. Many states have done so.
The repeal of Section 14-B would have the effect of voiding all right-to-work laws. By itself, the repeal would not require workers to be union members, but in states that now have right-to-work laws, the repeal would open the way to contracts requiring union membership. See **closed shop** for definitions of various agreements that require union membership.

- **right wing** (n.) But: *right-wing* (adj.), *right-winger* (n.).

- **Ringling Brothers and Barnum and Bailey Circus**
Headquarters is in Washington.

- **Rio Grande** Not *Rio Grande River*. (*Rio* means river.)

- **rip off** (v.) **rip-off** (n., adj.) Use this term sparingly.

- **river** Capitalize as part of a proper name: *the Mississippi River*. Lowercase in other uses: *the river, the Mississippi and Missouri rivers*.

- **road** Do not abbreviate. See **addresses**.

- **Roaring 20's** See **decades**.

- **robbery** See the **burglary, larceny, robbery, theft** entry.

- **rock 'n' roll** *Rock-and-roll* is better.

- **Rocky Mountains** Or simply: *the Rockies*.

- **roll call** (n.) **roll-call** (adj.)

- **roll over** (v.) **rollover** (n.) The selling of new securities to pay off old ones coming due, or the refinancing of an existing loan.

- **Rolls-Royce** Note the hyphen in this trademark for a make of automobile.

- **roly-poly**

- **ROM** An acronym for *read-only memory*, a form of computer memory that is programmed by the manufacturer and cannot be programmed by the user. Spell it out.

- **Roman Catholic Church** The church traces its origin to Christ's choice of the apostle Peter to lead his church on earth and his promise that "whatever you bind on earth shall be bound in heaven and whatever you loose on earth shall be loosed in heaven."
The church teaches that its bishops have been established as the legitimate successors of the apostles through generations of ceremonies in which authority was passed down by a laying on of hands.
Responsibility for teaching the faithful and administering the church rests with the bishops. However, the church holds that the pope has final authority over their actions because he is the bishop of Rome, the office that it teaches was held by Peter at his death.
The shared teaching power—often called collegiality—of the bishops is particularly manifest when a pope summons an ecumenical council, a meeting of all bishops to regulate church worship and define new expressions of its

teachings. Council actions must be approved by the pope, however, before they can take effect.

Although the pope is empowered to speak infallibly on faith and morals, he does so only in formal pronouncements that specifically state he is speaking from the chair (*ex cathedra*) of St. Peter. This rarely used prerogative was most recently invoked in 1950, when Pope Pius XII declared that Mary was assumed bodily into heaven.

The Curia serves as a form of governmental cabinet. Its members, appointed by the pope, handle both administrative and judicial functions.

The pope also chooses members of the College of Cardinals, who serve as his principal counselors. When a new pope must be chosen, they meet in a conclave to select a new pope by majority vote. In practice, cardinals are bishops, but there is no requirement that a cardinal be a bishop.   In the Latin Rite used by Catholics in the Western world, there are no national "churches" in the sense that applies in other denominations. Bishops in various nations do, however, organize conferences that develop programs to further the needs of the church in their nations. The National Conference of Catholic Bishops is the national organization of Roman Catholic bishops in the United States. Its administrative arm is the United States Catholic Conference, with offices in Washington.

In the Eastern Rite, followed by many Roman Catholics who live in the Middle East or trace their origins to it, there are national churches. They and the archbishops (often called *patriarchs*) who head them have considerable autonomy in ritual and discipline, but they acknowledge the authority of the pope. See **Eastern Rite churches**.

In the United States, the church's principal organizational units are archdioceses and dioceses. They are headed, respectively, by archbishops and bishops, who have final responsibility for many activities within their jurisdictions and report directly to Rome. Although the seat of an archdiocese once served as a meeting place for the bishops of other dioceses within a region, there is little practical difference between the two in the Latin Rite. An archbishop, however, is required to report to Rome if he believes that abuses have occurred in a diocese within his region.

The church counts more than 600 million members worldwide. In the United States it has more than 48 million members, making it the largest single body of Christians in the nation.

Beliefs: Roman Catholics believe in the Trinity—that there is one God who exists as three divine persons, the Father, the Son and the Holy Spirit. They believe that the Son became man as Jesus Christ.

Other beliefs include salvation through Christ, and everlasting heaven and hell.

The essential elements of belief are contained in the Bible and in "tradition," the body of teachings passed on both orally and in writing by the apostles and their successors.

The Mass is the central act of worship. Christ is believed to be present in the Holy Eucharist, which is consecrated during Mass.

In addition to the Holy Eucharist, there are six other sacraments—baptism, confirmation, penance (often called the sacrament of reconciliation), matrimony, holy orders, and the sacrament of the sick (formerly extreme unction).

Clergy: Ranks below the pope are, in descending order, cardinal, archbishop, bishop, monsignor, priest and deacon. In religious orders, some men who are not priests have the title *brother*.

Capitalize *pope* when used as a formal title before a name: *Pope John Paul the Second.* Lowercase in all other uses. See **titles**.

The first-reference forms for other titles follow. Use only last names on second reference.

Cardinals: *Cardinal Timothy Manning.* The usage *Timothy Cardinal Manning*, a practice traceable to the nobility's custom of identifications such as *William, Duke of Norfolk,* is still used in formal documents but otherwise is considered archaic.

Archbishops: *Archbishop Joseph Bernardin,* or *the Most Reverend Joseph Bernardin, archbishop of Cincinnati.*

Bishops: *Bishop Bernard Flanagan,* or *the Most Reverend Bernard Flanagan, bishop of Worcester.*

Monsignors: *Monsignor Joseph Vogt.* Do not use the abbreviation *Msgr.* or *the Right Reverend* or *the Very Reverend*—this distinction between types of monsignors no longer is made.

Priests: *the Reverend John Paret.* When necessary in quotations on second reference: *Father Paret.* See **religious titles**.

- **Romania** Not *Rumania.*

- **Romanian Orthodox Church** The Romanian Orthodox Church in America is an autonomous archdiocese of the Romanian Orthodox Church. The Romanian Orthodox Episcopate of America is an autonomous archdiocese within the Orthodox Church in America. See **Eastern Orthodox Churches**.

- **Roman numerals** Don't use them. See **numerals**.

- **Rome** The city in Italy stands alone in datelines.

- **room numbers** Follow the rules for **numerals** and capitalize: *Room Two, Room 222.*

- **Roquefort cheese, Roquefort dressing** A certification mark for a type of blue cheese cured in Roquefort, France. It is not a trademark.

- **rosary** It is *recited* or *said*, never *read.* Always lowercase.

- **Rosh Hashana** (rohsh ha-SHAH'-nah) A two-day holiday celebrating the Jewish new year and the start of the High Holy Days. Occurs in September or October.

- **rostrum** See the **lectern, podium, pulpit, rostrum** entry.

- **R-O-T-C** Acceptable in all references for *Reserved Officers' Training Corps.* See that entry.

- **round up** (v.) **round-up** (n.)

- **route numbers** Do not abbreviate *route*. See **highway designations**.

- **Royal Dutch-Shell Group of Companies** This holding company, based in London and The Hague, owns substantial portions of the stock in numerous corporations that specialize in petroleum and related products. Most have *Shell* in their names.

  Among them is Shell Oil Company, an American corporation, with headquarters in Houston.

- **royal titles** See **nobility**.

- **R-S-V-P** The abbreviation for the French *repondez s'il vous plait*, it means *please reply.*

- **Right Reverend** See the entry for the individual denomination.

- **rubber stamp** (n.) **rubber-stamp** (v. and adj.)

- **rubella** (roo-BEL'-uh) Also known as *German measles.*

- **runner-up, runners-up**

- **running mate**

- **rush hour** (n.) **rush-hour** (adj.)

- **Russia** See **Soviet Union**.

- **Russian names** When a first name in Russian has a close phonetic equivalent in English, use the equivalent in translating the name: *Alexander Solzhenitsyn* rather than *Aleksandr*, the spelling that would result from a transliteration of the Russian letters into the English alphabet.

  When a first name has no close phonetic equivalent in English, express it with an English spelling that approximates the sound in Russian: *Nikita*, for example.

  For last names, use the English spelling that most closely approximates the pronunciation in Russian.

  If an individual has a preference for an English spelling that is different from the one that would result by applying these guidelines, follow the individual's preference.

  Women's last names have feminine endings. But use them only if the woman is not married or if she is known under that name: *the ballerina Maya Plissetskaya*. Otherwise, use the masculine form: *Victoria Brezhnev*, not *Brezhneva*.

  Russian names never end in *off*, except for common mistransliterations such as *Rachmaninoff*. Instead, the transliterations should end in *ov*: *Romanov*.

  Always use pronouncers.

- **Russian Orthodox Church** See **Eastern Orthodox Churches**.

- **Russian Revolution** Also: *The Bolshevik Revolution.*

- **Sabbath** Capitalize in religious references; lowercase to mean a period of rest.

- **Sabena** (suh-BEE'-nuh) **Belgian World Airlines** A *Sabena airliner* is acceptable in any reference. Headquarters is in Brussels, Belgium.

- **saboteur**

- **sacraments** Capitalize the proper names used for a sacramental rite that commemorates the life of Jesus Christ or signifies a belief in his presence: *the Lord's Supper, Holy Communion, Holy Eucharist.*
  Lowercase the names of other sacraments: *baptism, confirmation, penance* (now often called *the sacrament of reconciliation*), *matrimony, holy orders* and *the sacrament of anointing the sick* (formerly *extreme unction*). See entries for the major religious denominations and **religious references**.

- **sacrilegious**

- **Safeway Stores, Incorporated** Headquarters is in Oakland, Calif.

- **saint** Abbreviate as *St.* in the names of saints, cities and other places: *St. Jude; St. Paul, Minn.; the St. Lawrence Seaway.* But see the entries for **Saint John** and **Sault Ste. Marie.**

- **Saint John** The spelling for the city in New Brunswick, to distinguish it from *St. John's, Newfoundland.*

- **salable**

- **sales** See **profit terminology**.

- **SALT** See **Strategic Arms Limitation Talks**.

- **Salt Lake City** Stands alone in datelines.

- **SALT-TWO** See **Strategic Arms Limitation Talks**.

- **salvo, salvos**

- **SAM, SAMs** Note lack of apostrophe in plural form. Acceptable on second reference for *surface-to-air missile(s)*.

- **San`a** The capital of Yemen. Note that the symbol between the *n* and the *a* is not an apostrophe. It is a reverse apostrophe, or a single open quote mark (').

- **sandbag** (n.) The verbs: *sandbagged, sandbagging*. And: *sandbagger*.

- **San Diego** The city in California stands alone in datelines.

- **sandstorm** See **weather terms**.

- **sandwich**

- **Sanforized** A trademark denoting that a fabric has been preshrunk according to a particular standard.
  A related trademark, *Sanforset*, describes a Sanforized fabric that has been treated to meet standards for smoothness.

- **San Francisco** The city in California stands alone in datelines.

- **sanitarium, sanitariums**

- **San Marino** Use alone in datelines on stories from the Republic of San Marino.

- **Santa Claus**

- **Sardinia** Use instead of *Italy* in datelines on stories from communities on this island.

- **Saskatchewan** A province of Canada north of Montana and North Dakota. Do not abbreviate. See **datelines.**

- **Satan** But lowercase *devil* and *satanic*.

- **satellite communications** The following are some generally used technical terms dealing with satellite communications.
  uplink: An earth station that transmits the signal from the ground to the satellite. The word also is used to describe the transmission itself.
  downlink: An earth station that receives the signal from the satellite. The word also is used to describe the transmission itself.
  earth station: Ground equipment that either sends to or receives from the satellite. An earth station has an antenna—a satellite dish—capable of communicating with the satellite.

footprint: The area on the ground in which a transmission from the satellite can be received.

geosynchronous: An orbit in which the satellite matches the earth's orbit, so that it appears always to be in the same place in reference to the ground. Most satellites are in geosynchronous orbits. Another term for this is *geostationary*.

transponder: The equipment on the satellite that sends and receives signals from the ground. A satellite usually has a number of transponders.

- **satellites** See **spacecraft designations**.

- **Saturday** See **days of the week**.

- **"Saturday night special"** Note quotation marks. See **weapons**.

- **Saudi Arabian Oil Company** The informal name *Saudi Aramco (uh-RAM'-koh)* is acceptable on second reference. Headquarters is in Dhahran (dah-RAHN'), Saudi Arabia.

- **Saulte Ste. Marie** (soo saynt muh-REE'), **Michigan; Saulte Ste. Marie, Ontario** The abbreviation is *Ste.* instead of *St.* because the full name is *Saulte Sainte Marie*.

- **savings and loan associations** They are not banks. Use *the S-and-L* or *the association* on second reference.

- **savior** Use this spelling for all senses, rather than the alternate form, *saviour*.

- **Scandinavian Airlines System** *S-A-S* is acceptable in all references. Headquarters is in Stockholm, Sweden.

- **scene numbers** Follow the rules for **numerals** and capitalize: *Scene Two. Act Two, Scene Four.*
  But: *the second scene.*

- **scener** A report from the actual scene of an event, with the sound of the event in the background.
  Whether live or taped, a scener must be done while the sounds in the background actually are taking place. The idea is to give a real-time description of what is happening.
  If you play back tape of an event behind your voice in a studio, that is *not* a scener —it's a voicer.
  Sceners run the same length as voicers —35 seconds maximum. See the entries under **actuality; natural sound; q&a; voicer** and **wrap**.

- **scheme** Do not use as a synonym for *plan* or *project*.

- **school** Capitalize when part of a proper name: *Public School Three* (follow the rules for **numerals**), *Madison Elementary School, Thomas Jefferson High School.*

• **scissors** Takes plural verbs and pronouns: *The scissors are on the table. Leave them there.*

• **scores** Use hyphens and the word *to*, and, in an exception to the rules in **numerals**, use figures only: *The Mets beat the Giants 6-to-5. It was a 12-to-3 victory.*

However, when reporting one team's score in the text of the story, follow the rules for **numerals**: *The six-run effort; the Yankees scored a total of seven runs; the Packers rolled up 24 points.* But: *It was Boston 6, Baltimore 5.* See the entries for individual sports for details on scoring formats.

• **Scot, Scots, Scottish** A native of Scotland is a *Scot.* The people are the *Scots*, not the *Scotch.* Somebody or something is *Scottish.*

• **scotch barley, scotch broth, scotch salmon, scotch sour**

• **Scotch tape** A trademark for a brand of transparent tape.

• **Scotch whisky** A type of whiskey distilled in Scotland from malted barley. The malt is dried over a peat fire.

Capitalize *Scotch* and use the spelling *whisky* only when the two words are used together.

Lowercase *scotch* when standing alone: *Does it make a good mix with scotch?*

Use the spelling *whiskey* for generic references to the beverage, which may be distilled from any of several grains.

The verb *to scotch* means to stamp out, put an end to.

• **Scotland** Use *Scotland* after the names of Scottish communities in datelines. See **datelines** and **United Kingdom.**

• **Scripture, Scriptures** Capitalize when referring to religious writings in the bible. See **Bible.**

• **scuba** Lowercase acronym for *self-contained underwater breathing apparatus.*

• **sculptor** Use for both men and women.

• **scurrilous**

• **Seaboard World Airlines** Headquarters is in New York.

• **Sea Islands** A chain of islands off the coasts of South Carolina, Georgia and Florida.

Islands within the boundaries of South Carolina include Parris Island, Port Royal Island, and St. Helena Island.

Those within Georgia include Cumberland Island (largest in the chain), St. Simons Island and St. Catherines Island (no apostrophes), and Sea Island.

Amelia Island is within the boundaries of Florida.

Several communities have names taken from the island name—Port Royal is a town on Port Royal Island, Sea Island is a resort on Sea Island, and St. Simons Island is a village on St. Simons Island.

In datelines:

(Port Royal, South Carolina) --

(St. Simons Island, Georgia) --

- **seaman** See **military titles**.

- **Sears, Roebuck and Company** Headquarters is in Chicago.

- **seasons** lowercase *spring, summer, fall, winter* and derivatives such as *springtime* unless part of a formal name: *Dartmouth Winter Carnival, Winter Olympics, Summer Olympics.*

- **Seattle** The city in the state of Washington stands alone in datelines.

- **second-guess** (v.) The noun form: *second guess.* Also: *second-guesser.*

- **second hand** (n.) **second-hand** (adj. and adv.) The hyphen is for readability.
Second-hand Rose had a watch with a second hand that she bought second-hand.

- **second-rate** (adj.) All uses: *A second-rate play. The play is second-rate.*

- **second reference** When used in this handbook, the term applies to all references other than the primary reference to an organization or individual within a story.

Generally speaking, the first reference to a subject comes in the lead of the story, and the second reference covers all subsequent mentions. But where the full reference to a subject can make the lead impossibly cumbersome, the writer may choose to lead with the second reference form of the name or term, and treat the subsequent mention as the primary reference. For example:

The U-A-W is on strike. Members of the United Auto Workers Union walked off car assembly lines across the country at midnight.

In cases where the second-reference term is used in the lead, be sure to use the full reference in the next sentence.

Acceptable abbreviations and acronyms for organizations frequently in the news are listed under the organization's full name. A few prominent acronyms acceptable on first reference also are listed alphabetically according to the letters of the acronym.

The listing of an acceptable term for second reference does not mean that it always must be used after the first reference. Often a generic word such as *the agency, the commission* or *the company* is more appropriate and less jarring to the listener. At other times, the full name may need to be repeated for clarity.

For additional guidelines that apply to organizations, see **abbreviations** and **acronyms**.

For additional guidelines that apply to individuals, see **courtesy titles** and **titles**.

- **secretary-general** Note hyphen.
  Capitalize as part of a formal title before a name. See **titles**.

- **secretary of state** Capitalize as a formal title before a name. See **titles**.

- **secretary-treasurer** Note hyphen.
  Capitalize as part of a formal title before a name. See **titles**.

- **Secret Service** A federal agency administered by the Treasury Department.
  The *Secret Service Uniformed Division,* which protects the president's residence and offices and the embassies in Washington, formerly was known as the *Executive Protective Service.*

- **section** Follow the rules for **numerals** and capitalize when referring to a part of a law or bill: *Section 14-B of the Taft-Hartley Act. Section Five of the Jones Act.*

- **Securities and Exchange Commission** *S-E-C* is acceptable on second reference. The related legislation is the *Securities Exchange Act.* Note: no *and.*

- **Security Council (U-N)** Precede it with *U-N* or *United Nations* on first reference.
  Retain capitalization of *Security Council* in subsequent references. Lowercase *council* whenever it stands alone.

- **Seeing Eye dog** No hyphen. A trademark for a guide dog.

- **see-saw** The hyphen is for readability.

- **self-** Always hyphenate:

self-assured   self-defense   self-government

- **sell out** (v.) **sell-out** (n.) The hyphen is for readability.

- **semi-** Hyphenate, except when the unhyphenated form is so familiar that the hyphenated form would look unusual. This is for readability.

Some examples:

semicolon   semi-official   semi-tropical

But: *semifinal.*

*   **semi-annual** The hyphen is for readability. It means twice a year—and is best said that way.
    Biannual means the same thing—and ought to be similarly avoided.
    Biennial means once every two years. Avoid it, too.

*   **semicolon** Use to indicate a greater separation of thought and information than a comma can convey but less than a period provides. It should be only rarely used in news copy.
    The basic guidelines:
    To clarify a series: Semicolons can separate elements of a series when individual segments contain material that must also be set off by commas:

    He leaves a son, John Smith of Kansas City, Missouri; a daughter, Jane Smith of Kansas City, Kansas; and a brother, Joe Smith of East St. Louis, Illinois.

    Note that the semicolon is used before the final *and* in such a series.
    Another application of this principle may be seen in the cross-references at the end of entries in this book. Because some entries themselves have a comma, a semicolon is used to separate references to multiple entries, as in: *See the entries for **felony, misdemeanor; pardon, parole, probation** and **prison, jail**.*
    To link independent clauses: A semicolon can be used when a coordinating conjunction such as *and, but* or *for* is not present: *The package was due last week; it arrived today.* See the **comma; double dash** and **ellipsis** entries for alternate forms of punctuation, which often are preferable.
    Placement with quotes: Place a semicolon outside quotation marks.

*   **senate** Capitalize all specific references to governmental legislative bodies, regardless of whether the name of the nation or state is used: *the United States Senate, the Senate, the Virginia Senate, the state Senate, the Senate.*
    Lowercase plural uses: *the Virginia and North Carolina senates.* See **governmental bodies**.
    The same principles apply to foreign bodies. See **foreign legislative bodies**.
    Lowercase references to non-governmental bodies: *the student senate at Yale.*

*   **senator** Do not use the abbreviation *Sen.* in any reference. See **legislative titles** and **party affiliation**.

*   **senatorial** Always lowercase.

*   **send off** (v.) **send-off** (n.)

- **senior** See the **junior, senior** entry.

- **senior citizen** Use the term sparingly. See **elderly**.

- **sentences** Capitalize the first word of every sentence, including quoted statements and direction questions: *Patrick Henry put it this way: "I know not what course others may take, but as for me, give me liberty or give me death."*
  Capitalize the first word of a quoted statement if it constitutes a sentence, even if it was part of a larger sentence in the original: *Patrick Henry said, "Give me liberty or give me death."*
  Also, capitalize the first word of a direct question that constitutes a full sentence, even without quotation marks: *The report tries to answer the question, Will the economy improve?* See **ellipsis**.

- **September** See **months**.

- **sergeant** See **military titles**.

- **serial numbers** Use them in stories only when they are essential. Usually, they are best reserved for an advisory at the bottom of the story.
  In copy, use figures and hyphens. If there is a space between a string of letters or numbers, use a comma: *A013467* should be expressed as *serial number A-o-1-3-4-6-7*, while *Ao9 87b* should be expressed as *A-o-9, 8-7-b*. The comma is the visual cue to pause.
  If a list of serial numbers is sent, do not use hyphens or commas:

  (Washington) — Here is a list of the toys recalled in an agreement announced by the Consumer Product Safety Commission today:

  > **``Talking baby'' doll, model 12876B**
  > **Race car, model 846105S**
  > **Rocking horse, model 35X**

- **serviceable**

- **service clubs** See the **fraternal organizations and service clubs** entry.

- **serviceman, servicewoman**

- **service mark** A brand, symbol or word used by a supplier of services and protected by law to prevent a competitor from using it: *Realtor*, for a member of the National Association of Realtors, for example.
  When a service mark is used, capitalize it.
  The preferred form, however, is to use a generic term unless the service mark is essential to the story. See **brand names** and **trademark**.

- **sesquicentennial** Every 150 years. Say it that way.

- **set up** (v.) **set-up** (n. and adj.) The hyphen is for readability.

- **Seven Seas** Arabian Sea, Atlantic Ocean, Bay of Bengal, Mediterranean Sea, Persian Gulf, Red Sea, South China Sea.

- **Seven Sisters** The colleges are: Barnard, Bryn Mawr, Mount Holyoke, Radcliffe, Smith, Vassar and Wellesley.
  Also, an old nickname for the world's largest privately operated oil companies: British Petroleum, Exxon, Gulf, Mobil, Royal Dutch-Shell, Texaco and Chevron (formerly Standard Oil Company of California). Chevron has taken over Gulf, reducing the number to six.

- **Seventh-day Adventist Church** The denomination is traceable to the preaching of William Miller of New Hampton, N.Y., a Baptist layman who said his study of the Book of Daniel showed that the end of the world would come in the mid 1840s.
  When the prediction did not come true, the Millerites split into smaller groups. One, influenced by visions described by Ellen Harmon, later Mrs. James White, is the precursor of Seventh-day Adventist practice today.
  The church has four constituent levels:
  - Local churches.
  - Local conferences of churches for a state or part of a state.
  - Union conferences of a number of local conferences.
  - The General Conference.

  The General Conference in Session, which meets every five years, and the General Conference Executive Committee are the highest administrative authorities.
  The office of the General Conference, located in Washington, lists American membership at 627,000, and worldwide membership at 5.2 million.
  Beliefs: The description *adventist* is based on the belief that a second coming of Christ is near. Believers hold that events leading to the coming began in the mid 1840s and will continue until the completion of a process that will identify those worthy of joining in the resurrection at the second coming of Christ.
  Seventh-day derives from the contention that the Bible permits no deviation from observing the seventh day of the week as the Sabbath.
  Baptism, by immersion, is reserved for those old enough to understand its meaning. Baptism and the Lord's Supper are the only sacraments.
  Clergy: The head of the General Conference holds the formal title of *president.* The formal titles for ministers are *pastor* or *elder.* Capitalize them when used immediately before a name on first reference. Do not carry the title to subsequent references.
  The designation *the Reverend* is not used. See **religious titles**.

- **Seven Wonders of the World** The Egyptian pyramids, the hanging gardens of Babylon, the Mausoleum at Halicarnassus, the temple of Artemis at Ephesus, the Colossus of Rhodes, the statue of Zeus by Phidias at Olympia and the Pharos or lighthouse at Alexandria.

- **sewage, sewerage** *Sewage* is waste matter.
  Sewerage is the drainage system and is not a word most people use.

- **sex changes** Follow these guidelines in using proper names or personal pronouns when referring to an individual who has had a sex-change operation:
  - If the reference is to an action before the operation, use the proper name and gender of the individual at that time.
  - If the reference is to an action after the operation, use the new proper name and gender.

  For example:
  Dr. Richard Raskind was a first-rate amateur tennis player. He won several tournaments. Ten years later, when Dr. Renee Richards applied to play in tournaments, many women players objected on the ground that she was the former Richard Raskind, who had undergone a sex-change operation. Richards said she was entitled to compete as a woman. See **courtesy titles**.

- **sexism** Avoid constructions that force personal pronouns to be gender-specific when the sentence actually refers to people of both sexes. See **man, mankind** and **women**.

  Similarly, avoid the use of gender-specific references in connection with storms or ships that carry names usually associated with men or women. See **hurricanes** and **she**.

- **shah** Capitalize when used as a title before a name: *Shah Mohammed Reza Pahlavi of Iran.*

  The Shah of Iran commonly was known only by his title, which is, in effect, an alternative name. Capitalize *Shah of Iran* in references to the holder of the title; lowercase subsequent references as *the shah.* This practice is based on the guidelines in the **nobility** entry.

- **shake up** (v.) **shake-up** (n. and adj.)

- **shall, will** Few people use the word *shall* in normal conversation. It is reserved for formal occasions and expressions of extreme determination: *We shall overcome. We shall hold a meeting.*

  Use *will* in most constructions: *We will hold a meeting. Officials say they will announce their decision today. The Mets will take on the Padres tonight.* See the **should, would** entry and **subjunctive mood**.

- **shape up** (v.) **shape-up** (n. and adj.)

- **Shariah** (shuh-REE'-uh) The legal code of Islam. It is roughly comparable to the Talmudic tradition in Judaism.

- **Shavuot** (shuh-VOO'-oht) The Jewish Feast of Weeks, commemorating the receiving of the Ten Commandments. Occurs in May or June.

- **she** Do not use this pronoun in references to ships or nations. Use *it* instead.

- **Sheet Metal Workers International Association** The shortened form *Sheet Metal Workers union* is acceptable in all references. Headquarters is in Washington.

- **Sheetrock** A trademark for a brand of gypsum wallboard.

- **shell** See **weapons**.

- **Shell Oil Company** This American company, with headquarters in Houston, is part of the Royal Dutch-Shell Group of Companies. The group owns more than half of the stock in Shell Oil.

- **sheriff** Capitalize when used as a formal title before a name. See **titles**.

- **ships** See the **boat, ship** entry and **she**.

- **shirt sleeve, shirt sleeves** (n.) **shirt-sleeve** (adj.)

- **shoeshine, shoestring**

- **shopworn**

- **short** An investment term used to describe the position held by individuals who sell stock they do not yet own. They do so by borrowing the stock from their broker in order to deliver to the purchaser. A person selling short is betting that the price of the stock will fall, so the cost of replacing the borrowed stock will be lower.

- **shortchange**

- **short covering** The purchase of a security to to repay shares borrowed from a broker. See **short**.

- **short-lived** (adj.) *A short-lived plan. The plan was short-lived.*

- **short sale** A sale of securities that are not owned by the seller at the time of sale. The seller intends to purchase or borrow the securities in time to make delivery, hoping that the price will drop in the interim. See **short**.

- **short ton** Equal to 2,000 pounds. See **ton**.

- **shot** See **weapons**.

- **shotgun** See **weapons**.

- **should, would** Use *should* to express an obligation. *We should help the needy.*

Use *would* to express a customary action: *In the summer we would spend hours by the seashore.*

Use *would* also in constructing a conditional past tense, but be careful:

Wrong: *If Soderholm would not have injured his foot, Thompson would not have been in the lineup.*

Right: *If Soderholm hadn't injured his foot, Thompson would not have been in the lineup.* See **subjunctive mood**.

- **showcase, showroom**

- **show off** (v.) **show-off** (n.)

- **shut down** (v.) **shut-down** (n.)

- **shut-in**

- **shut off** (v.) **shut-off** (n.)

- **shut out** (v.) **shutout** (n.)

- **(sic)** Do not use *(sic)* to indicate an error, peculiar usage or spelling. Instead, put an advisory at the bottom of the copy. See **correction** and **parentheses**.

- **Sicily** Use instead of *Italy* in datelines on stories from communities on this island.

- **side by side, side-by-side** *They walked side by side. The stories received side-by-side display.*

- **Sierra Nevada, the** Not *Sierra Nevada Mountains. Sierra* means mountains.
  Not *Sierras* or *Sierra Nevadas. Sierra* is plural.

- **sightseeing, sightseer**

- **Simoniz** (SY'-muh-nyz) A trademark for a brand of auto wax.

- **Sinai** (SY'-ny) Not *the Sinai.* But: *the Sinai Desert, the Sinai Peninsula.*

- **Singapore** Stands alone in datelines.

- **single-handed, single-handedly**

- **sir** See **nobility**.

- **sister** Capitalize in all references before the names of nuns.
  If no surname is given, the name is the same in all references: *Sister Agnes Rita.*

If a surname is used on first reference, drop the given name on second reference: *Sister Clair Regina Torpy* on first reference, *Sister Torpy* in subsequent references.

Use *Mother* the same way when referring to a woman who heads a group of nuns. See **religious titles.**

- **sister-in-law, sisters-in-law**

- **sit down** (v.) **sit-down** (n. and adj)

- **sit in** (v.) **sit-in** (n. and adj.)

- **situation** An overused word that usually can be eliminated—or replaced with something better.
  Generally, when the word *situation* is preceded by an adjective (as in *hostage situation* or, in reference to a slowdown, *economic situation*), the word isn't needed at all.
  Better would be *hostage stand-off* or *the holdout*; and *the recession* or, simply, *the economy.*

- **sizable**

- **skeptic** See the **cynic, skeptic** entry.

- **ski, skis, skier, skied, skiing** Also: *ski jump, ski jumping.*

- **Skid Road, Skid Row** The term originated as *Skid Road* in the Seattle area, where dirt roads were used to skid logs to the mill. Over the years, *Skid Road* became a synonym for the area where loggers gathered, usually down among the rooming houses and saloons. In time, the term spread to other cities as a description for sections, such as the Bowery in New York, that are havens for derelicts. In the process, *row* replaced *road* in many references.
  Use *Skid Road* for this section in Seattle; either *Skid Road* or *Skid Row* for other areas.

- **skillful**

- **slang** In general, be conversational while avoiding slang, the highly informal language that is outside conventional or standard usage. See **colloquialisms; dialect** and **word selection.**

- **slaying** See the **homicide, murder, manslaughter** entry.

- **sledgehammer**

- **sleet** See **weather terms.**

- **sleight of hand**

- **slowdown**

- **slumlord**

- **slush fund**

- **small-arms fire**

- **small-business man, small-business woman**

- **smash up (v.)**

- **smash-up** (n. and adj.) The hyphen is for readability.

- **Smithfield Ham** A trademark for a ham that is dry-cured, smoked and aged in Smithfield, Va.

- **Smithsonian Institution** Not *Smithsonian Institute.*

- **smoke bomb, smoke screen**

- **Smokey** Or *Smokey Bear.* Not *Smokey the Bear.*
  But: *A smoky room, the Smoky Mountains.*

- **snowdrift, snowfall, snowflake, snowman, snowplow, snowshoe, snowstorm, snowsuit**

- **so called** (adv.) **so-called** (adj.)

- **socialist, socialism** See the **political parties and philosophies** entry.

- **Social Security** Capitalize all references to the American system.
  Lowercase generic uses such as: *There is a social security program in Britain.*

- **social titles** See **courtesy titles**.

- **Society for the Prevention of Cruelty to Animals** S-P-C-A is
  acceptable on second reference.
  The *American Society for the Prevention of Cruelty to Animals* is limited to the five boroughs of New York City.
  The autonomous chapters in other cities ordinarily precede the organization by the name of the city: On first reference, *the Philadelphia Society for the Prevention of Cruelty to Animals;* on second, *the Philadelphia S-P-C-A* or *S-P-C-A,* as appropriate in the context.

- **Society of Friends** See **Quakers**.

- **Society of Professional Journalists** On second reference, *S-P-J*.
This organization is no longer called *the Society of Professional Journalists,
Sigma Delta Chi.*

- **soft-spoken**

- **solicitor** See **lawyer**.

- **Solid South** Those Southern states traditionally regarded as supporters of
the Democratic Party.

- **soliloquy, soliloquies**

- **song titles** See **music** and **composition titles**. For treatment of the
names of musical performing groups, see **musical performers**.

- **son-in-law, sons-in law**

- **S-O-S** The distress signal.
S.O.S (no final period) is a trademark for a brand of soap pad.

- **sound barrier** The speed of sound, no longer a true barrier because
aircraft have exceeded it. See **Mach number**.

- **South** As defined by the Census Bureau, the 16-state region is broken into
three divisions.
The four *East South-Central* states are Alabama, Kentucky, Mississippi and
Tennessee.
The eight *South Atlantic* states are Delaware, Florida, Georgia, Maryland,
North Carolina, South Carolina, Virginia and West Virginia.
The four *West South-Central* states are Arkansas, Louisiana, Oklahoma and
Texas. See **North-Central region; Northeast region** and **West** for the
bureau's other regional breakdowns.

- **south, southern, southeast, southwest** See the **directions and
regions** entry.

- **South America** See **Western Hemisphere**.

- **South Carolina** See **state names**.

- **South Dakota** See **state names**.

- **Southeast Asia** The nations of the Indochinese Peninsula and the islands
southeast of it: Burma, Cambodia, Indonesia, Laos, Malaysia, Papua New Guinea,

the Philippines, Singapore, Thailand and Vietnam. See **Asian subcontinent** and **Far East**.

• **Southeast Asia Treaty Organization** *SEATO* is acceptable on second reference.

• **Southeastern Conference** Alabama, Arkansas, Auburn, Florida, Georgia, Kentucky, Louisiana State, Mississippi, Mississippi State, South Carolina, Tennessee, Vanderbilt.

• **Southwest Conference** Baylor, Houston, Rice, Southern Methodist, Texas, Texas A-and-M, Texas Christian, Texas Tech.

• **Soviet Union** It no longer exists. The *Soviet Union* has broken into a number of independent countries.

The *Commonwealth of Independent States* was founded on Dec. 8, 1991, as a federation of 11 of the 15 former republics of the Soviet Union.

Russia is the largest and richest of the former republics. Latvia, Lithuania and Estonia became independent nations before the mid-1991 breakup of the Soviet Union.

The republics, with their adjective forms and pronouncers:

Armenia	Armenian
Azerbaijan (a-zuhr-by-JAHN')	Azerbaijani
Belarus	Belarussian
Estonia	Estonian
Georgia	Georgian
Kazakstan (KAH'-zak-stahn)	Kazakh
Kyrgyzstan (KEER'-gih-stahn)	Kyrgyz
Latvia	Latvian
Lithuania	Lithuanian
Moldova (mohl-DOH'-vuh)	Moldovan
Russia	Russian
Tajikistan (tah-JEEK'-ee-stahn)	Tajik
Turkmenistan (turk-MEN'-ih-stahn)	Turkmen
Ukraine (no *the*)	Ukrainian
Uzbekistan (ooz-BEK'-ee-stahn)	Uzbek

Datelines: *Moscow* stands alone. Follow all other datelines with the name of the state:

(Alma-Ata, Kazakstan) —

• **Space Age** It began on Oct. 4, 1957, with the launching of the Soviets' *Sputnik-One* satellite.

• **space agency** See **National Aeronautics and Space Administration**.

• **space centers**   See **John F. Kennedy Space Center and Lyndon B. Johnson Space Center**.

• **spacecraft**   The plural also is *spacecraft.*

• **spacecraft designations**   Follow the rules for **numerals** and capitalize, but do not use quotation marks: *Gemini Seven, Apollo Eleven, Soyuz (SOY'-yooz) 35.*
   But use quotation marks around the proper name of a spacecraft: *the space shuttle "Challenger."*

• **spaceship**

• **space shuttle**   Lowercase *space shuttle* but capitalize a proper name and put it in quotes: *the space shuttle "Discovery."*
   The shuttle is a reusable winged aircraft capable of carrying scientists and cargo into Earth orbit. It is designed to take off vertically with the aid of booster rockets. After an orbital mission, re-entry begins with the firing of engines that send the craft back into Earth's atmosphere. The final leg of the return trip is a powerless glide to a landing strip.

• **spacewalk**

• **Spanish-American War**

• **Spanish and Portuguese names**   The family names of both the father and mother usually are considered part of a person's full name. In everyday use, customs vary widely with individuals and countries.
   The normal sequence is given name, father's family name, mother's family name: *Jose Lopez Portillo.*
   On second reference, use only the father's family name (*Lopez*), unless the individual prefers or is widely known by a multiple last name (*Lopez Portillo*).
   Some individuals use a *y* (for *and* pronounced *ee*) between the two surnames: *Jose Lopez y Portillo.* Include the *y* on second reference only if both names are used: *Lopez y Portillo.*
   In the Portuguese practice common in Portugal and Brazil, some individuals use only the mother's family name on second reference. If the individual's preference is not known, use both family names on second reference: *Humberto Castello Branco* on first reference, *Castello Branco on second.*
   A married woman frequently uses her father's family name followed by the particle *de* (for *of*) and her husband's name. A woman named *Irma Perez* who married a man named *Anibal Gutierrez* would be known as *Irma Perez de Gutierrez.* Use *Mrs. Gutierrez* on second reference.

• **speaker**   Capitalize as a formal title before a name. Generally, it is a formal title only for the speaker of a legislative body: *House Speaker Thomas O'Neill.* See **titles**.

- **special contexts** When this term is used in this handbook, it means that the material described may be used in a regular program devoted to a specialized subject or when a particular literary effect is suitable.

Special literary effects generally are suitable only in feature copy, but even there they should be used with care. Most feature material should follow the same style norms that apply to regular news copy.

The most frequent difference between special contexts and general news programs is the use of terms specific to the context. In, for example, a feature about computers, terms such as *RAM* and *ROM* may be familiar to the audience, and can be used with less explanation than in general news copy.

In addition, some programs appeal to an audience with narrower tastes than the general radio or television audience. A regular feature aimed at rock audiences, for example, will deal with topics and use terms that might be deemed offensive by the audience of a religious station.

When dealing with special contexts, however, remember that the broadcaster is a federal licensee and must follow certain legal guidelines with regard to language, subject matter and taste. Remember, too, that no copy should be so technical that it could be understood only by an expert.

- **species** Same in singular and plural. Use singular or plural verbs and pronouns depending on the sense: *The species has been unable to maintain itself. Both species are extinct.*

- **speeches** Capitalize and use quotation marks for their formal titles, as described in **composition titles**.

- **speechmaker, speechmaking**

- **speed of sound** See **Mach number** and **sound barrier**.

- **speeds** Follow the rules for **numerals**: *The car slowed to seven miles-per-hour. Winds of 70 to 75 miles-per-hour.*

In the adjective form, use a hyphen to connect the number to the unit of speed: *There was a 15-mile-per-hour wind blowing.*

- **speed up** (v.) **speed-up** (n. and adj.) The hyphen is for readability.

- **spelling** The basic rule when in doubt is to consult this handbook followed by, if necessary, a dictionary under conditions described in the **dictionaries** entry.

Memory aid: Noah Webster developed the following rule of thumb for the frequently vexing question of whether to double a final consonant in forming the present participle and past tense of a verb:
  - If the stress in pronunciation is on the first syllable, do not double the consonant: *combat, combating, combated; cancel, canceling, canceled.*
  - If the stress in pronunciation is on the second syllable, double the consonant: *control, controlling, controlled; refer, referring, referred.*

- If the word is only one syllable, double a consonant unless confusion would result: *jut, jutted, jutting.* An exception to avoid confusion with *buss,* is *bus, bused, busing.*

- **spill, spilled, spilling**   Not *spilt* in the past tense.

- **spinoff** (n.)   A distribution that occurs when the company forms a separate company out of a division, a subsidiary or other holdings. The shares of the new company are distributed proportionately to the holders in the parent company.

- **split infinitive**   See **verbs**.

- **spokesman, spokeswoman**   But not *spokesperson.* Use *a representative* if you do not know the gender of the individual.

- **sports sponsorship**   For the titles or names of sports events, use the commercial sponsor's name only if there is no other, previously established name commonly accepted for the event. For example, *Sugar Bowl,* not *U-S-F-and-G Sugar Bowl; Winston 500,* but not *Pepsi Firecracker 400.*

- **spot market**   A market for buying or selling commodities or foreign exchange for immediate delivery and for cash payment.

- **spot price**   The price of a commodity available for immediate sale and delivery. The term also is used to refer to foreign exchange transactions.

- **spouse**   Use when some of the people involved may be men. For example: *physicians and their spouses,* not *physicians and their wives.*

- **spring**   See **seasons**.

- **springtime**

- **sputnik**   Usually lowercase, but capitalize when followed by a **numeral** as part of a proper name: *Sputnik One.* It is Russian for *satellite.*

- **squall**   See **weather terms**.

- **square**   Do not abbreviate. Capitalize as part of a proper name: *Trafalgar Square.*

- **squinting modifier**   A misplaced adverb that can be interpreted as modifying either of two words: *Those who lie often are found out.*
  Place the adverb where there can be no confusion, even if a compound verb must be split: *Those who often lie are found out.* Or if that was not the sense: *Those who lie are often found out.*

- **Sri Lanka** (shree LAHN'-kuh) Formerly *Ceylon.* Use *Sri Lanka* in datelines and other references to the nation. The people may be called either *Sri Lankans* or *Ceylonese.*

    Before the nation was called Ceylon, it was Serendip, whence comes the word *serendipity.*

- **S-R-O** Do not use as an abbreviation for *standing room only.*

- **S.S. Kresge Company** Now known as *K-mart.* Headquarters is in Troy, Mich.

- **S-S-T** Acceptable in all references for a *supersonic transport.*

- **stadium, stadiums** Capitalize only when part of a proper name: *Yankee Stadium.*

- **Stalin, Josef** Not *Joseph.*

- **stanch, staunch** *Stanch* is a verb: *He stanched the flow of blood.* *Staunch* is an adjective: *She is a staunch supporter of equality.*

- **Standard and Poor's Register of Corporations** The source for determining the formal name of a business. See **company names**. The register is published by *Standard and Poor's Corporation of New York.*

- **standard-bearer**

- **Standard Oil Company(Indiana)** Now known as *Amoco Corporation.* Headquarters is in Chicago.

- **Standard Oil Company (New Jersey)** Now known as *Exxon Corporation.* Headquarters is in New York.

- **Standard Oil Company of California** Now known as *Chevron Corporation.* Headquarters is in San Francisco.

- **Standard Oil Company (Ohio)** Now known as *Standard Oil Company.* Headquarters is in Cleveland.

- **standard time** Capitalize *Eastern Standard Time, Pacific Standard Time.* etc., but lowercase *standard time* when standing alone. See **time zones**.

- **stand in** (v.) **stand-in** (n. and adj.)

- **standing room only** Do not use the abbreviation *S-R-O.*

- **stand off** (v.) **stand-off** (n. and adj.)

- **stand out** (v.) **standout** (n. and adj.)

- **starboard** Nautical for *right*. See **port, starboard**.

- **"The Star-Spangled Banner"** But lowercase *the national anthem*.

- **START** See Strategic Arms Reduction Treaty.

- **state** Lowercase in all *state of* constructions: *the state of Maine, the states of Maine and Vermont.*
  Four states—Kentucky, Massachusetts, Pennsylvania and Virginia—legally are commonwealths rather than states. But the distinction is necessary only in formal uses: *The Commonwealth of Kentucky filed a suit*. For usual geographic references, these states may be handled as all the others are.
  Do not capitalize *state* when used simply as an adjective to specify a level of jurisdiction: *state Representative William Smith, the state Transportation Department, state funds.*
  Apply the same principle to phrases such as *the city of Chicago, the town of Auburn*, etc. See also **state names**.

- **statehouse** Capitalize all references to a specific statehouse, with or without the name of the state: *the Vermont Statehouse is in Montpelier. The governor will visit the Statehouse today.*
  Lowercase plural uses: *the Massachusetts and Rhode Island statehouses.*

- **state names** Some guidelines:
  Abbreviations: Don't use them in the body of the story or the dateline.
  Punctuation: Place one comma between the city and the state name, and another after the state name, unless ending a sentence: *He was traveling from Nashville, Tennessee, to Austin, Texas, to Show Low, Arizona. She said Cook County, Illinois, was Mayor Daley's stronghold.*
  Miscellaneous: Use *New York City* or *New York state* when the distinction is necessary.
  Use the *state of Washington* or *Washington state* when confusion with Washington, D.C., would otherwise result. See **Washington D-C**.

- **State of the Union** Capitalize all references to the president's annual address.
  Lowercase other uses: *A new report says the state of the union is excellent.*

- **state police** Capitalize with a state name if part of the formal description for a police agency: *the New York State Police, the Virginia State Police.*
  In most cases, *state police* standing alone is a shorthand reference for *state police officers* rather than a reference to the agency. For consistency and to avoid hairline distinctions about whether the reference is to the agency or the officers, lowercase the words *state police* whenever they are not preceded by the state name. See **highway patrol**.

- **states' rights**

- **statewide**

- **stationary, stationery** To stand still is to be *stationary.* Writing paper is *stationery.*

- **station wagon**

- **statute mile** It equals 5,280 feet, or roughly 1.6 kilometers. To convert to approximate nautical miles, multiply the number of statue miles by .869. See **kilometer; knot; mile** and **nautical mile.**

- **staunch** See the **stanch, staunch** entry.

- **steady-state theory** See **big-bang theory.**

- **stealth** When used in connection with military aircraft, ships and vehicles, it means the equipment is masked from various types of electronic detection. *Stealth equipment* can range from radar wave absorbing paint to electronic jamming devices. Like the *cruise* missile, always lowercase, with no quotation marks.

- **stepbrother, stepfather, stepmother, stepsister**

- **steppingstone**

- **stifling**

- **St. John's** The city in the Canadian province of Newfoundland. Not to be confused with *Saint John, New Brunswick.*

- **St. Louis** The city in Missouri stands alone in datelines.

- **stock** See the **common stock, preferred stock** entry.

- **stockbroker**

- **stock index futures** Futures contracts valued on the basis of indexes that track the prices of a specific group of stocks. The most widely traded is the future based on the Standard & Poor's 500-stock index. Speculators also trade options on index futures.

- **stock market prices** Spell out any fractions or decimals— fractions are preferred. Follow the rules for **numerals; fractions;** and **decimals.**
  Some examples: *The stock went up three-quarters of a point. It has risen one and a-half points over the past week. A-T-and-T was up six and five-eighths.*

• **stock markets** Stocks are traded in a number of forums across the United States, but the two most prominent markets are the New York Stock Exchange and the Nasdaq (NAZ'-dak) Stock Market.

The New York Stock Exchange handles the largest dollar volume of any stock exchange in the country. It and the Nasdaq Stock Market handle approximately the same volume of trades each day.

NYSE has a trading floor on Wall Street in New York City. Trades are executed by floor traders known as *NYSE specialists*. There is a limit of one specialist per stock on the NYSE exchange. The exchange handles a total of more than 2,000 issues.

Nasdaq has no trading floor; it is a computer network of dealers called *market makers*. These dealers are authorized by Nasdaq to trade in a given stock. There is no limit to the number of market makers Nasdaq will authorize for a stock. Nasdaq handles about 4,000 stocks.

The customary measure of NYSE activity is the Dow Jones Industrial Average, which takes into account the prices of 30 blue-chip industrial corporations.

The customary measure of Nasdaq activity is the Nasdaq Composite Index, representing all 4,000 stocks traded on the network.

• **stockmen's advisory** See **weather terms**.

• **stopgap**

• **storm** See **weather terms**.

• **straight-laced, strait-laced** Use *straight-laced* for someone strict or severe in behavior or moral views. Be careful in using the term, though: It is judgmental.

Strait-laced describes the notion of confinement, as in a corset, and is best avoided.

• **strait** Capitalize as part of a proper name: *Bering Strait, Strait of Gibraltar.* But: *the Bosporus* and *the Dardanelles.* Neither is followed by *Strait.*

• **straitjacket** Not *straight-jacket.*

• **Strategic Air Command** Do not use the acronym *SAC.*

• **Strategic Arms Limitation Talks** (Treaty) *SALT* or *SALT-Two* are acceptable on the second reference, but be sure to make clear whether you are referring to the treaties or the negotiations that led up to them.

There are two treaties, one of which has not been ratified.

• **Strategic Arms Reduction Treaty** *START* is acceptable on first reference to the treaty as long as it is made immediately clear which is being referred to. Use the *strategic arms treaty*, or *the treaties* in some references to avoid alphabet soup.

There are two treaties, START-One (1991) and START-Two (1993).
Do not confuse with the *Strategic Arms Limitation Treaty* of 1979, known as *SALT*.

- **Strategic Defense Initiaitve** This is the official name of the research and development work on defense against a nuclear attack.
S-D-I is the abbreviation and is acceptable on second reference.
"Star Wars" has become synonymous with both and was derived from the movie series. It also is acceptable on second reference, but must be kept within quotation marks.

- **street** Do not abbreviate. See **addresses**.

- **strikebreaker**

- **strong-arm** (v. and adj.)

- **strong-willed**

- **student** See the **pupil, student** entry.

- **Styrofoam** A trademark for a brand of plastic foam. Use the term *plastic foam* unless referring specifically to the trademark product.

- **sub-** The rules in prefixes apply, but in general, no hyphen. Some examples:

sub-basement	subculture	submachine gun	subtotal
subcommittee	subdivision	sub-orbital	sub-zero

- **subcommittee** Lowercase when used with the name of a legislative body's full committee: *a Ways and Means subcommittee.*
Capitalize when a subcommittee has a proper name of its own: *the Senate Permanent Subcommittee on Investigations.*
Spelling out the full name and affiliation of a congressional subcommittee can mean the death of an otherwise lively sentence. Therefore, informalize where possible: *The Health and Research Subcommittee of the Senate Health and Labor Committee* is best referred to as either *a senate health subcommittee* or *the health and research subcommittee.*
Generally, subcommittee action is required before a full congressional committee will report a bill to the floor. Be sure to make the distinction between subcommittee action and full committee action.

- **subject** See the **citizen, resident, subject, national, native** entry.

- **subjunctive mood** Use the subjunctive mood of a verb for contrary-to-fact conditions, and expressions of doubts, wishes or regrets:
If I were a rich man, I wouldn't have to work hard.

I doubt that more money would be the answer.
I wish it were possible to take back my words.
Sentences that express a contingency or hypothesis may use either the subjunctive or the indicative mood depending on the context. In general, use the subjunctive if there is little likelihood that a contingency might come true:
If I were to marry a millionaire, I wouldn't have to worry about money.
If the bill should overcome the opposition against it, it would provide extensive tax relief.
But:
If I marry my millionaire beau, I won't have to worry about money.
If the bill passes as expected, it will provide an immediate tax cut. See the **should, would** entry.

- **submachine gun**   See **weapons**.

- **subpoena, subpoenaed, subpoenaing**

- **subs**   A wire substitution is sent following a bulletin kill or bulletin elimination. Wire subs must be so slugged and contain an advisory as to what has been fixed in the story. For the specific format, see Chapter 8, "Kills and Correctives."

- **Sucaryl** (SOO'-kuh-ril)   A trademark for a brand of non-caloric sweetener.

- **successor**

- **suffixes**   See separate listings for commonly used suffixes.
  Follow Webster's New World Dictionary for words not in this book.
  If a word combination is not listed in Webster's New World, use two words for the verb form; hyphenate any noun or adjective forms.

- **suit** (soot), **suite** (sweet)   You may have a *suit* of clothes, a *suit* of cards, or be faced with a *lawsuit*.
  There are *suites* of music, rooms and furniture.

- **Sukkot** (SOO'-koht)   The Jewish Feast of Tabernacles, celebrating the fall harvest and commemorating the desert wandering of the Jews during the Exodus. Occurs in September or October.

- **summer**   See **seasons**.

- **summertime**

- **sun**   Lowercase. See **heavenly bodies**.

- **sunbathe**   The verb forms: *sunbathed, sunbathing.* Also: *sunbather.*

- **Sun Belt** Generally, those states in the South and West, ranging from Florida and Georgia through the Gulf states into California.

- **Sunday** See **days of the week**.

- **super** Avoid the slang tendency to use it in place of *excellent* or *wonderful*.

- **super-** The rules in prefixes apply, but in general, no hyphen. Some frequently used words:

superagency	supercharge	superpower	supertanker
supercarrier	superhighway		

   As with all prefixes, however, use a hyphen if the word that follows is a proper noun: *super-Republican.*

- **Super Bowl**

- **super-conducting super collider** Note the hyphen in the first word; it is for readability.

- **superintendent** Do not abbreviate. Capitalize when used as a formal title before a name. See **titles.**

- **superior court** See **court names.**

- **supersede**

- **supersonic** See **Mach number** and **sound barrier.**

- **supersonic transport** *S-S-T* is acceptable in all references.

- **supra-** The rules in prefixes apply, but in general, use a hyphen for readability. Some examples:

   supra-governmental   supra-national

   The prefix is not in common use, and should be used only when central to the story.

- **Supreme Court of the United States** Capitalize *U-S Supreme Court* and also *the Supreme Court* when the context makes the *U-S* designation unnecessary.
   The chief justice is properly the *chief justice of the United States*, not *of the Supreme Court: Chief Justice William Rehnquist.*
   The proper title for the eight other members of the court is *associate justice.* When used as a formal title before a name, it should be shortened to *justice*

unless there are special circumstances: *Justice Sandra Day O'Connor, Associate Justice Sandra Day O'Connor.* See **judge**.

- **supreme courts of the states** Capitalize with the state name: *the New York Supreme Court.* Capitalize without the state name when the context makes the name unnecessary: *the state Supreme Court, the Supreme Court.*

  If a court with this name is not a state's highest tribunal, the fact should be noted. In New York, for example, the Supreme Court is a trial court. Appeals are directed to the Appellate Division of the Supreme Court. The state's highest court is the Court of Appeals.

- **surface-to-air missile(s)** *SAM* and *SAMs* may be used on second reference. But avoid the redundant *SAM missiles*.

- **suspensive hyphenation** The form: *The report says five- and six-year-olds need more time in school.*

- **swastika**

- **sweat pants, sweat shirt, sweat suit**

- **swimming** Scoring is in minutes, if appropriate, seconds and tenths of a second. Extend to hundredths if available.

  Events in the United States frequently are measured in yards. Olympic contests and other international events are measured in metric units.

  Identify events as *100-yard freestyle, women's 100-meter backstroke*, etc., on first reference. Condense to *men's 100 freestyle, women's 100 backstroke* on second reference.

- **Swissair** Headquarters is in Zurich, Switzerland.

- **syllabus, syllabuses**

- **synagogue** Capitalize only when part of a formal name.

- **Synagogue Council of America** See **Jewish congregations**.

- **synod** A council of churches or church officials. See the entry for the denomination in question.

- **Syrian Catholic Church** See **Eastern Rite churches**.

- **Tabasco** A trademark for a brand of hot pepper sauce.

- **tablecloth**

- **tablespoon, tablespoonfuls** Equal to three teaspoons or one-half fluid ounce.
  The metric equivalent is approximately 15 milliliters. See **liter**.

- **table tennis** See **pingpong**.

- **tabular matter** Tabular matter on broadcast wires serves two purposes. For radio, it provides material for ad-libbing. For television, it provides material for the composition of graphics. In both industries, tabular material also provides detailed information for writing a local version of the story.
  Tabular material is not fully scripted and is not intended to be read directly on the air in its tabular form. It therefore does not follow the rules intended to reduce the chances of stumbling. Instead, follow these guidelines:
  Numbers: Do not spell them out. Use figures, decimal points and, if appropriate, fractions.
  Pronouncers: Do not use them.
  Abbreviations: Standard abbreviations may be used in lists. State names, for example, may be abbreviated. In all abbreviations, follow the rules of AP print style as spelled out in The Associated Press Stylebook.
  Ages: Don't spell them out. They may follow the person's name and be set off by commas.
  Addresses: Use figures, according to AP print style.

- **tail-spin** The hyphen is for readability.

- **tail wind**

- **Taiwan** Use *Taiwan*, not *Formosa*, in references to the Nationalist government on Taiwan and to the island itself. See **China**.

- **take-home pay**

- **take off** (v.) **take-off** (n. and adj.) The hyphen is for readability.

- **take out** (v.) **take-out** (n. and adj.) The hyphen is for readability.

- **take over** (v.) **takeover** (n. and adj.)

- **takes** To make the copy as easy to handle as possible, long stories are broken into pages, called *takes*. The number of takes in a script should be kept to the minimum to reduce the chance of any single take getting lost or delayed in transmission.

  Generally, a take should run no more than 40 lines, and the first take of a multitake script should indicate the total number of takes in the slug:

  The Sunriser (three takes)

  Subsequent takes should also be numbered in the slug:

  The Sunriser, take 2

- **take up** (v.) **take-up** (n. and adj.)

- **Talmud** (TAHL'-mud) The collection of writings that constitute the Jewish civil and religious law.

- **Tammany, Tammany Hall, Tammany Society**

- **tanks** Follow the rules for **hyphen** and **numerals**. Do not put generic names in quotation marks: *M-60, M-60's.*

- **tape recording** The noun. Do not use the verb *tape-record.* Use *tape* instead.

- **Tass** A news agency in Russia. It once was the Soviet government's news agency but became independent when the Soviet Union collapsed.

- **tattletale**

- **teachers college** No apostrophe.

- **team** See **collective nouns**.

- **teammate**

- **teamster** Capitalize *teamster* only if the intended meaning is that the individual is a member of the International Brotherhood of Teamsters, Chauffeurs, Warehousemen and Helpers of America.

- **Teamsters union** Note the lowercase *u*. Acceptable in all references to the **International Brotherhood of Teamsters, Chauffeurs, Warehousemen and Helpers of America**. See the entry under that name.

• **tear gas** Two words. See also **Chemical Mace**.

• **teaspoon** Equal to one-sixth of a fluid ounce, or one-third of a tablespoon. The metric equivalent is about five milliliters. See **liter**.

• **teaspoonful, teaspoonfuls** Not *teaspoonsful*.

• **Technicolor** A trademark for a process of making color motion pictures.

• **teen, teen-ager** (n.) **teenage** (adj.)

• **Teflon** A trademark for a type of non-stick coating.

• **telecast** (n.) **televise** (v.) *Telecast* is an outdated word that is best avoided. Many *televised* events—most televised presidential speeches, for example—also are carried on radio.
 Broadcast is therefore often the better word: *The president will make a broadcast address.*

• **telephone numbers** Use them only when vital to the story, or, in feature material, when they will provide the listener with extra information that would be useful.
 Wire stories should generally move such numbers in an advisory sent with the story, so members have the option of not using them. Use this form:

 (News directors: The toll-free number is (800) 555-1234.)

 When using telephone numbers in the copy, use figures and hyphens. Between the exchange and the second set of numbers, use a space, a hyphen and a space: *2-6-2 - 4-0-0-0.* If an area code is used, indicate so in the text: *area code 2-1-2, 2-6-2 - 4-0-0-0* or *the area code is 2-1-2 and the number is 2-6-2 - 4-0-0-0.* Area codes which are expressed as numbers instead of individual digits—800, for example—should be written without hypens: *The number is 800, 2-7-3 - 1-2-3-4.*
 Do not put the telephone numbers in parentheses in the copy.
 Wrong: *The group has set up a toll-free number (800 555-1234).*
 Right: *The group has set up a toll-free number. It is area code 800, 5-5-5 - 1-2-3-4.*
 But the best form is to leave the number out of the story and put it in an advisory at the bottom of the copy.

• **TelePrompTer** A trademark for a type of cuing device. It is no relation to Teleprompter Corp., a cable television company with headquarters in New York.

• **Teletype** A trademark for a brand of teleprinter and teletypewriter.

• **television program titles** Follow the guidelines in **composition titles**. Put quotation marks around *show* only if it is part of the formal name. The word *show* may be dropped when it would be cumbersome, such as in a set of listings.

Treat programs named for the star in any of the following ways as appropriate in text or listing: *"The Mary Tyler Moore Show," "Mary Tyler Moore,"* or *the Mary Tyler Moore show*. But be consistent in a story or set of listings.

Use quotation marks also for the title of an episode: *"Chuckles Bites the Dust,"* an episode of "The Mary Tyler Moore Show."

- **television stations** See **call letters**.

- **telex, Telex** A communications system.
Use lowercase when not referring to a specific company. Use uppercase only when referring to the company.

- **telltale**

- **temblor** See **earthquakes**.

- **temperature-humidity index** See **weather terms**.

- **temperatures** Follow the rules for **numerals**. Use a word, not a minus sign, for temperatures below zero.
Some examples:
The day's low was minus ten. It hit ten below zero at noon. It's 65 degrees all across the country.
It will be in the 70's in the Southwest.
Temperatures get *higher* or *lower* — not *warmer* or *cooler*.
Wrong: *Cold temperatures dominated the Northwest.*
Right: *Low temperatures dominated the Northwest.* Or: *Cold weather dominated the Northwest.* See **Fahrenheit; Celsius** and **weather terms**.

- **Ten Commandments**

- **tenderhearted**

- **ten-fold** The hyphen is for readability.

- **Tennessee** See **state names**.

- **Tennessee Valley Authority** *T-V-A* is acceptable on second reference. Headquarters is in Knoxville, Tenn.

- **tennis** The scoring units are *points, games, sets* and *matches.*
A player wins a point if the opponent fails to return the ball, hits it into the net or hits it out of bounds. A player also wins a point if the opponent is serving and fails to put the ball into play after two attempts (a *double fault,* in tennis terms).
A player must win four points to win a game. In tennis scoring, both players

begin at *love* and advance to *15, 30, 40* and *game.* (The numbers *15, 30* and *40* have no point value as such—they simply are tennis terminology for *one point, two points* and *three points.*)

The server's score is always called out first.

If a game is tied at 40-all, or *deuce,* play continues until one player has a two-point margin.

A set is won if a player wins six games before the opponent has won five. If a set becomes tied at five games apiece, it goes to the first player to win seven games. If two players who were tied at five games apiece also tie at six games apiece, they normally play a tiebreaker—a game that goes to the first player to win seven points. In some cases, however, the rules call for a player to win by two games.

A match may be either a best-of-three contest that goes to the first player or team to win two sets, or a best-of-five contest that goes to the first player or team to win three sets.

Scores: Tennis scores are reported without the word *to.* Use figures (an exception to the rules in **numerals**) and a hyphen: *Chris Evert won the first set from Sue Barker 6-Love, lost the second 3-6 and won the third 7-6. Chris Evert won her match, defeating Sue Barker 6-0, 3-6, 7-6.*

- **tera-** A prefix denoting 1 trillion units of a measure. Move a decimal point 12 places to the right, adding zeros if necessary, to convert to the basic unit: 5.5 tera-tons equals 5.5 trillion tons.

  Always use a hyphen between *tera* and the root word, since this prefix is unfamiliar to most people.

- **terrace** Do not abbreviate. See **addresses.**

- **Texaco, Incorporated** Headquarters is in Harrison, N.Y.

- **Texas** The state with the second-most land in terms of total area: 262,134 square miles. See **state names.**

- **texts, transcripts** Transcripts are used only rarely on broadcast wires, since the sound usually tells the story. When they are used, they generally are quite brief.

  Follow normal style guidelines for capitalization in handling a text or a transcript. But follow AP print style for numbers and hyphenation.

  Use quotation marks only for words that were quoted by the person who spoke.

  Identify a change in speakers by starting a new paragraph with the new speaker's name and a colon. Use normal second-reference forms if the speaker has been identified earlier; provide a full name and identification if the individual is being mentioned for the first time.

  Use *Q:* for *question* and *A:* for *answer* at the start of paragraphs when these notations are adequate to identify a change in speakers. See **ellipsis** for guidelines on condensing texts and transcripts.

- **Thai** A native or the language of Thailand. *Siam* and *Siamese* are historical only. Use *siamese* for the cat.

- **Thanksgiving, Thanksgiving Day** The fourth Thursday in November.

- **that** (conjunction) Use the conjunction *that* to introduce a dependent clause if the sentence sounds or looks awkward without it. There are no hard-and-fast rules, but in general:
  "To say:" *That* usually may be omitted when a dependent clause immediately follows a form of the verb *to say*: *The president said he had signed the bill.*
  Time element: *That* should be used when a time element intervenes between the verb and the dependent clause: *The president said Monday that he had signed the bill.* However avoid this construction whenever possible.
  Specified verbs: *That* usually is necessary after certain verbs. They include: *advocate, assert, contend, declare, estimate, make clear, point out, propose,* and *state.*
  Subordinate clauses: *That* is required before subordinate clauses beginning with conjunctions such as *after, although, because, before, in addition to, until* and *while*: *Haldeman said that after he learned of Nixon's intention to resign, he sought pardons for all connected with Watergate.*
  When in doubt, include *that.* Omission can hurt. Inclusion never does.

- **that, which, who, whom** (pronouns) Use *who* and *whom* in referring to people and to animals with a name: *John Jones is the man who helped me.* See the **who, whom** entry.
  Use *that* and *which* in referring to inanimate objects and to animals without a name. See the **essential clauses, non-essential clauses** entry for guidelines on using *that* and *which* to introduce phrases and clauses.

- **theater** Use this spelling except in some proper names: *Shubert Theatre.*

- **theft** See the **burglary, larceny, robbery, theft** entry.

- **their, there, they're** *Their* is a possessive pronoun: *They went to their house.*
  There is an adverb indicating direction: *We went there for dinner.*
  There also is used with the force of a pronoun for impersonal constructions in which the real subject follows the verb: *There is no food on the table.*
  They're is a contraction for *they are*: *They're going to their house.*

- **theretofore** Use *until then.*

- **Thermo-Fax** A trademark for a brand of photocopy machine.

- **thermos** Formerly a trademark, now a generic term for any vacuum bottle, although one manufacturer still uses the word as a brand name.

Lowercase *thermos* when it is used to mean any vacuum bottle; use *Thermos* when referring to the specific brand.

• **Third World** The economically developing nations of Africa, Asia and Latin America. Do not confuse with *non-aligned*, which is a political term. See **non-aligned**.

• **three-D**

• **3-M** An exception to the rules for **numerals**. The name of the company is *Minnesota Mining and Manufacturing*. Its products are known under the names *3-M* and *Scotch*. The company is popularly known as *3-M*, which is acceptable in all references. Headquarters is in St. Paul, Minn.

• **three R's** They are: *reading, 'riting* and *'rithmetic.*

• **threesome**

• **throw-away** (n. and adj.) The hyphen is for readability.

• **thunderstorm** See **weather terms**.

• **Thursday** See **days of the week**.

• **tidbit**

• **tie, tied, tying**

• **tie in** (v.) **tie-in** (n. and adj.)

• **tie up** (v.) **tie-up** (n. and adj.)

• **time element** Write in the present tense, especially in leads. Always put the latest information at the top of the story.
  These two rules will go far in determining the time element in your copy.
  Use *today, this morning, this afternoon, tonight* and similar terms as appropriate. Do not use the day of the week for references to *yesterday* or *tomorrow* except during those hours when it is past midnight in some time zones but not in others. See **today**.
  In references to days within the past seven or within the upcoming seven (a total span of 14 days), use the day of the week without *last* or *next.* The tense— past or future—will serve to indicate which day of the week you mean: *He made the statement Tuesday. He will make the next announcement Tuesday.*
  Avoid awkward placements of the time element, particularly those that suggest the day of the week is the object of a transitive verb: *The police jailed Tuesday.* Potential remedies include the use of the word *on* (see the **on** entry), rephrasing the sentence, or placing the time element in a different sentence.

• **time of day** The exact time of day that an event has happened or will happen is not necessary in most stories. Follow these guidelines to determine when it should be included and in what form:

When to be specific: There are circumstances under which a specific clock reference is called for. In these cases, use the *local* time and include the time zone if appropriate:

• Whenever it gives the audience a better picture of the scene: Did the earthquake occur when people were likely to be home asleep or at work? A clock reading for the time in the datelined community is acceptable, although *predawn hours* or *rush hour* often is more graphic and eliminates the need for a cumbersome time zone reference.

• Whenever the time is critical to the story: When will the rocket be launched? When will a major political address be broadcast? What is the deadline for meeting a demand?

Deciding on clock time: When giving a clock reading, use the time in the community where the story occurred— usually the datelined community—and say so in the body of the story: *It was 3 a-m in London when the first blast occurred.*

Any story or table that involves national television or radio programs should use Eastern time, and indicate so. If the program will not be broadcast simultaneously across the nation, indicate the differing local transmission times.

Zone abbreviations: When adding a zone abbreviation to a time, use a comma: *8 a-m, E-D-T. 9:30 p-m, E-D-T.* But when an *a-m* or *p-m* designation is not made, do not use a comma: *tomorrow morning at 9 E-D-T.* The same guidelines apply when spelling out such terms as Eastern time, Pacific Daylight Time. See

a-m, p-m.

Such zonal references should be used only if:

• The story involves travel or other activities, such as the closing hour for polling places or the time of an event likely to affect people or developments in more than one time zone. This includes national events such as presidential addresses, shuttle launches, etc.

• The item involves radio or television programs (see above).

• The item is an advisory.

Converting to Eastern time: Do not convert clock times from other time zones in the continental United States to Eastern time. If the time is critical in a story from outside the continental United States, provide a conversion to Eastern time using this form: *The kidnappers set a deadline of 9 a-m — that's 3 a-m, Eastern time.* See **time zones**.

For guidance on specific forms, see the next entry.

• **times** Use figures, except for *noon* and *midnight*. Use a colon to separate hours from minutes, and hyphenate *a-m* or *p-m*: *11 a-m, 12:30 p-m.* Avoid such redundancies as *10 a-m this morning* or *10 p-m tomorrow night.*

The construction *4 o'clock* is acceptable, but listings with *a-m* or *p-m* are preferred. See **midnight** and **time zones**.

- **time sequences** Spell them out in all contexts: *2:30:21.65* should be expressed as *two hours, 30 minutes and 21-point-65 seconds,* or *two and a-half hours, 21-point-65 seconds.*

  Tenths and hundredths of a second may be expressed that way—instead of as decimals. See **numerals; decimals; fractions.**

- **Time Warner, Incorporated** Headquarters is in New York.

- **time zones** Capitalize the full name of the time in force within a particular zone: *Eastern Standard Time, Eastern Daylight Time, Central Standard Time.*

  Lowercase all but the region in short forms: *Eastern time, the Eastern time zone, Mountain time.* See **time of day** for guidelines on when to use the clock time and when to use the zonal reference.

  Time zones should be spelled out when not accompanied by a clock reading: *Chicago is in the Central time zone.*

  When the time zone is abbreviated, capitalize and use hyphens. If the clock reading includes *a-m* or *p-m,* set off the zone with a comma: *9 E-D-T* but *9 a-m, E-D-T.*

  Any references to time zones outside of the continental United States are best informalized: *It's 6 a-m in Anchorage* as opposed to *6 a-m, Alaska Standard Time.* Do not abbreviate such time zones.

  One exception: *Greenwich Mean Time* may be abbreviated *G-M-T* on the second reference.

- **tiptop**

- **titleholder**

- **titles** Minimize the use of long formal titles, since they tend to make sentences long and cumbersome. When possible, use the informal version of a title. This often is accomplished by flip-flopping the words and eliminating *of: Secretary of the Treasury* becomes *Treasury Secretary.*

  When even the informal title is too long, separate it from the name: *The speaker was Charles Robinson. He's the undersecretary of state for economic affairs.* Or: *The State Department's top economist, Charles Robinson.*

  In general, confine capitalization to formal titles used directly before a person's name.

  Some guidelines:

  Lowercase: Lowercase titles when they are not used directly before an individual's name: *The president is speaking. The pope gave his blessing.*

  Lowercase titles in constructions that set them off from the name with commas: *The vice president, Nelson Rockefeller, says he won't run again.* But avoid these constructions.

  Abbreviated titles: The only titles that should be abbreviated are *Mr., Mrs., Ms.* and *Dr.* Spell out all others.

  Courtesy titles: See **courtesy titles** for guidance on when to use *Miss, Ms., Mrs.* or *Mr.*

  Formal titles: Capitalize formal titles when they are used immediately before one or more names: *Pope John Paul, President Washington, Vice Presidents Al Gore and Dan Quayle.* A formal title generally is one that denotes a scope of authority, professional activity or academic accomplishment so specific that the designation becomes almost as much an integral part of an individual's identity as a proper name itself: *President Reagan, Mayor Ed Koch, Dr. Marcus Welby.*

Other titles serve primarily as occupational descriptions: *astronaut John Glenn, movie star Ronald Reagan, peanut farmer Jimmy Carter.*

A final determination on whether a title is formal or occupational depends on the practice of the governmental or private organization that confers it. If there is doubt about the status of a title and the practice of the organization cannot be determined, use a construction that informalizes the title.

Nobility: Capitalize a full title when it serves as an alternative name. See **nobility**.

Past and future titles: Use *former,* not *ex-,* for one who no longer holds the title. One who is about to take on a job is the *designate: Secretary of State designate Christopher,* or *President-elect Clinton.* In all cases, when used immediately before a name, capitalize the title but not the qualifying word.

Royal titles: Capitalize *king, queen,* etc. when used directly before a name. See individual entries and **nobility**.

Unique titles: If a title applies to only one person in an organization, it should be preceded by *the: George Bush is the vice president.* See **composition titles; legislative titles; military titles** and **religious titles**.

- **T-N-T** Acceptable in all references for *trinitrotoluene.*

- **tobacco, tobaccos**

- **Tobago** See the **Trinidad and Tobago** entry.

- **today** Use it. Also use *yesterday, last night, tomorrow* and *tonight.* But be careful about making your copy too time-zone specific: When it's *tonight* in New York, it's *this afternoon* in Hawaii.

  Do not use *today, tomorrow* or *yesterday* for stories transmitted between midnight Eastern time and 3 a.m. Eastern time. Instead, use the day of week, to avoid confusion when it's past midnight in some time zones but not in others.

  Do not use *today* as an excuse to write a past-tense lead: *Mayor Jones spoke today.* Instead, use the present perfect tense: *Mayor Jones has spoken.*

- **Tokyo** Stands alone in datelines.

- **tollhouse, tollhouse cookies**

- **Tommy gun** Alternative trademark for a Thompson submachine gun. See **weapons**.

- **tomorrow** See **today**.

- **ton** There are three types:
  A *short ton* is equal to 2,000 pounds.
  A *long ton*, also known as a *British ton*, is equal to 2,240 pounds.
  A *metric ton* is equal to one-thousand kilograms—roughly 2,204.62 pounds.

Tonnage Conversion Equations

Short to long: Multiply by .89
5 short tons x .89 = 4.45 long tons

Short to metric: Multiply by .9
5 short tons x .9 = 4.5 metric tons

Long to short: Multiply by 1.12
5 long tons x 1.12 = 5.6 short tons

Long to metric: Multiply by 1.02
5 long tons x 1.02 =5.1 metric tons

Metric to short: Multiply by 1.1
5 metric tons x 1.1 =5.5 short tons

Metric to long: Multiply by.98
5 metric tons x .98 = 4.9 long tons

See **metric system**. See **kiloton, kilotonnage** for units used to measure the power of nuclear explosions. See **oil** for formulas to convert the tonnage of oil shipments to gallons.

- **tonight** All that's necessary is *8 tonight*, or *8 p-m*. Avoid the redundant *8 p-m tonight.* See **today.**

- **(Tops)** Capitalize and place in parentheses after the story's slug. A *tops* is a separate that provides significant new material on a story already covered in the day's report. After a story breaks, it may be topped out several times. If a story's first use is in a summary, and it is updated then with a separate, that can be slugged tops:

  Hostages (Tops)

  If the updating material is of an urgent nature, give the story an *URGENT* designation, but no *(Tops)*:

  Hostages URGENT

- **tornado** See **weather terms**.

- **Toronto** The city in Canada stands alone in datelines.

- **Tory, Tories** An exception to the normal practice when forming the plural of a proper name ending in *y*. The words are acceptable on second reference to the Conservative Party in Britain and its members.

- **total, totaled, totaling** The phrase *a total of* often is redundant. It may be used, however, to avoid a figure at the start of a sentence: *A total of 650 people were killed in holiday traffic accidents.*

- **Touch-Tone** A trademark of AT&T for its push-button dialing service.

- **toward** Not *towards*.

- **town** Apply the capitalization principles in **cities and towns**.

- **town council** Apply the capitalization principles in **city council**.

- **track and field** Scoring is in distance or time, depending on the event. Most events are measured in metric units. For those meets that include feet, make sure the measurement is clearly stated, as in *men's 100-meter dash, women's 880-yard run*.
  Spell out all times in the body of the story. Extend times to hundredths if available: *six seconds; seven and 45 hundredths; four hours, 35 minutes; 24 and three-tenths seconds*. Follow the rules for **numerals; decimals** and **fractions**.

- **trade in** (v.) **trade-in** (n. and adj.)

- **trademark** A trademark is a brand, symbol or word used by a manufacturer or dealer and protected by law to prevent a competitor from using it: *AstroTurf*, for a type of artificial grass, for example. In general, use a generic equivalent unless the trademark name is essential to the story. Many trademarks are listed separately in this book, together with generic equivalents.
  The U.S. Trademark Association, located in New York, is a helpful source of information about trademarks. See **brand names** and **service mark**.

- **trade off** (v.) **trade-off** (n. and adj.)

- **traffic, trafficked, trafficking**

- **trampoline** Formerly a trademark, now a generic term.

- **trans-** The rules in **prefixes** apply, but in general no hyphen. Some examples:

transcontinental	transoceanic	trans-ship	trans-Siberian
transmigrate	transsexual		

Also: *trans-Atlantic* and *trans-Pacific*. These are exceptions to Webster's New World in keeping with the general rule that a hyphen is needed when a prefix precedes a capitalized word.

- **transfer, transferred, transferring**

- **Transjordan** An earlier name for *Jordan*.

- **Transportation Communications International Union**

Formerly the *Brotherhood of Railway, Airline and Steamship Clerks, Freight Handlers, Express and Station Employees.*

Do not use the abbreviation *T-C-U.* Use *the union, the transportation union* or *the railway workers union* on second reference. Headquarters is in Rockville, Md.

* **transsexuals** See **sex changes.**

* **Trans World Airlines** A *T-W-A airliner* is acceptable in any reference. Headquarters is in New York.

* **travel, traveled, traveling, traveler**

* **travelogue** Not *travelog.*

* **treasurer** Capitalize when used as a formal title immediately before a name. See **titles.**

   Note: The secretary of the U.S. Department of the Treasury is not the same person as the U.S. treasurer.

* **treasury bills, treasury bonds, treasury notes** See **loan terminology.**

* **trees** See **plants.**

* **tribes** See **nationalities and races.**

* **trigger-happy** Use the term with caution; it is judgmental.

* **TriMotor** The proper name of a three-engine airplane once made by Ford Motor Co.

* **Trinidad and Tobago** In datelines on stories from this island nation, use a community name followed by either *Trinidad* or *Tobago*—but not both— depending on where the community is located.

* **TriStar** The proper name that Lockheed Martin uses for its *L-Ten-Eleven* jetliner.

* **Trojan horse, Trojan War**

* **troop, troops, troupe** A *troop* is a group of people or animals. *Troops* mean several such groups, particularly groups of soldiers. Use *troupe* only for ensembles of actors, dancers, singers, and the like.

* **tropical depression** See **weather terms.**

* **Truman, Harry S.** With a period after the initial. Truman once said there

was no need for the period because the *S* did not stand for a name. Asked in the early 1960s about his preference, he replied, "It makes no difference to me." AP style has called for the period since that time.

- **trustee** (truhs-TEE') A person to whom another's property or the management of another's property is entrusted. Do not capitalize if used before a name.

- **trusty** (TRUHS'-tee) A prison inmate granted special privileges as a trustworthy person. Do not capitalize if used before a name.

- **try out** (v.) **tryout** (n.)

- **tsar** Use *czar*.

- **T-shirt**

- **tuberculosis** *T-B* is acceptable on second reference.

- **Tuesday** See **days of the week**.

- **tune up** (v.) **tuneup** (n. and adj.)

- **turboprop** See **aircraft terms**.

- **turnpike** Capitalize as part of a proper name: *the Pennsylvania Turnpike.* Lowercase *turnpike* when it stands alone. See **highway designations**.

- **T-V** Acceptable as an adjective or in such constructions as *cable T-V.* But say *television* instead of *T-V* unless part of a quotation.

- **Twelve Apostles** The disciples of Jesus. An exception to the normal practice of using a figure for numerals above 11.

- **20th Century Fox, Twentieth Century Fund, Twentieth Century Limited** Follow an organization's practice. See **company names**.

- **typhoons** Use *it* or *its*—not *he* or *she* or *her* or *his*—when referring to typhoons.
  Capitalize the word *typhoon* and put the proper name of the storm in quotation marks: *Typhoon "Alexis."* Lowercase *typhoon* when it stands alone.
  And do not let the presence of a woman's name, when it is used, provide an excuse for the use of sexist images in describing the behavior of the storm. See **weather terms**.

- **U** In Burmese names, *U* is an honorific prefix. It means something akin to *Mr.* and is used for adult males only. Do not use it. *U Nu* is only *Nu* in all references. Women retain their given names after marriage. No courtesy titles apply.

- **U-boat** A German submarine. Anything referring to a submarine should be *submarine* unless directly referring to a German vessel of World War I or World War II vintage.

- **U-F-O, U-F-O's** Acceptable in all references to *unidentified flying object(s).*

- **U-H-F** Acceptable in all references for *ultrahigh frequency.* Television stations that transmit on channels numbered higher than 13 are *U-H-F stations.*

- **Ukraine** Note: no *the.* Formerly the *Ukrainian Soviet Socialist Republic,* it is now an independent state. See **Soviet Union**.

- **Ukrainian Catholic Church** See **Eastern Rite churches**.

- **ukulele**

- **Ulster** A colloquial synonym for *Northern Ireland.* See **United Kingdom.**

- **ultra-** The rules in **prefixes** apply, but in general, no hyphen. Some examples:

ultramodern   ultra-nationalism   ultrasonic   ultraviolet

- **ultrahigh frequency** *U-H-F* is acceptable in all references.

- **un-** The rules in **prefixes** apply, but in general, no hyphen. Some examples:

un-American   unarmed   unnecessary   unshaven

- **U-N** Acceptable in all references to the *United Nations.* See **United Nations**.

- ## Uncle Sam

- ## Uncle Tom   A term of contempt applied to a black person, taken from the main character in Harriet Beecher Stowe's novel "Uncle Tom's Cabin." It describes the practice of kowtowing to whites to curry favor.

  Do not apply it to an individual. It carries potentially libelous connotations of having sold one's convictions for money, prestige or political influence.

- **under-**   The rules in **prefixes** apply, but in general, no hyphen. Some examples:

underdog   underground   undersheriff   undersold

- **undersecretary**   One word. See **titles**.

- **under way**   Two words in virtually all uses: *The project is under way. The naval maneuvers are under way.*

  One word only when used as an adjective before a noun in a nautical sense: *an underway flotilla*, which is a construction that should be avoided in any case.

- **unemployment rate**   In the United States, this estimate of the number of unemployed residents seeking work is compiled monthly by the Bureau of Labor Statistics, an agency of the Labor Department. Each month the bureau selects a nationwide cross section of the population and conducts interviews to determine the size of the work force.

  The work force is defined as the number of people with jobs and the number looking for jobs. It does not include people who previously could not find jobs and gave up looking.

  The unemployment rate is expressed as a percentage figure. The essential calculation involves dividing the total work force into the number of people looking for jobs, followed by adjustments to reflect variable factors such as seasonal trends. In reporting the unemployment rate, follow the rules for **percentages**.

- **UNESCO**   Acceptable on second reference for the *United Nations Educational, Scientific and Cultural Organization.*

- **UNICEF**   Acceptable in all references for the *United Nations Children's Fund.* The words *International* and *Emergency,* originally part of the name, have been dropped.

- **unidentified flying objects**   *U-F-O* and *U-F-O's* are acceptable in all references.

- ## Uniform Code of Military Justice   The laws covering members of the U.S. armed forces.

- **uninterested** See **disinterested, uninterested.**

- **union** Capitalize when used as a proper name for the Northern states during the Civil War: *The Union defeated the Confederacy.*

- **union names** The formal names of unions may be condensed to conventionally accepted short forms. Capitalize the characteristic words from the full name followed by *union* in lowercase.
  Follow union practice in the use of the word *worker* in shortened forms. Among major unions, all except the *United Steelworkers* use two words: *United Auto Workers, United Mine Workers.*
  When *worker* is used generically, make *autoworkers* one word in keeping with widespread practice; use two words for other job descriptions: *bakery workers, mine workers, steel workers.*
  See the **local (union)** entry and the individual entries for more information on many of these unions frequently in the news:

Amalgamated Clothing and Textile Workers Union of America
Amalgamated Transit Union
American Federation of Government Employees
American Federation of Labor and Congress of Industrial Organizations
American Federation of Musicians
American Federation of State, County and Municipal Employees
American Federation of Teachers
American Federation of Television and Radio Artists
American Postal Workers Union
Bakery and Confectionary Workers' International Union of America
Bricklayers, Masons and Plasterers' International Union of America
Brotherhood of Railway, Airline and Steamship Clerks, Freight Handlers, Express and Station Employees
Communications Workers of America
Hotel and Restaurant Employees and Bartenders International Union
International Association of Machinists and Aerospace Workers
International Brotherhood of Electrical Workers
International Brotherhood of Painters and Allied Trades of the United States and Canada

International Brotherhood of Teamsters, Chauffeurs, Warehousemen and Helpers of America
International Ladies' Garment Workers Union
International Longshoremen's and Warehousemen's Union
International Longshoremen's Association
Laborers' International Union of North America
National Association of Letter Carriers
Newspaper Guild, The
Oil, Chemical and Atomic Workers International Union
Sheet Metal Workers International Association
Transportation Communication International Union
United Automobile, Aerospace and Agricultural Implement Workers of America
United Brotherhood of Carpenters and Joiners of America
United Electrical, Radio and Machine Workers of America
United Food and Commercial Workers International Union
United Mine Workers of America
United Rubber, Cork, Linoleum and Plastic Workers of America
United Steelworkers of America

- **Union of American Hebrew Congregations** See **Jewish congregations**.

- **Union of Orthodox Jewish Congregations of America** See **Jewish congregations**.

- **Union of Soviet Socialist Republics** It no longer exists. See **Soviet Union**.

- **union shop** See **closed shop**.

- **unique** It means one of a kind. Do not describe something as *rather unique* or *very unique*.

- **United Airlines** A subsidiary of UAL Corp. Headquarters is in Chicago.

- **United Arab Emirates** Do not abbreviate in any context. Generally, on second reference, *the Emirates*.

- **United Automobile, Aerospace and Agricultural Implement Workers of America** The shortened forms *United Auto Workers* and *United Auto Workers union* are acceptable in all references.
  U-A-W and *the Auto Workers* are acceptable on second reference.
  Use *autoworker* or *autoworkers*—one word, lowercase—in generic references to workers in the auto industry. Headquarters is in Detroit.

- **United Brotherhood of Carpenters and Joiners of America** The shortened form *Carpenters union* is acceptable in all references. Headquarters is in Washington.

- **United Church of Christ** See **Congregationalist churches**.

- **United Electrical, Radio and Machine Workers of America** The shortened form *Electrical Workers union* is acceptable in all references. Headquarters is in New York.

- **United Food and Commercial Workers International Union** Formed by the merger of the Retail Clerks International Union and the Amalgamated Meat Cutters and Butcher Workmen of North America.
  The shortened form *Food and Commercial Workers union* is acceptable in all references. Headquarters is in Washington.

- **United Kingdom** It consists of Great Britain and Northern Ireland. Great Britain (or Britain) consists of England, Scotland and Wales. Ireland is independent of the United Kingdom.
  Northern Ireland is physically a part of the same island as Ireland, but is a province of Great Britain. See **datelines** and **Ireland**.

- **United Methodist Church** See **Methodist churches**.

- **United Mine Workers of America** The shortened forms *United Mine Workers* and *United Mine Workers union* are acceptable in all references.
U-M-W and *the Mine Workers* are acceptable on second reference.
Use *mine workers* or *miners*, lowercase, in generic references to workers in the industry. Headquarters is in Washington.

- **United Nations** The abbreviation *U-N* may be used in copy as a noun or adjective, but spell out *United Nations* in datelines:

   (United Nations) - -

   Use *U-N General Assembly*, *U-N Secretariat* and *U-N Security Council* on the first reference. The *U-N* can be dropped, with capitalization retained, in subsequent references.
Lowercase *the assembly* and *the council* when they stand alone.
Only the Security Council has the power of enforcement in the United Nations. But it also is subject to the veto power of the five permanent members: the United States, Britain, France, China and Russia. See **UNESCO** and **UNICEF**.

- **United Presbyterian Church in the United States of America** It no longer exists. See **Presbyterian churches**.

- **United Press International** A privately owned news agency formed in 1958 in a merger of the United Press and the International News Service.
Use the full name on the first reference. *U-P-I* is acceptable on second reference.

- **United Rubber, Cork, Linoleum and Plastic Workers of America** The shortened forms *United Rubber Workers* and *United Rubber Workers union* are acceptable in all references.
Use *rubber workers*, lowercase, in generic references to workers in the rubber industry. Headquarters is in Akron, Ohio.

- **United Service Organizations** *U-S-O* is acceptable on second reference.

- **United States** Spell it out as a noun. *U-S* is acceptable as an adjective, although *American* is preferred.
For organizations with names beginning with the words *United States*, see entries alphabetized under **U-S**.

- **United Steelworkers of America** The shortened forms *United Steelworkers* and *United Steelworkers union* are acceptable in all references. Headquarters is in Pittsburgh.
Use *steel workers*—two words, lowercase—in generic references to workers in the steel industry. Many *Steelworkers* are employed in other industries and thus are not *steel workers*.

- **United Synagogue of America** *Not synagogues.* See **Jewish congregations**.

- **up-** The rules in **prefixes** apply, but in general, no hyphen. Some examples:

up-end	upstate	upgrade	uptown

- **-up** Follow Webster's New World Dictionary. Hyphenate if not listed there. Some frequently used words (all are nouns, some also are used as adjectives):

breakup	crackup	mix-up	shake-up
build-up	follow-up	mock-up	shape-up
call-up	frame-up	pileup	smashup
change-up	grown-up	push-up	speedup
checkup	holdup	roundup	tie-up
cleanup	letup	runners-up	walk-up
close-up	lineup	setup	windup
cover-up	makeup		

Use two words when any of these occurs as a verb. See **suffixes**.

- **updates** These are story-related advisories that contain the same computer category code as the stories to which they pertain. They are not full air-ready scripts, and are designed solely to inform newsrooms of incremental new developments on an expedited basis—before a story can be written.

> **Clinton News Conference UPDATE**
>
> **President Clinton has begun his news conference.**
>
> **AP Broadcast News Center**

The information in an update is related to a developing story. Major developments should be handled as **urgents** orX **bulletins**. An **advisory** provides information about upcoming coverage or features on the wire, radio network, APTV, SNTV or in GraphicsBank.

- **U-P-I** Acceptable on second reference for *United Press International*.

- **uppercase** One word (n., v., adj.) when referring to the use of capital letters. An exception to Webster's New World.

- **upside down** (adv.) **upside-down** (adj.) *The cat turned upside down. She made an upside-down cake. The book is upside-down.*

- **upstate** Always lowercase: *upstate New York.*

- **upward** Not *upwards*.

- **urgents** An urgent is a short, separate story providing important new information on a story of importance and urgency. Generally, urgents are sent when expected developments occur in major stories, or when new stories of high—but not overwhelming—importance break.
  Extremely important stories take bulletin treatment. Transcendant stories are treated as flash material. These are quite rare.
  The form for urgents:

  Clinton Cabinet URGENT

  (Little Rock) -- Senator Lloyd Bentsen of Texas is President-elect Clinton's choice for Treasury Secretary.

  Urgents always take a U priority code and the category code for the type of story. When an urgent updates a story already on the wire, delete the (Tops) designation from the slug. See **bulletin** and **flash**.

- **U-S** Acceptable as an adjective for *United States*, though *American* is preferred.

- **U-S-Airways** Formerly *Allegheny Airlines*. Allegheny Commuter airlines operate under contracts with *U-S-Air*. Headquarters is in Washington.

- **U-S Air Force** See **air force; military academies; military titles**.

- **U-S Army** See **army; military academies; military titles**.

- **U-S Coast Guard** See **coast guard; military academies; military titles**.

- **U-S Conference of Mayors** The members are mayors of cities with 30,000 or more residents. See **National League of Cities**. Use *the conference* or *the mayors conference* on second reference.
  There is no organization with the name *National Mayors' Conference*.

- **U-S Court of Appeals** The court is divided into 13 circuits, as follows:
  District of Columbia Circuit.
  Federal Circuit.
  First Circuit: Maine, Massachusetts, New Hampshire, Rhode Island, Puerto Rico. Based in Boston.
  Second Circuit: Connecticut, New York, Vermont. Based in New York.
  Third Circuit: Delaware, New Jersey, Pennsylvania, Virgin Islands. Based in Philadelphia.
  Fourth Circuit: Maryland, North Carolina, South Carolina, Virginia, West Virginia. Based in Richmond, Va.

Fifth Circuit: Louisiana, Mississippi, Texas. Based in New Orleans.
Sixth Circuit: Kentucky, Michigan, Ohio, Tennessee. Based in Cincinnati.
Seventh Circuit: Illinois, Indiana, Wisconsin. Based in Chicago.
Eighth Circuit: Arkansas, Iowa, Minnesota, Missouri, Nebraska, North Dakota, South Dakota. Based in St. Louis.
Ninth Circuit: Alaska, Arizona, California, Hawaii, Idaho, Montana, Nevada, Oregon, Washington, Guam. Based in San Francisco.
Tenth Circuit: Colorado, Kansas, New Mexico, Oklahoma, Utah, Wyoming. Based in Denver.
Eleventh Circuit: Alabama, Florida and Georgia. Based in Atlanta.
The courts do not always sit in cities where they are based. Sessions may be held in other major cities within each region.
Reference Forms: A phrase such as *a federal appeals court* is acceptable on first reference.
On first reference to the full name, use *U-S Court of Appeals* or a full name: *Eighth U-S Circuit Court of Appeals* or *the U-S Court of Appeals for the Eighth Circuit.*
U-S Circuit Court of Appeals without a circuit number is a misnomer and should not be used.
In shortened and subsequent references: *the Court of Appeals, the Second Circuit, the appeals court, the appellate court(s), the circuit court(s), the court.*
Do not create non-existent entities such as *San Francisco Court of Appeals.* Make it *the U-S Court of Appeals in San Francisco.*
Jurists: The formal title for the jurists on the court is *judge: U-S Circuit Judge Homer Thornberry* is preferred to *U-S Appeals Judge Homer Thornberry,* but either is acceptable. See **judge.**

• U-S Court of Appeals for the Federal Circuit It replaced the *U-S-Court of Claims* and the *U-S Court of Customs and Patent Appeals.* It handles suits against the federal government and appeals involving customs, patents and copyright. It is based in Washington.

• U-S Court of Military Appeals This court, not a part of the judicial branch, is a civilian body established by Congress to hear appeals from actions of the Defense Department. It is based in Washington.

• U-S Customs Court This court, based in New York City, handles disputes over customs duties that arise at any U.S. port of entry.

• U-S District Courts There are 94. In shortened and subsequent references,: *the District Court, the District Courts, the court.*
Judge is the formal title for District Court jurists: *U-S District Judge Frank Johnson.* See **judge.**

• user friendly An already overworked term. Avoid it.
For example: *The system is easy to use,* not *the system is user friendly.*

- **usher** Use for both men and women.

- **U-S Information Agency** The abbreviation *U-S-I-A* is acceptable on second reference.

- **U-S Military Academy** See **military academies**.

- **U-S Navy** See **military academies; military titles** and **navy.**

- **U-S Postal Service** The *Postal Service* is acceptable on any reference. Lowercase *the service* when it stands alone. Lowercase *post office* in generic references to the agency and to an individual post office: *I went to the post office.*

- **U-S Postal Service Directory of Post Offices** The reference for U.S. place names not covered in this book.

- **U-S-S** Stands for *United States Ship, Steamer* or *Steamship.* It is used before the name of a vessel and is preceded by *the*: the U-S-S "Enterprise." Note that *U-S-S* does not go inside the quotation marks.
  In datelines:

  (Aboard the U-S-S "Iowa") - -

- **U-S Supreme Court** See **Supreme Court of the United States.**

- **U-S Tax Court** This is an administrative body within the U.S. Treasury Department rather than part of the judicial branch. It handles appeals in tax cases.

- **U-S-X Corporation** Formerly *U-S Steel.*

- **Utah** See **state names.**

- **U-turn** (n. and adj.)

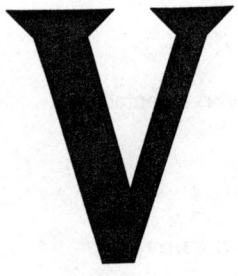

- **v.** See **verbs.**

- **vacuum**

- **Valium** A trademark for a brand of tranquilizer and muscle relaxant. It also may be called *diazepam (dy-AZ'-uh-pam).*

- **valley** Capitalize as part of a full name: *the Mississippi Valley.* Lowercase in plural uses: *the Mississippi and Missouri valleys.*

- **Vandyke beard, Vandyke collar**

- **Varig Brazilian Airlines** Headquarters is in Rio de Janeiro.

- **Vaseline** A trademark for a brand of petroleum jelly.

- **Vatican City** Stands alone in datelines.

- **V-C-R** Acceptable in all references to a *videocassette recorder.*

- **V-D-T** An abbreviation for *video display terminal.* Spell it out or use *video monitor* or *screen* instead.

- **V-E day** May 8, 1945, the day the surrender of Germany was announced, officially ending the European fighting in World War II.

- **vegetables** See **food.**

- **V-Eight** An engine configuration.

- **Velcro** A trademark for a nylon material that can be pressed together or pulled apart for easy fastening and unfastening.

- **vendor**

- **venereal disease** *V-D* is acceptable on second reference.

- **verbal** See the **oral, verbal, written** entry.

- **verbs** The abbreviation *v.* is used in this book to identify the spelling of the verb forms of words frequently misspelled.

   Split forms: In general, avoid awkward constructions that split infinitive forms of a verb (*to leave, to help,* etc.) or compound forms (*had left, are found out,* etc.).

   Awkward: *She was ordered to immediately leave on an assignment.*

   Preferred: *She was ordered to leave immediately on an assignment.*

   Awkward: *There stood the wagon that we had early last autumn left by the barn.*

   Preferred: *There stood the wagon that we had left by the barn early last autumn.*

   Occasionally, however, a split is not awkward and is necessary to convey the meaning: *He wanted to really help his mother. Those who lie are often found out. How has your health been? The budget was tentatively approved.*

- **Vermont** See **state names**.

- **vernacular** The native language of a country or place. A vernacular term that has achieved widespread recognition may be used without explanation if appropriate in the context.

   Terms not widely known should be explained when used. In general, they are appropriate only when illustrating vernacular speech. See **colloquialisms; dialect**.

- **versus** Do not abbreviate.

- **vertical take-off aircraft** See the **V-STOL** and **VTOL** entries.

- **very high frequency** *V-H-F* is acceptable in all references. Television stations that broadcast on channel 13 and below are *V-H-F stations*.

- **Very Reverend** See **Epsicopal Church; religious titles** and **Roman Catholic Church**.

- **Veterans Affairs** No apostrophe. Formerly the *Veterans Administration,* it became a Cabinet-level agency in March 1989. The full title is *Department of Veterans Affairs.*

   V-A may be used on second reference.

- **Veterans Day** Formerly *Armistice Day,* November 11, the anniversary of the armistice that ended World War I in 1918. The armistice went into effect at 11 a.m. on November 11—11th hour of the 11th day of the 11th month.

   The federal legal holiday observed on the fourth Monday in October during the mid-70s reverted to November 11 in 1978.

- **Veterans of Foreign Wars** *V-F-W* is acceptable on the second reference. Headquarters is in Kansas City, Mo.

- **veto, vetoes** (n.) The verb forms: *vetoed, vetoing.*

- **V-H-F** Acceptable in all references for *very high frequency.*

- **vice-** Use two words: *vice admiral, vice chairman, vice chancellor, vice consul, vice president, vice principal, vice regent, vice secretary.*
  Several are exceptions to Webster's New World. The two-word rule has been adopted for consistency in handling the similar terms.

- **vice president** Capitalize or lowercase following the same rules that apply to **president**.
  The first name of the vice president of the United States may be dropped on first reference.

- **vice-versa**

- **Victrola** A trademark for a brand of record player.

- **videocassette recorder** *V-C-R* is acceptable in all references.

- **videodisc** Like *compact disc*, an exception to the spelling of *disk.*

- **videotape** (n. and v.)

- **videotex, teletex** Not *videotext*. *Videotex* is the generic term for two-way interactive data systems that transmit text and sometimes graphics via telephone lines or cable. A user can specify desired information and communicate with a host computer or other users through a terminal keyboard or similar controller.
  Teletex is a one-way system that transmits text material or graphics via a television or F-M broadcast signal or cable television system. The user can select material desired but cannot communicate with other users.

- **vie, vied, vying**

- **vienna bread, vienna coffee, vienna sausages** See **food**.

- **Viet Cong**

- **Vietnam** Not *Viet Nam.*

- **Vietnam War**

- **village** Apply the capitalization rules in **city**.

- **V-I-P, V-I-P's** Acceptable in all references to *very important people*.

- **Virginia** Legally a commonwealth, not a state. See **state** and **state names**.

- **Virgin Islands** Use with a community name in datelines on stories from the U.S. Virgin Islands. Do not abbreviate. Identify an individual island in the text if relevant. See **datelines** and **British Virgin Islands**.

- **viscount, viscountess** See **nobility**.

- **vitamins** Lowercase *vitamin*, use a hyphen, follow the rules for **numerals** and, if a letter stands alone, capitalize it: *vitamin B-12, vitamin A.*

- **V-J day** The day of victory for the Allied Forces over Japan in World War II. It can be marked on two days: August 15, 1945, the day fighting ended, or September 2, 1945, the day Japan officially surrendered.

- **V-neck** (n. and adj.)

- **Voice of America** *V-O-A* is acceptable on second reference.

- **voicer** A self-contained radio correspondent report. Voicers run no more than 35 seconds and end in a lockout. See the entries under **actuality; lockouts; natural sound; q&a; scener** and **wrap**.

- **volatile** Something that evaporates rapidly. It may or may not be explosive.

- **Volkswagen of America, Incorporated** The name of the American subsidiary of the German carmaker known as *Volkswagen A-G*. American headquarters is in Englewood Cliffs, N.J.

- **volley, volleys**

- **Volunteers in Service to America** *VISTA* is acceptable on second reference.

- **von** See **foreign particles**.

- **voodoo**

- **vote-getter**

- **vote tabulations** For treatment of voter returns in the body of a story, see **election returns**.
   When reporting returns in tabular form, always use figures.

   Here are the latest nationwide election returns in the race for president, with 67 percent of the nation's precincts reporting.

   Clinton 30,521,194 — 44 percent
   Has won 29 states and the District of Columbia with 349 electoral votes.
   Leads in 2 states with 17 electoral votes.

   Bush 27,002,298 — 39 percent
   Has won 10 states with 74 electoral votes.
   Leads in 8 states with 95 electoral votes.

   Perot 12,473,912 — 18 percent
   Has won 0 states with 0 electoral votes.
   Leads in 0 states with 0 electoral votes

   In general, vote tabulations should be expressed in the simplest possible terms, whether the subject is the general election or the defeat of a bill in the state legislature.
   Follow the rules for **numerals**, use hyphens and the word *to*: *Clinton is leading Bush by a 44-to-38 margin. The bill passed 230-to-205.*

- **V-STOL** (VEE'-stawl) Do not use this acronym for aircraft capable of *vertical or short take-off or landing*. Instead, describe the aircraft's capabilities in the copy.

- **VTOL** (VEE'-tawl) Do not use this acronym for aircraft capable of *vertical take-off or landing*. Instead, describe the aircraft's capabilities in the copy.

- **vulgarities** See the **obscenities, profanities, vulgarities** entry.

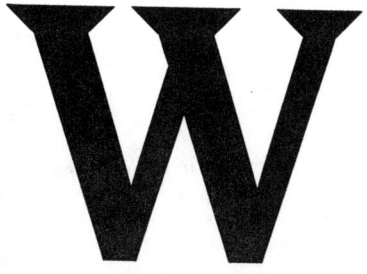

- **Wac, WAC** *Wac* (note lowercase) is no longer used by the military but is an acceptable term in a reference to a woman who served in what used to be the *Women's Army Corps.*

  WAC is acceptable on second reference to the corps.

- **Waf, WAF** *Waf* (note lowercase) no longer is used by the military but is acceptable in a reference to a woman who served in the Air Force.

  WAF is acceptable on second reference to the *Women in the Air Force,* an unofficial organizational distinction formerly made by the Air Force but never authorized by Congress.

- **waiter** (male) **waitress** (female)

- **Wales** Use *Wales* after the names of Welsh communities in datelines. See **datelines** and **United Kingdom**.

- **walk up** (v.) **walk-up** (n. and adj.)

- **Wall Street** Although *Wall Street* is commonly used to denote the national stock market in general, it actually is the site of only the New York Stock Exchange and the American Stock Exchange.

  A construction such as *on the financial markets* or *among stocks* is preferred to *on Wall Street* when referring to stock trading beyond the New York and American stock exchanges. See **stock markets**.

- **war** Capitalize when used as part of the name of a specific conflict: *the Civil War, the Cold War, the Korean War, the Vietnam War, the War of 1812, World War II, the Gulf War, the Persian Gulf War,* etc.

- **warden** Capitalize as a formal title before a name. See **titles**.

- **wards** Follow the rules for **numerals**. See **political divisions**.

- **warhead**

- **war horse, warhorse** Two words for a horse used in battle. One word for a veteran of many battles: *He is a political warhorse.*

- **war-like** The hyphen is for readability.

- **warlord**

- **Warner Brothers** This is the motion picture division of *Time Warner, Incorporated.*

- **warrant officer** See **military titles**.

- **wartime**

- **washed-up** (adj.)

- **Washington** Use *Washington state* or *state of Washington* if necessary to distinguish between the state and *Washington D-C* See **state; state names**.

- **Washington's Birthday** Capitalize *birthday* in reference to the holiday.
The date he was born is calculated as February 22. The federal legal holiday is the third Monday in February. Some states and some organizations refer to it as *Presidents Day* (no apostrophe), but the formal name has not changed.

- **Washington D-C** No comma. *Washington* is acceptable in all references unless there might be confusion with the state of Washington. See **Washington**.

- **wastebasket**

- **waterspout** See **weather terms**.

- **Wave, WAVES** *Wave* is no longer used by the military, but is acceptable in a reference to a woman who served in the Navy.
WAVES is acceptable on second reference to the *Women's Auxiliary Volunteer Emergency Service*, an organizational distinction made for women in the Navy during World War II but subsequently discontinued.

- **weak-kneed** Use only as a description of a physical condition.

- **weapons** Gun: An acceptable term for any firearm. Note the following definitions and forms in dealing with weapons and ammunition:
anti-aircraft: A heavy-caliber cannon that fires explosive shells. It is designed for defense against air attack. The form: *a 105-millimeter anti-aircraft gun.*
artillery: A carriage-mounted cannon.
automatic: A kind of pistol designed for automatic or semiautomatic firing. Its cartridges are held in a *magazine.* The form: *a 22-caliber automatic.*
buckshot: See **shot** in this section.
bullet: The projectile fired by a rifle, pistol or machine gun. Together with metal casing, primer and propellant, it forms a *cartridge.*

caliber: A measurement of the diameter of the inside of a gun barrel except for most shotguns. Measurement is in either millimeters or decimal fractions of an inch. The word *caliber* is not used when giving the metric measurement. The forms: *a nine-millimeter pistol, a 22-caliber rifle.*

cannon: A large-caliber weapon, usually supported on some type of carriage, that fires explosive projectiles. The form: *a 105-millimeter cannon.*

carbine: A short-barreled rifle. The form: *an M-Three carbine.*

cartridge: See **bullet** above.

colt: Named for Samuel Colt, it designates a make of weapon or ammunition developed for Colt handguns. The forms: *a Colt 45-caliber revolver, a Colt-45,* and *45 Long Colt ammunition.*

gauge: This word describes the size of a shotgun. Gauge is expressed in terms of the number per pound of round lead balls with a diameter equal to the size of the barrel. The bigger the number, the smaller the shotgun. Some common shotgun gauges:

Gauge	Interior Diameter
10	.775 inches
12	.729 inches
16	.662 inches
20	.615 inches
28	.550 inches
410	.410 inches

The 410 actually is a caliber, but commonly is called a gauge. The forms: *a 12-gauge shotgun, a 410-gauge shotgun.*

howitzer: A cannon shorter than a gun of the same caliber employed to fire projectiles at relatively high angles at a target, such as opposing forces behind a ridge. The form: *a 105-millimeter howitzer.*

machine gun: An automatic gun, usually mounted on a support, that fires as long as the trigger is depressed. The forms: *a 50-caliber Browning machine gun.*

Magnum: A trademark for a type of high-powered cartridge with a larger case and a larger powder charge than other cartridges of approximately the same caliber. The form: *a 357-caliber Magnum, a 44-caliber Magnum.*

M-One, M-16: These and similar combinations of a letter and numerals designate rifles used by the military. The forms: *an M-One rifle, an M-16 carbine.*

musket: A heavy, smooth-bore, large-caliber shoulder firearm fired by means of a matchlock, a wheel lock, a flintlock or a percussion lock. Its ammunition is a musket ball.

pistol: A hand weapon. It may be a *revolver* or an *automatic.* Its measurements are in calibers. The form: *a 38-caliber pistol.*

revolver: A kind of pistol. Its cartridges are held in chambers in a cylinder that revolves. The form: *a 45-caliber revolver.*

rifle: A firearm with a rifled bore. It uses bullets or cartridges for ammunition. Its size is measured in calibers. The form: *a 22-caliber rifle.*

Saturday night special: The popular name for the type of cheap pistol used for impulsive crimes, often committed Saturday nights.

shell: The word applies to military or naval ammunition and to shotgun ammunition.

shot: Small lead or steel pellets fired by shotguns. A shotgun shell usually contains one to two ounces of shot. Do not use *shot* interchangeably with *buckshot*, which refers only to the largest shot sizes.

shotgun: A small-arms gun with a smooth bore, sometimes double-barreled. Its ammunition is shot. Its size is measured in gauges. The form: *a 12-gauge shotgun.*

submachine gun: A lightweight automatic gun firing small-arms ammunition.

• **weather-beaten**

• **weather bureau** See **National Weather Service**.

• **weatherman** The preferred term is *forecaster.*

• **weather terms** The following are based on definitions used by the National Weather Service. All temperatures are Fahrenheit.

blizzard: Wind speeds of 35 miles-an-hour and considerable falling and or blowing of snow with visibility near zero.

coastal waters: The waters within about 20 miles of the coast, including bays, harbors and sounds.

cyclone: A storm with strong winds rotating about a moving center of low atmospheric pressure.

The word sometimes is used in the United States to mean *tornado* and in the Indian Ocean area to mean *hurricane.* Because of the confusion that can result, use the more precise words.

degree-day: A degree-day is a computation that gauges the amount of heating or cooling needed for a building. An uninsulated building will maintain an inside temperature of 70 degrees if the outside temperature is 65 degrees. A degree-day is a one-degree difference in this equilibrium for one day (a temperature of 64 degrees for 24 hours), or its equivalent such as a two-degree difference for half a day (a temperature of 63 for 12 hours).

A temperature of 10 below zero for 24 hours yields 75 degree-days. A temperature of 85 degrees for six hours yields five degree-days.

dust storm: Visibility of one-half mile or less due to dust and wind speeds of 30 miles-an-hour or more.

flash flood: A sudden, violent flood. It typically occurs after a heavy rain or the melting of a heavy snow.

flash flood warning: Warns that flash flooding is imminent or in progress. People in the affected area should take necessary precautions immediately.

flash flood watch: Alerts the public that flash flooding is possible. Those in the affected area are urged to be ready to take additional precautions if a flash flood warning is issued or if flooding is observed.

flood: Stories about floods usually tell how high the water is and where it is expected to crest. Such a story should also, for comparison, list flood stage and how high the water is above, or below, flood stage.

Wrong: *The river is expected to crest at 39 feet.*

Right: *The river is expected to crest at 39 feet, 12 feet above flood stage.*

freeze: Describes conditions when the temperature at or near the surface is expected to be below 32 degrees during the growing season. Adjectives such as *severe* or *hard* are used if a cold spell exceeding two days is expected.

A freeze may or may not be accompanied by the formation of frost. However, use of the term *freeze* usually is restricted for occasions when wind or other conditions prevent frost.

freezing drizzle, freezing rain: Each is a synonym for *ice storm.*

frost: Describes the formation of thin ice crystals, which might develop under conditions similar to dew except for the minimum temperatures involved. Phrases such as *frost in low places* or *scattered light frost* are used when appropriate. The term *frost* seldom appears in state forecasts unless rather heavy frost is expected over an extensive area.

funnel cloud: A violent, rotating column of air that does not touch the ground, usually a pendant from a cumulonimbus (kyoo-myoo-loh-NIM'-buhs) cloud.

gale: Sustained winds within the range of 39 to 54 miles-an-hour—34 to 47 knots.

heavy snow: It generally means:
- A fall accumulating to four inches or more in 12 hours, or
- One accumulating to six inches or more in 24 hours.

high wind: Normally indicates that sustained winds of 39 miles-per-hour or greater are expected to persist for one hour or longer.

hurricane or typhoon: A warm-core tropical cyclone in which the minimum sustained surface wind is 74 miles-an-hour or more.

Hurricanes are east of the international date line. Typhoons develop west of that line. Both are known as *cyclones* in the Indian Ocean.

When a hurricane or typhoon loses strength—as measured by its wind speed— it is reduced to a *tropical storm.* Generally, these storms tend to gain strength over open water and lose strength over land.

hurricane categories: Hurricanes are ranked one to five according to what is known as the Saffir-Simpson scale of strength:
- A *Category One* hurricane has a central barometric pressure of 28.94 inches or more and winds of 74 to 95 miles-per-hour, is accompanied by a 4 to 5 foot storm surge and causes minimal damage.
- A *Category Two* hurricane has a central barometric pressure of 28.5 to 28.93 inches and winds of 96 to 110 miles-per-hour, is accompanied by a 6 to 8 foot storm surge and causes moderate damage.
- A *Category Three* hurricane has a central barometric pressure of 27.91 to 28.49 inches and winds of 111 to 130 miles-per-hour, is accompanied by a 9 to 12 foot storm surge and causes extensive damage.
- A *Category Four* hurricane has a central barometric pressure of 27.17 to 27.90 inches and winds of 131 to 155 miles-per-hour, is accompanied by a 13 to 18 foot storm surge and causes extreme damage.
- A *Category Five* hurricane has a central barometric pressure of less than 27.17 inches and winds greater than 155 miles-per-hour, is accompanied by a storm surge higher than 18 feet and causes catastrophic damage.

Only two *Category Five* storms have hit the United States since record-keeping began: the 1935 Labor Day hurricane that hit the Florida Keys and killed 405 people and Hurricane Camille, which devastated the Mississippi coast in 1969, killing 265 and leaving $1.4 billion in damage.

hurricane eye: The relatively calm area in the center of the storm. In this area, winds are light and the sky is often covered only partly by clouds.

hurricane season: The portion of the year that has a relatively high incidence of hurricanes. In the Atlantic, Caribbean and Gulf of Mexico, it is from June through November. In the eastern Pacific, it is June through November 15. In the central Pacific, it is June through October.

hurricane tide: Same as **storm tide**. See entry in this section.

hurricane warning: Warns that one or both of these dangerous effects of a hurricane are expected in a specified coastal area in 24 hours or less:

- Sustained winds of 74 miles-an-hour— 64 knots—or higher.
- Dangerously high water or a combination of dangerously high water and exceptionally high waves, even though winds expected may be less than hurricane force.

hurricane watch: An announcement for specific areas that a hurricane or incipient hurricane conditions may pose a threat to coastal and inland communities.

ice storm, freezing drizzle, freezing rain: Describes the freezing of drizzle or rain on objects as it strikes them. *Freezing drizzle* and *freezing rain* are synonyms for *ice storm.*

ice storm warning: Reserved for occasions when significant, and possibly damaging, accumulations of ice are expected.

National Hurricane Center: The National Weather Service's National Hurricane Center in Miami has overall responsibility for tracking and providing information about tropical depressions, tropical storms and hurricanes in the Atlantic Ocean, Gulf of Mexico and Caribbean Sea.

The service's Eastern Pacific Hurricane Center in San Francisco is responsible for hurricane information in the Pacific Ocean area north of the equator and east of 140 degrees west longitude.

The service's Central Pacific Hurricane Center in Honolulu is responsible for hurricane information in the Pacific Ocean area north of the equator from 140 degrees west longitude to 180 degrees.

nearshore waters: The waters extending to five miles from shore.

offshore waters: The waters extending to about 250 miles from shore.

sandstorm: Visibility of one-half mile or less due to sand blown by winds of 30 miles-an-hour or more.

severe blizzard: Wind speeds of 45 miles-an-hour or more, great density of falling or blowing snow with visibility frequently near zero and a temperature of 10 degrees or lower.

severe thunderstorm: Describes either of the following:

- Thunderstorm-related surface winds sustained or gusts 50 knots or greater.
- Surface hail three-quarters of an inch in diameter or larger. The word *hail* in a watch implies hail at the surface and aloft unless qualifying phrases such as *hail aloft* are used.

sleet: One form of ice pellet. Describes generally solid grains of ice formed by the freezing of raindrops or the refreezing of largely melted snowflakes. Sleet, like small hail, usually bounces when hitting a hard surface.

sleet (heavy): Heavy sleet is a fairly rare event in which the ground is covered to a depth of significance to motorists and others.

snow avalanche bulletin: Snow avalanche bulletins are issued by the U.S. Forest Service for avalanche-prone areas in the western United States.

squall: A sudden increase of wind speed by at least 16 knots and rising to 25 knots or more and lasting for at least one minute.

stockmen's advisory: Alerts the public that livestock may require protection because of certain combinations of cold, wet and windy weather, specifically cold rain or snow with temperatures 45 degrees or lower and winds of 25 miles-per-hour or higher. If the temperature is in the mid-30s or lower, the wind speed criterion is lowered to about 15 miles-per-hour.

storm tide: Directional waves caused by a severe atmospheric disturbance. A *tidal wave* radiates from the center of an earthquake.

temperature-humidity index: The *T-H-I* indicates the combined effect of heat and air moisture on human comfort. A reading of 70 or below indicates no discomfort. A reading of 75 would indicate discomfort in half the population. All would feel uncomfortable with a reading of 79. The National Weather Service issues the *T-H-I* between June 15 and September 15.

tornado: A violent rotating column of air forming a pendant, usually from a cumulonimbus cloud, and touching the ground. It usually starts as a funnel cloud and is accompanied by a loud roaring noise. On a local scale, it is the most destructive of all atmospheric phenomena.

tornado warning: Warns the public of an existing tornado or one suspected to be in existence.

tornado watch: Alerts the public to the possibility of a tornado.

traveler's advisory: Alerts the public that difficult traveling or hazardous road conditions are expected to be widespread.

tropical depression: A tropical cyclone in which the maximum sustained surface wind is 38 miles-per-hour—33 knots—or less.

tropical storm: A warm-core tropical cyclone in which the maximum sustained surface wind ranges from 39 to 73 miles-per-hour—34 to 63 knots.

typhoon: See **hurricane** or **typhoon** in this listing.

waterspout: A tornado over water.

wind chill index: No hyphen. It is a calculation that describes the combined effect of the wind and low temperatures on exposed skin. The wind chill index would be minus 22, for example, if the temperature was 15 degrees and the wind was blowing at 25 miles per hour—in other words, the combined effect would be the same as a temperature of 22 below zero with no wind.

The higher the wind at a given temperature, the lower the wind chill reading, although wind speeds above 40 miles-per-hour have little additional chilling effect.

wind shear: A sudden shift in wind direction and speed. It is caused when a mass of cooled air rushes downward out of a thunderstorm in what is called a *microburst*, hits the ground and rushes outward in all directions.

A plane flying through a microburst at low altitude, as on final approach or takeoff, would at first experience a strong headwind and increased lift, followed by a strong tailwind and sharply decreased lift.

winter storm warning: Notifies the public that severe winter weather conditions are almost certain to occur.

winter storm watch: Alerts the public to the possibility of severe winter weather conditions.

• **weather vane**

• **Webster's New World Dictionary**   Note: No quotation marks, since it is a reference work as explained under the rules in **composition titles**. See **dictionaries**.

• **Webster's Third New International Dictionary**   See **dictionaries**.

• **Wednesday**   See **days of the week**.

• **weekend**

• **week-long**   The hyphen is for readability.

• **weights**   Follow the rules for **numerals**: *The baby weighs nine pounds, seven ounces. They had a nine-pound, seven-ounce boy.*

• **weird, weirdo**

• **Welcome Wagon**   A trademark of Welcome Wagon International, Incorporated.

• **well**   Hyphenate as part of a compound modifier: *It is a well-known area. It is well-known.* See the **hyphen** entry for guidelines on compound modifiers.

• **well-being**

• **well-to-do**

• **well-wishers**   The hyphen is for readability.

• **west, western**   See the **directions and regions** entry.

• **West**   As defined by the U.S. Census Bureau, the 13-state region is broken into two divisions.

The eight *Mountain division* states are Arizona, Colorado, Idaho, Montana, Nevada, New Mexico, Utah and Wyoming.

The five *Pacific division* states are Alaska, California, Hawaii, Oregon and

Washington. See **North-Central region; Northeast region** and **South** for the bureau's other three regional breakdowns.

• **Western Athletic Conference** Air Force, Brigham Young, Colorado State, Fresno State, Hawaii, New Mexico, San Diego State, Texas-El Paso, Utah, Wyoming.

• **Western Hemisphere** The continents of North and South America, and the islands near them. It frequently is subdivided as follows:

Caribbean: The islands from the tip of Florida to the continent of South America, plus, particularly in a political sense, French Guiana, Guyana and Suriname on the northeastern coast of South America.

Major island elements are the Bahamas, Cuba, Hispaniola (the island shared by the Dominican Republic and Haiti), Jamaica, Puerto Rico and the West Indies islands.

Central America: The narrow strip of land between Mexico and Colombia. Located there are Belize, Costa Rica, El Salvador, Guatemala, Honduras, Nicaragua and Panama.

Latin America: The area of the Americas south of the United States where Romance languages (those derived from Latin) are dominant. It applies to most of the region south of the United States except areas with a British heritage: The Bahamas, Barbados, Belize, Grenada, Guyana, Jamaica, Trinidad and Tobago and various islands in the West Indies. Suriname, the former Dutch Guiana, is an additional exception.

North America: Canada, Mexico, the United States and the Danish territory of Greenland. When the term is used in more than its continental sense, it also may include the islands of the Caribbean.

South America: Argentina, Bolivia, Brazil, Chile, Colombia, Ecuador, Paraguay, Peru, Uruguay, Venezuela, and in a purely continental sense, French Guiana, Guyana and Suriname. Politically and psychologically, however, the latter three regard themselves as part of the Caribbean.

West Indies: The term no longer is used extensively, but it applies to the Caribbean islands east of Puerto Rico southward to South America.

Major island elements are the nations of Barbados, Grenada, and Trinidad and Tobago, plus smaller islands dependent in various degrees on:

- Britain: British Virgin Islands, Anguilla, and the West Indies Associated States, including Antigua, Dominica, St. Lucia, St. Vincent and St. Christopher-Nevis.
- France: Guadeloupe (composed of islands known as Basse-Terre and Grande-Terre, plus five other islands) and Martinique.
- Netherlands: Netherlands Antilles, composed of Aruba, Bonaire, Curacao, Saba, St. Eustatius and the southern portion of St. Martin Island (the northern half is held by France and is part of Guadeloupe).
- United States: U.S. Virgin Islands, principally St. Croix, St. John and St. Thomas.

• **West Germany** It no longer exists. See **Germany**.

• **West Indies** An island chain extending in an eastward arc between the southeastern United States and the northern shore of South America , separating the Caribbean Sea from the Atlantic Ocean and including the Bahamas, the Greater Antilles and the Lesser Antilles. See **Western Hemisphere**.

• **West Point** Acceptable on second reference to the *U-S Military Academy*. See **military academies**.
   In datelines:

   (West Point, New York) - -

• **West Virginia** See **state names**.

• **wheat** It is measured in bushels domestically, in metric tons for international trade. There are 36.7 bushels of wheat in a metric ton.

• **wheelchair**

• **wheeler-dealer**

• **whereabouts** Takes a singular verb: *His whereabouts is a mystery.*

• **wherever**

• **which** See the **essential clauses, non-essential clauses** entry; the **that, which, who, whom** entry; and the **who, whom** entry.

• **whip** Capitalize when used as a formal title before a name. See **legislative titles** and **titles**.

• **whiskey, whiskeys** Use the spelling *whisky* only in conjunction with *Scotch*. See the **Scotch whisky** entry.

• **white-collar** (adj.)

• **white paper** Two words, lowercase, when used to refer to a special report.

• **whitewash** (n., v. and adj.)

• **who, whom** Use *who* and *whom* for references to human beings and to animals with a name. Use *that* and *which* for inanimate objects and animals without a name.
   Who is the word when someone is the subject of a sentence, clause or phrase: *The woman who rented the room left the window open. Who is there?*
   Whom is the word when someone is the object of a verb or preposition: *The woman to whom the room was rented left the window open. Whom do you wish to see?* See the **essential clauses, non-ssential clauses** entry for guidelines on how

to punctuate clauses introduced by *who, whom, that* and *which.*

- **whole-hearted** The hyphen is for readability.

- **wholesale price index** See **producer price index.**

- **whole-wheat**

- **who's, whose** *Who's* is a contraction for *who is*, not a possessive: *Who's there?*
  Whose is the possessive: *I do not know whose coat it is.*

- **wide-** Usually hyphenated. Some examples:

wide-angle	wide-brimmed	wide-eyed	wide-open
wide-awake			

  Exception: *widespread.*

- **-wide** Usually, no hyphen. Some examples:

citywide	countrywide	nationwide	worldwide
continentwide	industrywide	statewide	

- **widow, widower** In obituaries: A man is *survived by his wife*, or *leaves his wife*. A woman is *survived by her husband*, or *leaves her husband*.
  Guard against the redundant *widow of the late*. Use *wife of the late* or *widow of.*

- **widths** See **dimensions.**

- **wildlife**

- **Wilkes-Barre** (wilks bayr), **Pennsylvania**

- **will** See the **shall, will** entry and **subjunctive mood.**

- **Wilson's disease** After Samuel Wilson, an English neurologist. A disease characterized by abnormal accumulation of copper in the brain, liver and other organs.

- **Windbreaker** A trademark for a brand of wind-resistant sports jacket.

- **wind chill index** See **weather terms.**

- **window dressing** The noun. But as a verb: *window-dress.*

- **wind-swept**

- **wind up** (v.) **windup** (n. and adj.)

- **wingspan**

- **winter** See **seasons**.

- **wintertime**

- **wiretap, wiretapper** The verb forms: *wiretap, wiretapped, wiretapping.*

- **Wisconsin** See **state names**.

- **-wise** No hyphen when it means *in the direction of* or *with regard to.* Some examples:

| clockwise | lengthwise | otherwise | slantwise |

Avoid contrived combinations such as *moneywise, religionwise.*

The word *penny-wise* is spelled with a hyphen because it is a compound adjective in which *wise* means smart, not an application of the suffix *-wise.* The same for *street-wise*, as in *street-wise youth.*

- **Woman's Christian Temperance Union** Not *Women's.*

- **women** Women should receive the same treatment as men in all areas of coverage. Physical descriptions, sexist references, demeaning stereotypes and condescending phrases should not be used.

To cite some examples, this means that:

- Copy should not assume maleness when both genders are involved, as in *Jackson told newsmen* or in *the taxpayer ... he* when it easily can be said *Jackson told reporters* or *taxpayers ... they.*
- Copy should not relate a woman's appearance to her professional capabilities, as in: *Mary Smith doesn't look the part, but she's an authority on ...*
- Copy should not gratuitously mention family relationships when there is no relevance to the subject, as in: *Golda Meir, a doughty grandmother, told the Egyptians ...*
- Use the same standards for men and women in deciding whether to include specific mention of personal appearance or marital and family situation.

In other words, treatment of the sexes should be even-handed and free of assumptions and stereotypes. This does not mean that valid and acceptable words such as *mankind* or *humanity* cannot be used. They are proper. See **courtesy titles; divorcee; man, mankind** and the **-persons** entries.

- **Women's Army Corps** See the **Wac, WAC** entry.

- **Woolworth's** Acceptable in all references for *F.W. Woolworth Company.*

- **word-of-mouth** (n. and adj.)

- **words as words** The meaning of this phrase, which appears occasionally in this handbook and similar manuals that deal with words, is best illustrated by an example: In this sentence, *woman* appears solely as a word rather than as the means of representing the concept normally associated with the word.

  When italics are available, a word used as a word should be italicized. Entries in this book use italics when a word or phrase is discussed in this sense. Note, for example, the italics used on *woman* in this sentence and in the example sentence.

  Italics are not available to highlight this type of word usage on the news wires. When a news story must use a word as a word, place quotation marks around it instead. See **plurals**.

- **word selection** In general, any word with a meaning that is universally understood is acceptable unless it is offensive or below the normal standards for literate writing. Choose words and constructions that are in common conversational use and evoke clear images.

  This handbook lists many words with cautionary notes about how they should be used. The entries in Webster's New World provide cautionary notes, comparisons and usage guidelines to help a writer choose the correct word for a particular context.

  Any word listed in Webster's New World may be used for the definitions given unless this handbook restricts its use to only some of the definitions recorded by the dictionary or specifies that the word be confined to certain contexts. If the dictionary cautions that a particular usage is objected to by some linguists or is not accepted widely, be wary of the usage unless there is a reason in the context.

  The dictionary uses the description *substandard* to identify words below the norms for literate writing. The dictionary provides guidance on many idiomatic expressions under the principal word in the expression. The definition and spelling of *under way*, for example, are found in the "way" entry.

  If it is necessary to use an archaic word or an archaic sense of a word, explain the meaning. Additional guidance on the acceptability of words is provided in this book under:

Americanisms	**jargon**
colloquialisms	**special contexts**
dialect	**vernacular**
foreign words	

  See also the **obscenities, profanities, vulgarities** entry.

- **workday**

- **work force**

- **working class** (n.) **working-class** (adj.)

- **workout**

- **workweek**

- **World Bank** Acceptable in all references for the *International Bank for Reconstruction and Development.*

- **World Council of Churches** This is the main international, interdenominational cooperative body of Anglican, Eastern Orthodox, Protestant, and old or national Catholic churches.
  Roman Catholicism is not a member but cooperates with the council in various programs. Headquarters is in Geneva, Switzerland.

- **World Court** This was an alternate name for the *Permanent Court of International Justice* set up by the League of Nations.
  See the entry for the **International Court of Justice,** which has replaced it.

- **World Health Organization** *W-H-O* is acceptable on second reference. Headquarters is in Geneva, Switzerland.

- **World Series** Or *the Series* on second reference. A rare exception to the general principles under **capitalization.**

- **World War One, World War Two**

- **worldwide**

- **worn-out**

- **worship, worshiped, worshiping, worshiper**

- **worthwhile**

- **would** See the **should, would** entry.

- **wrack** See the **rack, wrack** entry.

- **wrap** A radio voice report that includes both the correspondent and a newsmaker actuality. A wrap runs no more than 40 seconds and ends in a lockout.
  The actuality generally should be no shorter than 10 seconds and no longer than 15. It also should be fed separately.
  See also the entries for **actuality; lockouts; natural sound; q&a; scener** and **voicer.**

- **wrestling** Identify events by weight divisions. The key words to indicate winners are *pinned* and *outpointed.*

- **write in** (v.) **write-in** (n. and adj.)

- **wrongdoing**

- **Wyoming** See **state names**.

- **X** No longer in use as a motion picture rating. It has been replaced by **N-C-17**. See **movie ratings.**

- **Xerox** A trademark for a brand of photocopy machine. Never a verb. Use *copy* or *photocopy* instead.

- **X-ray** (n., v. and adj.) Use for both the photographic process and the radiation particles themselves.

- **yam** Botanically, yams and sweet potatoes are not related, although several varieties of moist-fleshed sweet potatoes are popularly called *yams* in some parts of the United States.

- **yard** Three feet.
  The metric equivalent is about .91 meters.
  To convert to meters, multiply the number of yards by .91: 5 yards times .91 equals 4.55 meters. See **foot; meter** and **distances**.

- **yard lines** Follow the rules for **numerals** when indicating the dividing lines on football fields and the distance traveled: *The five-yard line, the 40-yard line, he plunged in from the two, it was a six-yard run, he gained seven yards.*

- **year-end** (adj.)

- **yearling** An animal one year old or in its second year. The birthdays of all thoroughbred horses arbitrarily are set at January 1. On that date, any foal born in the preceding year is reckoned one year old—a *yearling.*

- **year-long** The hyphen is for readability.

- **years** Use figures, without commas: *1975.*
  Use an *s* with an apostrophe to indicate spans of decades or centuries: *the 1890's, the 1800's.*
  Years are the lone exception to the general rule in **numerals** that a figure is not used to start a sentence: *1976 was a very good year.* See **A-D; B-C; decades** and **months**.

- **yellow journalism** The use of cheaply sensational methods to attract or influence readers. The term comes from the "Yellow Kid," a comic strip in the New York World in 1895.

- **yeoman** (YOH'-muhn) See **military titles**.

- **yesteryear**

- **yield** In a financial sense, the annual rate of return on an investment, as paid in dividends or interest. It is expressed as a percentage obtained by dividing the market price for a stock or bond into the dividend or interest paid in the preceding 12 months. See **profit terminology**.

- **Yom Kippur** (yohm kee-POOR') The Jewish Day of Atonement. It is the holiest day of the Jewish year and occurs in September or October.

- **Young Men's Christian Association** *Y-M-C-A* is acceptable in all references. Headquarters is in New York.

- **Young Women's Christian Association** *Y-W-C-A* is acceptable in all references. Headquarters is in New York.

- **youth** Don't use it; people don't talk that way.
Use *man* or *woman* for individuals 18 and older, *teenager, boy* or *girl* for people aged 13 to 18.

- **yo-yo** Formerly a trademark, now a generic term.

- **Yukon** A territorial section of Canada. Use in datelines after the names of communities in the territory. See **Canada**.

- **yule, yuletide**

Z

- **zero, zeroes**

- **zero-base budgeting** A process that requires an agency, department or division to justify budget requests as if its programs were starting from scratch, or from a base of zero. In theory, this ensures a review of all programs at budget time.

- **zigzag**

- **Zionism** The effort of the Jews to regain and retain their biblical homeland. It is based on the promise of God in Book of Genesis that Israel would forever belong to Abraham and his descendants as a nation.
  The term is named for Mount Zion, the site of the ancient temple in Jerusalem. The Bible also frequently uses *Zion* in a general sense to denote the place where God is especially present with his people.

- **ZIP codes** Use all-caps *ZIP* for *Zone Improvement Program*, but lowercase the word *code*.
  Hyphenate the five-digit codes, setting them off with the word *ZIP* or *the ZIP code is*: *ZIP 1-0-0-2-0, the ZIP code is 1-0-0-2-0.*

STYLEBOOK ORDER FORM

Copies of The Associated Press Stylebook and Libel Manual can be ordered from t
AP Newsfeatures Department at the following rates:

AP member newspapers, broadcast members and journalism departmen
of member schools—$7.75 per copy, plus postage. A special assessment will be ma
for the charges.

Bookstores serving AP member schools—$9.75 per copy. Payment
full must accompany these orders.

All others—$10.75 per copy. Payment in full must accompany these orders.

For shipping and handling, add $2.50 for up to five books, $5.00 for orde
of six or more.

Orders should be placed for no more copies than are needed, as the
cannot accept returns. Orders requiring prepayment must be accompani
by a check or money order for the full amount or they will be returned a
the order delayed.

Mail to: **Stylebook**, AP Newsfeatures
50 Rockefeller Plaza, New York, NY 10020

Please send _____ copies of the AP Stylebook.   ❑ Payment enclosed.
❑ Please assess;
we are AP members.

Name _____

Organization _____

Mailing address _____

City _____ State _____ Zip code _____

Make all checks payable to **AP Stylebook.**
(Do not send cash or stamps)

THE WORD

There's only one writing guide that is a must for every new and veteran writer—**THE WORD.**

The updated and expanded **THE WORD:** An Associated Press Guide to Good Newswriting is the perfect companion volume to the **AP Stylebook and Libel Manual.**

In this revised, second edition of **THE WORD,** author Jack Cappon, AP general news editor, offers plenty of sound advice for journalists and journalists-to-be. Included in the book are guidelines on such topics as writing introductions, using quotes, organizing a story, and avoiding wordiness.

AP members may order **THE WORD** at the price of $4.50 per copy, plus postage. An assessment will be made for the charges. All others may order **The Word** at $6.00 per copy, prepaid.

For shipping and handling, add $1.00 for up to five books, $2.00 for six or more.

Mail to:
The Word
AP Newsfeatures
50 Rockefeller Plaza
New York, NY 10020

Please send me _____ copies of The Word
( ) Payment enclosed
( ) We are AP members. Please assess.

Name _____

Organization _____

Mailing Address _____

City _____ State _____ Zip Code _____

Mail all checks payable to THE WORD.
               (Do not send cash or stamps)

THE PICTURE

The Picture: A Guide to Good News Photography is written for phot
journalists—or would-be photojournalists.

A perfect photo companion to **The Word,** it is a book about picking the rig
angles, the right film, lighting and the philosophies of profession
photographers on how they cover a broad range of assignments, from news ar
sports to features and portraits. Each section is illustrated.

The 143-page guide was written by Brian Horton, veteran AP New
photos editor.

Cost of the book to AP member newspapers is $6.95 per copy, plus posta
or shipping, on orders of up to 10 books; $6.50 per book on orders of more tha
10. Cost to non-members is $8.95.

For shipping and handling, add $1.00 for up to five books, $2.00 for six
more.

Mail to: **The Picture,** AP Newsfeatures
50 Rockefeller Plaza, New York, NY 10020

Please send _____ copies of The Picture.   ❏ Payment enclosed.
❏ Please assess;
we are AP members.

Name _____

Organization _____

Mailing address _____

City _____ State _____ Zip code _____

Make all checks payable to **The Picture.**
(Do not send cash or stamps)

MANUAL DE TECNICAS

Manual de Tecnicas de Redaccion Periodistica is a handbook of writing techniques designed for Spanish-language print and broadcast journalists.

An important guide for anyone who writes professionally in Spanish—or wants to learn how the professionals do it—**Manual de Tecnicas** covers the fundamentals of journalism: writing the lead, sources and quotes, structure and connections, writing with "color," basic vocabulary, often misused terms, use and overuse of data, and much, much more.

The spiral-bound book, written in Spanish by the same rules it preaches, is a practical guide backed by AP's long and prestigious experience in journalism.

AP members can order **Manual de Tecnicas** for $11.95 a copy, including shipping. (Members will be assessed directly.)

All others may order the book for $13.95, plus $2.95 shipping for up to 10 copies; $5.95 for more than 10. Prepayment is required.

Mail to:
Manual de Tecnicas
AP Newsfeatures
50 Rockefeller Plaza
New York, NY 10020

Please send me _____ copies of Manual de Tecnicas
( ) Payment enclosed
( ) We are AP members; please assess.

Name _____

Organization _____

Mailing Address _____

City _____ State _____ Zip Code _____

Make all checks payable to **The Associated Press.**
(Do not send cash or stamps)

Visa/Master card No. _____

Expiration date _____

Signature _____

BROADCAST NEWS HANDBOOK

Additional copies of the AP Broadcast News Handbook can b
ordered from The Associated Press at $14.95 a copy, includin
shipping.

All orders require prepayment.

Mail to: **Broadcast Handbook,**
AP Newsfeatures
50 Rockefeller Plaza,
New York, NY 10020

Please send _____ copies of The Broadcast News Handbook.

❑ Payment enclosed.   ❑ Please assess; we are AP members.

Name _____

Organization _____

Mailing address _____

City _____ State _____ Zip code _____

Make all checks payable to **AP Broadcast News Handbook.**
(Do not send cash or stamps)